CCNA
200-301

Official Cert Guide, Volume 1

WENDELL ODOM, CCIE No. 1624 Emeritus

Cisco Press

221 River St. (3D11C)
Hoboken, NJ 07030

CCNA 200-301 Official Cert Guide, Volume 1

Wendell Odom

Published by:
Cisco Press

1 2019

Library of Congress Control Number: 2019908180

ISBN-13: 978-0-13-579273-5
ISBN-10: 0-13-579273-8

Warning and Disclaimer

This book is designed to provide information about the Cisco CCNA 200-301 exam. Every effort has been made to make this book as complete and as accurate as possible, but no warranty or fitness is implied.

The information is provided on an "as is" basis. The authors, Cisco Press, and Cisco Systems, Inc. shall have neither liability nor responsibility to any person or entity with respect to any loss or damages arising from the information contained in this book or from the use of the discs or programs that may accompany it.

The opinions expressed in this book belong to the author and are not necessarily those of Cisco Systems, Inc.

Trademark Acknowledgments

All terms mentioned in this book that are known to be trademarks or service marks have been appropriately capitalized. Cisco Press or Cisco Systems, Inc., cannot attest to the accuracy of this information. Use of a term in this book should not be regarded as affecting the validity of any trademark or service mark.

Special Sales

For information about buying this title in bulk quantities, or for special sales opportunities (which may include electronic versions; custom cover designs; and content particular to your business, training goals, marketing focus, or branding interests), please contact our corporate sales department at corpsales@pearsoned.com or (800) 382-3419.

For government sales inquiries, please contact governmentsales@pearsoned.com.

For questions about sales outside the U.S., please contact intlcs@pearson.com.

Feedback Information

At Cisco Press, our goal is to create in-depth technical books of the highest quality and value. Each book is crafted with care and precision, undergoing rigorous development that involves the unique expertise of members from the professional technical community.

Readers' feedback is a natural continuation of this process. If you have any comments regarding how we could improve the quality of this book, or otherwise alter it to better suit your needs, you can contact us through email at feedback@ciscopress.com. Please make sure to include the book title and ISBN in your message.

We greatly appreciate your assistance.

Editor-in-Chief: Mark Taub

Business Operation Manager, Cisco Press: Ronald Fligge

Director ITP Product Management: Brett Bartow

Managing Editor: Sandra Schroeder

Development Editor: Christopher Cleveland

Senior Project Editor: Tonya Simpson

Copy Editor: Chuck Hutchinson

Technical Editor: Elan Beer

Editorial Assistant: Cindy Teeters

Cover Designer: Chuti Prasertsith

Composition: Tricia Bronkella

Indexer: Ken Johnson

Proofreader: Debbie Williams

Americas Headquarters
Cisco Systems, Inc.
San Jose, CA

Asia Pacific Headquarters
Cisco Systems (USA) Pte. Ltd.
Singapore

Europe Headquarters
Cisco Systems International BV
Amsterdam, The Netherlands

Cisco has more than 200 offices worldwide. Addresses, phone numbers, and fax numbers are listed on the Cisco Website at **www.cisco.com/go/offices**.

CCDE, CCENT, Cisco Eos, Cisco HealthPresence, the Cisco logo, Cisco Lumin, Cisco Nexus, Cisco StadiumVision, Cisco TelePresence, Cisco WebEx, DCE, and Welcome to the Human Network are trademarks; Changing the Way We Work, Live, Play, and Learn and Cisco Store are service marks; and Access Registrar, Aironet, AsyncOS, Bringing the Meeting To You, Catalyst, CCDA, CCDP, CCIE, CCIP, CCNA, CCNP, CCSP, CCVP, Cisco, the Cisco Certified Internetwork Expert logo, Cisco IOS, Cisco Press, Cisco Systems, Cisco Systems Capital, the Cisco Systems logo, Cisco Unity, Collaboration Without Limitation, EtherFast, EtherSwitch, Event Center, Fast Step, Follow Me Browsing, FormShare, GigaDrive, HomeLink, Internet Quotient, IOS, iPhone, iQuick Study, IronPort, the IronPort logo, LightStream, Linksys, MediaTone, MeetingPlace, MeetingPlace Chime Sound, MGX, Networkers, Networking Academy, Network Registrar, PCNow, PIX, PowerPanels, ProConnect, ScriptShare, SenderBase, SMARTnet, Spectrum Expert, StackWise, The Fastest Way to Increase Your Internet Quotient, TransPath, WebEx, and the WebEx logo are registered trademarks of Cisco Systems, Inc. and/or its affiliates in the United States and certain other countries.

All other trademarks mentioned in this document or website are the property of their respective owners. The use of the word partner does not imply a partnership relationship between Cisco and any other company. (0812R)

About the Author

Wendell Odom, CCIE No. 1624 Emeritus, has been in the networking industry since 1981. He has worked as a network engineer, consultant, systems engineer, instructor, and course developer; he currently works writing and creating certification study tools. This book is his 28th edition of some product for Pearson, and he is the author of all editions of the CCNA Cert Guides about Routing and Switching from Cisco Press. He has written books about topics from networking basics, certification guides throughout the years for CCENT, CCNA R&S, CCNA DC, CCNP ROUTE, CCNP QoS, and CCIE R&S. He maintains study tools, links to his blogs, and other resources at www.certskills.com.

About the Contributing Author

David Hucaby, CCIE No. 4594, CWNE No. 292, is a network engineer for University of Kentucky Healthcare. He has been authoring Cisco Press titles for 20 years, with a focus on wireless and LAN switching topics. David has bachelor of science and master of science degrees in electrical engineering. He lives in Kentucky with his wife, Marci, and two daughters.

About the Technical Reviewer

Elan Beer, CCIE No. 1837, is a senior consultant and Cisco instructor specializing in data center architecture and multiprotocol network design. For the past 27 years, Elan has designed networks and trained thousands of industry experts in data center architecture, routing, and switching. Elan has been instrumental in large-scale professional service efforts designing and troubleshooting internetworks, performing data center and network audits, and assisting clients with their short- and long-term design objectives. Elan has a global perspective of network architectures via his international clientele. Elan has used his expertise to design and troubleshoot data centers and internetworks in Malaysia, North America, Europe, Australia, Africa, China, and the Middle East. Most recently, Elan has been focused on data center design, configuration, and troubleshooting as well as service provider technologies. In 1993, Elan was among the first to obtain the Cisco Certified System Instructor (CCSI) certification, and in 1996, he was among the first to attain the Cisco System highest technical certification, the Cisco Certified Internetworking Expert. Since then, Elan has been involved in numerous large-scale data center and telecommunications networking projects worldwide.

Acknowledgments

Brett Bartow and I have been a team for a few decades. His support and wisdom have been a big help through what is the most significant change to the Cisco CCNA and CCNP certifications since their beginnings back in 1998. He's always a great partner on working through big picture direction as well as features to make the books the best they can be for our readers. Once again he's the starting point of the team! (And one of the things he does is gather the rest of the team that you see below...)

I don't mean this to sound too melodramatic, but I am too psyched: I got Dave Hucaby to join my team as a coauthor for this edition of the book! Dave's been writing about LAN switching, wireless LANs, and security topics for Cisco Press almost as long as I have, and I've always loved the accuracy and style of his books. Cisco added more than a little wireless LAN content to CCNA this time around. One thing led to another, I wondered if Dave might be willing to join in, and now we get Dave on the wireless chapters! I hope you'll enjoy those chapters as much as I did when preparing the book.

Chris Cleveland did the development editing for the very first Cisco Press exam certification guide way back in 1998, and he still can't seem to get away from us! Seriously, when Brett and I first discuss any new book, the first question is whether Chris has time to develop the book. It's always a pleasure working with you, Chris, for what seems like the 20th time or so by now.

The second question for Brett when starting a new book is whether we might be able to get Elan Beer to do the tech editing. Elan has the right wiring, skills, and experience to do a great job for us with all aspects of the tech editing process. Fantastic job as usual; thanks, Elan.

Sometimes, with a short book timeline as with this book, I don't know who's working on the project for the production group until I've written these notes, but I heard Sandra's and Tonya's names early this time. Knowing they would be on the project again really did give me a chance to exhale, and I have to say that knowing they would be on the project gave me a great sense of calm going into the production phase of the book.

Thanks to Sandra Schroeder, Tonya Simpson, and all the production team for making the magic happen. Not to sound too much like a broken record, but getting to work with familiar people who have been a great help in the past really does help reduce the stress when writing, besides getting the highest-quality product out the door in print and e-book forms. From fixing all my grammar and passive-voice sentences to pulling the design and layout together, they do it all; thanks for putting it all together and making it look easy. And Tonya got to juggle two books of mine at the same time (again)—thanks for managing the whole production process again.

Mike Tanamachi, illustrator and mind reader, did a great job on the figures again. I use a different process with the figures than most authors, with Mike drawing new figures as soon as I outline a new section or chapter. It means more edits when I change my mind and lots of mind reading of what Wendell really wanted versus what I drew poorly on my iPad. Mike came through again with some beautiful finished products.

I could not have made the timeline for this book without Chris Burns of Certskills Professional. Chris owns much of the PTP question support and administration process, works on the labs we put on my blog, and then catches anything I need to toss over my shoulder so I can focus on the books. Chris, you are the man!

A special thank you to you readers who write in with suggestions and possible errors, and especially those of you who post online at the Cisco Learning Network and at my blog (blog.certskills.com). Without question, the comments I receive directly and over-hear by participating at CLN made this edition a better book.

Thanks to my wonderful wife, Kris, who helps make this sometimes challenging work lifestyle a breeze. I love walking this journey with you, doll. Thanks to my daughter Hannah, launching to college just as this book releases! And thanks to Jesus Christ, Lord of everything in my life.

Contents at a Glance

Online Appendixes

Contents

Online Appendixes

Reader Services

To access additional content for this book, simply register your product. To start the registration process, go to www.ciscopress.com/register and log in or create an account[*]. Enter the product ISBN 9780135792735 and click Submit. After the process is complete, you will find any available bonus content under Registered Products.

*Be sure to check the box that you would like to hear from us to receive exclusive discounts on future editions of this product.

Icons Used in This Book

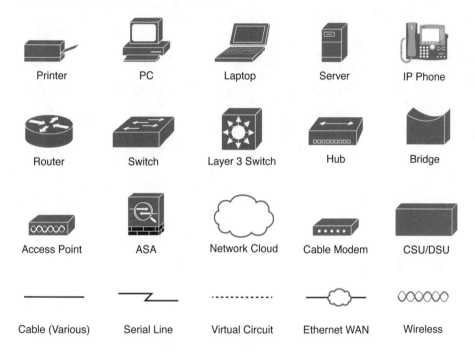

Printer	PC	Laptop	Server	IP Phone
Router	Switch	Layer 3 Switch	Hub	Bridge
Access Point	ASA	Network Cloud	Cable Modem	CSU/DSU
Cable (Various)	Serial Line	Virtual Circuit	Ethernet WAN	Wireless

Command Syntax Conventions

The conventions used to present command syntax in this book are the same conventions used in the IOS Command Reference. The Command Reference describes these conventions as follows:

- **Boldface** indicates commands and keywords that are entered literally as shown. In actual configuration examples and output (not general command syntax), boldface indicates commands that are manually input by the user (such as a **show** command).

- *Italic* indicates arguments for which you supply actual values.

- Vertical bars (|) separate alternative, mutually exclusive elements.
- Square brackets ([ ]) indicate an optional element.
- Braces ({ }) indicate a required choice.
- Braces within brackets ([{ }]) indicate a required choice within an optional element.

Introduction

About Cisco Certifications and CCNA

Congratulations! If you're reading far enough to look at this book's Introduction, you've probably already decided to go for your Cisco certification, and the CCNA certification is the one place to begin that journey. If you want to succeed as a technical person in the networking industry at all, you need to know Cisco. Cisco has a ridiculously high market share in the router and switch marketplace, with more than 80 percent market share in some markets. In many geographies and markets around the world, networking equals Cisco. If you want to be taken seriously as a network engineer, Cisco certification makes perfect sense.

The first few pages of this Introduction explain the core features of Cisco's Career Certification program, of which the Cisco Certified Network Associate (CCNA) serves as the foundation for all the other certifications in the program. This section begins with a comparison of the old to the new certifications due to some huge program changes in 2019. It then gives the key features of CCNA, how to get it, and what's on the exam.

The Big Changes to Cisco Certifications in 2019

Cisco announced sweeping changes to its career certification program around mid-year 2019. Because so many of you will have read and heard about the old versions of the CCNA certification, this intro begins with a few comparisons between the old and new CCNA as well as some of the other Cisco career certifications.

First, consider Cisco's career certifications before 2019 as shown in Figure I-1. At that time, Cisco offered 10 separate CCNA certifications in different technology tracks. Cisco also had eight Professional-level (CCNP, or Cisco Certified Network Professional) certifications.

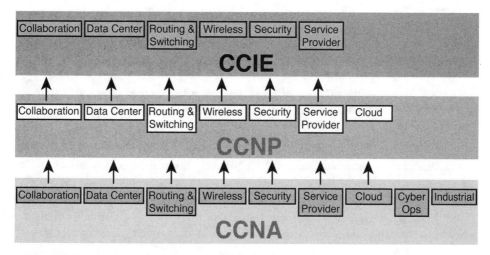

Figure I-1 *Old Cisco Certification Silo Concepts*

Why so many? Cisco began with one track—Routing and Switching—back in 1998. Over time, Cisco identified more and more technology areas that had grown to have enough content to justify another set of CCNA and CCNP certifications on those topics, so Cisco added more tracks. Many of those also grew to support expert level topics with CCIE (Cisco Certified Internetwork Expert).

In 2019, Cisco consolidated the tracks and moved the topics around quite a bit, as shown in Figure I-2.

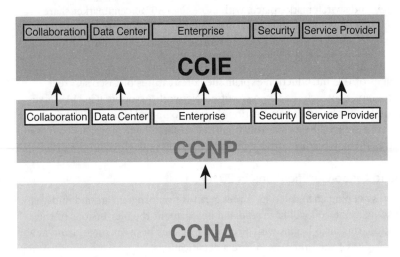

Figure I-2 *New Cisco Certification Tracks and Structure*

All the tracks now begin with the content in the one remaining CCNA certification. For CCNP, you now have a choice of five technology areas for your next steps, as shown in Figure I-2. (Note that Cisco replaced "Routing and Switching" with the term "Enterprise.")

Cisco made the following changes with the 2019 announcements:

CCENT: Retired the only Entry-level certification (CCENT, or Cisco Certified Entry Network Technician), with no replacement.

CCNA: Retired all the CCNA certifications except what was then known as "CCNA Routing and Switching," which became simply "CCNA."

CCNP: Consolidated the Professional level (CCNP) certifications to five tracks, including merging CCNP Routing and Switching and CCNP Wireless into CCNP Enterprise.

CCIE: Achieved better alignment with CCNP tracks through the consolidations.

Cisco needed to move many of the individual exam topics from one exam to another because of the number of changes. For instance, Cisco retired nine CCNA certifications plus the CCDA (Design Associate) certification—but those technologies didn't disappear! Cisco just moved the topics around to different exams in different certifications.

Consider wireless LANs as an example. The 2019 announcements retired both CCNA Wireless and CCNP Wireless as certifications. Some of the old CCNA Wireless topics landed in the new CCNA, while others landed in the two CCNP Enterprise exams about wireless LANs.

For those of you who want to learn more about the transition, check out my blog (blog.certskills.com) and look for posts in the News category from around June 2019. Now on to the details about CCNA as it exists starting in 2019!

How to Get Your CCNA Certification

As you saw in Figure I-2, all career certification paths now begin with CCNA. So how do you get it? Today, you have one and only one option to achieve CCNA certification:

Take and pass one exam: The Cisco 200-301 CCNA exam.

To take the 200-301 exam, or any Cisco exam, you will use the services of Pearson VUE (vue.com). The process works something like this:

1. Establish a login at https://home.pearsonvue.com/ (or use your existing login).

2. Register for, schedule a time and place, and pay for the Cisco 200-301 exam, all from the VUE website.

3. Take the exam at the VUE testing center.

4. You will receive a notice of your score, and whether you passed, before you leave the testing center.

Types of Questions on CCNA 200-301 Exam

The Cisco CCNA and CCNP exams all follow the same general format, with these types of questions:

- Multiple-choice, single-answer

- Multiple-choice, multiple-answer

- Testlet (one scenario with multiple multiple-choice questions)

- Drag-and-drop

- Simulated lab (sim)

- Simlet

Although the first four types of questions in the list should be somewhat familiar to you from other tests in school, the last two are more common to IT tests and Cisco exams in particular. Both use a network simulator to ask questions so that you control and use simulated Cisco devices. In particular:

Sim questions: You see a network topology and lab scenario, and can access the devices. Your job is to fix a problem with the configuration.

Simlet questions: This style combines sim and testlet question formats. As with a sim question, you see a network topology and lab scenario, and can access the devices. However, as with a testlet, you also see multiple multiple-choice questions. Instead of changing/fixing the configuration, you answer questions about the current state of the network.

These two question styles with the simulator give Cisco the ability to test your configuration skills with sim questions, and your verification and troubleshooting skills with simlet questions.

Before taking the test, learn the exam user interface by watching some videos Cisco provides about the exam user interface. To find the videos, just go to cisco.com and search for "Cisco Certification Exam Tutorial Videos."

CCNA 200-301 Exam Content, Per Cisco

Ever since I was in grade school, whenever the teacher announced that we were having a test soon, someone would always ask, "What's on the test?" We all want to know, and we all want to study what matters and avoid studying what doesn't matter.

Cisco tells the world the topics on each of its exams. Cisco wants the public to know the variety of topics and get an idea about the kinds of knowledge and skills required for each topic for every Cisco certification exam. To find the details, go to www.cisco.com/go/certifications, look for the CCNA page, and navigate until you see the exam topics.

This book also lists those same exam topics in several places. From one perspective, every chapter sets about to explain a small set of exam topics, so each chapter begins with the list of exam topics covered in that chapter. However, you might want to also see the exam topics in one place, so Appendix R, "Exam Topics Cross Reference," lists all the exam topics. You may want to download Appendix R in PDF form and keep it handy. The appendix lists the exam topics with two different cross references:

- A list of exam topics and the chapter(s) that covers each topic

- A list of chapters and the exam topics covered in each chapter

Exam Topic Verbs and Depth

Reading and understanding the exam topics, especially deciding the depth of skills required for each exam topic, require some thought. Each exam topic mentions the name of some technology, but it also lists a verb that implies the depth to which you must master the topic. The primary exam topics each list one or more verbs that describe the skill level required. For example, consider the following exam topic:

Configure and **verify** IPv4 addressing and subnetting

Note that this one exam topic has two verbs (*configure* and *verify*). Per this exam topic, you should be able to not only configure IPv4 addresses and subnets, but you should understand them well enough to verify that the configuration works. In contrast, the following exam topic asks you to describe a technology but does not ask you to configure it:

Describe the purpose of first hop redundancy protocol

The *describe* verb tells you to be ready to describe whatever a "first hop redundancy protocol" is. That exam topic also implies that you do not then need to be ready to configure or verify any first hop redundancy protocols (HSRP, VRRP, and GLBP).

Finally, note that the configure and verify exam topics imply that you should be able to describe and explain and otherwise master the concepts so that you understand what you have configured. The earlier "Configure and verify IPv4 addressing and subnetting" does not mean that you should know how to type commands but have no clue as to what you configured. You must first master the conceptual exam topic verbs. The progression runs something like this:

Describe, Identify, Explain, Compare/Contrast, Configure, Verify, Troubleshoot

For instance, an exam topic that lists "compare and contrast" means that you should be able to describe, identify, and explain the technology. Also, an exam topic with "configure and verify" tells you to also be ready to describe, explain, and compare/contrast.

The Context Surrounding the Exam Topics

Take a moment to navigate to www.cisco.com/go/certifications and find the list of exam topics for the CCNA 200-301 exam. Did your eyes go straight to the list of exam topics? Or did you take the time to read the paragraphs above the exam topics first?

That list of exam topics for the CCNA 200-301 exam includes a little over 50 primary exam topics and about 50 more secondary exam topics. The primary topics have those verbs as just discussed, which tell you something about the depth of skill required. The secondary topics list only the names of more technologies to know.

However, the top of the web page that lists the exam topics also lists some important information that tells us some important facts about the exam topics. In particular, that leading text, found at the beginning of Cisco exam topic pages of most every exam, tells us

- The guidelines may change over time.

- The exam topics are general guidelines about what may be on the exam.

- The actual exam may include "other related topics."

Interpreting these three facts in order, I would not expect to see a change to the published list of exam topics for the exam. I've been writing the Cisco Press CCNA Cert Guides since Cisco announced CCNA back in 1998, and I've never seen Cisco change the official exam topics in the middle of an exam—not even to fix typos. But the introductory words say that they might change the exam topics, so it's worth checking.

As for the second item in the preceding list, even before you know what the acronyms mean, you can see that the exam topics give you a general but not detailed idea about each topic. The exam topics do not attempt to clarify every nook and cranny or to list every command and parameter; however, this book serves as a great tool in that it acts as a much more detailed interpretation of the exam topics. We examine every exam topic, and if we think a concept or command is possibly within an exam topic, we put it into the book. So, the exam topics give us general guidance, and these books give us much more detailed guidance.

The third item in the list uses literal wording that runs something like this: "However, other related topics may also appear on any specific delivery of the exam." That one statement can be a bit jarring to test takers, but what does it really mean? Unpacking the statement, it says that such questions may appear on any one exam but may not; in other words, they don't set about to ask every test taker some questions that include concepts not mentioned in the exam topics. Second, the phrase "...other **related** topics..." emphasizes that any such questions would be related to some exam topic, rather than being far afield—a fact that helps us in how we respond to this particular program policy.

For instance, the CCNA 200-301 exam includes configuring and verifying the OSPF routing protocol, but it does not mention the EIGRP routing protocol. I personally would be unsurprised to see an OSPF question that required a term or fact not specifically mentioned in the exam topics. I would be surprised to see one that (in my opinion) ventures far away from the OSPF features in the exam topics. Also, I would not expect to see a question about how to configure and verify EIGRP.

And just as one final side point, note that Cisco does on occasion ask a test taker some unscored questions, and those may appear to be in this vein of questions from outside topics. When you sit down to take the exam, the small print mentions that you may see unscored questions and you won't know which ones are unscored. (These questions give Cisco a way to test possible new questions.) But some of these might be ones that fall into the "other related topics" category, but then not affect your score.

You should prepare a little differently for any Cisco exam, in comparison to say an exam back in school, in light of Cisco's "other related questions" policy:

- Do not approach an exam topic with an "I'll learn the core concepts and ignore the edges" approach.

- Instead, approach each exam topic with a "pick up all the points I can" approach by mastering each exam topic, both in breadth and in depth.

- Go beyond each exam topic when practicing configuration and verification by taking a little extra time to look for additional show commands and configuration options, and make sure you understand as much of the show command output that you can.

By mastering the known topics, and looking for places to go a little deeper, you will hopefully pick up the most points you can from questions about the exam topics. Then the extra practice you do with commands may happen to help you learn beyond the exam topics in a way that can help you pick up other points as well.

CCNA 200-301 Exam Content, Per This Book

When we created the Official Cert Guide content for the CCNA 200-301 exam, we considered a few options for how to package the content, and we landed on releasing a two-book set. Figure I-3 shows the setup of the content, with roughly 60 percent of the content in Volume 1 and the rest in Volume 2.

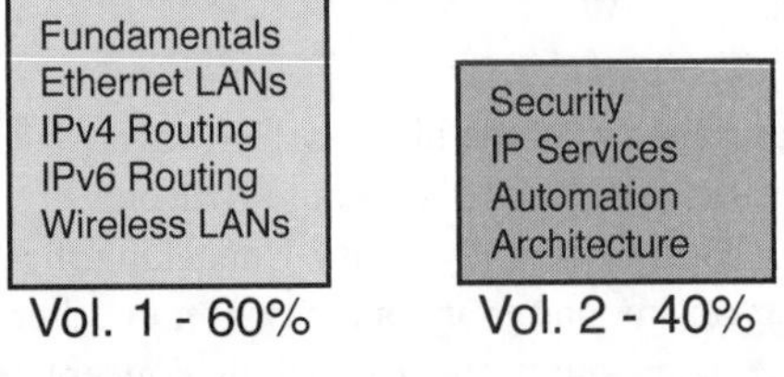

Fundamentals
Ethernet LANs
IPv4 Routing
IPv6 Routing
Wireless LANs

Security
IP Services
Automation
Architecture

Vol. 1 - 60%   Vol. 2 - 40%

Figure I-3 *Two Books for CCNA 200-301*

The two books together cover all the exam topics in the CCNA 200-301 exam. Each chapter in each book develops the concepts and commands related to an exam topic, with clear and detailed explanations, frequent figures, and many examples that build your understanding of how Cisco networks work.

As for choosing what content to put into the books, note that we begin and finish with Cisco's exam topics, but with an eye toward predicting as many of the "other related topics" as we can. We start with the list of exam topics and apply a fair amount of experience, discussion, and other secret sauce to come up with an interpretation of what specific concepts and commands are worthy of being in the books or not. At the end of the writing process, the books should cover all the published exam topics, with additional depth and breadth that I choose based on the analysis of the exam. As we have done from the very first edition of the *CCNA Official Cert Guide*, we intend to cover each and every topic in depth. But as you would expect, we cannot predict every single fact on the exam given the nature of the exam policies, but we do our best to cover all known topics.

Book Features

This book includes many study features beyond the core explanations and examples in each chapter. This section acts as a reference to the various features in the book.

Chapter Features and How to Use Each Chapter

Each chapter of this book is a self-contained short course about one small topic area, organized for reading and study, as follows:

"Do I Know This Already?" quizzes: Each chapter begins with a pre-chapter quiz.

Foundation Topics: This is the heading for the core content section of the chapter.

Chapter Review: This section includes a list of study tasks useful to help you remember concepts, connect ideas, and practice skills-based content in the chapter.

Figure I-4 shows how each chapter uses these three key elements. You start with the DIKTA quiz. You can use the score to determine whether you already know a lot, or not so much, and determine how to approach reading the Foundation Topics (that is, the technology content in the chapter). When finished, use the Chapter Review tasks to start working on mastering your memory of the facts and skills with configuration, verification, and troubleshooting.

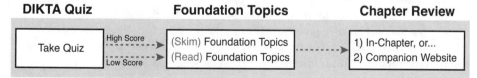

Figure I-4 *Three Primary Tasks for a First Pass Through Each Chapter*

In addition to these three main chapter features, each "Chapter Review" section uses a variety of other book features, including the following:

■ **Review Key Topics:** Inside the "Foundation Topics" section, the Key Topic icon appears next to the most important items, for the purpose of later review and mastery. While all content matters, some is, of course, more important to learn, or needs more review to master, so these items are noted as key topics. The Chapter Review lists the key topics in a table; scan the chapter for these items to review them. Or review the key topics interactively using the companion website.

■ **Complete Tables from Memory:** Instead of just rereading an important table of information, you will find some tables have been turned into memory tables, an interactive exercise found on the companion website. Memory tables repeat the table, but with parts of the table removed. You can then fill in the table to exercise your memory, and click to check your work.

■ **Key Terms You Should Know:** You do not need to be able to write a formal definition of all terms from scratch; however, you do need to understand each term well enough to understand exam questions and answers. The Chapter Review lists the key terminology from the chapter. Make sure you have a good understanding of each term and use the Glossary to cross-check your own mental definitions. You can also review key terms with the "Key Terms Flashcards" app on the companion website.

■ **Labs:** Many exam topics use verbs such as *configure* and *verify*; all these refer to skills you should practice at the user interface (CLI) of a router or switch. The Chapter and Part Reviews refer you to these other tools. The upcoming section titled "About Building Hands-On Skills" discusses your options.

■ **Command References:** Some book chapters cover a large number of router and switch commands. The Chapter Review includes reference tables for the commands used in that chapter, along with an explanation. Use these tables for reference, but also use them for study. Just cover one column of the table, and see how much you can remember and complete mentally.

■ **Review DIKTA Questions:** Although you have already seen the DIKTA questions from the chapters, re-answering those questions can prove a useful way to review facts. The Part Review suggests that you repeat the DIKTA questions but using the Pearson Test Prep (PTP) exam.

■ **Subnetting Exercises:** Chapters 12, 13, 14, 22, and 24 ask you to perform some math processes related to either IPv4 or IPv6 addressing. The Chapter Review asks you to do additional practice problems. The problems can be found in Appendices D through H, in PDF form, on the companion website. The website also includes interactive versions of most of the exercises from those appendices.

Part Features and How to Use the Part Review

The book organizes the chapters into parts for the purpose of helping you study for the exam. Each part groups a small number of related chapters together. Then the study process (described just before Chapter 1) suggests that you pause after each part to do a review of all chapters in the part. Figure I-5 lists the titles of the eight parts and the chapters in those parts (by chapter number) for this book.

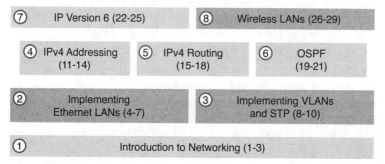

Figure I-5 *The Book Parts (by Title), and Chapter Numbers in Each Part*

The Part Review that ends each part acts as a tool to help you with spaced review sessions. Spaced reviews—that is, reviewing content several times over the course of your study—help improve retention. The Part Review activities include many of the same kinds of activities seen in the Chapter Review. Avoid skipping the Part Review, and take the time to do the review; it will help you in the long run.

The Companion Website for Online Content Review

We created an electronic version of every Chapter and Part Review task that could be improved though an interactive version of the tool. For instance, you can take a "Do I Know This Already?" quiz by reading the pages of the book, but you can also use our testing software. As another example, when you want to review the key topics from a chapter, you can find all those in electronic form as well.

All the electronic review elements, as well as other electronic components of the book, exist on this book's companion website. The companion website gives you a big advantage: you can do most of your Chapter and Part Review work from anywhere using the interactive tools on the site. The advantages include

- **Easier to use:** Instead of having to print out copies of the appendixes and do the work on paper, you can use these new apps, which provide you with an easy-to-use, interactive experience that you can easily run over and over.

- **Convenient:** When you have a spare 5–10 minutes, go to the book's website and review content from one of your recently finished chapters.

- **Untethered from the book:** You can access your review activities from anywhere—no need to have the book with you.

- **Good for tactile learners:** Sometimes looking at a static page after reading a chapter lets your mind wander. Tactile learners might do better by at least typing answers into an app, or clicking inside an app to navigate, to help keep you focused on the activity.

The interactive Chapter Review elements should improve your chances of passing as well. Our in-depth reader surveys over the years show that those who do the Chapter and Part Reviews learn more. Those who use the interactive versions of the review elements also tend to do more of the Chapter and Part Review work. So take advantage of the tools and maybe you will be more successful as well. Table I-1 summarizes these interactive applications and the traditional book features that cover the same content.

Table I-1 *Book Features with Both Traditional and App Options*

Feature	Traditional	App
Key Topic	Table with list; flip pages to find	Key Topics Table app
Config Checklist	Just one of many types of key topics	Config Checklist app
Key Terms	Listed in each "Chapter Review" section, with the Glossary in the back of the book	Glossary Flash Cards app
Subnetting Practice	Appendixes D–H, with practice problems and answers	A variety of apps, one per problem type

The companion website also includes links to download, navigate, or stream for these types of content:

■ Pearson Sim Lite Desktop App

■ Pearson Test Prep (PT) Desktop App

■ Pearson Test Prep (PT) Web App

■ Videos as mentioned in book chapters

How to Access the Companion Website

To access the companion website, which gives you access to the electronic content with this book, start by establishing a login at www.ciscopress.com and register your book. To do so, simply go to www.ciscopress.com/register and enter the ISBN of the print book: 9780135792735. After you have registered your book, go to your account page and click the **Registered Products** tab. From there, click the **Access Bonus Content** link to get access to the book's companion website.

Note that if you buy the *Premium Edition eBook and Practice Test* version of this book from Cisco Press, your book will automatically be registered on your account page. Simply go to your account page, click the **Registered Products** tab, and select **Access Bonus Content** to access the book's companion website.

How to Access the Pearson Test Prep (PTP) App

You have two options for installing and using the Pearson Test Prep application: a web app and a desktop app.

To use the Pearson Test Prep application, start by finding the registration code that comes with the book. You can find the code in these ways:

- **Print book:** Look in the cardboard sleeve in the back of the book for a piece of paper with your book's unique PTP code.

- **Premium Edition:** If you purchase the Premium Edition eBook and Practice Test directly from the Cisco Press website, the code will be populated on your account page after purchase. Just log in at www.ciscopress.com, click **account** to see details of your account, and click the **digital purchases** tab.

- **Amazon Kindle:** For those who purchase a Kindle edition from Amazon, the access code will be supplied directly from Amazon.

- **Other Bookseller E-books:** Note that if you purchase an e-book version from any other source, the practice test is not included because other vendors to date have not chosen to vend the required unique access code.

NOTE Do not lose the activation code because it is the only means with which you can access the QA content with the book.

Once you have the access code, to find instructions about both the PTP web app and the desktop app, follow these steps:

Step 1. Open this book's companion website, as was shown earlier in this Introduction under the heading "How to Access the Companion Website."

Step 2. Click the **Practice Exams** button.

Step 3. Follow the instructions listed there both for installing the desktop app and for using the web app.

Note that if you want to use the web app only at this point, just navigate to www.pearsontestprep.com, establish a free login if you do not already have one, and register this book's practice tests using the registration code you just found. The process should take only a couple of minutes.

NOTE Amazon eBook (Kindle) customers: It is easy to miss Amazon's email that lists your PTP access code. Soon after you purchase the Kindle eBook, Amazon should send an email. However, the email uses very generic text, and makes no specific mention of PTP or practice exams. To find your code, read every email from Amazon after you purchase the book. Also do the usual checks for ensuring your email arrives like checking your spam folder.

NOTE Other eBook customers: As of the time of publication, only the publisher and Amazon supply PTP access codes when you purchase their eBook editions of this book.

Feature Reference

The following list provides an easy reference to get the basic idea behind each book feature:

- **Practice exam:** The book gives you the rights to the Pearson Test Prep (PTP) testing software, available as a web app and desktop app. Use the access code on a piece of cardboard in the sleeve in the back of the book, and use the companion website to download the desktop app or navigate to the web app (or just go to www.pearsontestprep.com).

- **E-book:** Pearson offers an e-book version of this book that includes extra practice tests. If interested, look for the special offer on a coupon card inserted in the sleeve in the back of the book. This offer enables you to purchase the *CCNA 200-301 Official Cert Guide, Volume 1, Premium Edition eBook and Practice Test* at a 70 percent discount off the list price. The product includes three versions of the e-book, PDF (for reading on your computer), EPUB (for reading on your tablet, mobile device, or Nook or other e-reader), and Mobi (the native Kindle version). It also includes additional practice test questions and enhanced practice test features.

- **Subnetting videos:** The companion website contains a series of videos that show you how to calculate various facts about IP addressing and subnetting (in particular, using the shortcuts described in this book).

- **Mentoring videos:** The companion website also includes a number of videos about other topics as mentioned in individual chapters.

- **Subnetting practice apps:** The companion website contains appendixes with a set of subnetting practice problems and answers. This is a great resource to practice building subnetting skills. You can also do these same practice problems with applications from the "Chapter and Part Review" section of the companion website.

- **CCNA 200-301 Network Simulator Lite:** This lite version of the best-selling CCNA Network Simulator from Pearson provides you with a means, right now, to experience the Cisco command-line interface (CLI). No need to go buy real gear or buy a full simulator to start learning the CLI. Just install it from the companion website.

- **CCNA Simulator:** If you are looking for more hands-on practice, you might want to consider purchasing the CCNA Network Simulator. You can purchase a copy of this software from Pearson at http://pearsonitcertification.com/networksimulator or other retail outlets. To help you with your studies, Pearson has created a mapping guide that maps each of the labs in the simulator to the specific sections in each volume of the CCNA Cert Guide. You can get this mapping guide free on the Extras tab on the book product page: www.ciscopress.com/title/9780135792735.

- **PearsonITCertification.com:** The website www.pearsonitcertification.com is a great resource for all things IT-certification related. Check out the great CCNA articles, videos, blogs, and other certification preparation tools from the industry's best authors and trainers.

- **Author's website and blogs:** The author maintains a website that hosts tools and links useful when studying for CCNA. In particular, the site has a large number of free lab exercises about CCNA content, additional sample questions, and other exercises. Additionally, the site indexes all content so you can study based on the book chapters and parts. To find it, navigate to blog.certskills.com.

Book Organization, Chapters, and Appendixes

This book contains 29 core chapters, with each chapter covering a subset of the topics on the CCNA exam. The book organizes the chapters into parts of three to five chapters. The core chapters cover the following topics:

- **Part I: Introduction to Networking**

    - **Chapter 1, "Introduction to TCP/IP Networking,"** introduces the central ideas and terms used by TCP/IP, and contrasts the TCP/IP networking model with the OSI model.

    - **Chapter 2, "Fundamentals of Ethernet LANs,"** introduces the concepts and terms used when building Ethernet LANs.

    - **Chapter 3, "Fundamentals of WANs and IP Routing,"** covers the basics of the data-link layer for WANs in the context of IP routing but emphasizes the main network layer protocol for TCP/IP. This chapter introduces the basics of IPv4, including IPv4 addressing and routing.

- **Part II: Implementing Ethernet LANs**

    - **Chapter 4, "Using the Command-Line Interface,"** explains how to access the text-based user interface of Cisco Catalyst LAN switches.

    - **Chapter 5, "Analyzing Ethernet LAN Switching,"** shows how to use the Cisco CLI to verify the current status of an Ethernet LAN and how it switches Ethernet frames.

    - **Chapter 6, "Configuring Basic Switch Management,"** explains how to configure Cisco switches for basic management features, such as remote access using Telnet and SSH.

    - **Chapter 7, "Configuring and Verifying Switch Interfaces,"** shows how to configure a variety of switch features that apply to interfaces, including duplex/speed.

- **Part III: Implementing VLANs and STP**

    - **Chapter 8, "Implementing Ethernet Virtual LANs,"** explains the concepts and configuration surrounding virtual LANs, including VLAN trunking.

    - **Chapter 9, "Spanning Tree Protocol Concepts,"** discusses the concepts behind IEEE Spanning Tree Protocol (STP), including Rapid STP (RSTP) and how they make some switch interfaces block frames to prevent frames from looping continuously around a redundant switched LAN.

    - **Chapter 10, "RSTP and EtherChannel Configuration,"** shows how to configure and verify RSTP and Layer 2 EtherChannels on Cisco switches.

- Part IV: IPv4 Addressing

  - Chapter 11, "Perspectives on IPv4 Subnetting," walks you through the entire concept of subnetting, from starting with a Class A, B, or C network to a completed subnetting design as implemented in an enterprise IPv4 network.

  - Chapter 12, "Analyzing Classful IPv4 Networks," explains how IPv4 addresses originally fell into several classes, with unicast IP addresses being in Class A, B, and C. This chapter explores all things related to address classes and the IP network concept created by those classes.

  - Chapter 13, "Analyzing Subnet Masks," shows how an engineer can analyze the key facts about a subnetting design based on the subnet mask. This chapter shows how to look at the mask and IP network to determine the size of each subnet and the number of subnets.

  - Chapter 14, "Analyzing Existing Subnets," describes how most troubleshooting of IP connectivity problems starts with an IP address and mask. This chapter shows how to take those two facts and find key facts about the IP subnet in which that host resides.

- Part V: IPv4 Routing

  - Chapter 15, "Operating Cisco Routers," is like Chapter 8, focusing on basic device management, but it focuses on routers instead of switches.

  - Chapter 16, "Configuring IPv4 Addressing and Static Routes," discusses how to add IPv4 address configuration to router interfaces and how to configure static IPv4 routes.

  - Chapter 17, "IP Routing in the LAN," shows how to configure and troubleshoot different methods of routing between VLANs, including Router-on-a-Stick (ROAS), Layer 3 switching with SVIs, Layer 3 switching with routed ports, and using Layer 3 EtherChannels.

  - Chapter 18, "Troubleshooting IPv4 Routing," focuses on how to use two key troubleshooting tools to find routing problems: the **ping** and **traceroute** commands.

- Part VI: OSPF

  - Chapter 19, "Understanding OSPF Concepts," introduces the fundamental operation of the Open Shortest Path First (OSPF) protocol, focusing on link state fundamentals, neighbor relationships, flooding link state data, and calculating routes based on the lowest cost metric.

  - Chapter 20, "Implementing OSPF," takes the concepts discussed in the previous chapter and shows how to configure and verify those same features.

  - Chapter 21, "OSPF Network Types and Neighbors," takes the next steps in OSPF configuration and verification by looking in more depth at the concepts of how routers enable OSPF on interfaces, and the conditions that must be true before two routers will succeed in becoming OSPF neighbors.

- Part VII: IP Version 6

  - Chapter 22, "Fundamentals of IP Version 6," discusses the most basic concepts of IP version 6, focusing on the rules for writing and interpreting IPv6 addresses.

- Chapter 23, "IPv6 Addressing and Subnetting," works through the two branches of unicast IPv6 addresses—global unicast addresses and unique local addresses—that act somewhat like IPv4 public and private addresses, respectively.

- Chapter 24, "Implementing IPv6 Addressing on Routers," shows how to configure IPv6 routing and addresses on routers, while discussing a variety of special IPv6 addresses.

- Chapter 25, "Implementing IPv6 Routing," shows how to add static routes to an IPv6 router's routing table.

- Part VIII: Wireless LANs

  - Chapter 26, "Fundamentals of Wireless Networks," introduces the foundational concepts of wireless 802.11 LANs, including wireless topologies and basic wireless radio communications protocols.

  - Chapter 27, "Analyzing Cisco Wireless Architectures," turns your attention to the questions related to systematic and architectural issues surrounding how to build wireless LANs and explains the primary options available for use.

  - Chapter 28, "Securing Wireless Networks," explains the unique security challenges that exist in a wireless LAN and the protocols and standards used to prevent different kinds of attacks.

  - Chapter 29, "Building a Wireless LAN," shows how to configure and secure a wireless LAN using a Wireless LAN Controller (WLC).

- Part IX: Print Appendixes

  - Appendix A, "Numeric Reference Tables," lists several tables of numeric information, including a binary-to-decimal conversion table and a list of powers of 2.

  - Appendix B, "CCNA 200-301, Volume 1 Exam Updates," is a place for the author to add book content mid-edition. Always check online for the latest PDF version of this appendix; the appendix lists download instructions.

  - Appendix C, "Answers to the 'Do I Know This Already?' Quizzes," includes the explanations to all the "Do I Know This Already" quizzes.

  - The Glossary contains definitions for all the terms listed in the "Key Terms You Should Know" sections at the conclusion of the chapters.

- Part X: Online Appendixes

- Practice Appendixes

The following appendixes are available in digital format from the companion website. These appendixes provide additional practice for several networking processes that use some math.

- Appendix D, "Practice for Chapter 12: Analyzing Classful IPv4 Networks"

- Appendix E, "Practice for Chapter 13: Analyzing Subnet Masks"

- Appendix F, "Practice for Chapter 14: Analyzing Existing Subnets"

- Appendix G, "Practice for Chapter 22: Fundamentals of IP Version 6"

■ Appendix H, "Practice for Chapter 24: Implementing IPv6 Addressing on Routers"

■ Content from Previous Editions

Although the publisher restarts numbering at edition "1" each time, the name of the related exam changes in a significant way. In function, this book is in effect part of the 9th edition of the CCNA Cert Guide materials from Cisco Press. From edition to edition, some readers over the years have asked that we keep some select chapters with the book. Keeping content that Cisco removed from the exam, but that may still be useful, can help the average reader as well as instructors who use the materials to teach courses with this book. The following appendices hold this edition's content from previous editions:

■ Appendix J, "Topics from Previous Editions," is a collection of small topics from prior editions. None of the topics justify a complete appendix by themselves, so we collect the small topics into this single appendix.

■ Appendix K, "Analyzing Ethernet LAN Designs," examines various ways to design Ethernet LANs, discussing the pros and cons, and explains common design terminology.

■ Appendix L, "Subnet Design," takes a design approach to subnetting. This appendix begins with a classful IPv4 network and asks why a particular mask might be chosen, and if chosen, what subnet IDs exist.

■ Appendix M, "Practice for Appendix L: Subnet Design"

■ Appendix N, "Variable-Length Subnet Masks," moves away from the assumption of one subnet mask per network to multiple subnet masks per network, which makes subnetting math and processes much more challenging. This appendix explains those challenges.

■ Appendix O, "Spanning Tree Protocol Implementation," shows how to configure and verify STP on Cisco switches.

■ Appendix P, "LAN Troubleshooting," examines the most common LAN switching issues and how to discover those issues when troubleshooting a network. The appendix includes troubleshooting topics for STP/RSTP, Layer 2 EtherChannel, LAN switching, VLANs, and VLAN trunking.

■ Appendix Q, "Troubleshooting IPv4 Routing Protocols," walks through the most common problems with IPv4 routing protocols, while alternating between OSPF examples and EIGRP examples.

■ Miscellaneous Appendixes

    ■ Appendix I, "Study Planner," is a spreadsheet with major study milestones, where you can track your progress through your study.

    ■ Appendix R, "Exam Topics Cross Reference," provides some tables to help you find where each exam objective is covered in the book.

About Building Hands-On Skills

You need skills in using Cisco routers and switches, specifically the Cisco command-line interface (CLI). The Cisco CLI is a text-based command-and-response user interface; you type a command, and the device (a router or switch) displays messages in response. To answer sim and simlet questions on the exams, you need to know a lot of commands, and you need to be able to navigate to the right place in the CLI to use those commands.

This next section walks through the options of what is included in the book, with a brief description of lab options outside the book.

Config Lab Exercises

Some router and switch features require multiple configuration commands. Part of the skill you need to learn is to remember which configuration commands work together, which ones are required, and which ones are optional. So, the challenge level goes beyond just picking the right parameters on one command. You have to choose which commands to use, in which combination, typically on multiple devices. And getting good at that kind of task requires practice.

Each Config Lab lists details about a straightforward lab exercise for which you should create a small set of configuration commands for a few devices. Each lab presents a sample lab topology, with some requirements, and you have to decide what to configure on each device. The answer then shows a sample configuration. Your job is to create the configuration and then check your answer versus the supplied answer.

Config Lab content resides outside the book at the author's blog site (blog.certskills. com). You can navigate to the Config Lab in a couple of ways from the site, or just go directly to https://blog.certskills.com/category/hands-on/config-lab/ to reach a list of all Config Labs. Figure I-6 shows the logo that you will see with each Config Lab.

Figure I-6 *Config Lab Logo in the Author's Blogs*

These Config Labs have several benefits, including the following:

Untethered and responsive: Do them from anywhere, from any web browser, from your phone or tablet, untethered from the book or DVD.

Designed for idle moments: Each lab is designed as a 5- to 10-minute exercise if all you are doing is typing in a text editor or writing your answer on paper.

Two outcomes, both good: Practice getting better and faster with basic configuration, or if you get lost, you have discovered a topic that you can now go back and reread to complete your knowledge. Either way, you are a step closer to being ready for the exam!

Blog format: The format allows easy adds and changes by me and easy comments by you.

Self-assessment: As part of final review, you should be able to do all the Config Labs, without help, and with confidence.

Note that the blog organizes these Config Lab posts by book chapter, so you can easily use these at both Chapter Review and Part Review. See the "Your Study Plan" element that follows the Introduction for more details about those review sections.

A Quick Start with Pearson Network Simulator Lite

The decision of how to get hands-on skills can be a little scary at first. The good news: You have a free and simple first step to experience the CLI: install and use the Pearson Network Simulator Lite (or NetSim Lite) that comes with this book.

This book comes with a lite version of the best-selling CCNA Network Simulator from Pearson, which provides you with a means, right now, to experience the Cisco CLI. No need to go buy real gear or buy a full simulator to start learning the CLI. Just install it from the companion website.

This latest version of NetSim Lite includes labs associated with Part II of this book, plus a few more from Part III. Part I includes concepts only, with Part II being the first part with commands. So, make sure to use the NetSim Lite to learn the basics of the CLI to get a good start.

Of course, one reason that you get access to the NetSim Lite is that the publisher hopes you will buy the full product. However, even if you do not use the full product, you can still learn from the labs that come with NetSim Lite while deciding about what options to pursue.

The Pearson Network Simulator

The Config Labs and the Pearson Network Simulator Lite both fill specific needs, and they both come with the book. However, you need more than those two tools.

The single best option for lab work to do along with this book is the paid version of the Pearson Network Simulator. This simulator product simulates Cisco routers and switches so that you can learn for CCNA certification. But more importantly, it focuses on learning for the exam by providing a large number of useful lab exercises. Reader surveys tell us that those people who use the Simulator along with the book love the learning process and rave about how the book and Simulator work well together.

Of course, you need to make a decision for yourself and consider all the options. Thankfully, you can get a great idea of how the full Simulator product works by using the Pearson Network Simulator Lite product included with the book. Both have the same base code, same user interface, and same types of labs. Try the Lite version to decide if you want to buy the full product.

Note that the Simulator and the books work on a different release schedule. For a time in 2019 (and probably into 2020), the Simulator will be the one created for the previous versions of the exams (ICND1 100-101, ICND2 200-101, and CCNA 200-120).

Interestingly, Cisco did not add a large number of new topics that require CLI skills to the CCNA 200-301 exam as compared with its predecessor, so the old Simulator covers most of the CLI topics. So, during the interim before the products based on the 200-301 exam come out, the old Simulator products should be quite useful.

On a practical note, when you want to do labs when reading a chapter or doing Part Review, the Simulator organizes the labs to match the book. Just look for the Sort by Chapter tab in the Simulator's user interface. However, during the months in 2019 for which the Simulator is the older edition listing the older exams in the title, you will need to refer to a PDF that lists those labs versus this book's organization. You can find that PDF on the book product page under the Downloads tab here: www.ciscopress.com/title/9780135792735.

More Lab Options

If you decide against using the full Pearson Network Simulator, you still need hands-on experience. You should plan to use some lab environment to practice as much CLI as possible.

First, you can use real Cisco routers and switches. You can buy them, new or used, or borrow them at work. You can rent them for a fee. If you have the right mix of gear, you could even do the Config Lab exercises from my blog on that gear or try to re-create examples from the book.

Cisco also makes a simulator that works very well as a learning tool: Cisco Packet Tracer. Cisco now makes Packet Tracer available for free. However, unlike the Pearson Network Simulator, it does not include lab exercises that direct you as to how to go about learning each topic. If interested in more information about Packet Tracer, check out my series about using Packet Tracer at my blog (blog.certskills.com); just search for "Packet Tracer."

Cisco offers a virtualization product that lets you run router and switch operating system (OS) images in a virtual environment. This tool, the Virtual Internet Routing Lab (VIRL), lets you create a lab topology, start the topology, and connect to real router and switch OS images. Check out http://virl.cisco.com for more information.

You can even rent virtual Cisco router and switch lab pods from Cisco, in an offering called Cisco Learning Labs (https://learningnetworkstore.cisco.com/cisco-learning-labs).

This book does not tell you what option to use, but you should plan on getting some hands-on practice somehow. The important thing to know is that most people need to practice using the Cisco CLI to be ready to pass these exams.

For More Information

If you have any comments about the book, submit them via www.ciscopress.com. Just go to the website, select **Contact Us**, and type your message.

Cisco might make changes that affect the CCNA certification from time to time. You should always check www.cisco.com/go/ccna for the latest details.

The *CCNA 200-301 Official Cert Guide, Volume 1*, helps you attain CCNA certification. This is the CCNA certification book from the only Cisco-authorized publisher. We at Cisco Press believe that this book certainly can help you achieve CCNA certification, but the real work is up to you! I trust that your time will be well spent.

Your Study Plan

You just got this book. You have probably already read (or quickly skimmed) the Introduction. You are probably now wondering whether to start reading here or skip ahead to Chapter 1, "Introduction to TCP/IP Networking."

Stop to read this section about how to create your own study plan for the CCNA 200-301 exam. Your study will go much better if you take time (maybe 15 minutes) to think about a few key points about how to study before starting on this journey. That is what this section will help you do.

A Brief Perspective on Cisco Certification Exams

Cisco sets the bar pretty high for passing the CCNA 200-301 exam. Most anyone can study and pass the exam, but it takes more than just a quick read through the book and the cash to pay for the exam.

The challenge of the exam comes from many angles. First, the exam covers a lot of concepts and many commands specific to Cisco devices. Beyond knowledge, all these Cisco exams also require deep skills. You must be able to analyze and predict what really happens in a network, and you must be able to configure Cisco devices to work correctly in those networks.

The more challenging questions on these exams work a lot like a jigsaw puzzle, but with four out of every five puzzle pieces not even in the room. To solve the puzzle, you have to mentally re-create the missing pieces. To do that, you must know each networking concept and remember how the concepts work together.

For instance, you might encounter a question that asks you why two routers cannot exchange routing information using the OSPF routing protocol. The question would supply some of the information, like some pieces of the jigsaw puzzle, as represented with the white pieces in Figure 1. You have to apply your knowledge of IPv4 routing, IPv4 addressing, and the OSPF protocol to the scenario in the question to come up with some of the other pieces of the puzzle. For a given question, some pieces of the puzzle might remain a mystery, but with enough of the puzzle filled in, you should be able to answer the question. And some pieces will just remain unknown for a given question.

These skills require that you prepare by doing more than just reading and memorizing. Of course, you need to read many pages in this book to learn many individual facts and how these facts relate to each other. But a big part of this book lists exercises that require more than just simply reading, exercises that help you build the skills to solve these networking puzzles.

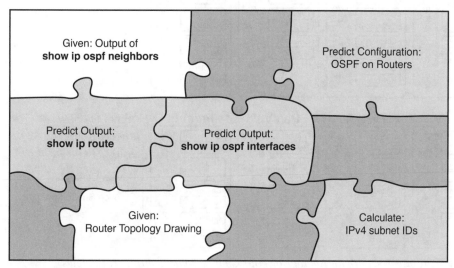

Figure 1 *Filling In Puzzle Pieces with Your Analysis Skills*

Five Study Plan Steps

What do you need to do to be ready to pass, beyond reading and remembering all the facts? You need to develop skills. You need to mentally link each idea with other related ideas. Doing that requires additional work. To help you along the way, the next few pages give you five key planning steps to take so that you can more effectively build those skills and make those connections, before you dive into this exciting but challenging world of learning networking on Cisco gear.

Step 1: Think in Terms of Parts and Chapters

The first step in your study plan is to get the right mindset about the size and nature of the task you have set out to accomplish. This is a large book, and to be ready for the CCNA 200-301 exam, you need to complete it and then the *CCNA 200-301 Official Cert Guide, Volume 2*. You cannot think about these two books as one huge task, or you might get discouraged. So break the task down into smaller tasks.

The good news here is that the book is designed with obvious breakpoints and built-in extensive review activities. In short, the book is more of a study system than a book.

The first step in your study plan is to visualize this book not as one large book but as components. First, visualize the book as eight smaller parts. Then, within each part, visualize each part as three or four chapters. Your study plan has you working through the chapters in each part and then reviewing the material in that part before moving on, as shown in Figure 2.

Now your plan has the following:

1 large task: Read and master all content in the book.

8 medium tasks/book: Read and master a part.

4 small tasks/part: Read and master a chapter.

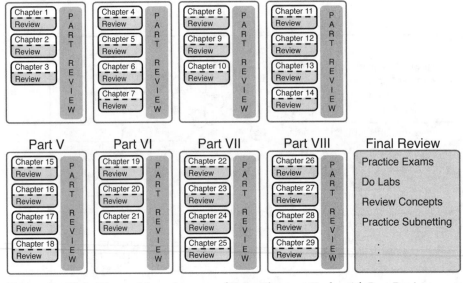

Figure 2   *Eight Parts, with an Average of Four Chapters Each, with Part Reviews*

Step 2: Build Your Study Habits Around the Chapter

For your second step, possibly the most important step, approach each chapter with the same process as shown in Figure 3. The chapter pre-quiz (called a DIKTA quiz, or "Do I Know This Already?" quiz) helps you decide how much time to spend reading versus skimming the core of the chapter, called the "Foundation Topics." The "Chapter Review" section then gives you instructions about how to study and review what you just read.

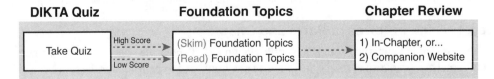

Figure 3   *Suggested Approach to Each Chapter*

The book has no long chapters, on purpose. They average about 20 pages for the Foundation Topics (which is the part of the chapter with new content). Because we kept the size reasonable, you can complete all of a chapter in one or two short study sessions. For instance, when you begin a new chapter, if you have an hour or an hour and a half, you should be able to complete a first reading of the chapter and at least make a great start on it. And even if you do not have enough time to read the entire chapter, look for the major headings inside the chapter; each chapter has two to three major headings, and those make a great place to stop reading when you need to wait to complete the reading in the next study sessions.

The Chapter Review tasks are very important to your exam-day success. Doing these tasks after you've read the chapter really does help you get ready. Do not put off using these tasks until later! The chapter-ending review tasks help you with the first phase of deepening your knowledge and skills of the key topics, remembering terms, and linking the concepts together in your brain so that you can remember how it all fits together. The following list describes most of the activities you will find in the "Chapter Review" sections:

- Review key topics
- Review key terms
- Answer the DIKTA questions
- Re-create config checklists
- Review command tables
- Review memory tables
- Do lab exercises
- Watch video
- Do subnetting exercises

Step 3: Use Book Parts for Major Milestones

Studies show that to master a concept and/or skill, you should plan to go through multiple study sessions to review the concept and to practice the skill. The "Chapter Review" section at the end of each chapter is the first such review, while the Part Review, at the end of each part, acts as that second review.

Plan time to do the Part Review task at the end of each part, using the Part Review elements found at the end of each part. You should expect to spend about as much time on one Part Review as you would on one entire chapter. So in terms of planning your time, think of the Part Review itself as another chapter.

Figure 4 lists the names of the parts in this book, with some color coding. Note that Parts II and III are related (Ethernet), and Parts IV through VII are also related (IP version 4 and IP Version 6). Each part ends with a Part Review section of two to four pages, with notes about what tools and activities to use.

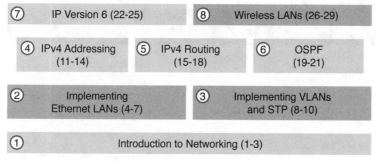

Figure 4 *Parts as Major Milestones*

Also, consider setting a goal date for finishing each part of the book (and a reward, as well). Plan a break, some family time, some time out exercising, eating some good food, whatever helps you get refreshed and motivated for the next part.

Step 4: Use Volume 2's Final Review Chapter

Your fourth step has one overall task: perform the details outlined in the "Final Exam Review" chapter at the end of the *CCNA 200-301 Official Cert Guide, Volume 2*. Note that you have no exam to take at the end of this Volume 1 book, so keep working with Volume 2 when you complete this book. Once you're finished with both books, Volume 2's "Final Exam Review" will direct you.

Step 5: Set Goals and Track Your Progress

Your fifth study plan step spans the entire timeline of your study effort. Before you start reading the book and doing the rest of these study tasks, take the time to make a plan, set some goals, and be ready to track your progress.

While making lists of tasks may or may not appeal to you, depending on your personality, goal setting can help everyone studying for these exams. And to do the goal setting, you need to know what tasks you plan to do.

> **NOTE**   If you read this, and decide that you want to try to do better with goal setting beyond your exam study, check out a blog series I wrote about planning your networking career here: http://blog.certskills.com/tag/development-plan/.

As for the list of tasks to do when studying, you do not have to use a detailed task list. (You could list every single task in every chapter-ending "Chapter Review" section, every task in the Part Reviews, and every task in the "Final Review" chapter.) However, listing the major tasks can be enough.

You should track at least two tasks for each typical chapter: reading the "Foundation Topics" section and doing the Chapter Review at the end of the chapter. And, of course, do not forget to list tasks for Part Reviews and Final Review. Table 1 shows a sample for Part I of this book.

Table 1   Sample Excerpt from a Planning Table

Element	Task	Goal Date	First Date Completed	Second Date Completed (Optional)
Chapter 1	Read Foundation Topics			
Chapter 1	Do Chapter Review tasks			
Chapter 2	Read Foundation Topics			
Chapter 2	Do Chapter Review tasks			
Chapter 3	Read Foundation Topics			
Chapter 3	Do Chapter Review tasks			
Part I Review	Do Part Review activities			

> **NOTE** Appendix I, "Study Planner," on the companion website, contains a complete planning checklist like Table 1 for the tasks in this book. This spreadsheet allows you to update and save the file to note your goal dates and the tasks you have completed.

Use your goal dates as a way to manage your study, and not as a way to get discouraged if you miss a date. Pick reasonable dates that you can meet. When setting your goals, think about how fast you read and the length of each chapter's "Foundation Topics" section, as listed in the table of contents. Then, when you finish a task sooner than planned, move up the next few goal dates.

If you miss a few dates, do *not* start skipping the tasks listed at the ends of the chapters! Instead, think about what is impacting your schedule—real life, commitment, and so on—and either adjust your goals or work a little harder on your study.

Things to Do Before Starting the First Chapter

Now that you understand the big ideas behind a good study plan for the book, take a few more minutes for a few overhead actions that will help. Before leaving this section, look at some other tasks you should do either now or around the time you are reading the first few chapters to help make a good start in the book.

Bookmark the Companion Website

The companion website contains links to all the tools you need for chapter and part review. In fact, it includes a chapter-by-chapter and part-by-part breakdown of all the review activities. Before you finish the first chapter, make sure and follow the instructions in the Introduction's section titled "The Companion Website for Online Content Review," get access, and bookmark the page.

Also, if you did not yet read about the companion website in the Introduction or explore the site, take a few minutes to look at the resources available on the site.

Bookmark/Install Pearson Test Prep

This book, like many other Cisco Press books, includes the rights to use the Pearson Test Prep (PTP) software, along with rights to use some exam questions related to this book. PTP has many useful study features:

- Both a web and desktop version for your convenience and choice
- History tracking of your simulated exam attempts, synchronized between web and desktop
- Study mode, which lets you see the correct answers with each question and the related explanations
- Practice exam mode, which simulates exam conditions, hiding answers/explanations and timing the exam event
- Filters to let you choose questions based on chapter(s) and/or part(s)

You should take a few minutes to set up your PTP installation. Refer to the section titled "How to Access the Pearson Test Prep (PTP) App" in the Introduction for details.

Understand This Book's PTP Databases and Modes

When you activate a product in PTP, you gain the rights to that product's exams. Understanding those exams helps you choose when to use them and when to delay using different exams to save those questions for later. The retail version of this book comes with four exams, as shown in Figure 5; the premium edition adds exams 3 and 4, which are similar in purpose to exams 1 and 2.

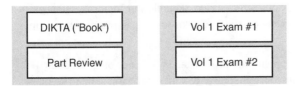

Figure 5 *PTP Exams/Exam Databases and When to Use Them*

When using PTP, you can choose to use any of these exam databases at any time, both in study mode and practice exam mode. However, many people find it best to avoid using some exams until you do your final exam review at the end of reading the *CCNA 200-301 Official Cert Guide, Volume 2*. So, consider using this plan:

■ During Chapter Review, use PTP to review the DIKTA questions for that chapter, using study mode.

■ During Part Review, use the questions built specifically for Part Review (the Part Review questions) for that part of the book, using study mode.

■ Save the remaining exams to use with the "Final Review" chapter at the end of the Volume 2 book.

Alternatively, use exams 1 and 2 at any time during your study, and consider buying the premium edition of the book to add two more exams. For instance, you could review each chapter by answering the questions from that chapter in exams 1 and 2, and wait to use exams 3 and 4 until your final exam review at the end of Volume 2.

NOTE The *CCNA 200-301 Official Cert Guide, Volume 2*, includes several CCNA exams as well—exams that include questions from Volume 1 and Volume 2. You can use those exams during final review to practice simulated CCNA 200-301 exams.

Additionally, take the time to experiment with the study modes in the PTP applications:

Study mode: Study mode works best when you are still working on understanding and learning the content. In study mode, you can see the answers immediately, so you can study the topics more easily.

Practice mode: This mode lets you practice an exam event somewhat like the actual exam. It gives you a preset number of questions, from all chapters, with a timed event. Practice exam mode also gives you a score for that timed event.

Practice Viewing Per-Chapter DIKTA Questions

Take a few minutes to experiment with and understand how to use PTP to answer questions from a single chapter's DIKTA quiz, as follows:

Step 1.   Start the PTP web or desktop app.

Step 2.   From the main (home) menu, select the item for this product, with a name like *CCNA 200-301 Official Cert Guide, Volume 1*, and click **Open Exam**.

Step 3.   The top of the next window that appears should list some exams. Check the **Book Questions** box, and uncheck the other boxes. This selects the "book" questions (that is, the DIKTA questions from the beginning of each chapter).

Step 4.   On this same window, click at the bottom of the screen to deselect all objectives (chapters). Then select the box beside each chapter in the part of the book you are reviewing.

Step 5.   Select any other options on the right side of the window.

Step 6.   Click **Start** to start reviewing the questions.

Practice Viewing Per-Part Review Questions

Your PTP access also includes a Part Review exam created solely for study during the Part Review process. To view these questions, follow the same process as you did with DIKTA/book questions, but select the Part Review database rather than the book database. PTP has a clear name for this database: Part Review Questions.

Join the Cisco Learning Network CCNA Study Group

Register (for free) at the Cisco Learning Network (CLN, http://learningnetwork.cisco.com) and join the CCNA study group. This group allows you to both lurk and participate in discussions about topics related to the CCNA exam. Register (for free), join the groups, and set up an email filter to redirect the messages to a separate folder. Even if you do not spend time reading all the posts yet, later, when you have time to read, you can browse through the posts to find interesting topics (or just search the posts from the CLN website).

Getting Started: Now

Now dive in to your first of many short, manageable tasks: reading the relatively short Chapter 1. Enjoy!

This first part of the book introduces the fundamentals of the most important topics in TCP/IP networking. Chapter 1 provides a broad look at TCP/IP, introducing the common terms, big concepts, and major protocols for TCP/IP. Chapter 2 then examines local-area networks (LAN), which are networks that connect devices that are located near each other; for instance, in the same building. Chapter 3 then shows how to connect those LANs across long distances with wide-area networks (WAN) with a focus on how routers connect LANs and WANs to forward data between any two devices in the network.

Part I

Introduction to Networking

Introduction to TCP/IP Networking

This chapter covers the following exam topics:

1.0 Network Fundamentals

1.3 Compare physical interface and cabling types

1.3.a Single-mode fiber, multimode fiber, copper

1.3.b Connections (Ethernet shared media and point-to-point)

Welcome to the first chapter in your study for CCNA! This chapter begins Part I, which focuses on the basics of networking.

Networks work correctly because the various devices and software follow the rules. Those rules come in the form of standards and protocols, which are agreements of a particular part of how a network should work. However, the sheer number of standards and protocols available can make it difficult for the average network engineer to think about and work with networks—so the world of networking has used several networking models over time. Networking models define a structure and different categories (layers) of standards and protocols. As new standards and protocols emerge over time, networkers can think of those new details in the context of a working model.

You can think of a networking model as you think of a set of architectural plans for building a house. A lot of different people work on building your house, such as framers, electricians, bricklayers, painters, and so on. The blueprint helps ensure that all the different pieces of the house work together as a whole. Similarly, the people who make networking products, and the people who use those products to build their own computer networks, follow a particular networking model. That networking model defines rules about how each part of the network should work, as well as how the parts should work together so that the entire network functions correctly.

Today, TCP/IP rules as the most pervasive networking model in use. You can find support for TCP/IP on practically every computer operating system (OS) in existence today, from mobile phones to mainframe computers. Every network built using Cisco products today supports TCP/IP. And not surprisingly, the CCNA exam focuses heavily on TCP/IP. This chapter uses TCP/IP for one of its main purposes: to present various concepts about networking using the context of the different roles and functions in the TCP/IP model.

"Do I Know This Already?" Quiz

Take the quiz (either here or use the PTP software) if you want to use the score to help you decide how much time to spend on this chapter. The letter answers are listed at the bottom of the page following the quiz. Appendix C, found both at the end of the book as well as on the companion website, includes both the answers and explanations. You can also find both answers and explanations in the PTP testing software.

Table 1-1 "Do I Know This Already?" Foundation Topics Section-to-Question Mapping

Foundation Topics Section	Questions
Perspectives on Networking	None
TCP/IP Networking Model	1–4
Data Encapsulation Terminology	5–7

1. Which of the following protocols are examples of TCP/IP transport layer protocols? (Choose two answers.)

   a. Ethernet

   b. HTTP

   c. IP

   d. UDP

   e. SMTP

   f. TCP

2. Which of the following protocols are examples of TCP/IP data-link layer protocols? (Choose two answers.)

   a. Ethernet

   b. HTTP

   c. IP

   d. UDP

   e. SMTP

   f. TCP

   g. PPP

3. The process of HTTP asking TCP to send some data and making sure that it is received correctly is an example of what?

   a. Same-layer interaction

   b. Adjacent-layer interaction

   c. OSI model

   d. All of these answers are correct.

4. The process of TCP on one computer marking a TCP segment as segment 1, and the receiving computer then acknowledging the receipt of TCP segment 1 is an example of what?

   a. Data encapsulation

   b. Same-layer interaction

   c. Adjacent-layer interaction

   d. OSI model

   e. All of these answers are correct.

5. The process of a web server adding a TCP header to the contents of a web page, followed by adding an IP header and then adding a data-link header and trailer, is an
   example of what?

   a. Data encapsulation

   b. Same-layer interaction

   c. OSI model

   d. All of these answers are correct.

6. Which of the following terms is used specifically to identify the entity created when
   encapsulating data inside data-link layer headers and trailers?

   a. Data

   b. Chunk

   c. Segment

   d. Frame

   e. Packet

7. Which OSI encapsulation term can be used instead of the term frame?

   a. Layer 1 PDU

   b. Layer 2 PDU

   c. Layer 3 PDU

   d. Layer 5 PDU

   e. Layer 7 PDU

Foundation Topics

Perspectives on Networking

So, you are new to networking. Like many people, your perspective about networks might
be that of a user of the network, as opposed to the network engineer who builds networks.
For some, your view of networking might be based on how you use the Internet, from home,
using a high-speed Internet connection like digital subscriber line (DSL) or cable TV, as
shown in Figure 1-1.

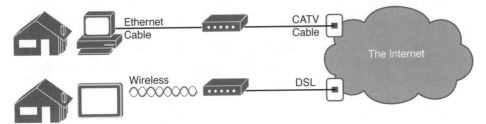

Figure 1-1 *End-User Perspective on High-Speed Internet Connections*

The top part of the figure shows a typical high-speed cable Internet user. The PC connects to a cable modem using an Ethernet cable. The cable modem then connects to a cable TV (CATV) outlet in the wall using a round coaxial cable—the same kind of cable used to connect your TV to the CATV wall outlet. Because cable Internet services provide service continuously, the user can just sit down at the PC and start sending email, browsing websites, making Internet phone calls, and using other tools and applications.

The lower part of the figure uses two different technologies. First, the tablet computer uses wireless technology that goes by the name wireless local-area network (wireless LAN), or Wi-Fi, instead of using an Ethernet cable. In this example, the router uses a different technology, DSL, to communicate with the Internet.

Both home-based networks and networks built for use by a company make use of similar networking technologies. The Information Technology (IT) world refers to a network created by one corporation, or enterprise, for the purpose of allowing its employees to communicate, as an *enterprise network*. The smaller networks at home, when used for business purposes, often go by the name small office/home office (SOHO) networks.

Users of enterprise networks have some idea about the enterprise network at their company or school. People realize that they use a network for many tasks. PC users might realize that their PC connects through an Ethernet cable to a matching wall outlet, as shown at the top of Figure 1-2. Those same users might use wireless LANs with their laptop when going to a meeting in the conference room as well. Figure 1-2 shows these two end-user perspectives on an enterprise network.

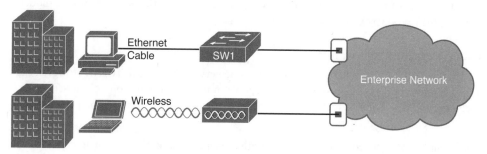

Figure 1-2   *Example Representation of an Enterprise Network*

NOTE   In networking diagrams, a cloud represents a part of a network whose details are not important to the purpose of the diagram. In this case, Figure 1-2 ignores the details of how to create an enterprise network.

Some users might not even have a concept of the network at all. Instead, these users just enjoy the functions of the network—the ability to post messages to social media sites, make phone calls, search for information on the Internet, listen to music, and download countless apps to their phones—without caring about how it works or how their favorite device connects to the network.

Regardless of how much you already know about how networks work, this book and the related certification help you learn how networks do their job. That job is simply this: moving data from one device to another. The rest of this chapter, and the rest of this first part of the book, reveals the basics of how to build enterprise networks so that they can deliver data between two devices.

TCP/IP Networking Model

A *networking model*, sometimes also called either a *networking architecture* or *networking blueprint*, refers to a comprehensive set of documents. Individually, each document describes one small function required for a network; collectively, these documents define everything that should happen for a computer network to work. Some documents define a *protocol*, which is a set of logical rules that devices must follow to communicate. Other documents define some physical requirements for networking. For example, a document could define the voltage and current levels used on a particular cable when transmitting data.

You can think of a networking model as you think of an architectural blueprint for building a house. Sure, you can build a house without the blueprint. However, the blueprint can ensure that the house has the right foundation and structure so that it will not fall down, and it has the correct hidden spaces to accommodate the plumbing, electrical, gas, and so on. Also, the many different people that build the house using the blueprint—such as framers, electricians, bricklayers, painters, and so on—know that if they follow the blueprint, their part of the work should not cause problems for the other workers.

Similarly, you could build your own network—write your own software, build your own networking cards, and so on—to create a network. However, it is much easier to simply buy and use products that already conform to some well-known networking model or blueprint. Because the networking product vendors build their products with some networking model in mind, their products should work well together.

History Leading to TCP/IP

Today, the world of computer networking uses one networking model: TCP/IP. However, the world has not always been so simple. Once upon a time, networking protocols didn't exist, including TCP/IP. Vendors created the first networking protocols; these protocols supported only that vendor's computers.

For example, IBM, the computer company with the largest market share in many markets back in the 1970s and 1980s, published its Systems Network Architecture (SNA) networking model in 1974. Other vendors also created their own proprietary networking models. As a result, if your company bought computers from three vendors, network engineers often had to create three different networks based on the networking models created by each company, and then somehow connect those networks, making the combined networks much more complex. The left side of Figure 1-3 shows the general idea of what a company's enterprise network might have looked like back in the 1980s, before TCP/IP became common in enterprise internetworks.

Answers to the "Do I Know This Already?" quiz:

1 D and F **2** A and G **3** B **4** B **5** A **6** D **7** B

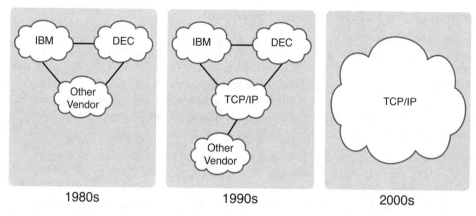

Figure 1-3 *Historical Progression: Proprietary Models to the Open TCP/IP Model*

Although vendor-defined proprietary networking models often worked well, having an open, vendor-neutral networking model would aid competition and reduce complexity. The International Organization for Standardization (ISO) took on the task to create such a model, starting as early as the late 1970s, beginning work on what would become known as the Open Systems Interconnection (OSI) networking model. ISO had a noble goal for the OSI model: to standardize data networking protocols to allow communication among all computers across the entire planet. ISO worked toward this ambitious and noble goal, with participants from most of the technologically developed nations on Earth participating in the process.

A second, less-formal effort to create an open, vendor-neutral, public networking model sprouted forth from a U.S. Department of Defense (DoD) contract. Researchers at various universities volunteered to help further develop the protocols surrounding the original DoD work. These efforts resulted in a competing open networking model called TCP/IP.

During the 1990s, companies began adding OSI, TCP/IP, or both to their enterprise networks. However, by the end of the 1990s, TCP/IP had become the common choice, and OSI fell away. The center part of Figure 1-3 shows the general idea behind enterprise networks in that decade—still with networks built upon multiple networking models but including TCP/IP.

Here in the twenty-first century, TCP/IP dominates. Proprietary networking models still exist, but they have mostly been discarded in favor of TCP/IP. The OSI model, whose development suffered in part because of a slower formal standardization process as compared with TCP/IP, never succeeded in the marketplace. And TCP/IP, the networking model originally created almost entirely by a bunch of volunteers, has become the most prolific network model ever, as shown on the right side of Figure 1-3.

In this chapter, you will read about some of the basics of TCP/IP. Although you will learn some interesting facts about TCP/IP, the true goal of this chapter is to help you understand what a networking model or networking architecture really is and how it works.

Also in this chapter, you will learn about some of the jargon used with OSI. Will any of you ever work on a computer that is using the full OSI protocols instead of TCP/IP? Probably not. However, you will often use terms relating to OSI.

Overview of the TCP/IP Networking Model

The TCP/IP model both defines and references a large collection of protocols that allow computers to communicate. To define a protocol, TCP/IP uses documents called *Requests For Comments* (RFC). (You can find these RFCs using any online search engine.) The TCP/IP model also avoids repeating work already done by some other standards body or vendor consortium by simply referring to standards or protocols created by those groups. For example, the Institute of Electrical and Electronic Engineers (IEEE) defines Ethernet LANs; the TCP/IP model does not define Ethernet in RFCs, but refers to IEEE Ethernet as an option.

The TCP/IP model creates a set of rules that allows us all to take a computer (or mobile device) out of the box, plug in all the right cables, turn it on, and connect to and use the network. You can use a web browser to connect to your favorite website, use most any app, and it all works. How? Well, the OS on the computer implements parts of the TCP/IP model. The Ethernet card, or wireless LAN card, built in to the computer implements some LAN standards referenced by the TCP/IP model. In short, the vendors that created the hardware and software implemented TCP/IP.

To help people understand a networking model, each model breaks the functions into a small number of categories called *layers*. Each layer includes protocols and standards that relate to that category of functions, as shown in Figure 1-4.

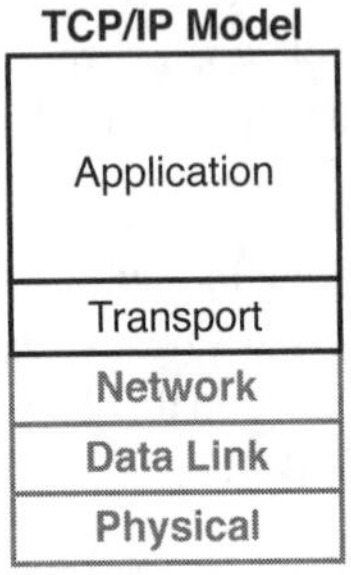

TCP/IP Model

Application
Transport
Network
Data Link
Physical

Figure 1-4   *The TCP/IP Networking Models*

The TCP/IP model shows the more common terms and layers used when people talk about TCP/IP today. The bottom layer focuses on how to transmit bits over each individual link. The data-link layer focuses on sending data over one type of physical link: for instance, networks use different data-link protocols for Ethernet LANs versus wireless LANs. The network layer focuses on delivering data over the entire path from the original sending computer to the final destination computer. And the top two layers focus more on the applications that need to send and receive data.

> **NOTE**   A slightly different four-layer original version of the TCP/IP model exists in RFC 1122, but for the purposes of both real networking and for today's CCNA, use the five-layer model shown here in Figure 1-4.

Many of you will have already heard of several TCP/IP protocols, like the examples listed in Table 1-2. Most of the protocols and standards in this table will be explained in more detail as you work through this book. Following the table, this section takes a closer look at the layers of the TCP/IP model.

Table 1-2   TCP/IP Architectural Model and Example Protocols

TCP/IP Architecture Layer	Example Protocols
Application	HTTP, POP3, SMTP
Transport	TCP, UDP
Internet	IP, ICMP
Data Link & Physical	Ethernet, 802.11 (Wi-Fi)

TCP/IP Application Layer

TCP/IP application layer protocols provide services to the application software running on a computer. The application layer does not define the application itself, but it defines services that applications need. For example, application protocol HTTP defines how web browsers can pull the contents of a web page from a web server. In short, the application layer provides an interface between software running on a computer and the network itself.

Arguably, the most popular TCP/IP application today is the web browser. Many major software vendors either have already changed or are changing their application software to support access from a web browser. And thankfully, using a web browser is easy: You start a web browser on your computer and select a website by typing the name of the website, and the web page appears.

HTTP Overview

What really happens to allow that web page to appear on your web browser?

Imagine that Bob opens his browser. His browser has been configured to automatically ask for web server Larry's default web page, or *home page*. The general logic looks like Figure 1-5.

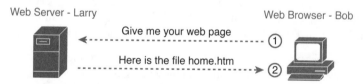

Figure 1-5   *Basic Application Logic to Get a Web Page*

So, what really happened? Bob's initial request actually asks Larry to send his home page back to Bob. Larry's web server software has been configured to know that the default web page is contained in a file called home.htm. Bob receives the file from Larry and displays the contents of the file in Bob's web browser window.

HTTP Protocol Mechanisms

Taking a closer look, this example shows how applications on each endpoint computer—specifically, the web browser application and web server application—use a TCP/IP application layer protocol. To make the request for a web page and return the contents of the web page, the applications use the Hypertext Transfer Protocol (HTTP).

HTTP did not exist until Tim Berners-Lee created the first web browser and web server in the early 1990s. Berners-Lee gave HTTP functionality to ask for the contents of web pages, specifically by giving the web browser the ability to request files from the server and giving the server a way to return the content of those files. The overall logic matches what was shown in Figure 1-5; Figure 1-6 shows the same idea, but with details specific to HTTP.

NOTE   The full version of most web addresses—also called Uniform Resource Locators (URL) or Universal Resource Identifiers (URI)—begins with the letters *http*, which means that HTTP is used to transfer the web pages.

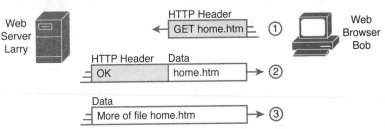

Figure 1-6   *HTTP GET Request, HTTP Reply, and One Data-Only Message*

To get the web page from Larry, at Step 1, Bob sends a message with an HTTP header. Generally, protocols use headers as a place to put information used by that protocol. This HTTP header includes the request to "get" a file. The request typically contains the name of the file (home.htm, in this case), or if no filename is mentioned, the web server assumes that Bob wants the default web page.

Step 2 in Figure 1-6 shows the response from web server Larry. The message begins with an HTTP header, with a return code (200), which means something as simple as "OK" returned in the header. HTTP also defines other return codes so that the server can tell the browser whether the request worked. (Here is another example: If you ever looked for a web page that was not found, and then received an HTTP 404 "not found" error, you received an HTTP return code of 404.) The second message also includes the first part of the requested file.

Step 3 in Figure 1-6 shows another message from web server Larry to web browser Bob, but this time without an HTTP header. HTTP transfers the data by sending multiple messages, each with a part of the file. Rather than wasting space by sending repeated HTTP headers that list the same information, these additional messages simply omit the header.

TCP/IP Transport Layer

Although many TCP/IP application layer protocols exist, the TCP/IP transport layer includes a smaller number of protocols. The two most commonly used transport layer protocols are the Transmission Control Protocol (TCP) and the User Datagram Protocol (UDP).

Transport layer protocols provide services to the application layer protocols that reside one layer higher in the TCP/IP model. How does a transport layer protocol provide a service to a higher-layer protocol? This section introduces that general concept by focusing on a single service provided by TCP: error recovery. The *CCNA 200-301 Official Cert Guide*, Volume 2, includes a chapter, "Introduction to TCP/IP Transport and Applications," which examines the transport layer.

TCP Error Recovery Basics

To appreciate what the transport layer protocols do, you must think about the layer above the transport layer, the application layer. Why? Well, each layer provides a service to the layer above it, like the error-recovery service provided to application layer protocols by TCP.

For example, in Figure 1-5, Bob and Larry used HTTP to transfer the home page from web server Larry to Bob's web browser. But what would have happened if Bob's HTTP GET request had been lost in transit through the TCP/IP network? Or, what would have happened if Larry's response, which included the contents of the home page, had been lost? Well, as you might expect, in either case, the page would not have shown up in Bob's browser.

TCP/IP needs a mechanism to guarantee delivery of data across a network. Because many application layer protocols probably want a way to guarantee delivery of data across a network, the creators of TCP included an error-recovery feature. To recover from errors, TCP uses the concept of acknowledgments. Figure 1-7 outlines the basic idea behind how TCP notices lost data and asks the sender to try again.

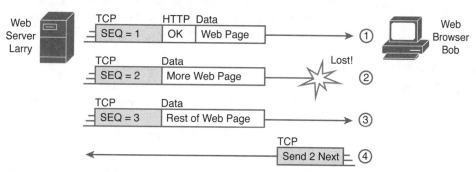

Figure 1-7   *TCP Error-Recovery Services as Provided to HTTP*

Figure 1-7 shows web server Larry sending a web page to web browser Bob, using three separate messages. Note that this figure shows the same HTTP headers as Figure 1-6, but it also shows a TCP header. The TCP header shows a sequence number (SEQ) with each message. In this example, the network has a problem, and the network fails to deliver the TCP message (called a segment) with sequence number 2. When Bob receives messages with sequence numbers 1 and 3, but does not receive a message with sequence number 2, Bob realizes that message 2 was lost. That realization by Bob's TCP logic causes Bob to send a TCP segment back to Larry, asking Larry to send message 2 again.

Same-Layer and Adjacent-Layer Interactions

Figure 1-7 also demonstrates a function called *adjacent-layer interaction*, which refers to the concepts of how adjacent layers in a networking model, on the same computer, work together. In this example, the higher-layer protocol (HTTP) wants error recovery, so it uses the next lower-layer protocol (TCP) to perform the service of error recovery; the lower layer provides a service to the layer above it.

Figure 1-7 also shows an example of a similar function called *same-layer interaction*. When a particular layer on one computer wants to communicate with the same layer on another computer, the two computers use headers to hold the information that they want to communicate. For example, in Figure 1-7, Larry set the sequence numbers to 1, 2, and 3 so that Bob could notice when some of the data did not arrive. Larry's TCP process created that TCP header with the sequence number; Bob's TCP process received and reacted to the TCP segments.

Table 1-3 summarizes the key points about how adjacent layers work together on a single computer and how one layer on one computer works with the same networking layer on another computer.

Table 1-3   Summary: Same-Layer and Adjacent-Layer Interactions

Concept	Description
Same-layer interaction on different computers	The two computers use a protocol to communicate with the same layer on another computer. The protocol defines a header that communicates what each computer wants to do.
Adjacent-layer interaction on the same computer	On a single computer, one lower layer provides a service to the layer just above. The software or hardware that implements the higher layer requests that the next lower layer perform the needed function.

TCP/IP Network Layer

The application layer includes many protocols. The transport layer includes fewer protocols, most notably, TCP and UDP. The TCP/IP network layer includes a small number of protocols, but only one major protocol: the Internet Protocol (IP). In fact, the name TCP/IP is simply the names of the two most common protocols (TCP and IP) separated by a /.

IP provides several features, most importantly, addressing and routing. This section begins by comparing IP's addressing and routing with another commonly known system that uses addressing and routing: the postal service. Following that, this section introduces IP addressing and routing. (More details follow in Chapter 3, "Fundamentals of WANs and IP Routing.")

Internet Protocol and the Postal Service

Imagine that you just wrote two letters: one to a friend on the other side of the country and one to a friend on the other side of town. You addressed the envelopes and put on the stamps, so both are ready to give to the postal service. Is there much difference in how you treat each letter? Not really. Typically, you would just put them in the same mailbox and expect the postal service to deliver both letters.

The postal service, however, must think about each letter separately, and then make a decision of where to send each letter so that it is delivered. For the letter sent across town, the people in the local post office probably just need to put the letter on another truck.

For the letter that needs to go across the country, the postal service sends the letter to another post office, then another, and so on, until the letter gets delivered across the country. At each post office, the postal service must process the letter and choose where to send it next.

To make it all work, the postal service has regular routes for small trucks, large trucks, planes, boats, and so on, to move letters between postal service sites. The service must be able to receive and forward the letters, and it must make good decisions about where to send each letter next, as shown in Figure 1-8.

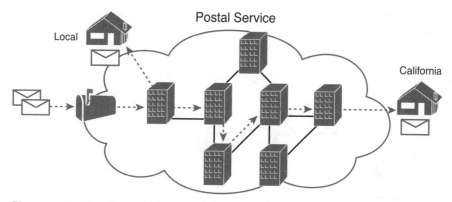

Figure 1-8 *Postal Service Forwarding (Routing) Letters*

Still thinking about the postal service, consider the difference between the person sending the letter and the work that the postal service does. The person sending the letters expects that the postal service will deliver the letter most of the time. However, the person sending the letter does not need to know the details of exactly what path the letters take. In contrast, the postal service does not create the letter, but it accepts the letter from the customer. Then, the postal service must know the details about addresses and postal codes that group addresses into larger groups, and it must have the ability to deliver the letters.

The TCP/IP application and transport layers act like the person sending letters through the postal service. These upper layers work the same way regardless of whether the endpoint host computers are on the same LAN or are separated by the entire Internet. To send a message, these upper layers ask the layer below them, the network layer, to deliver the message.

The lower layers of the TCP/IP model act more like the postal service to deliver those messages to the correct destinations. To do so, these lower layers must understand the underlying physical network because they must choose how to best deliver the data from one host to another.

So, what does this all matter to networking? Well, the network layer of the TCP/IP networking model, primarily defined by the Internet Protocol (IP), works much like the postal service. IP defines that each host computer should have a different IP address, just as the postal service defines addressing that allows unique addresses for each house, apartment, and business. Similarly, IP defines the process of routing so that devices called routers can work like the post office, forwarding packets of data so that they are delivered to the correct destinations. Just as the postal service created the necessary infrastructure to deliver letters—post offices, sorting machines, trucks, planes, and personnel—the network layer defines the details of how a network infrastructure should be created so that the network can deliver data to all computers in the network.

Internet Protocol Addressing Basics

IP defines addresses for several important reasons. First, each device that uses TCP/IP—each TCP/IP *host*—needs a unique address so that it can be identified in the network. IP also defines how to group addresses together, just like the postal system groups addresses based on postal codes (like ZIP codes in the United States).

To understand the basics, examine Figure 1-9, which shows the familiar web server Larry and web browser Bob; but now, instead of ignoring the network between these two computers, part of the network infrastructure is included.

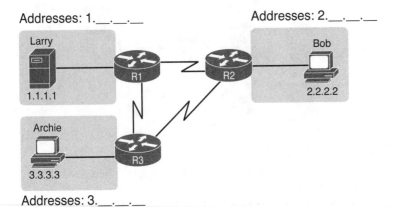

Addresses: 1.__.__.__

Addresses: 2.__.__.__

Addresses: 3.__.__.__

Figure 1-9   *Simple TCP/IP Network: Three Routers with IP Addresses Grouped*

First, note that Figure 1-9 shows some sample IP addresses. Each IP address has four numbers, separated by periods. In this case, Larry uses IP address 1.1.1.1, and Bob uses 2.2.2.2. This style of number is called a dotted-decimal notation (DDN).

Figure 1-9 also shows three groups of addresses. In this example, all IP addresses that begin with 1 must be on the upper left, as shown in shorthand in the figure as 1.__.__.__. All addresses that begin with 2 must be on the right, as shown in shorthand as 2.__.__.__. Finally, all IP addresses that begin with 3 must be at the bottom of the figure.

In addition, Figure 1-9 introduces icons that represent IP routers. Routers are networking devices that connect the parts of the TCP/IP network together for the purpose of routing (forwarding) IP packets to the correct destination. Routers do the equivalent of the work done by each post office site: They receive IP packets on various physical interfaces, make decisions based on the IP address included with the packet, and then physically forward the packet out some other network interface.

IP Routing Basics

The TCP/IP network layer, using the IP protocol, provides a service of forwarding IP packets from one device to another. Any device with an IP address can connect to the TCP/IP network and send packets. This section shows a basic IP routing example for perspective.

> **NOTE**   The term *IP host* refers to any device, regardless of size or power, that has an IP address and connects to any TCP/IP network.

Figure 1-10 repeats the familiar case in which web server Larry wants to send part of a web page to Bob, but now with details related to IP. On the lower left, note that server Larry has the familiar application data, HTTP header, and TCP header ready to send. In addition, the message now contains an IP header. The IP header includes a source IP address of Larry's IP address (1.1.1.1) and a destination IP address of Bob's IP address (2.2.2.2).

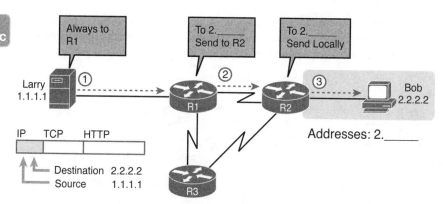

Figure 1-10 *Basic Routing Example*

Step 1, on the left of Figure 1-10, begins with Larry being ready to send an IP packet. Larry's IP process chooses to send the packet to some router—a nearby router on the same LAN—with the expectation that the router will know how to forward the packet. (This logic is much like you or me sending all our letters by putting them in a nearby mailbox.) Larry doesn't need to know anything more about the topology or the other routers.

At Step 2, Router R1 receives the IP packet, and R1's IP process makes a decision. R1 looks at the destination address (2.2.2.2), compares that address to its known IP routes, and chooses to forward the packet to Router R2. This process of forwarding the IP packet is called *IP routing* (or simply *routing*).

At Step 3, Router R2 repeats the same kind of logic used by Router R1. R2's IP process will compare the packet's destination IP address (2.2.2.2) to R2's known IP routes and make a choice to forward the packet to the right, on to Bob.

You will learn IP in more depth than any other protocol while preparing for CCNA. More than half the chapters in this book discuss some feature that relates to addressing, IP routing, and how routers perform routing.

TCP/IP Data-Link and Physical Layers

The TCP/IP model's data-link and physical layers define the protocols and hardware required to deliver data across some physical network. The two work together quite closely; in fact, some standards define both the data-link and physical layer functions. The physical layer defines the cabling and energy (for example, electrical signals) that flow over the cables. Some rules and conventions exist when sending data over the cable; however, those rules exist in the data-link layer of the TCP/IP model.

Focusing on the data-link layer for a moment, just like every layer in any networking model, the TCP/IP data-link layer provides services to the layer above it in the model (the network layer). When a host's or router's IP process chooses to send an IP packet to another router or host, that host or router then uses link-layer details to send that packet to the next host/router.

Because each layer provides a service to the layer above it, take a moment to think about the IP logic related to Figure 1-10. In that example, host Larry's IP logic chooses to send the IP packet to a nearby router (R1). However, while Figure 1-10 shows a simple line between Larry and router R1, that drawing means that some Ethernet LAN sits between the two. Figure 1-11 shows four steps of what occurs at the link layer to allow Larry to send the IP packet to R1.

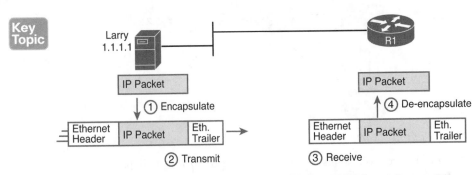

Figure 1-11 *Larry Using Ethernet to Forward an IP Packet to Router R1*

NOTE Figure 1-11 depicts the Ethernet as a series of lines. Networking diagrams often use this convention when drawing Ethernet LANs, in cases where the actual LAN cabling and LAN devices are not important to some discussion, as is the case here. The LAN would have cables and devices, like LAN switches, which are not shown in this figure.

Figure 1-11 shows four steps. The first two occur on Larry, and the last two occur on Router R1, as follows:

Step 1. Larry encapsulates the IP packet between an Ethernet header and Ethernet trailer, creating an Ethernet *frame*.

Step 2. Larry physically transmits the bits of this Ethernet frame, using electricity flowing over the Ethernet cabling.

Step 3. Router R1 physically receives the electrical signal over a cable and re-creates the same bits by interpreting the meaning of the electrical signals.

Step 4. Router R1 de-encapsulates the IP packet from the Ethernet frame by removing and discarding the Ethernet header and trailer.

By the end of this process, Larry and R1 have worked together to deliver the packet from Larry to Router R1.

NOTE Protocols define both headers and trailers for the same general reason, but headers exist at the beginning of the message and trailers exist at the end.

The data-link and physical layers include a large number of protocols and standards. For example, the link layer includes all the variations of Ethernet protocols and wireless LAN protocols discussed throughout this book.

In short, the TCP/IP physical and data-link layers include two distinct functions, respectively: functions related to the physical transmission of the data, plus the protocols and rules that control the use of the physical media.

Data Encapsulation Terminology

As you can see from the explanations of how HTTP, TCP, IP, and Ethernet do their jobs, when sending data, each layer adds its own header (and for data-link protocols, also a trailer) to the data supplied by the higher layer. The term *encapsulation* refers to the process of putting headers (and sometimes trailers) around some data.

Many of the examples in this chapter show the encapsulation process. For example, web server Larry encapsulated the contents of the home page inside an HTTP header in Figure 1-6. The TCP layer encapsulated the HTTP headers and data inside a TCP header in Figure 1-7. IP encapsulated the TCP headers and the data inside an IP header in Figure 1-10. Finally, the Ethernet link layer encapsulated the IP packets inside both a header and a trailer in Figure 1-11.

The process by which a TCP/IP host sends data can be viewed as a five-step process. The first four steps relate to the encapsulation performed by the four TCP/IP layers, and the last step is the actual physical transmission of the data by the host. In fact, if you use the five-layer TCP/IP model, one step corresponds to the role of each layer. The steps are summarized in the following list:

Step 1.   **Create and encapsulate the application data with any required application layer headers.** For example, the HTTP OK message can be returned in an HTTP header, followed by part of the contents of a web page.

Step 2.   **Encapsulate the data supplied by the application layer inside a transport layer header.** For end-user applications, a TCP or UDP header is typically used.

Step 3.   **Encapsulate the data supplied by the transport layer inside a network layer (IP) header.** IP defines the IP addresses that uniquely identify each computer.

Step 4.   **Encapsulate the data supplied by the network layer inside a data-link layer header and trailer.** This layer uses both a header and a trailer.

Step 5.   **Transmit the bits.** The physical layer encodes a signal onto the medium to transmit the frame.

The numbers in Figure 1-12 correspond to the five steps in this list, graphically showing the same concepts. Note that because the application layer often does not need to add a header, the figure does not show a specific application layer header, but the application layer will also at times add a header as well.

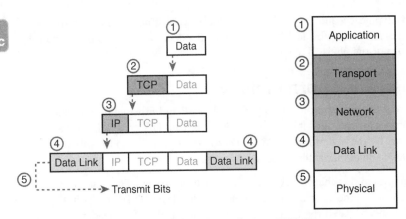

Figure 1-12   *Five Steps of Data Encapsulation: TCP/IP*

Names of TCP/IP Messages

One reason this chapter takes the time to show the encapsulation steps in detail has to do with terminology. When talking and writing about networking, people use *segment*, *packet*, and *frame* to refer to the messages shown in Figure 1-13 and the related list. Each term has a specific meaning, referring to the headers (and possibly trailers) defined by a particular layer and the data encapsulated following that header. Each term, however, refers to a different layer: segment for the transport layer, packet for the network layer, and frame for the link layer. Figure 1-13 shows each layer along with the associated term.

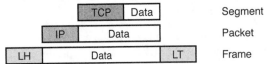

Figure 1-13   *Perspectives on Encapsulation and "Data"**

* The letters LH and LT stand for link header and link trailer, respectively, and refer to the data-link layer header and trailer.

Figure 1-13 also shows the encapsulated data as simply "data." When focusing on the work done by a particular layer, the encapsulated data typically is unimportant. For example, an IP packet can indeed have a TCP header after the IP header, an HTTP header after the TCP header, and data for a web page after the HTTP header. However, when discussing IP, you probably just care about the IP header, so everything after the IP header is just called data. So, when drawing IP packets, everything after the IP header is typically shown simply as data.

OSI Networking Model and Terminology

At one point in the history of the OSI model, many people thought that OSI would win the battle of the networking models discussed earlier. If that had occurred, instead of running TCP/IP on every computer in the world, those computers would be running with OSI.

However, OSI did not win that battle. In fact, OSI no longer exists as a networking model that could be used instead of TCP/IP, although some of the original protocols referenced by the OSI model still exist.

So, why is OSI even in this book? Terminology. During those years in which many people thought the OSI model would become commonplace in the world of networking (mostly in the late 1980s and early 1990s), many vendors and protocol documents started using terminology from the OSI model. That terminology remains today. So, while you will never need to work with a computer that uses OSI, to understand modern networking terminology, you need to understand something about OSI.

Comparing OSI and TCP/IP Layer Names and Numbers

The OSI model has many similarities to the TCP/IP model from a basic conceptual perspective. It has layers, and each layer defines a set of typical networking functions. As with TCP/IP, the OSI layers each refer to multiple protocols and standards that implement the functions specified by each layer. In other cases, just as for TCP/IP, the OSI committees did not create new protocols or standards, but instead referenced other protocols that were already defined. For example, the IEEE defines Ethernet standards, so the OSI committees did not waste time specifying a new type of Ethernet; it simply referred to the IEEE Ethernet standards.

Today, the OSI model can be used as a standard of comparison to other networking models. Figure 1-14 compares the seven-layer OSI model with both the four-layer and five-layer TCP/IP models.

	OSI		TCP/IP
7	Application		
6	Presentation	5 - 7	Application
5	Session		
4	Transport	4	Transport
3	Network	3	Network
2	Data Link	2	Data Link
1	Physical	1	Physical

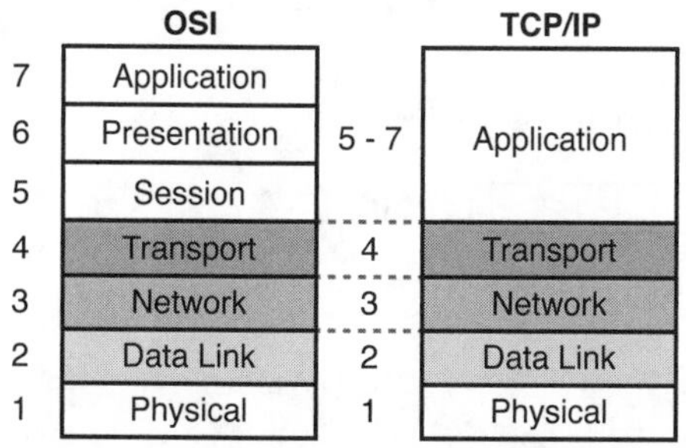

Figure 1-14 *OSI Model Compared to the Two TCP/IP Models*

Note that the TCP/IP model in use today, on the right side of the figure, uses the exact same layer names as OSI at the lower layers. The functions generally match as well, so for the purpose of discussing networking, and reading networking documentation, think of the bottom four layers as equivalent, in name, in number, and in meaning.

Even though the world uses TCP/IP today rather than OSI, we tend to use the numbering from the OSI layer. For instance, when referring to an application layer protocol in a TCP/IP network, the world still refers to the protocol as a "Layer 7 protocol." Also, while TCP/IP includes more functions at its application layer, OSI breaks those intro session, presentation, and application layers. Most of the time, no one cares much about the distinction, so you will see references like "Layer 5–7 protocol," again using OSI numbering.

For the purposes of this book, know the mapping between the five-layer TCP/IP model and the seven-layer OSI model shown in Figure 1-14, and know that layer number references to Layer 7 really do match the application layer of TCP/IP as well.

OSI Data Encapsulation Terminology

Like TCP/IP, each OSI layer asks for services from the next lower layer. To provide the services, each layer makes use of a header and possibly a trailer. The lower layer encapsulates the higher layer's data behind a header.

OSI uses a more generic term to refer to messages, rather than frame, packet, and segment. OSI uses the term *protocol data unit* (PDU). A PDU represents the bits that include the headers and trailers for that layer, as well as the encapsulated data. For example, an IP packet, as shown in Figure 1-13, using OSI terminology, is a PDU, more specifically a *Layer 3 PDU* (abbreviated L3PDU) because IP is a Layer 3 protocol. OSI simply refers to the Layer *x* PDU (LxPDU), with *x* referring to the number of the layer being discussed, as shown in Figure 1-15.

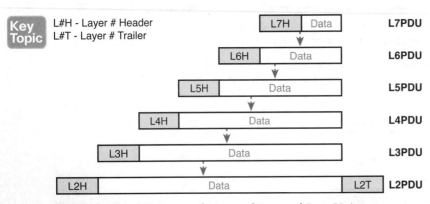

Figure 1-15   *OSI Encapsulation and Protocol Data Units*

Chapter Review

The "Your Study Plan" element, just before Chapter 1, discusses how you should study and practice the content and skills for each chapter before moving on to the next chapter. That element introduces the tools used here at the end of each chapter. If you haven't already done so, take a few minutes to read that section. Then come back here and do the useful work of reviewing the chapter to help lock into memory what you just read.

Review this chapter's material using either the tools in the book or the interactive tools for the same material found on the book's companion website. Table 1-4 outlines the key review elements and where you can find them. To better track your study progress, record when you completed these activities in the second column.

Table 1-4   Chapter Review Tracking

Review Element	Review Date(s)	Resource Used
Review key topics		Book, website
Review key terms		Book, website
Answer DIKTA questions		Book, PTP Online

Review All the Key Topics

Table 1-5   Key Topics for Chapter 1

Key Topic Elements	Description	Page Number
Table 1-3	Provides definitions of same-layer and adjacent-layer interaction	22
Figure 1-10	Shows the general concept of IP routing	25
Figure 1-11	Depicts the data-link services provided to IP for the purpose of delivering IP packets from host to host	26
Figure 1-12	Five steps to encapsulate data on the sending host	28
Figure 1-13	Shows the meaning of the terms *segment*, *packet*, and *frame*	28
Figure 1-14	Compares the OSI and TCP/IP network models	29
Figure 1-15	Terminology related to encapsulation	30

Key Terms You Should Know

adjacent-layer interaction, de-encapsulation, encapsulation, frame, networking model, packet, protocol data unit (PDU), same-layer interaction, segment

CHAPTER 2

Fundamentals of Ethernet LANs

This chapter covers the following exam topics:

1.0 Network Fundamentals

1.1 Explain the role and function of network components

1.1.b L2 and L3 Switches

1.2 Describe characteristics of network topology architectures

1.2.e Small office/home office (SOHO)

1.3 Compare physical interface and cabling types

1.3.a Single-mode fiber, multimode fiber, copper

1.3.b Connections (Ethernet shared media and point-to-point)

Most enterprise computer networks can be separated into two general types of technology: local-area networks (LANs) and wide-area networks (WANs). LANs typically connect nearby devices: devices in the same room, in the same building, or in a campus of buildings. In contrast, WANs connect devices that are typically relatively far apart. Together, LANs and WANs create a complete enterprise computer network, working together to do the job of a computer network: delivering data from one device to another.

Many types of LANs have existed over the years, but today's networks use two general types of LANs: Ethernet LANs and wireless LANs. Ethernet LANs happen to use cables for the links between nodes, and because many types of cables use copper wires, Ethernet LANs are often called *wired LANs*. Ethernet LANs also make use of fiber-optic cabling, which includes a fiberglass core that devices use to send data using light. In comparison to Ethernet, wireless LANs do not use wires or cables, instead using radio waves for the links between nodes; Part V of this book discusses Wireless LANs at length.

This chapter introduces Ethernet LANs, with more detailed coverage in Parts II and III of this book.

"Do I Know This Already?" Quiz

Take the quiz (either here or use the PTP software) if you want to use the score to help you decide how much time to spend on this chapter. The letter answers are listed at the bottom of the page following the quiz. Appendix C, found both at the end of the book as well as on the companion website, includes both the answers and explanations. You can also find both answers and explanations in the PTP testing software.

Table 2-1 "Do I Know This Already?" Foundation Topics Section-to-Question Mapping

Foundation Topics Section	Questions
An Overview of LANs	1–2
Building Physical Ethernet LANs with UTP	3–4
Building Physical Ethernet LANs with Fiber	5
Sending Data in Ethernet Networks	6–9

1. In the LAN for a small office, some user devices connect to the LAN using a cable, while others connect using wireless technology (and no cable). Which of the following is true regarding the use of Ethernet in this LAN?

    a. Only the devices that use cables are using Ethernet.

    b. Only the devices that use wireless are using Ethernet.

    c. Both the devices using cables and those using wireless are using Ethernet.

    d. None of the devices are using Ethernet.

2. Which of the following Ethernet standards defines Gigabit Ethernet over UTP cabling?

    a. 10GBASE-T

    b. 100BASE-T

    c. 1000BASE-T

    d. None of the other answers is correct.

3. Which of the following is true about Ethernet crossover cables for Fast Ethernet?

    a. Pins 1 and 2 are reversed on the other end of the cable.

    b. Pins 1 and 2 on one end of the cable connect to pins 3 and 6 on the other end of the cable.

    c. Pins 1 and 2 on one end of the cable connect to pins 3 and 4 on the other end of the cable.

    d. The cable can be up to 1000 meters long to cross over between buildings.

    e. None of the other answers is correct.

4. Each answer lists two types of devices used in a 100BASE-T network. If these devices were connected with UTP Ethernet cables, which pairs of devices would require a straight-through cable? (Choose three answers.)

    a. PC and router

    b. PC and switch

    c. Hub and switch

    d. Router and hub

    e. Wireless access point (Ethernet port) and switch

5. Which of the following are advantages of using multimode fiber for an Ethernet link instead of UTP or single-mode fiber?

   a. To achieve the longest distance possible for that single link.

   b. To extend the link beyond 100 meters while keeping initial costs as low as possible.

   c. To make use of an existing stock of laser-based SFP/SFP+ modules.

   d. To make use of an existing stock of LED-based SFP/SFP+ modules.

6. Which of the following is true about the CSMA/CD algorithm?

   a. The algorithm never allows collisions to occur.

   b. Collisions can happen, but the algorithm defines how the computers should notice a collision and how to recover.

   c. The algorithm works with only two devices on the same Ethernet.

   d. None of the other answers is correct.

7. Which of the following is true about the Ethernet FCS field?

   a. Ethernet uses FCS for error recovery.

   b. It is 2 bytes long.

   c. It resides in the Ethernet trailer, not the Ethernet header.

   d. It is used for encryption.

8. Which of the following are true about the format of Ethernet addresses? (Choose three answers.)

   a. Each manufacturer puts a unique OUI code into the first 2 bytes of the address.

   b. Each manufacturer puts a unique OUI code into the first 3 bytes of the address.

   c. Each manufacturer puts a unique OUI code into the first half of the address.

   d. The part of the address that holds this manufacturer's code is called the MAC.

   e. The part of the address that holds this manufacturer's code is called the OUI.

   f. The part of the address that holds this manufacturer's code has no specific name.

9. Which of the following terms describe Ethernet addresses that can be used to send one frame that is delivered to multiple devices on the LAN? (Choose two answers.)

   a. Burned-in address

   b. Unicast address

   c. Broadcast address

   d. Multicast address

Foundation Topics

An Overview of LANs

The term *Ethernet* refers to a family of LAN standards that together define the physical and data-link layers of the world's most popular wired LAN technology. The standards, defined by the Institute of Electrical and Electronics Engineers (IEEE), define the cabling, the connectors on the ends of the cables, the protocol rules, and everything else required to create an Ethernet LAN.

Typical SOHO LANs

To begin, first think about a small office/home office (SOHO) LAN today, specifically a LAN that uses only Ethernet LAN technology. First, the LAN needs a device called an Ethernet *LAN switch*, which provides many physical ports into which cables can be connected. An Ethernet uses *Ethernet cables*, which is a general reference to any cable that conforms to any of several Ethernet standards. The LAN uses Ethernet cables to connect different Ethernet devices or nodes to one of the switch's Ethernet ports.

Figure 2-1 shows a drawing of a SOHO Ethernet LAN. The figure shows a single LAN switch, five cables, and five other Ethernet nodes: three PCs, a printer, and one network device called a *router*. (The router connects the LAN to the WAN, in this case to the Internet.)

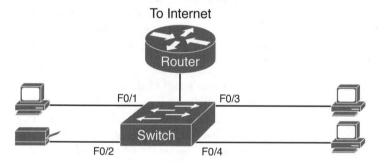

Figure 2-1 *Typical Small Ethernet-Only SOHO LAN*

Although Figure 2-1 shows the switch and router as separate devices, many SOHO Ethernet LANs today combine the router and switch into a single device. Vendors sell consumer-grade integrated networking devices that work as a router and Ethernet switch, as well as doing other functions. These devices typically have "router" on the packaging, but many models also have four-port or eight-port Ethernet LAN switch ports built in to the device.

Typical SOHO LANs today also support wireless LAN connections. You can build a single SOHO LAN that includes both Ethernet LAN technology as well as wireless LAN technology, which is also defined by the IEEE. Wireless LANs, defined by the IEEE using standards that begin with 802.11, use radio waves to send the bits from one node to the next.

Most wireless LANs rely on yet another networking device: a wireless LAN access point (AP). The AP acts somewhat like an Ethernet switch, in that all the wireless LAN nodes communicate with the wireless AP. If the network uses an AP that is a separate physical device, the AP then needs a single Ethernet link to connect the AP to the Ethernet LAN, as shown in Figure 2-2.

Note that Figure 2-2 shows the router, Ethernet switch, and wireless LAN access point as three separate devices so that you can better understand the different roles. However, most SOHO networks today would use a single device, often labeled as a "wireless router," that does all these functions.

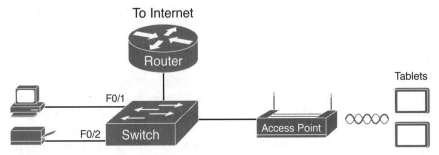

Figure 2-2 *Typical Small Wired and Wireless SOHO LAN*

Typical Enterprise LANs

Enterprise networks have similar needs compared to a SOHO network, but on a much larger scale. For example, enterprise Ethernet LANs begin with LAN switches installed in a wiring closet behind a locked door on each floor of a building. The electricians install the Ethernet cabling from that wiring closet to cubicles and conference rooms where devices might need to connect to the LAN. At the same time, most enterprises also support wireless LANs in the same space, to allow people to roam around and still work and to support a growing number of devices that do not have an Ethernet LAN interface.

Figure 2-3 shows a conceptual view of a typical enterprise LAN in a three-story building. Each floor has an Ethernet LAN switch and a wireless LAN AP. To allow communication between floors, each per-floor switch connects to one centralized distribution switch. For example, PC3 can send data to PC2, but it would first flow through switch SW3 to the first floor to the distribution switch (SWD) and then back up through switch SW2 on the second floor.

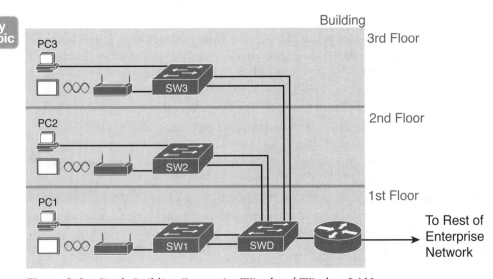

Figure 2-3 *Single-Building Enterprise Wired and Wireless LAN*

Answers to the "Do I Know This Already?" quiz:

1 A **2** C **3** B **4** B, D, and E **5** B **6** B **7** C **8** B, C, and E **9** C and D

The figure also shows the typical way to connect a LAN to a WAN using a router. LAN switches and wireless access points work to create the LAN itself. Routers connect to both the LAN and the WAN. To connect to the LAN, the router simply uses an Ethernet LAN interface and an Ethernet cable, as shown on the lower right of Figure 2-3.

The rest of this chapter focuses on Ethernet in particular.

The Variety of Ethernet Physical Layer Standards

The term *Ethernet* refers to an entire family of standards. Some standards define the specifics of how to send data over a particular type of cabling, and at a particular speed. Other standards define protocols, or rules, that the Ethernet nodes must follow to be a part of an Ethernet LAN. All these Ethernet standards come from the IEEE and include the number 802.3 as the beginning part of the standard name.

Ethernet supports a large variety of options for physical Ethernet links given its long history over the last 40 or so years. Today, Ethernet includes many standards for different kinds of optical and copper cabling, and for speeds from 10 megabits per second (Mbps) up to 400 gigabits per second (Gbps). The standards also differ as far as the types and length of the cables.

The most fundamental cabling choice has to do with the materials used inside the cable for the physical transmission of bits: either copper wires or glass fibers. Devices using UTP cabling transmit data over electrical circuits via the copper wires inside the cable. Fiber-optic cabling, the more expensive alternative, allows Ethernet nodes to send light over glass fibers in the center of the cable. Although more expensive, optical cables typically allow longer cabling distances between nodes.

To be ready to choose the products to purchase for a new Ethernet LAN, a network engineer must know the names and features of the different Ethernet standards supported in Ethernet products. The IEEE defines Ethernet physical layer standards using a couple of naming conventions. The formal name begins with 802.3 followed by some suffix letters. The IEEE also uses more meaningful shortcut names that identify the speed, as well as a clue about whether the cabling is UTP (with a suffix that includes *T*) or fiber (with a suffix that includes *X*). Table 2-2 lists a few Ethernet physical layer standards. First, the table lists enough names so that you get a sense of the IEEE naming conventions.

Table 2-2   Examples of Types of Ethernet

Speed	Common Name	Informal IEEE Standard Name	Formal IEEE Standard Name	Cable Type, Maximum Length
10 Mbps	Ethernet	10BASE-T	802.3	Copper, 100 m
100 Mbps	Fast Ethernet	100BASE-T	802.3u	Copper, 100 m
1000 Mbps	Gigabit Ethernet	1000BASE-LX	802.3z	Fiber, 5000 m
1000 Mbps	Gigabit Ethernet	1000BASE-T	802.3ab	Copper, 100 m
10 Gbps	10 Gig Ethernet	10GBASE-T	802.3an	Copper, 100 m

> **NOTE** Fiber-optic cabling contains long thin strands of fiberglass. The attached Ethernet nodes send light over the glass fiber in the cable, encoding the bits as changes in the light.

> **NOTE** You might expect that a standard that began at the IEEE almost 40 years ago would be stable and unchanging, but the opposite is true. The IEEE, along with active industry partners, continues to develop new Ethernet standards with longer distances, different cabling options, and faster speeds. Check out the Ethernet Alliance web page (www.EthernetAlliance.org) and look for the roadmap for some great graphics and tables about the latest happenings with Ethernet.

Consistent Behavior over All Links Using the Ethernet Data-Link Layer

Although Ethernet includes many physical layer standards, Ethernet acts like a single LAN technology because it uses the same data-link layer standard over all types of Ethernet physical links. That standard defines a common Ethernet header and trailer. (As a reminder, the header and trailer are bytes of overhead data that Ethernet uses to do its job of sending data over a LAN.) No matter whether the data flows over a UTP cable or any kind of fiber cable, and no matter the speed, the data-link header and trailer use the same format.

While the physical layer standards focus on sending bits over a cable, the Ethernet data-link protocols focus on sending an *Ethernet frame* from source to destination Ethernet node. From a data-link perspective, nodes build and forward frames. As first defined in Chapter 1, "Introduction to TCP/IP Networking," the term *frame* specifically refers to the header and trailer of a data-link protocol, plus the data encapsulated inside that header and trailer. The various Ethernet nodes simply forward the frame, over all the required links, to deliver the frame to the correct destination.

Figure 2-4 shows an example of the process. In this case, PC1 sends an Ethernet frame to PC3. The frame travels over a UTP link to Ethernet switch SW1, then over fiber links to Ethernet switches SW2 and SW3, and finally over another UTP link to PC3. Note that the bits actually travel at four different speeds in this example: 10 Mbps, 1 Gbps, 10 Gbps, and 100 Mbps, respectively.

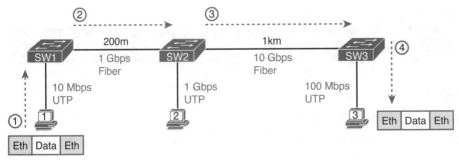

Figure 2-4   *Ethernet LAN Forwards a Data-Link Frame over Many Types of Links*

So, what is an Ethernet LAN? It is a combination of user devices, LAN switches, and different kinds of cabling. Each link can use different types of cables, at different speeds.

However, they all work together to deliver Ethernet frames from the one device on the LAN to some other device.

The rest of this chapter takes these concepts a little deeper. The next section examines how to build a physical Ethernet network using UTP cabling, followed by a similar look at using fiber cabling to build Ethernet LANs. The chapter ends with some discussion of the rules for forwarding frames through an Ethernet LAN.

Building Physical Ethernet LANs with UTP

The next section of this chapter focuses on the individual physical links between any two Ethernet nodes, specifically those that use Unshielded Twisted Pair (UTP) cabling. Before the Ethernet network as a whole can send Ethernet frames between user devices, each node must be ready and able to send data over an individual physical link.

This section focuses on the three most commonly used Ethernet standards: 10BASE-T (Ethernet), 100BASE-T (Fast Ethernet, or FE), and 1000BASE-T (Gigabit Ethernet, or GE). Specifically, this section looks at the details of sending data in both directions over a UTP cable. It then examines the specific wiring of the UTP cables used for 10-Mbps, 100-Mbps, and 1000-Mbps Ethernet.

Transmitting Data Using Twisted Pairs

While it is true that Ethernet sends data over UTP cables, the physical means to send the data uses electricity that flows over the wires inside the UTP cable. To better understand how Ethernet sends data using electricity, break the idea down into two parts: how to create an electrical circuit and then how to make that electrical signal communicate 1s and 0s.

First, to create one electrical circuit, Ethernet defines how to use the two wires inside a single twisted pair of wires, as shown in Figure 2-5. The figure does not show a UTP cable between two nodes, but instead shows two individual wires that are inside the UTP cable. An electrical circuit requires a complete loop, so the two nodes, using circuitry on their Ethernet ports, connect the wires in one pair to complete a loop, allowing electricity to flow.

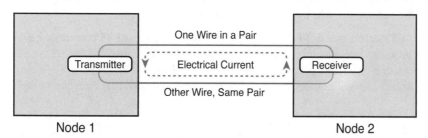

Figure 2-5   *Creating One Electrical Circuit over One Pair to Send in One Direction*

To send data, the two devices follow some rules called an *encoding scheme*. The idea works a lot like when two people talk using the same language: The speaker says some words in a particular language, and the listener, because she speaks the same language, can understand the spoken words. With an encoding scheme, the transmitting node changes the electrical signal over time, while the other node, the receiver, using the same rules, interprets those changes as either 0s or 1s. (For example, 10BASE-T uses an encoding scheme that encodes a binary 0 as a transition from higher voltage to lower voltage during the middle of a 1/10,000,000th-of-a-second interval.)

Note that in an actual UTP cable, the wires will be twisted together, instead of being parallel as shown in Figure 2-5. The twisting helps solve some important physical transmission issues. When electrical current passes over any wire, it creates electromagnetic interference (EMI) that interferes with the electrical signals in nearby wires, including the wires in the same cable. (EMI between wire pairs in the same cable is called *crosstalk*.) Twisting the wire pairs together helps cancel out most of the EMI, so most networking physical links that use copper wires use twisted pairs.

Breaking Down a UTP Ethernet Link

The term *Ethernet link* refers to any physical cable between two Ethernet nodes. To learn about how a UTP Ethernet link works, it helps to break down the physical link into those basic pieces, as shown in Figure 2-6: the cable itself, the connectors on the ends of the cable, and the matching ports on the devices into which the connectors will be inserted.

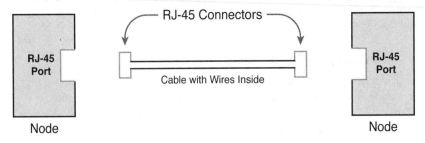

Figure 2-6 *Basic Components of an Ethernet Link*

First, think about the UTP cable itself. The cable holds some copper wires, grouped as twisted pairs. The 10BASE-T and 100BASE-T standards require two pairs of wires, while the 1000BASE-T standard requires four pairs. Each wire has a color-coded plastic coating, with the wires in a pair having a color scheme. For example, for the blue wire pair, one wire's coating is all blue, while the other wire's coating is blue-and-white striped.

Many Ethernet UTP cables use an RJ-45 connector on both ends. The RJ-45 connector has eight physical locations into which the eight wires in the cable can be inserted, called *pin positions*, or simply *pins*. These pins create a place where the ends of the copper wires can touch the electronics inside the nodes at the end of the physical link so that electricity can flow.

NOTE If available, find a nearby Ethernet UTP cable and examine the connectors closely. Look for the pin positions and the colors of the wires in the connector.

To complete the physical link, the nodes each need an RJ-45 *Ethernet port* that matches the RJ-45 connectors on the cable so that the connectors on the ends of the cable can connect to each node. PCs often include this RJ-45 Ethernet port as part of a network interface card (NIC), which can be an expansion card on the PC or can be built in to the system itself.

Switches typically have many RJ-45 ports because switches give user devices a place to connect to the Ethernet LAN. Figure 2-7 shows photos of the cables, connectors, and ports.

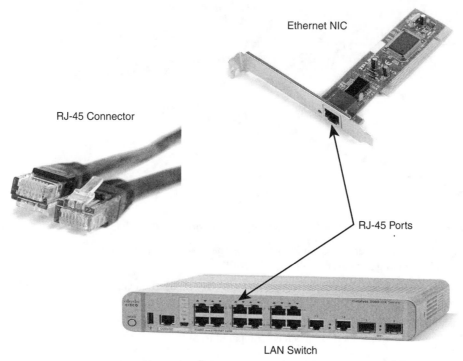

Figure 2-7 *RJ-45 Connectors and Ports (Ethernet NIC © Oleg Begunenko/123RF, RJ-45 Connector © Anton Samsonov/123RF)*

The figure shows a connector on the left and ports on the right. The left shows the eight pin positions in the end of the RJ-45 connector. The upper right shows an Ethernet NIC that is not yet installed in a computer. The lower-right part of the figure shows the side of a Cisco switch, with multiple RJ-45 ports, allowing multiple devices to easily connect to the Ethernet network.

Finally, while RJ-45 connectors with UTP cabling can be common, Cisco LAN switches often support other types of connectors as well. When you buy one of the many models of Cisco switches, you need to think about the mix and numbers of each type of physical ports you want on the switch.

To give its customers flexibility as to the type of Ethernet links, even after the customer has bought the switch, Cisco switches include some physical ports whose port hardware (the transceiver) can be changed later, after you purchase the switch.

For example, Figure 2-8 shows a photo of a Cisco switch with one of the swappable transceivers. In this case, the figure shows an enhanced small form-factor pluggable (SFP+) transceiver, which runs at 10 Gbps, just outside two SFP+ slots on a Cisco 3560CX switch. The SFP+ itself is the silver-colored part below the switch, with a black cable connected to it.

Figure 2-8   *10-Gbps SFP+ with Cable Sitting Just Outside a Catalyst 3560CX Switch*

Gigabit Ethernet Interface Converter (GBIC): The original form factor for a removable transceiver for Gigabit interfaces; larger than SFPs

Small Form Pluggable (SFP): The replacement for GBICs, used on Gigabit interfaces, with a smaller size, taking less space on the side of the networking card or switch.

Small Form Pluggable Plus (SFP+): Same size as the SFP, but used on 10-Gbps interfaces. (The Plus refers to the increase in speed compared to SFPs.)

UTP Cabling Pinouts for 10BASE-T and 100BASE-T

So far in this section, you have learned about the equivalent of how to drive a truck on a 1000-acre ranch: You could drive the truck all over the ranch, any place you wanted to go, and the police would not mind. However, as soon as you get on the public roads, the police want you to behave and follow the rules. Similarly, so far this chapter has discussed the general principles of how to send data, but it has not yet detailed some important rules for Ethernet cabling: the rules of the road so that all the devices send data using the right wires inside the cable.

This next topic discusses some of those rules, specifically for the 10-Mbps 10BASE-T and the 100-Mbps 100BASE-T. Both use UTP cabling in similar ways (including the use of only two wire pairs). A short comparison of the wiring for 1000BASE-T (Gigabit Ethernet), which uses four pairs, follows.

Straight-Through Cable Pinout

10BASE-T and 100BASE-T use two pairs of wires in a UTP cable, one for each direction, as shown in Figure 2-9. The figure shows four wires, all of which sit inside a single UTP cable that connects a PC and a LAN switch. In this example, the PC on the left transmits using the top pair, and the switch on the right transmits using the bottom pair.

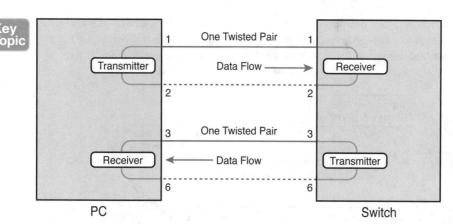

Figure 2-9 *Using One Pair for Each Transmission Direction with 10- and 100-Mbps Ethernet*

For correct transmission over the link, the wires in the UTP cable must be connected to the correct pin positions in the RJ-45 connectors. For example, in Figure 2-9, the transmitter on the PC on the left must know the pin positions of the two wires it should use to transmit. Those two wires must be connected to the correct pins in the RJ-45 connector on the switch so that the switch's receiver logic can use the correct wires.

To understand the wiring of the cable—which wires need to be in which pin positions on both ends of the cable—you need to first understand how the NICs and switches work. As a rule, Ethernet NIC transmitters use the pair connected to pins 1 and 2; the NIC receivers use a pair of wires at pin positions 3 and 6. LAN switches, knowing those facts about what Ethernet NICs do, do the opposite: Their receivers use the wire pair at pins 1 and 2, and their transmitters use the wire pair at pins 3 and 6.

To allow a PC NIC to communicate with a switch, the UTP cable must also use a *straight-through cable pinout*. The term *pinout* refers to the wiring of which color wire is placed in each of the eight numbered pin positions in the RJ-45 connector. An Ethernet straight-through cable connects the wire at pin 1 on one end of the cable to pin 1 at the other end of the cable; the wire at pin 2 needs to connect to pin 2 on the other end of the cable; pin 3 on one end connects to pin 3 on the other, and so on, as seen in Figure 2-10. Also, it uses the wires in one wire pair at pins 1 and 2, and another pair at pins 3 and 6.

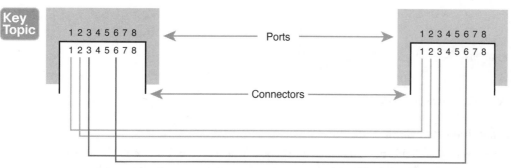

Figure 2-10 *10BASE-T and 100BASE-T Straight-Through Cable Pinout*

Figure 2-11 shows one final perspective on the straight-through cable pinout. In this case, PC Larry connects to a LAN switch. Note that the figure again does not show the UTP cable, but instead shows the wires that sit inside the cable, to emphasize the idea of wire pairs and pins.

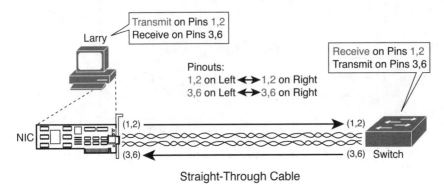

Figure 2-11 *Ethernet Straight-Through Cable Concept*

A straight-through cable works correctly when the nodes use opposite pairs for transmitting data. However, when two like devices connect to an Ethernet link, they both transmit on the same pins. In that case, you then need another type of cabling pinout called a *crossover cable*. The crossover cable pinout crosses the pair at the transmit pins on each device to the receive pins on the opposite device.

While that previous sentence is true, this concept is much clearer with a figure such as Figure 2-12. The figure shows what happens on a link between two switches. The two switches both transmit on the pair at pins 3 and 6, and they both receive on the pair at pins 1 and 2. So, the cable must connect a pair at pins 3 and 6 on each side to pins 1 and 2 on the other side, connecting to the other node's receiver logic. The top of the figure shows the literal pinouts, and the bottom half shows a conceptual diagram.

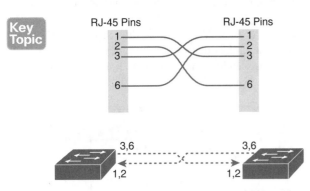

Figure 2-12 *Crossover Ethernet Cable*

Choosing the Right Cable Pinouts

For the exam, you should be well prepared to choose which type of cable (straight-through or crossover) is needed in each part of the network. The key is to know whether a device acts like a PC NIC, transmitting at pins 1 and 2, or like a switch, transmitting at pins 3 and 6. Then, just apply the following logic:

> **Crossover cable:** If the endpoints transmit on the same pin pair

> **Straight-through cable:** If the endpoints transmit on different pin pairs

Table 2-3 lists the devices and the pin pairs they use, assuming that they use 10BASE-T and 100BASE-T.

Table 2-3   10BASE-T and 100BASE-T Pin Pairs Used

Transmits on Pins 1,2	Transmits on Pins 3,6
PC NICs	Hubs
Routers	Switches
Wireless access point (Ethernet interface)	—

For example, Figure 2-13 shows a campus LAN in a single building. In this case, several straight-through cables are used to connect PCs to switches. In addition, the cables connecting the switches require crossover cables.

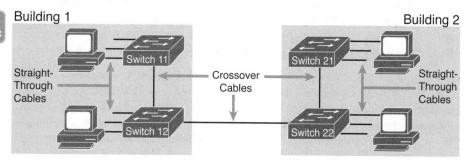

Figure 2-13   *Typical Uses for Straight-Through and Crossover Ethernet Cables*

> **NOTE**   If you have some experience with installing LANs, you might be thinking that you have used the wrong cable before (straight-through or crossover), but the cable worked. Cisco switches have a feature called *auto-mdix* that notices when the wrong cable is used and automatically changes its logic to make the link work. However, for the exams, be ready to identify whether the correct cable is shown in the figures.

UTP Cabling Pinouts for 1000BASE-T

1000BASE-T (Gigabit Ethernet) differs from 10BASE-T and 100BASE-T as far as the cabling and pinouts. First, 1000BASE-T requires four wire pairs. Second, it uses more advanced electronics that allow both ends to transmit and receive simultaneously on each wire pair. However, the wiring pinouts for 1000BASE-T work almost identically to the earlier standards, adding details for the additional two pairs.

The straight-through cable for 1000BASE-T uses the four wire pairs to create four circuits, but the pins need to match. It uses the same pinouts for two pairs as do the 10BASE-T and

100BASE-T standards, and it adds a pair at pins 4 and 5 and the final pair at pins 7 and 8, as shown in Figure 2-14.

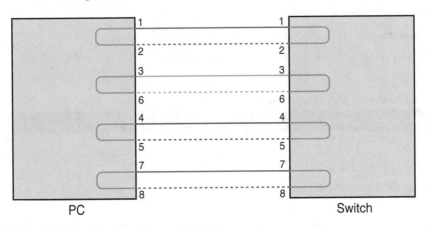

Figure 2-14   *Four-Pair Straight-Through Cable to 1000BASE-T*

The Gigabit Ethernet crossover cable crosses the same two-wire pairs as the crossover cable for the other types of Ethernet (the pairs at pins 1,2 and 3,6). It also crosses the two new pairs as well (the pair at pins 4,5 with the pair at pins 7,8).

Building Physical Ethernet LANs with Fiber

The capability of many UTP-based Ethernet standards to use a cable length up to 100 meters means that the majority of Ethernet cabling in an enterprise uses UTP cables. The distance from an Ethernet switch to every endpoint on the floor of a building will likely be less than 100m. In some cases, however, an engineer might prefer to use fiber cabling for some links in an Ethernet LAN, first to reach greater distances, but for other reasons as well. This next section examines a few of the tradeoffs after discussing the basics of how to transmit data over fiber cabling.

Fiber Cabling Transmission Concepts

Fiber-optic cabling uses glass as the medium through which light passes, varying that light over time to encode 0s and 1s. It might seem strange at first to use glass given that most of us think of glass in windows. Window glass is hard, unbending, and if you hit or bend it enough, the glass will probably shatter—all bad characteristics for a cabling material.

Instead, fiber-optic cables use fiberglass, which allows a manufacturer to spin a long thin string (fiber) of flexible glass. A fiber-optic cable holds the fiber in the middle of the cable, allowing the light to pass through the glass—which is a very important attribute for the purposes of sending data.

Although sending data through a glass fiber works well, the glass fiber by itself needs some help. The glass could break, so the glass fiber needs some protection and strengthening. Figure 2-15 shows a cutout with the components of a fiber cable for perspective.

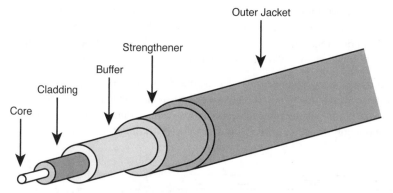

Figure 2-15 *Components of a Fiber-Optic Cable*

The three outer layers of the cable protect the interior of the cable and make the cables easier to install and manage, while the inner *cladding* and *core* work together to create the environment to allow transmission of light over the cable. A light source, called the *optical transmitter*, shines a light into the core. Light can pass through the core; however, light reflects off the cladding back into the core. Figure 2-16 shows an example with a light emitting diode (LED) transmitter. You can see how the cladding reflects the light back into the core as it travels through the core.

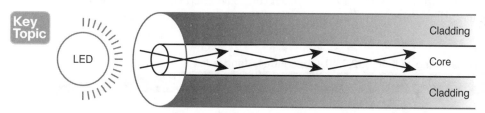

Figure 2-16 *Transmission on Multimode Fiber with Internal Reflection*

The figure shows the normal operation of a multimode fiber, characterized by the fact that the cable allows for multiple angles (modes) of light waves entering the core.

In contrast, single-mode fiber uses a smaller-diameter core, around one-fifth the diameter of common multimode cables (see Figure 2-17). To transmit light into a much smaller core, a laser-based transmitter sends light at a single angle (hence the name *single-mode*).

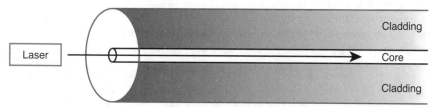

Figure 2-17 *Transmission on Single-Mode Fiber with Laser Transmitter*

Both multimode and single-mode cabling have important roles in Ethernet and meet different needs. Multimode improves the maximum distances over UTP, and it uses less expensive transmitters as compared with single-mode. Standards do vary; for instance, the standards for 10 Gigabit Ethernet over Fiber allow for distances up to 400m, which would often allow for connection of devices in different buildings in the same office park. Single-mode allows distances into the tens of kilometers, but with slightly more expensive SFP/SFP+ hardware.

To transmit between two devices, you need two cables, one for each direction, as shown in Figure 2-18. The concept works much like having two electrical circuits with the original UTP Ethernet standards. Note that the transmit port on one device connects to a cable that connects to a receive port on the other device, and vice versa with the other cable.

Figure 2-18   *Two Fiber Cables with Tx Connected to Rx on Each Cable*

Using Fiber with Ethernet

To use fiber with Ethernet switches, you need to use a switch with either built-in ports that support a particular optical Ethernet standard, or a switch with modular ports that allow you to change the Ethernet standard used on the port. Refer back to Figure 2-8, which shows a photo of a switch with two SFP+ ports, into which you could insert any of the supported SFP+ modules. Those SFP+ ports support a variety of 10-Gbps standards like those listed in Table 2-4.

Table 2-4   A Sampling of IEEE 802.3 10-Gbps Fiber Standards

Standard	Cable Type	Max Distance*
10GBASE-S	MM	400m
10GBASE-LX4	MM	300m
10GBASE-LR	SM	10km
10GBASE-E	SM	30km

* The maximum distances are based on the IEEE standards with no repeaters.

For instance, to build an Ethernet LAN in an office park, you might need to use some multimode and single-mode fiber links. In fact, many office parks might already have fiber cabling installed for the expected future use by the tenants in the buildings. If each building was within a few hundred meters of at least one other building, you could use multimode fiber between the buildings and connect switches to create your LAN.

NOTE   Outside the need to study for CCNA, if you need to look more deeply at fiber Ethernet and SFP/SFP+, check out tmgmatrix.cisco.com as a place to search for and learn about compatible SFP/SFP+ hardware from Cisco.

Although distance might be the first criterion to consider when thinking about whether to use UTP or fiber cabling, a few other tradeoffs exist as well. UTP wins again on cost, because the cost goes up as you move from UTP, to multimode, and then to single-mode, due to the extra cost for the transmitters like the SFP and SFP+ modules. UTP has some negatives, however. First, UTP might work poorly in some electrically noisy environments such as factories, because UTP can be affected by electromagnetic interference (EMI). Also, UTP cables emit a faint signal outside the cable, so highly secure networks may choose to use fiber, which does not create similar emissions, to make the network more secure. Table 2-5 summarizes these tradeoffs.

Table 2-5   Comparisons Between UTP, MM, and SM Ethernet Cabling

Criteria	UTP	Multimode	Single-Mode
Relative Cost of Cabling	Low	Medium	Medium
Relative Cost of a Switch Port	Low	Medium	High
Approximate Max Distance	100m	500m	40km
Relative Susceptibility to Interference	Some	None	None
Relative Risk of Copying from Cable Emissions	Some	None	None

Sending Data in Ethernet Networks

Although physical layer standards vary quite a bit, other parts of the Ethernet standards work the same regardless of the type of physical Ethernet link. Next, this final major section of this chapter looks at several protocols and rules that Ethernet uses regardless of the type of link. In particular, this section examines the details of the Ethernet data-link layer protocol, plus how Ethernet nodes, switches, and hubs forward Ethernet frames through an Ethernet LAN.

Ethernet Data-Link Protocols

One of the most significant strengths of the Ethernet family of protocols is that these protocols use the same data-link standard. In fact, the core parts of the data-link standard date back to the original Ethernet standards.

The Ethernet data-link protocol defines the Ethernet frame: an Ethernet header at the front, the encapsulated data in the middle, and an Ethernet trailer at the end. Ethernet actually defines a few alternate formats for the header, with the frame format shown in Figure 2-19 being commonly used today.

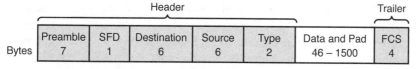

Figure 2-19   *Commonly Used Ethernet Frame Format*

While all the fields in the frame matter, some matter more to the topics discussed in this book. Table 2-6 lists the fields in the header and trailer and a brief description for reference, with the upcoming pages including more detail about a few of these fields.

Table 2-6   IEEE 802.3 Ethernet Header and Trailer Fields

Field	Bytes	Description
Preamble	7	Synchronization.
Start Frame Delimiter (SFD)	1	Signifies that the next byte begins the Destination MAC Address field.
Destination MAC Address	6	Identifies the intended recipient of this frame.
Source MAC Address	6	Identifies the sender of this frame.
Type	2	Defines the type of protocol listed inside the frame; today, most likely identifies IP version 4 (IPv4) or IP version 6 (IPv6).
Data and Pad[*]	46– 1500	Holds data from a higher layer, typically an L3PDU (usually an IPv4 or IPv6 packet). The sender adds padding to meet the minimum length requirement for this field (46 bytes).
Frame Check Sequence (FCS)	4	Provides a method for the receiving NIC to determine whether the frame experienced transmission errors.

* The IEEE 802.3 specification limits the data portion of the 802.3 frame to a minimum of 46 and a maximum of 1500 bytes. The *term maximum transmission unit* (MTU) defines the maximum Layer 3 packet that can be sent over a medium. Because the Layer 3 packet rests inside the data portion of an Ethernet frame, 1500 bytes is the largest IP MTU allowed over an Ethernet.

Ethernet Addressing

The source and destination Ethernet address fields play a huge role in how Ethernet LANs work. The general idea for each is relatively simple: the sending node puts its own address in the source address field and the intended Ethernet destination device's address in the destination address field. The sender transmits the frame, expecting that the Ethernet LAN, as a whole, will deliver the frame to that correct destination.

Ethernet addresses, also called Media Access Control (MAC) addresses, are 6-byte-long (48-bit-long) binary numbers. For convenience, most computers list MAC addresses as 12-digit hexadecimal numbers. Cisco devices typically add some periods to the number for easier readability as well; for example, a Cisco switch might list a MAC address as 0000.0C12.3456.

Most MAC addresses represent a single NIC or other Ethernet port, so these addresses are often called a *unicast* Ethernet address. The term *unicast* is simply a formal way to refer to the fact that the address represents one interface to the Ethernet LAN. (This term also contrasts with two other types of Ethernet addresses, *broadcast* and *multicast*, which will be defined later in this section.)

The entire idea of sending data to a destination unicast MAC address works well, but it works only if all the unicast MAC addresses are unique. If two NICs tried to use the same MAC address, there could be confusion. (The problem would be like the confusion caused to the postal service if you and I both tried to use the same mailing address—would the postal service deliver mail to your house or mine?) If two PCs on the same Ethernet tried to use the same MAC address, to which PC should frames sent to that MAC address be delivered?

Ethernet solves this problem using an administrative process so that, at the time of manufacture, all Ethernet devices are assigned a universally unique MAC address. Before a manufacturer can build Ethernet products, it must ask the IEEE to assign the manufacturer a universally unique 3-byte code, called the organizationally unique identifier (OUI). The manufacturer agrees to give all NICs (and other Ethernet products) a MAC address that begins with its assigned 3-byte OUI. The manufacturer also assigns a unique value for the last 3 bytes, a number that manufacturer has never used with that OUI. As a result, the MAC address of every device in the universe is unique.

> **NOTE**   The IEEE also calls these universal MAC addresses global MAC addresses.

Figure 2-20 shows the structure of the unicast MAC address, with the OUI.

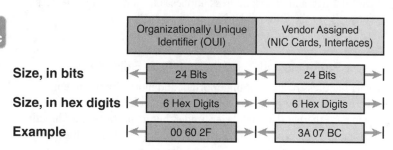

Figure 2-20   *Structure of Unicast Ethernet Addresses*

Ethernet addresses go by many names: LAN address, Ethernet address, hardware address, burned-in address, physical address, universal address, or MAC address. For example, the term burned-in address (BIA) refers to the idea that a permanent MAC address has been encoded (burned into) the ROM chip on the NIC. As another example, the IEEE uses the term *universal address* to emphasize the fact that the address assigned to a NIC by a manufacturer should be unique among all MAC addresses in the universe.

In addition to unicast addresses, Ethernet also uses group addresses. *Group addresses* identify more than one LAN interface card. A frame sent to a group address might be delivered to a small set of devices on the LAN, or even to all devices on the LAN. In fact, the IEEE defines two general categories of group addresses for Ethernet:

Broadcast address: Frames sent to this address should be delivered to all devices on the Ethernet LAN. It has a value of FFFF.FFFF.FFFF.

Multicast addresses: Frames sent to a multicast Ethernet address will be copied and forwarded to a subset of the devices on the LAN that volunteers to receive frames sent to a specific multicast address.

Table 2-7 summarizes most of the details about MAC addresses.

Table 2-7   LAN MAC Address Terminology and Features

LAN Addressing Term or Feature	Description
MAC	Media Access Control. 802.3 (Ethernet) defines the MAC sublayer of IEEE Ethernet.
Ethernet address, NIC address, LAN address	Other names often used instead of MAC address. These terms describe the 6-byte address of the LAN interface card.
Burned-in address	The 6-byte address assigned by the vendor making the card.
Unicast address	A term for a MAC address that represents a single LAN interface.
Broadcast address	An address that means "all devices that reside on this LAN right now."
Multicast address	On Ethernet, a multicast address implies some subset of all devices currently on the Ethernet LAN.

Identifying Network Layer Protocols with the Ethernet Type Field

While the Ethernet header's address fields play an important and more obvious role in Ethernet LANs, the Ethernet Type field plays a much less obvious role. The Ethernet Type field, or EtherType, sits in the Ethernet data-link layer header, but its purpose is to directly help the network processing on routers and hosts. Basically, the Type field identifies the type of network layer (Layer 3) packet that sits inside the Ethernet frame.

First, think about what sits inside the data part of the Ethernet frame shown earlier in Figure 2-14. Typically, it holds the network layer packet created by the network layer protocol on some device in the network. Over the years, those protocols have included IBM Systems Network Architecture (SNA), Novell NetWare, Digital Equipment Corporation's DECnet, and Apple Computer's AppleTalk. Today, the most common network layer protocols are both from TCP/IP: IP version 4 (IPv4) and IP version 6 (IPv6).

The original host has a place to insert a value (a hexadecimal number) to identify the type of packet encapsulated inside the Ethernet frame. However, what number should the sender put in the header to identify an IPv4 packet as the type? Or an IPv6 packet? As it turns out, the IEEE manages a list of EtherType values, so that every network layer protocol that needs a unique EtherType value can have a number. The sender just has to know the list. (Anyone can view the list; just go to www.ieee.org and search for *EtherType*.)

For example, a host can send one Ethernet frame with an IPv4 packet and the next Ethernet frame with an IPv6 packet. Each frame would have a different Ethernet Type field value, using the values reserved by the IEEE, as shown in Figure 2-21.

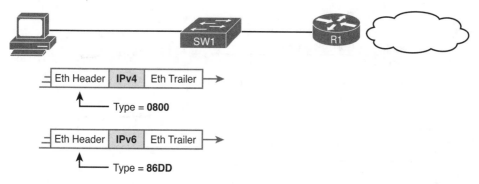

Figure 2-21   *Use of Ethernet Type Field*

Error Detection with FCS

Ethernet also defines a way for nodes to find out whether a frame's bits changed while cross-ing over an Ethernet link. (Usually, the bits could change because of some kind of electrical interference, or a bad NIC.) Ethernet, like most data-link protocols, uses a field in the data-link trailer for the purpose of error detection.

The Ethernet Frame Check Sequence (FCS) field in the Ethernet trailer—the only field in the Ethernet trailer—gives the receiving node a way to compare results with the sender, to discover whether errors occurred in the frame. The sender applies a complex math formula to the frame before sending it, storing the result of the formula in the FCS field. The receiver applies the same math formula to the received frame. The receiver then compares its own results with the sender's results. If the results are the same, the frame did not change; other-wise, an error occurred, and the receiver discards the frame.

Note that *error detection* does not also mean *error recovery*. Ethernet defines that the errored frame should be discarded, but Ethernet does not attempt to recover the lost frame. Other pro-tocols, notably TCP, recover the lost data by noticing that it is lost and sending the data again.

Sending Ethernet Frames with Switches and Hubs

Ethernet LANs behave slightly differently depending on whether the LAN has mostly mod-ern devices, in particular, LAN switches instead of some older LAN devices called LAN hubs. Basically, the use of more modern switches allows the use of full-duplex logic, which is much faster and simpler than half-duplex logic, which is required when using hubs. The final topic in this chapter looks at these basic differences.

Sending in Modern Ethernet LANs Using Full Duplex

Modern Ethernet LANs use a variety of Ethernet physical standards, but with standard Ethernet frames that can flow over any of these types of physical links. Each individual link can run at a different speed, but each link allows the attached nodes to send the bits in the frame to the next node. They must work together to deliver the data from the sending Ethernet node to the destination node.

The process is relatively simple, on purpose; the simplicity lets each device send a large number of frames per second. Figure 2-22 shows an example in which PC1 sends an Ethernet frame to PC2.

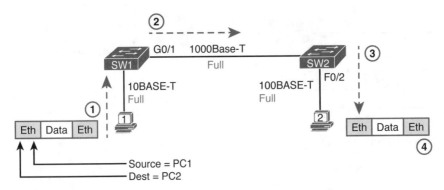

Figure 2-22   *Example of Sending Data in a Modern Ethernet LAN*

Following the steps in the figure:

1.   PC1 builds and sends the original Ethernet frame, using its own MAC address as the source address and PC2's MAC address as the destination address.

2.   Switch SW1 receives and forwards the Ethernet frame out its G0/1 interface (short for Gigabit interface 0/1) to SW2.

3.   Switch SW2 receives and forwards the Ethernet frame out its F0/2 interface (short for Fast Ethernet interface 0/2) to PC2.

4.   PC2 receives the frame, recognizes the destination MAC address as its own, and processes the frame.

The Ethernet network in Figure 2-22 uses full duplex on each link, but the concept might be difficult to see.

Full duplex means that that the NIC or switch port has no half-duplex restrictions. So, to understand full duplex, you need to understand half duplex, as follows:

Half duplex: The device must wait to send if it is currently receiving a frame; in other words, it cannot send and receive at the same time.

Full duplex: The device does not have to wait before sending; it can send and receive at the same time.

So, with all PCs and LAN switches, and no LAN hubs, all the nodes can use full duplex. All nodes can send and receive on their port at the same instant in time. For example, in Figure 2-22, PC1 and PC2 could send frames to each other simultaneously, in both directions, without any half-duplex restrictions.

Using Half Duplex with LAN Hubs

To understand the need for half-duplex logic in some cases, you have to understand a little about an older type of networking device called a LAN hub. When the IEEE first introduced 10BASE-T in 1990, Ethernet switches did not exist yet; instead, networks used a device called a LAN hub. Like a switch, a LAN hub provided a number of RJ-45 ports as a place to connect links to PCs; however, hubs used different rules for forwarding data.

LAN hubs forward data using physical layer standards rather than data-link standards and are therefore considered to be Layer 1 devices. When an electrical signal comes in one hub port, the hub repeats that electrical signal out all other ports (except the incoming port). By doing so, the data reaches all the rest of the nodes connected to the hub, so the data hopefully reaches the correct destination. The hub has no concept of Ethernet frames, of addresses, making decisions based on those addresses, and so on.

The downside of using LAN hubs is that if two or more devices transmitted a signal at the same instant, the electrical signal collides and becomes garbled. The hub repeats all received electrical signals, even if it receives multiple signals at the same time. For example, Figure 2-23 shows the idea, with PCs Archie and Bob sending an electrical signal at the same instant of time (at Steps 1A and 1B) and the hub repeating both electrical signals out toward Larry on the left (Step 2).

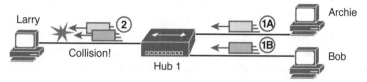

Figure 2-23   *Collision Occurring Because of LAN Hub Behavior*

NOTE   For completeness, note that the hub floods each frame out all other ports (except the incoming port). So, Archie's frame goes to both Larry and Bob; Bob's frame goes to Larry and Archie.

If you replace the hub in Figure 2-23 with a LAN switch, the switch prevents the collision on the left. The switch operates as a Layer 2 device, meaning that it looks at the data-link header and trailer. A switch would look at the MAC addresses, and even if the switch needed to forward both frames to Larry on the left, the switch would send one frame and queue the other frame until the first frame was finished.

Now back to the issue created by the hub's logic: collisions. To prevent these collisions, the Ethernet nodes must use half-duplex logic instead of full-duplex logic. A problem occurs only when two or more devices send at the same time; half-duplex logic tells the nodes that if someone else is sending, wait before sending.

For example, back in Figure 2-23, imagine that Archie began sending his frame early enough so that Bob received the first bits of that frame before Bob tried to send his own frame. Bob, at Step 1B, would notice that he was receiving a frame from someone else, and using half-duplex logic, would simply wait to send the frame listed at Step 1B.

Nodes that use half-duplex logic actually use a relatively well-known algorithm called carrier sense multiple access with collision detection (CSMA/CD). The algorithm takes care of the obvious cases but also the cases caused by unfortunate timing. For example, two nodes could check for an incoming frame at the exact same instant, both realize that no other node is sending, and both send their frames at the exact same instant, causing a collision. CSMA/CD covers these cases as well, as follows:

Step 1.   A device with a frame to send listens until the Ethernet is not busy.

Step 2.   When the Ethernet is not busy, the sender begins sending the frame.

Step 3. The sender listens while sending to discover whether a collision occurs; collisions might be caused by many reasons, including unfortunate timing. If a collision occurs, all currently sending nodes do the following:

   A. They send a jamming signal that tells all nodes that a collision happened.

   B. They independently choose a random time to wait before trying again, to avoid unfortunate timing.

   C. The next attempt starts again at Step 1.

Although most modern LANs do not often use hubs and therefore do not need to use half duplex, enough old hubs still exist in enterprise networks so that you need to be ready to understand duplex issues. Each NIC and switch port has a duplex setting. For all links between PCs and switches, or between switches, use full duplex. However, for any link connected to a LAN hub, the connected LAN switch and NIC port should use half duplex. Note that the hub itself does not use half-duplex logic, instead just repeating incoming signals out every other port.

Figure 2-24 shows an example, with full-duplex links on the left and a single LAN hub on the right. The hub then requires SW2's F0/2 interface to use half-duplex logic, along with the PCs connected to the hub.

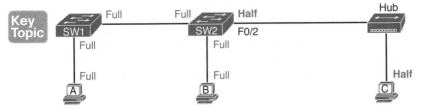

Figure 2-24   *Full and Half Duplex in an Ethernet LAN*

Before closing the chapter, note that the discussion of full and half duplex connects to two specific terms from CCNA exam topic 1.3.b, but those connections may not be obvious. First, the term *Ethernet shared media* (from the exam topic) refers to designs that use hubs, require CSMA/CD, and therefore share the bandwidth. The idea behind the term comes from the fact that the devices connected to the hub share the network because they must use CSMA/CD, and CSMA/CD enforces rules that allow only one device to successfully send a frame at any point in time.

By contrast, the term *Ethernet point-to-point* in that same exam topic emphasizes the fact that in a network built with switches, each (point-to-point) link works independently of the others. Because of the full-duplex logic discussed in this section, a frame can be sent on every point-to-point link in an Ethernet at the same time.

Chapter Review

One key to doing well on the exams is to perform repetitive spaced review sessions. Review this chapter's material using either the tools in the book or interactive tools for the same material found on the book's companion website. Refer to the "Your Study Plan" element for more details. Table 2-8 outlines the key review elements and where you can find them. To better track your study progress, record when you completed these activities in the second column.

Table 2-8   Chapter Review Tracking

Review Element	Review Date(s)	Resource Used
Review key topics		Book, website
Review key terms		Book, website
Answer DIKTA questions		Book, PTP
Review memory tables		Book, website

Review All the Key Topics

Table 2-9   Key Topics for Chapter 2

Key Topic Element	Description	Page Number
Figure 2-3	Drawing of a typical wired and wireless enterprise LAN	36
Table 2-2	Several types of Ethernet LANs and some details about each	37
Figure 2-9	Conceptual drawing of transmitting in one direction each over two different electrical circuits between two Ethernet nodes	43
Figure 2-10	10- and 100-Mbps Ethernet straight-through cable pinouts	43
Figure 2-12	10- and 100-Mbps Ethernet crossover cable pinouts	44
Table 2-3	List of devices that transmit on wire pair 1,2 and pair 3,6	45
Figure 2-13	Typical uses for straight-through and crossover Ethernet cables	45
Figure 2-16	Physical transmission concepts in a multimode cable	47
Table 2-5	Comparison between UTP, MM, and SM Ethernet Cabling	49
Figure 2-20	Format of Ethernet MAC addresses	51
List	Definitions of half duplex and full duplex	54
Figure 2-24	Examples of which interfaces use full duplex and which interfaces use half duplex	56

Key Terms You Should Know

Ethernet, IEEE, wired LAN, wireless LAN, Ethernet frame, 10BASE-T, 100BASE-T, 1000BASE-T, Fast Ethernet, Gigabit Ethernet, Ethernet link, RJ-45, Ethernet port, network interface card (NIC), straight-through cable, crossover cable, Ethernet address, MAC address, unicast address, broadcast address, Frame Check Sequence, transceiver, Multimode (MM), single-mode (SM), electromagnetic Interference (EMI), core, cladding, fiber-optic cable

CHAPTER 3

Fundamentals of WANs and IP Routing

This chapter covers the following exam topics:

1.0 Network Fundamentals

1.1 Explain the role and function of network components

1.1.a Routers

1.2 Describe characteristics of network topology architectures

1.2.d WAN

This chapter introduces WANs and the various features of the TCP/IP network layer.

First, for WANs, note that the current CCNA blueprint does not examine WANs in detail as an end to themselves. However, to understand IP routing, you need to understand the basics of the two types of WAN links introduced in the first major section of this chapter: serial links and Ethernet WAN links. In their most basic form, these WAN links connect routers that sit at sites that can be miles to hundreds of miles apart, allowing communications between remote sites.

The rest of the chapter then turns to the TCP/IP Network layer, with IP as the center of the discussion. The second section of the chapter discusses the major features of IP: routing, addressing, and routing protocols. The final section of the chapter examines a few protocols other than IP that also help the TCP/IP Network layer create a network that allows end-to-end communication between endpoints.

"Do I Know This Already?" Quiz

Take the quiz (either here or use the PTP software) if you want to use the score to help you decide how much time to spend on this chapter. The letter answers are listed at the bottom of the page following the quiz. Appendix C, found both at the end of the book as well as on the companion website, includes both the answers and explanations. You can also find both answers and explanations in the PTP testing software.

Table 3-1 "Do I Know This Already?" Foundation Topics Section-to-Question Mapping

Foundation Topics Section	Questions
Wide-Area Networks	1, 2
IP Routing	3–6
Other Network Layer Functions	7

1. Which of the following fields in the HDLC header used by Cisco routers does Cisco add, beyond the ISO standard HDLC?

   a. Flag

   b. Type

   c. Address

   d. FCS

2. Two routers, R1 and R2, connect using an Ethernet over MPLS service. The service provides point-to-point service between these two routers only, as a Layer 2 Ethernet service. Which of the following are the most likely to be true about this WAN? (Choose two answers.)

   a. R1 will connect to a physical Ethernet link, with the other end of the cable connected to R2.

   b. R1 will connect to a physical Ethernet link, with the other end of the cable connected to a device at the WAN service provider point of presence.

   c. R1 will forward data-link frames to R2 using an HDLC header/trailer.

   d. R1 will forward data-link frames to R2 using an Ethernet header/trailer.

3. Imagine a network with two routers that are connected with a point-to-point HDLC serial link. Each router has an Ethernet, with PC1 sharing the Ethernet with Router1 and PC2 sharing the Ethernet with Router2. When PC1 sends data to PC2, which of the following is true?

   a. Router1 strips the Ethernet header and trailer off the frame received from PC1, never to be used again.

   b. Router1 encapsulates the Ethernet frame inside an HDLC header and sends the frame to Router2, which extracts the Ethernet frame for forwarding to PC2.

   c. Router1 strips the Ethernet header and trailer off the frame received from PC1, which is exactly re-created by Router2 before forwarding data to PC2.

   d. Router1 removes the Ethernet, IP, and TCP headers and rebuilds the appropriate headers before forwarding the packet to Router2.

4. Which of the following does a router normally use when making a decision about routing TCP/IP packets?

   a. Destination MAC address

   b. Source MAC address

   c. Destination IP address

   d. Source IP address

   e. Destination MAC and IP addresses

5. Which of the following are true about a LAN-connected TCP/IP host and its IP routing (forwarding) choices?

    a. The host always sends packets to its default gateway.

    b. The host never sends packets to its default gateway.

    c. The host sends packets to its default gateway if the destination IP address is in a different subnet than the host.

    d. The host sends packets to its default gateway if the destination IP address is in the same subnet as the host.

6. Which of the following are functions of a routing protocol? (Choose two answers.)

    a. Advertising known routes to neighboring routers

    b. Learning routes for subnets directly connected to the router

    c. Learning routes and putting those routes into the routing table for routes advertised to the router by its neighboring routers

    d. Forwarding IP packets based on a packet's destination IP address

7. A company implements a TCP/IP network, with PC1 sitting on an Ethernet LAN. Which of the following protocols and features requires PC1 to learn information from some other server device?

    a. ARP

    b. ping

    c. DNS

    d. None of these answers is correct.

Foundation Topics

Wide-Area Networks

Imagine a typical day at the branch office at some enterprise. The user sits at some endpoint device: a PC, tablet, phone, and so on. It connects to a LAN, either via an Ethernet cable or using a wireless LAN. However, the user happens to be checking information on a website, and that web server sits at the home office of the company. To make that work, the data travels over one or more wide-area network (WAN) links.

WAN technologies define the physical (Layer 1) standards and data-link (Layer 2) protocols used to communicate long distances. This first section examines two such technologies: leased-line WANs and Ethernet WANs. Leased-line WANs have been an option for networks for half a century, are becoming much less common today, but you may still see some leased-line WAN links in the exam. Ethernet WAN links do use the same data-link protocols as Ethernet LANs, but they use additional features to make the links work over the much longer distances required for WANs. The next few pages examine leased-line WANs first, followed by Ethernet WANs.

Leased-Line WANs

To connect LANs using a WAN, the internetwork uses a router connected to each LAN, with a WAN link between the routers. First, the enterprise's network engineer would order some kind of WAN link. A router at each site connects to both the WAN link and the LAN, as shown in Figure 3-1. Note that a crooked line between the routers is the common way to represent a leased line when the drawing does not need to show any of the physical details of the line.

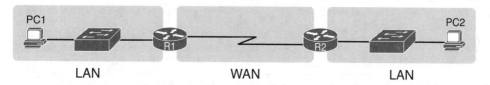

Figure 3-1   *Small Enterprise Network with One Leased Line*

This section begins by examining the physical details of leased lines, followed by a discussion of the default data-link protocol for leased lines (HDLC).

Physical Details of Leased Lines

The leased line service delivers bits in both directions, at a predetermined speed, using full-duplex logic. In fact, conceptually it acts as if you had a full-duplex crossover Ethernet link between two routers, as shown in Figure 3-2. The leased line uses two pairs of wires, one pair for each direction of sending data, which allows full-duplex operation.

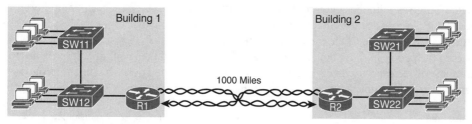

Figure 3-2   *Conceptual View of the Leased-Line Service*

Of course, leased lines have many differences compared to an Ethernet crossover cable. To create such possibly long links, or circuits, a leased line does not actually exist as a single long cable between the two sites. Instead, the telephone company (telco) that creates the leased line installs a large network of cables and specialized switching devices to create its own computer network. The telco network creates a service that acts like a crossover cable between two points, but the physical reality is hidden from the customer.

Leased lines come with their own set of terminology as well. First, the term *leased line* refers to the fact that the company using the leased line does not own the line but instead pays a monthly lease fee to use it. Table 3-2 lists some of the many names for leased lines, mainly so that in a networking job, you have a chance to translate from the terms each person uses with a basic description as to the meaning of the name.

Table 3-2   Different Names for a Leased Line

Name	Meaning or Reference
Leased circuit, Circuit	The words *line* and *circuit* are often used as synonyms in telco terminology; *circuit* makes reference to the electrical circuit between the two endpoints.
Serial link, Serial line	The words *link* and *line* are also often used as synonyms. *Serial* in this case refers to the fact that the bits flow serially and that routers use serial interfaces.
Point-to-point link, Point-to-point line	These terms refer to the fact that the topology stretches between two points, and two points only. (Some older leased lines allowed more than two devices.)
T1	This specific type of leased line transmits data at 1.544 megabits per second (1.544 Mbps).
WAN link, Link	Both of these terms are very general, with no reference to any specific technology.
Private line	This term refers to the fact that the data sent over the line cannot be copied by other telco customers, so the data is private.

To create a leased line, some physical path must exist between the two routers on the ends of the link. The physical cabling must leave the customer buildings where each router sits. However, the telco does not simply install one cable between the two buildings. Instead, it uses what is typically a large and complex network that creates the appearance of a cable between the two routers.

Figure 3-3 gives a little insight into the cabling that could exist inside the telco for a short leased line. Telcos put their equipment in buildings called central offices (CO). The telco installs cables from the CO to most every other building in the city, expecting to sell services to the people in those buildings one day. The telco would then configure its switches to use some of the capacity on each cable to send data in both directions, creating the equivalent of a crossover cable between the two routers.

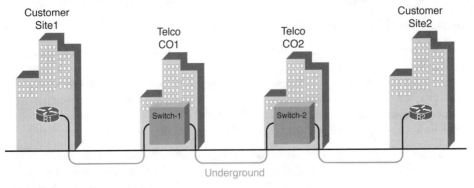

Figure 3-3   *Possible Cabling Inside a Telco for a Short Leased Line*

Answers to the "Do I Know This Already?" quiz:

1 B **2** B, D **3** A **4** C **5** C **6** A, C **7** C

Although the customer does not need to know all the details of how a telco creates a particular leased line, enterprise engineers do need to know about the parts of the link that exist inside the customer's building at the router. However, for the purposes of CCNA, you can think of any serial link as a point-to-point connection between two routers.

HDLC Data-Link Details of Leased Lines

A leased line provides a Layer 1 service. In other words, it promises to deliver bits between the devices connected to the leased line. However, the leased line itself does not define a data-link layer protocol to be used on the leased line.

Because leased lines define only the Layer 1 transmission service, many companies and standards organizations have created data-link protocols to control and use leased lines. Today, the two most popular data-link layer protocols used for leased lines between two routers are High-Level Data Link Control (HDLC) and Point-to-Point Protocol (PPP).

All data-link protocols perform a similar role: to control the correct delivery of data over a physical link of a particular type. For example, the Ethernet data-link protocol uses a destination address field to identify the correct device that should receive the data and an FCS field that allows the receiving device to determine whether the data arrived correctly. HDLC provides similar functions.

HDLC has less work to do than Ethernet because of the simple point-to-point topology of a leased line. When one router sends an HDLC frame, the frame can go only one place: to the other end of the link. So, while HDLC has an address field, the destination is implied, and the actual address is unimportant. The idea is sort of like when I have lunch with my friend Gary, and only Gary. I do not need to start every sentence with "Hey, Gary"—he knows I am talking to him.

HDLC has other fields and functions similar to Ethernet as well. Table 3-3 lists the HDLC fields, with the similar Ethernet header/trailer field, just for the sake of learning HDLC based on something you have already learned about (Ethernet).

Table 3-3   Comparing HDLC Header Fields to Ethernet

HDLC Field	Ethernet Equivalent	Description
Flag	Preamble, SFD	Lists a recognizable bit pattern so that the receiving nodes realize that a new frame is arriving.
Address	Destination Address	Identifies the destination device.
Control	N/A	Mostly used for purposes no longer in use today for links between routers.
Type	Type	Identifies the type of Layer 3 packet encapsulated inside the frame.
FCS	FCS	Identifies a field used by the error detection process. (It is the only trailer field in this table.)

HDLC exists today as a standard of the International Organization for Standardization (ISO), the same organization that brought us the OSI model. However, ISO standard HDLC does not have a Type field, and routers need to know the type of packet inside the frame. So, Cisco routers use a Cisco-proprietary variation of HDLC that adds a Type field, as shown in Figure 3-4.

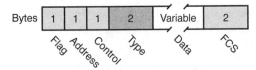

Figure 3-4   *HDLC Framing*

How Routers Use a WAN Data Link

Leased lines connect to routers, and routers focus on delivering packets to a destination host. However, routers physically connect to both LANs and WANs, with those LANs and WANs requiring that data be sent inside data-link frames. So, now that you know a little about HDLC, it helps to think about how routers use the HDLC protocol when sending data.

First, the TCP/IP network layer focuses on forwarding IP packets from the sending host to the destination host. The underlying LANs and WANs just act as a way to move the packets to the next router or end-user device. Figure 3-5 shows that network layer perspective.

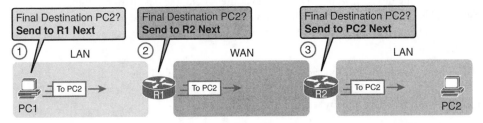

Figure 3-5   *IP Routing Logic over LANs and WANs*

Following the steps in the figure, for a packet sent by PC1 to PC2's IP address:

1. PC1's network layer (IP) logic tells it to send the packet to a nearby router (R1).

2. Router R1's network layer logic tells it to forward (route) the packet out the leased line to Router R2 next.

3. Router R2's network layer logic tells it to forward (route) the packet out the LAN link to PC2 next.

While Figure 3-5 shows the network layer logic, the PCs and routers must rely on the LANs and WANs in the figure to actually move the bits in the packet. Figure 3-6 shows the same figure, with the same packet, but this time showing some of the data-link layer logic used by the hosts and routers. Basically, three separate data-link layer steps encapsulate the packet, inside a data-link frame, over three hops through the internetwork: from PC1 to R1, from R1 to R2, and from R2 to PC2.

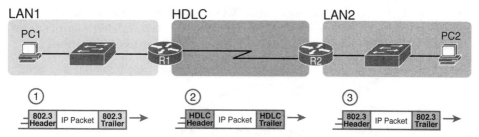

Figure 3-6 *General Concept of Routers De-encapsulating and Re-encapsulating IP Packets*

Following the steps in the figure, again for a packet sent by PC1 to PC2's IP address:

1. To send the IP packet to Router R1 next, PC1 encapsulates the IP packet in an Ethernet frame that has the destination MAC address of R1.

2. Router R1 de-encapsulates (removes) the IP packet from the Ethernet frame, encapsulates the packet into an HDLC frame using an HDLC header and trailer, and forwards the HDLC frame to Router R2 next.

3. Router R2 de-encapsulates (removes) the IP packet from the HDLC frame, encapsulates the packet into an Ethernet frame that has the destination MAC address of PC2, and forwards the Ethernet frame to PC2.

In summary, a leased line with HDLC creates a WAN link between two routers so that they can forward packets for the devices on the attached LANs. The leased line itself provides the physical means to transmit the bits, in both directions. The HDLC frames provide the means to encapsulate the network layer packet correctly so that it crosses the link between routers.

Leased lines have many benefits that have led to their relatively long life in the WAN marketplace. These lines are simple for the customer, are widely available, are of high quality, and are private. However, they do have some negatives as well compared to newer WAN technologies, including a higher cost and typically longer lead times to get the service installed. Additionally, by today's standards, leased-line LANs are slow, with faster speeds in the tens of megabits per second (Mbps). New faster WAN technology has been replacing leased lines for a long time, including the second WAN technology discussed in this book: Ethernet.

Ethernet as a WAN Technology

For the first several decades of the existence of Ethernet, Ethernet was only appropriate for LANs. The restrictions on cable lengths and devices might allow a LAN that stretched a kilometer or two, to support a campus LAN, but that was the limit.

As time passed, the IEEE improved Ethernet standards in ways that made Ethernet a reasonable WAN technology. For example, the 1000BASE-LX standard uses single-mode fiber cabling, with support for a 5-km cable length; the 1000BASE-ZX standard supports an even longer 70-km cable length. As time went by, and as the IEEE improved cabling distances for fiber Ethernet links, Ethernet became a reasonable WAN technology.

Today, many WAN service providers (SP) offer WAN services that take advantage of Ethernet. SPs offer a wide variety of these Ethernet WAN services, with many different names. But all of them use a similar model, with Ethernet used between the customer site and the SP's network, as shown in Figure 3-7.

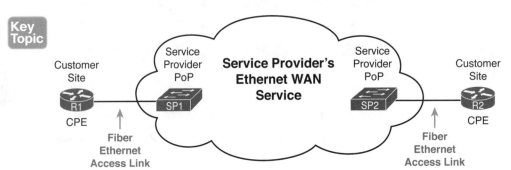

Figure 3-7   *Fiber Ethernet Link to Connect a CPE Router to a Service Provider's WAN*

The model shown in Figure 3-7 has many of the same ideas of how a telco creates a leased line, as shown earlier in Figure 3-3, but now with Ethernet links and devices. The customer connects to an Ethernet link using a router interface. The (fiber) Ethernet link leaves the customer building and connects to some nearby SP location called a point of presence (PoP). Instead of a telco switch as shown in Figure 3-3, the SP uses an Ethernet switch. Inside the SP's network, the SP uses any technology that it wants to create the specific Ethernet WAN services.

Ethernet WANs That Create a Layer 2 Service

Ethernet WAN services include a variety of specific services that vary in ways that change how routers use those services. However, for the purposes of CCNA, you just need to understand the most basic Ethernet WAN service, one that works much like an Ethernet crossover cable—just over a WAN. In other words:

■ Logically, behaves like a point-to-point connection between two routers

■ Physically, behaves as if a physical fiber Ethernet link existed between the two routers

> **NOTE**   For perspective about the broad world of the service provider network shown in Figure 3-7, look for more information about the Cisco CCNA, CCNP Service Provider, and CCIE Service Provider certifications. See www.cisco.com/go/certifications for more details.

This book refers to this particular Ethernet WAN service with a couple of the common names:

Ethernet WAN: A generic name to differentiate it from an Ethernet LAN.

Ethernet Line Service (E-Line): A term from the Metro Ethernet Forum (MEF) for the kind of point-to-point Ethernet WAN service shown throughout this book.

Ethernet emulation: A term emphasizing that the link is not a literal Ethernet link from end to end.

Ethernet over MPLS (EoMPLS): A term that refers to Multiprotocol Label Switching (MPLS), a technology that can be used to create the Ethernet service for the customer.

So, if you can imagine two routers, with a single Ethernet link between the two routers, you understand what this particular EoMPLS service does, as shown in Figure 3-8. In this case, the two routers, R1 and R2, connect with an EoMPLS service instead of a serial link. The routers use Ethernet interfaces, and they can send data in both directions at the same time. Physically, each router actually connects to some SP PoP, as shown earlier in Figure 3-7, but logically, the two routers can send Ethernet frames to each other over the link.

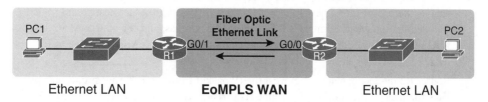

Figure 3-8   *EoMPLS Acting Like a Simple Ethernet Link Between Two Routers*

How Routers Route IP Packets Using Ethernet Emulation

WANs, by their very nature, give IP routers a way to forward IP packets from a LAN at one site, over the WAN, and to another LAN at another site. Routing over an EoMPLS WAN link still uses the WAN like a WAN, as a way to forward IP packets from one site to another. However, the WAN link happens to use the same Ethernet protocols as the Ethernet LAN links at each site.

The EoMPLS link uses Ethernet for both Layer 1 and Layer 2 functions. That means the link uses the same familiar Ethernet header and trailer, as shown in the middle of Figure 3-9. Note that the figure shows a small cloud over the Ethernet link as a way to tell us that the link is an Ethernet WAN link, rather than an Ethernet LAN link.

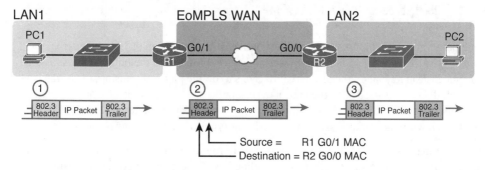

Figure 3-9   *Routing over an EoMPLS Link*

NOTE   The 802.3 headers/trailers in the figure are different at each stage! Make sure to notice the reasons in the step-by-step explanations that follow.

The figure shows the same three routing steps as shown with the serial link in the earlier Figure 3-6. In this case, all three routing steps use the same Ethernet (802.3) protocol. However, note that each frame's data-link header and trailer are different. Each router discards the old data-link header/trailer and adds a new set, as described in these steps. Focus mainly on Step 2, because compared to the similar example shown in Figure 3-6, Steps 1 and 3 are unchanged:

1. To send the IP packet to Router R1 next, PC1 encapsulates the IP packet in an Ethernet frame that has the destination MAC address of R1.

2. Router R1 de-encapsulates (removes) the IP packet from the Ethernet frame and encapsulates the packet into a new Ethernet frame, with a new Ethernet header and trailer. The destination MAC address is R2's G0/0 MAC address, and the source MAC address is R1's G0/1 MAC address. R1 forwards this frame over the EoMPLS service to R2 next.

3. Router R2 de-encapsulates (removes) the IP packet from the Ethernet frame, encapsulates the packet into an Ethernet frame that has the destination MAC address of PC2, and forwards the Ethernet frame to PC2.

Throughout this book, the WAN links (serial and Ethernet) will connect routers as shown here, with the focus being on the LANs and IP routing. The rest of the chapter turns our attention to a closer look at IP routing.

IP Routing

Many protocol models have existed over the years, but today the TCP/IP model dominates. And at the network layer of TCP/IP, two options exist for the main protocol around which all other network layer functions revolve: IP version 4 (IPv4) and IP version 6 (IPv6). Both IPv4 and IPv6 define the same kinds of network layer functions, but with different details. This chapter introduces these network layer functions for IPv4.

> **NOTE** All references to IP in this chapter refer to the older and more established IPv4.

Internet Protocol (IP) focuses on the job of routing data, in the form of IP packets, from the source host to the destination host. IP does not concern itself with the physical transmission of data, instead relying on the lower TCP/IP layers to do the physical transmission of the data. Instead, IP concerns itself with the logical details, rather than physical details, of delivering data. In particular, the network layer specifies how packets travel end to end over a TCP/IP network, even when the packet crosses many different types of LAN and WAN links.

This next major section of the chapter examines IP routing in more depth. First, IP defines what it means to route an IP packet from sending host to destination host, while using successive data-link protocols. This section then examines how IP addressing rules help to make IP routing much more efficient by grouping addresses into subnets. This section closes by looking at the role of IP routing protocols, which give routers a means by which to learn routes to all the IP subnets in an internetwork.

Network Layer Routing (Forwarding) Logic

Routers and end-user computers (called *hosts* in a TCP/IP network) work together to perform IP routing. The host operating system (OS) has TCP/IP software, including the software that implements the network layer. Hosts use that software to choose where to send IP packets, often to a nearby router. Those routers make choices of where to send the IP packet next. Together, the hosts and routers deliver the IP packet to the correct destination, as shown in the example in Figure 3-10.

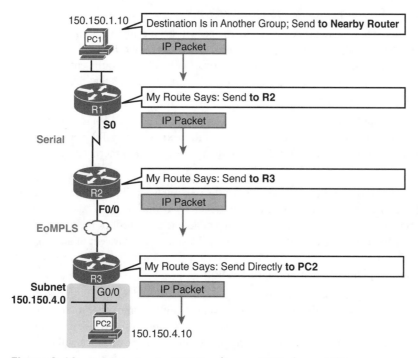

Figure 3-10 *Routing Logic: PC1 Sending an IP Packet to PC2*

The IP packet, created by PC1, goes from the top of the figure all the way to PC2 at the bottom of the figure. The next few pages discuss the network layer routing logic used by each device along the path.

> **NOTE** The term *path selection* is sometimes used to refer to the routing process shown in Figure 3-10. At other times, it refers to routing protocols, specifically how routing protocols select the best route among the competing routes to the same destination.

Host Forwarding Logic: Send the Packet to the Default Router

In this example, PC1 does some basic analysis and then chooses to send the IP packet to the router so that the router will forward the packet. PC1 analyzes the destination address and realizes that PC2's address (150.150.4.10) is not on the same LAN as PC1. So PC1's logic tells it to send the packet to a device whose job it is to know where to route data: a nearby router, on the same LAN, called PC1's default router.

To send the IP packet to the default router, the sender sends a data-link frame across the medium to the nearby router; this frame includes the packet in the data portion of the frame. That frame uses data-link layer (Layer 2) addressing in the data-link header to ensure that the nearby router receives the frame.

> **NOTE**   The *default router* is also referred to as the *default gateway*.

R1 and R2's Logic: Routing Data Across the Network

All routers use the same general process to route the packet. Each router keeps an *IP routing table*. This table lists IP address *groupings*, called *IP networks* and *IP subnets*. When a router receives a packet, it compares the packet's destination IP address to the entries in the routing table and makes a match. This matching entry also lists directions that tell the router where to forward the packet next.

In Figure 3-10, R1 would have matched the destination address (150.150.4.10) to a routing table entry, which in turn told R1 to send the packet to R2 next. Similarly, R2 would have matched a routing table entry that told R2 to send the packet, over an Ethernet WAN link, to R3 next.

The routing concept works a little like driving down the freeway when approaching a big interchange. You look up and see signs for nearby towns, telling you which exits to take to go to each town. Similarly, the router looks at the IP routing table (the equivalent of the road signs) and directs each packet over the correct next LAN or WAN link (the equivalent of a road).

R3's Logic: Delivering Data to the End Destination

The final router in the path, R3, uses almost the same logic as R1 and R2, but with one minor difference. R3 needs to forward the packet directly to PC2, not to some other router. On the surface, that difference seems insignificant. In the next section, when you read about how the network layer uses LANs and WANs, the significance of the difference will become obvious.

How Network Layer Routing Uses LANs and WANs

While the network layer routing logic ignores the physical transmission details, the bits still have to be transmitted. To do that work, the network layer logic in a host or router must hand off the packet to the data-link layer protocols, which, in turn, ask the physical layer to actually send the data. The data-link layer adds the appropriate header and trailer to the packet, creating a frame, before sending the frames over each physical network.

The routing process forwards the network layer packet from end to end through the network, while each data-link frame only takes a smaller part of the trip. Each successive data-link layer frame moves the packet to the next device that thinks about network layer logic. In short, the network layer thinks about the bigger view of the goal, like "Send this packet to the specified next router or host…," while the data-link layer thinks about the specifics, like "Encapsulate the packet in a data-link frame and transmit it." The following list summarizes the major steps in a router's internal network layer routing for each packet beginning with the a frame arriving in a router interface:

Step 1.   Use the data-link Frame Check Sequence (FCS) field to ensure that the frame had no errors; if errors occurred, discard the frame.

Step 2.   Assuming that the frame was not discarded at Step 1, discard the old data-link header and trailer, leaving the IP packet.

Step 3. Compare the IP packet's destination IP address to the routing table, and find the route that best matches the destination address. This route identifies the outgoing interface of the router and possibly the next-hop router IP address.

Step 4. Encapsulate the IP packet inside a new data-link header and trailer, appropriate for the outgoing interface, and forward the frame.

Figure 3-11 works through a repeat example of a packet sent by PC1 to PC2, followed by a detailed analysis of each device's routing logic. Each explanation includes the details about how PC1 and each of the three routers builds the appropriate new data-link headers.

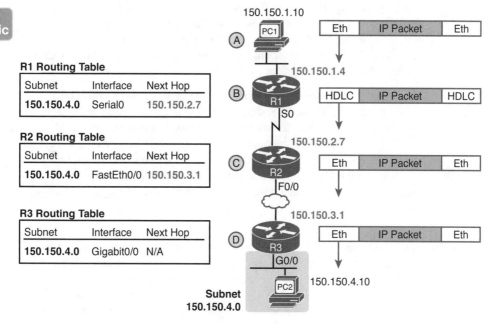

Figure 3-11 *Network Layer and Data-Link Layer Encapsulation*

The following list explains the forwarding logic at each router, focusing on how the routing integrates with the data link.

Step A. **PC1 sends the packet to its default router.** PC1's network layer logic builds the IP packet, with a destination address of PC2's IP address (150.150.4.10). The network layer also performs the analysis to decide that 150.150.4.10 is not in the local IP subnet, so PC1 needs to send the packet to R1 (PC1's default router). PC1 places the IP packet into an Ethernet data-link frame, with a destination Ethernet address of R1's Ethernet address. PC1 sends the frame on to the Ethernet.

Step B. **R1 processes the incoming frame and forwards the packet to R2.** Because the incoming Ethernet frame has a destination MAC of R1's Ethernet MAC, R1 decides to process the frame. R1 checks the frame's FCS for errors, and if none, R1 discards the Ethernet header and trailer. Next, R1 compares the packet's destination address (150.150.4.10) to its routing table and finds the entry for subnet 150.150.4.0. Because the destination address of 150.150.4.10 is in that subnet, R1 forwards the packet out the interface listed in that matching route (Serial0) to next-hop Router R2 (150.150.2.7). R1 must first encapsulate the IP packet into an HDLC frame.

Step C.   **R2 processes the incoming frame and forwards the packet to R3.** R2 repeats the same general process as R1 when R2 receives the HDLC frame. R2 checks the FCS field and finds that no errors occurred and then discards the HDLC header and trailer. Next, R2 compares the packet's destination address (150.150.4.10) to its routing table and finds the entry for subnet 150.150.4.0, a route that directs R2 to send the packet out interface Fast Ethernet 0/0 to next-hop router 150.150.3.1 (R3). But first, R2 must encapsulate the packet in an Ethernet header. That header uses R2's MAC address and R3's MAC address on the Ethernet WAN link as the source and destination MAC address, respectively.

Step D.   **R3 processes the incoming frame and forwards the packet to PC2.** Like R1 and R2, R3 checks the FCS, discards the old data-link header and trailer, and matches its own route for subnet 150.150.4.0. R3's routing table entry for 150.150.4.0 shows that the outgoing interface is R3's Ethernet interface, but there is no next-hop router because R3 is connected directly to subnet 150.150.4.0. All R3 has to do is encapsulate the packet inside a new Ethernet header and trailer, but with a destination Ethernet address of PC2's MAC address.

Because the routers build new data-link headers and trailers, and because the new headers contain data-link addresses, the PCs and routers must have some way to decide what data-link addresses to use. An example of how the router determines which data-link address to use is the IP Address Resolution Protocol (ARP). *ARP dynamically learns the data-link address of an IP host connected to a LAN.* For example, at the last step, at the bottom of Figure 3-11, Router R3 would use ARP once to learn PC2's MAC address before sending any packets to PC2.

How IP Addressing Helps IP Routing

IP defines network layer addresses that identify any host or router interface that connects to a TCP/IP network. The idea basically works like a postal address: Any interface that expects to receive IP packets needs an IP address, just like you need a postal address before receiving mail from the postal service. This next short topic introduces the idea of IP networks and subnets, which are the groups of addresses defined by IP.

NOTE   IP defines the word *network* to mean a very specific concept. To avoid confusion when writing about IP addressing, this book (and others) often avoids using the term *network* for other uses. In particular, this book uses the term *internetwork* to refer more generally to a network made up of routers, switches, cables, and other equipment.

Rules for Groups of IP Addresses (Networks and Subnets)

TCP/IP groups IP addresses together so that IP addresses used on the same physical network are part of the same group. IP calls these address groups an *IP network* or an *IP subnet*. Using that same postal service analogy, each IP network and IP subnet works like a postal code (or in the United States, a ZIP code). All nearby postal addresses are in the same postal code (ZIP code), while all nearby IP addresses must be in the same IP network or IP subnet.

IP defines specific rules about which IP address should be in the same IP network or IP subnet. Numerically, the addresses in the same group have the same value in the first part of the addresses. For example, Figures 3-10 and 3-11 could have used the following conventions:

- Hosts on the top Ethernet: Addresses start with 150.150.1

- Hosts on the R1–R2 serial link: Addresses start with 150.150.2

- Hosts on the R2–R3 EoMPLS link: Addresses start with 150.150.3

- Hosts on the bottom Ethernet: Addresses start with 150.150.4

From the perspective of IP routing, the grouping of IP addresses means that the routing table can be much smaller. A router can list one routing table entry for each IP network or subnet, instead of one entry for every single IP address.

While the list shows just one example of how IP addresses may be grouped, the rules for how to group addresses using subnets will require some work to master the concepts and math. Part III of this book details IP addressing and subnetting, and you can find other subnetting video and practice products listed in the Introduction to the book. However, the brief version of two of the foundational rules of subnetting can be summarized as follows:

- Two IP addresses, not separated from each other by a router, must be in the same group (subnet).

- Two IP addresses, separated from each other by at least one router, must be in different groups (subnets).

It's similar to the USPS ZIP code system and how it requires local governments to assign addresses to new buildings. It would be ridiculous to have two houses next door to each other, whose addresses had different postal/ZIP codes. Similarly, it would be silly to have people who live on opposite sides of the country to have addresses with the same postal/ZIP code.

The IP Header

The routing process also makes use of the IPv4 header, as shown in Figure 3-12. The header lists a 32-bit source IP address, as well as a 32-bit destination IP address. The header, of course, has other fields, a few of which matter for other discussions in this book. The book will refer to this figure as needed, but otherwise, be aware of the 20-byte IP header and the existence of the source and destination IP address fields. Note that in the examples so far in this chapter, while routers remove and add data-link headers each time it routes a packet, the IP header remains, with the IP addresses unchanged by the IP routing process.

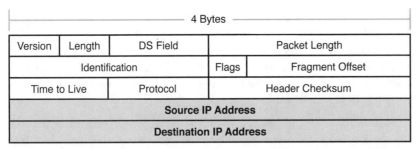

Figure 3-12 *IPv4 Header, Organized as 4 Bytes Wide for a Total of 20 Bytes*

How IP Routing Protocols Help IP Routing

For routing logic to work on both hosts and routers, each host and router needs to know something about the TCP/IP internetwork. Hosts need to know the IP address of their default router so that hosts can send packets to remote destinations. Routers, however, need to know routes so they forward packets to each and every reachable IP network and IP subnet.

The best method for routers to know all the useful routes is to configure the routers to use the same IP routing protocol. Alternately, a network engineer could configure (type) all the required routes, on every router. However, if you enable the same routing protocol on all the routers in a TCP/IP internetwork, with the correct settings, the routers will send routing protocol messages to each other. As a result, all the routers will learn routes for all the IP networks and subnets in the TCP/IP internetwork.

IP supports a small number of different IP routing protocols. All use some similar ideas and processes to learn IP routes, but different routing protocols do have some internal differences; otherwise, you would not need more than one routing protocol. However, many routing protocols use the same general steps for learning routes:

Step 1. Each router, independent of the routing protocol, adds a route to its routing table for each subnet directly connected to the router.

Step 2. Each router's routing protocol tells its neighbors about the routes in its routing table, including the directly connected routes and routes learned from other routers.

Step 3. After learning a new route from a neighbor, the router's routing protocol adds a route to its IP routing table, with the next-hop router of that route typically being the neighbor from which the route was learned.

Also, note that at the final step, routers may have to choose between multiple routes to reach a single subnet. When that happens, routers place the best currently available route to reach a subnet (based on a measurement called a metric) into the routing table.

Figure 3-13 shows an example of how a routing protocol works, using the same diagram as in Figures 3-10 and 3-11. In this case, IP subnet 150.150.4.0, which consists of all addresses that begin with 150.150.4.0, sits on the Ethernet at the bottom of the figure. The figure shows the advertisement of routes for subnet 150.150.4.0 from bottom to top, as described in detail following the figure.

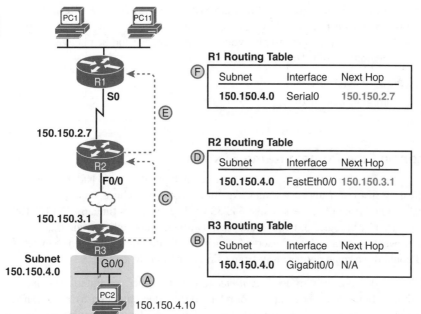

Figure 3-13   *Example of How Routing Protocols Advertise About Networks and Subnets*

Follow items A through F shown in the figure to see how each router learns its route to 150.150.4.0.

Step A.   Subnet 150.150.4.0 exists as a subnet at the bottom of the figure, connected to Router R3.

Step B.   R3 adds a connected route for 150.150.4.0 to its IP routing table; this happens without help from the routing protocol.

Step C.   R3 sends a routing protocol message, called a *routing update*, to R2, causing R2 to learn about subnet 150.150.4.0.

Step D.   R2 adds a route for subnet 150.150.4.0 to its routing table.

Step E.   R2 sends a similar routing update to R1, causing R1 to learn about subnet 150.150.4.0.

Step F.   R1 adds a route for subnet 150.150.4.0 to its routing table. The route lists R1's own Serial0 as the outgoing interface and R2 as the next-hop router IP address (150.150.2.7).

Other Network Layer Features

The TCP/IP network layer defines many functions beyond IP. Sure, IP plays a huge role in networking today, defining IP addressing and IP routing. However, other protocols and standards, defined in other Requests For Comments (RFC), play an important role for network layer functions as well. For example, routing protocols like Open Shortest Path First (OSPF) exist as separate protocols, defined in separate RFCs.

This last short section of the chapter introduces three other network layer features that should be helpful to you when reading through the rest of this book. These last three topics just help fill in a few holes, helping to give you some perspective and helping you make sense of later discussions as well. The three topics are

■ Domain Name System (DNS)

■ Address Resolution Protocol (ARP)

■ Ping

Using Names and the Domain Name System

Can you imagine a world in which every time you used an application, you had to refer to it by IP address? Instead of using easy names like google.com or facebook.com, you would have to remember and type IP addresses, like 64.233.177.100. (At press time, 64.233.177.100 was an address used by Google, and you could reach Google's website by typing that address in a browser.) Certainly, asking users to remember IP addresses would not be user friendly and could drive some people away from using computers at all.

Thankfully, TCP/IP defines a way to use *hostnames* to identify other computers. The user either never thinks about the other computer or refers to the other computer by name. Then, protocols dynamically discover all the necessary information to allow communications based on that name.

For example, when you open a web browser and type in the hostname **www.google.com**, your computer does not send an IP packet with destination IP address www.google.com; it sends an IP packet to an IP address used by the web server for Google. TCP/IP needs a way to let a computer find the IP address used by the listed hostname, and that method uses the Domain Name System (DNS).

Enterprises use the DNS process to resolve names into the matching IP address, as shown in the example in Figure 3-14. In this case, PC11, on the left, needs to connect to a server named Server1. At some point, the user either types in the name Server1 or some application on PC11 refers to that server by name. At Step 1, PC11 sends a DNS message—a DNS query—to the DNS server. At Step 2, the DNS server sends back a DNS reply that lists Server1's IP address. At Step 3, PC11 can now send an IP packet to destination address 10.1.2.3, the address used by Server1.

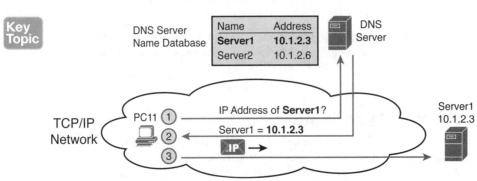

Figure 3-14 *Basic DNS Name Resolution Request*

Note that the example in Figure 3-14 shows a cloud for the TCP/IP network because the details of the network, including routers, do not matter to the name resolution process. Routers treat the DNS messages just like any other IP packet, routing them based on the destination IP address. For example, at Step 1 in the figure, the DNS query will list the DNS server's IP address as the destination address, which any routers will use to forward the packet.

Finally, DNS defines much more than just a few messages. DNS defines protocols, as well as standards for the text names used throughout the world, and a worldwide set of distributed DNS servers. The domain names that people use every day when web browsing, which look like www.example.com, follow the DNS naming standards. Also, no single DNS server knows all the names and matching IP addresses, but the information is distributed across many DNS servers. So, the DNS servers of the world work together, forwarding queries to each other, until the server that knows the answer supplies the desired IP address information.

The Address Resolution Protocol

As discussed in depth throughout this chapter, IP routing logic requires that hosts and routers encapsulate IP packets inside data-link layer frames. For Ethernet interfaces, how does a router know what MAC address to use for the destination? It uses ARP.

On Ethernet LANs, whenever a host or router needs to encapsulate an IP packet in a new Ethernet frame, the host or router knows all the important facts to build that header—except for the destination MAC address. The host knows the IP address of the next device, either another host IP address or the default router IP address. A router knows the IP route used for forwarding the IP packet, which lists the next router's IP address. However, the hosts and routers do not know those neighboring devices' MAC addresses beforehand.

TCP/IP defines the Address Resolution Protocol (ARP) as the method by which any host or router on a LAN can dynamically learn the MAC address of another IP host or router on the same LAN. ARP defines a protocol that includes the *ARP Request*, which is a message that makes the simple request "if this is your IP address, please reply with your MAC address." ARP also defines the *ARP Reply* message, which indeed lists both the original IP address and the matching MAC address.

Figure 3-15 shows an example that uses the same router and host from the bottom part of the earlier Figure 3-13. The figure shows the ARP Request sent by router R3, on the left of the figure, as a LAN broadcast. All devices on the LAN will then process the received frame. On the right, at Step 2, host PC2 sends back an ARP Reply, identifying PC2's MAC address. The text beside each message shows the contents inside the ARP message itself, which lets PC2 learn R3's IP address and matching MAC address, and R3 learn PC2's IP address and matching MAC address.

Note that hosts and routers remember the ARP results, keeping the information in their *ARP cache* or *ARP table*. A host or router only needs to use ARP occasionally, to build the ARP cache the first time. Each time a host or router needs to send a packet encapsulated in an Ethernet frame, it first checks its ARP cache for the correct IP address and matching MAC address. Hosts and routers will let ARP cache entries time out to clean up the table, so occasional ARP Requests can be seen.

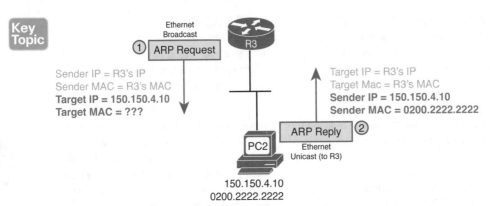

Figure 3-15 *Sample ARP Process*

> **NOTE**   You can see the contents of the ARP cache on most PC operating systems by using the **arp -a** command from a command prompt.

ICMP Echo and the ping Command

After you have implemented a TCP/IP internetwork, you need a way to test basic IP connectivity without relying on any applications to be working. The primary tool for testing basic network connectivity is the **ping** command.

Ping (Packet Internet Groper) uses the Internet Control Message Protocol (ICMP), sending a message called an *ICMP echo request* to another IP address. The computer with that IP address should reply with an *ICMP echo reply*. If that works, you successfully have tested the IP network. In other words, you know that the network can deliver a packet from one host to the other and back. ICMP does not rely on any application, so it really just tests basic IP connectivity—Layers 1, 2, and 3 of the OSI model. Figure 3-16 outlines the basic process.

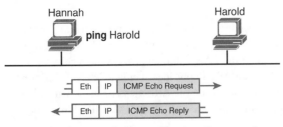

Figure 3-16 *Sample Network, ping Command*

Note that while the **ping** command uses ICMP, ICMP does much more. ICMP defines many messages that devices can use to help manage and control the IP network.

Chapter Review

The "Your Study Plan" element, just before Chapter 1, discusses how you should study and practice the content and skills for each chapter before moving on to the next chapter. That element introduces the tools used here at the end of each chapter. If you haven't already done so, take a few minutes to read that section. Then come back here and do the useful work of reviewing the chapter to help lock into memory what you just read.

Review this chapter's material using either the tools in the book or interactive tools for the same material found on the book's companion website. Table 3-4 outlines the key review elements and where you can find them. To better track your study progress, record when you completed these activities in the second column.

Table 3-4   Chapter Review Tracking

Review Element	Review Date(s)	Resource Used
Review key topics		Book, website
Review key terms		Book, website
Answer DIKTA questions		Book, PTP
Review memory tables		Book, website

Review All the Key Topics

Table 3-5   Key Topics for Chapter 3

Key Topic Element	Description	Page Number
Figure 3-7	Ethernet over MPLS—physical connections	66
List	Four-step process of how routers route (forward) packets	70
Figure 3-11	IP Routing and Encapsulation	71
List	Two statements about how IP expects IP addresses to be grouped into networks or subnets	73
List	Three-step process of how routing protocols learn routes	74
Figure 3-13	IP Routing Protocol Basic Process	75
Figure 3-14	Example that shows the purpose and process of DNS name resolution	76
Figure 3-15	Example of the purpose and process of ARP	78

Key Terms You Should Know

leased line, wide-area network (WAN), telco, serial interface, HDLC, Ethernet over MPLS, Ethernet Line Service (E-Line), default router (default gateway), routing table, IP network, IP subnet, IP packet, routing protocol, dotted-decimal notation (DDN), IPv4 address, unicast IP address, subnetting, hostname, DNS, ARP, ping

Part I Review

Keep track of your part review progress with the checklist shown in Table P1-1. Details on each task follow the table.

Table P1-1 Part I Review Checklist

Activity	1st Date Completed	2nd Date Completed
Repeat All DIKTA Questions		
Answer Part Review Questions		
Review Key Topics		

Repeat All DIKTA Questions

For this task, answer the "Do I Know This Already?" questions again for the chapters in this part of the book, using the PTP software. Refer to the Introduction to this book, the section titled "How to View Only DIKTA Questions by Chapter or Part," for help with how to make the PTP software show you DIKTA questions for this part only.

Answer Part Review Questions

For this task, answer the Part Review questions for this part of the book, using the PTP software. Refer to the Introduction to this book, the section titled "How to View Part Review Questions," for help with how to make the PTP software show you Part Review questions for this part only. (Note that if you use the questions but then want even more, get the Premium Edition of the book, as detailed in the Introduction, in the section "Other Features," under the item labeled "eBook.")

Review Key Topics

Browse back through the chapters and look for the Key Topic icons. If you do not remember some details, take the time to reread those topics, or use the Key Topics application(s) found on the companion website.

Use Per-Chapter Interactive Review Elements

Using the companion website, browse through the interactive review elements, like memory tables and key term flashcards, to review the content from each chapter.

Part I provided a broad look at the fundamentals of all parts of networking, focusing on Ethernet LANs, WANs, and IP routing. Parts II and III now drill into depth about the details of Ethernet, which was introduced in Chapter 2, "Fundamentals of Ethernet LANs."

Part II begins that journey by discussing the basics of building a small Ethernet LAN with Cisco Catalyst switches. The journey begins by showing how to access the user interface of a Cisco switch so that you can see evidence of what the switch is doing and configure the switch to act in the ways you want it to act. At this point, you should start using whatever lab practice option you chose in the "Your Study Plan" section that preceded Chapter 1, "Introduction to TCP/IP Networking." (And if you have not yet finalized your plan for how to practice your hands-on skills, now is the time.)

After you complete Chapter 4 and see how to get into the command-line interface (CLI) of a switch, the next three chapters step through some important foundations of how to implement LANs—foundations used by every company that builds LANs with Cisco gear. Chapter 5 takes a close look at Ethernet switching—that is, the logic used by a switch—and how to know what a particular switch is doing. Chapter 6 shows the ways to configure a switch for remote access with Telnet and Secure Shell (SSH), along with a variety of other useful commands that will help you when you work with any real lab gear, simulator, or any other practice tools. Chapter 7, the final chapter in Part II, shows how to configure and verify the operation of switch interfaces for several important features, including speed, duplex, and autonegotiation.

Part II

Implementing Ethernet LANs

CHAPTER 4

Using the Command-Line Interface

This chapter covers the following exam topics:

None

This chapter explains foundational skills required before you can learn about the roughly 15 exam topics that use the verbs *configure* and *verify*. However, Cisco does not list the foundational skills described in this chapter as a separate exam topic, so there are no specific exam topics included in this chapter.

To create an Ethernet LAN, network engineers start by planning. They consider the requirements, create a design, buy the switches, contract to install cables, and configure the switches to use the right features.

The CCNA exam focuses on skills like understanding how LANs work, configuring different switch features, verifying that those features work correctly, and finding the root cause of the problem when a feature is not working correctly. The first skill you need to learn before doing all the configuration and verification tasks is to learn how to access and use the user interface of the switch, called the command-line interface (CLI).

This chapter begins that process by showing the basics of how to access the switch's CLI. These skills include how to access the CLI and how to issue verification commands to check on the status of the LAN. This chapter also includes the processes of how to configure the switch and how to save that configuration.

Note that this chapter focuses on processes that provide a foundation for most every exam topic that includes the verbs *configure* and/or *verify*. Most of the rest of the chapters in Parts II and III of this book then go on to include details of the particular commands you can use to verify and configure different switch features.

"Do I Know This Already?" Quiz

Take the quiz (either here or use the PTP software) if you want to use the score to help you decide how much time to spend on this chapter. The letter answers are listed at the bottom of the page following the quiz. Appendix C, found both at the end of the book as well as on the companion website, includes both the answers and explanations. You can also find both answers and explanations in the PTP testing software.

Table 4-1 "Do I Know This Already?" Foundation Topics Section-to-Question Mapping

Foundation Topics Section	Questions
Accessing the Cisco Catalyst Switch CLI	1–3
Configuring Cisco IOS Software	4–6

1. In what modes can you type the command **show mac address-table** and expect to get a response with MAC table entries? (Choose two answers.)

   a. User mode

   b. Enable mode

   c. Global configuration mode

   d. Interface configuration mode

2. In which of the following modes of the CLI could you type the command **reload** and expect the switch to reboot?

   a. User mode

   b. Enable mode

   c. Global configuration mode

   d. Interface configuration mode

3. Which of the following is a difference between Telnet and SSH as supported by a Cisco switch?

   a. SSH encrypts the passwords used at login, but not other traffic; Telnet encrypts nothing.

   b. SSH encrypts all data exchange, including login passwords; Telnet encrypts nothing.

   c. Telnet is used from Microsoft operating systems, and SSH is used from UNIX and Linux operating systems.

   d. Telnet encrypts only password exchanges; SSH encrypts all data exchanges.

4. What type of switch memory is used to store the configuration used by the switch when it is up and working?

   a. RAM

   b. ROM

   c. Flash

   d. NVRAM

   e. Bubble

5. What command copies the configuration from RAM into NVRAM?

   a. **copy running-config tftp**

   b. **copy tftp running-config**

   c. **copy running-config start-up-config**

   d. **copy start-up-config running-config**

   e. **copy startup-config running-config**

   f. **copy running-config startup-config**

6. A switch user is currently in console line configuration mode. Which of the following would place the user in enable mode? (Choose two answers.)

   a. Using the **exit** command once

   b. Using the **end** command once

   c. Pressing the Ctrl+Z key sequence once

   d. Using the **quit** command

Foundation Topics

Accessing the Cisco Catalyst Switch CLI

Cisco uses the concept of a command-line interface (CLI) with its router products and most of its Catalyst LAN switch products. The CLI is a text-based interface in which the user, typically a network engineer, enters a text command and presses Enter. Pressing Enter sends the command to the switch, which tells the device to do something. The switch does what the command says, and in some cases, the switch replies with some messages stating the results of the command.

Cisco Catalyst switches also support other methods to both monitor and configure a switch. For example, a switch can provide a web interface so that an engineer can open a web browser to connect to a web server running in the switch. Switches also can be controlled and operated using network management software.

This book discusses only Cisco Catalyst enterprise-class switches, and in particular, how to use the Cisco CLI to monitor and control these switches. This first major section of the chapter first examines these Catalyst switches in more detail and then explains how a network engineer can get access to the CLI to issue commands.

Cisco Catalyst Switches

Within the Cisco Catalyst brand of LAN switches, Cisco produces a wide variety of switch series or families. Each switch series includes several specific models of switches that have similar features, similar price-versus-performance tradeoffs, and similar internal components.

For example, at the time this book was published, the Cisco 2960-XR series of switches was a current switch model series. Cisco positions the 2960-XR series (family) of switches as full-featured, low-cost wiring closet switches for enterprises. That means that you would expect to use 2960-XR switches as access switches in a typical campus LAN design.

Figure 4-1 shows a photo of 10 different models from the 2960-XR switch model series from Cisco. Each switch series includes several models, with a mix of features. For example, some of the switches have 48 RJ-45 unshielded twisted-pair (UTP) 10/100/1000 ports, meaning that these ports can autonegotiate the use of 10BASE-T (10 Mbps), 100BASE-T (100 Mbps), or 1000BASE-T (1 Gbps) Ethernet.

Figure 4-1 *Cisco 2960-XR Catalyst Switch Series*

Cisco refers to a switch's physical connectors as either *interfaces* or *ports*, with an interface type and interface number. The interface type, as used in commands on the switch, is either Ethernet, Fast Ethernet, Gigabit Ethernet, and so on for faster speeds. For Ethernet interfaces that support running at multiple speeds, the permanent name for the interface refers to the fastest supported speed. For example, a 10/100/1000 interface (that is, an interface that runs at 10 Mbps, 100 Mbps, or 1000 Mbps) would be called Gigabit Ethernet no matter what speed is currently in use.

To uniquely number each different interface, some Catalyst switches use a two-digit interface number (*x/y*), while others have a three-digit number (*x/y/z*). For instance, two 10/100/1000 ports on many older Cisco Catalyst switches would be called GigabitEthernet 0/0 and GigabitEthernet 0/1, while on the newer 2960-XR series, two interfaces would be GigabitEthernet 1/0/1 and GigabitEthernet 1/0/2.

Accessing the Cisco IOS CLI

Like any other piece of computer hardware, Cisco switches need some kind of operating system software. Cisco calls this OS the Internetwork Operating System (IOS).

Cisco IOS Software for Catalyst switches implements and controls logic and functions performed by a Cisco switch. Besides controlling the switch's performance and behavior, Cisco IOS also defines an interface for humans called the CLI. The Cisco IOS CLI allows the user to use a terminal emulation program, which accepts text entered by the user. When the user presses Enter, the terminal emulator sends that text to the switch. The switch processes the text as if it is a command, does what the command says, and sends text back to the terminal emulator.

The switch CLI can be accessed through three popular methods—the console, Telnet, and Secure Shell (SSH). Two of these methods (Telnet and SSH) use the IP network in which the switch resides to reach the switch. The console is a physical port built specifically to allow access to the CLI. Figure 4-2 depicts the options.

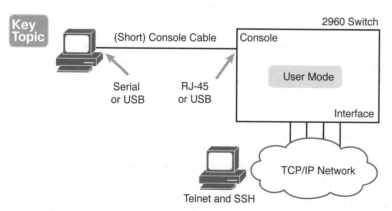

Figure 4-2 *CLI Access Options*

Console access requires both a physical connection between a PC (or other user device) and the switch's console port, as well as some software on the PC. Telnet and SSH require software on the user's device, but they rely on the existing TCP/IP network to transmit data. The next few pages detail how to connect the console and set up the software for each method to access the CLI.

Cabling the Console Connection

The physical console connection, both old and new, uses three main components: the physical console port on the switch, a physical serial port on the PC, and a cable that works with the console and serial ports. However, the physical cabling details have changed slowly over time, mainly because of advances and changes with serial interfaces on PC hardware. For this next topic, the text looks at three cases: newer connectors on both the PC and the switch, older connectors on both, and a third case with the newer (USB) connector on the PC but with an older connector on the switch.

Most PCs today use a familiar standard USB cable for the console connection. Cisco has been including USB ports as console ports in newer routers and switches as well. All you have to do is look at the switch to make sure you have the correct style of USB cable end to match the USB console port. In the simplest form, you can use any USB port on the PC, with a USB cable, connected to the USB console port on the switch or router, as shown on the far right side of Figure 4-3.

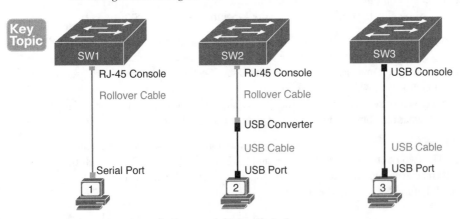

Figure 4-3   *Console Connection to a Switch*

Older console connections use a PC serial port that pre-dates USB, a UTP cable, and an RJ-45 console port on the switch, as shown on the left side of Figure 4-3. The PC serial port typically has a D-shell connector (roughly rectangular) with nine pins (often called a DB-9). The console port looks like any Ethernet RJ-45 port (but is typically colored in blue and with the word *console* beside it on the switch).

The cabling for this older-style console connection can be simple or require some effort, depending on what cable you use. You can use the purpose-built console cable that ships with new Cisco switches and routers and not think about the details. However, you can make

---

Answers to the "Do I Know This Already?" quiz:

1 A, B **2** B **3** B **4** A **5** F **6** B, C

your own cable with a standard serial cable (with a connector that matches the PC), a standard RJ-45 to DB-9 converter plug, and a UTP cable. However, the UTP cable does not use the same pinouts as Ethernet; instead, the cable uses rollover cable pinouts rather than any of the standard Ethernet cabling pinouts. The rollover pinout uses eight wires, rolling the wire at pin 1 to pin 8, pin 2 to pin 7, pin 3 to pin 6, and so on.

As it turns out, USB ports became common on PCs before Cisco began commonly using USB for its console ports. So, you also have to be ready to use a PC that has only a USB port and not an old serial port, but a router or switch that has the older RJ-45 console port (and no USB console port). The center of Figure 4-3 shows that case. To connect such a PC to a router or switch console, you need a USB converter that converts from the older console cable to a USB connector, and a rollover UTP cable, as shown in the middle of Figure 4-3.

> **NOTE** When using the USB options, you typically also need to install a software driver so that your PC's OS knows that the device on the other end of the USB connection is the console of a Cisco device. Also, you can easily find photos of these cables and components online, with searches like "cisco console cable," "cisco usb console cable," or "console cable converter."

The 2960-XR series, for instance, supports both the older RJ-45 console port and a USB console port. Figure 4-4 points to the two console ports; you would use only one or the other. Note that the USB console port uses a mini-B port rather than the more commonly seen rectangular standard USB Type A port.

USB Console (Mini-B)

RJ-45 Console

Figure 4-4   *A Part of a 2960-XR Switch with Console Ports Shown*

After the PC is physically connected to the console port, a terminal emulator software package must be installed and configured on the PC. The terminal emulator software treats all data as text. It accepts the text typed by the user and sends it over the console connection to the switch. Similarly, any bits coming into the PC over the console connection are displayed as text for the user to read.

The emulator must be configured to use the PC's serial port to match the settings on the switch's console port settings. The default console port settings on a switch are as follows. Note that the last three parameters are referred to collectively as 8N1:

- 9600 bits/second
- No hardware flow control
- 8-bit ASCII
- No parity bits
- 1 stop bit

Figure 4-5 shows one such terminal emulator. The image shows the window created by the emulator software in the background, with some output of a **show** command. The foreground, in the upper right, shows a settings window that lists the default console settings as listed just before this paragraph.

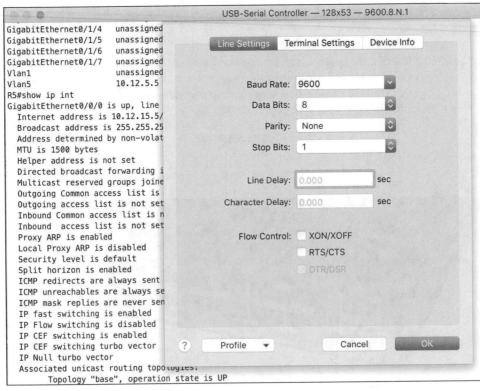

Figure 4-5   *Terminal Settings for Console Access*

Accessing the CLI with Telnet and SSH

For many years, terminal emulator applications have supported far more than the ability to communicate over a serial port to a local device (like a switch's console). Terminal emulators support a variety of TCP/IP applications as well, including Telnet and SSH. Telnet and SSH both allow the user to connect to another device's CLI, but instead of connecting through a console cable to the console port, the traffic flows over the same IP network that the networking devices are helping to create.

Telnet uses the concept of a Telnet client (the terminal application) and a Telnet server (the switch in this case). A *Telnet client*, the device that sits in front of the user, accepts keyboard input and sends those commands to the *Telnet server*. The Telnet server accepts the text, interprets the text as a command, and replies back.

Cisco Catalyst switches enable a Telnet server by default, but switches need a few more configuration settings before you can successfully use Telnet to connect to a switch. Chapter 6, "Configuring Basic Switch Management," covers switch configuration to support Telnet and SSH in detail.

Using Telnet in a lab today makes sense, but Telnet poses a significant security risk in production networks. Telnet sends all data (including any username and password for login to the switch) as clear-text data. SSH gives us a much better option.

Think of SSH as the much more secure Telnet cousin. Outwardly, you still open a terminal emulator, connect to the switch's IP address, and see the switch CLI, no matter whether you use Telnet or SSH. The differences exist behind the scenes: SSH encrypts the contents of all messages, including the passwords, avoiding the possibility of someone capturing packets in the network and stealing the password to network devices.

User and Enable (Privileged) Modes

All three CLI access methods covered so far (console, Telnet, and SSH) place the user in an area of the CLI called *user EXEC mode*. User EXEC mode, sometimes also called *user mode*, allows the user to look around but not break anything. The "EXEC mode" part of the name refers to the fact that in this mode, when you enter a command, the switch executes the command and then displays messages that describe the command's results.

NOTE   If you have not used the CLI before, you might want to experiment with the CLI from the Sim Lite product, or view the video about CLI basics. You can find these resources on the companion website as mentioned in the Introduction.

Cisco IOS supports a more powerful EXEC mode called *enable* mode (also known as *privileged* mode or *privileged EXEC* mode). Enable mode gets its name from the **enable** command, which moves the user from user mode to enable mode, as shown in Figure 4-6. The other name for this mode, *privileged mode*, refers to the fact that powerful (or privileged) commands can be executed there. For example, you can use the **reload** command, which tells the switch to reinitialize or reboot Cisco IOS, only from enable mode.

NOTE   If the command prompt lists the hostname followed by a >, the user is in user mode; if it is the hostname followed by the #, the user is in enable mode.

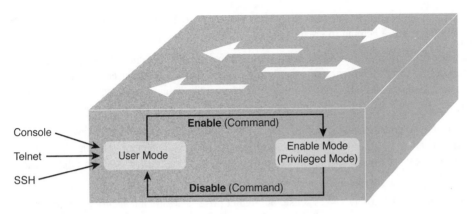

Figure 4-6   *User and Privileged Modes*

Example 4-1 demonstrates the differences between user and enable modes. The example shows the output that you could see in a terminal emulator window, for instance, when connecting from the console. In this case, the user sits at the user mode prompt ("Certskills1>") and tries the **reload** command. The **reload** command tells the switch to reinitialize or reboot Cisco IOS, so IOS allows this powerful command to be used only from enable mode. IOS rejects the **reload** command when used in user mode. Then the user moves to enable mode—also called privileged mode—(using the **enable** EXEC command). At that point, IOS accepts the **reload** command now that the user is in enable mode.

Example 4-1   *Example of Privileged Mode Commands Being Rejected in User Mode*

```
Press RETURN to get started.


User Access Verification


Password:
Certskills1>
Certskills1> reload
Translating "reload"
% Unknown command or computer name, or unable to find computer address
Certskills1> enable
Password:
Certskills1#
Certskills1# reload


Proceed with reload? [confirm] y
00:08:42: %SYS-5-RELOAD: Reload requested by console. Reload Reason: Reload Command.
```

NOTE   The commands that can be used in either user (EXEC) mode or enable (EXEC) mode are called EXEC commands.

This example is the first instance of this book showing you the output from the CLI, so it is worth noting a few conventions. The bold text represents what the user typed, and the non-bold text is what the switch sent back to the terminal emulator. Also, the typed passwords do not show up on the screen for security purposes. Finally, note that this switch has been preconfigured with a hostname of Certskills1, so the command prompt on the left shows that hostname on each line.

Password Security for CLI Access from the Console

A Cisco switch, with default settings, remains relatively secure when locked inside a wiring closet, because by default, a switch allows console access only. By default, the console requires no password at all, and no password to reach enable mode for users that happened to connect from the console. The reason is that if you have access to the physical console port of the switch, you already have pretty much complete control over the switch. You could literally get out your screwdriver and walk off with it, or you could unplug the power, or follow well-published procedures to go through password recovery to break into the CLI and then configure anything you want to configure.

However, many people go ahead and set up simple password protection for console users. Simple passwords can be configured at two points in the login process from the console: when the user connects from the console, and when any user moves to enable mode (using the **enable** EXEC command). You may have noticed that back in Example 4-1, the user saw a password prompt at both points.

Example 4-2 shows the additional configuration commands that were configured prior to collecting the output in Example 4-1. The output holds an excerpt from the EXEC command **show running-config**, which lists the current configuration in the switch.

Example 4-2 *Nondefault Basic Configuration*

```
Certskills1# show running-config
! Output has been formatted to show only the parts relevant to this discussion
hostname Certskills1
!
enable secret love
!
line console 0
 login
 password faith
! The rest of the output has been omitted
Certskills1#
```

Working from top to bottom, note that the first configuration command listed by the **show running-config** command sets the switch's hostname to Certskills1. You might have noticed that the command prompts in Example 4-1 all began with Certskills1, and that's why the command prompt begins with the hostname of the switch.

Next, note that the lines with a ! in them are comment lines, both in the text of this book and in the real switch CLI.

The **enable secret love** configuration command defines the password that all users must use to reach enable mode. So, no matter whether users connect from the console, Telnet, or SSH, they would use the password love when prompted for a password after typing the **enable** EXEC command.

Finally, the last three lines configure the console password. The first line (**line console 0**) is the command that identifies the console, basically meaning "these next commands apply to the console only." The **login** command tells IOS to perform simple password checking (at the console). Remember, by default, the switch does not ask for a password for console users. Finally, the **password faith** command defines the password the console user must type when prompted.

This example just scratches the surface of the kinds of security configuration you might choose to configure on a switch, but it does give you enough detail to configure switches in your lab and get started (which is the reason I put these details in this first chapter of Part II). Note that Chapter 6 shows the configuration steps to add support for Telnet and SSH (including password security), and Chapter 5 of the *CCNA 200-301 Official Cert Guide*, *Volume 2*, "Securing Network Devices," shows additional security configuration as well.

CLI Help Features

If you printed the Cisco IOS Command Reference documents, you would end up with a stack of paper several feet tall. No one should expect to memorize all the commands—and no one does. You can use several very easy, convenient tools to help remember commands and save time typing. As you progress through your Cisco certifications, the exams will cover progressively more commands. However, you should know the methods of getting command help.

Table 4-2 summarizes command-recall help options available at the CLI. Note that, in the first column, *command* represents any command. Likewise, *parm* represents a command's parameter. For example, the second row lists *command* **?**, which means that commands such as **show ?** and **copy ?** would list help for the **show** and **copy** commands, respectively.

Table 4-2 Cisco IOS Software Command Help

What You Enter	What Help You Get
?	Provides help for all commands available in this mode.
command ?	With a space between the command and the ?, the switch lists text to describe all the first parameter options for the command.
com?	Lists commands that start with **com**.
command parm?	Lists all parameters beginning with the **parameter typed so far**. (Notice that there is no space between *parm* and the ?.)
command parm<Tab>	Pressing the Tab key causes IOS to spell out the rest of the word, assuming that you have typed enough of the word so there is only one option that begins with that string of characters.
command parm1 ?	If a space is inserted before the question mark, the CLI lists all the next parameters and gives a brief explanation of each.

When you enter the **?**, the Cisco IOS CLI reacts immediately; that is, you don't need to press the Enter key or any other keys. The device running Cisco IOS also redisplays what you entered before the **?** to save you some keystrokes. If you press Enter immediately after the **?**, Cisco IOS tries to execute the command with only the parameters you have entered so far.

The information supplied by using help depends on the CLI mode. For example, when **?** is entered in user mode, the commands allowed in user mode are displayed, but commands available only in enable mode (not in user mode) are not displayed. Also, help is available in configuration mode, which is the mode used to configure the switch. In fact, configuration mode has many different subconfiguration modes, as explained in the section "Configuration Submodes and Contexts," later in this chapter. So, you can get help for the commands available in each configuration submode as well. (Note that this might be a good time to use the free Sim Lite product on the companion website—open any lab, use the question mark, and try some commands.)

Cisco IOS stores the commands that you enter in a history buffer, storing ten commands by default. The CLI allows you to move backward and forward in the historical list of commands and then edit the command before reissuing it. These key sequences can help you use the CLI more quickly on the exams. Table 4-3 lists the commands used to manipulate previously entered commands.

Table 4-3 Key Sequences for Command Edit and Recall

Keyboard Command	What Happens
Up arrow or Ctrl+P	This displays the most recently used command. If you press it again, the next most recent command appears, until the history buffer is exhausted. (The *P* stands for previous.)
Down arrow or Ctrl+N	If you have gone too far back into the history buffer, these keys take you forward to the more recently entered commands. (The *N* stands for next.)
Left arrow or Ctrl+B	This moves the cursor backward in the currently displayed command without deleting characters. (The *B* stands for back.)
Right arrow or Ctrl+F	This moves the cursor forward in the currently displayed command without deleting characters. (The *F* stands for forward.)
Backspace	This moves the cursor backward in the currently displayed command, deleting characters.

The debug and show Commands

By far, the single most popular Cisco IOS command is the **show** command. The **show** command has a large variety of options, and with those options, you can find the status of almost every feature of Cisco IOS. Essentially, the **show** command lists the currently known facts about the switch's operational status. The only work the switch does in reaction to **show** commands is to find the current status and list the information in messages sent to the user.

For example, consider the output from the **show mac address-table dynamic** command listed in Example 4-3. This **show** command, issued from user mode, lists the table the switch uses to make forwarding decisions. A switch's MAC address table basically lists the data a switch uses to do its primary job.

Example 4-3   *Nondefault Basic Configuration*

```
Certskills1> show mac address-table dynamic
 Mac Address Table
-------------------------------------------


Vlan    Mac Address       Type        Ports
----    -----------       --------    -----
  31    0200.1111.1111    DYNAMIC     Gi0/1
  31    0200.3333.3333    DYNAMIC     Fa0/3
  31    1833.9d7b.0e9a    DYNAMIC     Gi0/1
  10    1833.9d7b.0e9a    DYNAMIC     Gi0/1
  10    30f7.0d29.8561    DYNAMIC     Gi0/1
   1    1833.9d7b.0e9a    DYNAMIC     Gi0/1
  12    1833.9d7b.0e9a    DYNAMIC     Gi0/1
Total Mac Addresses for this criterion: 7
Certskills1>
```

The **debug** command also tells the user details about the operation of the switch. However, while the **show** command lists status information at one instant of time—more like a photograph—the **debug** command acts more like a live video camera feed. Once you issue a **debug** command, IOS remembers, issuing messages that any switch user can choose to see. The console sees these messages by default. Most of the commands used throughout this book to verify operation of switches and routers are **show** commands.

Configuring Cisco IOS Software

You will want to configure every switch in an Enterprise network, even though the switches will forward traffic even with default configuration. This section covers the basic configuration processes, including the concept of a configuration file and the locations in which the configuration files can be stored. Although this section focuses on the configuration process, and not on the configuration commands themselves, you should know all the commands covered in this chapter for the exams, in addition to the configuration processes.

Configuration mode is another mode for the Cisco CLI, similar to user mode and privileged mode. User mode lets you issue nondisruptive commands and displays some information. Privileged mode supports a superset of commands compared to user mode, including commands that might disrupt switch operations. However, not one of the commands in user or privileged mode changes the switch's configuration. Configuration mode accepts *configuration commands*—commands that tell the switch the details of what to do and how to do it. Figure 4-7 illustrates the relationships among configuration mode, user EXEC mode, and privileged EXEC mode.

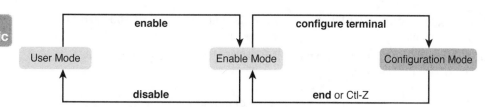

Figure 4-7 *CLI Configuration Mode Versus EXEC Modes*

Commands entered in configuration mode update the active configuration file. *These changes to the configuration occur immediately each time you press the Enter key at the end of a command.* Be careful when you enter a configuration command!

Configuration Submodes and Contexts

Configuration mode itself contains a multitude of commands. To help organize the configuration, IOS groups some kinds of configuration commands together. To do that, when using configuration mode, you move from the initial mode—global configuration mode—into subcommand modes. *Context-setting commands* move you from one configuration subcommand mode, or context, to another. These context-setting commands tell the switch the topic about which you will enter the next few configuration commands. More importantly, the context tells the switch the topic you care about right now, so when you use the ? to get help, the switch gives you help about that topic only.

> **NOTE** *Context-setting* is not a Cisco term. It is just a description used here to help make sense of configuration mode.

The best way to learn about configuration submodes is to use them, but first, take a look at these upcoming examples. For instance, the **interface** command is one of the most commonly used context-setting configuration commands. For example, the CLI user could enter interface configuration mode by entering the **interface FastEthernet 0/1** configuration command. Asking for help in interface configuration mode displays only commands that are useful when configuring Ethernet interfaces. Commands used in this context are called *subcommands*—or, in this specific case, *interface subcommands.* When you begin practicing with the CLI with real equipment, the navigation between modes can become natural. For now, consider Example 4-4, which shows the following:

- Movement from enable mode to global configuration mode by using the **configure terminal** EXEC command

- Using a **hostname Fred** global configuration command to configure the switch's name

- Movement from global configuration mode to console line configuration mode (using the **line console 0** command)

- Setting the console's simple password to **hope** (using the **password hope** line subcommand)

- Movement from console configuration mode to interface configuration mode (using the **interface** *type number* command)

- Setting the speed to 100 Mbps for interface Fa0/1 (using the **speed 100** interface subcommand)

- Movement from interface configuration mode back to global configuration mode (using the **exit** command)

Example 4-4 *Navigating Between Different Configuration Modes*

```
Switch# configure terminal
Switch(config)# hostname Fred
Fred(config)# line console 0
Fred(config-line)# password hope
Fred(config-line)# interface FastEthernet 0/1
Fred(config-if)# speed 100
Fred(config-if)# exit
Fred(config)#
```

The text inside parentheses in the command prompt identifies the configuration mode. For example, the first command prompt after you enter configuration mode lists (config), meaning global configuration mode. After the **line console 0** command, the text expands to (config-line), meaning line configuration mode. Each time the command prompt changes within config mode, you have moved to another configuration mode.

Table 4-4 shows the most common command prompts in configuration mode, the names of those modes, and the context-setting commands used to reach those modes.

Table 4-4 Common Switch Configuration Modes

Prompt	Name of Mode	Context-Setting Command(s) to Reach This Mode
hostname(config)#	Global	None—first mode after **configure terminal**
hostname(config-line)#	Line	**line console 0** **line vty 0 15**
hostname(config-if)#	Interface	**interface** *type number*
hostname(vlan)#	VLAN	**vlan** *number*

You should practice until you become comfortable moving between the different configuration modes, back to enable mode, and then back into the configuration modes. However, you can learn these skills just doing labs about the topics in later chapters of the book. For now, Figure 4-8 shows most of the navigation between global configuration mode and the four configuration submodes listed in Table 4-4.

NOTE You can also move directly from one configuration submode to another, without first using the **exit** command to move back to global configuration mode. Just use the commands listed in bold in the center of the figure.

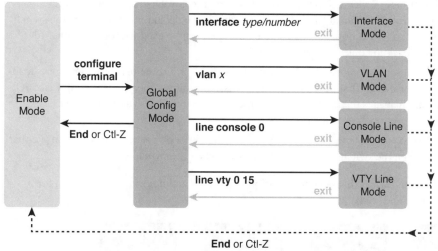

Figure 4-8 *Navigation In and Out of Switch Configuration Modes*

You really should stop and try navigating around these configuration modes. If you have not yet decided on a lab strategy, install the Pearson Sim Lite software from the companion website. It includes the simulator and a couple of lab exercises. Start any lab, ignore the instructions, and just get into configuration mode and move around between the configuration modes shown in Figure 4-8.

No set rules exist for what commands are global commands or subcommands. Generally, however, when multiple instances of a parameter can be set in a single switch, the command used to set the parameter is likely a configuration subcommand. Items that are set once for the entire switch are likely global commands. For example, the **hostname** command is a global command because there is only one hostname per switch. Conversely, the **speed** command is an interface subcommand that applies to each switch interface that can run at different speeds, so it is a subcommand, applying to the particular interface under which it is configured.

Storing Switch Configuration Files

When you configure a switch, it needs to use the configuration. It also needs to be able to retain the configuration in case the switch loses power. Cisco switches contain random-access memory (RAM) to store data while Cisco IOS is using it, but RAM loses its contents when the switch loses power or is reloaded. To store information that must be retained when the switch loses power or is reloaded, Cisco switches use several types of more permanent memory, none of which has any moving parts. By avoiding components with moving parts (such as traditional disk drives), switches can maintain better uptime and availability.

The following list details the four main types of memory found in Cisco switches, as well as the most common use of each type:

■ **RAM:** Sometimes called DRAM, for dynamic random-access memory, RAM is used by the switch just as it is used by any other computer: for working storage. The running (active) configuration file is stored here.

■ **Flash memory:** Either a chip inside the switch or a removable memory card, flash memory stores fully functional Cisco IOS images and is the default location where the switch gets its Cisco IOS at boot time. Flash memory also can be used to store any other files, including backup copies of configuration files.

■ **ROM:** Read-only memory (ROM) stores a bootstrap (or boothelper) program that is loaded when the switch first powers on. This bootstrap program then finds the full Cisco IOS image and manages the process of loading Cisco IOS into RAM, at which point Cisco IOS takes over operation of the switch.

■ **NVRAM:** Nonvolatile RAM (NVRAM) stores the initial or startup configuration file that is used when the switch is first powered on and when the switch is reloaded.

Figure 4-9 summarizes this same information in a briefer and more convenient form for memorization and study.

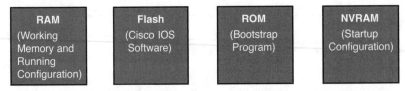

Figure 4-9   *Cisco Switch Memory Types*

Cisco IOS stores the collection of configuration commands in a *configuration file*. In fact, switches use multiple configuration files—one file for the initial configuration used when powering on, and another configuration file for the active, currently used running configuration as stored in RAM. Table 4-5 lists the names of these two files, their purpose, and their storage location.

Table 4-5   Names and Purposes of the Two Main Cisco IOS Configuration Files

Configuration Filename	Purpose	Where It Is Stored
startup-config	Stores the initial configuration used anytime the switch reloads Cisco IOS.	NVRAM
running-config	Stores the currently used configuration commands. This file changes dynamically when someone enters commands in configuration mode.	RAM

Essentially, when you use configuration mode, you change only the running-config file. This means that the configuration example earlier in this chapter (Example 4-4) updates only the running-config file. However, if the switch lost power right after that example, all that configuration would be lost. If you want to keep that configuration, you have to copy the running-config file into NVRAM, overwriting the old startup-config file.

Example 4-5 demonstrates that commands used in configuration mode change only the running configuration in RAM. The example shows the following concepts and steps:

Step 1.   The example begins with both the running and startup-config having the same hostname, per the **hostname hannah** command.

Step 2.   The hostname is changed in configuration mode using the **hostname harold** command.

Step 3.   The **show running-config** and **show startup-config** commands show the fact that the hostnames are now different, with the **hostname harold** command found only in the running-config.

Example 4-5 *How Configuration Mode Commands Change the Running-Config File, Not the Startup-Config File*

```
! Step 1 next (two commands)
!
hannah# show running-config
! (lines omitted)
hostname hannah
! (rest of lines omitted)

hannah# show startup-config
! (lines omitted)
hostname hannah
! (rest of lines omitted)
! Step 2 next. Notice that the command prompt changes immediately after
! the hostname command.

hannah# configure terminal
hannah(config)# hostname harold
harold(config)# exit
! Step 3 next (two commands)
!
harold# show running-config
! (lines omitted) - just showing the part with the hostname command
hostname harold
!
harold# show startup-config
! (lines omitted) - just showing the part with the hostname command
hostname hannah
```

Copying and Erasing Configuration Files

The configuration process updates the running-config file, which is lost if the router loses power or is reloaded. Clearly, IOS needs to provide us a way to copy the running configuration so that it will not be lost, so it will be used the next time the switch reloads or powers on. For instance, Example 4-5 ended with a different running configuration (with the **hostname harold** command) versus the startup configuration.

In short, the EXEC command **copy running-config startup-config** backs up the running-config to the startup-config file. This command overwrites the current startup-config file with what is currently in the running-configuration file.

In addition, in the lab, you may want to just get rid of all existing configuration and start over with a clean configuration. To do that, you can erase the startup-config file using three different commands:

```
write erase
erase startup-config
erase nvram:
```

Once the startup-config file is erased, you can reload or power off/on the switch, and it will boot with the now-empty startup configuration.

Note that Cisco IOS does not have a command that erases the contents of the running-config file. To clear out the running-config file, simply erase the startup-config file, and then **reload** the switch, and the running-config will be empty at the end of the process.

> **NOTE**   Cisco uses the term *reload* to refer to what most PC operating systems call rebooting or restarting. In each case, it is a re-initialization of the software. The **reload** EXEC command causes a switch to reload.

Chapter Review

One key to doing well on the exams is to perform repetitive spaced review sessions. Review this chapter's material using either the tools in the book or on the book's companion website. Refer to the "Your Study Plan" element section titled "Step 2: Build Your Study Habits Around the Chapter" for more details. Table 4-6 outlines the key review elements and where you can find them. To better track your study progress, record when you completed these activities in the second column.

Table 4-6   Chapter Review Tracking

Review Element	Review Date(s)	Resource Used
Review key topics		Book, website
Review key terms		Book, website
Repeat DIKTA questions		Book, PTP
Review memory tables		Book, website
Review command tables		Book

Review All the Key Topics

Table 4-7   Key Topics for Chapter 4

Key Topic Element	Description	Page Number
Figure 4-2	Three methods to access a switch CLI	87
Figure 4-3	Cabling options for a console connection	88
List	A Cisco switch's default console port settings	90
Figure 4-7	Navigation between user, enable, and global config modes	97
Table 4-4	A list of configuration mode prompts, the name of the configuration mode, and the command used to reach each mode	98
Figure 4-8	Configuration mode context-setting commands	99
Table 4-5	The names and purposes of the two configuration files in a switch or router	100

Key Terms You Should Know

command-line interface (CLI), Telnet, Secure Shell (SSH), enable mode, user mode, configuration mode, startup-config file, running-config file

Command References

Tables 4-8 and 4-9 list configuration and verification commands used in this chapter, respectively. As an easy review exercise, cover the left column in a table, read the right column, and try to recall the command without looking. Then repeat the exercise, covering the right column, and try to recall what the command does.

Table 4-8   Chapter 4 Configuration Commands

Command	Mode and Purpose
line console 0	Global command that changes the context to console configuration mode.
login	Line (console and vty) configuration mode. Tells IOS to prompt for a password (no username).
password *pass-value*	Line (console and vty) configuration mode. Sets the password required on that line for login if the **login** command (with no other parameters) is also configured.
interface *type port-number*	Global command that changes the context to interface mode— for example, **interface FastEthernet 0/1**.
hostname *name*	Global command that sets this switch's hostname, which is also used as the first part of the switch's command prompt.
exit	Moves back to the next higher mode in configuration mode.

Command	Mode and Purpose
end	Exits configuration mode and goes back to enable mode from any of the configuration submodes.
Ctrl+Z	This is not a command, but rather a two-key combination (pressing the Ctrl key and the letter Z) that together do the same thing as the **end** command.

Table 4-9   Chapter 4 EXEC Command Reference

Command	Purpose
no debug all undebug all	Enable mode EXEC command to disable all currently enabled debugs.
reload	Enable mode EXEC command that reboots the switch or router.
copy running-config startup-config	Enable mode EXEC command that saves the active config, replacing the startup-config file used when the switch initializes.
copy startup-config running-config	Enable mode EXEC command that merges the startup-config file with the currently active config file in RAM.
show running-config	Lists the contents of the running-config file.
write erase erase startup-config erase nvram:	These enable mode EXEC commands erase the startup-config file.
quit	EXEC command that disconnects the user from the CLI session.
show startup-config	Lists the contents of the startup-config (initial config) file.
enable	Moves the user from user mode to enable (privileged) mode and prompts for a password if one is configured.
disable	Moves the user from enable mode to user mode.
configure terminal	Enable mode command that moves the user into configuration mode.

CHAPTER 5

Analyzing Ethernet LAN Switching

This chapter covers the following exam topics:

1.0 Network Fundamentals

1.1 Explain the role and function of network components

1.1.b L2 and L3 Switches

1.13 Describe switching concepts

1.13.a MAC learning and aging

1.13.b Frame switching

1.13.c Frame flooding

1.13.d MAC address table

2.0 Network Access

2.5 Describe the need for and basic operations of Rapid PVST+ Spanning Tree Protocol and identify basic operations

When you buy a Cisco Catalyst Ethernet switch, the switch is ready to work. All you have to do is take it out of the box, power on the switch by connecting the power cable to the switch and a power outlet, and connect hosts to the switch using the correct unshielded twisted-pair (UTP) cables. You do not have to configure anything else, or connect to the console and login, or do anything: the switch just starts forwarding Ethernet frames.

In Part II of this book, you will learn how to build, configure, and verify the operation of Ethernet LANs. In Chapter 4, "Using the Command-Line Interface," you learned how to move around in the CLI, issue commands, and configure the switch. This chapter takes a short but important step in that journey by explaining the logic a switch uses when forwarding Ethernet frames.

This chapter breaks the content into two major sections. The first reviews and then further develops the concepts behind LAN switching, which were first introduced back in Chapter 2, "Fundamentals of Ethernet LANs." The second section then uses IOS show commands to verify that Cisco switches actually learned the MAC addresses, built the MAC address table, and forwarded frames.

"Do I Know This Already?" Quiz

Take the quiz (either here or use the PTP software) if you want to use the score to help you decide how much time to spend on this chapter. The letter answers are listed at the bottom of the page following the quiz. Appendix C, found both at the end of the book as well as on the companion website, includes both the answers and explanations. You can also find both answers and explanations in the PTP testing software.

Table 5-1 "Do I Know This Already?" Foundation Topics Section-to-Question Mapping

Foundation Topics Section	Questions
LAN Switching Concepts	1–4
Verifying and Analyzing Ethernet Switching	5–6

1. Which of the following statements describes part of the process of how a switch decides to forward a frame destined for a known unicast MAC address?

   a. It compares the unicast destination address to the bridging, or MAC address, table.

   b. It compares the unicast source address to the bridging, or MAC address, table.

   c. It forwards the frame out all interfaces in the same VLAN except for the incoming interface.

   d. It compares the destination IP address to the destination MAC address.

   e. It compares the frame's incoming interface to the source MAC entry in the MAC address table.

2. Which of the following statements describes part of the process of how a LAN switch decides to forward a frame destined for a broadcast MAC address?

   a. It compares the unicast destination address to the bridging, or MAC address, table.

   b. It compares the unicast source address to the bridging, or MAC address, table.

   c. It forwards the frame out all interfaces in the same VLAN except for the incoming interface.

   d. It compares the destination IP address to the destination MAC address.

   e. It compares the frame's incoming interface to the source MAC entry in the MAC address table.

3. Which of the following statements best describes what a switch does with a frame destined for an unknown unicast address?

   a. It forwards out all interfaces in the same VLAN except for the incoming interface.

   b. It forwards the frame out the one interface identified by the matching entry in the MAC address table.

   c. It compares the destination IP address to the destination MAC address.

   d. It compares the frame's incoming interface to the source MAC entry in the MAC address table.

4. Which of the following comparisons does a switch make when deciding whether a new MAC address should be added to its MAC address table?

   a. It compares the unicast destination address to the bridging, or MAC address, table.

   b. It compares the unicast source address to the bridging, or MAC address, table.

   c. It compares the VLAN ID to the bridging, or MAC address, table.

   d. It compares the destination IP address's ARP cache entry to the bridging, or MAC address, table.

5. A Cisco Catalyst switch has 24 10/100 ports, numbered 0/1 through 0/24. Ten PCs connect to the 10 lowest numbered ports, with those PCs working and sending data over the network. The other ports are not connected to any device. Which of the following answers lists facts displayed by the show interfaces status command?

    a. Port Ethernet 0/1 is in a connected state.

    b. Port Fast Ethernet 0/11 is in a connected state.

    c. Port Fast Ethernet 0/5 is in a connected state.

    d. Port Ethernet 0/15 is in a notconnected state.

6. Consider the following output from a Cisco Catalyst switch:

```
SW1# show mac address-table dynamic
          Mac Address Table
-------------------------------------------

Vlan    Mac Address      Type       Ports
----    -----------      --------   -----
   1    02AA.AAAA.AAAA   DYNAMIC    Gi0/1
   1    02BB.BBBB.BBBB   DYNAMIC    Gi0/2
   1    02CC.CCCC.CCCC   DYNAMIC    Gi0/3
Total Mac Addresses for this criterion: 3
```

Which of the following answers is true about this switch?

    a. The output proves that port Gi0/2 connects directly to a device that uses address 02BB.BBBB.BBBB.

    b. The switch has learned three MAC addresses since the switch powered on.

    c. The three listed MAC addresses were learned based on the destination MAC address of frames forwarded by the switch.

    d. 02CC.CCCC.CCCC was learned from the source MAC address of a frame that entered port Gi0/3.

Foundation Topics

LAN Switching Concepts

A modern Ethernet LAN connects user devices as well as servers into some switches, with the switches then connecting to each other, sometimes in a design like Figure 5-1. Part of the LAN, called a campus LAN, supports the end-user population as shown on the left of the figure. End-user devices connect to LAN switches, which in turn connect to other switches so that a path exists to the rest of the network. The campus LAN switches sit in wiring closets close to the end users. On the right, the servers used to provide information to the users also connect to the LAN. Those servers and switches often sit in a closed room called a *data center*, with connections to the campus LAN to support traffic to/from the users.

To forward traffic from a user device to a server and back, each switch performs the same kind of logic, independently from each other. The first half of this chapter examines the logic: how a switch chooses to forward an Ethernet frame, when the switch chooses to not forward the frame, and so on.

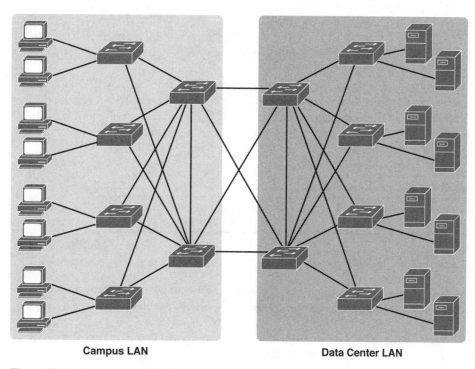

Campus LAN   **Data Center LAN**

Figure 5-1 *Campus LAN and Data Center LAN, Conceptual Drawing*

Overview of Switching Logic

Ultimately, the role of a LAN switch is to forward Ethernet frames. LANs exist as a set of user devices, servers, and other devices that connect to switches, with the switches connected to each other. The LAN switch has one primary job: to forward frames to the correct destination (MAC) address. And to achieve that goal, switches use logic—logic based on the source and destination MAC address in each frame's Ethernet header.

LAN switches receive Ethernet frames and then make a switching decision: either forward the frame out some other ports or ignore the frame. To accomplish this primary mission, switches perform three actions:

1. Deciding when to forward a frame or when to filter (not forward) a frame, based on the destination MAC address

2. Preparing to forward frames by learning MAC addresses by examining the source MAC address of each frame received by the switch

3. Preparing to forward only one copy of the frame to the destination by creating a (Layer 2) loop-free environment with other switches by using Spanning Tree Protocol (STP)

The first action is the switch's primary job, whereas the other two items are overhead functions.

NOTE   Throughout this book's discussion of LAN switches, the terms *switch port* and *switch interface* are synonymous.

Although Chapter 2's section titled "Ethernet Data-Link Protocols" already discussed the frame format, this discussion of Ethernet switching is pretty important, so reviewing the Ethernet frame at this point might be helpful. Figure 5-2 shows one popular format for an Ethernet frame. Basically, a switch would take the frame shown in the figure, make a decision of where to forward the frame, and send the frame out that other interface.

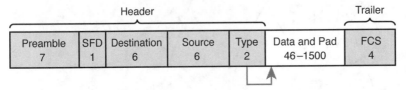

Figure 5-2   *IEEE 802.3 Ethernet Frame (One Variation)*

Most of the upcoming discussions and figures about Ethernet switching focus on the use of the destination and source MAC address fields in the header. All Ethernet frames have both a destination and source MAC address. Both are 6-bytes long (represented as 12 hex digits in the book) and are a key part of the switching logic discussed in this section. Refer back to Chapter 2's discussion of the header in detail for more info on the rest of the Ethernet frame.

NOTE   The companion website includes a video that explains the basics of Ethernet switching.

Now on to the details of how Ethernet switching works!

Forwarding Known Unicast Frames

To decide whether to forward a frame, a switch uses a dynamically built table that lists MAC addresses and outgoing interfaces. Switches compare the frame's destination MAC address to this table to decide whether the switch should forward a frame or simply ignore it. For example, consider the simple network shown in Figure 5-3, with Fred sending a frame to Barney.

In this figure, Fred sends a frame with destination address 0200.2222.2222 (Barney's MAC address). The switch compares the destination MAC address (0200.2222.2222) to the MAC address table, matching the bold table entry. That matched table entry tells the switch to forward the frame out port F0/2, and only port F0/2.

Answers to the "Do I Know This Already?" quiz:

1 A **2** C **3** A **4** B **5** C **6** D

NOTE   A switch's MAC address table is also called the *switching table*, or *bridging table*, or even the *Content-Addressable Memory (CAM) table*, in reference to the type of physical memory used to store the table.

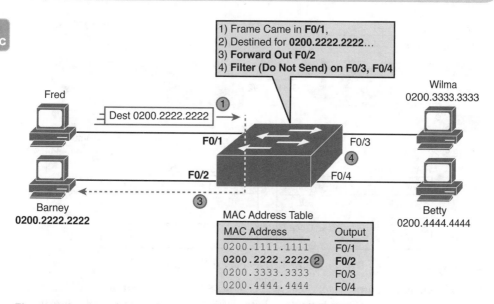

Figure 5-3   *Sample Switch Forwarding and Filtering Decision*

A switch's MAC address table lists the location of each MAC relative to that one switch. In LANs with multiple switches, each switch makes an independent forwarding decision based on its own MAC address table. Together, they forward the frame so that it eventually arrives at the destination.

For example, Figure 5-4 shows the first switching decision in a case in which Fred sends a frame to Wilma, with destination MAC 0200.3333.3333. The topology has changed versus the previous figure, this time with two switches, and Fred and Wilma connected to two different switches. Figure 5-3 shows the first switch's logic, in reaction to Fred sending the original frame. Basically, the switch receives the frame in port F0/1, finds the destination MAC (0200.3333.3333) in the MAC address table, sees the outgoing port of G0/1, so SW1 forwards the frame out its G0/1 port.

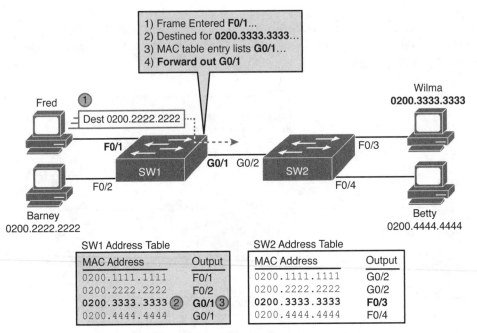

Figure 5-4 *Forwarding Decision with Two Switches: First Switch*

That same frame next arrives at switch SW2, entering SW2's G0/2 interface. As shown in Figure 5-5, SW2 uses the same logic steps, but using SW2's table. The MAC table lists the forwarding instructions for that switch only. In this case, switch SW2 forwards the frame out its F0/3 port, based on SW2's MAC address table.

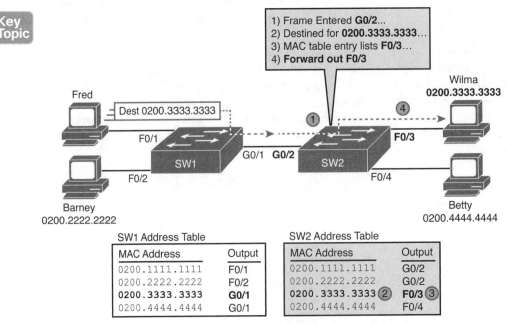

Figure 5-5 *Forwarding Decision with Two Switches: Second Switch*

NOTE   The forwarding choice by a switch was formerly called a *forward-versus-filter* decision, because the switch also chooses to not forward (to filter) frames, not sending the frame out some ports.

The examples so far use switches that happen to have a MAC table with all the MAC addresses listed. As a result, the destination MAC address in the frame is known to the switch. The frames are called known unicast frames, or simply known unicasts, because the destination address is a unicast address, and the destination is known. As shown in these examples, switches forward known unicast frames out one port: the port as listed in the MAC table entry for that MAC address.

Learning MAC Addresses

Thankfully, the networking staff does not have to type in all those MAC table entries. Instead, each switch does its second main function: to learn the MAC addresses and interfaces to put into its address table. With a complete MAC address table, the switch can make accurate forwarding and filtering decisions as just discussed.

Switches build the address table by listening to incoming frames and examining the *source MAC address* in the frame. If a frame enters the switch and the source MAC address is not in the MAC address table, the switch creates an entry in the table. That table entry lists the interface from which the frame arrived. Switch learning logic is that simple.

Figure 5-6 depicts the same single-switch topology network as Figure 5-3, but before the switch has built any address table entries. The figure shows the first two frames sent in this network—first a frame from Fred, addressed to Barney, and then Barney's response, addressed to Fred.

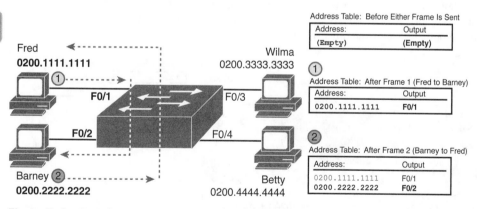

Figure 5-6   *Switch Learning: Empty Table and Adding Two Entries*

(Figure 5-6 depicts the MAC learning process only, and ignores the forwarding process and therefore ignores the destination MAC addresses.)

Focus on the learning process and how the MAC table grows at each step as shown on the right side of the figure. The switch begins with an empty MAC table, as shown in the upper-right part of the figure. Then Fred sends his first frame (labeled "1") to Barney, so the switch adds an entry for 0200.1111.1111, Fred's MAC address, associated with interface F0/1. Why F0/1? The frame sent by Fred entered the switch's F0/1 port. SW1's logic runs something like this: "The source is MAC 0200.1111.1111, the frame entered F0/1, so from my perspective, 0200.1111.1111 must be reachable out my port F0/1."

Continuing the example, when Barney replies in Step 2, the switch adds a second entry, this one for 0200.2222.2222, Barney's MAC address, along with interface F0/2. Why F0/2? The frame Barney sent entered the switch's F0/2 interface. Learning always occurs by looking at the source MAC address in the frame and adds the incoming interface as the associated port.

Flooding Unknown Unicast and Broadcast Frames

Now again turn your attention to the forwarding process, using the topology in Figure 5-5. What do you suppose the switch does with Fred's first frame, the one that occurred when there were no entries in the MAC address table? As it turns out, when there is no matching entry in the table, switches forward the frame out all interfaces (except the incoming interface) using a process called *flooding*. And the frame whose destination address is unknown to the switch is called an *unknown unicast frame*, or simply an *unknown unicast*.

Switches flood unknown unicast frames. Flooding means that the switch forwards copies of the frame out all ports, except the port on which the frame was received. The idea is simple: if you do not know where to send it, send it everywhere, to deliver the frame. And, by the way, that device will likely then send a reply—and then the switch can learn that device's MAC address and forward future frames out one port as a known unicast frame.

Switches also flood LAN broadcast frames (frames destined to the Ethernet broadcast address of FFFF.FFFF.FFFF) because this process helps deliver a copy of the frame to all devices in the LAN.

For example, Figure 5-7 shows the same first frame sent by Fred, when the switch's MAC table is empty. At step 1, Fred sends the frame. At step 2, the switch sends a copy of the frame out all three of the other interfaces.

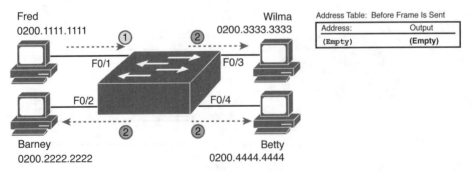

Figure 5-7 *Switch Flooding: Unknown Unicast Arrives, Floods Out Other Ports*

Avoiding Loops Using Spanning Tree Protocol

The third primary feature of LAN switches is loop prevention, as implemented by Spanning Tree Protocol (STP). Without STP, any flooded frames would loop for an indefinite period of time in Ethernet networks with physically redundant links. To prevent looping frames, STP blocks some ports from forwarding frames so that only one active path exists between any pair of LAN segments.

The result of STP is good: frames do not loop infinitely, which makes the LAN usable. However, STP has negative features as well, including the fact that it takes some work to balance traffic across the redundant alternate links.

A simple example makes the need for STP more obvious. Remember, switches flood unknown unicast frames and broadcast frames. Figure 5-8 shows an unknown unicast frame, sent by Larry to Bob, which loops forever because the network has redundancy but no STP. Note that the figure shows one direction of the looping frame only, just to reduce clutter, but a copy of the frame would also loop the other direction.

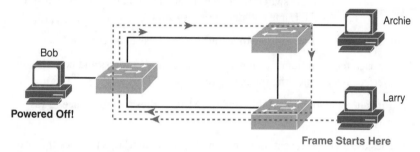

Figure 5-8 *Network with Redundant Links but Without STP: The Frame Loops Forever*

The flooding of this frame would result in the frame repeatedly rotating around the three switches, because none of the switches list Bob's MAC address in their address tables—so each switch floods the frame. And while the flooding process is a good mechanism for forwarding unknown unicasts and broadcasts, the continual flooding of traffic frames as in the figure can completely congest the LAN to the point of making it unusable.

A topology like Figure 5-8, with redundant links, is good, but we need to prevent the bad effect of those looping frames. To avoid Layer 2 loops, all switches need to use STP. STP causes each interface on a switch to settle into either a blocking state or a forwarding state. *Blocking* means that the interface cannot forward or receive data frames, while *forwarding* means that the interface can send and receive data frames. If a correct subset of the interfaces is blocked, only a single currently active logical path exists between each pair of LANs.

> **NOTE** STP behaves identically for a transparent bridge and a switch. Therefore, the terms *bridge*, *switch*, and *bridging device* all are used interchangeably when discussing STP.

Chapter 9 of this book, "Spanning Tree Protocol Concepts," examines STP in depth, including how STP prevents loops.

LAN Switching Summary

Switches use Layer 2 logic, examining the Ethernet data-link header to choose how to process frames. In particular, switches make decisions to forward and filter frames, learn MAC addresses, and use STP to avoid loops, as follows:

Step 1.   Switches forward frames based on the destination MAC address:

A. If the destination MAC address is a broadcast, multicast, or unknown destination unicast (a unicast not listed in the MAC table), the switch floods the frame.

B. If the destination MAC address is a known unicast address (a unicast address found in the MAC table):

i. If the outgoing interface listed in the MAC address table is different from the interface in which the frame was received, the switch forwards the frame out the outgoing interface.

ii. If the outgoing interface is the same as the interface in which the frame was received, the switch filters the frame, meaning that the switch simply ignores the frame and does not forward it.

Step 2.   Switches use the following logic to learn MAC address table entries:

A. For each received frame, examine the source MAC address and note the interface from which the frame was received.

B. If it is not already in the table, add the MAC address and interface it was learned on.

Step 3.   Switches use STP to prevent loops by causing some interfaces to block, meaning that they do not send or receive frames.

Verifying and Analyzing Ethernet Switching

A Cisco Catalyst switch comes from the factory ready to switch frames. All you have to do is connect the power cable, plug in the Ethernet cables, and the switch starts switching incoming frames. Connect multiple switches together, and they are ready to forward frames between the switches as well. And the big reason behind this default behavior has to do with the default settings on the switches.

Cisco Catalyst switches come ready to get busy switching frames because of settings like these:

- The interfaces are enabled by default, ready to start working once a cable is connected.
- All interfaces are assigned to VLAN 1.
- 10/100 and 10/100/1000 interfaces use autonegotiation by default.
- The MAC learning, forwarding, flooding logic all works by default.
- STP is enabled by default.

This second section of the chapter examines how switches will work with these default settings, showing how to verify the Ethernet learning and forwarding process.

Demonstrating MAC Learning

To see a switch's MAC address table, use the **show mac address-table** command. With no additional parameters, this command lists all known MAC addresses in the MAC table, including some overhead static MAC addresses that you can ignore. To see all the dynamically learned MAC addresses only, instead use the **show mac address-table dynamic** command.

The examples in this chapter use almost no configuration, as if you just unboxed the switch when you first purchased it. For the examples, the switches have no configuration other than the **hostname** command to set a meaningful hostname. Note that to do this in lab, all I did was

- Use the **erase startup-config** EXEC command to erase the startup-config file
- Use the **delete vlan.dat** EXEC command to delete the VLAN configuration details
- Use the **reload** EXEC command to reload the switch (thereby using the empty startup-config, with no VLAN information configured)
- Configure the **hostname SW1** command to set the switch hostname

Once done, the switch starts forwarding and learning MAC addresses, as demonstrated in Example 5-1.

Example 5-1   show mac address-table dynamic *for Figure 5-7*

```
SW1# show mac address-table dynamic
          Mac Address Table
-------------------------------------------

Vlan    Mac Address       Type        Ports
----    -----------       --------    -----
   1    0200.1111.1111    DYNAMIC     Fa0/1
   1    0200.2222.2222    DYNAMIC     Fa0/2
   1    0200.3333.3333    DYNAMIC     Fa0/3
   1    0200.4444.4444    DYNAMIC     Fa0/4
Total Mac Addresses for this criterion: 4
SW1#
```

First, focus on two columns of the table: the MAC Address and Ports columns of the table. The values should look familiar: they match the earlier single-switch example, as repeated here as Figure 5-9. Note the four MAC addresses listed, along with their matching ports, as shown in the figure.

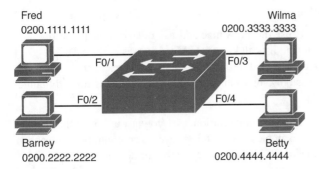

Figure 5-9 *Single Switch Topology Used in Verification Section*

Next, look at the Type field in the heading of the output table. The column tells us how the switch learned the MAC address as described earlier in this chapter; in this case, the switch learned all MAC addresses dynamically. You can also statically predefine MAC table entries using a couple of different features, including port security, and those would appear as Static in the Type column.

Finally, the VLAN column of the output gives us a chance to briefly discuss how VLANs impact switching logic. LAN switches forward Ethernet frames inside a VLAN. What that means is if a frame enters via a port in VLAN 1, then the switch will forward or flood that frame out other ports in VLAN 1 only, and not out any ports that happen to be assigned to another VLAN. Chapter 8, "Implementing Ethernet Virtual LANs," looks at all the details of how switches forward frames when using VLANs.

Switch Interfaces

The first example assumes that you installed the switch and cabling correctly, and that the switch interfaces work. Once you do the installation and connect to the Console, you can easily check the status of those interfaces with the **show interfaces status** command, as shown in Example 5-2.

Example 5-2 show interfaces status *on Switch SW1*

```
SW1# show interfaces status

Port      Name              Status       Vlan    Duplex  Speed Type
Fa0/1                       connected    1        a-full  a-100 10/100BaseTX
Fa0/2                       connected    1        a-full  a-100 10/100BaseTX
Fa0/3                       connected    1        a-full  a-100 10/100BaseTX
Fa0/4                       connected    1        a-full  a-100 10/100BaseTX
Fa0/5                       notconnect   1          auto    auto 10/100BaseTX
Fa0/6                       notconnect   1          auto    auto 10/100BaseTX
Fa0/7                       notconnect   1          auto    auto 10/100BaseTX
Fa0/8                       notconnect   1          auto    auto 10/100BaseTX
Fa0/9                       notconnect   1          auto    auto 10/100BaseTX
Fa0/10                      notconnect   1          auto    auto 10/100BaseTX
Fa0/11                      notconnect   1          auto    auto 10/100BaseTX
```

```
Fa0/12                       notconnect  1           auto    auto 10/100BaseTX
Fa0/13                       notconnect  1           auto    auto 10/100BaseTX
Fa0/14                       notconnect  1           auto    auto 10/100BaseTX
Fa0/15                       notconnect  1           auto    auto 10/100BaseTX
Fa0/16                       notconnect  1           auto    auto 10/100BaseTX
Fa0/17                       notconnect  1           auto    auto 10/100BaseTX
Fa0/18                       notconnect  1           auto    auto 10/100BaseTX
Fa0/19                       notconnect  1           auto    auto 10/100BaseTX
Fa0/20                       notconnect  1           auto    auto 10/100BaseTX
Fa0/21                       notconnect  1           auto    auto 10/100BaseTX
Fa0/22                       notconnect  1           auto    auto 10/100BaseTX
Fa0/23                       notconnect  1           auto    auto 10/100BaseTX
Fa0/24                       notconnect  1           auto    auto 10/100BaseTX
Gi0/1                        notconnect  1           auto    auto 10/100/1000BaseTX
Gi0/2                        notconnect  1           auto    auto 10/100/1000BaseTX
SW1#
```

Focus on the port column for a moment. As a reminder, Cisco Catalyst switches name their ports based on the fastest specification supported, so in this case, the switch has 24 interfaces named FastEthernet, and two named GigabitEthernet. Many commands abbreviate those terms, this time as Fa for FastEthernet and Gi for GigabitEthernet. (The example happens to come from a Cisco Catalyst switch that has 24 10/100 ports and two 10/100/1000 ports.)

The Status column, of course, tells us the status or state of the port. In this case, the lab switch had cables and devices connected to ports F0/1–F0/4 only, with no other cables connected. As a result, those first four ports have a state of connected, meaning that the ports have a cable and are functional. The notconnect state means that the port is not yet functioning. It may mean that there is no cable installed, but other problems may exist as well. (The section "Analyzing Switch Interface Status and Statistics," in Chapter 7, "Configuring and Verifying Switch Interfaces," works through the details of what causes a switch interface to fail.)

NOTE   You can see the status for a single interface in a couple of ways. For instance, for F0/1, the command **show interfaces f0/1 status** lists the status in a single line of output as in Example 5-2. The **show interfaces f0/1** command (without the **status** keyword) displays a detailed set of messages about the interface.

The **show interfaces** command has a large number of options. One particular option, the **counters** option, lists statistics about incoming and outgoing frames on the interfaces. In particular, it lists the number of unicast, multicast, and broadcast frames (both the in and out directions), and a total byte count for those frames. Example 5-3 shows an example, again for interface F0/1.

Example 5-3   show interfaces f0/1 counters *on Switch SW1*

```
SW1# show interfaces f0/1 counters

Port              InOctets      InUcastPkts      InMcastPkts      InBcastPkts
Fa0/1             1223303            10264              107               18


Port             OutOctets     OutUcastPkts     OutMcastPkts     OutBcastPkts
Fa0/1             3235055            13886            22940              437
```

Finding Entries in the MAC Address Table

With a single switch and only four hosts connected to it, you can just read the details of the MAC address table and find the information you want to see. However, in real networks, with lots of interconnected hosts and switches, just reading the output to find one MAC address can be hard to do. You might have hundreds of entries—page after page of output—with each MAC address looking like a random string of hex characters. (The book uses easy-to-recognize MAC addresses to make it easier to learn.)

Thankfully, Cisco IOS supplies several more options on the **show mac address-table** command to make it easier to find individual entries. First, if you know the MAC address, you can search for it—just type in the MAC address at the end of the command, as shown in Example 5-4. All you have to do is include the **address** keyword, followed by the actual MAC address. If the address exists, the output lists the address. Note that the output lists the exact same information in the exact same format, but it lists only the line for the matching MAC address.

Example 5-4   show mac address-table dynamic *with the* address *Keyword*

```
SW1# show mac address-table dynamic address 0200.1111.1111
          Mac Address Table
-------------------------------------------


Vlan    Mac Address      Type        Ports
----    -----------      --------    -----
   1    0200.1111.1111   DYNAMIC      Fa0/1
Total Mac Addresses for this criterion: 1
```

While this information is useful, often the engineer troubleshooting a problem does not know the MAC addresses of the devices connected to the network. Instead, the engineer has a topology diagram, knowing which switch ports connect to other switches and which connect to endpoint devices.

Sometimes you might be troubleshooting while looking at a network topology diagram and want to look at all the MAC addresses learned off a particular port. IOS supplies that option with the **show mac address-table dynamic interface** command. Example 5-5 shows one example, for switch SW1's F0/1 interface.

Example 5-5 show mac address-table dynamic *with the* interface *Keyword*

```
SW1# show mac address-table dynamic interface fastEthernet 0/1
          Mac Address Table
-------------------------------------------

Vlan    Mac Address      Type        Ports
----    -----------      --------    -----
   1    0200.1111.1111   DYNAMIC     Fa0/1
Total Mac Addresses for this criterion: 1
```

Finally, you may also want to find the MAC address table entries for one VLAN. You guessed it—you can add the **vlan** parameter, followed by the VLAN number. Example 5-6 shows two such examples from the same switch SW1 from Figure 5-7—one for VLAN 1, where all four devices reside, and one for a nonexistent VLAN 2.

Example 5-6   *The* show mac address-table vlan *Command*

```
SW1# show mac address-table dynamic vlan 1
          Mac Address Table
-------------------------------------------

Vlan    Mac Address      Type        Ports
----    -----------      --------    -----
   1    0200.1111.1111   DYNAMIC     Fa0/1
   1    0200.2222.2222   DYNAMIC     Fa0/2
   1    0200.3333.3333   DYNAMIC     Fa0/3
   1    0200.4444.4444   DYNAMIC     Fa0/4
Total Mac Addresses for this criterion: 4
SW1#
SW1# show mac address-table dynamic vlan 2
          Mac Address Table
-------------------------------------------

Vlan    Mac Address      Type        Ports
----    -----------      --------    -----
SW1#
```

Managing the MAC Address Table (Aging, Clearing)

This chapter closes with a few comments about how switches manage their MAC address tables. Switches do learn MAC addresses, but those MAC addresses do not remain in the table indefinitely. The switch will remove the entries due to age, due to the table filling, and you can remove entries using a command.

First, for aging out MAC table entries, switches remove entries that have not been used for a defined number of seconds (default of 300 seconds on many switches). To do that, switches look at every incoming frame and every source MAC address, and do something related to learning. If it is a new MAC address, the switch adds the correct entry to the table, of course. However, if that entry already exists, the switch still does something: it resets the inactivity timer back to 0 for that entry. Each entry's timer counts upward over time to measure how long the entry has been in the table. The switch times out (removes) any entries whose timer reaches the defined aging time.

Example 5-7 shows the aging timer setting for the entire switch. The aging time can be configured to a different time, globally and per-VLAN using the **mac address-table aging-time** *time-in-seconds* [**vlan** *vlan-number*] global configuration command. The example shows a case with all defaults, with the global setting of 300 seconds, and no per-VLAN overrides.

Example 5-7   *The MAC Address Default Aging Timer Displayed*

```
SW1# show mac address-table aging-time
Global Aging Time: 300
Vlan    Aging Time
----    ----------
SW1#


SW1# show mac address-table count

Mac Entries for Vlan 1:
-------------------------
Dynamic Address Count  : 4
Static  Address Count  : 0
Total Mac Addresses    : 4

Total Mac Address Space Available: 7299
```

Each switch also removes the oldest table entries, even if they are younger than the aging time setting, if the table fills. The MAC address table uses content-addressable memory (CAM), a physical memory that has great table lookup capabilities. However, the size of the table depends on the size of the CAM in a particular model of switch and based on some configurable settings in the switch. When a switch tries to add a new MAC table entry and finds the table full, the switch times out (removes) the oldest table entry to make space. For perspective, the end of Example 5-7 lists the size of a Cisco Catalyst switch's MAC table at about 8000 entries—the same four existing entries from the earlier examples, with space for 7299 more.

Finally, you can remove the dynamic entries from the MAC address table with the **clear mac address-table dynamic** command. Note that the **show** commands in this chapter can be executed from user and enable mode, but the **clear** command happens to be an enable mode command. The command also allows parameters to limit the types of entries cleared, as follows:

- By VLAN: **clear mac address-table dynamic vlan** *vlan-number*
- By Interface: **clear mac address-table dynamic interface** *interface-id*
- By MAC address: **clear mac address-table dynamic address** *mac-address*

MAC Address Tables with Multiple Switches

Finally, to complete the discussion, it helps to think about an example with multiple switches, just to emphasize how MAC learning, forwarding, and flooding happen independently on each LAN switch.

Consider the topology in Figure 5-10, and pay close attention to the port numbers. The ports were purposefully chosen so that neither switch used any of the same ports for this example. That is, switch SW2 does have a port F0/1 and F0/2, but I did not plug any devices into those ports when making this example. Also note that all ports are in VLAN 1, and as with the other examples in this chapter, all default configuration is used other than the hostname on the switches.

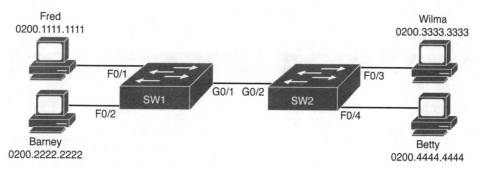

Figure 5-10   *Two-Switch Topology Example*

Think about a case in which both switches learn all four MAC addresses. For instance, that would happen if the hosts on the left communicate with the hosts on the right. SW1's MAC address table would list SW1's own port numbers (F0/1, F0/2, and G0/1) because SW1 uses that information to decide where SW1 should forward frames. Similarly, SW2's MAC table lists SW2's port numbers (F0/3, F0/4, G0/2 in this example). Example 5-8 shows the MAC address tables on both switches for that scenario.

Example 5-8   *The MAC Address Table on Two Switches*

```
SW1# show mac address-table dynamic
          Mac Address Table
-------------------------------------------


Vlan    Mac Address       Type        Ports
----    -----------       --------    -----
   1    0200.1111.1111    DYNAMIC     Fa0/1
   1    0200.2222.2222    DYNAMIC     Fa0/2
   1    0200.3333.3333    DYNAMIC     Gi0/1
   1    0200.4444.4444    DYNAMIC     Gi0/1
Total Mac Addresses for this criterion: 4

! The next output is from switch SW2
SW2# show mac address-table dynamic
   1    0200.1111.1111    DYNAMIC     Gi0/2
```

```
    1    0200.2222.2222    DYNAMIC    Gi0/2
    1    0200.3333.3333    DYNAMIC    Fa0/3
    1    0200.4444.4444    DYNAMIC    Fa0/4
Total Mac Addresses for this criterion: 4
```

Chapter Review

Review this chapter's material using either the tools in the book or interactive tools for the same material found on the book's companion website. Table 5-2 outlines the key review elements and where you can find them. To better track your study progress, record when you completed these activities in the second column.

Table 5-2 Chapter Review Tracking

Review Element	Review Date(s)	Resource Used
Review key topics		Book, website
Review key terms		Book, website
Repeat DIKTA questions		Book, PTP
Do labs		Book, Sim Lite, blog
Review command tables		Book

Review All the Key Topics

Table 5-3 Key Topics for Chapter 5

Key Topic Element	Description	Page Number
List	Three main functions of a LAN switch	109
Figure 5-3	Process to forward a known unicast frame	111
Figure 5-5	Process to forward a known unicast, second switch	112
Figure 5-6	Process to learn MAC addresses	113
List	Summary of switch forwarding logic	117
Example 5-1	The **show mac address-table dynamic** command	117

Do Labs

The Sim Lite software is a version of Pearson's full simulator learning product with a subset of the labs, included free with this book. The subset of labs mostly relate to this part of the book, so take the time to try some of the labs.

As always, also check the author's blog site pages for configuration exercises (Config Labs) at http://blog.certskills.com.

Key Terms You Should Know

broadcast frame, known unicast frame, Spanning Tree Protocol (STP), unknown unicast frame, MAC address table, forward, flood

Command References

Table 5-4 lists the verification commands used in this chapter. As an easy review exercise, cover the left column, read the right, and try to recall the command without looking. Then repeat the exercise, covering the right column, and try to recall what the command does.

Table 5-4   Chapter 5 EXEC Command Reference

Command	Mode/Purpose/Description
show mac address-table	Shows all MAC table entries of all types
show mac address-table dynamic	Shows all dynamically learned MAC table entries
show mac address-table dynamic vlan *vlan-id*	Shows all dynamically learned MAC table entries in that VLAN
show mac address-table dynamic address *mac-address*	Shows the dynamically learned MAC table entries with that MAC address
show mac address-table dynamic interface *interface-id*	Shows all dynamically learned MAC table entries associated with that interface
show mac address-table count	Shows the number of entries in the MAC table and the total number of remaining empty slots in the MAC table
show mac address-table aging-time	Shows the global and per-VLAN aging timeout for inactive MAC table entries
clear mac address-table dynamic	Empties the MAC table of all dynamic entries
show interfaces status	Lists one line per interface on the switch, with basic status and operating information for each
clear mac address-table dynamic [vlan *vlan-number*] [interface *interface-id*] [address *mac-address*]	Clears (removes) dynamic MAC table entries: either all (with no parameters), or a subset based on VLAN ID, interface ID, or a specific MAC address

Note that this chapter also includes reference to one configuration command, so it does not call for the use of a separate table. For review, the command is

mac address-table aging-time *time-in-seconds* [vlan *vlan-number*]

CHAPTER 6

Configuring Basic Switch Management

This chapter covers the following exam topics:

1.0 Network Fundamentals

1.6 Configure and verify IPv4 addressing and subnetting

4.0 IP Services

4.6 Configure and verify DHCP client and relay

4.8 Configure network devices for remote access using SSH

5.0 Security Fundamentals

5.3 Configure device access control using local passwords

The work performed by a networking device can be divided into three broad categories. The first and most obvious, called the data plane, is the work a switch does to forward frames generated by the devices connected to the switch. In other words, the data plane is the main purpose of the switch. Second, the control plane refers to the configuration and processes that control and change the choices made by the switch's data plane. The network engineer can control which interfaces are enabled and disabled, which ports run at which speeds, how Spanning Tree blocks some ports to prevent loops, and so on.

The third category, the management plane, is the topic of this chapter. The management plane deals with managing the device itself, rather than controlling what the device is doing. In particular, this chapter looks at the most basic management features that can be configured in a Cisco switch. The first section of the chapter works through the configuration of different kinds of login security. The second section shows how to configure IPv4 settings on a switch so it can be remotely managed. The last (short) section then explains a few practical matters that can make your life in the lab a little easier.

"Do I Know This Already?" Quiz

Take the quiz (either here or use the PTP software) if you want to use the score to help you decide how much time to spend on this chapter. The letter answers are listed at the bottom of the page following the quiz. Appendix C, found both at the end of the book as well as on the companion website, includes both the answers and explanations. You can also find both answers and explanations in the PTP testing software.

Table 6-1 "Do I Know This Already?" Foundation Topics Section-to-Question Mapping

Foundation Topics Section	Questions
Securing the Switch CLI	1–3
Enabling IP for Remote Access	4–5
Miscellaneous Settings Useful in Lab	6

1. Imagine that you have configured the **enable secret** command, followed by the **enable password** command, from the console. You log out of the switch and log back in at the console. Which command defines the password that you had to enter to access privileged mode?

   a. **enable password**

   b. **enable secret**

   c. Neither

   d. The **password** command, if it is configured

2. An engineer wants to set up simple password protection with no usernames for some switches in a lab, for the purpose of keeping curious coworkers from logging in to the lab switches from their desktop PCs. Which of the following commands would be a useful part of that configuration?

   a. A **login** vty mode subcommand

   b. A **password** *password* console subcommand

   c. A **login local** vty subcommand

   d. A **transport input ssh** vty subcommand

3. An engineer had formerly configured a Cisco 2960 switch to allow Telnet access so that the switch expected a password of **mypassword** from the Telnet user. The engineer then changed the configuration to support Secure Shell. Which of the following commands could have been part of the new configuration? (Choose two answers.)

   a. A **username** *name* **secret** *password* vty mode subcommand

   b. A **username** *name* **secret** *password* global configuration command

   c. A **login local** vty mode subcommand

   d. A **transport input ssh** global configuration command

4. An engineer's desktop PC connects to a switch at the main site. A router at the main site connects to each branch office through a serial link, with one small router and switch at each branch. Which of the following commands must be configured on the branch office switches, in the listed configuration mode, to allow the engineer to telnet to the branch office switches and supply only a password to login? (Choose three answers.)

    a. The **ip address** command in interface configuration mode

    b. The **ip address** command in global configuration mode

    c. The **ip default-gateway** command in VLAN configuration mode

    d. The **ip default-gateway** command in global configuration mode

    e. The **password** command in console line configuration mode

    f. The **password** command in vty line configuration mode

5. A Layer 2 switch configuration places all its physical ports into VLAN 2. The IP addressing plan shows that address 172.16.2.250 (with mask 255.255.255.0) is reserved for use by this new LAN switch and that 172.16.2.254 is already configured on the router connected to that same VLAN. The switch needs to support SSH connections into the switch from any subnet in the network. Which of the following commands are part of the required configuration in this case? (Choose two answers.)

    a. The **ip address 172.16.2.250 255.255.255.0** command in interface vlan 1 configuration mode.

    b. The **ip address 172.16.2.250 255.255.255.0** command in interface vlan 2 configuration mode.

    c. The **ip default-gateway 172.16.2.254** command in global configuration mode.

    d. The switch cannot support SSH because all its ports connect to VLAN 2, and the IP address must be configured on interface VLAN 1.

6. Which of the following line subcommands tells a switch to wait until a show command's output has completed before displaying log messages on the screen?

    a. **logging synchronous**

    b. **no ip domain-lookup**

    c. **exec-timeout 0 0**

    d. **history size 15**

Foundation Topics

Securing the Switch CLI

By default, a Cisco Catalyst switch allows anyone to connect to the console port, access user mode, and then move on to enable and configuration modes without any kind of security. That default makes sense, given that if you can get to the console port of the switch, you already have control over the switch physically. However, everyone needs to operate switches remotely, and the first step in that process is to secure the switch so that only the appropriate users can access the switch command-line interface (CLI).

This first topic in the chapter examines how to configure login security for a Cisco Catalyst switch. Securing the CLI includes protecting access to enable mode, because from enable mode, an attacker could reload the switch or change the configuration. Protecting user mode is also important, because attackers can see the status of the switch, learn about the network, and find new ways to attack the network.

Note that all remote access and management protocols require that the switch IP configuration be completed and working. A switch's IPv4 configuration has nothing to do with how a Layer 2 switch forwards Ethernet frames (as discussed in Chapter 5, "Analyzing Ethernet LAN Switching"). Instead, to support Telnet and Secure Shell (SSH) into a switch, the switch needs to be configured with an IP address. This chapter also shows how to configure a switch's IPv4 settings in the upcoming section "Enabling IPv4 for Remote Access."

In particular, this section covers the following login security topics:

■ Securing user mode and privileged mode with simple passwords

■ Securing user mode access with local usernames

■ Securing user mode access with external authentication servers

■ Securing remote access with Secure Shell (SSH)

Securing User Mode and Privileged Mode with Simple Passwords

By default, Cisco Catalyst switches allow full access from the console but no access via Telnet or SSH. Using default settings, a console user can move into user mode and then privileged mode with no passwords required; however, default settings prevent remote users from accessing even user mode.

The defaults work great for a brand new switch, but in production, you will want to secure access through the console as well as enable remote login via Telnet and/or SSH so you can sit at your desk and log in to all the switches in the LAN. Keep in mind, however, that you should not open the switch for just anyone to log in and change the configuration, so some type of secure login should be used.

Most people use a simple shared password for access to lab gear. This method uses a password only—with no username—with one password for console users and a different password for Telnet users. Console users must supply the *console password*, as configured in console line configuration mode. Telnet users must supply the *Telnet password*, also called the vty password, so called because the configuration sits in vty line configuration mode. Figure 6-1 summarizes these options for using shared passwords from the perspective of the user logging in to the switch.

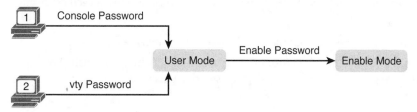

Figure 6-1 *Simple Password Security Concepts*

NOTE   This section refers to several passwords as *shared* passwords. Users share these pass-words in that all users must know and use that same password. In other words, each user does not have a unique username/password to use, but rather, all the appropriate staff knows and uses the same password.

In addition, Cisco switches protect enable mode (also called privileged mode) with yet another shared password called the *enable password*. From the perspective of the network engineer connecting to the CLI of the switch, once in user mode, the user types the **enable** EXEC command. This command prompts the user for this enable password; if the user types the correct password, IOS moves the user to enable mode.

Example 6-1 shows an example of the user experience of logging in to a switch from the console when the shared console password and the shared enable password have both been set. Note that before this example began, the user started the terminal emulator, physically connected a laptop to the console cable, and then pressed the Return key to make the switch respond as shown at the top of the example.

Example 6-1   *Console Login and Movement to Enable Mode*

```
(User now presses enter now to start the process. This line of text does not appear.)

User Access Verification

Password: faith
Switch> enable
Password: love
Switch#
```

Note that the example shows the password text as if typed (faith and love), along with the **enable** command that moves the user from user mode to enable mode. In reality, the switch hides the passwords when typed, to prevent someone from reading over your shoulder to see the passwords.

To configure the shared passwords for the console, Telnet, and for enable mode, you need to configure several commands. However, the parameters of the commands can be pretty intuitive. Figure 6-2 shows the configuration of all three of these passwords.

The configuration for these three passwords does not require a lot of work. First, the console and vty password configuration sets the password based on the context: console mode for the console (**line con 0**), and vty line configuration mode for the Telnet password (**line vty 0 15**). Then inside console mode and vty mode, respectively, the two commands in each mode are as follows:

> **password** *password-value*: Defines the actual password used on the console or vty
>
> **login**: Tells IOS to enable the use of a simple shared password (with no username) on this line (console or vty), so that the switch asks the user for a password

---

Answers to the "Do I Know This Already?" quiz:

1 B **2** A **3** B, C **4** A, D, F **5** B, C **6** A

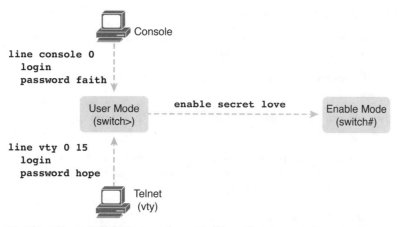

Figure 6-2   *Simple Password Security Configuration*

The configured enable password, shown on the right side of the figure, applies to all users, no matter whether they connect to user mode via the console, Telnet, or otherwise. The command to configure the enable password is a global configuration command: **enable secret** *password-value*.

> **NOTE**   Older IOS versions used the command **enable password** *password-value* to set the enable password, and that command still exists in IOS. However, the **enable secret** command is much more secure. In real networks, use **enable secret**. Chapter 5, "Securing Network Devices," in the *CCNA 200-301 Official Cert Guide, Volume 2*, explains more about the security levels of various password mechanisms, including a comparison of the **enable secret** and **enable password** commands.

To help you follow the process, and for easier study later, use the configuration checklist before the example. The configuration checklist collects the required and optional steps to configure a feature as described in this book. The configuration checklist for shared passwords for the console, Telnet, and enable passwords is

Step 1.   Configure the enable password with the **enable secret** *password-value* command.

Step 2.   Configure the console password:

    A.   Use the **line con 0** command to enter console configuration mode.

    B.   Use the **password** *password-value* subcommand to set the value of the console password.

    C.   Use the **login** subcommand to enable console password security using a simple password.

Step 3. Configure the Telnet (vty) password:

  A. Use the **line vty 0 15** command to enter vty configuration mode for all 16 vty lines (numbered 0 through 15).

  B. Use the **password** *password-value* subcommand to set the value of the console password.

  C. Use the **login** subcommand to enable console password security using a simple password.

Example 6-2 shows the configuration process as noted in the configuration checklist, along with setting the enable secret password. Note that the lines which begin with a ! are comment lines; they are there to guide you through the configuration.

Example 6-2 *Configuring Basic Passwords*

```
! Enter global configuration mode, set the enable password, and also
! set the hostname (just because it makes sense to do so)
!
Switch# configure terminal
Switch(config)# enable secret love
!
! At Step 2 in the checklist, enter console configuration mode, set the
! password value to "faith" and enable simple passwords for the console.
! The exit command moves the user back to global config mode.
!
Switch#(config)# line console 0
Switch#(config-line)# password faith
Switch#(config-line)# login
Switch#(config-line)# exit
!
! The next few lines do basically the same configuration, except it is
! for the vty lines. Telnet users will use "hope" to login.
!
Switch#(config)# line vty 0 15
Switch#(config-line)# password hope
Switch#(config-line)# login
Switch#(config-line)# end
Switch#
```

Example 6-3 shows the resulting configuration in the switch per the **show running-config** command. The gray lines highlight the new configuration. Note that many unrelated lines of output have been deleted from the output to keep focused on the password configuration.

Example 6-3 *Resulting Running-Config File (Subset) Per Example 6-2 Configuration*

```
Switch# show running-config
!
Building configuration...
```

```
Current configuration: 1333 bytes
!
version 12.2
!
enable secret 5 $1$OwtI$A58c2XgqWyDNeDnv51mNR.
!
interface FastEthernet0/1
!
interface FastEthernet0/2
!
! Several lines have been omitted here - in particular, lines for
! FastEthernet interfaces 0/3 through 0/23.
!
interface FastEthernet0/24
!
interface GigabitEthernet0/1
!
interface GigabitEthernet0/2
!
line con 0
 password faith
 login
!
line vty 0 4
 password hope
 login
!
line vty 5 15
 password hope
 login
```

NOTE   For historical reasons, the output of the **show running-config** command, in the last six lines of Example 6-3, separates the first five vty lines (0 through 4) from the rest (5 through 15).

Securing User Mode Access with Local Usernames and Passwords

Cisco switches support two other login security methods that both use per-user username/ password pairs instead of a shared password with no username. One method, referred to as local usernames and passwords, configures the username/password pairs locally—that is, in the switch's configuration. Switches support this local username/password option for the console, for Telnet, and even for SSH, but do not replace the enable password used to reach enable mode.

The configuration to migrate from using the simple shared passwords to instead using local usernames/passwords requires only some small configuration changes, as shown in Figure 6-3.

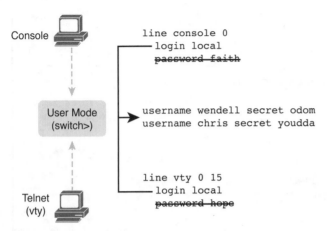

Figure 6-3 *Configuring Switches to Use Local Username Login Authentication*

Working through the configuration in the figure, first, the switch of course needs to know the list of username/password pairs. To create these, repeatedly use the **username** *name* **secret** *password* global configuration command. Then, to enable this different type of console or Telnet security, simply enable this login security method with the **login local** line. Basically, this command means "use the local list of usernames for login." You can also use the **no password** command (without even typing in the password) to clean up any remaining password subcommands from console or vty mode because these commands are not needed when using local usernames and passwords.

The following checklist details the commands to configure local username login, mainly as a method for easier study and review:

Step 1.   Use the **username** *name* **secret** *password* global configuration command to add one or more username/password pairs on the local switch.

Step 2.   Configure the console to use locally configured username/password pairs:

   A. Use the **line con 0** command to enter console configuration mode.

   B. Use the **login local** subcommand to enable the console to prompt for both username and password, checked versus the list of local usernames/passwords.

   C. (Optional) Use the **no password** subcommand to remove any existing simple shared passwords, just for good housekeeping of the configuration file.

Step 3.   Configure Telnet (vty) to use locally configured username/password pairs.

   A. Use the **line vty 0 15** command to enter vty configuration mode for all 16 vty lines (numbered 0 through 15).

   B. Use the **login local** subcommand to enable the switch to prompt for both username and password for all inbound Telnet users, checked versus the list of local usernames/passwords.

   C. (Optional) Use the **no password** subcommand to remove any existing simple shared passwords, just for good housekeeping of the configuration file.

When a Telnet user connects to the switch configured as shown in Figure 6-3, the user will be prompted first for a username and then for a password, as shown in Example 6-4. The username/password pair must be from the list of local usernames; otherwise, the login is rejected.

Example 6-4   *Telnet Login Process After Applying Configuration in Figure 6-3*

```
SW2# telnet 10.9.9.19
Trying 10.9.9.19 ... Open


User Access Verification

Username: wendell
Password:
SW1> enable
Password:
SW1# configure terminal
Enter configuration commands, one per line. End with CNTL/Z.
SW1(config)#^Z
SW1#
*Mar 1 02:00:56.229: %SYS-5-CONFIG_I: Configured from console by wendell on vty0
(10.9.9.19)
```

NOTE   Example 6-4 does not show the password value as having been typed because Cisco switches do not display the typed password for security reasons.

Securing User Mode Access with External Authentication Servers

The end of Example 6-4 points out one of the many security improvements when requiring each user to log in with their own username. The end of the example shows the user entering configuration mode (**configure terminal**) and then immediately leaving (**end**). Note that when a user exits configuration mode, the switch generates a log message. If the user logged in with a username, the log message identifies that username; note the "wendell" in the log message.

However, using a username/password configured directly on the switch causes some administrative headaches. For instance, every switch and router needs the configuration for all users who might need to log in to the devices. Then, when any changes need to happen, like an occasional change to the passwords for good security practices, the configuration of all devices must be changed.

A better option would be to use tools like those used for many other IT login functions. Those tools allow for a central place to securely store all username/password pairs, with tools to make users change their passwords regularly, tools to revoke users when they leave their current jobs, and so on.

Cisco switches allow exactly that option using an external server called an authentication, authorization, and accounting (AAA) server. These servers hold the usernames/passwords. Typically, these servers allow users to do self-service and forced maintenance to their passwords. Many production networks use AAA servers for their switches and routers today.

The underlying login process requires some additional work on the part of the switch for each user login, but once set up, the username/password administration is much less. When using a AAA server for authentication, the switch (or router) simply sends a message to the AAA server asking whether the username and password are allowed, and the AAA server replies. Figure 6-4 shows an example, with the user first supplying a username/password, the switch asking the AAA server, and the server replying to the switch stating that the username/password is valid.

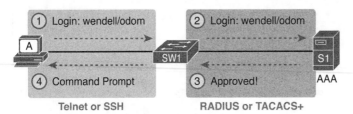

Figure 6-4 *Basic Authentication Process with an External AAA Server*

While the figure shows the general idea, note that the information flows with a couple of different protocols. On the left, the connection between the user and the switch or router uses Telnet or SSH. On the right, the switch and AAA server typically use either the RADIUS or TACACS+ protocol, both of which encrypt the passwords as they traverse the network.

Securing Remote Access with Secure Shell

So far, this chapter has focused on the console and on Telnet, mostly ignoring SSH. Telnet has one serious disadvantage: all data in the Telnet session flows as clear text, including the password exchanges. So, anyone that can capture the messages between the user and the switch (in what is called a man-in-the-middle attack) can see the passwords. SSH encrypts all data transmitted between the SSH client and server, protecting the data and passwords.

SSH can use the same local login authentication method as Telnet, with the locally configured username and password. (SSH cannot rely on authentication methods that do not include a username, like shared passwords.) So, the configuration to support local usernames for Telnet, as shown previously in Figure 6-3, also enables local username authentication for incoming SSH connections.

Figure 6-5 shows one example configuration of what is required to support SSH. The figure repeats the local username configuration as shown earlier in Figure 6-3, as used for Telnet. Figure 6-5 shows three additional commands required to complete the configuration of SSH on the switch.

SSH-Specific Configuration

```
hostname sw1
ip domain-name example.com
! Next Command Uses FQDN "sw1.example.com"
crypto key generate rsa
```

Local Username Configuration (Like Telnet)

```
username wendell secret odom
username chris secret youdda
!
line vty 0 15
  login local
```

Figure 6-5 *Adding SSH Configuration to Local Username Configuration*

IOS uses the three SSH-specific configuration commands in the figure to create the SSH encryption keys. The SSH server uses the fully qualified domain name (FQDN) of the switch as input to create that key. The switch creates the FQDN from the hostname and domain name of the switch. Figure 6-5 begins by setting both values (just in case they are not already configured). Then the third command, the **crypto key generate rsa** command, generates the SSH encryption keys.

The configuration in Figure 6-5 relies on two default settings that the figure therefore conveniently ignored. IOS runs an SSH server by default. In addition, IOS allows SSH connections into the vty lines by default.

Seeing the configuration happen in configuration mode, step by step, can be particularly helpful with SSH configuration. Note in particular that in this example, the **crypto key** command prompts the user for the key modulus; you could also add the parameters **modulus** *modulus-value* to the end of the **crypto key** command to add this setting on the command. Example 6-5 shows the commands in Figure 6-5 being configured, with the encryption key as the final step.

Example 6-5 *SSH Configuration Process to Match Figure 6-5*

```
SW1# configure terminal
Enter configuration commands, one per line. End with CNTL/Z.
!
! Step 1 next. The hostname is already set, but it is repeated just
! to be obvious about the steps.
!
SW1(config)# hostname SW1
SW1(config)# ip domain-name example.com
SW1(config)# crypto key generate rsa
The name for the keys will be: SW1.example.com
Choose the size of the key modulus in the range of 360 to 2048 for your
  General Purpose Keys. Choosing a key modulus greater than 512 may take
  a few minutes.
```

```
How many bits in the modulus [512]: 1024
% Generating 1024 bit RSA keys, keys will be non-exportable...
[OK] (elapsed time was 4 seconds)
SW1(config)#
!
! Optionally, set the SSH version to version 2 (only) - preferred
!
SW1(config)# ip ssh version 2
!
! Next, configure the vty lines for local username support, just like
! with Telnet
!
SW1(config)# line vty 0 15
SW1(config-line)# login local
SW1(config-line)# exit
!
! Define the local usernames, just like with Telnet
!
SW1(config)# username wendell password odom
SW1(config)# username chris password youdaman
SW1(config)# ^Z
SW1#
```

Earlier, I mentioned that one useful default was that the switch defaults to support both SSH and Telnet on the vty lines. However, because Telnet is a security risk, you could disable Telnet to enforce a tighter security policy. (For that matter, you can disable SSH support and allow Telnet on the vty lines as well.)

To control which protocols a switch supports on its vty lines, use the **transport input** {all | none | telnet | ssh} vty subcommand in vty mode, with the following options:

transport input all or **transport input telnet ssh:** Support both Telnet and SSH

transport input none: Support neither

transport input telnet: Support only Telnet

transport input ssh: Support only SSH

To complete this section about SSH, the following configuration checklist details the steps for one method to configure a Cisco switch to support SSH using local usernames. (SSH support in IOS can be configured in several ways; this checklist shows one simple way to configure it.) The process shown here ends with a comment to configure local username support on vty lines, as was discussed earlier in the section titled "Securing User Mode Access with Local Usernames and Passwords."

Step 1.   Configure the switch to generate a matched public and private key pair to use for encryption:

   A. If not already configured, use the **hostname** *name* in global configuration mode to configure a hostname for this switch.

B. If not already configured, use the **ip domain-name** *name* in global configuration mode to configure a domain name for the switch, completing the switch's FQDN.

C. Use the **crypto key generate rsa** command in global configuration mode (or the **crypto key generate rsa modulus** *modulus-value* command to avoid being prompted for the key modulus) to generate the keys. (Use at least a 768-bit key to support SSH version 2.)

Step 2. (Optional) Use the **ip ssh version 2** command in global configuration mode to override the default of supporting both versions 1 and 2, so that only SSHv2 connections are allowed.

Step 3. (Optional) If not already configured with the setting you want, configure the vty lines to accept SSH and whether to also allow Telnet:

A. Use the **transport input ssh** command in vty line configuration mode to allow SSH only.

B. Use the **transport input all** command (default) or **transport input telnet ssh** command in vty line configuration mode to allow both SSH and Telnet.

Step 4. Use various commands in vty line configuration mode to configure local username login authentication as discussed earlier in this chapter.

NOTE   Cisco routers often default to **transport input none**, so you must add the **transport input** line subcommand to enable Telnet and/or SSH into a router.

Two key commands give some information about the status of SSH on the switch. First, the **show ip ssh** command lists status information about the SSH server itself. The **show ssh** command then lists information about each SSH client currently connected into the switch. Example 6-6 shows samples of each, with user wendell currently connected to the switch.

Example 6-6 *Displaying SSH Status*

```
SW1# show ip ssh
SSH Enabled - version 2.0
Authentication timeout: 120 secs; Authentication retries: 3

SW1# show ssh
Connection Version Mode  Encryption  Hmac        State            Username
0          2.0     IN    aes126-cbc  hmac-sha1   Session started  wendell
0          2.0     OUT   aes126-cbc  hmac-sha1   Session started  wendell
%No SSHv1 server connections running.
```

Enabling IPv4 for Remote Access

To allow Telnet or SSH access to the switch, and to allow other IP-based management protocols (for example, Simple Network Management Protocol, or SNMP) to function as intended, the switch needs an IP address, as well as a few other related settings. The IP address has nothing to do with how switches forward Ethernet frames; it simply exists to support overhead management traffic.

This next topic begins by explaining the IPv4 settings needed on a switch, followed by the configuration. Note that although switches can be configured with IPv6 addresses with commands similar to those shown in this chapter, this chapter focuses solely on IPv4. All references to IP in this chapter imply IPv4.

Host and Switch IP Settings

A switch needs the same kind of IP settings as a PC with a single Ethernet interface. For perspective, a PC has a CPU, with the operating system running on the CPU. It has an Ethernet network interface card (NIC). The OS configuration includes an IP address associated with the NIC, either configured or learned dynamically with DHCP.

A switch uses the same ideas, except that the switch needs to use a virtual NIC inside the switch. Like a PC, a switch has a real CPU, running an OS (called IOS). The switch obviously has lots of Ethernet ports, but instead of assigning its management IP address to any of those ports, the switch then uses a NIC-like concept called a switched virtual interface (SVI), or more commonly, a VLAN interface, that acts like the switch's own NIC. Then the settings on the switch look something like a host, with the switch configuration assigning IP settings, like an IP address, to this VLAN interface, as shown in Figure 6-6.

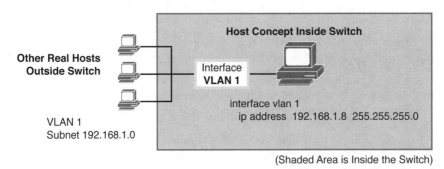

Figure 6-6 *Switch Virtual Interface (SVI) Concept Inside a Switch*

By using interface VLAN 1 for the IP configuration, the switch can then send and receive frames on any of the ports in VLAN 1. In a Cisco switch, by default, all ports are assigned to VLAN 1.

In most networks, switches configure many VLANs, so the network engineer has a choice of where to configure the IP address. That is, the management IP address does not have to be configured on the VLAN 1 interface (as configured with the **interface vlan 1** command seen in Figure 6-6).

A Layer 2 Cisco LAN switch needs only one IP address for management purposes. However, you can choose to use any VLAN to which the switch connects. The configuration then includes a VLAN interface for that VLAN number, with an appropriate IP address.

For example, Figure 6-7 shows a Layer 2 switch with some physical ports in two different VLANs (VLANs 1 and 2). The figure also shows the subnets used on those VLANs. The network engineer could choose to use either

- Interface VLAN 1, with an IP address in subnet 192.168.1.0
- Interface VLAN 2, with an IP address in subnet 192.168.2.0

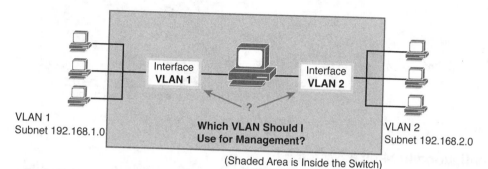

Figure 6-7   *Choosing One VLAN on Which to Configure a Switch IP Address*

Note that you should not try to use a VLAN interface for which there are no physical ports assigned to the same VLAN. If you do, the VLAN interface will not reach an up/up state, and the switch will not have the physical ability to communicate outside the switch.

> **NOTE**   Some Cisco switches can be configured to act as either a Layer 2 switch or a Layer 3 switch. When acting as a Layer 2 switch, a switch forwards Ethernet frames as discussed in depth in Chapter 5, "Analyzing Ethernet LAN Switching." Alternatively, a switch can also act as a *multilayer switch* or *Layer 3 switch*, which means the switch can do both Layer 2 switching and Layer 3 IP routing of IP packets, using the Layer 3 logic normally used by routers. This chapter assumes all switches are Layer 2 switches. Chapter 17, "IP Routing in the LAN," discusses Layer 3 switching in depth along with using multiple VLAN interfaces at the same time.

Configuring the IP address (and mask) on one VLAN interface allows the switch to send and receive IP packets with other hosts in a subnet that exists on that VLAN; however, the switch cannot communicate outside the local subnet without another configuration setting called the default gateway. The reason a switch needs a default gateway setting is the same reason that hosts need the same setting—because of how hosts think when sending IP packets. Specifically:

- To send IP packets to hosts in the same subnet, send them directly
- To send IP packets to hosts in a different subnet, send them to the local router; that is, the default gateway

Figure 6-8 shows the ideas. In this case, the switch (on the right) will use IP address 192.168.1.200 as configured on interface VLAN 1. However, to communicate with host A, on the far left of the figure, the switch must use Router R1 (the default gateway) to forward

IP packets to host A. To make that work, the switch needs to configure a default gateway setting, pointing to Router R1's IP address (192.168.1.1 in this case). Note that the switch and router both use the same mask, 255.255.255.0, which puts the addresses in the same subnet.

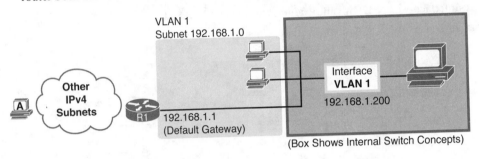

Figure 6-8 *The Need for a Default Gateway*

Configuring IPv4 on a Switch

A switch configures its IPv4 address and mask on this special NIC-like *VLAN interface*. The following steps list the commands used to configure IPv4 on a switch, assuming that the IP address is configured to be in VLAN 1, with Example 6-7 that follows showing an example configuration.

Step 1.   Use the **interface vlan 1** command in global configuration mode to enter interface VLAN 1 configuration mode.

Step 2.   Use the **ip address** *ip-address mask* command in interface configuration mode to assign an IP address and mask.

Step 3.   Use the **no shutdown** command in interface configuration mode to enable the VLAN 1 interface if it is not already enabled.

Step 4.   Add the **ip default-gateway** *ip-address* command in global configuration mode to configure the default gateway.

Step 5.   (Optional) Add the **ip name-server** *ip-address1 ip-address2 ...* command in global configuration mode to configure the switch to use Domain Name System (DNS) to resolve names into their matching IP address.

Example 6-7   *Switch Static IP Address Configuration*

```
Emma# configure terminal
Emma(config)# interface vlan 1
Emma(config-if)# ip address 192.168.1.200 255.255.255.0
Emma(config-if)# no shutdown
00:25:07: %LINK-3-UPDOWN: Interface Vlan1, changed state to up
00:25:08: %LINEPROTO-5-UPDOWN: Line protocol on Interface Vlan1, changed
 state to up
Emma(config-if)# exit
Emma(config)# ip default-gateway 192.168.1.1
```

On a side note, this example shows a particularly important and common command: the [no] **shutdown** command. To administratively enable an interface on a switch, use the **no shutdown** interface subcommand; to disable an interface, use the **shutdown** interface subcommand. This command can be used on the physical Ethernet interfaces that the switch uses to switch Ethernet messages in addition to the VLAN interface shown here in this example.

Also, pause long enough to look at the messages that appear just below the **no shutdown** command in Example 6-7. Those messages are syslog messages generated by the switch stating that the switch did indeed enable the interface. Switches (and routers) generate syslog messages in response to a variety of events, and by default, those messages appear at the console. Chapter 9, "Device Management Protocols," in the *CCNA 200-301 Official Cert Guide, Volume 2*, discusses syslog messages in more detail.

Configuring a Switch to Learn Its IP Address with DHCP

The switch can also use Dynamic Host Configuration Protocol (DHCP) to dynamically learn its IPv4 settings. Basically, all you have to do is tell the switch to use DHCP on the interface and enable the interface. Assuming that DHCP works in this network, the switch will learn all its settings. The following list details the steps, again assuming the use of interface VLAN 1, with Example 6-8 that follows showing an example:

Step 1.   Enter VLAN 1 configuration mode using the **interface vlan 1** global configuration command, and enable the interface using the **no shutdown** command as necessary.

Step 2.   Assign an IP address and mask using the **ip address dhcp** interface subcommand.

Example 6-8 *Switch Dynamic IP Address Configuration with DHCP*

```
Emma# configure terminal
Enter configuration commands, one per line. End with CNTL/Z.
Emma(config)# interface vlan 1
Emma(config-if)# ip address dhcp
Emma(config-if)# no shutdown
Emma(config-if)# ^Z
Emma#
00:38:20: %LINK-3-UPDOWN: Interface Vlan1, changed state to up
00:38:21: %LINEPROTO-5-UPDOWN: Line protocol on Interface Vlan1, changed state to up
```

Verifying IPv4 on a Switch

The switch IPv4 configuration can be checked in several places. First, you can always look at the current configuration using the **show running-config** command. Second, you can look at the IP address and mask information using the **show interfaces vlan** *x* command, which shows detailed status information about the VLAN interface in VLAN *x*. Finally, if using DHCP, use the **show dhcp lease** command to see the (temporarily) leased IP address and other parameters. (Note that the switch does not store the DHCP-learned IP configuration in the running-config file.) Example 6-9 shows sample output from these commands to match the configuration in Example 6-8.

Example 6-9 *Verifying DHCP-Learned Information on a Switch*

```
Emma# show dhcp lease
Temp IP addr: 192.168.1.101    for peer on Interface: Vlan1
Temp sub net mask: 255.255.255.0
   DHCP Lease server: 192.168.1.1, state: 3 Bound
   DHCP transaction id: 1966
   Lease: 86400 secs,  Renewal: 43200 secs,  Rebind: 75600 secs
Temp default-gateway addr: 192.168.1.1
   Next timer fires after: 11:59:45
   Retry count: 0   Client-ID: cisco-0019.e86a.6fc0-Vl1
   Hostname: Emma
Emma# show interfaces vlan 1
Vlan1 is up, line protocol is up
   Hardware is EtherSVI, address is 0019.e86a.6fc0 (bia 0019.e86a.6fc0)
   Internet address is 192.168.1.101/24
   MTU 1500 bytes, BW 1000000 Kbit, DLY 10 usec,
      reliability 255/255, txload 1/255, rxload 1/255
! lines omitted for brevity
Emma# show ip default-gateway
192.168.1.1
```

The output of the **show interfaces vlan 1** command lists two very important details related to switch IP addressing. First, this **show** command lists the interface status of the VLAN 1 interface—in this case, "up and up." If the VLAN 1 interface is not up, the switch cannot use its IP address to send and receive management traffic. Notably, if you forget to issue the **no shutdown** command, the VLAN 1 interface remains in its default shutdown state and is listed as "administratively down" in the **show** command output.

Second, note that the output lists the interface's IP address on the third line. If you statically configure the IP address, as in Example 6-7, the IP address will always be listed; however, if you use DHCP and DHCP fails, the **show interfaces vlan** *x* command will not list an IP address here. When DHCP works, you can see the IP address with the **show interfaces vlan 1** command, but that output does not remind you whether the address is either statically configured or DHCP leased. So it does take a little extra effort to make sure you know whether the address is statically configured or DHCP-learned on the VLAN interface.

Miscellaneous Settings Useful in the Lab

This last short section of the chapter touches on a couple of commands that can help you be a little more productive when practicing in a lab.

History Buffer Commands

When you enter commands from the CLI, the switch saves the last several commands in the history buffer. Then, as mentioned in Chapter 4, "Using the Command-Line Interface," you can use the up-arrow key or press Ctrl+P to move back in the history buffer to retrieve a command you entered a few commands ago. This feature makes it very easy and fast to use a set of commands repeatedly. Table 6-2 lists some of the key commands related to the history buffer.

Table 6-2 Commands Related to the History Buffer

Command	Description
show history	An EXEC command that lists the commands currently held in the history buffer.
terminal history size x	From EXEC mode, this command allows a single user to set, just for this one login session, the size of his or her history buffer.
history size x	A configuration command that, from console or vty line configuration mode, sets the default number of commands saved in the history buffer for the users of the console or vty lines, respectively.

The logging synchronous, exec-timeout, and no ip domain-lookup Commands

These next three configuration commands have little in common, other than the fact that they can be useful settings to reduce your frustration when using the console of a switch or router.

The console automatically receives copies of all unsolicited syslog messages on a switch. The idea is that if the switch needs to tell the network administrator some important and possibly urgent information, the administrator might be at the console and might notice the message.

Unfortunately, IOS (by default) displays these syslog messages on the console's screen at any time—including right in the middle of a command you are entering, or in the middle of the output of a **show** command. Having a bunch of text show up unexpectedly can be a bit annoying.

You could simply disable the feature that sends these messages to the console and then re-enable the feature later using the **no logging console** and **logging console** global configuration commands. For example, when working from the console, if you want to temporarily not be bothered by log messages, you can disable the display of these messages with the **no logging console** global configuration command, and then when finished, enable them again.

However, IOS supplies a reasonable compromise, telling the switch to display syslog messages only at more convenient times, such as at the end of output from a **show** command. To do so, just configure the **logging synchronous** console line subcommand, which basically tells IOS to synchronize the syslog message display with the messages requested using **show** commands.

Another way to improve the user experience at the console is to control timeouts of the login session from the console or when using Telnet or SSH. By default, the switch automatically disconnects console and vty (Telnet and SSH) users after 5 minutes of inactivity. The **exec-timeout** *minutes seconds* line subcommand enables you to set the length of that inactivity timer. In the lab (but not in production), you might want to use the special value of 0 minutes and 0 seconds meaning "never time out."

Finally, IOS has an interesting combination of features that can make you wait for a minute or so when you mistype a command. First, IOS tries to use DNS name resolution on IP hostnames—a generally useful feature. If you mistype a command, however, IOS thinks you want to telnet to a host by that name. With all default settings in the switch, the switch tries to resolve the hostname, cannot find a DNS server, and takes about a minute to time out and give you control of the CLI again.

To avoid this problem, configure the **no ip domain-lookup** global configuration command, which disables IOS's attempt to resolve the hostname into an IP address.

Example 6-10 collects all these commands into a single example, as a template for some good settings to add in a lab switch to make you more productive.

Example 6-10 *Commands Often Used in the Lab to Increase Productivity*

```
no ip domain-lookup
!
line console 0
 exec-timeout 0 0
 logging synchronous
 history size 20
!
line vty 0 15
 exec-timeout 0 0
 logging synchronous
 history size 20
```

Chapter Review

One key to doing well on the exams is to perform repetitive spaced review sessions. Review this chapter's material using either the tools in the book or interactive tools for the same material found on the book's companion website. Refer to the "Your Study Plan" element section titled "Step 2: Build Your Study Habits Around the Chapter" for more details. Table 6-3 outlines the key review elements and where you can find them. To better track your study progress, record when you completed these activities in the second column.

Table 6-3 Chapter Review Tracking

Review Element	Review Date(s)	Resource Used
Review key topics		Book, website
Review key terms		Book, website
Repeat DIKTA questions		Book, PTP
Review config checklists		Book, website
Do labs		Sim Lite, blog
Review command tables		Book

Review All the Key Topics

Table 6-4   Key Topics for Chapter 6

Key Topic Element	Description	Page Number
Example 6-2	Example of configuring password login security (no usernames)	132
Figure 6-5	SSH configuration commands with related username login security	137

Key Terms You Should Know

Telnet, Secure Shell (SSH), local username, AAA, AAA server, enable mode, default gateway, VLAN interface, history buffer, DNS, name resolution, log message

Do Labs

The Sim Lite software is a version of Pearson's full simulator learning product with a subset of the labs, included with this book for free. The subset of labs mostly relate to this part. Take the time to try some of the labs. As always, also check the author's blog site pages for configuration exercises (Config Labs) at https://blog.certskills.com.

Command References

Tables 6-5, 6-6, 6-7, and 6-8 list configuration and verification commands used in this chapter. As an easy review exercise, cover the left column in a table, read the right column, and try to recall the command without looking. Then repeat the exercise, covering the right column, and try to recall what the command does.

Table 6-5   Login Security Commands

Command	Mode/Purpose/Description
line console 0	Changes the context to console configuration mode.
line vty *1st-vty last-vty*	Changes the context to vty configuration mode for the range of vty lines listed in the command.
login	Console and vty configuration mode. Tells IOS to prompt for a password.
password *pass-value*	Console and vty configuration mode. Lists the password required if the **login** command (with no other parameters) is configured.
login local	Console and vty configuration mode. Tells IOS to prompt for a username and password, to be checked against locally configured **username** global configuration commands on this switch or router.
username *name* secret *pass-value*	Global command. Defines one of possibly multiple usernames and associated passwords, used for user authentication. Used when the **login local** line configuration command has been used.

Command	Mode/Purpose/Description
crypto key generate rsa [**modulus** *360..2048*]	Global command. Creates and stores (in a hidden location in flash memory) the keys required by SSH.
transport input {**telnet** | **ssh** | **all** | **none**}	vty line configuration mode. Defines whether Telnet/SSH access is allowed into this switch. Both values can be configured on one command to allow both Telnet and SSH access (the default).

Table 6-6   Switch IPv4 Configuration

Command	Mode/Purpose/Description
interface vlan *number*	Changes the context to VLAN interface mode. For VLAN 1, allows the configuration of the switch's IP address.
ip address *ip-address subnet-mask*	VLAN interface mode. Statically configures the switch's IP address and mask.
ip address dhcp	VLAN interface mode. Configures the switch as a DHCP client to discover its IPv4 address, mask, and default gateway.
ip default-gateway *address*	Global command. Configures the switch's default gateway IPv4 address. Not required if the switch uses DHCP.
ip name-server *server-ip-1 server-ip-2 ...*	Global command. Configures the IPv4 addresses of DNS servers, so any commands when logged in to the switch will use the DNS for name resolution.

Table 6-7   Other Switch Configuration

Command	Mode/Purpose/Description
hostname *name*	Global command. Sets this switch's hostname, which is also used as the first part of the switch's command prompt.
enable secret *pass-value*	Global command. Sets this switch's password that is required for any user to reach enable mode.
history size *length*	Line config mode. Defines the number of commands held in the history buffer, for later recall, for users of those lines.
logging synchronous	Console or vty mode. Tells IOS to send log messages to the user at natural break points between commands rather than in the middle of a line of output.
[no] logging console	Global command that disables or enables the display of log messages to the console.
exec-timeout *minutes* [*seconds*]	Console or vty mode. Sets the inactivity timeout, so that after the defined period of no action, IOS closes the current user login session.

Table 6-8   Chapter 6 EXEC Command Reference

Command	Purpose
show running-config	Lists the currently used configuration.
show running-config | begin line vty	Pipes (sends) the command output to the **begin** command, which only lists output beginning with the first line that contains the text "line vty."
show dhcp lease	Lists any information the switch acquires as a DHCP client. This includes IP address, subnet mask, and default gateway information.
show crypto key mypubkey rsa	Lists the public and shared key created for use with SSH using the **crypto key generate rsa** global configuration command.
show ip ssh	Lists status information for the SSH server, including the SSH version.
show ssh	Lists status information for current SSH connections into and out of the local switch.
show interfaces vlan *number*	Lists the interface status, the switch's IPv4 address and mask, and much more.
show ip default-gateway	Lists the switch's setting for its IPv4 default gateway.
terminal history size *x*	Changes the length of the history buffer for the current user only, only for the current login to the switch.
show history	Lists the commands in the current history buffer.

6

CHAPTER 7

Configuring and Verifying Switch Interfaces

This chapter covers the following exam topics:

1.0 Network Fundamentals

1.1 Explain the role and function of network components

1.1.b L2 and L3 switches

1.4 Describe switching concepts

So far in this part, you have learned the skills to navigate the command-line interface (CLI) and use commands that configure and verify switch features. You learned about the primary purpose of a switch—forwarding Ethernet frames—and learned how to see that process in action by looking at the switch MAC address table. After learning about the switch data plane in Chapter 5, "Analyzing Ethernet LAN Switching," you learned a few management plane features in Chapter 6, "Configuring Basic Switch Management," like how to configure the switch to support Telnet and Secure Shell (SSH) by configuring IP address and login security.

This chapter focuses on switch interfaces in two major sections. The first section shows how you can configure and change the operation of switch interfaces: how to change the speed, duplex, or even disable the interface. The second half then focuses on how to use show commands on a switch to verify switch interface status and how to interpret the output to find some of the more common issues with switch interfaces.

"Do I Know This Already?" Quiz

Take the quiz (either here or use the PTP software) if you want to use the score to help you decide how much time to spend on this chapter. The letter answers are listed at the bottom of the page following the quiz. Appendix C, found both at the end of the book as well as on the companion website, includes both the answers and explanations. You can also find both answers and explanations in the PTP testing software.

Table 7-1 "Do I Know This Already?" Foundation Topics Section-to-Question Mapping

Foundation Topics Section	Questions
Configuring Switch Interfaces	1–3
Analyzing Switch Interface Status and Statistics	4–6

1. Which of the following describes a way to disable IEEE standard autonegotiation on a 10/100 port on a Cisco switch?

    a. Configure the **negotiate disable** interface subcommand

    b. Configure the **no negotiate** interface subcommand

    c. Configure the **speed 100** interface subcommand

    d. Configure the **duplex half** interface subcommand

    e. Configure the **duplex full** interface subcommand

    f. Configure the **speed 100** and **duplex full** interface subcommands

2. In which of the following modes of the CLI could you configure the duplex setting for interface Fast Ethernet 0/5?

    a. User mode

    b. Enable mode

    c. Global configuration mode

    d. VLAN mode

    e. Interface configuration mode

3. A Cisco Catalyst switch connects with its Gigabit0/1 port to an end user's PC. The end user, thinking the user is helping, manually sets the PC's OS to use a speed of 1000 Mbps and to use full duplex, and disables the use of autonegotiation. The switch's G0/1 port has default settings for speed and duplex. What speed and duplex settings will the switch decide to use? (Choose two answers.)

    a. Full duplex

    b. Half duplex

    c. 10 Mbps

    d. 1000 Mbps

4. The output of the **show interfaces status** command on a 2960 switch shows interface Fa0/1 in a "disabled" state. Which of the following is true about interface Fa0/1? (Choose three answers.)

    a. The interface is configured with the **shutdown** command.

    b. The **show interfaces fa0/1** command will list the interface with two status codes of administratively down and line protocol down.

    c. The **show interfaces fa0/1** command will list the interface with two status codes of up and down.

    d. The interface cannot currently be used to forward frames.

    e. The interface can currently be used to forward frames.

5.   Switch SW1 uses its Gigabit 0/1 interface to connect to switch SW2's Gigabit 0/2 interface. SW2's Gi0/2 interface is configured with the **speed 1000** and **duplex full** commands. SW1 uses all defaults for interface configuration commands on its Gi0/1 interface. Which of the following are true about the link after it comes up? (Choose two answers.)

   a.   The link works at 1000 Mbps (1 Gbps).

   b.   SW1 attempts to run at 10 Mbps because SW2 has effectively disabled IEEE standard autonegotiation.

   c.   The link runs at 1 Gbps, but SW1 uses half duplex and SW2 uses full duplex.

   d.   Both switches use full duplex.

6.   Switch SW1 connects via a cable to switch SW2's G0/1 port. Which of the following conditions is the most likely to cause SW1's late collision counter to continue to increment?

   a.   SW2's G0/1 has been configured with a **shutdown** interface subcommand.

   b.   The two switches have been configured with different values on the **speed** interface subcommand.

   c.   A duplex mismatch exists with SW1 set to full duplex.

   d.   A duplex mismatch exists with SW1 set to half duplex.

Foundation Topics

Configuring Switch Interfaces

IOS uses the term *interface* to refer to physical ports used to forward data to and from other devices. Each interface can be configured with several settings, each of which might differ from interface to interface. IOS uses interface subcommands to configure these settings. Each of these settings may be different from one interface to the next, so you would first identify the specific interface, and then configure the specific setting.

This section begins with a discussion of three relatively basic per-interface settings: the port speed, duplex, and a text description. Following that, the text takes a short look at a pair of the most common interface subcommands: the **shutdown** and **no shutdown** commands, which administratively disable and enable the interface, respectively. This section ends with a discussion about autonegotiation concepts, which in turn dictates what settings a switch chooses to use when using autonegotiation.

Configuring Speed, Duplex, and Description

Switch interfaces that support multiple speeds (10/100 and 10/100/1000 interfaces), by default, will autonegotiate what speed to use. However, you can configure the speed and duplex settings with the **duplex {auto | full | half}** and **speed {auto | 10 | 100 | 1000}** interface subcommands. Simple enough.

Most of the time, using autonegotiation makes good sense, so when you set the duplex and speed manually using these commands, you typically have a good reason to do so. For instance, maybe you want to set the speed to the fastest possible on links between switches just to avoid the chance that autonegotiation chooses a slower speed.

The **description** text interface subcommand lets you add a text description to the interface. For instance, if you have good reason to configure the speed and duplex on a port, maybe add a description that says why you did. Example 7-1 shows how to configure **duplex** and **speed**, as well as the **description** command, which is simply a text description that can be configured by the administrator.

Example 7-1 *Configuring* **speed, duplex,** *and* **description** *on Switch Emma*

```
Emma# configure terminal
Enter configuration commands, one per line. End with CNTL/Z.
Emma(config)# interface FastEthernet 0/1
Emma(config-if)# duplex full
Emma(config-if)# speed 100
Emma(config-if)# description Printer on 3rd floor, Preset to 100/full
Emma(config-if)# exit
Emma(config)# interface range FastEthernet 0/11 - 20
Emma(config-if-range)# description end-users connect here
Emma(config-if-range)# ^Z
Emma#
```

First, focus on the mechanics of moving around in configuration mode again by looking closely at the command prompts. The various **interface** commands move the user from global mode into interface configuration mode for a specific interface. For instance, the example configures the **duplex, speed,** and **description** commands all just after the **interface FastEthernet 0/1** command, which means that all three of those configuration settings apply to interface Fa0/1, and not to the other interfaces.

The **show interfaces status** command lists much of the detail configured in Example 7-1, even with only one line of output per interface. Example 7-2 shows an example, just after the configuration in Example 7-1 was added to the switch.

Example 7-2 *Displaying Interface Status*

```
Emma# show interfaces status
Port      Name                Status        Vlan    Duplex  Speed Type
Fa0/1     Printer on 3rd floo  notconnect   1       full     100  10/100BaseTX
Fa0/2                          notconnect   1       auto    auto  10/100BaseTX
Fa0/3                          notconnect   1       auto    auto  10/100BaseTX
Fa0/4                          connected    1       a-full  a-100 10/100BaseTX
Fa0/5                          notconnect   1       auto    auto  10/100BaseTX
Fa0/6                          connected    1       a-full  a-100 10/100BaseTX
Fa0/7                          notconnect   1       auto    auto  10/100BaseTX
Fa0/8                          notconnect   1       auto    auto  10/100BaseTX
Fa0/9                          notconnect   1       auto    auto  10/100BaseTX
Fa0/10                         notconnect   1       auto    auto  10/100BaseTX
Fa0/11    end-users connect    notconnect   1       auto    auto  10/100BaseTX
Fa0/12    end-users connect    notconnect   1       auto    auto  10/100BaseTX
Fa0/13    end-users connect    notconnect   1       auto    auto  10/100BaseTX
Fa0/14    end-users connect    notconnect   1       auto    auto  10/100BaseTX
```

7

Fa0/15	end-users connect	notconnect	1	auto	auto 10/100BaseTX
Fa0/16	end-users connect	notconnect	1	auto	auto 10/100BaseTX
Fa0/17	end-users connect	notconnect	1	auto	auto 10/100BaseTX
Fa0/18	end-users connect	notconnect	1	auto	auto 10/100BaseTX
Fa0/19	end-users connect	notconnect	1	auto	auto 10/100BaseTX
Fa0/20	end-users connect	notconnect	1	auto	auto 10/100BaseTX
Fa0/21		notconnect	1	auto	auto 10/100BaseTX
Fa0/22		notconnect	1	auto	auto 10/100BaseTX
Fa0/23		notconnect	1	auto	auto 10/100BaseTX
Fa0/24		notconnect	1	auto	auto 10/100BaseTX
Gi0/1		notconnect	1	auto	auto 10/100/1000BaseTX
Gi0/2		notconnect	1	auto	auto 10/100/1000BaseTX

Working through the output in the example:

FastEthernet 0/1 (Fa0/1): This output lists the first few characters of the configured description. It also lists the configured speed of 100 and duplex full per the **speed** and **duplex** commands in Example 7-1. However, it also states that Fa0/1 has a status of not-connect, meaning that the interface is not currently working. (That switch port did not have a cable connected when collecting this example, on purpose.)

FastEthernet 0/2 (Fa0/2): Example 7-1 did not configure this port at all. This port had all default configuration. Note that the "auto" text under the speed and duplex heading means that this port will attempt to autonegotiate both settings when the port comes up. However, this port also does not have a cable connected (again on purpose, for comparison).

FastEthernet 0/4 (Fa0/4): Like Fa0/2, this port has all default configuration but was cabled to another working device to give yet another contrasting example. This device completed the autonegotiation process, so instead of "auto" under the speed and duplex headings, the output lists the negotiated speed and duplex (**a-full** and **a-100**). Note that the text includes the **a-** to mean that the listed speed and duplex values were autonegotiated.

Configuring Multiple Interfaces with the interface range Command

The bottom of the configuration in Example 7-1 shows a way to shorten your configuration work when making the same setting on multiple consecutive interfaces. To do so, use the **interface range** command. In the example, the **interface range FastEthernet 0/11 - 20** command tells IOS that the next subcommand(s) apply to interfaces Fa0/11 through Fa0/20. You can define a range as long as all interfaces are the same type and are numbered consecutively.

> **NOTE**   This book spells out all parameters fully to avoid confusion. However, most everyone abbreviates what they type in the CLI to the shortest unique abbreviation. For instance, the configuration commands **int f0/1** and **int ran f0/11 - 20** would also be acceptable.

IOS does not actually put the **interface range** command into the configuration. Instead, it acts as if you had typed the subcommand under every single interface in the specified

---

Answers to the "Do I Know This Already?" quiz:

1 F **2** E **3** A, D **4** A, B, D **5** A, D **6** D

range. Example 7-3 shows an excerpt from the **show running-config** command, listing the configuration of interfaces F0/11–12 from the configuration in Example 7-1. The example shows the same description command on both interfaces; to save space, the example does not bother to show all 10 interfaces that have the same description text.

Example 7-3 *How IOS Expands the Subcommands Typed After* **interface range**

```
Emma# show running-config
! Lines omitted for brevity
interface FastEthernet0/11
 description end-users connect here
!
interface FastEthernet0/12
 description end-users connect here
! Lines omitted for brevity
```

Administratively Controlling Interface State with shutdown

As you might imagine, network engineers need a way to bring down an interface without having to travel to the switch and remove a cable. In short, we need to be able to decide which ports should be enabled and which should be disabled.

In an odd turn of phrase, Cisco uses two interface subcommands to configure the idea of administratively enabling and disabling an interface: the **shutdown** command (to disable) and the **no shutdown** command (to enable). While the **no shutdown** command might seem like an odd command to enable an interface at first, you will use this command a lot in the lab, and it will become second nature. (Most people, in fact, use the abbreviations **shut** and **no shut**.)

Example 7-4 shows an example of disabling an interface using the **shutdown** interface subcommand. In this case, switch SW1 has a working interface F0/1. The user connects at the console and disables the interface. IOS generates a log message each time an interface fails or recovers, and log messages appear at the console, as shown in the example.

Example 7-4 *Administratively Disabling an Interface with* **shutdown**

```
SW1# configure terminal
Enter configuration commands, one per line. End with CNTL/Z.
SW1(config)# interface fastEthernet 0/1
SW1(config-if)# shutdown
SW1(config-if)#
*Mar 2 03:02:19.701: %LINK-5-CHANGED: Interface FastEthernet0/1, changed state to
administratively down
*Mar 2 03:02:20.708: %LINEPROTO-5-UPDOWN: Line protocol on Interface FastEthernet0/1,
changed state to down
```

To bring the interface back up again, all you have to do is follow the same process but use the **no shutdown** command instead.

Before leaving the simple but oddly named **shutdown/no shutdown** commands, take a look at two important show commands that list the status of a shutdown interface. The **show**

interfaces status command lists one line of output per interface, and when shut down, lists the interface status as "disabled." That makes logical sense to most people. The **show interfaces** command (without the **status** keyword) lists many lines of output per interface, giving a much more detailed picture of interface status and statistics. With that command, the interface status comes in two parts, with one part using the phrase "administratively down," matching the highlighted log message in Example 7-4.

Example 7-5 shows an example of each of these commands. Note that both examples also use the F0/1 parameter (short for Fast Ethernet0/1), which limits the output to the messages about F0/1 only. Also note that F0/1 is still shut down at this point.

Example 7-5 *The Different Status Information About Shutdown in Two Different* **show** *Commands*

```
SW1# show interfaces f0/1 status

Port       Name            Status        Vlan      Duplex  Speed Type
Fa0/1                      disabled      1         auto    auto  10/100BaseTX


SW1# show interfaces f0/1
FastEthernet0/1 is administratively down, line protocol is down (disabled)
  Hardware is Fast Ethernet, address is 1833.9d7b.0e81 (bia 1833.9d7b.0e81)
  MTU 1500 bytes, BW 10000 Kbit/sec, DLY 1000 usec,
     reliability 255/255, txload 1/255, rxload 1/255
  Encapsulation ARPA, loopback not set
  Keepalive set (10 sec)
  Auto-duplex, Auto-speed, media type is 10/100BaseTX
  input flow-control is off, output flow-control is unsupported
  ARP type: ARPA, ARP Timeout 04:00:00
  Last input never, output 00:00:36, output hang never
  Last clearing of "show interface" counters never
  Input queue: 0/75/0/0 (size/max/drops/flushes); Total output drops: 0
  Queueing strategy: fifo
  Output queue: 0/40 (size/max)
  5 minute input rate 0 bits/sec, 0 packets/sec
  5 minute output rate 0 bits/sec, 0 packets/sec
     164 packets input, 13267 bytes, 0 no buffer
     Received 164 broadcasts (163 multicasts)
     0 runts, 0 giants, 0 throttles
     0 input errors, 0 CRC, 0 frame, 0 overrun, 0 ignored
     0 watchdog, 163 multicast, 0 pause input
     0 input packets with dribble condition detected
     66700 packets output, 5012302 bytes, 0 underruns
     0 output errors, 0 collisions, 1 interface resets
     0 unknown protocol drops
     0 babbles, 0 late collision, 0 deferred
     0 lost carrier, 0 no carrier, 0 pause output
     0 output buffer failures, 0 output buffers swapped out
```

Removing Configuration with the no Command

One purpose for the specific commands shown in Part II of the book is to teach you about that command. In some cases, the commands are not the end goal, and the text is attempting to teach you something about how the CLI works. This next short topic is more about the process than about the commands.

With some IOS configuration commands (but not all), you can revert to the default setting by issuing a **no** version of the command. What does that mean? Let me give you a few examples:

- If you earlier had configured **speed 100** on an interface, the **no speed** command on that same interface reverts to the default speed setting (which happens to be **speed auto**).

- Same idea with the **duplex** command: an earlier configuration of **duplex half** or **duplex full**, followed by **no duplex** on the same interface, reverts the configuration back to the default of duplex auto.

- If you had configured a **description** command with some text, to go back to the default state of having no **description** command at all for that interface, use the **no description** command.

Example 7-6 shows the process. In this case, switch SW1's F0/2 port has been configured with **speed 100**, **duplex half**, **description link to 2901-2**, and **shutdown**. You can see evidence of all four settings in the command that begins the example. (This command lists the running-config, but only the part for that one interface.) The example then shows the **no** versions of those commands and closes with a confirmation that all the commands have reverted to default.

Example 7-6 *Removing Various Configuration Settings Using the* no *Command*

```
SW1# show running-config interface f0/2
Building configuration...

Current configuration : 95 bytes
!
interface FastEthernet0/2
 description link to 2901-2
 shutdown
 speed 100
 duplex half
end

SW1# configure terminal
Enter configuration commands, one per line. End with CNTL/Z.
SW1(config)# interface fastethernet 0/2
SW1(config-if)# no speed
SW1(config-if)# no duplex
SW1(config-if)# no description
SW1(config-if)# no shutdown
```

```
SW1(config-if)# ^Z
SW1#
SW1# show running-config interface f0/2
Building configuration...
Current configuration : 33 bytes
!
interface FastEthernet0/2
end
SW1#
```

NOTE The **show running-config** and **show startup-config** commands typically do not display default configuration settings, so the absence of commands listed under interface F0/2 at the end of the example means that those commands now use default values.

Autonegotiation

For any 10/100 or 10/100/1000 interfaces—that is, interfaces that can run at different speeds—Cisco Catalyst switches default to a setting of **duplex auto** and **speed auto**. As a result, those interfaces attempt to automatically determine the speed and duplex setting to use. Alternatively, you can configure most devices, switch interfaces included, to use a specific speed and/or duplex.

In practice, using autonegotiation is easy: just leave the speed and duplex at the default setting, and let the switch port negotiate what settings to use on each port. However, problems can occur due to unfortunate combinations of configuration. Therefore, this next topic walks through more detail about the concepts behind autonegotiation, so you know better how to interpret the meaning of the switch **show** commands and when to choose to use a particular configuration setting.

Autonegotiation Under Working Conditions

Ethernet devices on the ends of a link must use the same standard; otherwise, they cannot correctly send data. For example, a NIC cannot use 100BASE-T, which uses a two-pair UTP cable with a 100-Mbps speed, while the switch port on the other end of the link uses 1000BASE-T. Even if you used a cable that works with Gigabit Ethernet, the link would not work with one end trying to send at 100 Mbps while the other tried to receive the data at 1000 Mbps.

Upgrading to new and faster Ethernet standards becomes a problem because both ends have to use the same standard. For example, if you replace an old PC with a new one, the old one might have been using 100BASE-T while the new one uses 1000BASE-T. The switch port on the other end of the link needs to now use 1000BASE-T, so you upgrade the switch. If that switch had ports that would use only 1000BASE-T, you would need to upgrade all the other PCs connected to the switch. So, having both PC network interface cards (NIC) and switch ports that support multiple standards/speeds makes it much easier to migrate to the next better standard.

The IEEE autonegotiation protocol helps makes it much easier to operate a LAN when NICs and switch ports support multiple speeds. IEEE autonegotiation (IEEE standard 802.3u) defines a protocol that lets the two UTP-based Ethernet nodes on a link negotiate so that they each choose to use the same speed and duplex settings. The protocol messages flow outside the normal Ethernet electrical frequencies as out-of-band signals over the UTP cable. Basically, each node states what it can do, and then each node picks the best options that both nodes support: the fastest speed and the best duplex setting, with full duplex being better than half duplex.

NOTE   Autonegotiation relies on the fact that the IEEE uses the same wiring pinouts for 10BASE-T and 100BASE-T, and that 1000BASE-T simply adds to those pinouts, adding two pairs.

Many networks use autonegotiation every day, particularly between user devices and the access layer LAN switches, as shown in Figure 7-1. The company installed four-pair cabling of the right quality to support 1000BASE-T, to be ready to support Gigabit Ethernet. As a result, the wiring supports 10-Mbps, 100-Mbps, and 1000-Mbps Ethernet options. Both nodes on each link send autonegotiation messages to each other. The switch in this case has all 10/100/1000 ports, while the PC NICs support different options.

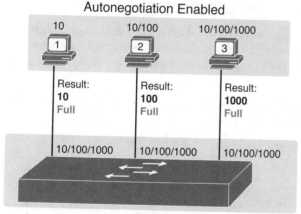

Figure 7-1   *IEEE Autonegotiation Results with Both Nodes Working Correctly*

The following list breaks down the logic, one PC at a time:

PC1: The switch port claims it can go as fast as 1000 Mbps, but PC1's NIC claims a top speed of 10 Mbps. Both the PC and the switch choose the fastest speed that each supports (10 Mbps) and the best duplex that each supports (full).

PC2: PC2 claims a best speed of 100 Mbps, which means it can use 10BASE-T or 100BASE-T. The switch port and NIC negotiate to use the best speed of 100 Mbps and full duplex.

PC3: It uses a 10/100/1000 NIC, supporting all three speeds and standards, so both the NIC and switch port choose 1000 Mbps and full duplex.

Autonegotiation Results When Only One Node Uses Autonegotiation

Figure 7-1 shows the IEEE autonegotiation results when both nodes use the process. However, most Ethernet devices can disable autonegotiation, so it is just as important to know what happens when a node tries to use autonegotiation but the node gets no response.

Disabling autonegotiation is not always a bad idea. For instance, many network engineers disable autonegotiation on links between switches and simply configure the desired speed and duplex on both switches. However, mistakes can happen when one device on an Ethernet predefines speed and duplex (and disables autonegotiation), while the device on the other end attempts autonegotiation. In that case, the link might not work at all, or it might just work poorly.

> **NOTE** Configuring both the speed and duplex on a Cisco Catalyst switch interface disables autonegotiation.

IEEE autonegotiation defines some rules (defaults) that nodes should use as defaults when autonegotiation fails—that is, when a node tries to use autonegotiation but hears nothing from the device. The rules:

- **Speed:** Use your slowest supported speed (often 10 Mbps).
- **Duplex:** If your speed = 10 or 100, use half duplex; otherwise, use full duplex.

Cisco switches can make a better choice than that base IEEE speed default because Cisco switches can actually sense the speed used by other nodes, even without IEEE autonegotiation. As a result, Cisco switches use this slightly different logic to choose the speed when autonegotiation fails:

- **Speed:** Sense the speed (without using autonegotiation), but if that fails, use the IEEE default (slowest supported speed, often 10 Mbps).
- **Duplex:** Use the IEEE defaults: If speed = 10 or 100, use half duplex; otherwise, use full duplex.

> **NOTE** Ethernet interfaces using speeds faster than 1 Gbps always use full duplex.

Figure 7-2 shows three examples in which three users change their NIC settings and disable autonegotiation, while the switch (with all 10/100/1000 ports) attempts autonegotiation. That is, the switch ports all default to **speed auto** and **duplex auto**. The top of the figure shows the configured settings on each PC NIC, with the choices made by the switch listed next to each switch port.

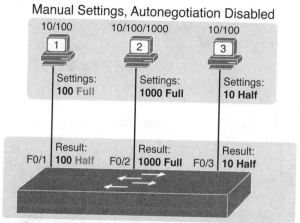

Figure 7-2 *IEEE Autonegotiation Results with Autonegotiation Disabled on One Side*

Reviewing each link, left to right:

- **PC1:** The switch receives no autonegotiation messages, so it senses the electrical signal to learn that PC1 is sending data at 100 Mbps. The switch uses the IEEE default duplex based on the 100 Mbps speed (half duplex).

- **PC2:** The switch uses the same steps and logic as with the link to PC1, except that the switch chooses to use full duplex because the speed is 1000 Mbps.

- **PC3:** The user picks poorly, choosing the slower speed (10 Mbps) and the worse duplex setting (half). However, the Cisco switch senses the speed without using IEEE autonegotiation and then uses the IEEE duplex default for 10-Mbps links (half duplex).

PC1 shows a classic and unfortunately common end result: a *duplex mismatch*. The two nodes (PC1 and SW1's port G0/1) both use 100 Mbps, so they can send data. However, PC1, using full duplex, does not attempt to use carrier sense multiple access with collision detection (CSMA/CD) logic and sends frames at any time. Switch port F0/1, with half duplex, does use CSMA/CD. As a result, switch port F0/1 will believe collisions occur on the link, even if none physically occur. The switch port will stop transmitting, back off, resend frames, and so on. As a result, the link is up, but it performs poorly. The upcoming section titled "Interface Speed and Duplex Issues" will revisit this problem with a focus on how to recognize the symptoms of a duplex mismatch.

Autonegotiation and LAN Hubs

LAN hubs also impact how autonegotiation works. Basically, hubs do not react to autonegotiation messages, and they do not forward the messages. As a result, devices connected to a hub must use the IEEE rules for choosing default settings, which often results in the devices using 10 Mbps and half duplex.

Figure 7-3 shows an example of a small Ethernet LAN that uses a 20-year-old 10BASE-T hub. In this LAN, all devices and switch ports are 10/100/1000 ports. The hub supports only 10BASE-T.

Figure 7-3 *IEEE Autonegotiation with a LAN Hub*

Note that the devices on the right need to use half duplex because the hub requires the use of the CSMA/CD algorithm to avoid collisions.

> **NOTE** If you would like to learn more about collision domains and the impact of these older LAN hubs, look to the companion website for Appendix K, "Analyzing Ethernet LAN Designs," to the section titled "Ethernet Collision Domains."

Analyzing Switch Interface Status and Statistics

Now that you have seen some of the ways to configure switch interfaces, the rest of the chapter takes a closer look at how to verify the interfaces work correctly. This section also looks at those more unusual cases in which the interface is working but not working well, as revealed by different interface status codes and statistics.

Interface Status Codes and Reasons for Nonworking States

Cisco switches actually use two different sets of interface status codes—one set of two codes (words) that use the same conventions as do router interface status codes, and another set with a single code (word). Both sets of status codes can determine whether an interface is working.

The switch **show interfaces** and **show interfaces description** commands list the two-code status named the *line status* and *protocol status*. The line status *generally* refers to whether Layer 1 is working, with protocol status generally referring to whether Layer 2 is working.

> **NOTE** This book refers to these two status codes in shorthand by just listing the two codes with a slash between them, such as *up/up*.

The single-code interface status corresponds to different combinations of the traditional two-code interface status codes and can be easily correlated to those codes. For example, the **show interfaces status** command lists a single-word state of *connected* state for working interfaces, with the same meaning as the two-word *up/up* state seen with the **show interfaces** and **show interfaces description** commands. Table 7-2 lists the code combinations and some root causes that could have caused a particular interface status.

Table 7-2   LAN Switch Interface Status Codes

Line Status	Protocol Status	Interface Status	Typical Root Cause
administratively down	down	disabled	The **shutdown** command is configured on the interface.
down	down	notconnect	No cable; bad cable; wrong cable pinouts; speed mismatch; neighboring device is (a) powered off, (b) **shutdown**, or (c) error disabled.
up	down	notconnect	Not expected on LAN switch physical interfaces.
down	down (err-disabled)	err-disabled	Port security has disabled the interface.
up	up	connected	The interface is working.

Examining the notconnect state for a moment, note that this state has many causes that have been mentioned through this book. For example, using incorrect cabling pinouts, instead of the correct pinouts explained in Chapter 2, "Fundamentals of Ethernet LANs," causes a problem. However, one topic can be particularly difficult to troubleshoot—the possibility for both speed and duplex mismatches, as explained in the next section.

As you can see in the table, having a bad cable is just one of many reasons for the down/down state (or notconnect, per the **show interfaces status** command). Some examples of the root causes of cabling problems include the following:

■ The installation of any equipment that uses electricity, even non-IT equipment, can interfere with the transmission on the cabling and make the link fail.

■ The cable could be damaged, for example, if it lies under carpet. If the user's chair keeps squashing the cable, eventually the electrical signal can degrade.

■ Although optical cables do not suffer from electromagnetic interference (EMI), someone can try to be helpful and move a fiber-optic cable out of the way—bending it too much. A bend into too tight a shape can prevent the cable from transmitting bits (called *macrobending*).

For the other interface states listed in Table 7-2, only the up/up (connected) state needs more discussion. An interface can be in a working state, and it might really be working—or it might be working in a degraded state. The next few topics discuss how to examine an up/up (connected) interface to find out whether it is working well or having problems.

Interface Speed and Duplex Issues

To discuss some of the speed and duplex issues, first consider the output from the **show interfaces status** and **show interfaces** commands as demonstrated in Example 7-7. The first of these commands lists a one-line summary of the interface status, while the second command gives many details—but surprisingly, the briefer **show interfaces status** command tells us more about autonegotiation.

Example 7-7 *Displaying Speed and Duplex Settings on Switch Interfaces*

```
SW1# show interfaces status

Port      Name                 Status       Vlan    Duplex  Speed Type
Fa0/1                          notconnect   1         auto   auto 10/100BaseTX
Fa0/2                          notconnect   1         auto   auto 10/100BaseTX
Fa0/3                          notconnect   1         auto   auto 10/100BaseTX
Fa0/4                          connected    1       a-full  a-100 10/100BaseTX
Fa0/5                          connected    1       a-full  a-100 10/100BaseTX
Fa0/6                          notconnect   1         auto   auto 10/100BaseTX
Fa0/7                          notconnect   1         auto   auto 10/100BaseTX
Fa0/8                          notconnect   1         auto   auto 10/100BaseTX
Fa0/9                          notconnect   1         auto   auto 10/100BaseTX
Fa0/10                         notconnect   1         auto   auto 10/100BaseTX
Fa0/11                         connected    1       a-full     10 10/100BaseTX
Fa0/12                         connected    1         half    100 10/100BaseTX
Fa0/13                         connected    1       a-full  a-100 10/100BaseTX
Fa0/14                         disabled     1         auto   auto 10/100BaseTX
! Lines omitted for brevity


SW1# show interfaces fa0/13
FastEthernet0/13 is up, line protocol is up (connected)
    Hardware is Fast Ethernet, address is 0019.e86a.6f8d (bia 0019.e86a.6f8d)
    MTU 1500 bytes, BW 100000 Kbit, DLY 100 usec,
       reliability 255/255, txload 1/255, rxload 1/255
    Encapsulation ARPA, loopback not set
    Keepalive set (10 sec)
    Full-duplex, 100Mbps, media type is 10/100BaseTX
    input flow-control is off, output flow-control is unsupported
    ARP type: ARPA, ARP Timeout 04:00:00
    Last input 00:00:05, output 00:00:00, output hang never
    Last clearing of "show interface" counters never
    Input queue: 0/75/0/0 (size/max/drops/flushes); Total output drops: 0
    Queueing strategy: fifo
    Output queue: 0/40 (size/max)
    5 minute input rate 0 bits/sec, 0 packets/sec
    5 minute output rate 0 bits/sec, 0 packets/sec
       85022 packets input, 10008976 bytes, 0 no buffer
       Received 284 broadcasts (0 multicast)
       0 runts, 0 giants, 0 throttles
       0 input errors, 0 CRC, 0 frame, 0 overrun, 0 ignored
       0 watchdog, 281 multicast, 0 pause input
       0 input packets with dribble condition detected
       95226 packets output, 10849674 bytes, 0 underruns
       0 output errors, 0 collisions, 1 interface resets
```

```
0 unknown protocol drops
0 babbles, 0 late collision, 0 deferred
0 lost carrier, 0 no carrier, 0 PAUSE output
0 output buffer failures, 0 output buffers swapped out
```

Although both commands in the example can be useful, only the **show interfaces status** command implies how the switch determined the speed and duplex settings. The command output lists autonegotiated settings with a prefix of **a-** and the manually set values without the **a-** prefix.

For example, consider ports Fa0/12 and Fa0/13 in the output of the **show interfaces status** command. For Fa0/13, **a-full** means full duplex as autonegotiated, whereas **half** on Fa0/12 means half duplex but as manually configured. The example shades the command output that implies that the switch's Fa0/12 interface's speed and duplex were not found through autonegotiation, but Fa0/13 did use autonegotiation.

In comparison, note that the **show interfaces fa0/13** command (without the **status** option) simply lists the speed and duplex for interface Fast Ethernet 0/13, with nothing implying that the values were learned through autonegotiation.

When the IEEE autonegotiation process works on both devices—that is, both are sending autonegotiation messages—both devices agree to the fastest speed and best duplex supported by both devices. However, when one device uses autonegotiation and the other disables it, the first device must resort to default settings as detailed earlier in section "Autonegotiation Results When Only One Node Uses Autonegotiation." As a reminder, those defaults are

- **Speed:** Sense the speed (without using autonegotiation), but if that fails, use the IEEE default (slowest supported speed, often 10 Mbps).
- **Duplex:** Use the IEEE defaults: If speed = 10 or 100, use half duplex; otherwise, use full duplex.

When a switch must use its defaults, it should get the speed correct, but it may choose the wrong duplex setting, creating a duplex mismatch.

For example, in Figure 7-4, imagine that SW2's Gi0/2 interface was configured with the **speed 100** and **duplex full** commands (these settings are not recommended on a Gigabit-capable interface, by the way). On Cisco switches, configuring both the **speed** and **duplex** commands disables IEEE autonegotiation on that port. If SW1's Gi0/1 interface tries to use autonegotiation, SW1 would also use a speed of 100 Mbps, but default to use half duplex. Example 7-8 shows the results of this specific case on SW1.

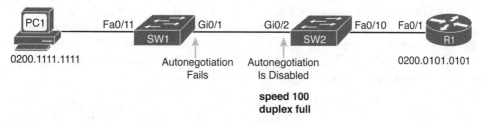

Figure 7-4 *Conditions to Create a Duplex Mismatch Between SW1 and SW2*

Example 7-8 *Confirming Duplex Mismatch on Switch SW1*

```
SW1# show interfaces gi0/1 status


Port       Name            Status     Vlan    Duplex  Speed Type
Gi0/1                      connected  trunk   a-half  a-100 10/100/1000BaseTX
```

First, note that even though SW1 had to use an autonegotiation default, the **show interfaces status** command still shows the speed and duplex with the **a-** prefix. SW2's port was manually set to 100/Full, so SW1 sensed the speed and runs at 100 Mbps; however, the autonegotiation rules then tell SW1 to use half duplex, as confirmed by the output in Example 7-8.

The output does not identify the duplex mismatch in any way; in fact, finding a duplex mismatch can be much more difficult than finding a speed mismatch. For instance, if you purposefully set the speed on the link in Figure 7-4 to be 10 Mbps on one switch and 100 Mbps on the other, both switches would list the port in a down/down or notconnect state. However, in the case shown in Example 7-8, with a duplex mismatch, *if the duplex settings do not match on the ends of an Ethernet segment, the switch interface will still be in a connected (up/up) or connected state.*

Not only does the **show** command give an appearance that the link has no issues, but the link will likely work poorly, with symptoms of intermittent problems. The reason is that the device using half duplex (SW1 in this case) uses carrier sense multiple access collision detect (CSMA/CD) logic, waiting to send when receiving a frame, believing collisions occur when they physically do not—and actually stopping sending a frame because the switch thinks a collision occurred. With enough traffic load, the interface could be in a connect state, but it's extremely inefficient for passing traffic.

To identify duplex mismatch problems, check the duplex setting on each end of the link to see if the values mismatch. You can also watch for incrementing collision and late collision counters, as explained in the next section.

Common Layer 1 Problems on Working Interfaces

When the interface reaches the connect (up/up) state, the switch considers the interface to be working. The switch, of course, tries to use the interface, and at the same time, the switch keeps various interface counters. These interface counters can help identify problems that can occur even though the interface is in a connect state, like issues related to the duplex mismatch problem that was just described. This section explains some of the related concepts and a few of the most common problems.

Whenever the physical transmission has problems, the receiving device might receive a frame whose bits have changed values. These frames do not pass the error detection logic as implemented in the FCS field in the Ethernet trailer, as covered in Chapter 2. The receiving device discards the frame and counts it as some kind of *input error*. Cisco switches list this error as a CRC error, as highlighted in Example 7-9. (Cyclic redundancy check [CRC] is a term related to how the frame check sequence [FCS] math detects an error.)

Example 7-9 *Interface Counters for Layer 1 Problems*

```
SW1# show interfaces fa0/13
! lines omitted for brevity
    Received 284 broadcasts (0 multicast)
    0 runts, 0 giants, 0 throttles
    0 input errors, 0 CRC, 0 frame, 0 overrun, 0 ignored
    0 watchdog, 281 multicast, 0 pause input
    0 input packets with dribble condition detected
    95226 packets output, 10849674 bytes, 0 underruns
    0 output errors, 0 collisions, 1 interface resets
    0 unknown protocol drops
    0 babbles, 0 late collision, 0 deferred
    0 lost carrier, 0 no carrier, 0 PAUSE output
    0 output buffer failures, 0 output buffers swapped out
```

The number of input errors and the number of CRC errors are just a few of the counters in the output of the **show interfaces** command. The challenge is to decide which counters you need to think about, which ones show that a problem is happening, and which ones are normal and of no concern.

The example highlights several of the counters as examples so that you can start to understand which ones point to problems and which ones are just counting normal events that are not problems. The following list shows a short description of each highlighted counter, in the order shown in the example:

Runts: Frames that did not meet the minimum frame size requirement (64 bytes, including the 18-byte destination MAC, source MAC, type, and FCS). Can be caused by collisions.

Giants: Frames that exceed the maximum frame size requirement (1518 bytes, including the 18-byte destination MAC, source MAC, type, and FCS).

Input Errors: A total of many counters, including runts, giants, no buffer, CRC, frame, overrun, and ignored counts.

CRC: Received frames that did not pass the FCS math; can be caused by collisions.

Frame: Received frames that have an illegal format, for example, ending with a partial byte; can be caused by collisions.

Packets Output: Total number of packets (frames) forwarded out the interface.

Output Errors: Total number of packets (frames) that the switch port tried to transmit, but for which some problem occurred.

Collisions: Counter of all collisions that occur when the interface is transmitting a frame.

Late Collisions: The subset of all collisions that happen after the 64th byte of the frame has been transmitted. (In a properly working Ethernet LAN, collisions should occur within the first 64 bytes; late collisions today often point to a duplex mismatch.)

Note that many of these counters occur as part of the CSMA/CD process used when half duplex is enabled. Collisions occur as a normal part of the half-duplex logic imposed by CSMA/CD, so a switch interface with an increasing collisions counter might not even have a problem. However, one problem, called late collisions, points to the classic duplex mismatch problem.

If a LAN design follows cabling guidelines, all collisions should occur by the end of the 64th byte of any frame. When a switch has already sent 64 bytes of a frame, and the switch receives a frame on that same interface, the switch senses a collision. In this case, the collision is a late collision, and the switch increments the late collision counter in addition to the usual CSMA/CD actions to send a jam signal, wait a random time, and try again.

With a duplex mismatch, like the mismatch between SW1 and SW2 in Figure 7-4, the half-duplex interface will likely see the late collisions counter increment. Why? The half-duplex interface sends a frame (SW1), but the full-duplex neighbor (SW2) sends at any time, even after the 64th byte of the frame sent by the half-duplex switch. So, just keep repeating the **show interfaces** command, and if you see the late collisions counter incrementing on a half-duplex interface, you might have a duplex mismatch problem.

A working interface (in an up/up state) can still suffer from issues related to the physical cabling as well. The cabling problems might not be bad enough to cause a complete failure, but the transmission failures result in some frames failing to pass successfully over the cable. For example, excessive interference on the cable can cause the various input error counters to keep growing larger, especially the CRC counter. In particular, if the CRC errors grow, but the collisions counters do not, the problem might simply be interference on the cable. (The switch counts each collided frame as one form of input error as well.)

Chapter Review

One key to doing well on the exams is to perform repetitive spaced review sessions. Review this chapter's material using either the tools in the book or interactive tools for the same material found on the book's companion website. Refer to the "Your Study Plan" element section titled "Step 2: Build Your Study Habits Around the Chapter" for more details. Table 7-3 outlines the key review elements and where you can find them. To better track your study progress, record when you completed these activities in the second column.

Table 7-3   Chapter Review Tracking

Review Element	Review Date(s)	Resource Used
Review key topics		Book, website
Review key terms		Book, website
Answer DIKTA questions		Book, PTP
Review command tables		Book
Review memory tables		Website
Do labs		Sim Lite, blog

Review All the Key Topics

Table 7-4   Key Topics for Chapter 7

Key Topic Element	Description	Page Number
Example 7-1	Example of configuring **speed**, **duplex**, and **description**	153
Example 7-4	Example of disabling an interface using the **shutdown** command	155
List	Key decision rules for autonegotiation on Cisco switches when the other device does not participate	160
Table 7-2	Two types of interface state terms and their meanings	163
Example 7-7	Example that shows how to find the speed and duplex settings, as well as whether they were learned through autonegotiation	164
List	Defaults for IEEE autonegotiation	165
List	Explanations of different error statistics on switch interfaces	167

Key Terms You Should Know

port security, autonegotiation, full duplex, half duplex, 10/100, 10/100/1000

Do Labs

The Sim Lite software is a version of Pearson's full simulator learning product with a subset of the labs, included free with this book. The subnet of labs mostly relate to this part. Take the time to try some of the labs. As always, also check the author's blog site pages for configuration exercises (Config Labs) at https://blog.certskills.com.

Command References

Tables 7-5 and 7-6 list configuration and verification commands used in this chapter. As an easy review exercise, cover the left column in a table, read the right column, and try to recall the command without looking. Then repeat the exercise, covering the right column, and try to recall what the command does.

Table 7-5   Switch Interface Configuration

Command	Mode/Purpose/Description
interface *type port-number*	Changes context to interface mode. The type is typically Fast Ethernet or Gigabit Ethernet. The possible port numbers vary depending on the model of switch—for example, Fa0/1, Fa0/2, and so on.
interface range *type port-number - end-port-number*	Changes the context to interface mode for a range of consecutively numbered interfaces. The subcommands that follow then apply to all interfaces in the range.

Command	Mode/Purpose/Description
shutdown | no shutdown	Interface mode. Disables or enables the interface, respectively.
speed {10 | 100 | 1000 | auto}	Interface mode. Manually sets the speed to the listed speed or, with the auto setting, automatically negotiates the speed.
duplex {auto | full | half}	Interface mode. Manually sets the duplex to half or full, or to autonegotiate the duplex setting.
description *text*	Interface mode. Lists any information text that the engineer wants to track for the interface, such as the expected device on the other end of the cable.
no duplex no speed no description	Reverts to the default setting for each interface subcommand of **speed auto**, **duplex auto**, and the absence of a **description** command.

Table 7-6   Chapter 7 EXEC Command Reference

Command	Purpose
show running-config	Lists the currently used configuration
show running-config | interface *type number*	Displays the running-configuration excerpt of the listed interface and its subcommands only
show mac address-table dynamic [interface *type number*] [vlan *vlan-id*]	Lists the dynamically learned entries in the switch's address (forwarding) table, with subsets by interface and/or VLAN
show mac address-table static [interface *type number*]	Lists static MAC addresses and MAC addresses learned or defined with port security
show interfaces [*type number*] status	Lists one output line per interface (or for only the listed interface if included), noting the description, operating state, and settings for duplex and speed on each interface
show interfaces [*type number*]	Lists detailed status and statistical information about all interfaces (or the listed interface only)
show interfaces description	Displays one line of information per interface, with a two-item status (similar to the **show interfaces** command status), and includes any description that is configured on the interfaces

Part II Review

Keep track of your part review progress with the checklist shown in Table P2-1. Details on each task follow the table.

Table P2-1   Part II Part Review Checklist

Activity	1st Date Completed	2nd Date Completed
Repeat All DIKTA Questions		
Answer Part Review Questions		
Review Key Topics		
Do Labs		
Review Appendix P on the Companion Website		
Videos		

Repeat All DIKTA Questions

For this task, answer the "Do I Know This Already?" questions again for the chapters in this part of the book, using the PCPT software.

Answer Part Review Questions

For this task, answer the Part Review questions for this part of the book, using the PTP software.

Review Key Topics

Review all key topics in all chapters in this part, either by browsing the chapters or by using the Key Topics application on the companion website.

Labs

Depending on your chosen lab tool, here are some suggestions for what to do in lab:

Pearson Network Simulator: If you use the full Pearson ICND1 or CCNA simulator, focus more on the configuration scenario and troubleshooting scenario labs associated with the topics in this part of the book. These types of labs include a larger set of topics and work well as Part Review activities. (See the Introduction for some details about how to find which labs are about topics in this part of the book.)

Blog: Config Labs: The author's blog includes a series of configuration-focused labs that you can do on paper, each in 10–15 minutes. Review and perform the labs for this part of the book, as found at http://blog.certskills.com. Then navigate to the Hands-on Config labs.

Other: If using other lab tools, as a few suggestions: Make sure to experiment heavily with VLAN configuration and VLAN trunking configuration. Also, spend some time changing interface settings like **speed** and **duplex** on a link between two switches, to make sure that you understand which cases would result in a duplex mismatch.

Review Appendix P on the Companion Website

The previous edition of the CCNA exam blueprint included the word "troubleshoot" as applied to Ethernet and VLANs, while the current CCNA exam blueprint does not. Appendix P on the companion website contains a chapter from the previous edition of the book that focused on troubleshooting. That appendix, named "LAN Troubleshooting," can be useful as a tool to review the topics in this part of the book. (Note that if you use this extra appendix, you can ignore the mentions of Port Security until you have reached that topic in the *CCNA 200-301 Official Cert Guide, Volume 2*.)

Watch Videos

Chapters 4 and 5 each recommend a video that can be helpful to anyone who is just learning about the Cisco CLI and basic switching concepts. If you have not watched those videos yet, take a moment to navigate to the companion website and watch the videos (listed under Chapters 4 and 5).

Part II of this book introduces the basics of Ethernet LANs, both in concept and in how to implement the features. However, the two primary features discussed in Part III of this book—Virtual LANs (VLANs) and Spanning Tree Protocol (STP)—impact almost everything you have learned about Ethernet so far. VLANs allow a network engineer to create separate Ethernet LANs through simple configuration choices. The ability to separate some switch ports into one VLAN and other switch ports into another VLAN gives network designers a powerful tool for creating networks. Once created, VLANs also have a huge impact on how a switch works, which then impacts how you verify and troubleshoot the operation of a campus LAN.

STP—and the related and similar Rapid STP (RSTP)—acts to prevent frames from looping around a LAN. Without STP or RSTP, in LANs with redundant links, broadcasts and some other frames would be forwarded around and around the LAN, eventually clogging the LAN so much as to make it unusable.

The current CCNA 200-301 exam blueprint includes exam topics for the configuration and verification of VLANs and related topics. However, the CCNA exam topics only mention RSTP concepts rather than configuration/verification. To that end, Part III opens with Chapter 8, which goes to the configuration/verification depth with VLAN topics, followed by Chapter 9, which introduces the concepts of STP and RSTP.

Part III closes with Chapter 10, which includes some RSTP configuration, along with Layer 2 EtherChannel configuration.

Other Resources

As one additional suggestion for those who intend to move on to CCNP Enterprise, consider skimming or reading Appendix P, "LAN Troubleshooting," found on the online companion website. This appendix, a copy of a chapter from the previous edition of the book, takes a troubleshooting approach to many of the topics found in Parts II and III of this book. Although Cisco completely removed the word *troubleshoot* from the CCNA exam blueprint in its current CCNA 200-301 version, the topics still remain relevant and can be a help for reviewing and refining what you learned in Parts II and III of this book.

Part III

Implementing VLANs and STP

CHAPTER 8

Implementing Ethernet Virtual LANs

This chapter covers the following exam topics:

1.0 Network Fundamentals

1.13 Describe switching concepts

1.13.a MAC learning and aging

1.13.b Frame switching

1.13.c Frame flooding

1.13.d MAC address table

2.0 Network Access

2.1 Configure and verify VLANs (normal range) spanning multiple switches

2.1.a Access ports (data and voice)

2.1.b Default VLAN

2.1.c Connectivity

2.2 Configure and verify interswitch connectivity

2.2.a Trunk ports

2.2.b 802.1Q

2.2.c Native VLAN

So far in this book, you have learned that Ethernet switches receive Ethernet frames, make decisions, and then forward (switch) those Ethernet frames. That core logic revolves around MAC addresses, the interface in which the frame arrives, and the interfaces out which the switch forwards the frame.

While true, that logic omits any consideration of virtual LANs (VLANs). VLANs impact the switching logic for each frame because each VLAN acts as a subset of the switch ports in an Ethernet LAN. Switches believe each Ethernet frame to be received in an identifiable VLAN, forwarded based on MAC table entries for that VLAN, and forwarded out ports in that VLAN. This chapter explores those concepts and others related to VLANs.

As for the organization of the chapter, the first major section of the chapter explains the core concepts. These concepts include how VLANs work on a single switch, how to use VLAN trunking to create VLANs that span across multiple switches, and how to forward traffic between VLANs using a router. The second major section shows how to configure VLANs and VLAN trunks: how to statically assign interfaces to a VLAN. The final major section discusses some issues that can arise when using VLANs and trunks and how to avoid those issues.

"Do I Know This Already?" Quiz

Take the quiz (either here or use the PTP software) if you want to use the score to help you decide how much time to spend on this chapter. The letter answers are listed at the bottom of the page following the quiz. Appendix C, found both at the end of the book as well as on the companion website, includes both the answers and explanations. You can also find both answers and explanations in the PTP testing software.

Table 8-1 "Do I Know This Already?" Foundation Topics Section-to-Question Mapping

Foundation Topics Section	Questions
Virtual LAN Concepts	1–3
VLAN and VLAN Trunking Configuration and Verification	4–6
Troubleshooting VLANs and VLAN Trunks	7–8

1. In a LAN, which of the following terms best equates to the term VLAN?

   a. Collision domain

   b. Broadcast domain

   c. Subnet

   d. Single switch

   e. Trunk

2. Imagine a switch with three configured VLANs. How many IP subnets are required, assuming that all hosts in all VLANs want to use TCP/IP?

   a. 0

   b. 1

   c. 2

   d. 3

   e. You cannot tell from the information provided.

3. Switch SW1 sends a frame to switch SW2 using 802.1Q trunking. Which of the answers describes how SW1 changes or adds to the Ethernet frame before forwarding the frame to SW2?

   a. Inserts a 4-byte header and does change the MAC addresses

   b. Inserts a 4-byte header and does not change the MAC addresses

   c. Encapsulates the original frame behind an entirely new Ethernet header

   d. None of the other answers are correct

4. Imagine that you are told that switch 1 is configured with the **dynamic auto** parameter for trunking on its Fa0/5 interface, which is connected to switch 2. You have to configure switch 2. Which of the following settings for trunking could allow trunking to work? (Choose two answers.)

   a. on

   b. dynamic auto

   c. dynamic desirable

   d. access

   e. None of the other answers are correct.

5. A switch has just arrived from Cisco. The switch has never been configured with any VLANs, but VTP has been disabled. An engineer configures the **vlan 22** and **name Hannahs-VLAN** commands and then exits configuration mode. Which of the following are true? (Choose two answers.)

   a. VLAN 22 is listed in the output of the **show vlan brief** command.

   b. VLAN 22 is listed in the output of the **show running-config** command.

   c. VLAN 22 is not created by this process.

   d. VLAN 22 does not exist in that switch until at least one interface is assigned to that VLAN.

6. Which of the following commands identify switch interfaces as being trunking interfaces: interfaces that currently operate as VLAN trunks? (Choose two answers.)

   a. show interfaces

   b. show interfaces switchport

   c. show interfaces trunk

   d. show trunks

7. In a switch that disables VTP, an engineer configures the commands **vlan 30** and **shutdown vlan 30**. Which answers should be true about this switch? (Choose two answers.)

   a. The **show vlan brief** command should list VLAN 30.

   b. The **show running-config** command should list VLAN 30.

   c. The switch should forward frames that arrive in access ports in VLAN 30.

   d. The switch should forward frames that arrive in trunk ports tagged with VLAN 30.

8. The **show interfaces g0/1 trunk** command provides three lists of VLAN IDs. Which items would limit the VLANs that appear in the first of the three lists of VLANs?

   a. A **shutdown vlan 30** global command

   b. A **switchport trunk allowed vlan** interface subcommand

   c. An STP choice to block on G0/1

   d. A **no vlan 30** global command

Foundation Topics

Virtual LAN Concepts

Before understanding VLANs, you must first have a specific understanding of the definition of a LAN. For example, from one perspective, a LAN includes all the user devices, servers, switches, routers, cables, and wireless access points in one location. However, an alternative narrower definition of a LAN can help in understanding the concept of a virtual LAN:

A LAN includes all devices in the same broadcast domain.

A broadcast domain includes the set of all LAN-connected devices, so that when any of the devices sends a broadcast frame, all the other devices get a copy of the frame. So, from one perspective, you can think of a LAN and a broadcast domain as being basically the same thing.

Using only default settings, a switch considers all its interfaces to be in the same broadcast domain. That is, for one switch, when a broadcast frame entered one switch port, the switch forwards that broadcast frame out all other ports. With that logic, to create two different LAN broadcast domains, you had to buy two different Ethernet LAN switches, as shown in Figure 8-1.

Figure 8-1   *Creating Two Broadcast Domains with Two Physical Switches and No VLANs*

By using two VLANs, a single switch can accomplish the same goals of the design in Figure 8-1—to create two broadcast domains—with a single switch. With VLANs, a switch can configure some interfaces into one broadcast domain and some into another, creating multiple broadcast domains. These individual broadcast domains created by the switch are called *virtual LANs* (VLAN).

For example, in Figure 8-2, the single switch creates two VLANs, treating the ports in each VLAN as being completely separate. The switch would never forward a frame sent by Dino (in VLAN 1) over to either Wilma or Betty (in VLAN 2).

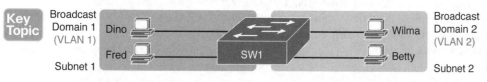

Figure 8-2   *Creating Two Broadcast Domains Using One Switch and VLANs*

Designing campus LANs to use more VLANs, each with a smaller number of devices, often helps improve the LAN in many ways. For example, a broadcast sent by one host in a VLAN will be received and processed by all the other hosts in the VLAN—but not by hosts in a different VLAN. Limiting the number of hosts that receive a single broadcast frame reduces the number of hosts that waste effort processing unneeded broadcasts. It also reduces security risks because fewer hosts see frames sent by any one host. These are just a few reasons for separating hosts into different VLANs. The following list summarizes the most common reasons for choosing to create smaller broadcast domains (VLANs):

- To reduce CPU overhead on each device, improving host performance, by reducing the number of devices that receive each broadcast frame

- To reduce security risks by reducing the number of hosts that receive copies of frames that the switches flood (broadcasts, multicasts, and unknown unicasts)

- To improve security for hosts through the application of different security policies per VLAN

- To create more flexible designs that group users by department, or by groups that work together, instead of by physical location

- To solve problems more quickly, because the failure domain for many problems is the same set of devices as those in the same broadcast domain

- To reduce the workload for the Spanning Tree Protocol (STP) by limiting a VLAN to a single access switch

The rest of this chapter looks closely at the mechanics of how VLANs work across multiple Cisco switches, including the required configuration. To that end, the next section examines VLAN trunking, a feature required when installing a VLAN that exists on more than one LAN switch.

Creating Multiswitch VLANs Using Trunking

Configuring VLANs on a single switch requires only a little effort: you simply configure each port to tell it the VLAN number to which the port belongs. With multiple switches, you have to consider additional concepts about how to forward traffic between the switches.

When you are using VLANs in networks that have multiple interconnected switches, the switches need to use *VLAN trunking* on the links between the switches. VLAN trunking causes the switches to use a process called *VLAN tagging*, by which the sending switch adds another header to the frame before sending it over the trunk. This extra trunking header includes a *VLAN identifier* (VLAN ID) field so that the sending switch can associate the frame with a particular VLAN ID, and the receiving switch can then know in what VLAN each frame belongs.

Figure 8-3 shows an example that demonstrates VLANs that exist on multiple switches, but it does not use trunking. First, the design uses two VLANs: VLAN 10 and VLAN 20. Each switch has two ports assigned to each VLAN, so each VLAN exists in both switches. To forward traffic in VLAN 10 between the two switches, the design includes a link between switches, with that link fully inside VLAN 10. Likewise, to support VLAN 20 traffic between switches, the design uses a second link between switches, with that link inside VLAN 20.

The design in Figure 8-3 functions perfectly. For example, PC11 (in VLAN 10) can send a frame to PC14. The frame flows into SW1, over the top link (the one that is in VLAN 10) and over to SW2.

Answers to the "Do I Know This Already?" quiz:

1 B **2** D **3** B **4** A, C **5** A, B **6** B, C **7** A, B **8** B

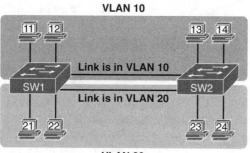

Figure 8-3 *Multiswitch VLAN Without VLAN Trunking*

The design shown in Figure 8-3 works, but it simply does not scale very well. It requires one physical link between switches to support every VLAN. If a design needed 10 or 20 VLANs, you would need 10 or 20 links between switches, and you would use 10 or 20 switch ports (on each switch) for those links.

VLAN Tagging Concepts

VLAN trunking creates one link between switches that supports as many VLANs as you need. As a VLAN trunk, the switches treat the link as if it were a part of all the VLANs. At the same time, the trunk keeps the VLAN traffic separate, so frames in VLAN 10 would not go to devices in VLAN 20, and vice versa, because each frame is identified by VLAN number as it crosses the trunk. Figure 8-4 shows the idea, with a single physical link between the two switches.

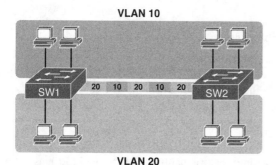

Figure 8-4 *Multiswitch VLAN with Trunking*

The use of trunking allows switches to forward frames from multiple VLANs over a single physical connection by adding a small header to the Ethernet frame. For example, Figure 8-5 shows PC11 sending a broadcast frame on interface Fa0/1 at Step 1. To flood the frame, switch SW1 needs to forward the broadcast frame to switch SW2. However, SW1 needs to let SW2 know that the frame is part of VLAN 10, so that after the frame is received, SW2 will flood the frame only into VLAN 10, and not into VLAN 20. So, as shown at Step 2, before sending the frame, SW1 adds a VLAN header to the original Ethernet frame, with the VLAN header listing a VLAN ID of 10 in this case.

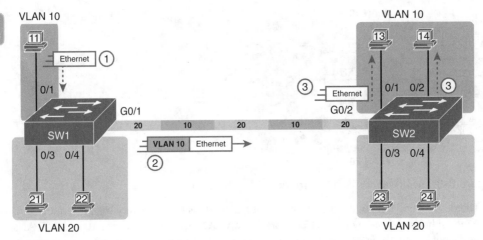

Figure 8-5   *VLAN Trunking Between Two Switches*

When SW2 receives the frame, it understands that the frame is in VLAN 10. SW2 then removes the VLAN header, forwarding the original frame out its interfaces in VLAN 10 (Step 3).

For another example, consider the case when PC21 (in VLAN 20) sends a broadcast. SW1 sends the broadcast out port Fa0/4 (because that port is in VLAN 20) and out Gi0/1 (because it is a trunk, meaning that it supports multiple different VLANs). SW1 adds a trunking header to the frame, listing a VLAN ID of 20. SW2 strips off the trunking header after determining that the frame is part of VLAN 20, so SW2 knows to forward the frame out only ports Fa0/3 and Fa0/4, because they are in VLAN 20, and not out ports Fa0/1 and Fa0/2, because they are in VLAN 10.

The 802.1Q and ISL VLAN Trunking Protocols

Cisco has supported two different trunking protocols over the years: Inter-Switch Link (ISL) and IEEE 802.1Q. Cisco created the ISL years before 802.1Q, in part because the IEEE had not yet defined a VLAN trunking standard. Today, 802.1Q has become the more popular trunking protocol, with Cisco not even bothering to support ISL in many of its switch models today.

While both ISL and 802.1Q tag each frame with the VLAN ID, the details differ. 802.1Q inserts an extra 4-byte 802.1Q VLAN header into the original frame's Ethernet header, as shown at the top of Figure 8-6. As for the fields in the 802.1Q header, only the 12-bit VLAN ID field inside the 802.1Q header matters for topics discussed in this book. This 12-bit field supports a theoretical maximum of 2^{12} (4096) VLANs, but in practice it supports a maximum of 4094. (Both 802.1Q and ISL use 12 bits to tag the VLAN ID, with two reserved values [0 and 4095].)

Cisco switches break the range of VLAN IDs (1–4094) into two ranges: the normal range and the extended range. All switches can use normal-range VLANs with values from 1 to 1005. Only some switches can use extended-range VLANs with VLAN IDs from 1006 to 4094. The rules for which switches can use extended-range VLANs depend on the configuration of the VLAN Trunking Protocol (VTP), which is discussed briefly in the section "VLAN Trunking Configuration," later in this chapter.

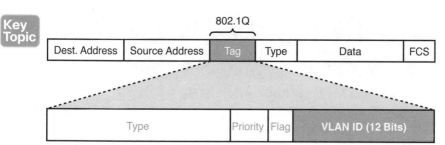

Figure 8-6 *802.1Q Trunking*

802.1Q also defines one special VLAN ID on each trunk as the *native VLAN* (defaulting to use VLAN 1). By definition, 802.1Q simply does not add an 802.1Q header to frames in the native VLAN. When the switch on the other side of the trunk receives a frame that does not have an 802.1Q header, the receiving switch knows that the frame is part of the native VLAN. Note that because of this behavior, both switches must agree on which VLAN is the native VLAN.

The 802.1Q native VLAN provides some interesting functions, mainly to support connections to devices that do not understand trunking. For example, a Cisco switch could be cabled to a switch that does not understand 802.1Q trunking. The Cisco switch could send frames in the native VLAN—meaning that the frame has no trunking header—so that the other switch would understand the frame. The native VLAN concept gives switches the capability of at least passing traffic in one VLAN (the native VLAN), which can allow some basic functions, like reachability to telnet into a switch.

Forwarding Data Between VLANs

If you create a campus LAN that contains many VLANs, you typically still need all devices to be able to send data to all other devices. This next topic discusses some concepts about how to route data between those VLANs.

The Need for Routing Between VLANs

LAN switches that forward data based on Layer 2 logic, as discussed so far in this book, often go by the name *Layer 2 switch*. For example, Chapter 5, "Analyzing Ethernet LAN Switching," discussed how LAN switches receive Ethernet frames (a Layer 2 concept), look at the destination Ethernet MAC address (a Layer 2 address), and forward the Ethernet frame out some other interface. All those concepts are defined by Layer 2 protocols, hence the name Layer 2 switch.

Layer 2 switches perform their logic per VLAN. For example, in Figure 8-7, the two PCs on the left sit in VLAN 10, in subnet 10. The two PCs on the right sit in a different VLAN (20), with a different subnet (20). Note that the figure repeats earlier Figure 8-2, but with the switch broken into halves, to emphasize the point that Layer 2 switches will not forward data between two VLANs.

As shown in the figure, when configured with some ports in VLAN 10 and others in VLAN 20, the switch acts like two separate switches in which it will forward traffic. In fact, one goal of VLANs is to separate traffic in one VLAN from another, preventing frames in one VLAN from leaking over to other VLANs. For example, when Dino (in VLAN 10) sends any Ethernet frame, if SW1 is a Layer 2 switch, that switch will not forward the frame to the PCs on the right in VLAN 20.

Figure 8-7 *Layer 2 Switch Does Not Route Between the VLANs*

Routing Packets Between VLANs with a Router

When including VLANs in a campus LAN design, the devices in a VLAN need to be in the same subnet. Following the same design logic, devices in different VLANs need to be in different subnets.

To forward packets between VLANs, the network must use a device that acts as a router. You can use an actual router, as well as some other switches that can perform some functions like a router. These switches that also perform Layer 3 routing functions go by the name *multilayer switch* or *Layer 3 switch*. This section first discusses how to forward data between VLANs when using Layer 2 switches and ends with a brief discussion of how to use Layer 3 switches.

For example, Figure 8-8 shows a router that can route packets between subnets 10 and 20. The figure shows the same Layer 2 switch as shown in Figure 8-7, with the same perspective of the switch being split into parts with two different VLANs, and with the same PCs in the same VLANs and subnets. Now Router R1 has one LAN physical interface connected to the switch and assigned to VLAN 10, and a second physical interface connected to the switch and assigned to VLAN 20. With an interface connected to each subnet, the Layer 2 switch can keep doing its job—forwarding frames inside a VLAN, while the router can do its job—routing IP packets between the subnets.

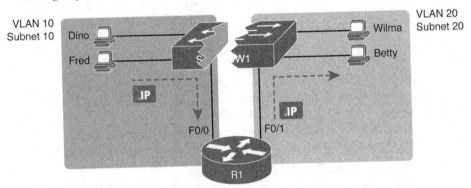

Figure 8-8 *Routing Between Two VLANs on Two Physical Interfaces*

The figure shows an IP packet being routed from Fred, which sits in one VLAN/subnet, to Betty, which sits in the other. The Layer 2 switch forwards two different Layer 2 Ethernet frames: one in VLAN 10, from Fred to R1's F0/0 interface, and the other in VLAN 20, from R1's F0/1 interface to Betty. From a Layer 3 perspective, Fred sends the IP packet to its default router (R1), and R1 routes the packet out another interface (F0/1) into another subnet where Betty resides.

The design in Figure 8-8 works, but there are several different solutions for routing packets between VLANs. This chapter shows the option of using a separate physical router, with a separate link per VLAN, because it can be the easiest of the options to understand and visualize. Chapter 17, "IP Routing in the LAN," works through those other features for routing packets between VLANs.

VLAN and VLAN Trunking Configuration and Verification

Cisco switches do not require any configuration to work. You can purchase Cisco switches, install devices with the correct cabling, turn on the switches, and they work. You would never need to configure the switch, and it would work fine, even if you interconnected switches, until you needed more than one VLAN. But if you want to use VLANs—and most enterprise networks do—you need to add some configuration.

This chapter separates the VLAN configuration details into two major sections. The first section looks at how to configure static access interfaces: switch interfaces configured to be in one VLAN only, therefore not using VLAN trunking. The second part shows how to configure interfaces that do use VLAN trunking.

Creating VLANs and Assigning Access VLANs to an Interface

This section shows how to create a VLAN, give the VLAN a name, and assign interfaces to a VLAN. To focus on these basic details, this section shows examples using a single switch, so VLAN trunking is not needed.

For a Cisco switch to forward frames in a particular VLAN, the switch must be configured to believe that the VLAN exists. In addition, the switch must have nontrunking interfaces (called *access interfaces*, or *static access interfaces*) assigned to the VLAN, and/or trunks that support the VLAN. The configuration steps for access interfaces are as follows:

Step 1.   To configure a new VLAN, follow these steps:

   A. From configuration mode, use the **vlan** *vlan-id* command in global configuration mode to create the VLAN and to move the user into VLAN configuration mode.

   B. (Optional) Use the **name** *name* command in VLAN configuration mode to list a name for the VLAN. If not configured, the VLAN name is VLANZZZZ, where ZZZZ is the four-digit decimal VLAN ID.

Step 2.   For each access interface, follow these steps:

   A. Use the **interface** *type number* command in global configuration mode to move into interface configuration mode for each desired interface.

   B. Use the **switchport access vlan** *id-number* command in interface configuration mode to specify the VLAN number associated with that interface.

   C. (Optional) Use the **switchport mode access** command in interface configuration mode to make this port always operate in access mode (that is, to not trunk).

While the list might look a little daunting, the process on a single switch is actually pretty simple. For example, if you want to put the switch's ports in three VLANs—11, 12, and

13—you first add three **vlan** commands: **vlan 11**, **vlan 12**, and **vlan 13**. Then, for each interface, add a **switchport access vlan 11** (or **12** or **13**) command to assign that interface to the proper VLAN.

> **NOTE** The term *default VLAN* (as shown in the exam topics) refers to the default setting on the **switchport access vlan** *vlan-id* command, and that default is VLAN ID 1. In other words, by default, each port is assigned to access VLAN 1.

VLAN Configuration Example 1: Full VLAN Configuration

Examples 8-1, 8-2, and 8-3 work through one scenario with VLAN configuration and verification. To begin, Example 8-1 begins by showing the VLANs in switch SW1 in Figure 8-9, with all default settings related to VLANs.

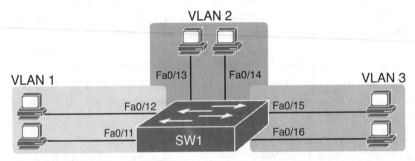

Figure 8-9   *Network with One Switch and Three VLANs*

Example 8-1   *Configuring VLANs and Assigning VLANs to Interfaces*

```
SW1# show vlan brief
VLAN Name                             Status    Ports
---- -------------------------------- --------- -------------------------------
1    default                          active    Fa0/1, Fa0/2, Fa0/3, Fa0/4
                                                Fa0/5, Fa0/6, Fa0/7, Fa0/8
                                                Fa0/9, Fa0/10, Fa0/11, Fa0/12
                                                Fa0/13, Fa0/14, Fa0/15, Fa0/16
                                                Fa0/17, Fa0/18, Fa0/19, Fa0/20
                                                Fa0/21, Fa0/22, Fa0/23, Fa0/24
                                                Gi0/1, Gi0/2
1002 fddi-default                     act/unsup
1003 token-ring-default               act/unsup
1004 fddinet-default                  act/unsup
1005 trnet-default                    act/unsup
```

The example begins with the **show vlan brief** command, confirming the default settings of five nondeletable VLANs, with all interfaces assigned to VLAN 1. VLAN 1 cannot be deleted but can be used. VLANs 1002–1005 cannot be deleted and cannot be used as access VLANs today. In particular, note that this 2960 switch has 24 Fast Ethernet ports (Fa0/1– Fa0/24) and two Gigabit Ethernet ports (Gi0/1 and Gi0/2), all of which are listed as being in

VLAN 1 per that first command's output, confirming that by default, Cisco switches assign all ports to VLAN 1.

Next, Example 8-2 shows steps that mirror the VLAN configuration checklist, namely the configuration of VLAN 2, plus the assignment of VLAN 2 as the access VLAN on two ports: Fa0/13 and Fa0/14.

Example 8-2 *Configuring VLANs and Assigning VLANs to Interfaces*

```
SW1# configure terminal
Enter configuration commands, one per line. End with CNTL/Z.
SW1(config)# vlan 2
SW1(config-vlan)# name Freds-vlan
SW1(config-vlan)# exit
SW1(config)# interface range fastethernet 0/13 - 14
SW1(config-if)# switchport access vlan 2
SW1(config-if)# switchport mode access
SW1(config-if)# end

SW1# show vlan brief

VLAN Name                             Status    Ports
---- -------------------------------- --------- -------------------------------
1    default                          active    Fa0/1, Fa0/2, Fa0/3, Fa0/4
                                                Fa0/5, Fa0/6, Fa0/7, Fa0/8
                                                Fa0/9, Fa0/10, Fa0/11, Fa0/12
                                                Fa0/15, Fa0/16, Fa0/17, Fa0/18
                                                Fa0/19, Fa0/20, Fa0/21, Fa0/22
                                                Fa0/23, Fa0/24, Gi0/1, Gi0/2
2    Freds-vlan                       active    Fa0/13, Fa0/14
1002 fddi-default                     act/unsup
1003 token-ring-default               act/unsup
1004 fddinet-default                  act/unsup
1005 trnet-default                    act/unsup
```

Take a moment to compare the output of the **show vlan brief** commands in Example 8-2 (after adding the configuration) versus Example 8-1. Example 8-2 shows new information about VLAN 2, with ports Fa0/13 and Fa0/14 no longer being listed with VLAN 1, but now listed as assigned to VLAN 2.

To complete this scenario, Example 8-3 shows a little more detail about the VLAN itself. First, the **show running-config** command lists both the **vlan 2** and **switchport access vlan 2** commands as configured in Example 8-2. Also, note that earlier Example 8-2 uses the **interface range** command, with one instance of the **switchport access vlan 2** interface subcommand. However, Example 8-3 shows how the switch actually applied that command to both Fa0/13 and Fa0/14. Example 8-3 ends with the **show vlan id 2** command, which confirms the operational status that ports Fa0/13 and Fa0/14 are assigned to VLAN 2.

Example 8-3 *Configuring VLANs and Assigning VLANs to Interfaces*

```
SW1# show running-config
! Many lines omitted for brevity
! Early in the output:
vlan 2
 name Freds-vlan
!
! more lines omitted for brevity
interface FastEthernet0/13
 switchport access vlan 2
 switchport mode access
!
interface FastEthernet0/14
 switchport access vlan 2
 switchport mode access
!


SW1# show vlan id 2
VLAN Name                             Status    Ports
---- -------------------------------- --------- -------------------------------
2    Freds-vlan                       active    Fa0/13, Fa0/14


VLAN Type  SAID       MTU   Parent RingNo BridgeNo Stp  BrdgMode Trans1 Trans2
---- ----- ---------- ----- ------ ------ -------- ---- -------- ------ ------
2    enet  100010     1500  -      -      -        -    -        0      0


Remote SPAN VLAN
----------------
Disabled


Primary Secondary Type             Ports
------- --------- ---------------- -----------------------------------------
```

The example surrounding Figure 8-9 uses six switch ports, all of which need to operate as access ports. That is, each port should not use trunking but instead should be assigned to a single VLAN, as assigned by the **switchport access vlan** *vlan-id* command. For ports that should always act as access ports, add the optional interface subcommand **switchport mode access**. This command tells the switch to always be an access interface and disables the protocol that negotiates trunking (Dynamic Trunking Protocol [DTP]) with the device on the other end of the link. (The upcoming section "VLAN Trunking Configuration" discusses more details about the commands that allow a port to negotiate whether it should use trunking.)

NOTE The book includes a video that works through a different VLAN configuration example as well. You can find the video on the companion website.

VLAN Configuration Example 2: Shorter VLAN Configuration

Example 8-2 shows how to configure a VLAN and add two ports to the VLAN as access ports. Example 8-4 does the same, this time with VLAN 3, and this time with a much briefer alternative configuration. The configuration completes the configuration of the design shown in Figure 8-9, by adding two ports to VLAN 3.

Example 8-4   *Shorter VLAN Configuration Example (VLAN 3)*

```
SW1# configure terminal
Enter configuration commands, one per line. End with CNTL/Z.
SW1(config)# interface range Fastethernet 0/15 - 16
SW1(config-if-range)# switchport access vlan 3
% Access VLAN does not exist. Creating vlan 3
SW1(config-if-range)# ^Z


SW1# show vlan brief

VLAN Name                             Status    Ports
---- -------------------------------- --------- -------------------------------
1    default                          active    Fa0/1, Fa0/2, Fa0/3, Fa0/4
                                                Fa0/5, Fa0/6, Fa0/7, Fa0/8
                                                Fa0/9, Fa0/10, Fa0/11, Fa0/12
                                                Fa0/17, Fa0/18, Fa0/19, Fa0/20
                                                Fa0/21, Fa0/22, Fa0/23, Fa0/24
                                                Gi0/1, Gi0/2
2    Freds-vlan                       active    Fa0/13, Fa0/14
3    VLAN0003                         active    Fa0/15, Fa0/16
1002 fddi-default                     act/unsup
1003 token-ring-default               act/unsup
1004 fddinet-default                  act/unsup
1005 trnet-default                    act/unsup
```

Example 8-2 shows how a switch can dynamically create a VLAN—the equivalent of the **vlan** *vlan-id* global config command—when the **switchport access vlan** interface subcommand refers to a currently unconfigured VLAN. This example begins with SW1 not knowing about VLAN 3. With the addition of the **switchport access vlan 3** interface subcommand, the switch realized that VLAN 3 did not exist, and as noted in the shaded message in the example, the switch created VLAN 3, using a default name (VLAN0003). The engineer did not need to type the **vlan 3** global command to create VLAN 3; the switch did that automatically. No other steps are required to create the VLAN. At the end of the process, VLAN 3 exists in the switch, and interfaces Fa0/15 and Fa0/16 are in VLAN 3, as noted in the shaded part of the **show vlan brief** command output.

VLAN Trunking Protocol

Before showing more configuration examples, you also need to know something about a Cisco protocol and tool called the VLAN Trunking Protocol (VTP). VTP is a Cisco proprietary tool on Cisco switches that advertises each VLAN configured in one switch (with the **vlan** *number* command) so that all the other switches in the campus learn about that VLAN.

This book does not discuss VTP as an end to itself for a few different reasons. First, the current CCNA 200-301 exam blueprint ignores VTP, as do the CCNP Enterprise Core and CCNP Enterprise Advanced Routing blueprints. Additionally, many enterprises choose to disable VTP.

Also, you can easily disable VTP so that it has no impact on your switches in the lab, which is exactly what I did when building all the examples in this book.

However, VTP has some small impact on how every Cisco Catalyst switch works, even if you do not try to use VTP. This brief section introduces enough details of VTP so that you can see these small differences in VTP that cannot be avoided.

First, all examples in this book (and in Volume 2) use switches that disable VTP in some way. Interestingly, for much of VTP's decades of existence, most switches did not allow VTP to be disabled completely; on those switches, to effectively disable VTP, the engineer would set the switch to use VTP transparent mode (with the **vtp mode transparent** global command). Some switches now have an option to disable VTP completely with the **vtp mode off** global command. For the purposes of this book, configuring a switch with either transparent mode or off mode disables VTP.

Note that both transparent and off modes prevent VTP from learning and advertising about VLAN configuration. Those modes allow a switch to configure all VLANs, including standard- and extended-range VLANs. Additionally, switches using transparent or off modes list the **vlan** configuration commands in the running-config file.

Finally, on a practical note, if you happen to do lab exercises with real switches or with simulators, and you see unusual results with VLANs, check the VTP status with the **show vtp status** command. If your switch uses VTP server or client mode, you will find

- The server switches can configure VLANs in the standard range only (1–1005).
- The client switches cannot configure VLANs.
- Both servers and clients may be learning new VLANs from other switches and seeing their VLANs deleted by other switches because of VTP.
- The **show running-config** command does not list any **vlan** commands; you must use other **show** commands to find out about the configured VLANs.

If possible in the lab, switch to disable VTP and ignore VTP for your switch configuration practice until you decide to learn more about VTP for other purposes.

NOTE Do not change VTP settings on any switch that also connects to the production network until you know how VTP works and you talk with experienced colleagues. Doing so can cause real harm to your LAN. For example, if the switch you configure connects to other switches, which in turn connect to switches used in the production LAN, you could accidentally change the VLAN configuration in other switches with serious impact to the operation of the network. You could delete VLANs and cause outages. Be careful and never experiment with VTP settings on a switch unless it and the other switches connected to it have absolutely no physical links connected to the production LAN.

VLAN Trunking Configuration

Trunking configuration between two Cisco switches can be very simple if you just statically configure trunking. For example, most Cisco Catalyst switches today support only 802.1Q and not ISL. You could literally add one interface subcommand for the switch interface on each side of the link (**switchport mode trunk**), and you would create a VLAN trunk that supported all the VLANs known to each switch.

However, trunking configuration on Cisco switches includes many more options, including several options for dynamically negotiating various trunking settings. The configuration can either predefine different settings or tell the switch to negotiate the settings, as follows:

- **The type of trunking:** IEEE 802.1Q, ISL, or negotiate which one to use, on switches that support both types of trunking.

- **The administrative mode:** Whether to always trunk, always not trunk, or negotiate whether to trunk or not.

First, consider the type of trunking. Cisco switches that support ISL and 802.1Q can negotiate which type to use, using the Dynamic Trunking Protocol (DTP). If both switches support both protocols, they use ISL; otherwise, they use the protocol that both support. Today, many Cisco switches do not support the older ISL trunking protocol. Switches that support both types of trunking use the **switchport trunk encapsulation {dot1q | isl | negotiate}** interface subcommand to either configure the type or allow DTP to negotiate the type.

DTP can also negotiate whether the two devices on the link agree to trunk at all, as guided by the local switch port's administrative mode. The administrative mode refers to the configuration setting for whether trunking should be used. Each interface also has an *operational* mode, which refers to what is currently happening on the interface and might have been chosen by DTP's negotiation with the other device. Cisco switches use the **switchport mode** interface subcommand to define the administrative trunking mode, as listed in Table 8-2.

Table 8-2 Trunking Administrative Mode Options with the **switchport mode** Command

Command Option	Description
access	Always act as an access (nontrunk) port
trunk	Always act as a trunk port
dynamic desirable	Initiates negotiation messages and responds to negotiation messages to dynamically choose whether to start using trunking
dynamic auto	Passively waits to receive trunk negotiation messages, at which point the switch will respond and negotiate whether to use trunking

For example, consider the two switches shown in Figure 8-10. This figure expands the design shown earlier in Figure 8-9, with a trunk to a new switch (SW2) and with parts of VLANs 1 and 3 on ports attached to SW2. The two switches use a Gigabit Ethernet link for the trunk. In this case, the trunk does not dynamically form by default because both (2960) switches default to an administrative mode of *dynamic auto*, meaning that neither switch initiates the trunk negotiation process. When one switch is changed to use *dynamic desirable* mode, which does initiate the negotiation, the switches negotiate to use trunking, specifically 802.1Q because the 2960s support only 802.1Q.

8

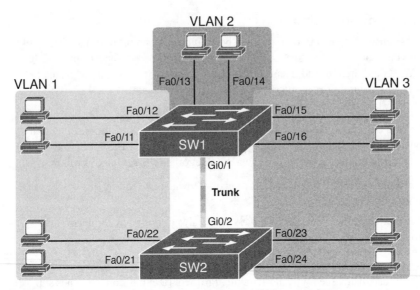

Figure 8-10 *Network with Two Switches and Three VLANs*

Example 8-5 begins with SW1 configured as shown in Examples 8-2 and 8-4—that is, SW1 has two ports each assigned to VLANs 1, 2, and 3. However, both SW1 and SW2 currently have all default settings on the interfaces that connect the two switches. With the default setting of **switchport mode dynamic auto**, the two switches do not trunk.

Example 8-5 *Initial (Default) State: Not Trunking Between SW1 and SW2*

```
SW1# show interfaces gigabit 0/1 switchport
Name: Gi0/1
Switchport: Enabled
Administrative Mode: dynamic auto
Operational Mode: static access
Administrative Trunking Encapsulation: dot1q
Operational Trunking Encapsulation: native
Negotiation of Trunking: On
Access Mode VLAN: 1 (default)
Trunking Native Mode VLAN: 1 (default)
Administrative Native VLAN tagging: enabled
Voice VLAN: none
Access Mode VLAN: 1 (default)
Trunking Native Mode VLAN: 1 (default)
Administrative Native VLAN tagging: enabled
Voice VLAN: none
Administrative private-vlan host-association: none
Administrative private-vlan mapping: none
Administrative private-vlan trunk native VLAN: none
Administrative private-vlan trunk Native VLAN tagging: enabled
Administrative private-vlan trunk encapsulation: dot1q
```

```
Administrative private-vlan trunk normal VLANs: none
Administrative private-vlan trunk private VLANs: none
Operational private-vlan: none
Trunking VLANs Enabled: ALL
Pruning VLANs Enabled: 2-1001
Capture Mode Disabled
Capture VLANs Allowed: ALL

Protected: false
Unknown unicast blocked: disabled
Unknown multicast blocked: disabled
Appliance trust: none

! Note that the next command results in a single empty line of output.
SW1# show interfaces trunk
SW1#
```

First, focus on the highlighted items from the output of the **show interfaces switchport** command at the beginning of Example 8-3. The output lists the default administrative mode setting of dynamic auto. Because SW2 also defaults to dynamic auto, the command lists SW1's operational status as "access," meaning that it is not trunking. ("Dynamic auto" tells both switches to sit there and wait on the other switch to start the negotiations.) The third shaded line points out the only supported type of trunking (802.1Q). (On a switch that supports both ISL and 802.1Q, this value would by default list "negotiate," to mean that the type of encapsulation is negotiated.) Finally, the operational trunking type is listed as "native," which is a reference to the 802.1Q native VLAN.

The end of the example shows the output of the **show interfaces trunk** command, but with no output. This command lists information about all interfaces that currently operationally trunk; that is, it lists interfaces that currently use VLAN trunking. With no interfaces listed, this command also confirms that the link between switches is not trunking.

Next, consider Example 8-6, which shows the new configuration that enables trunking. In this case, SW1 is configured with the **switchport mode dynamic desirable** command, which asks the switch to both negotiate as well as to begin the negotiation process, rather than waiting on the other device. The example shows that as soon as the command is issued, log messages appear showing that the interface goes down and then back up again, which happens when the interface transitions from access mode to trunk mode.

Example 8-6 *SW1 Changes from Dynamic Auto to Dynamic Desirable*

```
SW1# configure terminal
Enter configuration commands, one per line. End with CNTL/Z.
SW1(config)# interface gigabit 0/1
SW1(config-if)# switchport mode dynamic desirable
SW1(config-if)# ^Z
SW1#
```

```
%LINEPROTO-5-UPDOWN: Line protocol on Interface GigabitEthernet0/1, changed state to
  down
%LINEPROTO-5-UPDOWN: Line protocol on Interface GigabitEthernet0/1, changed state to
  up
SW1# show interfaces gigabit 0/1 switchport
Name: Gi0/1
Switchport: Enabled
Administrative Mode: dynamic desirable
Operational Mode: trunk
Administrative Trunking Encapsulation: dot1q
Operational Trunking Encapsulation: dot1q
Negotiation of Trunking: On
Access Mode VLAN: 1 (default)
Trunking Native Mode VLAN: 1 (default)
! lines omitted for brevity
```

Example 8-6 repeats the **show interfaces gi0/1 switchport** command seen in Example 8-5, but after configuring VLAN trunking, so this time the output shows that SW1's G0/1 interface now operates as a trunk. Note that the command still lists the administrative settings, which denote the configured values along with the operational settings, which list what the switch is currently doing. SW1 now claims to be in an operational mode of *trunk*, with an operational trunking encapsulation of dot1Q.

Example 8-7 now repeats the same **show interfaces trunk** command that showed no output at all back in Example 8-5. Now that SW1 trunks on its G0/1 port, the output in Example 8-7 lists G0/1, confirming that G0/1 is now operationally trunking. The next section discusses the meaning of the output of this command. Also, note that the end of the example repeats the **show vlan id 2** command; of note, it includes the trunk port G0/1 in the output because the trunk port can forward traffic in VLAN 2.

Example 8-7   *A Closer Look at SW1's G0/1 Trunk Port*

```
SW1# show interfaces trunk

Port        Mode            Encapsulation  Status        Native vlan
Gi0/1       desirable       802.1q         trunking      1


Port        Vlans allowed on trunk
Gi0/1       1-4094


Port        Vlans allowed and active in management domain
Gi0/1       1-3


Port        Vlans in spanning tree forwarding state and not pruned
Gi0/1       1-3
```

```
SW1# show vlan id 2
VLAN Name                             Status    Ports
---- -------------------------------- --------- -------------------------------
2    Freds-vlan                       active    Fa0/13, Fa0/14, G0/1


VLAN Type  SAID       MTU   Parent RingNo BridgeNo Stp  BrdgMode Trans1 Trans2
---- ----- ---------- ----- ------ ------ -------- ---- -------- ------ ------
2    enet  100010     1500  -      -      -        -    -        0      0


Remote SPAN VLAN
----------------
Disabled


Primary Secondary Type              Ports
------- --------- ----------------- -------------------------------------------
```

For the exams, you should be ready to interpret the output of the **show interfaces switchport** command, realize the administrative mode implied by the output, and know whether the link should operationally trunk based on those settings. Table 8-3 lists the combinations of the trunking administrative modes and the expected operational mode (trunk or access) resulting from the configured settings. The table lists the administrative mode used on one end of the link on the left, and the administrative mode on the switch on the other end of the link across the top of the table.

Table 8-3 Expected Trunking Operational Mode Based on the Configured Administrative Modes

Administrative Mode	Access	Dynamic Auto	Trunk	Dynamic Desirable
access	Access	Access	Do Not Use[1]	Access
dynamic auto	Access	Access	Trunk	Trunk
trunk	Do Not Use[1]	Trunk	Trunk	Trunk
dynamic desirable	Access	Trunk	Trunk	Trunk

[1] When two switches configure a mode of "access" on one end and "trunk" on the other, problems occur. Avoid this combination.

Finally, before leaving the discussion of configuring trunks, Cisco recommends disabling trunk negotiation on most ports for better security. The majority of switch ports on most switches will be used to connect to users and configured with the command **switchport mode access**—which also disables DTP. For ports without the **switchport mode access** command—for instance, ports statically configured to trunk with the **switchport mode trunk** command—DTP still operates, but you can disable DTP negotiations altogether using the **switchport nonegotiate** interface subcommand.

8

Implementing Interfaces Connected to Phones

This next topic is strange, at least in the context of access links and trunk links. In the world of IP telephony, telephones use Ethernet ports to connect to an Ethernet network so they can use IP to send and receive voice traffic sent via IP packets. To make that work, the switch's Ethernet port acts like an access port, but at the same time, the port acts like a trunk in some ways. This last topic of the chapter works through those main concepts.

Data and Voice VLAN Concepts

Before IP telephony, a PC could sit on the same desk as a phone. The phone happened to use UTP cabling, with that phone connected to some voice device (often called a *voice switch* or a *private branch exchange [PBX]*). The PC, of course, connected using an unshielded twisted-pair (UTP) cable to the usual LAN switch that sat in the wiring closet—sometimes in the same wiring closet as the voice switch. Figure 8-11 shows the idea.

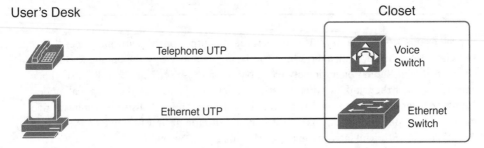

Figure 8-11 *Before IP Telephony: PC and Phone, One Cable Each, Connect to Two Different Devices*

The term *IP telephony* refers to the branch of networking in which the telephones use IP packets to send and receive voice as represented by the bits in the data portion of the IP packet. The phones connect to the network like most other end-user devices, using either Ethernet or Wi-Fi. These new IP phones did not connect via cable directly to a voice switch, instead connecting to the IP network using an Ethernet cable and an Ethernet port built in to the phone. The phones then communicated over the IP network with software that replaced the call setup and other functions of the PBX. (The current products from Cisco that perform this IP telephony control function are called *Cisco Unified Communication Manager*.)

The migration from using the already-installed telephone cabling to these new IP phones that needed UTP cables that supported Ethernet caused some problems in some offices. In particular:

- The older non-IP phones used a category of UTP cabling that often did not support 100-Mbps or 1000-Mbps Ethernet.

- Most offices had a single UTP cable running from the wiring closet to each desk, but now two devices (the PC and the new IP phone) both needed a cable from the desktop to the wiring closet.

- Installing a new cable to every desk would be expensive, plus you would need more switch ports.

To solve this problem, Cisco embedded small three-port switches into each phone.

IP telephones have included a small LAN switch, on the underside of the phone, since the earliest IP telephone products. Figure 8-12 shows the basic cabling, with the wiring closet cable connecting to one physical port on the embedded switch, the PC connecting with a short patch cable to the other physical port, and the phone's internal CPU connecting to an internal switch port.

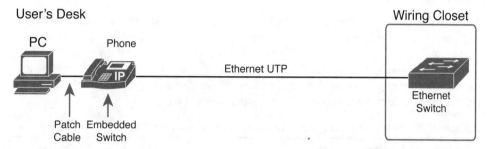

Figure 8-12 *Cabling with an IP Phone, a Single Cable, and an Integrated Switch*

Sites that use IP telephony, which includes almost every company today, now have two devices off each access port. In addition, Cisco best practices for IP telephony design tell us to put the phones in one VLAN and the PCs in a different VLAN. To make that happen, the switch port acts a little like an access link (for the PC's traffic), and a little like a trunk (for the phone's traffic). The configuration defines two VLANs on that port, as follows:

Data VLAN: Same idea and configuration as the access VLAN on an access port but defined as the VLAN on that link for forwarding the traffic for the device connected to the phone on the desk (typically the user's PC).

Voice VLAN: The VLAN defined on the link for forwarding the phone's traffic. Traffic in this VLAN is typically tagged with an 802.1Q header.

Figure 8-13 illustrates this design with two VLANs on access ports that support IP telephones.

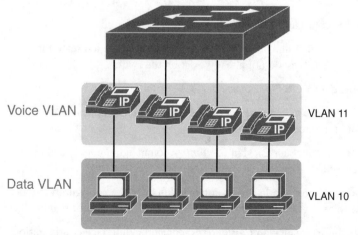

Figure 8-13 *A LAN Design, with Data in VLAN 10 and Phones in VLAN 11*

Data and Voice VLAN Configuration and Verification

Configuring a switch port to support IP phones, once you know the planned voice and data VLAN IDs, requires just a few easy commands. Making sense of the **show** commands once it is configured, however, can be a challenge. The port acts like an access port in many ways. However, with most configuration options, the voice frames flow with an 802.1Q header, so that the link supports frames in both VLANs on the link. But that makes for some different **show** command output.

Example 8-8 shows an example configuration. In this case, all four switch ports F0/1–F0/4 begin with default configuration. The configuration adds the new data and voice VLANs. The example then configures all four ports as access ports and defines the access VLAN, which is also called the *data VLAN* when discussing IP telephony. Finally, the configuration includes the **switchport voice vlan 11** command, which defines the voice VLAN used on the port. The example matches Figure 8-13, using ports F0/1–F0/4.

Example 8-8 *Configuring the Voice and Data VLAN on Ports Connected to Phones*

```
SW1# configure terminal
Enter configuration commands, one per line. End with CNTL/Z.
SW1(config)# vlan 10
SW1(config-vlan)# vlan 11
SW1(config-vlan)# interface range FastEthernet0/1 - 4
SW1(config-if)# switchport mode access
SW1(config-if)# switchport access vlan 10
SW1(config-if)# switchport voice vlan 11
SW1(config-if)#^Z
SW1#
```

NOTE CDP, which is discussed in the *CCNA 200-301 Official Cert Guide, Volume 2*, Chapter 9, "Device Management Protocols," must be enabled on an interface for a voice access port to work with Cisco IP phones. Cisco switches and routers enable CDP by default, so its configuration is not shown here.

The following list details the configuration steps for easier review and study:

Step 1. Use the **vlan** *vlan-id* command in global configuration mode to create the data and voice VLANs if they do not already exist on the switch.

Step 2. Configure the data VLAN like an access VLAN, as usual:

    A. Use the **interface** *type number* command global configuration mode to move into interface configuration mode.

    B. Use the **switchport access vlan** *id-number* command in interface configuration mode to define the data VLAN.

    C. Use the **switchport mode access** command in interface configuration mode to make this port always operate in access mode (that is, to not trunk).

Step 3. Use the **switchport voice vlan** *id-number* command in interface configuration mode to set the voice VLAN ID.

Verifying the status of a switch port configured like Example 8-8 shows some different output compared to the pure access port and pure trunk port configurations seen earlier in this chapter. For example, the **show interfaces switchport** command shows details about the operation of an interface, including many details about access ports. Example 8-9 shows those details for port F0/4 after the configuration in Example 8-8 was added.

Example 8-9   *Verifying the Data VLAN (Access VLAN) and Voice VLAN*

```
SW1# show interfaces FastEthernet 0/4 switchport
Name: Fa0/4
Switchport: Enabled
Administrative Mode: static access
Operational Mode: static access
Administrative Trunking Encapsulation: dot1q
Operational Trunking Encapsulation: native
Negotiation of Trunking: Off
Access Mode VLAN: 10 (VLAN0010)
Trunking Native Mode VLAN: 1 (default)
Administrative Native VLAN tagging: enabled
Voice VLAN: 11 (VLAN0011)
! The rest of the output is omitted for brevity
```

Working through the first three highlighted lines in the output, all those details should look familiar for any access port. The **switchport mode access** configuration command statically configures the administrative mode to be an access port, so the port of course operates as an access port. Also, as shown in the third highlighted line, the **switchport access vlan 10** configuration command defined the access mode VLAN as highlighted here.

The fourth highlighted line shows the one small new piece of information: the voice VLAN ID, as set with the **switchport voice vlan 11** command in this case. This small line of output is the only piece of information in the output that differs from the earlier access port examples in this chapter.

These ports act more like access ports than trunk ports. In fact, the **show interfaces** *type number* **switchport** command boldly proclaims, "Operational Mode: static access." However, one other **show** command reveals just a little more about the underlying operation with 802.1Q tagging for the voice frames.

As mentioned earlier, the **show interfaces trunk** command—that is, the command that does not include a specific interface in the middle of the command—lists the operational trunks on a switch. With IP telephony ports, the ports do not show up in the list of trunks either—providing evidence that these links are *not* treated as trunks. Example 8-10 shows just such an example.

However, the **show interfaces trunk** command with the interface listed in the middle of the command, as is also shown in Example 8-10, does list some additional information. Note that in this case, the **show interfaces F0/4 trunk** command lists the status as not-trunking, but with VLANs 10 and 11 allowed on the trunk. (Normally, on an access port, only the access VLAN is listed in the "VLANs allowed on the trunk" list in the output of this command.)

Example 8-10 *Allowed VLAN List and the List of Active VLANs*

```
SW1# show interfaces trunk
SW1# show interfaces F0/4 trunk


Port        Mode            Encapsulation  Status         Native vlan
Fa0/4       off             802.1q         not-trunking   1


Port        Vlans allowed on trunk
Fa0/4       10-11


Port        Vlans allowed and active in management domain
Fa0/4       10-11


Port        Vlans in spanning tree forwarding state and not pruned
Fa0/4       10-11
```

Summary: IP Telephony Ports on Switches

It might seem as though this short topic about IP telephony and switch configuration includes a lot of small twists and turns and trivia, and it does. The most important items to remember are as follows:

- Configure these ports like a normal access port to begin: Configure it as a static access port and assign it an access VLAN.

- Add one more command to define the voice VLAN (**switchport voice vlan** *vlan-id*).

- Look for the mention of the voice VLAN ID, but no other new facts, in the output of the **show interfaces** *type number* **switchport** command.

- Look for both the voice and data (access) VLAN IDs in the output of the **show interfaces** *type number* **trunk** command.

- Do not expect to see the port listed in the list of operational trunks as listed by the **show interfaces trunk** command.

Troubleshooting VLANs and VLAN Trunks

A switch's data plane forwarding processes depend in part on VLANs and VLAN trunking. This final section of the chapter focuses on issues related to VLANs and VLAN trunks that could prevent LAN switching from working properly, focusing on a few items not yet discussed in the chapter. In particular, this section examines these steps an engineer can take to avoid issues:

Step 1.   Confirm that all VLANs are both defined and active.

Step 2.   Check the allowed VLAN lists on both ends of each trunk to ensure that all VLANs intended to be used are included.

Step 3. Check for incorrect trunk configuration settings that result in one switch operating as a trunk, with the neighboring switch not operating as a trunk.

Step 4. Check the native VLAN settings on both ends of the trunk to ensure the settings match.

Access VLANs Undefined or Disabled

Switches do not forward frames for VLANs that are (a) not known because the VLAN is not configured or has not been learned with VTP or (b) the VLAN is known, but it is disabled (shut down). This next topic summarizes the best ways to confirm that a switch knows that a particular VLAN exists, and if it exists, determines the shutdown state of the VLAN.

First, on the issue of whether a VLAN exists on a switch, a VLAN can be defined to a switch in two ways: using the **vlan** *number* global configuration command, or it can be learned from another switch using VTP. As mentioned earlier in this chapter, the examples in this book assume that you are not using VTP. If you discover that a VLAN does not exist on a switch, simply configure the VLAN as discussed earlier in the section, "Creating VLANs and Assigning Access VLANs to an Interface."

In addition to checking the configuration, you can check for the status of the VLAN (as well as whether it is known to the switch) using the **show vlan** command. No matter the VTP mode, this command will list all VLANs known to the switch, plus one of two VLAN state values, depending on the current state: either *active* or *act/lshut*. The second of these states means that the VLAN is shut down. Shutting down a VLAN disables the VLAN on that switch only, so *the switch will not forward frames in that VLAN.*

Switch IOS gives you two similar configuration methods with which to disable (**shutdown**) and enable (**no shutdown**) a VLAN. Example 8-11 shows how, first by using the global command [**no**] **shutdown vlan** *number* and then using the VLAN mode subcommand [**no**] **shutdown**. The example shows the global commands enabling and disabling VLANs 10 and 20, respectively, and using VLAN subcommands to enable and disable VLANs 30 and 40, respectively.

Example 8-11 *Enabling and Disabling VLANs on a Switch*

```
SW2# show vlan brief

VLAN Name                             Status    Ports
---- -------------------------------- --------- -------------------------------
1    default                          active    Fa0/1, Fa0/2, Fa0/3, Fa0/4
                                                Fa0/5, Fa0/6, Fa0/7, Fa0/8
                                                Fa0/9, Fa0/10, Fa0/11, Fa0/12
                                                Fa0/14, Fa0/15, Fa0/16, Fa0/17
                                                Fa0/18, Fa0/19, Fa0/20, Fa0/21
                                                Fa0/22, Fa0/23, Fa0/24, Gi0/1
10   VLAN0010                         act/lshut Fa0/13
20   VLAN0020                         active
30   VLAN0030                         act/lshut
```

8

```
40     VLAN0040                          active
1002 fddi-default                        act/unsup
1003 token-ring-default                  act/unsup
1004 fddinet-default                     act/unsup
1005 trnet-default                       act/unsup


SW2# configure terminal
Enter configuration commands, one per line. End with CNTL/Z.
SW2(config)# no shutdown vlan 10
SW2(config)# shutdown vlan 20
SW2(config)# vlan 30
SW2(config-vlan)# no shutdown
SW2(config-vlan)# vlan 40
SW2(config-vlan)# shutdown
SW2(config-vlan)#
```

NOTE The output of the **show vlan brief** command also lists a state of "act/unsup" for the reserved VLAN IDs 1002–1005, with "unsup" meaning "unsupported."

Mismatched Trunking Operational States

Trunking can be configured correctly so that both switches use trunking. However, trunks can also be misconfigured, with a couple of different results: either both switches do not trunk, or one switch trunks and the other does not. Both results cause problems.

The most common incorrect configuration—which results in both switches not trunking—is a configuration that uses the **switchport mode dynamic auto** command on both switches on the link. The word *auto* just makes us all want to think that the link would trunk automatically, but this command is both automatic and passive. As a result, both switches passively wait on the other device on the link to begin negotiations. Example 8-12 highlights those parts of the output from the **show interfaces switchport** command that confirm both the configured and operational states. Note that the output lists the operational mode as "static access" rather than "trunking."

Example 8-12 *Operational Trunking State*

```
SW2# show interfaces gigabit0/2 switchport
Name: Gi0/2
Switchport: Enabled
Administrative Mode: dynamic auto
Operational Mode: static access
Administrative Trunking Encapsulation: dot1q
Operational Trunking Encapsulation: native
! lines omitted for brevity
```

A different incorrect trunking configuration has an even worse result: one switch trunks, sending tagged frames, while the neighboring switch does not trunk, so the neighboring switch discards any frames it receives that have a VLAN tag in the header. When this combination of events happens, the interface works in that the status on each end will be up/up or connected. Traffic in the native VLAN will actually cross the link successfully because those frames have no VLAN tags (headers). However, traffic in all the rest of the VLANs will not cross the link.

Figure 8-14 shows the incorrect configuration along with which side trunks and which does not. The side that trunks (SW1 in this case) enables trunking using the command **switchport mode trunk** but also disables Dynamic Trunking Protocol (DTP) negotiations using the **switchport nonegotiate** command. SW2's configuration also helps create the problem, by using one of the two trunking options that relies on DTP. Because SW1 has disabled DTP, SW2's DTP negotiations fail, and SW2 chooses to not trunk.

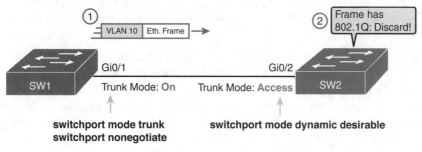

Figure 8-14   *Mismatched Trunking Operational States*

The figure shows what happens when using this incorrect configuration. At Step 1, SW1 could (for example) forward a frame in VLAN 10. However, SW2 would view any frame that arrives with an 802.1Q header as illegal because the frame has an 802.1Q header, and SW2 treats its G0/2 port as an access port. So, SW2 discards any 802.1Q frames received on that port.

The trunking issues shown here can be easily avoided by checking the configuration and by checking the trunk's operational state (mode) on both sides of the trunk. The best commands to check trunking-related facts are **show interfaces trunk** and **show interfaces switchport**. Just be aware that the switches do not prevent you from making these configuration mistakes.

The Supported VLAN List on Trunks

A Cisco switch can forward traffic for all defined and active VLANs. However, a particular VLAN trunk may not forward traffic for a defined and active VLAN for a variety of other reasons. You should learn how to identify which VLANs a particular trunk port currently supports and the reasons why the switch might not be forwarding frames for a VLAN on that trunk port.

The first category in this step can be easily done using the **show interfaces** *interface-id* **trunk** command, which only lists information about currently operational trunks. The best place to begin with this command is the last section of output, which lists the VLANs whose traffic will be forwarded over the trunk. Any VLANs that make it to this final list of VLANs in the command output meet the following criteria:

- The VLAN has not been removed from the *allowed VLAN list* on the trunk (as configured with the **switchport trunk allowed vlan** interface subcommand).

- The VLAN exists and is active on the local switch (as seen in the **show vlan** command).

- The VLAN has not been VTP-pruned from the trunk. (Because this book attempts to ignore VTP as much as possible, this section assumes that VTP is not used and this feature has no impact on any trunks.) The trunk is in an STP forwarding state in that VLAN (as also seen in the **show spanning-tree vlan** *vlan-id* command).

The **switchport trunk allowed vlan** interface subcommand gives the network engineer a method to administratively limit the VLANs whose traffic uses a trunk. If the engineer wants all defined VLANs to be supported on a trunk, the engineer simply does not configure this command. If the engineer would like to limit the trunk to support a subset of the VLANs known to the switch, however, the engineer can add one or more **switchport trunk allowed vlan** interface subcommands.

For instance, in a switch that has configured VLANs 1 through 100, but no others, by default the switch would allow traffic in all 100 VLANs. However, the trunk interface command **switchport trunk allowed vlan 1-60** would limit the trunk to forward traffic for VLANs 1 through 60, but not the rest of the VLANs. Example 8-13 shows a sample of the command output from the **show interfaces trunk** command, which confirms the first list of VLAN IDs now lists VLANs 1–60. Without the **switchport trunk allowed vlan** command, the first list would have included VLANs 1–4094.

Example 8-13 *Allowed VLAN List and List of Active VLANs*

```
SW1# show interfaces trunk

Port        Mode          Encapsulation    Status       Native vlan
Gi0/1       desirable     802.1q           trunking     1


Port        Vlans allowed on trunk
Gi0/1       1-60


Port        Vlans allowed and active in management domain
Gi0/1       1-59


Port        Vlans in spanning tree forwarding state and not pruned
Gi0/1       1-58
```

The output of the **show interfaces trunk** command creates three separate lists of VLANs, each under a separate heading. These three lists show a progression of reasons why a VLAN is not forwarded over a trunk. Table 8-4 summarizes the headings that precede each list and the reasons why a switch chooses to include or not include a VLAN in each list. For instance, in Example 8-13, VLAN 60 has been shut down, and VLAN 59 happens to be in an STP blocking state. (Chapter 9, "Spanning Tree Protocol Concepts," has more information about STP.)

Table 8-4 VLAN Lists in the **show interfaces trunk** Command

List Position	Heading	Reasons
First	VLANs allowed	VLANs 1–4094, minus those removed by the **switchport trunk allowed** command
Second	VLANs allowed and active...	The first list, minus VLANs not defined to the local switch (that is, there is not a **vlan** global configuration command or the switch has not learned of the VLAN with VTP), and also minus those VLANs in shutdown mode
Third	VLANs in spanning tree...	The second list, minus VLANs in an STP blocking state for that interface, and minus VLANs VTP pruned from that trunk

NOTE The companion website includes a video from the CCNA Exam Prep LiveLessons product, named "Troubleshooting VLANs Allowed on a Trunk #1," which works through the three lists of VLANs in the output of the **show interfaces** *interface-id* **trunk** command in more detail.

Mismatched Native VLAN on a Trunk

Unfortunately, it *is* possible to set the native VLAN ID to different VLANs on either end of the trunk, using the **switchport trunk native vlan** *vlan-id* command. If the native VLANs differ according to the two neighboring switches, the switches will cause frames sent in the native VLAN to jump from one VLAN to the other.

For example, if switch SW1 sends a frame using native VLAN 1 on an 802.1Q trunk, SW1 does not add a VLAN header, as is normal for the native VLAN. When switch SW2 receives the frame, noticing that no 802.1Q header exists, SW2 assumes that the frame is part of SW2's configured native VLAN. If SW2 has been configured to think VLAN 2 is the native VLAN on that trunk, SW2 will try to forward the received frame into VLAN 2. (This effect of a frame being sent in one VLAN but then being believed to be in a different VLAN is called *VLAN hopping*.)

Chapter Review

Review this chapter's material using either the tools in the book or the interactive tools for the same material found on the book's companion website. Table 8-5 outlines the key review elements and where you can find them. To better track your study progress, record when you completed these activities in the second column.

8

Table 8-5   Chapter Review Tracking

Review Element	Review Date(s)	Resource Used
Review key topics		Book, website
Review key terms		Book, website
Answer DIKTA questions		Book, PTP
Review config checklists		Book, website
Review command tables		Book
Review memory tables		Website
Do labs		Sim Lite, blog
Watch video		Website

Review All the Key Topics

Table 8-6   Key Topics for Chapter 8

Key Topic Element	Description	Page Number
Figure 8-2	Basic VLAN concept	179
List	Reasons for using VLANs	180
Figure 8-5	Diagram of VLAN trunking	182
Figure 8-6	802.1Q header	183
Table 8-2	Options of the **switchport mode** command	191
Table 8-3	Expected trunking results based on the configuration of the **switchport mode** command	195
List	Definitions of data VLAN and voice VLAN	197
List	Summary of data and voice VLAN concepts, configuration, and verification	200
Table 8-4	Analysis of the three VLAN lists in the output from the **show interfaces** *interface-id* **trunk** command	205

Key Terms You Should Know

802.1Q, trunk, trunking administrative mode, trunking operational mode, VLAN, VTP, VTP transparent mode, Layer 3 switch, access interface, trunk interface, data VLAN, voice VLAN, native VLAN, default VLAN, static access interface

Do Labs

The Sim Lite software is a version of Pearson's full simulator learning product with a subset of the labs, included free with this book. The Sim Lite with this book includes a couple of labs about VLANs. Also, check the author's blog site pages for configuration exercises (Config Labs) at https://blog.certskills.com.

Command References

Tables 8-7 and 8-8 list configuration and verification commands used in this chapter, respectively. As an easy review exercise, cover the left column in a table, read the right column, and try to recall the command without looking. Then repeat the exercise, covering the right column, and try to recall what the command does.

Table 8-7   Chapter 8 Configuration Command Reference

Command	Description
vlan *vlan-id*	Global config command that both creates the VLAN and puts the CLI into VLAN configuration mode
name *vlan-name*	VLAN subcommand that names the VLAN
[no] shutdown	VLAN mode subcommand that enables (**no shutdown**) or disables (**shutdown**) the VLAN
[no] shutdown vlan *vlan-id*	Global config command that has the same effect as the [no] **shutdown** VLAN mode subcommands
vtp mode {server | client | transparent | off}	Global config command that defines the VTP mode
switchport mode {access | dynamic {auto | desirable} | trunk}	Interface subcommand that configures the trunking administrative mode on the interface
switchport access vlan *vlan-id*	Interface subcommand that statically configures the interface into that one VLAN
switchport trunk encapsulation {dot1q | isl | negotiate}	Interface subcommand that defines which type of trunking to use, assuming that trunking is configured or negotiated
switchport trunk native vlan *vlan-id*	Interface subcommand that defines the native VLAN for a trunk port
switchport nonegotiate	Interface subcommand that disables the negotiation of VLAN trunking
switchport voice vlan *vlan-id*	Interface subcommand that defines the voice VLAN on a port, meaning that the switch uses 802.1Q tagging for frames in this VLAN
switchport trunk allowed vlan {add | all | except | remove} *vlan-list*	Interface subcommand that defines the list of allowed VLANs

8

Table 8-8   Chapter 8 EXEC Command Reference

Command	Description
show interfaces *interface-id* switchport	Lists information about any interface regarding administrative settings and operational state
show interfaces *interface-id* trunk	Lists information about all operational trunks (but no other interfaces), including the list of VLANs that can be forwarded over the trunk
show vlan [brief | id *vlan-id* | name *vlan-name* | summary]	Lists information about the VLAN
show vlan [*vlan*]	Displays VLAN information
show vtp status	Lists VTP configuration and status information

CHAPTER 9

Spanning Tree Protocol Concepts

This chapter covers the following exam topics:

2.0 Network Access

2.4 Configure and verify (Layer 2/Layer 3) EtherChannel (LACP)

2.5 Describe the need for and basic operations of Rapid PVST+ Spanning Tree Protocol and identify basic operations

2.5.a Root port, root bridge (primary/secondary), and other port names

2.5.b Port states (forwarding/blocking)

2.5.c PortFast benefits

Spanning Tree Protocol (STP) allows Ethernet LANs to have the added benefits of installing redundant links in a LAN, while overcoming the known problems that occur when adding those extra links. Using redundant links in a LAN design allows the LAN to keep working even when some links fail or even when some entire switches fail. Proper LAN design should add enough redundancy so that no single point of failure crashes the LAN; STP allows the design to use redundancy without causing some other problems.

Historically, the IEEE first standardized STP as part of the IEEE 802.1D standard back in 1990, with pre-standard versions working even before that time. Over time, the industry and IEEE improved STP, with the eventual replacement of STP with an improved protocol: Rapid Spanning Tree Protocol (RSTP). The IEEE first released RSTP as amendment 802.1w and, in 2004, integrated RSTP into the 802.1D standard.

An argument could be made to ignore STP today and instead focus solely on RSTP. Most modern networks use RSTP instead of STP. The most recent models and IOS versions of Cisco switches default to use RSTP instead of STP. Plus, the CCNA 200-301 exam topics mention RSTP by name, but not STP. However, STP and RSTP share many of the same mechanisms, and RSTP's improvements can be best understood in comparison to STP. For that reason, this chapter presents some details that apply only to STP, as a learning tool to help you understand RSTP.

This chapter organizes the material into three sections. The first section presents some core concepts about how both STP and RSTP discover a tree made of nodes (switches) and links so that no loops exist in a network. The second section then takes a brief look at the area for which STP differs the most from RSTP: in how STP reacts to changes in the network. This chapter ends with a third major section that details RSTP, including how RSTP works much better that STP when reacting to changes.

"Do I Know This Already?" Quiz

Take the quiz (either here or use the PTP software) if you want to use the score to help you decide how much time to spend on this chapter. The letter answers are listed at the bottom of the page following the quiz. Appendix C, found both at the end of the book as well as on the companion website, includes both the answers and explanations. You can also find both answers and explanations in the PTP testing software.

Table 9-1 "Do I Know This Already?" Foundation Topics Section-to-Question Mapping

Foundation Topics Section	Questions
STP and RSTP Basics	1–2
Details Specific to STP (and Not RSTP)	3–4
Rapid STP Concepts	5–7

1. Which of the following port states are stable states used when STP has completed convergence? (Choose two answers.)

   a. Blocking

   b. Forwarding

   c. Listening

   d. Learning

   e. Discarding

2. Which of the following bridge IDs wins election as root, assuming that the switches with these bridge IDs are in the same network?

   a. 32769:0200.1111.1111

   b. 32769:0200.2222.2222

   c. 4097:0200.1111.1111

   d. 4097:0200.2222.2222

   e. 40961:0200.1111.1111

3. Which of the following are transitory port states used only during the process of STP convergence? (Choose two answers.)

   a. Blocking

   b. Forwarding

   c. Listening

   d. Learning

   e. Discarding

4. Which of the following facts determines how often a nonroot bridge or switch sends an STP Hello BPDU message?

   a. The Hello timer as configured on that switch.

   b. The Hello timer as configured on the root switch.

   c. It is always every 2 seconds.

   d. The switch reacts to BPDUs received from the root switch by sending another BPDU 2 seconds after receiving the root BPDU.

5. Which of the following RSTP port states have the same name and purpose as a port state in traditional STP? (Choose two answers.)

    a. Blocking

    b. Forwarding

    c. Listening

    d. Learning

    e. Discarding

6. RSTP adds features beyond STP that enable ports to be used for a role if another port on the same switch fails. Which of the following statements correctly describe a port role that is waiting to take over for another port role? (Choose two answers.)

    a. An alternate port waits to become a root port.

    b. A backup port waits to become a root port.

    c. An alternate port waits to become a designated port.

    d. A backup port waits to become a designated port.

7. What STP feature causes an interface to be placed in the forwarding state as soon as the interface is physically active?

    a. STP

    b. EtherChannel

    c. Root Guard

    d. PortFast

Foundation Topics

STP and RSTP Basics

Without some mechanism like Spanning Tree Protocol (STP) or Rapid STP (RSTP), a LAN with redundant links would cause Ethernet frames to loop for an indefinite period of time. With STP or RSTP enabled, some switches block ports so that these ports do not forward frames. STP and RSTP intelligently choose which ports block, with two goals in mind:

■ All devices in a VLAN can send frames to all other devices. In other words, STP or RSTP does not block too many ports, cutting off some parts of the LAN from other parts.

■ Frames have a short life and do not loop around the network indefinitely.

STP and RSTP strike a balance, allowing frames to be delivered to each device, without causing the problems that occur when frames loop through the network over and over again.

> **NOTE** This first major section of the chapter explains details of both STP and RSTP, so this section uses the term *STP/RSTP* to refer to these protocols together. Note that this term is just a convenient shorthand. Later in the chapter, the text will point out differences between STP and RSTP and begin using the terms *STP* and *RSTP* separately, referring to only the specific protocol.

STP/RSTP prevents looping frames by adding an additional check on each interface before a switch uses it to send or receive user traffic. That check: If the port is in STP/RSTP forwarding state in that VLAN, use it as normal; if it is in STP/RSTP blocking state, however, block all user traffic and do not send or receive user traffic on that interface in that VLAN.

Note that these STP/RSTP states do not change the other information you already know about switch interfaces. The interface's state of connected/notconnect does not change. The interface's operational state as either an access or trunk port does not change. STP/RSTP adds this additional state, with the blocking state basically disabling the interface.

In many ways, those last two paragraphs sum up what STP/RSTP does. However, the details of how STP/RSTP does its work can take a fair amount of study and practice. This first major section of the chapter begins by explaining the need for STP/RSTP and the basic ideas of what STP/RSTP does to solve the problem of looping frames. The majority of this section then looks at how STP/RSTP goes about choosing which switch ports to block to accomplish its goals.

The Need for Spanning Tree

STP/RSTP prevents three common problems in Ethernet LANs. All three problems occur as a side effect of one fact: without STP/RSTP, some Ethernet frames would loop around the network for a long time (hours, days, literally forever if the LAN devices and links never failed).

Just one looping frame causes what is called a *broadcast storm*. Broadcast storms happen when any kind of Ethernet frames—broadcast frames, multicast frames, or unknown-destination unicast frames—loop around a LAN indefinitely. Broadcast storms can saturate all the links with copies of that one single frame, crowding out good frames, as well as significantly impacting end-user device performance by making the PCs process too many broadcast frames.

To help you understand how this occurs, Figure 9-1 shows a sample network in which Bob sends a broadcast frame. The dashed lines show how the switches forward the frame when STP/RSTP does not exist.

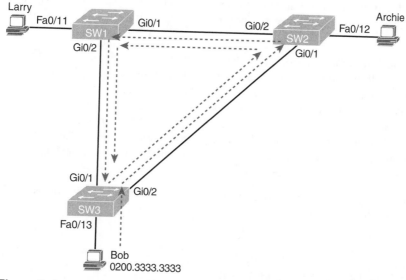

Figure 9-1   *Broadcast Storm*

NOTE Bob's original broadcast would also be forwarded around the other direction, with SW3 sending a copy of the original frame out its Gi0/1 port. To reduce clutter, Figure 9-1 does not show that frame.

Remember that LAN switch? That logic tells switches to flood broadcasts out all interfaces in the same VLAN except the interface in which the frame arrived. In Figure 9-1, that means SW3 forwards Bob's frame to SW2, SW2 forwards the frame to SW1, SW1 forwards the frame back to SW3, and SW3 forwards it back to SW2 again.

When broadcast storms happen, frames like the one in Figure 9-1 keep looping until something changes—someone shuts down an interface, reloads a switch, or does something else to break the loop. Also note that the same event happens in the opposite direction. When Bob sends the original frame, SW3 also forwards a copy to SW1, SW1 forwards it to SW2, and so on.

The storm also causes a much more subtle problem called *MAC table instability*. MAC table instability means that the switches' MAC address tables keep changing because frames with the same source MAC arrive on different ports. To see why, follow this example, in which SW3 begins Figure 9-1 with a MAC table entry for Bob, at the bottom of the figure, associated with port Fa0/13:

> 0200.3333.3333   Fa0/13   VLAN 1

However, now think about the switch-learning process that occurs when the looping frame goes to SW2, then SW1, and then back into SW3's Gi0/1 interface. SW3 thinks, "Hmm...the source MAC address is 0200.3333.3333, and it came in my Gi0/1 interface. Update my MAC table!" This results in the following entry on SW3, with interface Gi0/1 instead of Fa0/13:

> 0200.3333.3333   Gi0/1   VLAN 1

At this point, SW3 itself cannot correctly deliver frames to Bob's MAC address. At that instant, if a frame arrives at SW3 destined for Bob—a different frame than the looping frame that causes the problems—SW3 incorrectly forwards the frame out Gi0/1 to SW1, creating even more congestion.

The looping frames in a broadcast storm also cause a third problem: multiple copies of the frame arrive at the destination. Consider a case in which Bob sends a frame to Larry but none of the switches know Larry's MAC address. Switches flood frames sent to unknown destination unicast MAC addresses. When Bob sends the frame destined for Larry's MAC address, SW3 sends a copy to both SW1 and SW2. SW1 and SW2 also flood the frame, causing copies of the frame to loop. SW1 also sends a copy of each frame out Fa0/11 to Larry. As a result, Larry gets multiple copies of the frame, which may result in an application failure, if not more pervasive networking problems.

Table 9-2 summarizes the main three classes of problems that occur when STP/RSTP is not used in a LAN that has redundancy.

Answers to the "Do I Know This Already?" quiz:

1 A, B **2** C **3** C, D **4** B **5** B, D **6** A, D **7** D

Table 9-2   Three Classes of Problems Caused by Not Using STP in Redundant LANs

Problem	Description
Broadcast storms	The forwarding of a frame repeatedly on the same links, consuming significant parts of the links' capacities
MAC table instability	The continual updating of a switch's MAC address table with incorrect entries, in reaction to looping frames, resulting in frames being sent to the wrong locations
Multiple frame transmission	A side effect of looping frames in which multiple copies of one frame are delivered to the intended host, confusing the host

What Spanning Tree Does

STP/RSTP prevents loops by placing each switch port in either a forwarding state or a blocking state. Interfaces in the forwarding state act as normal, forwarding and receiving frames. However, interfaces in a blocking state do not process any frames except STP/RSTP messages (and some other overhead messages). Interfaces that block do not forward user frames, do not learn MAC addresses of received frames, and do not process received user frames.

Figure 9-2 shows a simple STP/RSTP tree that solves the problem shown in Figure 9-1 by placing one port on SW3 in the blocking state.

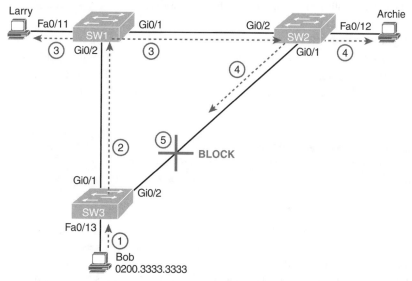

Figure 9-2   *What STP/RSTP Does: Blocks a Port to Break the Loop*

Now when Bob sends a broadcast frame, the frame does not loop. As shown in the steps in the figure:

Step 1.   Bob sends the frame to SW3.

Step 2.   SW3 forwards the frame only to SW1, but not out Gi0/2 to SW2, because SW3's Gi0/2 interface is in a blocking state.

Step 3. SW1 floods the frame out both Fa0/11 and Gi0/1.

Step 4. SW2 floods the frame out Fa0/12 and Gi0/1.

Step 5. SW3 physically receives the frame, but it ignores the frame received from SW2 because SW3's Gi0/2 interface is in a blocking state.

With the STP/RSTP topology in Figure 9-2, the switches simply do not use the link between SW2 and SW3 for traffic in this VLAN, which is the minor negative side effect of STP. However, if either of the other two links fails, STP/RSTP converges so that SW3 forwards instead of blocks on its Gi0/2 interface.

NOTE The term *STP convergence* refers to the process by which the switches collectively realize that something has changed in the LAN topology and determine whether they need to change which ports block and which ports forward.

That completes the description of what STP/RSTP does, placing each port into either a forwarding or blocking state. The more interesting question, and the one that takes a lot more work to understand, is how and why STP/RSTP makes its choices. How does STP/RSTP manage to make switches block or forward on each interface? And how does it converge to change state from blocking to forwarding to take advantage of redundant links in response to network outages? The following pages answer these questions.

How Spanning Tree Works

The STP/RSTP algorithm creates a spanning tree of interfaces that forward frames. The tree structure of forwarding interfaces creates a single path to and from each Ethernet link, just like you can trace a single path in a living, growing tree from the base of the tree to each leaf.

NOTE STP was created before LAN switches even existed, using LAN *bridges* to connect LANs. Today, switches play the same role as bridges, implementing STP/RSTP. However, many STP/RSTP terms still refer to bridge. For the purposes of STP/RSTP and this chapter, consider the terms *bridge* and *switch* synonymous.

The process used by STP, sometimes called the *spanning-tree algorithm* (STA), chooses the interfaces that should be placed into a forwarding state. For any interfaces not chosen to be in a forwarding state, STP/RSTP places the interfaces in blocking state. In other words, STP/RSTP simply picks which interfaces should forward, and any interfaces left over go to a blocking state.

STP/RSTP uses three criteria to choose whether to put an interface in forwarding state:

- STP/RSTP elects a root switch. STP puts all working interfaces on the root switch in forwarding state.

- Each nonroot switch considers one of its ports to have the least administrative cost between itself and the root switch. The cost is called that switch's *root cost*. STP/RSTP places its port that is part of the least root cost path, called that switch's *root port* (RP), in forwarding state.

■ Many switches can attach to the same Ethernet segment, but due to the fact that links connect two devices, a link would have at most two switches. With two switches on a link, the switch with the lowest root cost, as compared with the other switches attached to the same link, is placed in forwarding state. That switch is the designated switch, and that switch's interface, attached to that segment, is called the *designated port* (DP).

NOTE   The real reason the root switches place all working interfaces in a forwarding state (at step 1 in the list) is that all its interfaces on the root switch will become DPs. However, it is easier to just remember that all the root switches' working interfaces will forward frames.

All other interfaces are placed in blocking state. Table 9-3 summarizes the reasons STP/RSTP places a port in forwarding or blocking state.

Table 9-3   STP/RSTP: Reasons for Forwarding or Blocking

Characterization of Port	STP State	Description
All the root switch's ports	Forwarding	The root switch is always the designated switch on all connected segments.
Each nonroot switch's root port	Forwarding	The port through which the switch has the least cost to reach the root switch (lowest root cost).
Each LAN's designated port	Forwarding	The switch forwarding the Hello on to the segment, with the lowest root cost, is the designated switch for that segment.
All other working ports	Blocking	The port is not used for forwarding user frames, nor are any frames received on these interfaces considered for forwarding.

9

NOTE   STP/RSTP only considers working interfaces (those in a connected state). Failed interfaces (for example, interfaces with no cable installed) or administratively shutdown interfaces are instead placed into an STP/RSTP *disabled* state. So, this section uses the term *working ports* to refer to interfaces that could forward frames if STP/RSTP placed the interface into a forwarding state.

NOTE   STP and RSTP do differ slightly in the use of the names of some states like blocking and disabled, with RSTP using the status term *discarding*. However, those minor differences do not change the meaning of the discussions in this first section of the chapter. The upcoming section titled "Comparing STP and RSTP" discusses these differences, both important and minor.

The STP Bridge ID and Hello BPDU

The STA begins with an election of one switch to be the root switch. To better understand this election process, you need to understand the STP/RSTP messages sent between switches as well as the concept and format of the identifier used to uniquely identify each switch.

The STP/RSTP *bridge ID* (BID) is an 8-byte value unique to each switch. The bridge ID consists of a 2-byte priority field and a 6-byte system ID, with the system ID being based on a universal (burned-in) MAC address in each switch. Using a burned-in MAC address ensures that each switch's bridge ID will be unique.

STP/RSTP defines messages called *bridge protocol data units* (BPDU), also called configuration BPDUs, which switches use to exchange information with each other. The most common BPDU, called a Hello BPDU, lists many details, including the sending switch's BID. By listing its own unique BID, switches can tell which switch sent which Hello BPDU. Table 9-4 lists some of the key information in the Hello BPDU.

Table 9-4   Fields in the STP Hello BPDU

Field	Description
Root bridge ID	The bridge ID of the switch the sender of this Hello currently believes to be the root switch
Sender's bridge ID	The bridge ID of the switch sending this Hello BPDU
Sender's root cost	The STP/RSTP cost between this switch and the current root
Timer values on the root switch	Includes the Hello timer, MaxAge timer, and forward delay timer

For the time being, just keep the first three items from Table 9-4 in mind as the following sections work through the three steps in how STP/RSTP chooses the interfaces to place into a forwarding state. Next, the text examines the three main steps in the STP/RSTP process.

Electing the Root Switch

Switches elect a root switch based on the BIDs in the BPDUs. The root switch is the switch with the lowest numeric value for the BID. Because the two-part BID starts with the priority value, essentially the switch with the lowest priority becomes the root. For example, if one switch has priority 4096, and another switch has priority 8192, the switch with priority 4096 wins, regardless of what MAC address was used to create the BID for each switch.

If a tie occurs based on the priority portion of the BID, the switch with the lowest MAC address portion of the BID is the root. No other tiebreaker should be needed because switches use one of their own universal (burned-in) MAC addresses as the second part of their BIDs. So if the priorities tie, and one switch uses a MAC address of 0200.0000.0000 as part of the BID and the other uses 0811.1111.1111, the first switch (MAC 0200.0000.0000) becomes the root switch.

STP/RSTP elects a root switch in a manner not unlike a political election. The process begins with all switches claiming to be the root by sending Hello BPDUs listing their own BID as the root BID. If a switch hears a Hello that lists a better (lower) BID, that switch stops advertising itself as root and starts forwarding the superior Hello. The Hello sent by the better switch lists the better switch's BID as the root. It works like a political race in which a less-popular candidate gives up and leaves the race, throwing his support behind the more popular candidate. Eventually, everyone agrees which switch has the best (lowest) BID, and everyone supports the elected switch—which is where the political race analogy falls apart.

NOTE   A better Hello, meaning that the listed root's BID is better (numerically lower), is called a *superior Hello*; a worse Hello, meaning that the listed root's BID is not as good (numerically higher), is called an *inferior Hello*.

Figure 9-3 shows the beginning of the root election process. In this case, SW1 has advertised itself as root, as have SW2 and SW3. However, SW2 now believes that SW1 is a better root, so SW2 is now forwarding the Hello originating at SW1. So, at this point, the figure shows SW1 is saying Hello, claiming to be root; SW2 agrees and is forwarding SW1's Hello that lists SW1 as root; but SW3 is still claiming to be best, sending its own Hello BPDUs, listing SW3's BID as the root.

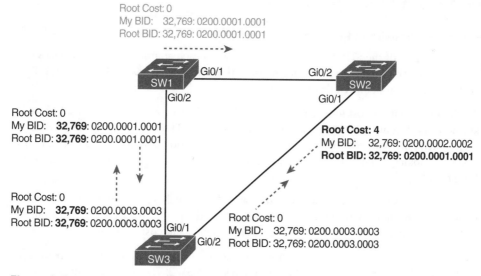

Figure 9-3   *Beginnings of the Root Election Process*

Two candidates still exist in Figure 9-3: SW1 and SW3. So, who wins? Well, from the BID, the lower-priority switch wins; if a tie occurs, the lower MAC address wins. As shown in the figure, SW1 has a lower BID (32769:0200.0001.0001) than SW3 (32769:0200.0003.0003), so SW1 wins, and SW3 now also believes that SW1 is the better switch. Figure 9-4 shows the resulting Hello messages sent by the switches.

Summarizing, the root election happens through each switch claiming to be root, with the best switch being elected based on the numerically lowest BID. Breaking down the BID into its components, the comparisons can be made as

- The lowest priority
- If that ties, the lowest switch MAC address

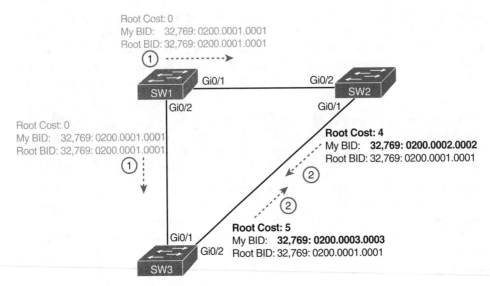

Figure 9-4 *SW1 Wins the Election*

Choosing Each Switch's Root Port

The second part of the STP/RSTP process occurs when each nonroot switch chooses its one and only *root port*. A switch's RP is its interface through which it has the least STP/RSTP cost to reach the root switch (least root cost).

The idea of a switch's cost to reach the root switch can be easily seen for humans. Just look at a network diagram that shows the root switch, lists the STP/RSTP cost associated with each switch port, and identifies the nonroot switch in question. Switches use a different process than looking at a network diagram, of course, but using a diagram can make it easier to learn the idea.

Figure 9-5 shows just such a figure, with the same three switches shown in the last several figures. SW1 has already won the election as root, and the figure considers the cost from SW3's perspective. (Note that the figure uses some nondefault cost settings.)

SW3 has two possible physical paths to send frames to the root switch: the direct path to the left and the indirect path to the right through switch SW2. The cost is the sum of the costs of all the *switch ports the frame would exit* if it flowed over that path. (The calculation ignores the inbound ports.) As you can see, the cost over the direct path out SW3's G0/1 port has a total cost of 5, and the other path has a total cost of 8. SW3 picks its G0/1 port as root port because it is the port that is part of the least-cost path to send frames to the root switch.

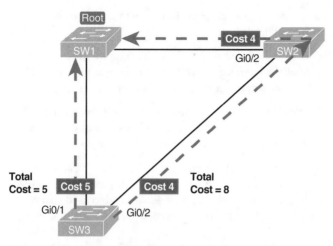

Figure 9-5 *How a Human Might Calculate STP/RSTP Cost from SW3 to the Root (SW1)*

Switches come to the same conclusion but using a different process. Instead, they add their local interface STP/RSTP cost to the root cost listed in each received Hello BPDU. The STP/RSTP port cost is simply an integer value assigned to each interface, per VLAN, for the purpose of providing an objective measurement that allows STP/RSTP to choose which interfaces to add to the STP/RSTP topology. The switches also look at their neighbor's root cost, as announced in Hello BPDUs received from each neighbor.

Figure 9-6 shows an example of how switches calculate their best root cost and then choose their root port, using the same topology and STP/RSTP costs as shown in Figure 9-5. STP/RSTP on SW3 calculates its cost to reach the root over the two possible paths by adding the advertised cost (in Hello messages) to the interface costs listed in the figure.

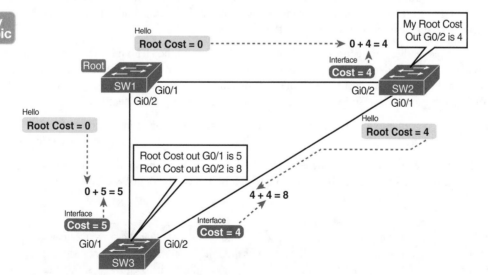

Figure 9-6 *How STP/RSTP Actually Calculates the Cost from SW3 to the Root*

Focus on the process for a moment. The root switch sends Hellos, with a listed root cost of 0. The idea is that the root's cost to reach itself is 0.

Next, look on the left of the figure. SW3 takes the received cost (0) from the Hello sent by SW1 and adds the interface cost (5) of the interface on which that Hello was received. SW3 calculates that the cost to reach the root switch, out that port (G0/1), is 5.

On the right side, SW2 has realized its best cost to reach the root is cost 4. So, when SW2 forwards the Hello toward SW3, SW2 lists a root cost 4. SW3's STP/RSTP port cost on port G0/2 is 4, so SW3 determines a total cost to reach root out its G0/2 port of 8.

As a result of the process depicted in Figure 9-6, SW3 chooses Gi0/1 as its RP because the cost to reach the root switch through that port (5) is lower than the other alternative (Gi0/2, cost 8). Similarly, SW2 chooses Gi0/2 as its RP, with a cost of 4 (SW1's advertised cost of 0 plus SW2's Gi0/2 interface cost of 4). Each switch places its root port into a forwarding state.

Switches need a tiebreaker to use in case the best root cost ties for two or more paths. If a tie occurs, the switch applies these three tiebreakers to the paths that tie, in order, as follows:

1. Choose based on the lowest neighbor bridge ID.

2. Choose based on the lowest neighbor port priority.

3. Choose based on the lowest neighbor internal port number.

Choosing the Designated Port on Each LAN Segment

STP/RSTP's final step to choose the STP/RSTP topology is to choose the designated port on each LAN segment. The designated port (DP) on each LAN segment is the switch port that advertises the lowest-cost Hello onto a LAN segment. When a nonroot switch forwards a Hello, the nonroot switch sets the root cost field in the Hello to that switch's cost to reach the root. In effect, the switch with the lower cost to reach the root, among all switches connected to a segment, becomes the DP on that segment.

For example, earlier Figure 9-4 shows in bold text the parts of the Hello messages from both SW2 and SW3 that determine the choice of DP on that segment. Note that both SW2 and SW3 list their respective cost to reach the root switch (cost 4 on SW2 and cost 5 on SW3). SW2 lists the lower cost, so SW2's Gi0/1 port is the designated port on that LAN segment.

All DPs are placed into a forwarding state; so in this case, SW2's Gi0/1 interface will be in a forwarding state.

If the advertised costs tie, the switches break the tie by choosing the switch with the lower BID. In this case, SW2 would also have won, with a BID of 32769:0200.0002.0002 versus SW3's 32769:0200.0003.0003.

NOTE Two additional tiebreakers are needed in some cases, although these would be unlikely today. A single switch can connect two or more interfaces to the same collision domain by connecting to a hub. In that case, the one switch hears its own BPDUs. So, if a switch ties with itself, two additional tiebreakers are used: the lowest interface STP/RSTP priority and, if that ties, the lowest internal interface number.

The only interface that does not have a reason to be in a forwarding state on the three switches in the examples shown in Figures 9-3 through 9-6 is SW3's Gi0/2 port. So, the STP/RSTP process is now complete. Table 9-5 outlines the state of each port and shows why it is in that state.

Table 9-5 State of Each Interface

Switch Interface	State	Reason Why the Interface Is in Forwarding State
SW1, Gi0/1	Forwarding	The interface is on the root switch, so it becomes the DP on that link.
SW1, Gi0/2	Forwarding	The interface is on the root switch, so it becomes the DP on that link.
SW2, Gi0/2	Forwarding	The root port of SW2.
SW2, Gi0/1	Forwarding	The designated port on the LAN segment to SW3.
SW3, Gi0/1	Forwarding	The root port of SW3.
SW3, Gi0/2	Blocking	Not the root port and not the designated port.

Note that the examples in this section focus on the links between the switches, but switch ports connected to endpoint devices should become DPs and settle into a forwarding state. Working through the logic, each switch will forward BPDUs on each port as part of the process to determine the DP on that LAN. Endpoints should ignore those messages because they do not run STP/RSTP, so the switch will win and become DP on every access port.

Configuring to Influence the STP Topology

STP/RSTP works by default on Cisco switches, so all the settings needed by a switch have a useful default. Switches have a default BID, based on a default priority value and adding a universal MAC address that comes with the switch hardware. Additionally, switch interfaces have default STP/RSTP costs based on the current operating speed of the switch interfaces.

Network engineers often want to change the STP/RSTP settings to then change the choices STP/RSTP makes in a given LAN. Two main tools available to the engineer are to configure the bridge ID and to change STP/RSTP port costs.

First, to change the BID, the engineer can set the priority used by the switch, while continuing to use the universal MAC address as the final 48 bits of the BID. For instance, giving a switch the lowest priority value among all switches will cause that switch to win the root election.

Port costs also have default values, per port, per VLAN. You can configure these port costs, which will in turn impact many switch's calculations of the root cost. For instance, to favor one link, give the ports on that link a lower cost, or to avoid a link, give the ports a higher cost.

Of course, it helps to know the default cost values so you can then choose alternative values as needed. Table 9-6 lists the default port costs suggested by IEEE. IOS on Cisco switches has long used the default settings as defined as far back as the 1998 version of the IEEE 802.1D standard. The latest IEEE standard to suggest RSTP default costs (as of the publication of this book), the 2018 publication of the 802.1Q standard, suggests values that are more useful when using links faster than 10 Gbps.

Table 9-6   Default Port Costs According to IEEE

Ethernet Speed	IEEE Cost: 1998 (and Before)	IEEE Cost: 2004 (and After)
10 Mbps	100	2,000,000
100 Mbps	19	200,000
1 Gbps	4	20,000
10 Gbps	2	2000
100 Gbps	N/A	200
1 Tbps	N/A	20

Of note in regards to these defaults, the cost defaults based on the operating speed of the link, not the maximum speed. That is, if a 10/100/1000 port runs at 10 Mbps for some reason, its default STP cost on a Cisco switch is 100, the default cost for an interface running at 10 Mbps. Also, if you prefer the defaults in the right-side column of Table 9-6, note that Cisco Catalyst switches can be configured to use those values as defaults with a single global configuration command on each switch (**spanning-tree pathcost method long**).

Details Specific to STP (and Not RSTP)

As promised in the introduction to this chapter, the first section showed features that apply to both STP and RSTP. This next heading acts as the turning point, with the next several pages being about STP only. The upcoming section titled "Rapid STP Concepts" then shows details specific to RSTP, in contrast to STP.

Once the engineer has finished all STP configuration, the STP topology should settle into a stable state and not change, at least until the network topology changes. This section examines the ongoing operation of STP while the network is stable, and then it covers how STP converges to a new topology when something changes.

Note that almost all the differences between STP and RSTP revolve around the activities of waiting for and reacting to changes in the topology. STP performed well for the era and circumstances in which it was created. The "rapid" in RSTP refers to the improvements to how fast RSTP could react when changes occur—so understanding how STP reacts will be useful to understand why RSTP reacts faster. These next few pages show the specifics of STP (and not RSTP) and how STP reacts to and manages convergence when changes happen in an Ethernet LAN.

STP Activity When the Network Remains Stable

An STP root switch sends a new Hello BPDU every 2 seconds by default. Each nonroot switch forwards the Hello on all DPs, but only after changing items listed in the Hello. (As a result, the Hello flows once over every working link in the LAN.)

When forwarding the Hello BPDU, each switch sets the root cost to that local switch's calculated root cost. The switch also sets the "sender's bridge ID" field to its own bridge ID. (The root's bridge ID field is not changed.)

Assuming a default Hello timer of 2 seconds on the root switch, each switch will forward the received (and changed) Hellos out all DPs so that all switches continue to receive Hellos every 2 seconds. The following steps summarize the steady-state operation when nothing is currently changing in the STP topology:

Step 1. The root creates and sends a Hello BPDU, with a root cost of 0, out all its working interfaces (those in a forwarding state).

Step 2. The nonroot switches receive the Hello on their root ports. After changing the Hello to list their own BID as the sender's BID and listing that switch's root cost, the switch forwards the Hello out all designated ports.

Step 3. Steps 1 and 2 repeat until something changes.

When a switch fails to receive a Hello, it knows a problem might be occurring in the network. Each switch relies on these periodically received Hellos from the root as a way to know that its path to the root is still working. When a switch ceases to receive the Hellos, or receives a Hello that lists different details, something has failed, so the switch reacts and starts the process of changing the spanning-tree topology.

STP Timers That Manage STP Convergence

For various reasons, the STP convergence process requires the use of three timers, listed in Table 9-7. Note that all switches use the timers as dictated by the root switch, which the root lists in its periodic Hello BPDU messages.

Table 9-7 STP Timers

Timer	Default Value	Description
Hello	2 seconds	The time period between Hellos created by the root.
MaxAge	10 times Hello	How long any switch should wait, after ceasing to hear Hellos, before trying to change the STP topology.
Forward delay	15 seconds	Delay that affects the process that occurs when an interface changes from blocking state to forwarding state. A port stays in an interim listening state, and then an interim learning state, for the number of seconds defined by the forward delay timer.

If a switch does not get an expected Hello BPDU within the Hello time, the switch continues as normal. However, if the Hellos do not show up again within MaxAge time, the switch reacts by taking steps to change the STP topology. With default settings, MaxAge is 20 seconds (10 times the default Hello timer of 2 seconds). So, a switch would go 20 seconds without hearing a Hello before reacting.

After MaxAge expires, the switch essentially makes all its STP choices again, based on any Hellos it receives from other switches. It reevaluates which switch should be the root switch. If the local switch is not the root, it chooses its RP. And it determines whether it is DP on each of its other links.

The best way to describe STP convergence is to show an example using the same familiar topology. Figure 9-7 shows the same familiar figure, with SW3's Gi0/2 in a blocking state, but SW1's Gi0/2 interface has just failed.

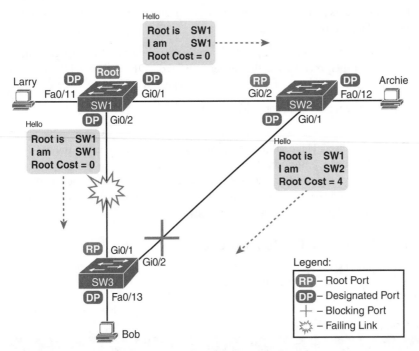

Figure 9-7   *Initial STP State Before SW1-SW3 Link Fails*

In the scenario shown in the figure, SW3 reacts to the change because SW3 fails to receive its expected Hellos on its Gi0/1 interface. However, SW2 does not need to react because SW2 continues to receive its periodic Hellos in its Gi0/2 interface. In this case, SW3 reacts either when MaxAge time passes without hearing the Hellos, or as soon as SW3 notices that interface Gi0/1 has failed. (If the interface fails, the switch can assume that the Hellos will not be arriving in that interface anymore.)

Now that SW3 can act, it begins by reevaluating the choice of root switch. SW3 still receives the Hellos from SW2, as forwarded from the root (SW1). SW1 still has a lower BID than SW3; otherwise, SW1 would not have already been the root. So, SW3 decides that SW1 wins the root election and that SW3 is not the root.

Next, SW3 reevaluates its choice of RP. At this point, SW3 is receiving Hellos on only one interface: Gi0/2. Whatever the calculated root cost, Gi0/2 becomes SW3's new RP. (The cost would be 8, assuming the STP costs had no changes since Figures 9-5 and 9-6.)

SW3 then reevaluates its role as DP on any other interfaces. In this example, no real work needs to be done. SW3 was already DP on interface Fa0/13, and it continues to be the DP because no other switches connect to that port.

Changing Interface States with STP

STP uses the idea of roles and states. *Roles*, like root port and designated port, relate to how STP analyzes the LAN topology. *States*, like forwarding and blocking, tell a switch whether to send or receive frames. When STP converges, a switch chooses new port roles, and the port roles determine the state (forwarding or blocking).

Switches using STP can simply move immediately from forwarding to blocking state, but they must take extra time to transition from blocking state to forwarding state. For instance, when switch SW3 in Figure 9-7 formerly used port G0/1 as its RP (a role), that port was in a forwarding state. After convergence, G0/1 might be neither an RP nor DP; the switch can immediately move that port to a blocking state.

However, when a port that formerly blocked needs to transition to forwarding, the switch first puts the port through two intermediate interface states. These temporary STP states help prevent temporary loops:

- **Listening:** Like the blocking state, the interface does not forward frames. The switch removes old stale (unused) MAC table entries for which no frames are received from each MAC address during this period. These stale MAC table entries could be the cause of the temporary loops.

- **Learning:** Interfaces in this state still do not forward frames, but the switch begins to learn the MAC addresses of frames received on the interface.

STP moves an interface from blocking to listening, then to learning, and then to forwarding state. STP leaves the interface in each interim state for a time equal to the forward delay timer, which defaults to 15 seconds. As a result, a convergence event that causes an interface to change from blocking to forwarding requires 30 seconds to transition from blocking to forwarding. In addition, a switch might have to wait MaxAge seconds (default 20 seconds) before even choosing to move an interface from blocking to forwarding state.

For example, follow what happens with an initial STP topology as shown in Figures 9-3 through 9-6, with the SW1-to-SW3 link failing as shown in Figure 9-7. If SW1 simply quit sending Hello messages to SW3, but the link between the two did not fail, SW3 would wait MaxAge seconds before reacting (20 seconds is the default). SW3 would actually quickly choose its ports' STP roles, but then wait 15 seconds each in listening and learning states on interface Gi0/2, resulting in a 50-second convergence delay.

Table 9-8 summarizes spanning tree's various interface states for easier review.

Table 9-8 IEEE STP (Not RSTP) States

State	Forwards Data Frames?	Learns MACs Based on Received Frames?	Transitory or Stable State?
Blocking	No	No	Stable
Listening	No	No	Transitory
Learning	No	Yes	Transitory
Forwarding	Yes	Yes	Stable
Disabled	No	No	Stable

Rapid STP Concepts

The original STP worked well given the assumptions about networks and networking devices in that era. However, as with any computing or networking standard, as time passes, hardware and software capabilities improve, so new protocols emerge to take advantage of those new capabilities. For STP, one of the most significant improvements over time has been the introduction of Rapid Spanning Tree Protocol (RSTP), introduced as standard IEEE 802.1w.

> **NOTE** Just to make sure you are clear about the terminology: Throughout the rest of the chapter, *STP* refers to the original STP standard only, and use of the term *RSTP* does not include STP.

Before getting into the details of RSTP, it helps to make sense of the standards numbers a bit. 802.1w was actually an amendment to the 802.1D standard. The IEEE first published 802.1D in 1990, and anew in 1998. After the 1998 version of 802.1D, the IEEE published the 802.1w amendment to 802.1D in 2001, which first standardized RSTP.

Over the years, other meaningful changes happened in the standards as well, although those changes probably do not impact most networkers' thinking when it comes to working with STP or RSTP. But to be complete, the IEEE replaced STP with RSTP in the revised 802.1D standard in 2004. In another move, in 2011 the IEEE moved all the RSTP details into a revised 802.1Q standard. As it stands today, RSTP actually sits in the 802.1Q standards document.

As a result, when reading about RSTP, you will see documents, books, videos, and the like that refer to RSTP and include various references to 802.1w, 802.1D, and 802.1Q—and they might all be correct based on timing and context. At the same time, many people refer to RSTP as 802.1w because that was the first IEEE document to define it. However, for the purposes of this book, focus instead on the RSTP acronym rather than the IEEE standards numbers used with RSTP over its history.

> **NOTE** The IEEE sells its standards, but through the "Get IEEE 802" program, you can get free PDFs of the current 802 standards. To read about RSTP today, you will need to download the 802.1Q standard, and then look for the sections about RSTP.

Now on to the details about RSTP in this chapter. As discussed throughout this chapter, RSTP and STP have many similarities, so this section next compares and contrasts the two. Following that, the rest of this section discusses the concepts unique to RSTP that are not found in STP—alternate root ports, different port states, backup ports, and the port roles used by RSTP.

Comparing STP and RSTP

RSTP works just like STP in several ways, as discussed in the first major section of the chapter. To review:

- RSTP and STP elect the root switch using the same rules and tiebreakers.
- RSTP and STP switches select their root ports with the same rules.
- RSTP and STP elect designated ports on each LAN segment with the same rules and tiebreakers.
- RSTP and STP place each port in either forwarding or blocking state, although RSTP calls the blocking state the *discarding* state.

In fact, RSTP works so much like STP that they can both be used in the same network. RSTP and STP switches can be deployed in the same network, with RSTP features working in switches that support it and traditional STP features working in the switches that support only STP.

With all these similarities, you might be wondering why the IEEE bothered to create RSTP in the first place. The overriding reason is convergence. STP takes a relatively long time to converge (50 seconds with the default settings when all the wait times must be followed). RSTP improves network convergence when topology changes occur, usually converging within a few seconds (or in slow conditions, in about 10 seconds).

RSTP changes and adds to STP in ways that avoid waiting on STP timers, resulting in quick transitions from forwarding to discarding (blocking) state and vice versa. Specifically, RSTP, compared to STP, defines more cases in which the switch can avoid waiting for a timer to expire, such as the following:

- RSTP adds a mechanism by which a switch can replace its root port, without any waiting to reach a forwarding state (in some conditions).
- RSTP adds a new mechanism to replace a designated port, without any waiting to reach a forwarding state (in some conditions).
- RSTP lowers waiting times for cases in which RSTP must wait for a timer.

For instance, imagine a failure case in which a link remains up, but for some reason, a non-root switch stops hearing the Hello BPDUs it had been hearing in the past. STP requires a switch to wait for MaxAge seconds, which STP defines based on 10 times the Hello timer, or 20 seconds, by default. RSTP shortens this timer, defining MaxAge as three times the Hello timer. Additionally, RSTP can send messages to the neighboring switch to inquire whether a problem has occurred rather than wait for timers.

The best way to get a sense for these mechanisms is to see how the RSTP alternate port and the backup port both work. RSTP uses the term *alternate port* to refer to a switch's other

9

ports that could be used as the root port if the root port ever fails. The *backup port* concept provides a backup port on the local switch for a designated port. (Note that backup ports apply only to designs that use hubs, so they are unlikely to be useful today.) However, both are instructive about how RSTP works. Table 9-9 lists these RSTP port roles.

Table 9-9   Port Roles in RSTP

Function	Port Role
Port that begins a nonroot switch's best path to the root	Root port
Port that replaces the root port when the root port fails	Alternate port
Switch port designated to forward onto a collision domain	Designated port
Port that replaces a designated port when a designated port fails	Backup port
Port that is administratively disabled	Disabled port

RSTP differs from STP in a few other ways as well. For instance, with STP, the root switch creates a Hello with all other switches, updating and forwarding the Hello. With RSTP, each switch independently generates its own Hellos. Additionally, RSTP allows for queries between neighbors, rather than waiting on timers to expire, as a means to avoid waiting to learn information. These types of protocol changes help RSTP-based switches isolate what has changed in a network and react quickly to choose a net RSTP topology.

The next few pages work through some of those overt RSTP features that differ from STP.

RSTP and the Alternate (Root) Port Role

With STP, each nonroot switch places one port in the STP root port (RP) role. RSTP follows that same convention, with the same exact rules for choosing the RP. RSTP then takes another step beyond STP, naming other possible RPs, identifying them as *alternate ports*.

To be an alternate port, both the RP and the alternate port must receive Hellos that identify the same root switch. For instance, in Figure 9-8, SW1 is the root. SW3 will receive Hello BPDUs on two ports: G0/1 and G0/2. Both Hellos list SW1's bridge ID (BID) as the root switch, so whichever port is not the root port meets the criteria to be an alternate port. SW3 picks G0/1 as its root port in this case and then makes G0/2 an alternate port.

An alternate port basically works like the second-best option for the root port. The alternate port can take over for the former root port, often very rapidly, without requiring a wait in other interim RSTP states. For instance, when the root port fails, or when Hellos stop arriving on the original root port, the switch changes the former root port's role and state: (a) the role from root port to a disabled port, and (b) the state from forwarding to discarding (the equivalent of STP's blocking state). Then, without waiting on any timers, the switch changes roles and state for the alternate port: its role changes to be the root port, with a forwarding state.

Notably, the new root port also does not need to spend time in other states, such as learning state, instead moving immediately to forwarding state.

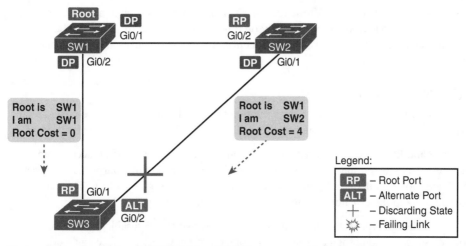

Figure 9-8 *Example of SW3 Making G0/2 Become an Alternate Port*

Figure 9-9 shows an example of RSTP convergence. SW3's root port before the failure shown in this figure is SW3's G0/1, the link connected directly to SW1 (the root switch). Then SW3's link to SW1 fails as shown in Step 1 of the figure.

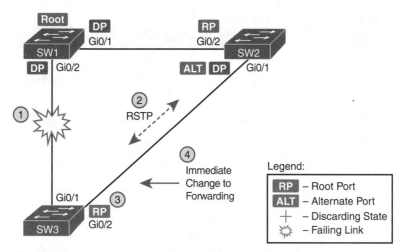

Figure 9-9 *Convergence Events with SW3 G0/1 Failure*

Following the steps in Figure 9-9:

Step 1. The link between SW1 and SW3 fails, so SW3's current root port (Gi0/1) fails.

Step 2. SW3 and SW2 exchange RSTP messages to confirm that SW3 will now transition its former alternate port (Gi0/2) to be the root port. This action causes SW2 to flush the required MAC table entries.

Step 3. SW3 transitions Gi0/1 to the disabled role and Gi0/2 to the root port role.

Step 4. SW3 transitions Gi0/2 to a forwarding state immediately, without using learning state, because this is one case in which RSTP knows the transition will not create a loop.

As soon as SW3 realizes its Gi0/1 interface has failed, the process shown in the figure takes very little time. None of the processes rely on timers, so as soon as the work can be done, the convergence completes. (This particular convergence example takes about 1 second in a lab.)

RSTP States and Processes

The depth of the previous example does not point out all details of RSTP, of course; however, the example does show enough details to discuss RSTP states and internal processes.

Both STP and RSTP use *port states*, but with some differences. First, RSTP keeps both the learning and forwarding states as compared with STP, for the same purposes. However, RSTP does not even define a listening state, finding it unnecessary. Finally, RSTP renames the blocking state to the discarding state and redefines its use slightly.

RSTP uses the discarding state for what STP defines as two states: disabled state and blocking state. Blocking should be somewhat obvious by now: the interface can work physically, but STP/RSTP chooses to not forward traffic to avoid loops. STP's disabled state simply meant that the interface was administratively disabled. RSTP just combines those into a single discarding state. Table 9-10 shows the list of STP and RSTP states for comparison purposes.

Table 9-10   Port States Compared: STP and RSTP

Function	STP State	RSTP State
Port is administratively disabled	Disabled	Discarding
Stable state that ignores incoming data frames and is not used to forward data frames	Blocking	Discarding
Interim state without MAC learning and without forwarding	Listening	Not used
Interim state with MAC learning and without forwarding	Learning	Learning
Stable state that allows MAC learning and forwarding of data frames	Forwarding	Forwarding

RSTP also changes some processes and message content (compared to STP) to speed convergence. For example, STP waits for a time (forward delay) in both listening and learning states. The reason for this delay in STP is that, at the same time, the switches have all been told to time out their MAC table entries. When the topology changes, the existing MAC table entries may actually cause a loop. With STP, the switches all tell each other (with BPDU messages) that the topology has changed and to time out any MAC table entries using the forward delay timer. This removes the entries, which is good, but it causes the need to wait in both listening and learning state for forward delay time (default 15 seconds each).

RSTP, to converge more quickly, avoids relying on timers. RSTP switches tell each other (using messages) that the topology has changed. Those messages also direct neighboring switches to flush the contents of their MAC tables in a way that removes all the potentially loop-causing entries, without a wait. As a result, RSTP creates more scenarios in which a formerly discarding port can immediately transition to a forwarding state, without waiting, and without using the learning state, as shown in the example in Figure 9-9.

RSTP and the Backup (Designated) Port Role

The RSTP backup port role acts as yet another new RSTP port role as compared to STP. As a reminder, the RSTP alternate port role creates a way for RSTP to quickly replace a switch's root port. Similarly, the RSTP backup port role creates a way for RSTP to quickly replace a switch's designated port on some LAN.

The need for a backup port can be a bit confusing at first because the need for the backup port role only happens in designs that are a little unlikely today. The reason is that a design must use hubs, which then allows the possibility that one switch connects more than one port to the same collision domain.

Figure 9-10 shows an example. SW3 and SW4 both connect to the same hub. SW4's port F0/1 happens to win the election as designated port (DP). The other port on SW4 that connects to the same collision domain, F0/2, acts as a backup port.

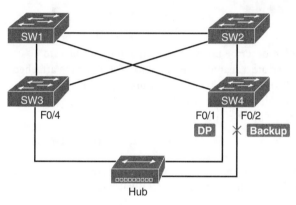

Figure 9-10   *RSTP Backup Port Example*

With a backup port, if the current designated port fails, SW4 can start using the backup port with rapid convergence. For instance, if SW4's F0/1 interface were to fail, SW4 could transition F0/2 to the designated port role, without any delay in moving from discarding state to a forwarding state.

RSTP Port Types

The final RSTP concept included here relates to some terms RSTP uses to refer to different types of ports and the links that connect to those ports.

To begin, consider the basic image in Figure 9-11. It shows several links between two switches. RSTP considers these links to be point-to-point links and the ports connected to them to be point-to-point ports because the link connects exactly two devices (points).

RSTP further classifies point-to-point ports into two categories. Point-to-point ports that connect two switches are not at the edge of the network and are simply called *point-to-point ports*. Ports that instead connect to a single endpoint device at the edge of the network, like a PC or server, are called *point-to-point edge ports*, or simply *edge ports*. In Figure 9-11, SW3's switch port connected to a PC is an edge port.

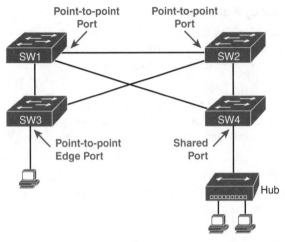

Figure 9-11 *RSTP Link Types*

Finally, RSTP defines the term *shared* to describe ports connected to a hub. The term *shared* comes from the fact that hubs create a shared Ethernet; hubs also force the attached switch port to use half-duplex logic. RSTP assumes that all half-duplex ports may be connected to hubs, treating ports that use half duplex as shared ports. RSTP converges more slowly on shared ports as compared to all point-to-point ports.

Optional STP Features

To close out the chapter, the last few topics introduce a few optional features that make STP work even better or be more secure: EtherChannel, PortFast, and BPDU Guard.

EtherChannel

One of the best ways to lower STP's convergence time is to avoid convergence altogether. EtherChannel provides a way to prevent STP convergence from being needed when only a single port or cable failure occurs.

EtherChannel combines multiple parallel segments of equal speed (up to eight) between the same pair of switches, bundled into an EtherChannel. The switches treat the EtherChannel as a single interface with regard to STP. As a result, if one of the links fails, but at least one of the links is up, STP convergence does not have to occur. For example, Figure 9-12 shows the familiar three-switch network, but now with two Gigabit Ethernet connections between each pair of switches.

With each pair of Ethernet links configured as an EtherChannel, STP treats each EtherChannel as a single link. In other words, both links to the same switch must fail for a switch to need to cause STP convergence. Without EtherChannel, if you have multiple parallel links between two switches, STP blocks all the links except one. With EtherChannel, all the parallel links can be up and working at the same time, while reducing the number of times STP must converge, which in turn makes the network more available.

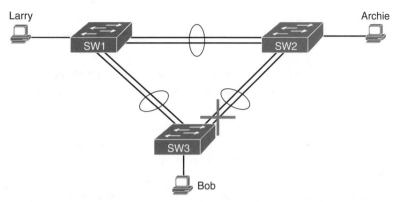

Figure 9-12 *Two-Segment EtherChannels Between Switches*

The current CCNA exam blueprint includes a topic for the configuration of both Layer 2 EtherChannels (as described here) as well as Layer 3 EtherChannels. Chapter 10, "RSTP and EtherChannel Configuration," shows how to configure Layer 2 EtherChannels, while Chapter 17, "IP Routing in the LAN," shows how to configure Layer 3 EtherChannels. Note that Layer 2 EtherChannels combine links that switches use as switch ports, with the switches using Layer 2 switching logic to forward and receive Ethernet frames over the EtherChannels. Layer 3 EtherChannels also combine links, but the switches use Layer 3 routing logic to forward packets over the EtherChannels.

PortFast

PortFast allows a switch to immediately transition from blocking to forwarding, bypassing listening and learning states. However, the only ports on which you can safely enable PortFast are ports on which you know that no bridges, switches, or other STP-speaking devices are connected. Otherwise, using PortFast risks creating loops, the very thing that the listening and learning states are intended to avoid.

PortFast is most appropriate for connections to end-user devices. If you turn on PortFast on ports connected to end-user devices, when an end-user PC boots, the switch port can move to an STP forwarding state and forward traffic as soon as the PC NIC is active. Without PortFast, each port must wait while the switch confirms that the port is a DP. With STP in particular (and not RSTP), the switch waits in the temporary listening and learning states before settling into the forwarding state.

As you might guess from the fact that PortFast speeds convergence, RSTP includes PortFast. You might recall the mention of RSTP port types, particularly point-to-point edge port types, around Figure 9-11. RSTP, by design of the protocol, converges quickly on these point-to-point edge type ports by bypassing the learning state, which is the same idea Cisco originally introduced with PortFast. In practice, Cisco switches enable RSTP point-to-point edge ports by enabling PortFast on the port.

9

BPDU Guard

STP and RSTP open up the LAN to several different types of possible security exposures. For example:

- An attacker could connect a switch to one of these ports, one with a low STP/RSTP priority value, and become the root switch. The new STP/RSTP topology could have worse performance than the desired topology.

- The attacker could plug into multiple ports, into multiple switches, become root, and actually forward much of the traffic in the LAN. Without the networking staff realizing it, the attacker could use a LAN analyzer to copy large numbers of data frames sent through the LAN.

- Users could innocently harm the LAN when they buy and connect an inexpensive consumer LAN switch (one that does not use STP/RSTP). Such a switch, without any STP/RSTP function, would not choose to block any ports and could cause a loop.

The *Cisco BPDU Guard* feature helps defeat these kinds of problems by disabling a port if any BPDUs are received on the port. So, this feature is particularly useful on ports that should be used only as an access port and never connected to another switch.

In addition, the BPDU Guard feature helps prevent problems with PortFast. PortFast should be enabled only on access ports that connect to user devices, not to other LAN switches. Using BPDU Guard on these same ports makes sense because if another switch connects to such a port, the local switch can disable the port before a loop is created.

Chapter Review

One key to doing well on the exams is to perform repetitive spaced review sessions. Review this chapter's material using either the tools in the book or interactive tools for the same material found on the book's companion website. Refer to the "Your Study Plan" element for more details. Table 9-11 outlines the key review elements and where you can find them. To better track your study progress, record when you completed these activities in the second column.

Table 9-11 Chapter Review Tracking

Review Element	Review Date(s)	Resource Used
Review key topics		Book, website
Review key terms		Book, website
Answer DIKTA questions		Book, PTP
Review memory tables		Website

Review All the Key Topics

Table 9-12   Key Topics for Chapter 9

Key Topic Element	Description	Page Number
Table 9-2	Lists the three main problems that occur when not using STP in a LAN with redundant links	215
Table 9-3	Lists the reasons why a switch chooses to place an interface into forwarding or blocking state	217
Table 9-4	Lists the most important fields in Hello BPDU messages	218
List	Logic for the root switch election	219
Figure 9-6	Shows how switches calculate their root cost	221
Table 9-6	Lists the original and current default STP port costs for various interface speeds	224
Step list	A summary description of steady-state STP operations	225
Table 9-7	STP timers	226
List	Definitions of what occurs in the listening and learning states	227
Table 9-8	Summary of 802.1D states	228
List	Key similarities between 802.1D STP and 802.1w RSTP	229
List	Methods RSTP uses to reduce convergence time	229
Table 9-9	List of 802.1w port roles	230
Table 9-10	Comparisons of port states with 802.1D and 802.1w	232

Key Terms You Should Know

blocking state, BPDU Guard, bridge ID, bridge protocol data unit (BPDU), designated port, EtherChannel, forward delay, forwarding state, Hello BPDU, learning state, listening state, MaxAge, PortFast, root port, root switch, root cost, Spanning Tree Protocol (STP), rapid STP (RSTP), alternate port, backup port, disabled port, discarding state

CHAPTER 10

RSTP and EtherChannel Configuration

This chapter covers the following exam topics:

2.0 Network Access

2.4 Configure and verify (Layer 2/Layer 3) EtherChannel (LACP)

2.5 Describe the need for and basic operations of Rapid PVST+ Spanning Tree Protocol and identify basic operations

2.5.a Root port, root bridge (primary/secondary), and other port names

2.5.b Port states (forwarding/blocking)

2.5.c PortFast benefits

This chapter shows how to configure Rapid Spanning Tree Protocol (RSTP) and Layer 2 EtherChannels. The EtherChannel content, in the second major section of the chapter, follows a typical flow for most configuration/verification topics in a certification guide: it reviews concepts, shows configurations, and provides show commands that point out the configuration settings and operational state. The details include how to manually configure a channel, how to cause a switch to dynamically create a channel, and how EtherChannel load distribution works.

The first section of the chapter explores RSTP implementation taking a different approach. Cisco mentions RSTP concepts, but not configuration/verification, in the CCNA exam topics. However, to get a real sense of RSTP concepts, especially some concepts specific to Cisco Catalyst switches, you need to work with RSTP configuration and verification. The first section of the chapter explores RSTP implementation, but as a means to the end of more fully understanding RSTP concepts.

For those of you who, like me, probably would want to go ahead and practice configuring RSTP, do some show commands, and understand more fully, you do have some options:

- Read Appendix O, "Spanning Tree Protocol Implementation," from this book's companion website. The appendix is a chapter from the previous edition of this book, with full details of configuration/verification of STP and RSTP.

- Use the STP/RSTP config labs on my blog site (as regularly listed in the Chapter Review section of each chapter).

"Do I Know This Already?" Quiz

Take the quiz (either here or use the PTP software) if you want to use the score to help you decide how much time to spend on this chapter. The letter answers are listed at the bottom of the page following the quiz. Appendix C, found both at the end of the book as well as on the companion website, includes both the answers and explanations. You can also find both answers and explanations in the PTP testing software.

Table 10-1 "Do I Know This Already?" Foundation Topics Section-to-Question Mapping

Foundation Topics Section	Questions
Understanding RSTP Through Configuration	1–3
Implementing EtherChannel	4–6

1. Which type value on the **spanning-tree mode** *type* global command enables the use of RSTP?

   a. rapid-pvst

   b. pvst

   c. rstp

   d. rpvst

2. Examine the following output from the **show spanning-tree vlan 5** command, which describes a root switch in a LAN. Which answers accurately describe facts related to the root's bridge ID?

   ```
   SW1# show spanning-tree vlan 5

   VLAN0005
       Spanning tree enabled protocol rstp
       Root ID  Priority     32773
                Address      1833.9d7b.0e80
                Cost         15
                Port         25 (GigabitEthernet0/1)
                Hello Time  2 sec Max Age 20 sec Forward Delay 15 sec
   ```

   a. The system ID extension value, in decimal, is 5.

   b. The root's configured priority value is 32773.

   c. The root's configured priority value is 32768.

   d. The system ID extension value, in hexadecimal, is 1833.9d7b.0e80.

3. With the Cisco RPVST+, which of the following action(s) does a switch take to identify which VLAN is described by a BPDU? (Choose three answers.)

   a. Adds a VLAN tag when forwarding a BPDU on trunks

   b. Adds the VLAN ID in an extra TLV in the BPDU

   c. Lists the VLAN ID as the middle 12 bits of the System ID field of the BPDU

   d. Lists the VLAN ID in the System ID Extension field of the BPDU

4. An engineer configures a switch to put interfaces G0/1 and G0/2 into the same Layer 2 EtherChannel. Which of the following terms is used in the configuration commands?

   a. EtherChannel

   b. PortChannel

   c. Ethernet-Channel

   d. Channel-group

5. Which combinations of keywords on the **channel-group** interface subcommand on two neighboring switches will cause the switches to use LACP and attempt to add the link to the EtherChannel? (Choose two answers.)

   a. desirable and active

   b. passive and active

   c. active and auto

   d. active and active

6. A Cisco Catalyst switch needs to send frames over a Layer 2 EtherChannel. Which answer best describes how the switch balances the traffic over the four active links in the channel?

   a. Breaks each frame into fragments of approximately one-fourth of the original frame, sending one fragment over each link

   b. Sends the entire frame over one link, alternating links in sequence for each successive frame

   c. Sends the entire frame over one link, choosing the link by applying some math to fields in each frame's headers

   d. Sends the entire frame over one link, using the link with the lowest percent utilization as the next link to use

Foundation Topics

Understanding RSTP Through Configuration

Cisco IOS switches today typically default to using RSTP rather than STP, with default settings so that RSTP works with no configuration. You can buy some Cisco switches and connect them with Ethernet cables in a redundant topology, and RSTP will ensure that frames do not loop. And even if some switches use RSTP and some use STP, the switches can interoperate and still build a working spanning tree—and you never even have to think about changing any settings!

Although RSTP works without any configuration, most medium-size to large-size campus LANs benefit from some STP configuration. For instance, Figure 10-1 shows a typical LAN design model, with two distribution layer switches (D1 and D2). The design may have dozens of access layer switches that connect to end users; the figure shows just three access switches (A1, A2, and A3). For a variety of reasons, most network engineers make the distribution layer switches be the root.

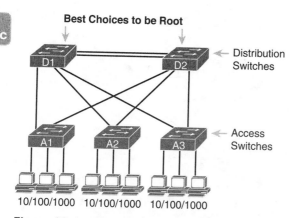

Figure 10-1   *Typical Configuration Choice: Making Distribution Switch Be Root*

> **NOTE**   Cisco uses the term *access switch* to refer to switches used to connect to endpoint devices. The term *distribution switch* refers to switches that do not connect to endpoints but rather connect to each access switch, providing a means to distribute frames throughout the LAN. If you want to read more about LAN design concepts and terms, refer to this book's companion website for Appendix K, "Analyzing Ethernet LAN Designs."

As discussed in the introduction to this chapter, this first section of the chapter examines a variety of STP/RSTP configuration topics, but with a goal of revealing a few more details about how STP and RSTP operate. Following this opening section about RSTP configuration, the next section examines how to configure Layer 2 EtherChannels, and how that impacts STP/RSTP.

The Need for Multiple Spanning Trees

The IEEE first standardized STP as the IEEE 802.1D standard, first published back in 1990. To put some perspective on that date, Cisco did not have a LAN switch product line at the time, and virtual LANs did not exist yet. Instead of multiple VLANs in a physical Ethernet LAN, the physical Ethernet LAN existed as one single broadcast domain, with one instance of STP.

By the mid 1990s, VLANs had appeared on the scene, along with LAN switches. The emergence of VLANs posed a challenge for STP—the only type of STP available at the time—because STP defined a single common spanning tree (CST) topology for the entire LAN. The IEEE needed an option to create multiple spanning trees so that traffic could be balanced across the available links, as shown in Figure 10-2. With two different STP instances, SW3 could block on a different interface in each VLAN, as shown in the figure.

10

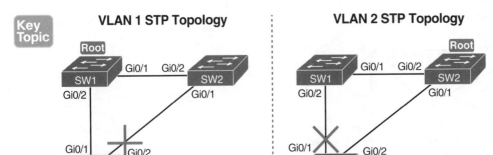

Figure 10-2   *Load Balancing with One Tree for VLAN 1 and Another for VLAN 2*

STP Modes and Standards

Because of the sequence of events over the history of the various STP family of protocols, vendors like Cisco needed to create their own proprietary features to create the per-VLAN spanning tree concept shown in Figure 10-2. That sequence resulted in the following:

■ When STP was the only STP standard back in the 1990s with 802.1D, Cisco created the STP-based Per VLAN Spanning Tree Plus (PVST+) protocol, which creates one spanning tree instance per VLAN.

■ When the IEEE introduced RSTP (in 802.1D amendment 802.1w, in the year 2001), Cisco also created the Rapid PVST+ (RPVST+) protocol. RPVST+ provided more features than standardized RSTP, including one tree per VLAN.

■ The IEEE did not adopt Cisco's PVST+ or RPVST+ into their standards to create multiple spanning trees. Instead, the IEEE created a different method: Multiple Spanning Tree Protocol (MSTP), originally defined in 802.1Q amendment 802.1s.

Figure 10-3 shows the features as a timeline for perspective.

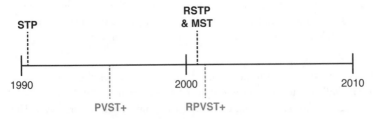

Figure 10-3   *Timeline of Per-VLAN and Multiple STP Features*

Today, Cisco Catalyst switches give us three options to configure on the **spanning-tree mode** command, which tells the switch which type of STP to use. Note that the switches do not support STP or RSTP with the single tree (CST). They can use either the Cisco-proprietary and STP-based PVST+, Cisco-proprietary and RSTP-based RPVST+, or the IEEE standard MSTP. Table 10-2 summarizes some of the facts about these standards and options,

Answers to the "Do I Know This Already?" quiz:
1 A **2** A, C **3** A, B, D **4** D **5** B, D **6** C

along with the keywords used on the **spanning-tree mode** global configuration command. Example 10-1, which follows, shows the command options in global configuration mode.

Table 10-2 STP Standards and Configuration Options

Name	Based on STP or RSTP?	# Trees	Original IEEE Standard	Config Parameter
STP	STP	1 (CST)	802.1D	N/A
PVST+	STP	1/VLAN	802.1D	**pvst**
RSTP	RSTP	1 (CST)	802.1w	N/A
Rapid PVST+	RSTP	1/VLAN	802.1w	**rapid-pvst**
MSTP	RSTP	1 or more*	802.1s	**mst**

* MSTP allows the definition of as many instances (multiple spanning tree instances, or MSTIs) as chosen by the network designer but does not require one per VLAN.

Example 10-1 *STP Status with Default STP Parameters on SW1 and SW2*

```
SW1(config)# spanning-tree mode ?
  mst         Multiple spanning tree mode
  pvst        Per-Vlan spanning tree mode
  rapid-pvst  Per-Vlan rapid spanning tree mode
SW1(config)#
```

The Bridge ID and System ID Extension

To support the idea of multiple spanning trees, whether one per VLAN or simply multiple as created with MSTP, the protocols must consider the VLANs and VLAN trunking. (That's one reason why RSTP and MSTP now exist as part of the 802.1Q standard, which defines VLANs and VLAN trunking.) To help make that work, the IEEE redefined the format of the original BID value to help make per-VLAN instances of STP/RSTP become a reality.

Originally, a switch's BID was formed by combining the switch's 2-byte priority and its 6-byte MAC address. The revised rules divide the original priority field into two separate fields, as shown in Figure 10-4: a 4-bit priority field and a 12-bit subfield called the *system ID extension* (which represents the VLAN ID).

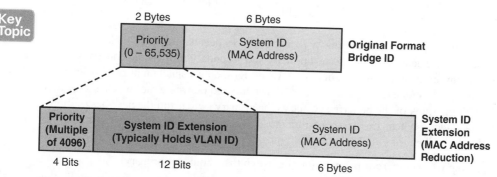

Figure 10-4 *STP System ID Extension*

10

Cisco switches let you configure the BID, but only the priority part. The switch fills in its universal (burned-in) MAC address as the system ID. It also plugs in the VLAN ID of a VLAN in the 12-bit system ID extension field; you cannot change that behavior either. The only part configurable by the network engineer is the 4-bit priority field.

However, configuring the number to put in the priority field may be one of the strangest things to configure on a Cisco router or switch. As shown at the top of Figure 10-4, the priority field was originally a 16-bit number, which represented a decimal number from 0 to 65,535. Because of that history, the configuration command (**spanning-tree vlan** *vlan-id* **priority** *x*) requires a decimal number between 0 and 65,535. But not just any number in that range will suffice; it must be a multiple of 4096, as emphasized in the help text shown in Example 10-2.

Example 10-2 *Help Shows Requirements for Using Increments of 4096 for Priority*

```
SW1(config)# spanning-tree vlan 1 priority ?
  <0-61440>  bridge priority in increments of 4096
SW1(config)#
```

Table 10-3 lists all the configurable values for the STP/RSTP priority. However, do not worry about memorizing the values. Instead, the table lists the values to emphasize two points about the binary values: the first 4 bits in each value differ, but the last 12 bits remain as 12 binary zeros.

Table 10-3 STP/RSTP Configurable Priority Values

Decimal Value	16-bit Binary Equivalent	Decimal Value	16-bit Binary Equivalent
0	0000 0000 0000 0000	32768	1000 0000 0000 0000
4096	0001 0000 0000 0000	36864	1001 0000 0000 0000
8192	0010 0000 0000 0000	40960	1010 0000 0000 0000
12288	0011 0000 0000 0000	45056	1011 0000 0000 0000
16384	0100 0000 0000 0000	49152	1100 0000 0000 0000
20480	0101 0000 0000 0000	53248	1101 0000 0000 0000
24576	0110 0000 0000 0000	57344	1110 0000 0000 0000
28672	0111 0000 0000 0000	61440	1111 0000 0000 0000

Note that while you can set the priority to any of the 16 decimal values in Table 10-3, Cisco provides a convenient means to create a primary and secondary root switch concept without configuring an actual number. In most LAN designs, only a small number of switches would be good candidates to ever be the root switch based on where the switches sit within the topology. Think of the preferred switch as the primary switch and the next-best option as the secondary switch. Then, to configure those two switches to be the two most likely switches to be the root switch, simply configure

spanning-tree vlan *x* **root primary** (on the switch that should be primary)

spanning-tree vlan *x* **root secondary** (on the switch that should be secondary)

These two commands cause the switch to make a choice of priority value but then store the chosen priority value in the **spanning-tree vlan** *x* **priority** *value* command. The command with **root primary** or **root secondary** does not appear in the configuration. When configuring **root primary**, the switch looks at the priority of the current root switch and chooses either (a) 24,576 or (b) 4096 less than the current root's priority (if the current root's priority is 24,576 or less) to the configuration instead. When configuring, **root secondary** always results in that switch using a priority of 28,672, with the assumption that the value will be less than other switches that use the default of 32,768, and higher than any switch configured as **root primary**.

How Switches Use the Priority and System ID Extension

Cisco Catalyst switches configure the priority value using a number that represents a 16-bit value; however, the system ID extension exists as the low-order 12 bits of that same number. This next topic works through connecting those ideas.

When the switch builds its BID to use for RSTP in a VLAN, it must combine the configured priority with the VLAN ID of that VLAN. Interestingly, the configured priority results in a 16-bit priority that always ends with 12 binary 0s. That fact makes the process of combining values to create the BID a little simpler for the switch and possibly a little simpler for network engineers once you understand it all.

First, consider the process shown in Figure 10-5. The top shows the configured priority value (decimal 32768), in 16-bit binary form, with a System ID Extension of 12 zeros. Moving down the figure, you see the binary version of a VLAN ID (decimal 9). At the last step, the switch replaces those last 12 bits of the System ID Extension with the value that matches the VLAN ID and uses that value as the first 16 bits of the BID.

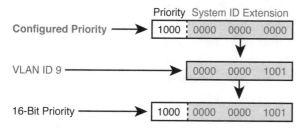

Figure 10-5 *Configured Priority (16-Bit) and System ID Extension (12-Bit) Added*

As it turns out, the process shown in Figure 10-5 is just the sum of the two numbers—both in binary and decimal. To see an example, refer to upcoming Example 10-3, which demonstrates the following details:

- The output shows details about VLAN 9.

- The root switch has been configured with the **spanning-tree vlan 9 priority 24576** command.

- The local switch (the switch on which the command was gathered) has been configured with the **spanning-tree vlan 9 priority 32768** command.

10

- Conveniently, the decimal equivalent of the two switches' first 16 bits—the original 16-bit priority field—can be easily calculated in decimal. In this example:

  - **Root Switch:** 24,576 (priority) + 9 (VLAN ID) = 24585

  - **Local Switch:** 32,768 (priority) + 9 (VLAN ID) = 32777

The output in Example 10-3 matches this logic. The top highlight shows the priority of the root switch (24585), which is the sum of the root switch's priority setting (configured as 24,576) plus 9 for the VLAN ID. The second highlight shows a value of 32,777, calculated as the local switch's priority setting of 32,768 plus 9 for the VLAN ID.

Example 10-3 *Examining the 16-bit Priority as Interpreted in Cisco* show *Commands*

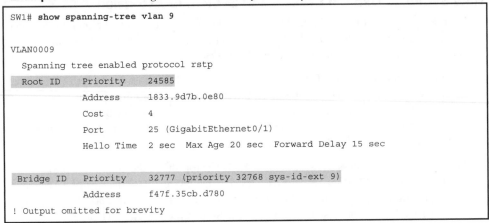

```
SW1# show spanning-tree vlan 9


VLAN0009
  Spanning tree enabled protocol rstp
  Root ID    Priority    24585
             Address     1833.9d7b.0e80
             Cost        4
             Port        25 (GigabitEthernet0/1)
             Hello Time  2 sec  Max Age 20 sec  Forward Delay 15 sec


  Bridge ID  Priority    32777 (priority 32768 sys-id-ext 9)
             Address     f47f.35cb.d780
! Output omitted for brevity
```

RSTP Methods to Support Multiple Spanning Trees

Although the history and configuration might make the BID priority idea seem a bit convoluted, having an extra 12-bit field in the BID works well in practice because it can be used to identify the VLAN ID. VLAN IDs range from 1 to 4094, requiring 12 bits.

For the purposes of discussion, focus on the standard RSTP and its Cisco-proprietary cousin RPVST+. Both use the RSTP mechanisms as discussed in Chapter 9, "Spanning Tree Protocol Concepts," but RPVST+ uses the mechanisms for every VLAN, while standard RSTP does not. So how do their methods differ?

- RSTP creates one tree—the Common Spanning Tree (CST)—while RPVST+ creates one tree for each and every VLAN.

- RSTP sends one set of RSTP messages (BPDUs) in the network, no matter the number of VLANs, while RPVST+ sends one set of messages per VLAN.

- RSTP and RPVST+ use different destination MAC addresses: RSTP with multicast address 0180.C200.0000 (an address defined in the IEEE standard), and RPVST+ with multicast address 0100.0CCC.CCCD (an address chosen by Cisco).

- When transmitting messages on VLAN trunks, RSTP sends the messages in the native VLAN with no VLAN header/tag. RPVST+ sends each VLAN's messages inside that VLAN—for instance, BPDUs about VLAN 9 have an 802.1Q header that lists VLAN 9.

- RPVST+ adds an extra type-length value (TLV) to the BPDU that identifies the VLAN ID, while RSTP does not (because it does not need to, as RSTP ignores VLANs.)

- Both view the 16-bit priority as having a 12-bit System ID Extension, with RSTP setting the value to 0000.0000.0000, meaning "no VLAN," while RPVST+ uses the VLAN ID.

In other words, standard RSTP behaves as if VLANs do not exist, while Cisco's RPVST+ integrates VLAN information into the entire process.

> **NOTE**   Some documents refer to the feature of sending BPDUs over trunks with VLAN tags matching the same VLAN as BPDU tunneling.

Other RSTP Configuration Options

This chapter does not attempt to work through all the configuration options available for RSTP. However, many of the configuration settings may be intuitive now that you know quite a bit about the protocol. This final topic in the first section of the chapter summarizes a few of the configuration concepts. As a reminder, for those interested in continuing on to CCNP Enterprise, you might be interested in reading more about RSTP configuration in the companion website's Appendix O, "Spanning Tree Protocol Implementation."

- **Switch Priority:** The global command **spanning-tree vlan** x **priority** y lets an engineer set the switch's priority in that VLAN.

- **Primary and Secondary Root Switches:** The global command **spanning-tree vlan** x **root primary | secondary** also lets you set the priority, but the switch decides on a value to make that switch likely to be the primary root switch (the root) or the secondary root switch (the switch that becomes root if the primary fails).

- **Port Costs:** The interface subcommand **spanning-tree [vlan** x**] cost** y lets an engineer set the switch's STP/RSTP cost on that port, either for all VLANs or for a specific VLAN on that port. Changing those costs then changes the root cost for some switches, which impacts the choice of root ports and designated ports.

That concludes this chapter's examination of RSTP configuration—now on to Layer 2 EtherChannel!

10

Configuring Layer 2 EtherChannel

As introduced in Chapter 9, two neighboring switches can treat multiple parallel links between each other as a single logical link called an *EtherChannel*. Without EtherChannel, a switch treats each physical port as an independent port, applying MAC learning, forwarding, and STP logic per physical port. With EtherChannel, the switch applies all those same processes to a group of physical ports as one entity: the EtherChannel. Without EtherChannel, with parallel links between two switches, STP/RSTP would block all links except one, but with EtherChannel, the switch can use all the links, load balancing the traffic over the links.

> **NOTE**   All references to EtherChannel in this chapter refer to Layer 2 EtherChannels, not to Layer 3 EtherChannels (as discussed in Chapter 17, "IP Routing in the LAN"). CCNA 200-301 exam topics include both Layer 2 and Layer 3 EtherChannels.

EtherChannel may be one of the most challenging switch features to make work. First, the configuration has several options, so you have to remember the details of which options work together. Second, the switches also require a variety of other interface settings to match among all the links in the channel, so you have to know those settings as well.

This section shows how to configure a Layer 2 EtherChannel, first through manual (static) configuration, and then by allowing dynamic protocols to create the channel. This section closes with some information about some common configuration issues that occur with Layer 2 EtherChannels.

Configuring a Manual Layer 2 EtherChannel

To configure a Layer 2 EtherChannel so that all the ports always attempt to be part of the channel, simply add the correct **channel-group** configuration command to each physical interface, on each switch, all with the **on** keyword, and all with the same number. The **on** keyword tells the switches to place a physical interface into an EtherChannel, and the number identifies the PortChannel interface number that the interface should be a part of.

Before getting into the configuration and verification, however, you need to start using three terms as synonyms: *EtherChannel*, *PortChannel*, and *Channel-group*. Oddly, IOS uses the **channel-group** configuration command, but then to display its status, IOS uses the **show etherchannel** command. Then the output of this **show** command refers to neither an "EtherChannel" nor a "Channel-group," instead using the term "PortChannel." So, pay close attention to these three terms in the example.

To configure an EtherChannel manually, follow these steps:

Step 1. Add the **channel-group** *number* **mode on** command in interface configuration mode under each physical interface that should be in the channel to add it to the channel.

Step 2. Use the same number for all commands on the same switch, but the channel-group number on the neighboring switch can differ.

Example 10-4 shows a simple example, with two links between switches SW1 and SW2, as shown in Figure 10-6. The configuration shows SW1's two interfaces placed into channel-group 1, with two **show** commands to follow.

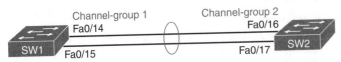

Figure 10-6 *Sample LAN Used in EtherChannel Example*

Example 10-4 *Configuring and Monitoring EtherChannel*

```
SW1# configure terminal
Enter configuration commands, one per line. End with CNTL/Z.
SW1(config)# interface fa 0/14
SW1(config-if)# channel-group 1 mode on
SW1(config)# interface fa 0/15
```

```
SW1(config-if)# channel-group 1 mode on
SW1(config-if)# ^Z


SW1# show spanning-tree vlan 3


VLAN0003
 Spanning tree enabled protocol ieee
 Root ID    Priority    28675
            Address     0019.e859.5380
            Cost        12
            Port        72 (Port-channel1)
            Hello Time 2 sec  Max Age 20 sec  Forward Delay 15 sec

 Bridge ID  Priority    28675 (priority 28672 sys-id-ext 3)
            Address     0019.e86a.6f80
            Hello Time   2 sec  Max Age 20 sec  Forward Delay 15 sec
            Aging Time  300


Interface           Role Sts Cost     Prio.Nbr Type
------------------- ---- --- --------- -------- --------------------------------
Po1                 Root FWD 12        128.64   P2p Peer(STP)


SW1# show etherchannel 1 summary
Flags:  D - down        P - bundled in port-channel
        I - stand-alone s - suspended
        H - Hot-standby (LACP only)
        R - Layer3      S - Layer2
        U - in use      N - not in use, no aggregation
        f - failed to allocate aggregator

        M - not in use, minimum links not met
        m - not in use, port not aggregated due to minimum links not met
        u - unsuitable for bundling
        w - waiting to be aggregated
        d - default port


        A - formed by Auto LAG

Number of channel-groups in use: 1
Number of aggregators:           1


Group  Port-channel  Protocol    Ports
------+-------------+-----------+-----------------------------------------------
1      Po1(SU)         -          Fa0/14(P) Fa0/15(P)
```

Take a few moments to look at the output in the two **show** commands in the example, as well. First, the **show spanning-tree** command lists Po1, short for PortChannel1, as an interface. This interface exists because of the **channel-group** commands using the 1 parameter. STP no longer operates on physical interfaces Fa0/14 and Fa0/15, instead operating on the PortChannel1 interface, so only that interface is listed in the output.

Next, note the output of the **show etherchannel 1 summary** command. It lists as a heading "Port-channel," with Po1 below it. It also lists both Fa0/14 and Fa0/15 in the list of ports, with a (P) beside each. Per the legend, the *P* means that the ports are bundled in the port channel, which is a code that means these ports have passed all the configuration checks and are valid to be included in the channel.

Configuring Dynamic EtherChannels

In addition to manual configuration, Cisco switches also support two different configuration options that then use a dynamic protocol to negotiate whether a particular link becomes part of an EtherChannel or not. Basically, the configuration enables a protocol for a particular channel-group number. At that point, the switch can use the protocol to send messages to/from the neighboring switch and discover whether their configuration settings pass all checks. If a given physical link passes, the link is added to the EtherChannel and used; if not, it is placed in a down state, and not used, until the configuration inconsistency can be resolved.

Most Cisco Catalyst switches support the Cisco-proprietary Port Aggregation Protocol (PAgP) and the IEEE standard Link Aggregation Control Protocol (LACP), based on IEEE standard 802.3ad. Although differences exist between the two, to the depth discussed here, they both accomplish the same task: negotiate so that only links that pass the configuration checks are actually used in an EtherChannel.

One difference of note is that LACP does support more links in a channel—16—as compared to PaGP's maximum of 8. With LACP, only 8 can be active at one time, with the others waiting to be used should any of the other links fail.

To configure either protocol, a switch uses the **channel-group** configuration commands on each switch, but with a keyword that either means "use this protocol and begin negotiations" or "use this protocol and wait for the other switch to begin negotiations." As shown in Figure 10-7, the **desirable** and **auto** keywords enable PAgP, and the **active** and **passive** keywords enable LACP. With these options, at least one side has to begin the negotiations. In other words, with PAgP, at least one of the two sides must use **desirable**, and with LACP, at least one of the two sides must use **active**.

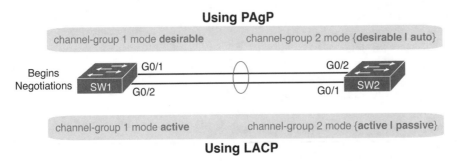

Figure 10-7 *Correct EtherChannel Configuration Combinations*

NOTE Do not use the **on** parameter on one end, and either **auto** or **desirable** (or for LACP, **active** or **passive**) on the neighboring switch. The **on** option uses neither PAgP nor LACP, so a configuration that uses **on**, with PAgP or LACP options on the other end, would prevent the EtherChannel from working.

For example, in the design shown in Figure 10-7, imagine both physical interfaces on both switches were configured with the **channel-group 2 mode desirable** interface subcommand. As a result, the two switches would negotiate and create an EtherChannel. Example 10-5 shows the verification of that configuration, with the command **show etherchannel 1 port-channel**. This command confirms the protocol in use (PAgP, because the **desirable** keyword was configured), and the list of interfaces in the channel.

Example 10-5 *EtherChannel Verification: PAgP Desirable Mode*

```
SW1# show etherchannel 1 port-channel
                Port-channels in the group:
                ---------------------------


Port-channel: Po1
------------
Age of the Port-channel   = 0d:00h:04m:04s
Logical slot/port   = 16/1            Number of ports = 2
GC                  = 0x00020001      HotStandBy port = null
Port state          = Port-channel Ag-Inuse
Protocol            = PAgP
Port security       = Disabled
Load share deferral = Disabled


Ports in the Port-channel:

Index   Load   Port    EC state          No of bits
------+------+------+------------------+-----------
  0     00     Gi0/1   Desirable-Sl        0
  0     00     Gi0/2   Desirable-Sl        0

Time since last port bundled: 0d:00h:03m:57s Gi0/2
```

Physical Interface Configuration and EtherChannels

Even when the **channel-group** commands have all been configured correctly, other configuration settings can prevent a switch from using a physical port in an EtherChannel—even physical ports manually configured to be part of the channel. The next topic examines those reasons.

First, before using a physical port in an EtherChannel, the switch compares the new physical port's configuration to the existing ports in the channel. That new physical interface's settings must be the same as the existing ports' settings; otherwise, the switch does not add the new link to the list of approved and working interfaces in the channel. That is, the physical interface remains configured as part of the PortChannel, but it is not used as part of the channel, often being placed into some nonworking state.

The list of items the switch checks includes the following:

- Speed
- Duplex
- Operational access or trunking state (all must be access, or all must be trunks)
- If an access port, the access VLAN
- If a trunk port, the allowed VLAN list (per the **switchport trunk allowed** command)
- If a trunk port, the native VLAN
- STP interface settings

In addition, switches check the settings on the neighboring switch. To do so, the switches either use PAgP or LACP (if already in use) or use Cisco Discovery Protocol (CDP) if using manual configuration. When checking neighbors, all settings except the STP settings must match.

As an example, SW1 and SW2 again use two links in one EtherChannel from Figure 10-7. Before configuring the EtherChannel, SW1's G0/2 was given a different RSTP port cost than G0/1. Example 10-6 picks up the story just after configuring the correct **channel-group** commands, when the switch is deciding whether to use G0/1 and G0/2 in this.

Example 10-6 *Local Interfaces Fail in EtherChannel Because of Mismatched STP Cost*

```
*Mar 1 23:18:56.132: %PM-4-ERR_DISABLE: channel-misconfig (STP) error detected on
Po1, putting Gi0/1 in err-disable state
*Mar 1 23:18:56.132: %PM-4-ERR_DISABLE: channel-misconfig (STP) error detected on
Po1, putting Gi0/2 in err-disable state
*Mar 1 23:18:56.132: %PM-4-ERR_DISABLE: channel-misconfig (STP) error detected on Po1,
putting Po1 in err-disable state
*Mar 1 23:18:58.120: %LINK-3-UPDOWN: Interface GigabitEthernet0/1, changed state to
down
*Mar 1 23:18:58.137: %LINK-3-UPDOWN: Interface Port-channel1, changed state to down
*Mar 1 23:18:58.137: %LINK-3-UPDOWN: Interface GigabitEthernet0/2, changed state to
down


SW1# show etherchannel summary
Flags:  D - down         P - bundled in port-channel
        I - stand-alone s - suspended
        H - Hot-standby (LACP only)
        R - Layer3       S - Layer2
        U - in use       N - not in use, no aggregation
        f - failed to allocate aggregator

        M - not in use, minimum links not met
        m - not in use, port not aggregated due to minimum links not met
        u - unsuitable for bundling
        w - waiting to be aggregated
```

```
        d - default port

        A - formed by Auto LAG

Number of channel-groups in use: 1
Number of aggregators: 1

Group  Port-channel  Protocol   Ports
------+-------------+----------+------------------------------------------------
1      Po1(SD)          -        Gi0/1(D) Gi0/2(D)
```

The messages at the top of the example specifically state what the switch does when determining whether the interface settings match. In this case, SW1 detects the different STP costs. SW1 does not use G0/1, does not use G0/2, and even places them into an err-disabled state. The switch also puts the PortChannel into err-disabled state. As a result, the PortChannel is not operational, and the physical interfaces are also not operational.

To solve this problem, you must reconfigure the physical interfaces to use the same STP settings. In addition, the PortChannel and physical interfaces must be **shutdown**, and then **no shutdown**, to recover from the err-disabled state. (Note that when a switch applies the **shutdown** and **no shutdown** commands to a PortChannel, it applies those same commands to the physical interfaces, as well; so, just do the **shutdown/no shutdown** on the PortChannel interface.)

EtherChannel Load Distribution

When using Layer 2 EtherChannels, a switch's MAC learning process associates MAC addresses with the PortChannel interfaces and not the underlying physical ports. Later, when a switch makes a forwarding decision to send a frame out a PortChannel interface, the switch must do more work: to decide out which specific physical port to use to forward the frame. IOS documentation refers to those rules as *EtherChannel load distribution* or *load balancing*. Figure 10-8 shows the main idea.

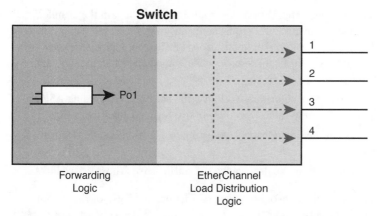

Figure 10-8 *Correct EtherChannel Configuration Combinations*

Configuration Options for EtherChannel Load Distribution

EtherChannel load distribution makes the choice for each frame based on various numeric values found in the Layer 2, 3, and 4 headers. The process uses one configurable setting as input: the load distribution method as defined with the **port-channel load-balance** *method* global command. The process then performs some match against the fields identified by the configured method.

Table 10-4 lists the most common methods. However, note that some switches may support only MAC-based methods, or only MAC- and IP-based methods, depending on the model and software version.

Table 10-4   EtherChannel Load Distribution Methods

Configuration Keyword	Math Uses...	Layer
src-mac	Source MAC address	2
dst-mac	Destination MAC address	2
src-dst-mac	Both source and destination MAC	2
src-ip	Source IP address	3
dst-ip	Destination IP address	3
src-dst-ip	Both source and destination IP	3
src-port	Source TCP or UDP port	4
dst-port	Destination TCP or UDP port	4
src-dst-port	Both source and destination TCP or UDP port	4

To appreciate why you might want to use different methods, you need to consider the results of how switches make their choice. (The discussion here focuses on the result, and not the logic, because the logic remains internal to the switch, and Cisco does not document how each switch model or IOS version works internally.) However, the various load distribution algorithms do share some common goals:

- To cause all messages in a single application flow to use the same link in the channel, rather than being sent over different links. Doing so means that the switch will not inadvertently reorder the messages sent in that application flow by sending one message over a busy link that has a queue of waiting messages, while immediately sending the next message out an unused link.

- To integrate the load distribution algorithm work into the hardware forwarding ASIC so that load distribution works just as quickly as the work to forward any other frame.

- To use all the active links in the EtherChannel, adjusting to the addition and removal of active links over time.

- Within the constraints of the other goals, balance the traffic across those active links.

In short, the algorithms first intend to avoid message reordering, make use of the switch forwarding ASICs, and use all the active links. However, the algorithm does not attempt to send the exact same number of bits over each link over time. The algorithm does try to balance the traffic, but always within the constraints of the other goals.

Whatever load distribution method you choose, the method identifies fields in the message headers. Any messages in the same application flow will then have the same values in the fields used by the load distribution algorithm and will always be forwarded over the same link. For example, when a user connects to a website, that web server may return thousands of packets to the client. Those thousands of packets should flow over the same link in the EtherChannel.

For instance, with the load distribution method of **src-mac** (meaning source MAC address), all frames with the same MAC address flow over one link. Figure 10-9 shows the idea with pseudo MAC addresses, with the load distribution sending frames with source MAC 1 over link 1, source MAC 2 over link 2, and source MAC 3 over link 3.

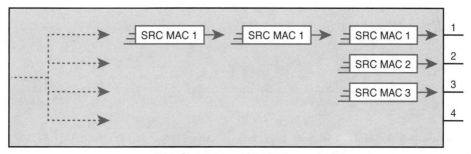

EtherChannel Load Distribution

Figure 10-9   *Distributing All Frames with Same Mac Out Same Interface*

Cisco provides a variety of load distribution options so that the engineer can examine the flows in the network with the idea of finding which fields have the most variety in their values: source and destination MAC, or IP address, or transport layer port numbers. The more variety in the values in the fields, the better the balancing effects, and the lower the chance of sending disproportionate amounts of traffic over one link.

NOTE   The algorithm focuses on the low-order bits in the fields in the headers because the low-order bits typically differ the most in real networks, while the high-order bits do not differ much. By focusing on the lower-order bits, the algorithm achieves better balancing of traffic over the links.

10

The Effects of the EtherChannel Load Distribution Algorithm

Figure 10-10 details a new EtherChannel that will be used in two examples to show the effects of load distribution. The examples will focus on frames sent by switch SW1 in the figure, showing the use of the **test etherchannel load-balance** EXEC command. That command asks the switch to consider some addresses or ports and answer the question: which link would you use when forwarding a message with those address/port values?

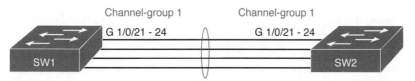

Figure 10-10   *Four-Link EtherChannel*

Example 10-7 shows how switch SW1 distributes traffic when using **src-mac** load distribution. The example lists the output from three of the **test etherchannel load-balance** commands, but note that all three commands use the same source MAC address. As a result, the answer from each command references the same interface (G1/0/22 in this case).

Example 10-7 *Testing with Identical Source MACs When Using* **src-mac** *Balancing*

```
SW1# show etherchannel load-balance
EtherChannel Load-Balancing Configuration:
        src-mac

EtherChannel Load-Balancing Addresses Used Per-Protocol:
Non-IP: Source MAC address
  IPv4: Source MAC address
  IPv6: Source MAC address


SW1# test etherchannel load-balance interface po1 mac 0200.0000.0001 0200.1111.1111
Would select Gi1/0/22 of Po1


SW1# test etherchannel load-balance interface po1 mac 0200.0000.0001 0200.1111.1112
Would select Gi1/0/22 of Po1


SW1# test etherchannel load-balance interface po1 mac 0200.0000.0001 0200.1111.1113
Would select Gi1/0/22 of Po1
```

Example 10-7 makes two important points:

- All three tests list the same outgoing physical interface because (1) the method uses only the source MAC address, and (2) all three tests use the same MAC addresses.

- All three tests use a different destination MAC address, with different low-order bits, but that had no impact on the choice because the method—**src-mac**—does not consider the destination MAC address.

In contrast on that first point, Example 10-8 repeats the **test** commands from Example 10-7. The switch still uses the **src-mac** balancing method, but now with different source MAC addresses in each test. Notice that the source MAC addresses used in the tests differ by just a few bit values in the low-order bits, so as a result, each test shows a different interface choice by SW1.

Example 10-8 *Testing with Source MACs with Low-Order Bit Differences*

```
SW1# test etherchannel load-balance interface po1 mac 0200.0000.0001 0200.1111.1111
Would select Gi1/0/22 of Po1


SW1# test etherchannel load-balance interface po1 mac 0200.0000.0002 0200.1111.1111
Would select Gi1/0/24 of Po1


SW1# test etherchannel load-balance interface po1 mac 0200.0000.0003 0200.1111.1111
Would select Gi1/0/23 of Po1
```

Example 10-9 shows yet a third variation, this time changing the load distribution method to **src-dst-mac**, which means that the switch will consider both source and destination MAC. The example repeats the exact same **test etherchannel** commands as Example 10-7, with the exact same MAC addresses: the source MAC addresses remain the same in all three tests, but the destination MAC addresses differ in the low-order bits. With the chosen destination MAC values differing slightly, switch SW1 happens to choose three different interfaces.

Example 10-9   *Evidence of Source and Destination MAC Load Distribution*

```
SW1# config t
Enter configuration commands, one per line.  End with CNTL/Z.
SW1(config)# port-channel load-balance src-dst-mac
SW1(config)# ^Z
SW1#
SW1# show etherchannel load-balance
EtherChannel Load-Balancing Configuration:
        src-dst-mac

EtherChannel Load-Balancing Addresses Used Per-Protocol:
Non-IP: Source XOR Destination MAC address
  IPv4: Source XOR Destination MAC address
  IPv6: Source XOR Destination MAC address


SW1# test etherchannel load-balance interface po1 mac 0200.0000.0001 0200.1111.1111
Would select Gi1/0/22 of Po1

SW1# test etherchannel load-balance interface po1 mac 0200.0000.0001 0200.1111.1112
Would select Gi1/0/24 of Po1

SW1# test etherchannel load-balance interface po1 mac 0200.0000.0001 0200.1111.1113
Would select Gi1/0/23 of Po1
```

Chapter Review

One key to doing well on the exams is to perform repetitive spaced review sessions. Review this chapter's material using either the tools in the book or interactive tools for the same material found on the book's companion website. Refer to the "Your Study Plan" element for more details. Table 10-5 outlines the key review elements and where you can find them. To better track your study progress, record when you completed these activities in the second column.

Table 10-5   Chapter Review Tracking

Review Element	Review Date(s)	Resource Used
Review key topics		Book, website
Review key terms		Book, website
Answer DIKTA questions		Book, PTP
Review config checklists		Book, website
Review command tables		Book
Review memory tables		Website
Do labs		Blog

Review All the Key Topics

Table 10-6   Key Topics for Chapter 10

Key Topic Element	Description	Page Number
Figure 10-1	Typical design choice for which switches should be made to be root	241
Figure 10-2	Conceptual view of load-balancing benefits of PVST+	242
Table 10-2	STP Standards and Configuration Options	243
Figure 10-4	Shows the format of the system ID extension of the STP priority field	243
List	Facts about RPVST+'s methods versus RSTP	246
List	Steps to manually configure an EtherChannel	248
List	Items a switch compares in a new physical port's configuration to the existing ports in the channel	252

Key Terms You Should Know

Rapid PVST+, PVST+, system ID extension, PAgP, LACP, PortChannel, Channel-group, EtherChannel, EtherChannel Load Distribution, primary root, secondary root

Command References

Tables 10-7 and 10-8 list configuration and verification commands used in this chapter. As an easy review exercise, cover the left column in a table, read the right column, and try to recall the command without looking. Then repeat the exercise, covering the right column, and try to recall what the command does.

Table 10-7   Chapter 10 Configuration Command Reference

Command	Description
spanning-tree mode {**pvst** | **rapid-pvst** | **mst**}	Global configuration command to set the STP mode.
spanning-tree [**vlan** *vlan-number*] **root primary**	Global configuration command that changes this switch to the root switch. The switch's priority is changed to the lower of either 24,576 or 4096 less than the priority of the current root bridge when the command was issued.
spanning-tree [**vlan** *vlan-number*] **root secondary**	Global configuration command that sets this switch's STP base priority to 28,672.
spanning-tree vlan *vlan-id* **priority** *priority*	Global configuration command that changes the bridge priority of this switch for the specified VLAN.
spanning-tree [**vlan** *vlan-number*] **cost** *cost*	Interface subcommand that changes the STP cost to the configured value.
spanning-tree [**vlan** *vlan-number*] **port-priority** *priority*	Interface subcommand that changes the STP port priority in that VLAN (0 to 240, in increments of 16).
channel-group *channel-group-number* **mode** {**auto** | **desirable** | **active** | **passive** | **on**}	Interface subcommand that enables EtherChannel on the interface.

Table 10-8   Chapter 10 EXEC Command Reference

Command	Description
show spanning-tree	Lists details about the state of STP on the switch, including the state of each port.
show spanning-tree vlan *vlan-id*	Lists STP information for the specified VLAN.
show etherchannel [*channel-group-number*] {**brief** | **detail** | **port** | **port-channel** | **summary**}	Lists information about the state of EtherChannels on this switch.

10

Part III Review

Keep track of your part review progress with the checklist shown in Table P3-1. Details on each task follow the table.

Table P3-1   Part III Part Review Checklist

Activity	1st Date Completed	2nd Date Completed
Repeat All DIKTA Questions		
Answer Part Review Questions		
Review Key Topics		
Do Labs		
Review Appendices		
Videos		

Repeat All DIKTA Questions

For this task, answer the "Do I Know This Already?" questions again for the chapters in this part of the book, using the PCPT software.

Answer Part Review Questions

For this task, answer the Part Review questions for this part of the book, using the PTP software.

Review Key Topics

Review all key topics in all chapters in this part, either by browsing the chapters or by using the Key Topics application on the companion website.

Labs

Depending on your chosen lab tool, here are some suggestions for what to do in lab:

Pearson Network Simulator: If you use the full Pearson ICND1 or CCNA simulator, focus more on the configuration scenario and troubleshooting scenario labs associated with the topics in this part of the book. These types of labs include a larger set of topics and work well as Part Review activities. (See the Introduction for some details about how to find which labs are about topics in this part of the book.) Note that the Sim Lite that comes with this book also has a couple of labs about VLANs.

Blog: Config Labs: The author's blog includes a series of configuration-focused labs that you can do on paper, each in 10–15 minutes. Review and perform the labs for this part of the book, as found at http://blog.certskills.com. Then navigate to the Hands-on Config labs.

Other: If using other lab tools, as a few suggestions: Make sure and experiment heavily with VLAN configuration and VLAN trunking configuration.

Dig Deeper with Appendices on the Companion Website

The chapters in Part III of the book recommended the following appendices for extra reading. If you care to read further, consider:

- **Appendix K, "Analyzing Ethernet LAN Designs":** A chapter from the previous edition that discusses design topologies and LAN design with two-tier and three-tier designs, including access and distribution switches.

- **Appendix O, "Spanning Tree Protocol Implementation":** A chapter that works through the configuration and verification commands for STP and RSTP.

- **Appendix P, "LAN Troubleshooting":** A chapter from the previous edition of the ICND2 Cert Guide. This chapter includes topics about VLANs, trunks, and STP and how to troubleshoot each.

Watch Videos

Chapter 8 recommends two videos, one about VLANs and another about the VLAN allowed list on trunks. If you have not watched those videos yet, take a moment to scan back to Chapter 8 on the companion website and watch the videos.

The book makes a big transition at this point. Part I gave you a broad introduction to networking, and Parts II and III went into some detail about the dominant LAN technology today: Ethernet. Part IV transitions from Ethernet to the network layer details that sit above Ethernet and WAN technology, specifically IP Version 4 (IPv4).

Thinking about the network layer requires engineers to shift how they think about addressing. Ethernet allows the luxury of using universal MAC addresses, assigned by the manufacturers, with no need to plan or configure addresses. Although the network engineer needs to understand MAC addresses, MAC already exists on each Ethernet NIC, and switches learn the Ethernet MAC addresses dynamically without even needing to be configured to do so. As a result, most people operating the network can ignore the specific MAC address values for most tasks.

Conversely, IP addressing gives us flexibility and allows choice, but those features require planning, along with a much deeper understanding of the internal structure of the addresses. People operating the network must be more aware of the network layer addresses when doing many tasks. To better prepare you for these Layer 3 addressing details, this part breaks down the addressing details into four chapters, with an opportunity to learn more in preparation for the CCNP Enterprise certification.

Part IV examines most of the basic details of IPv4 addressing and subnetting, mostly from the perspective of operating an IP network. Chapter 11 takes a grand tour of IPv4 addressing as implemented inside a typical enterprise network. Chapters 12, 13, and 14 look at some of the specific questions people must ask themselves when operating an IPv4 network.

Part IV

IPv4 Addressing

CHAPTER 11

Perspectives on IPv4 Subnetting

This chapter covers the following exam topics:

1.0 Network Fundamentals

1.6 Configure and verify IPv4 addressing and subnetting

1.7 Describe the need for private IPv4 addressing

Most entry-level networking jobs require you to operate and troubleshoot a network using a preexisting IP addressing and subnetting plan. The CCNA exam assesses your readiness to use preexisting IP addressing and subnetting information to perform typical operations tasks, such as monitoring the network, reacting to possible problems, configuring addresses for new parts of the network, and troubleshooting those problems.

However, you also need to understand how networks are designed and why. Anyone monitoring a network must continually ask the question, "Is the network working *as designed*?" If a problem exists, you must consider questions such as "What happens when the network works normally, and what is different right now?" Both questions require you to understand the intended design of the network, including details of the IP addressing and subnetting design.

This chapter provides some perspectives and answers for the bigger issues in IPv4 addressing. What addresses can be used so that they work properly? What addresses should be used? When told to use certain numbers, what does that tell you about the choices made by some other network engineer? How do these choices impact the practical job of configuring switches, routers, hosts, and operating the network on a daily basis? This chapter hopes to answer these questions while revealing details of how IPv4 addresses work.

"Do I Know This Already?" Quiz

Take the quiz (either here or use the PTP software) if you want to use the score to help you decide how much time to spend on this chapter. The letter answers are listed at the bottom of the page following the quiz. Appendix C, found both at the end of the book as well as on the companion website, includes both the answers and explanations. You can also find both answers and explanations in the PTP testing software.

Table 11-1 "Do I Know This Already?" Foundation Topics Section-to-Question Mapping

Foundation Topics Section	Questions
Analyze Requirements	1–3
Make Design Choices	4–7

1. Host A is a PC, connected to switch SW1 and assigned to VLAN 1. Which of the following are typically assigned an IP address in the same subnet as host A? (Choose two answers.)

   a. The local router's WAN interface

   b. The local router's LAN interface

   c. All other hosts attached to the same switch

   d. Other hosts attached to the same switch and also in VLAN 1

2. Why does the formula for the number of hosts per subnet ($2^H - 2$) require the subtraction of two hosts?

   a. To reserve two addresses for redundant default gateways (routers)

   b. To reserve the two addresses required for DHCP operation

   c. To reserve addresses for the subnet ID and default gateway (router)

   d. To reserve addresses for the subnet broadcast address and subnet ID

3. A Class B network needs to be subnetted such that it supports 100 subnets and 100 hosts/subnet. Which of the following answers list a workable combination for the number of network, subnet, and host bits? (Choose two answers.)

   a. Network = 16, subnet = 7, host = 7

   b. Network = 16, subnet = 8, host = 8

   c. Network = 16, subnet = 9, host = 7

   d. Network = 8, subnet = 7, host = 17

4. Which of the following are private IP networks? (Choose two answers.)

   a. 172.31.0.0

   b. 172.32.0.0

   c. 192.168.255.0

   d. 192.1.168.0

   e. 11.0.0.0

5. Which of the following are public IP networks? (Choose three answers.)

   a. 9.0.0.0

   b. 172.30.0.0

   c. 192.168.255.0

   d. 192.1.168.0

   e. 1.0.0.0

6. Before Class B network 172.16.0.0 is subnetted by a network engineer, what parts of the structure of the IP addresses in this network already exist, with a specific size? (Choose two answers.)

   a. Network

   b. Subnet

   c. Host

   d. Broadcast

7. A network engineer spends time thinking about the entire Class B network 172.16.0.0 and how to subnet that network. He then chooses how to subnet this Class B network and creates an addressing and subnetting plan, on paper, showing his choices. If you compare his thoughts about this network before subnetting the network to his thoughts about this network after mentally subnetting the network, which of the following occurred to the parts of the structure of addresses in this network?

   a. The subnet part got smaller.

   b. The host part got smaller.

   c. The network part got smaller.

   d. The host part was removed.

   e. The network part was removed.

Foundation Topics

Introduction to Subnetting

Say you just happened to be at the sandwich shop when it was selling the world's longest sandwich. You're pretty hungry, so you go for it. Now you have one sandwich, but because it's over 2 kilometers long, you realize it's a bit more than you need for lunch all by yourself. To make the sandwich more useful (and more portable), you chop the sandwich into meal-size pieces and give the pieces to other folks around you who are also ready for lunch.

Huh? Well, subnetting, at least the main concept, is similar to this sandwich story. You start with one network, but it is just one large network. As a single large entity, it might not be useful, and it is probably far too large. To make it useful, you chop it into smaller pieces, called subnets, and assign those subnets to be used in different parts of the enterprise internetwork.

This short first section of the chapter introduces IP subnetting. First, it shows the general ideas behind a completed subnet design that indeed chops (or subnets) one network into subnets. The rest of this section describes the many design steps that you would take to create just such a subnet design. By the end of this section, you should have the right context to then read through the subnetting design steps introduced throughout the rest of this chapter.

NOTE   All the chapters from this chapter up until Chapter 22, "Fundamentals of IP Version 6," focus on IPv4 rather than IPv6. All references to *IP* refer to IPv4 unless otherwise stated.

Subnetting Defined Through a Simple Example

An IP network—in other words, a Class A, B, or C network—is simply a set of consecutively numbered IP addresses that follows some preset rules. These Class A, B, and C rules define that for a given network, all the addresses in the network have the same value in some of the octets of the addresses. For example, Class B network 172.16.0.0 consists of all IP addresses that begin with 172.16: 172.16.0.0, 172.16.0.1, 172.16.0.2, and so on, through 172.16.255.255. Another example: Class A network 10.0.0.0 includes all addresses that begin with 10.

An IP subnet is simply a subset of a Class A, B, or C network. In fact, the word *subnet* is a shortened version of the phrase *subdivided network*. For example, one subnet of Class B network 172.16.0.0 could be the set of all IP addresses that begin with 172.16.1, and would include 172.16.1.0, 172.16.1.1, 172.16.1.2, and so on, up through 172.16.1.255. Another subnet of that same Class B network could be all addresses that begin with 172.16.2.

To give you a general idea, Figure 11-1 shows some basic documentation from a completed subnet design that could be used when an engineer subnets Class B network 172.16.0.0.

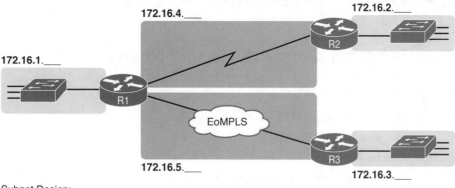

Subnet Design:

| Class B 172.16.0.0 |
| First 3 Octets are Equal |

Figure 11-1 *Subnet Plan Document*

The design shows five subnets—one for each of the three LANs and one each for the two WAN links. The small text note shows the rationale used by the engineer for the subnets: each subnet includes addresses that have the same value in the first three octets. For example, for the LAN on the left, the number shows 172.16.1.__, meaning "all addresses that begin with 172.16.1." Also, note that the design, as shown, does not use all the addresses in Class B network 172.16.0.0, so the engineer has left plenty of room for growth.

Operational View Versus Design View of Subnetting

Most IT jobs require you to work with subnetting from an operational view. That is, someone else, before you got the job, designed how IP addressing and subnetting would work for that particular enterprise network. You need to interpret what someone else has already chosen.

To fully understand IP addressing and subnetting, you need to think about subnetting from both a design and operational perspective. For example, Figure 11-1 simply states that in all these subnets, the first three octets must be equal. Why was that convention chosen? What alternatives exist? Would those alternatives be better for your internetwork today? All these questions relate more to subnetting design rather than to operation.

To help you see both perspectives, this chapter focuses more on design issues by moving through the entire design process for the purpose of introducing the bigger picture of IP subnetting. The next three chapters each take one topic from this chapter and examine it more closely but more from an operational perspective: how to use those ideas in real networks.

The remaining three main sections of this chapter examine each of the steps listed in Figure 11-2, in sequence.

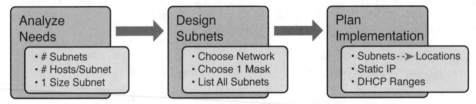

Figure 11-2   *Subnet Planning, Design, and Implementation Tasks*

Analyze Subnetting and Addressing Needs

This section discusses the meaning of four basic questions that can be used to analyze the addressing and subnetting needs for any new or changing enterprise network:

1. Which hosts should be grouped together into a subnet?
2. How many subnets does this internetwork require?
3. How many host IP addresses does each subnet require?
4. Will we use a single subnet size for simplicity, or not?

Rules About Which Hosts Are in Which Subnet

Every device that connects to an IP internetwork needs to have an IP address. These devices include computers used by end users, servers, mobile phones, laptops, IP phones, tablets, and networking devices like routers, switches, and firewalls. In short, any device that uses IP to send and receive packets needs an IP address.

> **NOTE**   In a discussion of IP addressing, the term *network* has specific meaning: a Class A, B, or C IP network. To avoid confusion with that use of the term *network*, this book uses the terms *internetwork* and *enterprise network* when referring to a collection of hosts, routers, switches, and so on.

Answers to the "Do I Know This Already?" quiz:

1 B, D **2** D **3** B, C **4** A, C **5** A, D, E **6** A, C **7** B

The IP addresses must be assigned according to some basic rules—and for good reasons. To make routing work efficiently, IP addressing rules group addresses into groups called subnets. The rules are as follows:

- Addresses in the same subnet are not separated by a router.
- Addresses in different subnets are separated by at least one router.

Figure 11-3 shows the general concept, with hosts A and B in one subnet and host C in another. In particular, note that hosts A and B are not separated from each other by any routers. However, host C, separated from A and B by at least one router, must be in a different subnet.

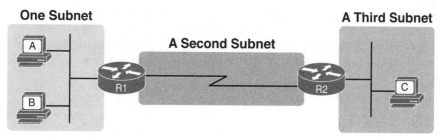

Figure 11-3 *PC A and B in One Subnet and PC C in a Different Subnet*

The idea that hosts on the same link must be in the same subnet is much like the postal code concept. All mailing addresses in the same town use the same postal code (ZIP codes in the United States). Addresses in another town, whether relatively nearby or on the other side of the country, have a different postal code. The postal code gives the postal service a better ability to automatically sort the mail to deliver it to the right location. For the same general reasons, hosts on the same LAN are in the same subnet, and hosts in different LANs are in different subnets.

Note that the point-to-point WAN link in the figure also needs a subnet. Figure 11-3 shows Router R1 connected to the LAN subnet on the left and to a WAN subnet on the right. Router R2 connects to that same WAN subnet. To do so, both R1 and R2 will have IP addresses on their WAN interfaces, and the addresses will be in the same subnet. (An Ethernet WAN link has the same IP addressing needs, with each of the two routers having an IP address in the same subnet.)

The Ethernet LANs in Figure 11-3 also show a slightly different style of drawing, using simple lines with no Ethernet switch. Drawings of Ethernet LANs when the details of the LAN switches do not matter simply show each device connected to the same line, as shown in Figure 11-3. (This kind of drawing mimics the original Ethernet cabling before switches and hubs existed.)

Finally, because the routers' main job is to forward packets from one subnet to another, routers typically connect to multiple subnets. For example, in this case, Router R1 connects to one LAN subnet on the left and one WAN subnet on the right. To do so, R1 will be configured with two different IP addresses, one per interface. These addresses will be in different subnets because the interfaces connect the router to different subnets.

Determining the Number of Subnets

To determine the number of subnets required, the engineer must think about the internetwork as documented and count the locations that need a subnet. To do so, the engineer requires access to network diagrams, VLAN configuration details, and details about WAN links. For the types of links discussed in this book, you should plan for one subnet for every

- VLAN
- Point-to-point serial link
- Ethernet WAN (Ethernet Line Service)

> **NOTE** Other WAN technologies outside the scope of the CCNA exam topics allow subnetting options other than one subnet per pair of routers on the WAN (as shown here). However, this book only uses point-to-point WAN technologies—serial links and Ethernet WAN links—that have one subnet for each point-to-point WAN connection between two routers.

For example, imagine that the network planner has only Figure 11-4 on which to base the subnet design.

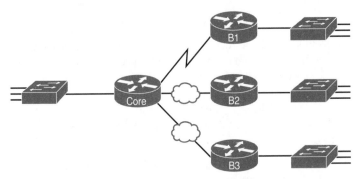

Figure 11-4 *Four-Site Internetwork with Small Central Site*

The number of subnets required cannot be fully predicted with only this figure. Certainly, three subnets will be needed for the WAN links, one per link. However, each LAN switch can be configured with a single VLAN or with multiple VLANs. You can be certain that you need at least one subnet for the LAN at each site, but you might need more.

Next, consider the more detailed version of the same figure shown in Figure 11-5. In this case, the figure shows VLAN counts in addition to the same Layer 3 topology (the routers and the links connected to the routers). It also shows that the central site has many more switches, but the key fact on the left, regardless of how many switches exist, is that the central site has a total of 12 VLANs. Similarly, the figure lists each branch as having two VLANs. Along with the same three WAN subnets, this internetwork requires 21 subnets.

Finally, in a real job, you would consider the needs today as well as how much growth you expect in the internetwork over time. Any subnetting plan should include a reasonable estimate of the number of subnets you need to meet future needs.

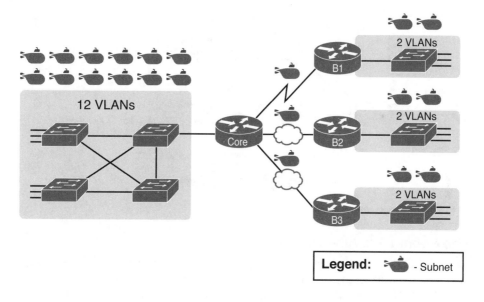

Figure 11-5   *Four-Site Internetwork with Larger Central Site*

Determining the Number of Hosts per Subnet

Determining the number of hosts per subnet requires knowing a few simple concepts and then doing a lot of research and questioning. Every device that connects to a subnet needs an IP address. For a totally new network, you can look at business plans—numbers of people at the site, devices on order, and so on—to get some idea of the possible devices. When expanding an existing network to add new sites, you can use existing sites as a point of comparison and then find out which sites will get bigger or smaller. And don't forget to count the router interface IP address in each subnet and the switch IP address used to remotely manage the switch.

Instead of gathering data for each and every site, planners often just use a few typical sites for planning purposes. For example, maybe you have some large sales offices and some small sales offices. You might dig in and learn a lot about only one large sales office and only one small sales office. Add that analysis to the fact that point-to-point links need a subnet with just two addresses, plus any analysis of more one-of-a-kind subnets, and you have enough information to plan the addressing and subnetting design.

For example, in Figure 11-6, the engineer has built a diagram that shows the number of hosts per LAN subnet in the largest branch, B1. For the two other branches, the engineer did not bother to dig to find out the number of required hosts. As long as the number of required IP addresses at sites B2 and B3 stays below the estimate of 50, based on larger site B1, the engineer can plan for 50 hosts in each branch LAN subnet and have plenty of addresses per subnet.

11

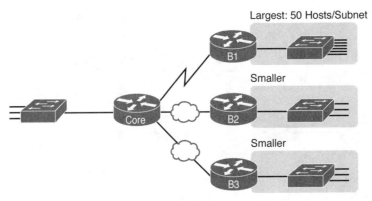

Figure 11-6   *Large Branch B1 with 50 Hosts/Subnet*

One Size Subnet Fits All—Or Not

The final choice in the initial planning step is to decide whether you will use a simpler design by using a one-size-subnet-fits-all philosophy. A subnet's size, or length, is simply the number of usable IP addresses in the subnet. A subnetting design can either use one size subnet or varied sizes of subnets, with pros and cons for each choice.

Defining the Size of a Subnet

Before you finish this book, you will learn all the details of how to determine the size of the subnet. For now, you just need to know a few specific facts about the size of subnets. Chapter 12, "Analyzing Classful IPv4 Networks," and Chapter 13, "Analyzing Subnet Masks," give you a progressively deeper knowledge of the details.

The engineer assigns each subnet a *subnet mask*, and that mask, among other things, defines the size of that subnet. The mask sets aside a number of *host bits* whose purpose is to number different host IP addresses in that subnet. Because you can number 2^x things with x bits, if the mask defines H host bits, the subnet contains 2^H unique numeric values.

However, the subnet's size is not 2^H. It's $2^H - 2$ because two numbers in each subnet are reserved for other purposes. Each subnet reserves the numerically lowest value for the *subnet number* and the numerically highest value as the *subnet broadcast address*. As a result, the number of usable IP addresses per subnet is $2^H - 2$.

> **NOTE** The terms *subnet number*, *subnet ID*, and *subnet address* all refer to the number that represents or identifies a subnet.

Figure 11-7 shows the general concept behind the three-part structure of an IP address, focusing on the host part and the resulting subnet size.

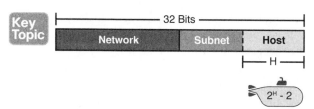

Figure 11-7   *Subnet Size Concepts*

One Size Subnet Fits All

To choose to use a single-size subnet in an enterprise network, you must use the same mask for all subnets because the mask defines the size of the subnet. But which mask?

One requirement to consider when choosing that one mask is this: that one mask must provide enough host IP addresses to support the largest subnet. To do so, the number of host bits (H) defined by the mask must be large enough so that $2^H - 2$ is larger than (or equal to) the number of host IP addresses required in the largest subnet.

For example, consider Figure 11-8. It shows the required number of hosts per LAN subnet. (The figure ignores the subnets on the WAN links, which require only two IP addresses each.) The branch LAN subnets require only 50 host addresses, but the main site LAN subnet requires 200 host addresses. To accommodate the largest subnet, you need at least 8 host bits. Seven host bits would not be enough because $2^7 - 2 = 126$. Eight host bits would be enough because $2^8 - 2 = 254$, which is more than enough to support 200 hosts in a subnet.

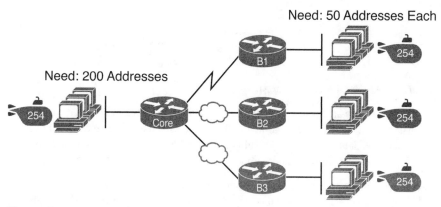

Figure 11-8   *Network Using One Subnet Size*

What's the big advantage when using a single-size subnet? Operational simplicity. In other words, keeping it simple. Everyone on the IT staff who has to work with networking can get used to working with one mask—and one mask only. Staff members will be able to answer all subnetting questions more easily because everyone gets used to doing subnetting math with that one mask.

The big disadvantage for using a single-size subnet is that it wastes IP addresses. For example, in Figure 11-8, all the branch LAN subnets support 254 addresses, while the largest branch subnet needs only 50 addresses. The WAN subnets only need two IP addresses, but each supports 254 addresses, again wasting more IP addresses.

The wasted IP addresses do not actually cause a problem in most cases, however. Most organizations use private IP networks in their enterprise internetworks, and a single Class A or Class B private network can supply plenty of IP addresses, even with the waste.

Multiple Subnet Sizes (Variable-Length Subnet Masks)

To create multiple sizes of subnets in one Class A, B, or C network, the engineer must create some subnets using one mask, some with another, and so on. Different masks mean different numbers of host bits, and a different number of hosts in some subnets based on the $2^H - 2$ formula.

For example, consider the requirements listed earlier in Figure 11-8. It showed one LAN subnet on the left that needs 200 host addresses, three branch subnets that need 50 addresses, and three WAN links that need two addresses. To meet those needs, but waste fewer IP addresses, three subnet masks could be used, creating subnets of three different sizes, as shown in Figure 11-9.

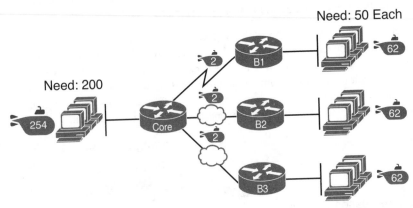

Figure 11-9 *Three Masks, Three Subnet Sizes*

The smaller subnets now waste fewer IP addresses compared to the design shown earlier in Figure 11-8. The subnets on the right that need 50 IP addresses have subnets with 6 host bits, for $2^6 - 2 = 62$ available addresses per subnet. The WAN links use masks with 2 host bits, for $2^2 - 2 = 2$ available addresses per subnet.

However, some are still wasted because you cannot set the size of the subnet as some arbitrary size. All subnets will be a size based on the $2^H - 2$ formula, with H being the number of host bits defined by the mask for each subnet.

One Mask for All Subnets, or More Than One

For the most part, this book explains subnetting using designs that use a single mask, creating a single subnet size for all subnets. Why? First, it makes the process of learning subnetting easier. Second, some types of analysis that you can do about a network—specifically, calculating the number of subnets in the classful network—only make sense when a single mask is used.

However, you still need to be ready to work with designs that use more than one mask in different subnets of the same Class A, B, or C network. In fact, a design that does just that is said to be using *variable-length subnet masks (VLSM)*. For example, the internetwork in Figure 11-10 shows 11 subnets, two with a mask of /30, and nine with a mask of /24. By using more than one mask among all the subnets of one Class A network (10.0.0.0), the design uses VLSM.

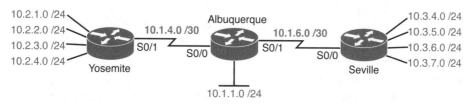

Figure 11-10   *Internetwork with VLSM: Network 10.0.0.0, >1 Mask*

For the current CCNA 200-301 exam, using VLSM causes no issues, although it does cause problems with some older routing protocols. The only routing protocol included in the CCNA blueprint (OSPF) works the same regardless of whether the design uses VLSM. Just be aware of the term and what it means and that it should not impact the features included in the current CCNA exam.

> **NOTE**   VLSM has been featured in the CCNA exam topics in the past. If you want to read a little more about VLSM, check out Appendix N, "Variable-Length Subnet Masks," on the companion website for this book.

Make Design Choices

Now that you know how to analyze the IP addressing and subnetting needs, the next major step examines how to apply the rules of IP addressing and subnetting to those needs and make some choices. In other words, now that you know how many subnets you need and how many host addresses you need in the largest subnet, how do you create a useful subnetting design that meets those requirements? The short answer is that you need to do the three tasks shown on the right side of Figure 11-11.

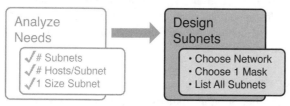

Figure 11-11   *Input to the Design Phase, and Design Questions to Answer*

Choose a Classful Network

In the original design for what we know of today as the Internet, companies used registered *public classful IP networks* when implementing TCP/IP inside the company. By the mid-1990s, an alternative became more popular: *private IP networks*. This section discusses the background behind these two choices because it impacts the choice of what IP network a company will then subnet and implement in its enterprise internetwork.

Public IP Networks

The original design of the Internet required that any company that connected to the Internet had to use a *registered public IP network*. To do so, the company would complete some paperwork, describing the enterprise's internetwork and the number of hosts existing, plus plans for growth. After submitting the paperwork, the company would receive an assignment of either a Class A, B, or C network.

Public IP networks—and the administrative processes surrounding them—ensure that all the companies that connect to the Internet all use unique IP addresses. In particular, after a public IP network is assigned to a company, only that company should use the addresses in that network. That guarantee of uniqueness means that Internet routing can work well because there are no duplicate public IP addresses.

For example, consider the example shown in Figure 11-12. Company 1 has been assigned public Class A network 1.0.0.0, and company 2 has been assigned public Class A network 2.0.0.0. Per the original intent for public addressing in the Internet, after these public network assignments have been made, no other companies can use addresses in Class A networks 1.0.0.0 or 2.0.0.0.

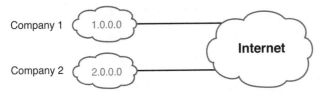

Figure 11-12 *Two Companies with Unique Public IP Networks*

This original address assignment process ensured unique IP addresses across the entire planet. The idea is much like the fact that your telephone number should be unique in the universe, your postal mailing address should also be unique, and your email address should also be unique. If someone calls you, your phone rings, but no one else's phone rings. Similarly, if company 1 is assigned Class A network 1.0.0.0, and the engineers at Company 1 assign address 1.1.1.1 to a particular PC, that address should be unique in the universe. A packet sent through the Internet to destination 1.1.1.1 should only arrive at this one PC inside company 1, instead of being delivered to some other host.

Growth Exhausts the Public IP Address Space

By the early 1990s, the world was running out of public IP networks that could be assigned. During most of the 1990s, the number of hosts newly connected to the Internet was growing at a double-digit pace *per month*. Companies kept following the rules, asking for public IP networks, and it was clear that the current address-assignment scheme could not continue without some changes. Simply put, the number of Class A, B, and C networks supported by the 32-bit address in IP version 4 (IPv4) was not enough to support one public classful network per organization, while also providing enough IP addresses in each company.

NOTE The universe has run out of public IPv4 addresses in a couple of significant ways. IANA, which assigns public IPv4 address blocks to the five Regional Internet Registries (RIR) around the globe, assigned the last of the IPv4 address spaces in early 2011. By 2015, ARIN, the RIR for North America, exhausted its supply of IPv4 addresses, so companies must return unused public IPv4 addresses to ARIN before they have more to assign to new companies. Try an online search for "ARIN depletion" to see pages about the current status of available IPv4 address space for just one RIR example.

The Internet community worked hard during the 1990s to solve this problem, coming up with several solutions, including the following:

- A new version of IP (IPv6), with much larger addresses (128 bit)
- Assigning a subset of a public IP network to each company, instead of an entire public IP network, to reduce waste, using a feature called "Classless Interdomain Routing" (CIDR)
- Network Address Translation (NAT), which allows the use of private IP networks

These three solutions matter to real networks today. However, to stay focused on the topic of subnet design, this chapter focuses on the third option, and in particular, the private IP networks that can be used by an enterprise when also using NAT. (Be aware that Chapter 10, "Network Address Translation" in *CCNA 200-301 Official Cert Guide, Volume 2*, gives more detail about the last two bullets in the list, while Part VII of this book discusses the first bullet item (IPv6) in more depth.)

Focusing on the third item in the bullet list, NAT allows multiple companies to use the exact same *private IP network*, using the same IP addresses as other companies while still connecting to the Internet. For example, Figure 11-13 shows the same two companies connecting to the Internet as in Figure 11-12, but now with both using the same private Class A network 10.0.0.0.

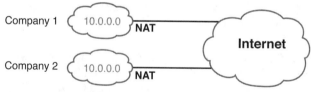

Figure 11-13 *Reusing the Same Private Network 10.0.0.0 with NAT*

Both companies use the same classful IP network (10.0.0.0). Both companies can implement their subnet design internal to their respective enterprise internetworks, without discussing their plans. The two companies can even use the exact same IP addresses inside network 10.0.0.0. And amazingly, at the same time, both companies can even communicate with each other through the Internet.

The technology called Network Address Translation makes it possible for companies to reuse the same IP networks, as shown in Figure 11-13. NAT does this by translating the IP addresses inside the packets as they go from the enterprise to the Internet, using a small number of public IP addresses to support tens of thousands of private IP addresses. That one bit of information is not enough to understand how NAT works; however, to keep the focus on subnetting, the book defers the discussion of how NAT works until *CCNA 200-301 Official Cert Guide, Volume 2*. For now, accept that most companies use NAT, and therefore, they can use private IP networks for their internetworks.

Private IP Networks

When using NAT—and almost every organization that connects to the Internet uses NAT—the company can simply pick one or more of the private IP networks from the list of reserved private IP network numbers. RFC 1918 defines the list of available private IP networks, which is summarized in Table 11-2.

Table 11-2   RFC 1918 Private Address Space

Class of Networks	Private IP Networks	Number of Networks
A	10.0.0.0	1
B	172.16.0.0 through 172.31.0.0	16
C	192.168.0.0 through 192.168.255.0	256

NOTE   According to an informal survey I ran on my blog a few years back, about half of the respondents said that their networks use private Class A network 10.0.0.0, as opposed to other private networks or public networks.

From the perspective of making IPv4 work for the entire world, private IP networks have helped preserve and extend IPv4 and its use in every enterprise and throughout the Internet. In particular, private networks have improved IPv4's implementation worldwide by

- **Avoiding Using Another Organization's Public Address Range for Private Networks:** Some organizations have a part of their networks that need zero Internet access. The hosts in that part of their network need IP addresses. RFC 1918 suggests that truly private networks—that is, networks with no need for Internet connectivity—use addresses from the RFC 1918 list of private networks.

- **Avoiding/Delaying IPv4 Address Exhaustion:** To delay the day in which all public IPv4 addresses were assigned to organizations as public addresses, RFC 1918 calls for the use of NAT along with private networks for the addresses internal to an organization.

- **Reducing Internet Routers' Routing Table Size:** Using private networks also helps reduce the size of the IP routing tables in Internet routers. For instance, routers in the Internet do not need routes for the private IP networks used inside organizations (in fact, ISPs filter those routes).

Choosing an IP Network During the Design Phase

Today, some organizations use private IP networks along with NAT, and some use public IP networks. Most new enterprise internetworks use private IP addresses throughout the network, along with NAT, as part of the connection to the Internet. Those organizations that already have registered public IP networks—often obtained before the addresses started running short in the early 1990s—can continue to use those public addresses throughout their enterprise networks.

After the choice to use a private IP network has been made, just pick one that has enough IP addresses. You can have a small internetwork and still choose to use private Class A network 10.0.0.0. It might seem wasteful to choose a Class A network that has over 16 million IP addresses, especially if you need only a few hundred. However, there's no penalty or problem with using a private network that is too large for your current or future needs.

For the purposes of this book, most examples use private IP network numbers. For the design step to choose a network number, just choose a private Class A, B, or C network from the list of RFC 1918 private networks.

Regardless, from a math and concept perspective, the methods to subnet a public IP network versus a private IP network are the same.

Choose the Mask

If a design engineer followed the topics in this chapter so far, in order, he would know the following:

- The number of subnets required
- The number of hosts/subnet required
- That a choice was made to use only one mask for all subnets so that all subnets are the same size (same number of hosts/subnet)
- The classful IP network number that will be subnetted

This section completes the design process, at least the parts described in this chapter, by discussing how to choose that one mask to use for all subnets. First, this section examines default masks, used when a network is not subnetted, as a point of comparison. Next, the concept of borrowing host bits to create subnet bits is explored. Finally, this section ends with an example of how to create a subnet mask based on the analysis of the requirements.

Classful IP Networks Before Subnetting

Before an engineer subnets a classful network, the network is a single group of addresses. In other words, the engineer has not yet subdivided the network into many smaller subsets called *subnets*.

When thinking about an unsubnetted classful network, the addresses in a network have only two parts: the network part and host part. Comparing any two addresses in the classful network:

- The addresses have the same value in the network part.
- The addresses have different values in the host part.

The actual sizes of the network and host part of the addresses in a network can be easily predicted, as shown in Figure 11-14.

11

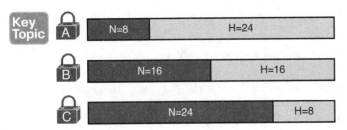

Figure 11-14 *Format of Unsubnetted Class A, B, and C Networks*

In Figure 11-14, N and H represent the number of network and host bits, respectively. Class rules define the number of network octets (1, 2, or 3) for Classes A, B, and C, respectively; the figure shows these values as a number of bits. The number of host octets is 3, 2, or 1, respectively.

Continuing the analysis of classful network before subnetting, the number of addresses in one classful IP network can be calculated with the same $2^H - 2$ formula previously discussed. In particular, the size of an unsubnetted Class A, B, or C network is as follows:

- **Class A:** $2^{24} - 2 = 16,777,214$
- **Class B:** $2^{16} - 2 = 65,534$
- **Class C:** $2^8 - 2 = 254$

Borrowing Host Bits to Create Subnet Bits

To subnet a network, the designer thinks about the network and host parts, as shown in Figure 11-15, and then the engineer adds a third part in the middle: the subnet part. However, the designer cannot change the size of the network part or the size of the entire address (32 bits). To create a subnet part of the address structure, the engineer borrows bits from the host part. Figure 11-15 shows the general idea.

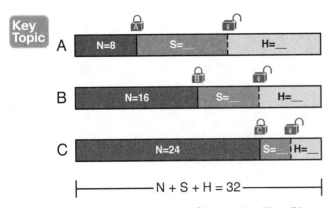

Figure 11-15 *Concept of Borrowing Host Bits*

Figure 11-15 shows a rectangle that represents the subnet mask. N, representing the number of network bits, remains locked at 8, 16, or 24, depending on the class. Conceptually, the designer moves a (dashed) dividing line into the host field, with subnet bits (S) between the network and host parts, and the remaining host bits (H) on the right. The three parts must add up to 32 because IPv4 addresses consist of 32 bits.

Choosing Enough Subnet and Host Bits

The design process requires a choice of where to place the dashed line shown in Figure 11-15. But what is the right choice? How many subnet and host bits should the designer choose? The answers hinge on the requirements gathered in the early stages of the planning process:

- Number of subnets required
- Number of hosts/subnet

The bits in the subnet part create a way to uniquely number the different subnets that the design engineer wants to create. With 1 subnet bit, you can number 2^1 or 2 subnets. With 2 bits, 2^2 or 4 subnets, with 3 bits, 2^3 or 8 subnets, and so on. The number of subnet bits must be large enough to uniquely number all the subnets, as determined during the planning process.

At the same time, the remaining number of host bits must also be large enough to number the host IP addresses in the largest subnet. Remember, in this chapter, we assume the use of a single mask for all subnets. This single mask must support both the required number of subnets and the required number of hosts in the largest subnet. Figure 11-16 shows the concept.

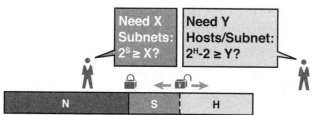

Figure 11-16 *Borrowing Enough Subnet and Host Bits*

Figure 11-16 shows the idea of the designer choosing a number of subnet (S) and host (H) bits and then checking the math. 2^S must be more than the number of required subnets, or the mask will not supply enough subnets in this IP network. Also, $2^H - 2$ must be more than the required number of hosts/subnet.

> **NOTE** The idea of calculating the number of subnets as 2^S applies only in cases where a single mask is used for all subnets of a single classful network, as is being assumed in this chapter.

To effectively design masks, or to interpret masks that were chosen by someone else, you need a good working memory of the powers of 2. Appendix A, "Numeric Reference Tables," lists a table with powers of 2 up through 2^{32} for your reference.

11

Example Design: 172.16.0.0, 200 Subnets, 200 Hosts

To help make sense of the theoretical discussion so far, consider an example that focuses on the design choice for the subnet mask. In this case, the planning and design choices so far tell us the following:

- Use a single mask for all subnets.
- Plan for 200 subnets.
- Plan for 200 host IP addresses per subnet.
- Use private Class B network 172.16.0.0.

To choose the mask, the designer asks this question:

How many subnet (S) bits do I need to number 200 subnets?

You can see that S = 7 is not large enough (2^7 = 128), but S = 8 is enough (2^8 = 256). So, you need *at least* 8 subnet bits.

Next, the designer asks a similar question, based on the number of hosts per subnet:

How many host (H) bits do I need to number 200 hosts per subnet?

The math is basically the same, but the formula subtracts 2 when counting the number of hosts/subnet. You can see that H = 7 is not large enough ($2^7 - 2$ = 126), but H = 8 is enough ($2^8 - 2$ = 254).

Only one possible mask meets all the requirements in this case. First, the number of network bits (N) must be 16 because the design uses a Class B network. The requirements tell us that the mask needs at least 8 subnet bits and at least 8 host bits. The mask only has 32 bits in it; Figure 11-17 shows the resulting mask.

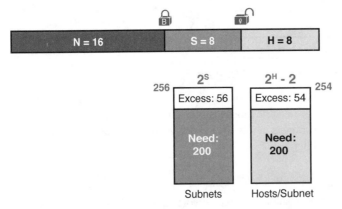

Figure 11-17   *Example Mask Choice, N = 16, S = 8, H = 8*

Masks and Mask Formats

Although engineers think about IP addresses in three parts when making design choices (network, subnet, and host), the subnet mask gives the engineer a way to communicate those design choices to all the devices in the subnet.

The subnet mask is a 32-bit binary number with a number of binary 1s on the left and with binary 0s on the right. By definition, the number of binary 0s equals the number of host bits; in fact, that is exactly how the mask communicates the idea of the size of the host part of the addresses in a subnet. The beginning bits in the mask equal binary 1, with those bit positions representing the combined network and subnet parts of the addresses in the subnet.

Because the network part always comes first, then the subnet part, and then the host part, the subnet mask, in binary form, cannot have interleaved 1s and 0s. Each subnet mask has one unbroken string of binary 1s on the left, with the rest of the bits as binary 0s.

After the engineer chooses the classful network and the number of subnet and host bits in a subnet, creating the binary subnet mask is easy. Just write down N 1s, S 1s, and then H 0s (assuming that N, S, and H represent the number of network, subnet, and host bits). Figure 11-18 shows the mask based on the previous example, which subnets a Class B network by creating 8 subnet bits, leaving 8 host bits.

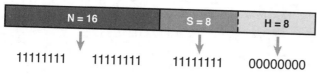

Figure 11-18 *Creating the Subnet Mask—Binary—Class B Network*

In addition to the binary mask shown in Figure 11-18, masks can also be written in two other formats: the familiar *dotted-decimal notation* (DDN) seen in IP addresses and an even briefer *prefix* notation. Chapter 13, "Analyzing Subnet Masks," discusses these formats and how to convert between the different formats.

Build a List of All Subnets

Building a list of all subnets, the final task of the subnet design step, determines the actual subnets that can be used, based on all the earlier choices. The earlier design work determined the Class A, B, or C network to use, and the (one) subnet mask to use that supplies enough subnets and enough host IP addresses per subnet. But what are those subnets? How do you identify or describe a subnet? This section answers these questions.

A subnet consists of a group of consecutive numbers. Most of these numbers can be used as IP addresses by hosts. However, each subnet reserves the first and last numbers in the group, and these two numbers cannot be used as IP addresses. In particular, each subnet contains the following:

Key Topic

- **Subnet number:** Also called the *subnet ID* or *subnet address*, this number identifies the subnet. It is the numerically smallest number in the subnet. It cannot be used as an IP address by a host.

- **Subnet broadcast:** Also called the *subnet broadcast address* or *directed broadcast address*, this is the last (numerically highest) number in the subnet. It also cannot be used as an IP address by a host.

- **IP addresses:** All the numbers between the subnet ID and the subnet broadcast address can be used as a host IP address.

11

For example, consider the earlier case in which the design results were as follows:

Network   172.16.0.0 (Class B)

Mask   255.255.255.0 (for all subnets)

With some math, the facts about each subnet that exists in this Class B network can be calculated. In this case, Table 11-3 shows the first 10 such subnets. It then skips many subnets and shows the last two (numerically largest) subnets.

Table 11-3   First 10 Subnets, Plus the Last Few, from 172.16.0.0, 255.255.255.0

Subnet Number	IP Addresses	Broadcast Address
172.16.0.0	172.16.0.1 – 172.16.0.254	172.16.0.255
172.16.1.0	172.16.1.1 – 172.16.1.254	172.16.1.255
172.16.2.0	172.16.2.1 – 172.16.2.254	172.16.2.255
172.16.3.0	172.16.3.1 – 172.16.3.254	172.16.3.255
172.16.4.0	172.16.4.1 – 172.16.4.254	172.16.4.255
172.16.5.0	172.16.5.1 – 172.16.5.254	172.16.5.255
172.16.6.0	172.16.6.1 – 172.16.6.254	172.16.6.255
172.16.7.0	172.16.7.1 – 172.16.7.254	172.16.7.255
172.16.8.0	172.16.8.1 – 172.16.8.254	172.16.8.255
172.16.9.0	172.16.9.1 – 172.16.9.254	172.16.9.255
Skipping many...		
172.16.254.0	172.16.254.1 – 172.16.254.254	172.16.254.255
172.16.255.0	172.16.255.1 – 172.16.255.254	172.16.255.255

After you have the network number and the mask, calculating the subnet IDs and other details for all subnets requires some math. In real life, most people use subnet calculators or subnet-planning tools. For the CCNA exam, you need to be ready to find this kind of information.

If you want to dig a little deeper in preparation for CCNP Enterprise or other studies related to IP routing, consider using Appendix L, "Subnet Design," on the book's companion website, which shows you how to find all the subnets of a given network.

Plan the Implementation

The next step, planning the implementation, is the last step before actually configuring the devices to create a subnet. The engineer first needs to choose where to use each subnet. For example, at a branch office in a particular city, which subnet from the subnet planning chart (Table 11-3) should be used for each VLAN at that site? Also, for any interfaces that require static IP addresses, which addresses should be used in each case? Finally, what range of IP addresses from inside each subnet should be configured in the DHCP server, to be dynamically leased to hosts for use as their IP address? Figure 11-19 summarizes the list of implementation planning tasks.

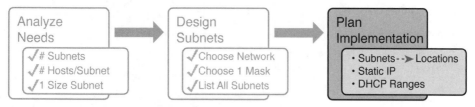

Figure 11-19   *Facts Supplied to the Plan Implementation Step*

Assigning Subnets to Different Locations

The job is simple: Look at your network diagram, identify each location that needs a subnet, and pick one from the table you made of all the possible subnets. Then, track it so that you know which ones you use where, using a spreadsheet or some other purpose-built subnet-planning tool. That's it! Figure 11-20 shows a sample of a completed design using Table 11-3, which happens to match the initial design sample shown way back in Figure 11-1.

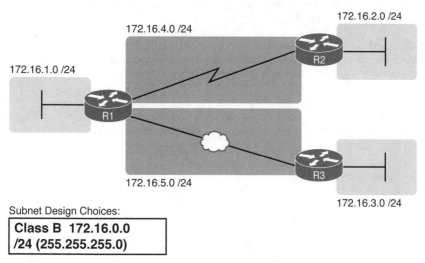

Figure 11-20   *Example of Subnets Assigned to Different Locations*

Although this design could have used any five subnets from Table 11-3, in real networks, engineers usually give more thought to some strategy for assigning subnets. For example, you might assign all LAN subnets lower numbers and WAN subnets higher numbers. Or you might slice off large ranges of subnets for different divisions of the company. Or you might follow that same strategy but ignore organizational divisions in the company, paying more attention to geographies.

For example, for a U.S.-based company with a smaller presence in both Europe and Asia, you might plan to reserve ranges of subnets based on continent. This kind of choice is particularly useful when later trying to use a feature called route summarization. Figure 11-21 shows the general benefit of placing addressing in the network for easier route summarization, using the same subnets from Table 11-3 again.

11

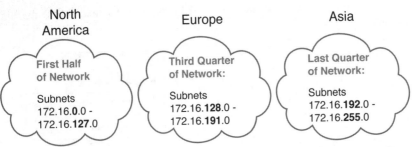

Figure 11-21 *Reserving 50 Percent of Subnets for North America and 25 Percent Each for Europe and Asia*

Choose Static and Dynamic Ranges per Subnet

Devices receive their IP address and mask assignment in one of two ways: dynamically by using Dynamic Host Configuration Protocol (DHCP) or statically through configuration. For DHCP to work, the network engineer must tell the DHCP server the subnets for which it must assign IP addresses. In addition, that configuration limits the DHCP server to only a subset of the addresses in the subnet. For static addresses, you simply configure the device to tell it what IP address and mask to use.

To keep things as simple as possible, most shops use a strategy to separate the static IP addresses on one end of each subnet, and the DHCP-assigned dynamic addresses on the other. It does not really matter whether the static addresses sit on the low end of the range of addresses or the high end.

For example, imagine that the engineer decides that, for the LAN subnets in Figure 11-20, the DHCP pool comes from the high end of the range, namely, addresses that end in .101 through .254. (The address that ends in .255 is, of course, reserved.) The engineer also assigns static addresses from the lower end, with addresses ending in .1 through .100. Figure 11-22 shows the idea.

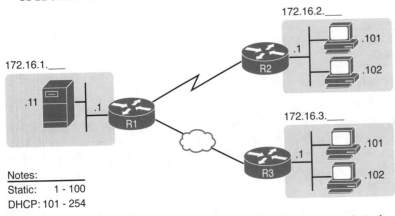

Figure 11-22 *Static from the Low End and DHCP from the High End*

Figure 11-22 shows all three routers with statically assigned IP addresses that end in .1. The only other static IP address in the figure is assigned to the server on the left, with address 172.16.1.11 (abbreviated simply as .11 in the figure).

On the right, each LAN has two PCs that use DHCP to dynamically lease their IP addresses. DHCP servers often begin by leasing the addresses at the bottom of the range of addresses, so in each LAN, the hosts have leased addresses that end in .101 and .102, which are at the low end of the range chosen by design.

Chapter Review

One key to doing well on the exams is to perform repetitive spaced review sessions. Review this chapter's material using either the tools in the book or interactive tools for the same material found on the book's companion website. Refer to the "Your Study Plan" element for more details. Table 11-4 outlines the key review elements and where you can find them. To better track your study progress, record when you completed these activities in the second column.

Table 11-4   Chapter Review Tracking

Review Element	Review Date(s)	Resource Used
Review key topics		Book, website
Review key terms		Book, website
Answer DIKTA questions		Book, PTP
Review memory tables		Website

Review All the Key Topics

Table 11-5   Key Topics for Chapter 11

Key Topic Element	Description	Page Number
List	Key facts about subnets	269
List	Rules about what places in a network topology need a subnet	270
Figure 11-7	Locations of the network, subnet, and host parts of an IPv4 address	273
List	Features that extended the life of IPv4	277
List	Motivations for using private IP networks	278
Figure 11-14	Formats of Class A, B, and C addresses when not subnetted	280
Figure 11-15	Formats of Class A, B, and C addresses when subnetted	280
Figure 11-16	General logic when choosing the size of the subnet and host parts of addresses in a subnet	281
List	Items that together define a subnet	283

11

Key Terms You Should Know

subnet, network, classful IP network, variable-length subnet masks (VLSM), network part, subnet part, host part, public IP network, private IP network, subnet mask

CHAPTER 12

Analyzing Classful IPv4 Networks

This chapter covers the following exam topics:

1.0 Network Fundamentals

1.6 Configure and verify IPv4 addressing and subnetting

When operating a network, you often start investigating a problem based on an IP address and mask. Based on the IP address alone, you should be able to determine several facts about the Class A, B, or C network in which the IP address resides.

This chapter lists the key facts about classful IP networks and explains how to discover these facts. Following that, this chapter lists some practice problems. Before moving to the next chapter, you should practice until you can consistently determine all these facts, quickly and confidently, based on an IP address.

"Do I Know This Already?" Quiz

Take the quiz (either here or use the PTP software) if you want to use the score to help you decide how much time to spend on this chapter. The letter answers are listed at the bottom of the page following the quiz. Appendix C, found both at the end of the book as well as on the companion website, includes both the answers and explanations. You can also find both answers and explanations in the PTP testing software.

Table 12-1 "Do I Know This Already?" Foundation Topics Section-to-Question Mapping

Foundation Topics Section	Questions
Classful Network Concepts	1–5

1. Which of the following are not valid Class A network IDs? (Choose two answers.)

   a. 1.0.0.0

   b. 130.0.0.0

   c. 127.0.0.0

   d. 9.0.0.0

2. Which of the following are not valid Class B network IDs?

   a. 130.0.0.0

   b. 191.255.0.0

   c. 128.0.0.0

   d. 150.255.0.0

   e. All are valid Class B network IDs.

3. Which of the following are true about IP address 172.16.99.45's IP network? (Choose two answers.)

    a. The network ID is 172.0.0.0.

    b. The network is a Class B network.

    c. The default mask for the network is 255.255.255.0.

    d. The number of host bits in the unsubnetted network is 16.

4. Which of the following are true about IP address 192.168.6.7's IP network? (Choose two answers.)

    a. The network ID is 192.168.6.0.

    b. The network is a Class B network.

    c. The default mask for the network is 255.255.255.0.

    d. The number of host bits in the unsubnetted network is 16.

5. Which of the following is a network broadcast address?

    a. 10.1.255.255

    b. 192.168.255.1

    c. 224.1.1.255

    d. 172.30.255.255

Foundation Topics

Classful Network Concepts

Imagine that you have a job interview for your first IT job. As part of the interview, you're given an IPv4 address and mask: 10.4.5.99, 255.255.255.0. What can you tell the interviewer about the classful network (in this case, the Class A network) in which the IP address resides?

This section, the first of two major sections in this chapter, reviews the concepts of *classful IP networks* (in other words, Class A, B, and C networks). In particular, this chapter examines how to begin with a single IP address and then determine the following facts:

■ Class (A, B, or C)

■ Default mask

■ Number of network octets/bits

■ Number of host octets/bits

■ Number of host addresses in the network

■ Network ID

■ Network broadcast address

■ First and last usable address in the network

IPv4 Network Classes and Related Facts

IP version 4 (IPv4) defines five address classes. Three of the classes, Classes A, B, and C, consist of unicast IP addresses. Unicast addresses identify a single host or interface so that the address uniquely identifies the device. Class D addresses serve as multicast addresses, so that one packet sent to a Class D multicast IPv4 address can actually be delivered to multiple hosts. Finally, Class E addresses were originally intended for experimentation but were changed to simply be reserved for future use. The class can be identified based on the value of the first octet of the address, as shown in Table 12-2.

Table 12-2   IPv4 Address Classes Based on First Octet Values

Class	First Octet Values	Purpose
A	1–126	Unicast (large networks)
B	128–191	Unicast (medium-sized networks)
C	192–223	Unicast (small networks)
D	224–239	Multicast
E	240–255	Reserved (formerly experimental)

After you identify the class of a unicast address as either A, B, or C, many other related facts can be derived just through memorization. Table 12-3 lists that information for reference and later study; each of these concepts is described in this chapter.

Table 12-3   Key Facts for Classes A, B, and C

	Class A	Class B	Class C
First octet range	1–126	128–191	192–223
Valid network numbers	1.0.0.0–126.0.0.0	128.0.0.0–191.255.0.0	192.0.0.0–223.255.255.0
Total networks	$2^7 - 2 = 126$	$2^{14} = 16,384$	$2^{21} = 2,097,152$
Hosts per network	$2^{24} - 2$	$2^{16} - 2$	$2^8 - 2$
Octets (bits) in network part	1 (8)	2 (16)	3 (24)
Octets (bits) in host part	3 (24)	2 (16)	1 (8)
Default mask	255.0.0.0	255.255.0.0	255.255.255.0

Note that the address ranges of all addresses that begin with 0 and all addresses that begin with 127 are reserved. Had they not been reserved since the creation of Class A networks, as listed in RFC 791 (published in 1981), then they might have been known as class A networks 0.0.0.0 and 127.0.0.0. Because they are reserved, however, the address space has 126 class A networks, and not 128. Also, note that there are no similar reserved ranges to begin/end the class B and C ranges.

In addition to the reservation of what would be class A networks 0.0.0.0 and 127.0.0.0 for other purposes, other newer RFCs have also reserved small pieces of the Class A, B, and C address space. So, tables like Table 12-3, with the count of the numbers of Class A, B, and C networks, are a good place to get a sense of the size of the number; however, the number of reserved networks does change slightly over time (albeit slowly) based on these other reserved address ranges.

> **NOTE**   If you are interested in seeing all the reserved IPv4 address ranges, just do an Internet search on "IANA IPv4 special-purpose address registry."

The Number and Size of the Class A, B, and C Networks

Table 12-3 lists the range of Class A, B, and C network numbers; however, some key points can be lost just referencing a table of information. This section examines the Class A, B, and C network numbers, focusing on the more important points and the exceptions and unusual cases.

First, the number of networks from each class significantly differs. Only 126 Class A networks exist: network 1.0.0.0, 2.0.0.0, 3.0.0.0, and so on, up through network 126.0.0.0. However, 16,384 Class B networks exist, with more than 2 million Class C networks.

Next, note that the size of networks from each class also significantly differs. Each Class A network is relatively large—over 16 million host IP addresses per network—so they were originally intended to be used by the largest companies and organizations. Class B networks are smaller, with over 65,000 hosts per network. Finally, Class C networks, intended for small organizations, have 254 hosts in each network. Figure 12-1 summarizes those facts.

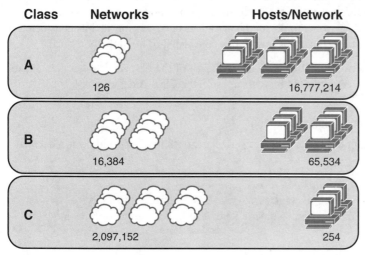

Figure 12-1   *Numbers and Sizes of Class A, B, and C Networks*

Address Formats

In some cases, an engineer might need to think about a Class A, B, or C network as if the network has not been subdivided through the subnetting process. In such a case, the addresses in the classful network have a structure with two parts: the *network part* (sometimes called the *prefix*) and the *host part*. Then, comparing any two IP addresses in one network, the following observations can be made:

The addresses in the same network have the same values in the network part.

The addresses in the same network have different values in the host part.

For example, in Class A network 10.0.0.0, by definition, the network part consists of the first octet. As a result, all addresses have an equal value in the network part, namely a 10 in the first octet. If you then compare any two addresses in the network, the addresses have a different value in the last three octets (the host octets). For example, IP addresses 10.1.1.1 and 10.1.1.2 have the same value (10) in the network part, but different values in the host part.

Figure 12-2 shows the format and sizes (in number of bits) of the network and host parts of IP addresses in Class A, B, and C networks, before any subnetting has been applied.

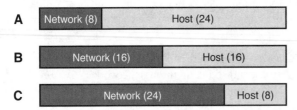

Figure 12-2 *Sizes (Bits) of the Network and Host Parts of Unsubnetted Classful Networks*

Default Masks

Although we humans can easily understand the concepts behind Figure 12-2, computers prefer numbers. To communicate those same ideas to computers, each network class has an associated *default mask* that defines the size of the network and host parts of an unsubnetted Class A, B, and C network. To do so, the mask lists binary 1s for the bits considered to be in the network part and binary 0s for the bits considered to be in the host part.

For example, Class A network 10.0.0.0 has a network part of the first single octet (8 bits) and a host part of the last three octets (24 bits). As a result, the Class A default mask is 255.0.0.0, which in binary is

11111111 00000000 00000000 00000000

Figure 12-3 shows default masks for each network class, both in binary and dotted-decimal format.

NOTE Decimal 255 converts to the binary value 11111111. Decimal 0, converted to 8-bit binary, is 00000000. See Appendix A, "Numeric Reference Tables," for a conversion table.

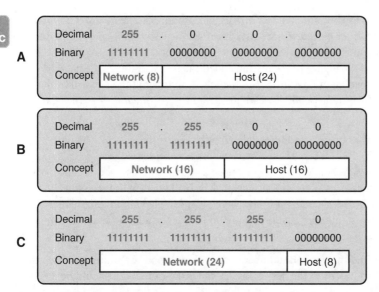

Figure 12-3 *Default Masks for Classes A, B, and C*

Number of Hosts per Network

Calculating the number of hosts per network requires some basic binary math. First, consider a case where you have a single binary digit. How many unique values are there? There are, of course, two values: 0 and 1. With 2 bits, you can make four combinations: 00, 01, 10, and 11. As it turns out, the total combination of unique values you can make with N bits is 2^N.

Host addresses—the IP addresses assigned to hosts—must be unique. The host bits exist for the purpose of giving each host a unique IP address by virtue of having a different value in the host part of the addresses. So, with H host bits, 2^H unique combinations exist.

However, the number of hosts in a network is not 2^H; instead, it is $2^H - 2$. Each network reserves two numbers that would have otherwise been useful as host addresses but have instead been reserved for special use: one for the network ID and one for the network broadcast address. As a result, the formula to calculate the number of host addresses per Class A, B, or C network is

$$2^H - 2$$

where H is the number of host bits.

Deriving the Network ID and Related Numbers

Each classful network has four key numbers that describe the network. You can derive these four numbers if you start with just one IP address in the network. The numbers are as follows:

- Network number
- First (numerically lowest) usable address
- Last (numerically highest) usable address
- Network broadcast address

12

First, consider both the network number and first usable IP address. The *network number*, also called the *network ID* or *network address*, identifies the network. By definition, the network number is the numerically lowest number in the network. However, to prevent any ambiguity, the people that made up IP addressing added the restriction that the network number cannot be assigned as an IP address. So, the lowest number in the network is the network ID. Then, the first (numerically lowest) host IP address is *one larger than* the network number.

Next, consider the network broadcast address along with the last (numerically highest) usable IP address. The TCP/IP RFCs define a network broadcast address as a special address in each network. This broadcast address could be used as the destination address in a packet, and the routers would forward a copy of that one packet to all hosts in that classful network. Numerically, a network broadcast address is always the highest (last) number in the network. As a result, the highest (last) number usable as an IP address is the address that is *one less than* the network broadcast address.

Simply put, if you can find the network number and network broadcast address, finding the first and last usable IP addresses in the network is easy. For the exam, you should be able to find all four values with ease; the process is as follows:

Step 1.   Determine the class (A, B, or C) based on the first octet.

Step 2.   Mentally divide the network and host octets based on the class.

Step 3.   To find the network number, change the IP address's host octets to 0.

Step 4.   To find the first address, add 1 to the fourth octet of the network ID.

Step 5.   To find the broadcast address, change the network ID's host octets to 255.

Step 6.   To find the last address, subtract 1 from the fourth octet of the network broadcast address.

The written process actually looks harder than it is. Figure 12-4 shows an example of the process, using Class A IP address 10.17.18.21, with the circled numbers matching the process.

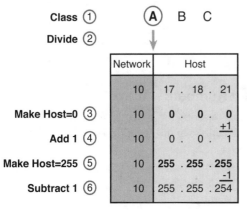

Figure 12-4   *Example of Deriving the Network ID and Other Values from 10.17.18.21*

Figure 12-4 shows the identification of the class as Class A (Step 1) and the number of network/host octets as 1 and 3, respectively. So, to find the network ID at Step 3, the figure copies only the first octet, setting the last three (host) octets to 0. At Step 4, just copy the network ID and add 1 to the fourth octet. Similarly, to find the broadcast address at Step 5, copy the network octets, but set the host octets to 255. Then, at Step 6, subtract 1 from the fourth octet to find the last (numerically highest) usable IP address.

Just to show an alternative example, consider IP address 172.16.8.9. Figure 12-5 shows the process applied to this IP address.

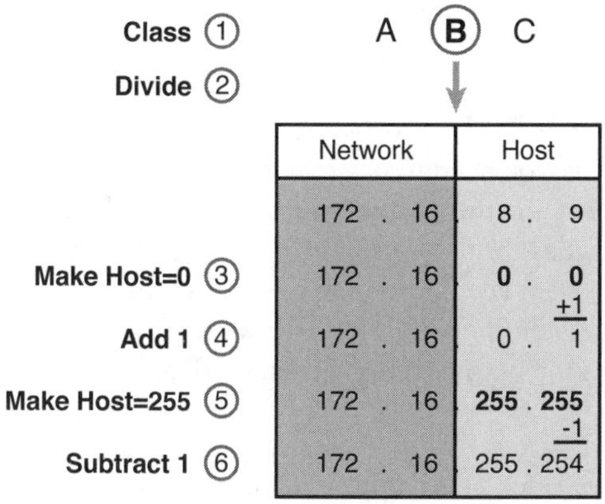

Figure 12-5 *Example Deriving the Network ID and Other Values from 172.16.8.9*

Figure 12-5 shows the identification of the class as Class B (Step 1) and the number of network/host octets as 2 and 2, respectively. So, to find the network ID at Step 3, the figure copies only the first two octets, setting the last two (host) octets to 0. Similarly, Step 5 shows the same action, but with the last two (host) octets being set to 255.

Unusual Network IDs and Network Broadcast Addresses

Some of the more unusual numbers in and around the range of Class A, B, and C network numbers can cause some confusion. This section lists some examples of numbers that make many people make the wrong assumptions about the meaning of the number.

For Class A, the first odd fact is that the range of values in the first octet omits the numbers 0 and 127. As it turns out, what would be Class A network 0.0.0.0 was originally reserved for some broadcasting requirements, so all addresses that begin with 0 in the first octet are reserved. What would be Class A network 127.0.0.0 is still reserved because of a special address used in software testing, called the loopback address (127.0.0.1).

For Class B (and C), some of the network numbers can look odd, particularly if you fall into a habit of thinking that 0s at the end means the number is a network ID, and 255s at the end means it's a network broadcast address. First, Class B network numbers range from 128.0.0.0 to 191.255.0.0, for a total of 2^{14} networks. However, even the very first (lowest number) Class B network number (128.0.0.0) looks a little like a Class A network number because it ends with three 0s. However, the first octet is 128, making it a Class B network with a two-octet network part (128.0).

12

For another Class B example, the high end of the Class B range also might look strange at first glance (191.255.0.0), but this is indeed the numerically highest of the valid Class B network numbers. This network's broadcast address, 191.255.255.255, might look a little like a Class A broadcast address because of the three 255s at the end, but it is indeed the broadcast address of a Class B network.

Similarly to Class B networks, some of the valid Class C network numbers do look strange. For example, Class C network 192.0.0.0 looks a little like a Class A network because of the last three octets being 0, but because it is a Class C network, it consists of all addresses that begin with three octets equal to 192.0.0. Similarly, 223.255.255.0, another valid Class C network, consists of all addresses that begin with 223.255.255.

Practice with Classful Networks

As with all areas of IP addressing and subnetting, you need to practice to be ready for the CCNA exam. You should practice some while reading this chapter to make sure that you understand the processes. At that point, you can use your notes and this book as a reference, with a goal of understanding the process. After that, keep practicing this and all the other subnetting processes. Before you take the exam, you should be able to always get the right answer, and with speed. Table 12-4 summarizes the key concepts and suggestions for this two-phase approach.

Table 12-4 Keep-Reading and Take-Exam Goals for This Chapter's Topics

	After Reading This Chapter	Before Taking the Exam
Focus on...	Learning how	Being correct and fast
Tools Allowed	All	Your brain and a notepad
Goal: Accuracy	90% correct	100% correct
Goal: Speed	Any speed	10 seconds

Practice Deriving Key Facts Based on an IP Address

Practice finding the various facts that can be derived from an IP address, as discussed throughout this chapter. To do so, complete Table 12-5.

Table 12-5 Practice Problems: Find the Network ID and Network Broadcast

	IP Address	Class	Network Octets	Host Octets	Network ID	Network Broadcast Address
1	1.1.1.1					
2	128.1.6.5					
3	200.1.2.3					
4	192.192.1.1					
5	126.5.4.3					

	IP Address	Class	Network Octets	Host Octets	Network ID	Network Broadcast Address
6	200.1.9.8					
7	192.0.0.1					
8	191.255.1.47					
9	223.223.0.1					

The answers are listed in the section "Answers to Earlier Practice Problems," later in this chapter.

Practice Remembering the Details of Address Classes

Tables 12-2 and 12-3, shown earlier in this chapter, summarized some key information about IPv4 address classes. Tables 12-6 and 12-7 show sparse versions of these same tables. To practice recalling those key facts, particularly the range of values in the first octet that identifies the address class, complete these tables. Then, refer to Tables 12-2 and 12-3 to check your answers. Repeat this process until you can recall all the information in the tables.

Table 12-6   Sparse Study Table Version of Table 12-2

Class	First Octet Values	Purpose
A		
B		
C		
D		
E		

Table 12-7   Sparse Study Table Version of Table 12-3

	Class A	Class B	Class C
First octet range			
Valid network numbers			
Total networks			
Hosts per network			
Octets (bits) in network part			
Octets (bits) in host part			
Default mask			

12

Chapter Review

One key to doing well on the exams is to perform repetitive spaced review sessions. Review this chapter's material using either the tools in the book or interactive tools for the same material found on the book's companion website. Refer to the "Your Study Plan" element for more details. Table 12-8 outlines the key review elements and where you can find them. To better track your study progress, record when you completed these activities in the second column.

Table 12-8   Chapter Review Tracking

Review Element	Review Date(s)	Resource Used
Review key topics		Book, website
Review key terms		Book, website
Answer DIKTA questions		Book, PTP
Review memory tables		Website
Practice analyzing classful IPv4 networks		Website, Appendix D

Review All the Key Topics

Table 12-9   Key Topics for Chapter 12

Key Topic Elements	Description	Page Number
Table 12-2	Address classes	290
Table 12-3	Key facts about Class A, B, and C networks	290
List	Comparisons of network and host parts of addresses in the same classful network	292
Figure 12-3	Default masks	293
Paragraph	Function to calculate the number of hosts per network	294
List	Steps to find information about a classful network	294

Key Terms You Should Know

network, classful IP network, network number, network ID, network address, network broadcast address, network part, host part, default mask

Additional Practice for This Chapter's Processes

For additional practice with analyzing classful networks, you may do a set of practice problems using your choice of tools:

Application: Use the Analyzing Classful IPv4 Networks application on the companion website.

PDF: Alternatively, practice the same problems using companion website Appendix D, "Practice for Chapter 12: Analyzing Classful IPv4 Networks."

Answers to Earlier Practice Problems

Table 12-5, shown earlier, listed several practice problems. Table 12-10 lists the answers.

Table 12-10   Practice Problems: Find the Network ID and Network Broadcast

	IP Address	Class	Network Octets	Host Octets	Network ID	Network Broadcast
1	1.1.1.1	A	1	3	1.0.0.0	1.255.255.255
2	128.1.6.5	B	2	2	128.1.0.0	128.1.255.255
3	200.1.2.3	C	3	1	200.1.2.0	200.1.2.255
4	192.192.1.1	C	3	1	192.192.1.0	192.192.1.255
5	126.5.4.3	A	1	3	126.0.0.0	126.255.255.255
6	200.1.9.8	C	3	1	200.1.9.0	200.1.9.255
7	192.0.0.1	C	3	1	192.0.0.0	192.0.0.255
8	191.255.1.47	B	2	2	191.255.0.0	191.255.255.255
9	223.223.0.1	C	3	1	223.223.0.0	223.223.0.255

The class, number of network octets, and number of host octets all require you to look at the first octet of the IP address to determine the class. If a value is between 1 and 126, inclusive, the address is a Class A address, with one network and three host octets. If a value is between 128 and 191 inclusive, the address is a Class B address, with two network and two host octets. If a value is between 192 and 223, inclusive, it is a Class C address, with three network octets and one host octet.

The last two columns can be found based on Table 12-3, specifically the number of network and host octets along with the IP address. To find the network ID, copy the IP address, but change the host octets to 0. Similarly, to find the network broadcast address, copy the IP address, but change the host octets to 255.

The last three problems can be confusing and were included on purpose so that you could see an example of these unusual cases, as follows.

12

Answers to Practice Problem 7 (from Table 12-5)

Consider IP address 192.0.0.1. First, 192 is on the lower edge of the first octet range for Class C; as such, this address has three network and one host octet. To find the network ID, copy the address, but change the single host octet (the fourth octet) to 0, for a network ID of 192.0.0.0. It looks strange, but it is indeed the network ID.

The network broadcast address choice for problem 7 can also look strange. To find the broadcast address, copy the IP address (192.0.0.1), but change the last octet (the only host octet) to 255, for a broadcast address of 192.0.0.255. In particular, if you decide that the broadcast should be 192.255.255.255, you might have fallen into the trap of logic, like "Change all 0s in the network ID to 255s," which is not the correct logic. Instead, change all host octets in the IP address (or network ID) to 255s.

Answers to Practice Problem 8 (from Table 12-5)

The first octet of problem 8 (191.255.1.47) sits on the upper edge of the Class B range for the first octet (128–191). As such, to find the network ID, change the last two octets (host octets) to 0, for a network ID of 191.255.0.0. This value sometimes gives people problems because they are used to thinking that 255 somehow means the number is a broadcast address.

The broadcast address, found by changing the two host octets to 255, means that the broadcast address is 191.255.255.255. It looks more like a broadcast address for a Class A network, but it is actually the broadcast address for Class B network 191.255.0.0.

Answers to Practice Problem 9 (from Table 12-5)

Problem 9, with IP address 223.223.0.1, is near the high end of the Class C range. As a result, only the last (host) octet is changed to 0 to form the network ID 223.223.0.0. It looks a little like a Class B network number at first glance because it ends in two octets of 0. However, it is indeed a Class C network ID (based on the value in the first octet).

CHAPTER 13

Analyzing Subnet Masks

This chapter covers the following exam topics:

1.0 Network Fundamentals

1.6 Configure and verify IPv4 addressing and subnetting

The subnet mask used in one or many subnets in an IP internetwork says a lot about the intent of the subnet design. First, the mask divides addresses into two parts: *prefix* and *host*, with the host part defining the size of the subnet. Then, the class (A, B, or C) further divides the structure of addresses in a subnet, breaking the prefix part into the *network* and *subnet* parts. The subnet part defines the number of subnets that could exist inside one classful IP network, assuming that one mask is used throughout the classful network.

The subnet mask holds the key to understanding several important subnetting design points. However, to analyze a subnet mask, you first need some basic math skills with masks. The math converts masks between the three different formats used to represent a mask:

- Binary
- Dotted-decimal notation (DDN)
- Prefix (also called classless interdomain routing [CIDR])

This chapter has two major sections. The first focuses on the mask formats and the math used to convert between the three formats. The second section explains how to take an IP address and its subnet mask and analyze those values. In particular, it shows how to determine the three-part format of the IPv4 address and describes the facts about the subnetting design that are implied by the mask.

"Do I Know This Already?" Quiz

Take the quiz (either here or use the PTP software) if you want to use the score to help you decide how much time to spend on this chapter. The letter answers are listed at the bottom of the page following the quiz. Appendix C, found both at the end of the book as well as on the companion website, includes both the answers and explanations. You can also find both answers and explanations in the PTP testing software.

Table 13-1 "Do I Know This Already?" Foundation Topics Section-to-Question Mapping

Foundation Topics Section	Questions
Subnet Mask Conversion	1–3
Defining the Format of IPv4 Addresses	4–7

1. Which of the following answers lists the prefix (CIDR) format equivalent of 255.255.254.0?

    a. /19

    b. /20

    c. /23

    d. /24

    e. /25

2. Which of the following answers lists the prefix (CIDR) format equivalent of 255.255.255.240?

    a. /26

    b. /28

    c. /27

    d. /30

    e. /29

3. Which of the following answers lists the dotted-decimal notation (DDN) equivalent of /30?

    a. 255.255.255.192

    b. 255.255.255.252

    c. 255.255.255.240

    d. 255.255.254.0

    e. 255.255.255.0

4. Working at the help desk, you receive a call and learn a user's PC IP address and mask (10.55.66.77, mask 255.255.255.0). When thinking about this using classful logic, you determine the number of network (N), subnet (S), and host (H) bits. Which of the following is true in this case?

    a. N=12

    b. S=12

    c. H=8

    d. S=8

    e. N=24

5. Working at the help desk, you receive a call and learn a user's PC IP address and mask (192.168.9.1/27). When thinking about this using classful logic, you determine the number of network (N), subnet (S), and host (H) bits. Which of the following is true in this case?

    a. N=24

    b. S=24

    c. H=8

    d. H=7

6. Which of the following statements is true about classless IP addressing concepts?

    a. Uses a 128-bit IP address

    b. Applies only for Class A and B networks

    c. Separates IP addresses into network, subnet, and host parts

    d. Ignores Class A, B, and C network rules

7. Which of the following masks, when used as the only mask within a Class B network, would supply enough subnet bits to support 100 subnets? (Choose two.)

    a. /24

    b. 255.255.255.252

    c. /20

    d. 255.255.252.0

Foundation Topics

Subnet Mask Conversion

This section describes how to convert between different formats for the subnet mask. You can then use these processes when you practice. If you already know how to convert from one format to the other, go ahead and move to the section "Practice Converting Subnet Masks," later in this chapter.

Three Mask Formats

Subnet masks can be written as 32-bit binary numbers, but not just any binary number. In particular, the binary subnet mask must follow these rules:

- The value must not interleave 1s and 0s.

- If 1s exist, they are on the left.

- If 0s exist, they are on the right.

For example, the following values would be illegal. The first is illegal because the value interleaves 0s and 1s, and the second is illegal because it lists 0s on the left and 1s on the right:

```
10101010 01010101 11110000 00001111
00000000 00000000 00000000 11111111
```

The following two binary values meet the requirements, in that they have all 1s on the left, followed by all 0s, with no interleaving of 1s and 0s:

```
11111111 00000000 00000000 00000000
11111111 11111111 11111111 00000000
```

Two alternative subnet mask formats exist so that we humans do not have to work with 32-bit binary numbers. One format, dotted-decimal notation (DDN), converts each set of 8 bits into the decimal equivalent. For example, the two previous binary masks would convert to the following DDN subnet masks because binary 11111111 converts to decimal 255, and binary 00000000 converts to decimal 0:

255.0.0.0

255.255.255.0

Although the DDN format has been around since the beginning of IPv4 addressing, the third mask format was added later, in the early 1990s: the *prefix* format. This format takes advantage of the rule that the subnet mask starts with some number of 1s, and then the rest of the digits are 0s. Prefix format lists a slash (/) followed by the number of binary 1s in the binary mask. Using the same two examples as earlier in this section, the prefix format equivalent masks are as follows:

/8

/24

Note that although the terms *prefix* or *prefix mask* can be used, the terms *CIDR mask* or *slash mask* can also be used. This newer prefix style mask was created around the same time as the classless interdomain routing (CIDR) specification back in the early 1990s, and the acronym CIDR grew to be used for anything related to CIDR, including prefix-style masks. In addition, the term *slash mask* is sometimes used because the value includes a slash mark (/).

You need to get comfortable working with masks in different formats. The rest of this section examines how to convert between the three formats.

Converting Between Binary and Prefix Masks

Converting between binary and prefix masks should be relatively intuitive after you know that the prefix value is simply the number of binary 1s in the binary mask. For the sake of completeness, the processes to convert in each direction are

Binary to prefix: Count the number of binary 1s in the binary mask, and write the total, in decimal, after a /.

Prefix to binary: Write P binary 1s, where P is the prefix value, followed by as many binary 0s as required to create a 32-bit number.

Tables 13-2 and 13-3 show some examples.

13

Table 13-2   Example Conversions: Binary to Prefix

Binary Mask	Logic	Prefix Mask
11111111 11111111 11000000 00000000	Count 8 + 8 + 2 = 18 binary 1s	/18
11111111 11111111 11111111 11110000	Count 8 + 8 + 8 + 4 = 28 binary 1s	/28
11111111 11111000 00000000 00000000	Count 8 + 5 = 13 binary 1s	/13

Table 13-3   Example Conversions: Prefix to Binary

Prefix Mask	Logic	Binary Mask
/18	Write 18 1s, then 14 0s, total 32	11111111 11111111 11000000 00000000
/28	Write 28 1s, then 4 0s, total 32	11111111 11111111 11111111 11110000
/13	Write 13 1s, then 19 0s, total 32	11111111 11111000 00000000 00000000

Converting Between Binary and DDN Masks

By definition, a dotted-decimal number (DDN) used with IPv4 addressing contains four decimal numbers, separated by dots. Each decimal number represents 8 bits. So, a single DDN shows four decimal numbers that together represent some 32-bit binary number.

Conversion from a DDN mask to the binary equivalent is relatively simple to describe but can be laborious to perform. First, to do the conversion, the process is as follows:

For each octet, perform a decimal-to-binary conversion.

However, depending on your comfort level with doing decimal-to-binary conversions, that process can be difficult or time-consuming. If you want to think about masks in binary for the exam, consider picking one of the following methods to do the conversion and practicing until you can do it quickly and accurately:

- Do the decimal-binary conversions, but practice your decimal-binary conversions to become faster. If you choose this path, consider the Cisco Binary Game, which you can find by searching its name at the Cisco Learning Network (CLN) (http://learningnetwork.cisco.com).

- Use the decimal-binary conversion chart in Appendix A, "Numeric Reference Tables." This lets you find the answer more quickly now, but you cannot use the chart on exam day.

- Memorize the nine possible decimal values that can be in a decimal mask, and practice using a reference table with those values.

The third method, which is the method recommended in this book, takes advantage of the fact that any and every DDN mask octet must be one of only nine values. Why? Well, remember how a binary mask cannot interleave 1s and 0s, and the 0s must be on the right? It turns out that only nine different 8-bit binary numbers conform to these rules. Table 13-4 lists the values, along with other relevant information.

Answers to the "Do I Know This Already?" quiz:

1 C **2** B **3** B **4** C **5** A **6** D **7** A, B

Table 13-4 Nine Possible Values in One Octet of a Subnet Mask

Binary Mask Octet	Decimal Equivalent	Number of Binary 1s
00000000	0	0
10000000	128	1
11000000	192	2
11100000	224	3
11110000	240	4
11111000	248	5
11111100	252	6
11111110	254	7
11111111	255	8

Many subnetting processes can be done with or without binary math. Some of those processes—mask conversion included—use the information in Table 13-4. You should plan to memorize the information in the table. I recommend making a copy of the table to keep handy while you practice. (You will likely memorize the contents of this table simply by practicing the conversion process enough to get both good and fast at the conversion.)

Using the table, the conversion processes in each direction with binary and decimal masks are as follows:

Binary to decimal: Organize the bits into four sets of eight. For each octet, find the binary value in the table and write down the corresponding decimal value.

Decimal to binary: For each octet, find the decimal value in the table and write down the corresponding 8-bit binary value.

Tables 13-5 and 13-6 show some examples.

Table 13-5 Conversion Example: Binary to Decimal

Binary Mask	Logic	Decimal Mask
11111111 11111111 11000000 00000000	11111111 maps to 255 11000000 maps to 192 00000000 maps to 0	255.255.192.0
11111111 11111111 11111111 11110000	11111111 maps to 255 11110000 maps to 240	255.255.255.240
11111111 11111000 00000000 00000000	11111111 maps to 255 11111000 maps to 248 00000000 maps to 0	255.248.0.0

13

Table 13-6 Conversion Examples: Decimal to Binary

Decimal Mask	Logic	Binary Mask
255.255.192.0	255 maps to 11111111 192 maps to 11000000 0 maps to 00000000	11111111 11111111 11000000 00000000
255.255.255.240	255 maps to 11111111 240 maps to 11110000	11111111 11111111 11111111 11110000
255.248.0.0	255 maps to 11111111 248 maps to 11111000 0 maps to 00000000	11111111 11111000 00000000 00000000

Converting Between Prefix and DDN Masks

When you are learning, the best way to convert between the prefix and decimal formats is to first convert to binary. For example, to move from decimal to prefix, first convert decimal to binary and then from binary to prefix.

For the exams, set a goal to master these conversions doing the math in your head. While learning, you will likely want to use paper. To train yourself to do all this without writing it down, instead of writing each octet of binary, just write the number of binary 1s in that octet.

Figure 13-1 shows an example with a prefix-to-decimal conversion. The left side shows the conversion to binary as an interim step. For comparison, the right side shows the binary interim step in shorthand that just lists the number of binary 1s in each octet of the binary mask.

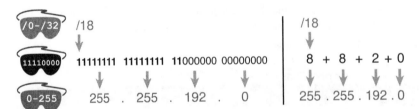

Figure 13-1 *Conversion from Prefix to Decimal: Full Binary Versus Shorthand*

Similarly, when converting from decimal to prefix, mentally convert to binary along the way, and as you improve, just think of the binary as the number of 1s in each octet. Figure 13-2 shows an example of such a conversion.

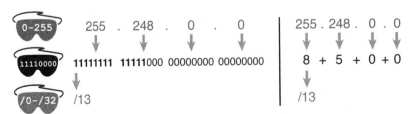

Figure 13-2 *Conversion from Decimal to Prefix: Full Binary Versus Shorthand*

Note that Appendix A has a table that lists all 33 legal subnet masks, with all three formats shown.

Practice Converting Subnet Masks

Before moving to the second half of this chapter, and thinking about what these subnet masks mean, first do some practice. Practice the processes discussed in this chapter until you get the right answer most of the time. Later, before taking the exam, practice more until you master the topics in this chapter and can move pretty fast, as outlined in the right column of Table 13-7.

Table 13-7 Keep-Reading and Take-Exam Goals for This Chapter's Topics

	Before Moving to the Next Section	Before Taking the Exam
Focus On...	Learning how	Being correct and fast
Tools Allowed	All	Your brain and a notepad
Goal: Accuracy	90% correct	100% correct
Goal: Speed	Any speed	10 seconds

Table 13-8 lists eight practice problems. The table has three columns, one for each mask format. Each row lists one mask, in one format. Your job is to find the mask's value in the other two formats for each row. Table 13-12, located in the section "Answers to Earlier Practice Problems," later in this chapter, lists the answers.

Table 13-8 Practice Problems: Find the Mask Values in the Other Two Formats

Prefix	Binary Mask	Decimal
	11111111 11111111 11000000 00000000	
		255.255.255.252
/25		
/16		
		255.0.0.0
	11111111 11111111 11111100 00000000	
		255.254.0.0
/27		

Identifying Subnet Design Choices Using Masks

Subnet masks have many purposes. In fact, if ten experienced network engineers were independently asked, "What is the purpose of a subnet mask?" the engineers would likely give a variety of true answers. The subnet mask plays several roles.

13

This chapter focuses on one particular use of a subnet mask: defining the prefix part of the IP addresses in a subnet. The prefix part must be the same value for all addresses in a subnet. In fact, a single subnet can be defined as all IPv4 addresses that have the same value in the prefix part of their IPv4 addresses.

While the previous paragraph might sound a bit formal, the idea is relatively basic, as shown in Figure 13-3. The figure shows a network diagram, focusing on two subnets: a subnet of all addresses that begin with 172.16.2 and another subnet made of all addresses that begin with 172.16.3. In this example, the prefix—the part that has the same value in all the addresses in the subnet—is the first three octets.

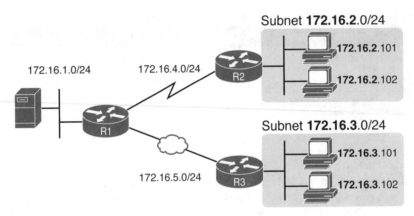

Figure 13-3   *Simple Subnet Design, with Mask /24*

While people can sit around a conference table and talk about how a prefix is three octets long, computers communicate that same concept using a subnet mask. In this case, the subnets use a subnet mask of /24, which means that the prefix part of the addresses is 24 bits (3 octets) long.

This section explains more about how to use a subnet mask to understand this concept of a prefix part of an IPv4 address, along with these other uses for a subnet mask. Note that this section discusses the first five items in the list.

- Defines the size of the prefix (combined network and subnet) part of the addresses in a subnet
- Defines the size of the host part of the addresses in the subnet
- Can be used to calculate the number of hosts in the subnet
- Provides a means for the network designer to communicate the design details—the number of subnet and host bits—to the devices in the network
- Under certain assumptions, can be used to calculate the number of subnets in the entire classful network
- Can be used in binary calculations of both the subnet ID and the subnet broadcast address

Masks Divide the Subnet's Addresses into Two Parts

The subnet mask subdivides the IP addresses in a subnet into two parts: the *prefix*, or *subnet part*, and the *host part*.

The prefix part identifies the addresses that reside in the same subnet because all IP addresses in the same subnet have the same value in the prefix part of their addresses. The idea is much like the postal code (ZIP codes in the United States) in mailing addresses. All mailing addresses in the same town have the same postal code. Likewise, all IP addresses in the same subnet have identical values in the prefix part of their addresses.

The host part of an address identifies the host uniquely inside the subnet. If you compare any two IP addresses in the same subnet, their host parts will differ, even though the prefix parts of their addresses have the same value. To summarize these key comparisons:

Prefix (subnet) part: Equal in all addresses in the same subnet.

Host part: Different in all addresses in the same subnet.

For example, imagine a subnet that, in concept, includes all addresses whose first three octets are 10.1.1. So, the following list shows several addresses in this subnet:

10.1.1.**1**

10.1.1.**2**

10.1.1.**3**

In this list, the prefix or subnet part (the first three octets of 10.1.1) are equal. The host part (the last octet [in bold]) is different. So, the prefix or subnet part of the address identifies the group, and the host part identifies the specific member of the group.

The subnet mask defines the dividing line between the prefix and the host part. To do so, the mask creates a conceptual line between the binary 1s in the binary mask and the binary 0s in the mask. In short, if a mask has P binary 1s, the prefix part is P bits long and the rest of the bits are host bits. Figure 13-4 shows the general concept.

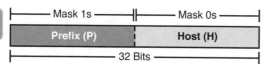

Figure 13-4 *Prefix (Subnet) and Host Parts Defined by Mask 1s and 0s*

The next figure, Figure 13-5, shows a specific example using mask 255.255.255.0. Mask 255.255.255.0 (/24) has 24 binary 1s, for a prefix length of 24 bits.

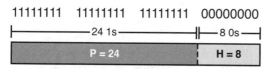

Figure 13-5 *Mask 255.255.255.0: P=24, H=8*

13

Masks and Class Divide Addresses into Three Parts

In addition to the two-part view of IPv4 addresses, you can also think about IPv4 addresses as having three parts. To do so, just apply Class A, B, and C rules to the address format to define the network part at the beginning of the address. This added logic divides the prefix into two parts: the *network* part and the *subnet* part. The class defines the length of the network part, with the subnet part simply being the rest of the prefix. Figure 13-6 shows the idea.

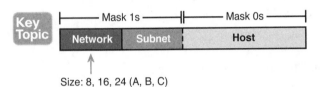

Size: 8, 16, 24 (A, B, C)

Figure 13-6   *Class Concepts Applied to Create Three Parts*

The combined network and subnet parts act like the prefix because all addresses in the same subnet must have identical values in the network and subnet parts. The size of the host part remains unchanged, whether viewing the addresses as having two parts or three parts.

To be complete, Figure 13-7 shows the same example as in the previous section, with the subnet of "all addresses that begin with 10.1.1." In that example, the subnet uses mask 255.255.255.0, and the addresses are all in Class A network 10.0.0.0. The class defines 8 network bits, and the mask defines 24 prefix bits, meaning that $24 - 8 = 16$ subnet bits exist. The host part remains as 8 bits per the mask.

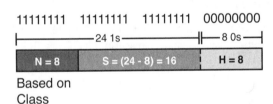

Based on
Class

Figure 13-7   *Subnet 10.1.1.0, Mask 255.255.255.0: N=8, S=16, H=8*

Classless and Classful Addressing

The terms *classless addressing* and *classful addressing* refer to the two different ways to think about IPv4 addresses as described so far in this chapter. Classful addressing means that you think about Class A, B, and C rules, so the prefix is separated into the network and subnet parts, as shown in Figures 13-6 and 13-7. Classless addressing means that you ignore the Class A, B, and C rules and treat the prefix part as one part, as shown in Figures 13-4 and 13-5. The following more formal definitions are listed for reference and study:

Classless addressing: The concept that an IPv4 address has two parts—the prefix part plus the host part—as defined by the mask, with *no consideration of the class* (A, B, or C).

Classful addressing: The concept that an IPv4 address has three parts—network, subnet, and host—as defined by the mask *and Class A, B, and C rules*.

NOTE Unfortunately, the networking world uses the terms *classless* and *classful* in a couple of different ways. In addition to the classless and classful addressing described here, each routing protocol can be categorized as either a *classless routing protocol* or a *classful routing protocol*. In another use, the terms *classless routing* and *classful routing* refer to some details of how Cisco routers forward (route) packets using the default route in some cases. As a result, these terms can be easily confused and misused. So, when you see the words *classless* and *classful*, be careful to note the context: addressing, routing, or routing protocols.

Calculations Based on the IPv4 Address Format

After you know how to break an address down using both classless and classful addressing rules, you can easily calculate a couple of important facts using some basic math formulas.

First, for any subnet, after you know the number of host bits, you can calculate the number of host IP addresses in the subnet. Next, if you know the number of subnet bits (using classful addressing concepts) and you know that only one subnet mask is used throughout the network, you can also calculate the number of subnets in the network. The formulas just require that you know the powers of 2:

Hosts in the subnet: $2^H - 2$, where H is the number of host bits.

Subnets in the network: 2^S, where S is the number of subnet bits. Only use this formula if only one mask is used throughout the network.

NOTE The section "Choose the Mask" in Chapter 11, "Perspectives on IPv4 Subnetting," details many concepts related to masks, including comments about this assumption of one mask throughout a single Class A, B, or C network.

The sizes of the parts of IPv4 addresses can also be calculated. The math is basic, but the concepts are important. Keeping in mind that IPv4 addresses are 32 bits long, the two parts with classless addressing must add up to 32 (P + H = 32), and with classful addressing, the three parts must add up to 32 (N + S + H = 32). Figure 13-8 shows the relationships.

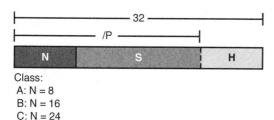

Class:
A: N = 8
B: N = 16
C: N = 24

Figure 13-8 *Relationship Between /P, N, S, and H*

You often begin with an IP address and mask, both when answering questions on the CCNA exam and when examining problems that occur in real networks. Based on the information in this chapter and earlier chapters, you should be able to find all the information in Figure 13-8 and then calculate the number of hosts/subnet and the number of subnets in the network.

13

For reference, the following process spells out the steps:

Step 1.   Convert the mask to prefix format (/P) as needed. (See the earlier section "Practice Converting Subnet Masks" for review.)

Step 2.   Determine N based on the class. (See Chapter 12, "Analyzing Classful IPv4 Networks," for review.)

Step 3.   Calculate S = P – N.

Step 4.   Calculate H = 32 – P.

Step 5.   Calculate hosts/subnet: $2^H - 2$.

Step 6.   Calculate number of subnets: 2^S.

For example, consider the case of IP address 8.1.4.5 with mask 255.255.0.0 by following this process:

Step 1.   255.255.0.0 = /16, so P=16.

Step 2.   8.1.4.5 is in the range 1–126 in the first octet, so it is Class A; so N=8.

Step 3.   S = P – N = 16 – 8 = 8.

Step 4.   H = 32 – P = 32 – 16 = 16.

Step 5. $2^{16} - 2 = 65,534$ hosts/subnet.

Step 6. $2^8 = 256$ subnets.

Figure 13-9 shows a visual analysis of the same problem.

Figure 13-9   *Visual Representation of Problem: 8.1.4.5, 255.255.0.0*

For another example, consider address 200.1.1.1, mask 255.255.255.252 by following this process:

Step 1.   255.255.255.252 = /30, so P=30.

Step 2.   200.1.1.1 is in the range 192–223 in the first octet, so it is Class C; so N=24.

Step 3.   S = P – N = 30 – 24 = 6.

Step 4.   H = 32 – P = 32 – 30 = 2.

Step 5. $2^2 - 2 = 2$ hosts/subnet.

Step 6. $2^6 = 64$ subnets.

This example uses a popular mask for serial links because serial links only require two host addresses, and the mask supports only two host addresses.

Practice Analyzing Subnet Masks

As with the other subnetting math in this book, using a two-phase approach may help. Take time now to practice until you feel as though you understand the process. Then, before the exam, make sure you master the math. Table 13-9 summarizes the key concepts and suggestions for this two-phase approach.

Table 13-9   Keep-Reading and Take-Exam Goals for This Chapter's Topics

	Before Moving to the Next Chapter	Before Taking the Exam
Focus On...	Learning how	Being correct and fast
Tools Allowed	All	Your brain and a notepad
Goal: Accuracy	90% correct	100% correct
Goal: Speed	Any speed	15 seconds

On a piece of scratch paper, answer the following questions. In each case:

- Determine the structure of the addresses in each subnet based on the class and mask, using classful IP addressing concepts. In other words, find the size of the network, subnet, and host parts of the addresses.
- Calculate the number of hosts in the subnet.
- Calculate the number of subnets in the network, assuming that the same mask is used throughout.

1. 8.1.4.5, 255.255.254.0
2. 130.4.102.1, 255.255.255.0
3. 199.1.1.100, 255.255.255.0
4. 130.4.102.1, 255.255.252.0
5. 199.1.1.100, 255.255.255.224

The answers are listed in the section "Answers to Earlier Practice Problems," later in this chapter.

Chapter Review

One key to doing well on the exams is to perform repetitive spaced review sessions. Review this chapter's material using either the tools in the book or interactive tools for the same material found on the book's companion website. Refer to the "Your Study Plan" element for more details. Table 13-10 outlines the key review elements and where you can find them. To better track your study progress, record when you completed these activities in the second column.

13

Table 13-10   Chapter Review Tracking

Review Element	Review Date(s)	Resource Used
Review key topics		Book, website
Review key terms		Book, website
Answer DIKTA questions		Book, PTP
Review memory tables		Website
Practice analyzing subnet masks		Website, Appendix E

Review All the Key Topics

Table 13-11   Key Topics for Chapter 13

Key Topic Element	Description	Page Number
List	Rules for binary subnet mask values	304
List	Rules to convert between binary and prefix masks	305
Table 13-4	Nine possible values in a decimal subnet mask	307
List	Rules to convert between binary and DDN masks	307
List	Some functions of a subnet mask	310
List	Comparisons of IP addresses in the same subnet	311
Figure 13-4	Two-part classless view of an IP address	311
Figure 13-6	Three-part classful view of an IP address	312
List	Definitions of classful addressing and classless addressing	312
List	Formal steps to analyze masks and calculate values	314

Key Terms You Should Know

binary mask, dotted-decimal notation (DDN), decimal mask, prefix mask, CIDR mask, classful addressing, classless addressing

Additional Practice for This Chapter's Processes

You can do more practice with the processes in this chapter with a pair of practice sets. One focuses on interpreting existing masks, while the other gives you practice with converting between mask formats. You may do each practice set using the following tools:

Application: Use the "Analyzing Subnet Masks" and "Converting Masks" applications on the companion website, listed under the Chapter Review for this chapter.

PDF: Alternatively, practice the same problems found in both these apps using companion website Appendix E, "Practice for Chapter 13: Analyzing Subnet Masks."

Answers to Earlier Practice Problems

Table 13-8, shown earlier, listed several practice problems for converting subnet masks; Table 13-12 lists the answers.

Table 13-12   Answers to Problems in Table 13-8

Prefix	Binary Mask	Decimal
/18	11111111 11111111 11000000 00000000	255.255.192.0
/30	11111111 11111111 11111111 11111100	255.255.255.252
/25	11111111 11111111 11111111 10000000	255.255.255.128
/16	11111111 11111111 00000000 00000000	255.255.0.0
/8	11111111 00000000 00000000 00000000	255.0.0.0
/22	11111111 11111111 11111100 00000000	255.255.252.0
/15	11111111 11111110 00000000 00000000	255.254.0.0
/27	11111111 11111111 11111111 11100000	255.255.255.224

Table 13-13 lists the answers to the practice problems from the earlier section "Practice Analyzing Subnet Masks."

Table 13-13   Answers to Problems from Earlier in the Chapter

	Problem	/P	Class	N	S	H	2^S	$2^H - 2$
1	8.1.4.5 255.255.254.0	23	A	8	15	9	32,768	510
2	130.4.102.1 255.255.255.0	24	B	16	8	8	256	254
3	199.1.1.100 255.255.255.0	24	C	24	0	8	N/A	254
4	130.4.102.1 255.255.252.0	22	B	16	6	10	64	1022
5	199.1.1.100 255.255.255.224	27	C	24	3	5	8	30

The following list reviews the problems:

1. For 8.1.4.5, the first octet (8) is in the 1–126 range, so it is a Class A address, with 8 network bits. Mask 255.255.254.0 converts to /23, so P – N = 15, for 15 subnet bits. H can be found by subtracting /P (23) from 32, for 9 host bits.

2. 130.4.102.1 is in the 128–191 range in the first octet, making it a Class B address, with N = 16 bits. 255.255.255.0 converts to /24, so the number of subnet bits is 24 – 16 = 8. With 24 prefix bits, the number of host bits is 32 – 24 = 8.

3. The third problem purposely shows a case where the mask does not create a subnet part of the address. The address, 199.1.1.100, has a first octet between 192 and 223, making it a Class C address with 24 network bits. The prefix version of the mask is /24, so the number of subnet bits is 24 – 24 = 0. The number of host bits is 32 minus

13

the prefix length (24), for a total of 8 host bits. So in this case, the mask shows that the network engineer is using the default mask, which creates no subnet bits and no subnets.

4. With the same address as the second problem, 130.4.102.1 is a Class B address with N = 16 bits. This problem uses a different mask, 255.255.252.0, which converts to /22. This makes the number of subnet bits 22 − 16 = 6. With 22 prefix bits, the number of host bits is 32 − 22 = 10.

5. With the same address as the third problem, 199.1.1.100 is a Class C address with N = 24 bits. This problem uses a different mask, 255.255.255.224, which converts to /27. This makes the number of subnet bits 27 − 24 = 3. With 27 prefix bits, the number of host bits is 32 − 27 = 5.

CHAPTER 14

Analyzing Existing Subnets

This chapter covers the following exam topics:

1.0 Network Fundamentals

1.6 Configure and verify IPv4 addressing and subnetting

Often, a networking task begins with the discovery of the IP address and mask used by some host. Then, to understand how the internetwork routes packets to that host, you must find key pieces of information about the subnet, specifically the following:

- Subnet ID
- Subnet broadcast address
- Subnet's range of usable unicast IP addresses

This chapter discusses the concepts and math to take a known IP address and mask, and then fully describe a subnet by finding the values in this list. These specific tasks might well be the most important IP skills in the entire IP addressing and subnetting topics in this book because these tasks might be the most commonly used tasks when operating and troubleshooting real networks.

"Do I Know This Already?" Quiz

Take the quiz (either here or use the PTP software) if you want to use the score to help you decide how much time to spend on this chapter. The letter answers are listed at the bottom of the page following the quiz. Appendix C, found both at the end of the book as well as on the companion website, includes both the answers and explanations. You can also find both answers and explanations in the PTP testing software.

Table 14-1 "Do I Know This Already?" Foundation Topics Section-to-Question Mapping

Foundation Topics Section	Questions
Defining a Subnet	1
Analyzing Existing Subnets: Binary	2
Analyzing Existing Subnets: Decimal	3–6

1. When you think about an IP address using classful addressing rules, an address can have three parts: network, subnet, and host. If you examined all the addresses in one subnet, in binary, which of the following answers correctly states which of the three parts of the addresses will be equal among all addresses? (Choose the best answer.)

   a. Network part only
   b. Subnet part only
   c. Host part only
   d. Network and subnet parts
   e. Subnet and host parts

2. Which of the following statements are true regarding the binary subnet ID, subnet broadcast address, and host IP address values in any single subnet? (Choose two answers.)

   a. The host part of the broadcast address is all binary 0s.

   b. The host part of the subnet ID is all binary 0s.

   c. The host part of a usable IP address can have all binary 1s.

   d. The host part of any usable IP address must not be all binary 0s.

3. Which of the following is the resident subnet ID for IP address 10.7.99.133/24?

   a. 10.0.0.0

   b. 10.7.0.0

   c. 10.7.99.0

   d. 10.7.99.128

4. Which of the following is the resident subnet for IP address 192.168.44.97/30?

   a. 192.168.44.0

   b. 192.168.44.64

   c. 192.168.44.96

   d. 192.168.44.128

5. Which of the following is the subnet broadcast address for the subnet in which IP address 172.31.77.201/27 resides?

   a. 172.31.201.255

   b. 172.31.255.255

   c. 172.31.77.223

   d. 172.31.77.207

6. A fellow engineer tells you to configure the DHCP server to lease the last 100 usable IP addresses in subnet 10.1.4.0/23. Which of the following IP addresses could be leased as a result of your new configuration?

   a. 10.1.4.156

   b. 10.1.4.254

   c. 10.1.5.200

   d. 10.1.7.200

   e. 10.1.255.200

Foundation Topics

Defining a Subnet

An IP subnet is a subset of a classful network, created by choice of some network engineer. However, that engineer cannot pick just any arbitrary subset of addresses; instead, the engineer must follow certain rules, such as the following:

- The subnet contains a set of consecutive numbers.

- The subnet holds 2^H numbers, where H is the number of host bits defined by the subnet mask.

- Two special numbers in the range cannot be used as IP addresses:

  - The first (lowest) number acts as an identifier for the subnet (*subnet ID*).

  - The last (highest) number acts as a *subnet broadcast address*.

- The remaining addresses, whose values sit between the subnet ID and subnet broadcast address, are used as *unicast IP addresses*.

This section reviews and expands the basic concepts of the subnet ID, subnet broadcast address, and range of addresses in a subnet.

An Example with Network 172.16.0.0 and Four Subnets

Imagine that you work at the customer support center, where you receive all initial calls from users who have problems with their computer. You coach the user through finding her IP address and mask: 172.16.150.41, mask 255.255.192.0. One of the first and most common tasks you will do based on that information is to find the subnet ID of the subnet in which that address resides. (In fact, this subnet ID is sometimes called the *resident subnet* because the IP address exists in or resides in that subnet.)

Before getting into the math, examine the mask (255.255.192.0) and classful network (172.16.0.0) for a moment. From the mask, based on what you learned in Chapter 13, "Analyzing Subnet Masks," you can find the structure of the addresses in the subnet, including the number of host and subnet bits. That analysis tells you that two subnet bits exist, meaning that there should be four (2^2) subnets. Figure 14-1 shows the idea.

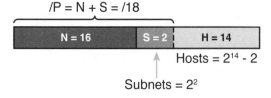

Figure 14-1 *Address Structure: Class B Network, /18 Mask*

Answers to the "Do I Know This Already?" quiz:

1 D **2** B, D **3** C **4** C **5** C **6** C

> **NOTE** This chapter, like the others in this part of the book, assumes that one mask is used throughout an entire classful network.

Because each subnet uses a single mask, all subnets of this single IP network must be the same size, because all subnets have the same structure. In this example, all four subnets will have the structure shown in the figure, so all four subnets will have $2^{14} - 2$ host addresses.

Next, consider the big picture of what happens with this example subnet design: the one Class B network now has four subnets of equal size. Conceptually, if you represent the entire Class B network as a number line, each subnet consumes one-fourth of the number line, as shown in Figure 14-2. Each subnet has a subnet ID—the numerically lowest number in the subnet—so it sits on the left of the subnet. And each subnet has a subnet broadcast address—the numerically highest number in the subnet—so it sits on the right side of the subnet.

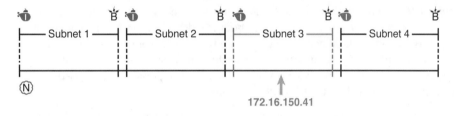

Legend:

(N) Network ID

Subnet ID

B Subnet Broadcast Address

Figure 14-2 *Network 172.16.0.0, Divided into Four Equal Subnets*

The rest of this chapter focuses on how to take one IP address and mask and discover the details about that one subnet in which the address resides. In other words, you see how to find the resident subnet of an IP address. Again, using IP address 172.16.150.41 and mask 255.255.192.0 as an example, Figure 14-3 shows the resident subnet, along with the subnet ID and subnet broadcast address that bracket the subnet.

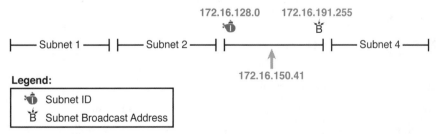

Legend:

Subnet ID

B Subnet Broadcast Address

Figure 14-3 *Resident Subnet for 172.16.150.41, 255.255.192.0*

Subnet ID Concepts

A subnet ID is simply a number used to succinctly represent a subnet. When listed along with its matching subnet mask, the subnet ID identifies the subnet and can be used to derive the subnet broadcast address and range of addresses in the subnet. Rather than having to write down all these details about a subnet, you simply need to write down the subnet ID and mask, and you have enough information to fully describe the subnet.

The subnet ID appears in many places, but it is seen most often in IP routing tables. For example, when an engineer configures a router with its IP address and mask, the router calculates the subnet ID and puts a route into its routing table for that subnet. The router typically then advertises the subnet ID/mask combination to neighboring routers with some IP routing protocol. Eventually, all the routers in an enterprise learn about the subnet—again using the subnet ID and subnet mask combination—and display it in their routing tables. (You can display the contents of a router's IP routing table using the **show ip route** command.)

Unfortunately, the terminology related to subnets can sometimes cause problems. First, the terms *subnet ID*, *subnet number*, and *subnet address* are synonyms. In addition, people sometimes simply say *subnet* when referring to both the idea of a subnet and the number that is used as the subnet ID. When talking about routing, people sometimes use the term *prefix* instead of *subnet*. The term *prefix* refers to the same idea as *subnet*; it just uses terminology from the classless addressing way to describe IP addresses, as discussed in Chapter 13's section "Classless and Classful Addressing."

The biggest terminology confusion arises between the terms *network* and *subnet*. In the real world, people often use these terms synonymously, and that is perfectly reasonable in some cases. In other cases, the specific meaning of these terms, and their differences, matter to what is being discussed.

For example, people often might say, "What is the network ID?" when they really want to know the subnet ID. In another case, they might want to know the Class A, B, or C network ID. So, when one engineer asks something like, "What's the net ID for 172.16.150.41 slash 18?" use the context to figure out whether he wants the literal classful network ID (172.16.0.0, in this case) or the literal subnet ID (172.16.128.0, in this case).

For the exams, be ready to notice when the terms *subnet* and *network* are used, and then use the context to figure out the specific meaning of the term in that case.

Table 14-2 summarizes the key facts about the subnet ID, along with the possible synonyms, for easier review and study.

Table 14-2   Summary of Subnet ID Key Facts

Definition	Number that represents the subnet
Numeric Value	First (smallest) number in the subnet
Literal Synonyms	Subnet number, subnet address, prefix, resident subnet
Common-Use Synonyms	Network, network ID, network number, network address
Typically Seen In...	Routing tables, documentation

Subnet Broadcast Address

The subnet broadcast address has two main roles: to be used as a destination IP address for the purpose of sending packets to all hosts in the subnet, and as a means to find the high end of the range of addresses in a subnet.

The original purpose for the subnet broadcast address was to give hosts a way to send one packet to all hosts in a subnet and to do so efficiently. For example, a host in subnet A could send a packet with a destination address of subnet B's subnet broadcast address. The routers would forward this one packet just like a packet sent to a host in subnet B. After the packet arrives at the router connected to subnet B, that last router would then forward the packet to all hosts in subnet B, typically by encapsulating the packet in a data-link layer broadcast frame. As a result, all hosts in host B's subnet would receive a copy of the packet.

The subnet broadcast address also helps you find the range of addresses in a subnet because the broadcast address is the last (highest) number in a subnet's range of addresses. To find the low end of the range, calculate the subnet ID; to find the high end of the range, calculate the subnet broadcast address.

Table 14-3 summarizes the key facts about the subnet broadcast address, along with the possible synonyms, for easier review and study.

Table 14-3   Summary of Subnet Broadcast Address Key Facts

Definition	A reserved number in each subnet that, when used as the destination address of a packet, causes the device to forward the packet to all hosts in that subnet
Numeric Value	Last (highest) number in the subnet
Literal Synonyms	Directed broadcast address
Broader-Use Synonyms	Network broadcast
Typically Seen In...	In calculations of the range of addresses in a subnet

Range of Usable Addresses

The engineers implementing an IP internetwork need to know the range of unicast IP addresses in each subnet. Before you can plan which addresses to use as statically assigned IP addresses, which to configure to be leased by the DHCP server, and which to reserve for later use, you need to know the range of usable addresses.

To find the range of usable IP addresses in a subnet, first find the subnet ID and the subnet broadcast address. Then, just add 1 to the fourth octet of the subnet ID to get the first (lowest) usable address, and subtract 1 from the fourth octet of the subnet broadcast address to get the last (highest) usable address in the subnet.

For example, Figure 14-3 showed subnet ID 172.16.128.0, mask /18. The first usable address is simply one more than the subnet ID (in this case, 172.16.128.1). That same figure showed a subnet broadcast address of 172.16.191.255, so the last usable address is one less, or 172.16.191.254.

Now that this section has described the concepts behind the numbers that collectively define a subnet, the rest of this chapter focuses on the math used to find these values.

Analyzing Existing Subnets: Binary

What does it mean to "analyze a subnet"? For this book, it means that you should be able to start with an IP address and mask and then define key facts about the subnet in which that address resides. Specifically, that means discovering the subnet ID, subnet broadcast address, and range of addresses. The analysis can also include the calculation of the number of addresses in the subnet as discussed in Chapter 13, but this chapter does not review those concepts.

Many methods exist to calculate the details about a subnet based on the address/mask. This section begins by discussing some calculations that use binary math, with the next section showing alternatives that use only decimal math. Although many people prefer the decimal method for going fast on the exams, the binary calculations ultimately give you a better understanding of IPv4 addressing. In particular, if you plan to move on to attain Cisco certifications beyond CCNA, you should take the time to understand the binary methods discussed in this section, even if you use the decimal methods for the exams.

Finding the Subnet ID: Binary

The two following statements summarize the logic behind the binary value of any subnet ID:

All numbers in the subnet (subnet ID, subnet broadcast address, and all usable IP addresses) have the same value in the prefix part of the numbers.

The subnet ID is the lowest numeric value in the subnet, so its host part, in binary, is all 0s.

To find the subnet ID in binary, you take the IP address in binary and change all host bits to binary 0. To do so, you need to convert the IP address to binary. You also need to identify the prefix and host bits, which can be easily done by converting the mask (as needed) to prefix format. (Note that Appendix A, "Numeric Reference Tables," includes a decimal-binary conversion table.) Figure 14-4 shows the idea, using the same address/mask as in the earlier examples in this chapter: 172.16.150.41, mask /18.

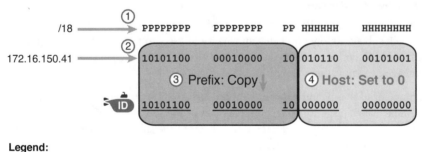

Legend:

 Subnet ID

Figure 14-4 *Binary Concept: Convert the IP Address to the Subnet ID*

Starting at the top of Figure 14-4, the format of the IP address is represented with 18 prefix (P) and 14 host (H) bits in the mask (Step 1). The second row (Step 2) shows the binary version of the IP address, converted from the dotted-decimal notation (DDN) value 172.16.150.41. (If you have not yet used the conversion table in Appendix A, it might be useful to double-check the conversion of all four octets based on the table.)

The next two steps show the action to copy the IP address's prefix bits (Step 3) and give the host bits a value of binary 0 (Step 4). This resulting number is the subnet ID (in binary).

The last step, not shown in Figure 14-4, is to convert the subnet ID from binary to decimal. This book shows that conversion as a separate step, in Figure 14-5, mainly because many people make a mistake at this step in the process. When converting a 32-bit number (like an IP address or IP subnet ID) back to an IPv4 DDN, you must follow this rule:

> Convert 8 bits at a time from binary to decimal, regardless of the line between the prefix and host parts of the number.

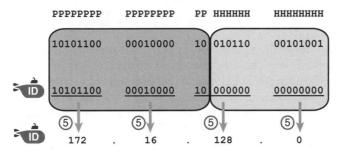

Figure 14-5 *Converting the Subnet ID from Binary to DDN*

Figure 14-5 shows this final step. Note that the third octet (the third set of 8 bits) has 2 bits in the prefix and 6 bits in the host part of the number, but the conversion occurs for all 8 bits.

NOTE You can do the numeric conversions in Figures 14-4 and 14-5 by relying on the conversion table in Appendix A. To convert from DDN to binary, for each octet, find the decimal value in the table and then write down the 8-bit binary equivalent. To convert from binary back to DDN, for each octet of 8 bits, find the matching binary entry in the table and write down the corresponding decimal value. For example, 172 converts to binary 10101100, and 00010000 converts to decimal 16.

Finding the Subnet Broadcast Address: Binary

Finding the subnet broadcast address uses a similar process. To find the subnet broadcast address, use the same binary process used to find the subnet ID, but instead of setting all the host bits to the lowest value (all binary 0s), set the host part to the highest value (all binary 1s). Figure 14-6 shows the concept.

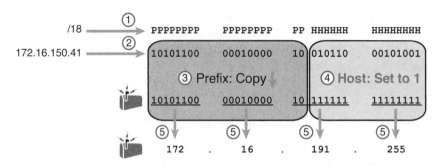

Legend:

 Broadcast Address

Figure 14-6 *Finding a Subnet Broadcast Address: Binary*

The process in Figure 14-6 demonstrates the same first three steps shown in Figure 14-4. Specifically, it shows the identification of the prefix and host bits (Step 1), the results of converting the IP address 172.16.150.41 to binary (Step 2), and the copying of the prefix bits (first 18 bits, in this case). The difference occurs in the host bits on the right, changing all host bits (the last 14, in this case) to the largest possible value (all binary 1s). The final step converts the 32-bit subnet broadcast address to DDN format. Also, remember that with any conversion from DDN to binary or vice versa, the process always converts using 8 bits at a time. In particular, in this case, the entire third octet of binary 10111111 is converted back to decimal 191.

Binary Practice Problems

Figures 14-4 and 14-5 demonstrate a process to find the subnet ID using binary math. The following process summarizes those steps in written form for easier reference and practice:

Step 1. Convert the mask to prefix format to find the length of the prefix (/P) and the length of the host part (32 − P).

Step 2. Convert the IP address to its 32-bit binary equivalent.

Step 3. Copy the prefix bits of the IP address.

Step 4. Write down 0s for the host bits.

Step 5. Convert the resulting 32-bit number, 8 bits at a time, back to decimal.

The process to find the subnet broadcast address is exactly the same, except in Step 4, you set the bits to 1s, as shown in Figure 14-6.

Take a few moments and run through the following five practice problems on scratch paper. In each case, find both the subnet ID and subnet broadcast address. Also, record the prefix style mask:

1. 8.1.4.5, 255.255.0.0

2. 130.4.102.1, 255.255.255.0

3. 199.1.1.100, 255.255.255.0

4.   130.4.102.1, 255.255.252.0

5.   199.1.1.100, 255.255.255.224

Tables 14-4 through 14-8 show the results for the five different examples. The tables show the host bits in bold, and they include the binary version of the address and mask and the binary version of the subnet ID and subnet broadcast address.

Table 14-4   Subnet Analysis for Subnet with Address 8.1.4.5, Mask 255.255.0.0

Prefix Length	/16	11111111 11111111 00000000 00000000
Address	8.1.4.5	00001000 00000001 00000100 00000101
Subnet ID	8.1.0.0	00001000 00000001 00000000 00000000
Broadcast Address	8.1.255.255	00001000 00000001 11111111 11111111

Table 14-5   Subnet Analysis for Subnet with Address 130.4.102.1, Mask 255.255.255.0

Prefix Length	/24	11111111 11111111 11111111 00000000
Address	130.4.102.1	10000010 00000100 01100110 00000001
Subnet ID	130.4.102.0	10000010 00000100 01100110 00000000
Broadcast Address	130.4.102.255	10000010 00000100 01100110 11111111

Table 14-6   Subnet Analysis for Subnet with Address 199.1.1.100, Mask 255.255.255.0

Prefix Length	/24	11111111 11111111 11111111 00000000
Address	199.1.1.100	11000111 00000001 00000001 01100100
Subnet ID	199.1.1.0	11000111 00000001 00000001 00000000
Broadcast Address	199.1.1.255	11000111 00000001 00000001 11111111

Table 14-7   Subnet Analysis for Subnet with Address 130.4.102.1, Mask 255.255.252.0

Prefix Length	/22	11111111 11111111 11111100 00000000
Address	130.4.102.1	10000010 00000100 01100110 00000001
Subnet ID	130.4.100.0	10000010 00000100 01100100 00000000
Broadcast Address	130.4.103.255	10000010 00000100 01100111 11111111

Table 14-8   Subnet Analysis for Subnet with Address 199.1.1.100, Mask 255.255.255.224

Prefix Length	/27	11111111 11111111 11111111 11100000
Address	199.1.1.100	11000111 00000001 00000001 01100100
Subnet ID	199.1.1.96	11000111 00000001 00000001 01100000
Broadcast Address	199.1.1.127	11000111 00000001 00000001 01111111

Shortcut for the Binary Process

The binary process described in this section so far requires that all four octets be converted to binary and then back to decimal. However, you can easily predict the results in at least three of the four octets, based on the DDN mask. You can then avoid the binary math in all but one octet and reduce the number of binary conversions you need to do.

First, consider an octet, and that octet only, whose DDN mask value is 255. The mask value of 255 converts to binary 11111111, which means that all 8 bits are prefix bits. Thinking through the steps in the process, at Step 2, you convert the address to some number. At Step 3, you copy the number. At Step 4, you convert the same 8-bit number back to decimal. All you did in those three steps, in this one octet, is convert from decimal to binary and convert the same number back to the same decimal value!

In short, the subnet ID (and subnet broadcast address) are equal to the IP address in octets for which the mask is 255.

For example, the resident subnet ID for 172.16.150.41, mask 255.255.192.0 is 172.16.128.0. The first two mask octets are 255. Rather than think about the binary math, you could just start by copying the address's value in those two octets: 172.16.

Another shortcut exists for octets whose DDN mask value is decimal 0, or binary 00000000. With a decimal mask value of 0, the math always results in a decimal 0 for the subnet ID, no matter the beginning value in the IP address. Specifically, just look at Steps 4 and 5 in this case: At Step 4, you would write down 8 binary 0s, and at Step 5, you would convert 00000000 back to decimal 0.

The following revised process steps take these two shortcuts into account. However, when the mask is neither 0 nor 255, the process requires the same conversions. At most, you have to do only one octet of the conversions. To find the subnet ID, apply the logic in these steps for each of the four octets:

Step 1. If the mask = 255, copy the decimal IP address for that octet.

Step 2. If the mask = 0, write down a decimal 0 for that octet.

Step 3. If the mask is neither 0 nor 255 in this octet, use the same binary logic as shown in the section "Finding the Subnet ID: Binary," earlier in this chapter.

Figure 14-7 shows an example of this process, again using 172.16.150.41, 255.255.192.0.

To find the subnet broadcast address, you can use a decimal shortcut similar to the one used to find the subnet ID: for DDN mask octets equal to decimal 0, set the decimal subnet broadcast address value to 255 instead of 0, as noted in the following list:

Step 1. If the mask = 255, copy the decimal IP address for that octet.

Step 2. If the mask = 0, write down a decimal 255 for that octet.

Step 3. If the mask is neither 0 nor 255 in this octet, use the same binary logic as shown in the section "Finding the Subnet Broadcast Address: Binary," earlier in this chapter.

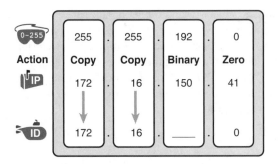

Legend:

DDN Mask   IP Address   Subnet ID

Figure 14-7 *Binary Shortcut Example*

Brief Note About Boolean Math

So far, this chapter has described how humans can use binary math to find the subnet ID and subnet broadcast address. However, computers typically use an entirely different binary process to find the same values, using a branch of mathematics called *Boolean algebra*. Computers already store the IP address and mask in binary form, so they do not have to do any conversions to and from decimal. Then, certain Boolean operations allow the computers to calculate the subnet ID and subnet broadcast address with just a few CPU instructions.

You do not need to know Boolean math to have a good understanding of IP subnetting. However, in case you are interested, computers use the following Boolean logic to find the subnet ID and subnet broadcast address, respectively:

Perform a *Boolean AND* of the IP address and mask. This process converts all host bits to binary 0.

Invert the mask, and then perform a *Boolean OR* of the IP address and inverted subnet mask. This process converts all host bits to binary 1s.

Finding the Range of Addresses

Finding the range of usable addresses in a subnet, after you know the subnet ID and subnet broadcast address, requires only simple addition and subtraction. To find the first (lowest) usable IP address in the subnet, simply add 1 to the fourth octet of the subnet ID. To find the last (highest) usable IP address, simply subtract 1 from the fourth octet of the subnet broadcast address.

Analyzing Existing Subnets: Decimal

Analyzing existing subnets using the binary process works well. However, some of the math takes time for most people, particularly the decimal-binary conversions. And you need to do the math quickly for the Cisco CCNA exam. For the exam, you really should be able to take an IP address and mask, and calculate the subnet ID and range of usable addresses within about 15 seconds. When using binary methods, most people require a lot of practice to be able to find these answers, even when using the abbreviated binary process.

This section discusses how to find the subnet ID and subnet broadcast address using only decimal math. Most people can find the answers more quickly using this process, at least after a little practice, as compared with the binary process. However, the decimal process does not tell you anything about the meaning behind the math. So, if you have not read the earlier section "Analyzing Existing Subnets: Binary," it is worthwhile to read it for the sake of understanding subnetting. This section focuses on getting the right answer using a method that, after you have practiced, should be faster.

Analysis with Easy Masks

With three easy subnet masks in particular, finding the subnet ID and subnet broadcast address requires only easy logic and literally no math. Three easy masks exist:

255.0.0.0

255.255.0.0

255.255.255.0

These easy masks have only 255 and 0 in decimal. In comparison, difficult masks have one octet that has neither a 255 nor a 0 in the mask, which makes the logic more challenging.

> **NOTE**   The terms *easy mask* and *difficult mask* are terms created for use in this book to describe the masks and the level of difficulty when working with each.

When the problem uses an easy mask, you can quickly find the subnet ID based on the IP address and mask in DDN format. Just use the following process for each of the four octets to find the subnet ID:

Step 1.   If the mask octet = 255, copy the decimal IP address.

Step 2.   If the mask octet = 0, write a decimal 0.

A similar simple process exists to find the subnet broadcast address, as follows:

Step 1.   If the mask octet = 255, copy the decimal IP address.

Step 2.   If the mask octet = 0, write a decimal 255.

Before moving to the next section, take some time to fill in the blanks in Table 14-9. Check your answers against Table 14-15 in the section "Answers to Earlier Practice Problems," later in this chapter. Complete the table by listing the subnet ID and subnet broadcast address.

Table 14-9   Practice Problems: Find Subnet ID and Broadcast Address, Easy Masks

	IP Address	Mask	Subnet ID	Broadcast Address
1	10.77.55.3	255.255.255.0		
2	172.30.99.4	255.255.255.0		
3	192.168.6.54	255.255.255.0		
4	10.77.3.14	255.255.0.0		
5	172.22.55.77	255.255.0.0		
6	1.99.53.76	255.0.0.0		

Predictability in the Interesting Octet

Although three masks are easier to work with (255.0.0.0, 255.255.0.0, and 255.255.255.0), the rest make the decimal math a little more difficult, so we call these masks difficult masks. With difficult masks, one octet is neither a 0 nor a 255. The math in the other three octets is easy and boring, so this book calls the one octet with the more difficult math the *interesting octet*.

If you take some time to think about different problems and focus on the interesting octet, you will begin to see a pattern. This section takes you through that examination so that you can learn how to predict the pattern, in decimal, and find the subnet ID.

First, the subnet ID value has a predictable decimal value because of the assumption that a single subnet mask is used for all subnets of a single classful network. The chapters in this part of the book assume that, for a given classful network, the design engineer chooses to use a single subnet mask for all subnets. (See the section "One Size Subnet Fits All—Or Not" in Chapter 11, "Perspectives on IPv4 Subnetting," for more details.)

To see that predictability, consider some planning information written down by a network engineer, as shown in Figure 14-8. The figure shows four different masks the engineer is considering using in an IPv4 network, along with Class B network 172.16.0.0. The figure shows the third-octet values for the subnet IDs that would be created when using mask 255.255.128.0, 255.255.192.0, 255.255.224.0, and 255.255.240.0, from top to bottom in the figure.

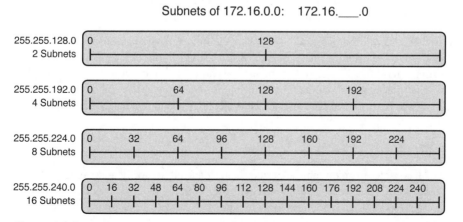

Figure 14-8   *Numeric Patterns in the Interesting Octet*

First, to explain the figure further, look at the top row of the figure. If the engineer uses 255.255.128.0 as the mask, the mask creates two subnets, with subnet IDs 172.16.0.0 and 172.16.128.0. If the engineer uses mask 255.255.192.0, the mask creates four subnets, with subnet IDs 172.16.0.0, 172.16.64.0, 172.16.128.0, and 172.16.192.0.

If you take the time to look at the figure, the patterns become obvious. In this case:

Mask: 255.255.128.0   Pattern: Multiples of 128

Mask: 255.255.192.0   Pattern: Multiples of 64

Mask: 255.255.224.0   Pattern: Multiples of 32

Mask: 255.255.240.0   Pattern: Multiples of 16

To find the subnet ID, you just need a way to figure out what the pattern is. If you start with an IP address and mask, just find the subnet ID closest to the IP address, without going over, as discussed in the next section.

Finding the Subnet ID: Difficult Masks

The following written process lists all the steps to find the subnet ID, using only decimal math. This process adds to the earlier process used with easy masks. For each octet:

Step 1.   If the mask octet = 255, copy the decimal IP address.

Step 2.   If the mask octet = 0, write a decimal 0.

Step 3.   If the mask is neither, refer to this octet as the *interesting octet*:

    A. Calculate the *magic number* as 256 – mask.

    B. Set the subnet ID's value to the multiple of the magic number that is closest to the IP address without going over.

The process uses two new terms created for this book: *magic number* and *interesting octet*. The term *interesting octet* refers to the octet identified at Step 3 in the process; in other words, it is the octet with the mask that is neither 255 nor 0. Step 3A then uses the term *magic number*, which is derived from the DDN mask. Conceptually, the magic number is the number you add to one subnet ID to get the next subnet ID in order, as shown in Figure 14-8. Numerically, it can be found by subtracting the DDN mask's value, in the interesting octet, from 256, as mentioned in Step 3A.

The best way to learn this process is to see it happen. In fact, if you can, stop reading now, use the companion website for this book, and watch the videos about finding the subnet ID with a difficult mask. These videos demonstrate this process. You can also use the examples on the next few pages that show the process being used on paper. Then follow the practice opportunities outlined in the section "Practice Analyzing Existing Subnets," later in this chapter.

Resident Subnet Example 1

For example, consider the requirement to find the resident subnet for IP address 130.4.102.1, mask 255.255.240.0. The process does not require you to think about prefix bits versus host bits, convert the mask, think about the mask in binary, or convert the IP address to and from binary. Instead, for each of the four octets, choose an action based on the value in the mask. Figure 14-9 shows the results; the circled numbers in the figure refer to the step numbers in the written process to find the subnet ID, as listed in the previous few pages.

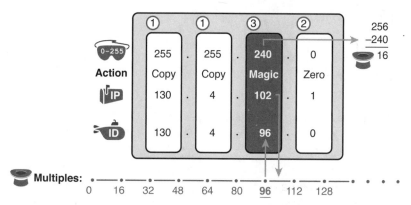

Figure 14-9 *Find the Subnet ID: 130.4.102.1, 255.255.240.0*

First, examine the three uninteresting octets (1, 2, and 4, in this example). The process keys on the mask, and the first two octets have a mask value of 255, so simply copy the IP address to the place where you intend to write down the subnet ID. The fourth octet has a mask value of 0, so write down a 0 for the fourth octet of the subnet ID.

The most challenging logic occurs in the interesting octet, which is the third octet in this example, because of the mask value 240 in that octet. For this octet, Step 3A asks you to calculate the magic number as 256 – mask. That means you take the mask's value in the interesting octet (240, in this case) and subtract it from 256: 256 – 240 = 16. The subnet ID's value in this octet must be a multiple of decimal 16, in this case.

Step 3B then asks you to find the multiples of the magic number (16, in this case) and choose the one closest to the IP address without going over. Specifically, that means that you should mentally calculate the multiples of the magic number, starting at 0. (Do not forget to start at 0!) Count, starting at 0: 0, 16, 32, 48, 64, 80, 96, 112, and so on. Then, find the multiple closest to the IP address value in this octet (102, in this case), without going over 102. So, as shown in Figure 14-9, you make the third octet's value 96 to complete the subnet ID of 130.4.96.0.

Resident Subnet Example 2

Consider another example: 192.168.5.77, mask 255.255.255.224. Figure 14-10 shows the results.

The three uninteresting octets (1, 2, and 3, in this case) require only a little thought. For each octet, each with a mask value of 255, just copy the IP address.

For the interesting octet, at Step 3A, the magic number is 256 – 224 = 32. The multiples of the magic number are 0, 32, 64, 96, and so on. Because the IP address value in the fourth octet is 77, in this case, the multiple must be the number closest to 77 without going over; therefore, the subnet ID ends with 64, for a value of 192.168.5.64.

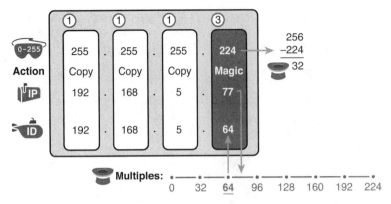

Figure 14-10 *Resident Subnet for 192.168.5.77, 255.255.255.224*

Resident Subnet Practice Problems

Before moving to the next section, take some time to fill in the blanks in Table 14-10. Check your answers against Table 14-16 in the section "Answers to Earlier Practice Problems," later in this chapter. Complete the table by listing the subnet ID in each case. The text following Table 14-16 also lists explanations for each problem.

Table 14-10 Practice Problems: Find Subnet ID, Difficult Masks

Problem	IP Address	Mask	Subnet ID
1	10.77.55.3	255.248.0.0	
2	172.30.99.4	255.255.192.0	
3	192.168.6.54	255.255.255.252	
4	10.77.3.14	255.255.128.0	
5	172.22.55.77	255.255.254.0	
6	1.99.53.76	255.255.255.248	

Finding the Subnet Broadcast Address: Difficult Masks

To find a subnet's broadcast address, a similar process can be used. For simplicity, this process begins with the subnet ID, rather than the IP address. If you happen to start with an IP address instead, use the processes in this chapter to first find the subnet ID, and then use the following process to find the subnet broadcast address for that same subnet. For each octet:

Step 1.   If the mask octet = 255, copy the subnet ID.

Step 2.   If the mask octet = 0, write 255.

Step 3.   If the mask is neither, identify this octet as the *interesting octet*:

    A. Calculate the *magic number* as 256 – mask.

    B. Take the subnet ID's value, add the magic number, and subtract 1 (ID + magic – 1).

As with the similar process used to find the subnet ID, you have several options for how to best learn and internalize the process. If you can, stop reading now, use the companion website for this book, and watch the videos listed for this chapter. Also, look at the examples in this section, which show the process being used on paper. Then, follow the practice opportunities outlined in the section "Additional Practice for This Chapter's Processes."

Subnet Broadcast Example 1

The first example continues the first example from the section "Finding the Subnet ID: Difficult Masks," earlier in this chapter, as demonstrated in Figure 14-9. That example started with the IP address/mask of 130.4.102.1, 255.255.240.0, and showed how to find subnet ID 130.4.96.0. Figure 14-11 now begins with that subnet ID and the same mask.

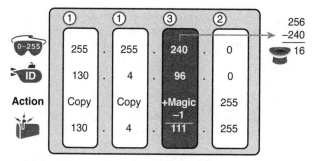

Figure 14-11 *Find the Subnet Broadcast: 130.4.96.0, 255.255.240.0*

First, examine the three uninteresting octets (1, 2, and 4). The process keys on the mask, and the first two octets have a mask value of 255, so simply copy the subnet ID to the place where you intend to write down the subnet broadcast address. The fourth octet has a mask value of 0, so write down a 255 for the fourth octet.

The logic related to the interesting octet occurs in the third octet in this example because of the mask value 240. First, Step 3A asks you to calculate the magic number, as 256 – mask. (If you had already calculated the subnet ID using the decimal process in this book, you should already know the magic number.) At Step 3B, you take the subnet ID's value (96), add the magic number (16), and subtract 1, for a total of 111. That makes the subnet broadcast address 130.4.111.255.

Subnet Broadcast Example 2

Again, this example continues an earlier example, from the section "Resident Subnet Example 2," as demonstrated in Figure 14-10. That example started with the IP address/mask of 192.168.5.77, mask 255.255.255.224 and showed how to find subnet ID 192.168.5.64. Figure 14-12 now begins with that subnet ID and the same mask.

First, examine the three uninteresting octets (1, 2, and 3). The process keys on the mask, and the first three octets have a mask value of 255, so simply copy the subnet ID to the place where you intend to write down the subnet broadcast address.

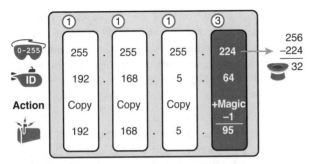

Figure 14-12   *Find the Subnet Broadcast: 192.168.5.64, 255.255.255.224*

The interesting logic occurs in the interesting octet, the fourth octet in this example, because of the mask value 224. First, Step 3A asks you to calculate the magic number, as 256 – mask. (If you had already calculated the subnet ID, it is the same magic number because the same mask is used.) At Step 3B, you take the subnet ID's value (64), add magic (32), and subtract 1, for a total of 95. That makes the subnet broadcast address 192.168.5.95.

Subnet Broadcast Address Practice Problems

Before moving to the next section, take some time to do several practice problems on a scratch piece of paper. Go back to Table 14-10, which lists IP addresses and masks, and practice by finding the subnet broadcast address for all the problems in that table. Then check your answers against Table 14-17 in the section "Answers to Earlier Practice Problems," later in this chapter.

Practice Analyzing Existing Subnets

As with the other subnetting math in this book, using a two-phase approach may help. Take time now to practice until you feel like you understand the process. Then, before the exam, make sure you master the math. Table 14-11 summarizes the key concepts and suggestions for this two-phase approach.

Table 14-11   Keep-Reading and Take-Exam Goals for This Chapter's Topics

	Before Moving to the Next Chapter	Before Taking the Exam
Focus On...	Learning how	Being correct and fast
Tools Allowed	All	Your brain and a notepad
Goal: Accuracy	90% correct	100% correct
Goal: Speed	Any speed	20–30 seconds

A Choice: Memorize or Calculate

As described in this chapter, the decimal processes to find the subnet ID and subnet broadcast address do require some calculation, including the calculation of the magic number (256 – mask). The processes also use a DDN mask, so if an exam question gives you a prefix-style mask, you need to convert to DDN format before using the process in this book.

Over the years, some people have told me they prefer to memorize a table to find the magic number. These tables could list the magic number for different DDN masks and prefix masks, so you avoid converting from the prefix mask to DDN. Table 14-12 shows an example of such a table. Feel free to ignore this table, use it, or make your own.

Table 14-12   Reference Table: DDN Mask Values, Binary Equivalent, Magic Numbers, and Prefixes

Prefix, interesting octet 2	/9	/10	/11	/12	/13	/14	/15	/16
Prefix, interesting octet 3	/17	/18	/19	/20	/21	/22	/23	/24
Prefix, interesting octet 4	/25	/26	/27	/28	/29	/30		
Magic number	128	64	32	16	8	4	2	1
DDN mask in the interesting octet	128	192	224	240	248	252	254	255

Chapter Review

One key to doing well on the exams is to perform repetitive spaced review sessions. Review this chapter's material using either the tools in the book or interactive tools for the same material found on the book's companion website. Refer to the "Your Study Plan" element for more details. Table 14-13 outlines the key review elements and where you can find them. To better track your study progress, record when you completed these activities in the second column.

Table 14-13   Chapter Review Tracking

Review Element	Review Date(s)	Resource Used
Review key topics		Book, website
Review key terms		Book, website
Answer DIKTA questions		Book, PTP
Review memory tables		Website
Practice mask analysis		Website, Appendix F
Practice analyzing existing subnets		Website, Appendix F

Review All the Key Topics

Table 14-14 Key Topics for Chapter 14

Key Topic Element	Description	Page Number
List	Definition of a subnet's key numbers	322
Table 14-2	Key facts about the subnet ID	324
Table 14-3	Key facts about the subnet broadcast address	325
List	Steps to use binary math to find the subnet ID	328
List	General steps to use binary and decimal math to find the subnet ID	330
List	Steps to use decimal and binary math to find the subnet broadcast address	330
List	Steps to use only decimal math to find the subnet ID	334
List	Steps to use only decimal math to find the subnet broadcast address	336

Key Terms You Should Know

resident subnet, subnet ID, subnet number, subnet address, subnet broadcast address

Additional Practice for This Chapter's Processes

You can do more practice with the processes in this chapter with a pair of practice sets. Both give you practice at analyzing existing subnets. You may do each practice set using the following tools:

Application: Use the "Analyzing Existing Subnets" exercises 1 and 2 on the companion website, listed under the Chapter Review for this chapter.

PDF: Alternatively, practice the same problems found in these apps using companion website Appendix F, "Practice for Chapter 14: Analyzing Existing Subnets."

Answers to Earlier Practice Problems

This chapter includes practice problems spread around different locations in the chapter. The answers are located in Tables 14-15, 14-16, and 14-17.

Table 14-15 Answers to Problems in Table 14-9

	IP Address	Mask	Subnet ID	Broadcast Address
1	10.77.55.3	255.255.255.0	10.77.55.0	10.77.55.255
2	172.30.99.4	255.255.255.0	172.30.99.0	172.30.99.255
3	192.168.6.54	255.255.255.0	192.168.6.0	192.168.6.255
4	10.77.3.14	255.255.0.0	10.77.0.0	10.77.255.255
5	172.22.55.77	255.255.0.0	172.22.0.0	172.22.255.255
6	1.99.53.76	255.0.0.0	1.0.0.0	1.255.255.255

Table 14-16   Answers to Problems in Table 14-10

	IP Address	Mask	Subnet ID
1	10.77.55.3	255.248.0.0	10.72.0.0
2	172.30.99.4	255.255.192.0	172.30.64.0
3	192.168.6.54	255.255.255.252	192.168.6.52
4	10.77.3.14	255.255.128.0	10.77.0.0
5	172.22.55.77	255.255.254.0	172.22.54.0
6	1.99.53.76	255.255.255.248	1.99.53.72

The following list explains the answers for Table 14-16:

1. The second octet is the interesting octet, with magic number 256 – 248 = 8. The multiples of 8 include 0, 8, 16, 24, ..., 64, 72, and 80. 72 is closest to the IP address value in that same octet (77) without going over, making the subnet ID 10.72.0.0.

2. The third octet is the interesting octet, with magic number 256 – 192 = 64. The multiples of 64 include 0, 64, 128, and 192. 64 is closest to the IP address value in that same octet (99) without going over, making the subnet ID 172.30.64.0.

3. The fourth octet is the interesting octet, with magic number 256 – 252 = 4. The multiples of 4 include 0, 4, 8, 12, 16, ..., 48, 52, and 56. 52 is the closest to the IP address value in that same octet (54) without going over, making the subnet ID 192.168.6.52.

4. The third octet is the interesting octet, with magic number 256 – 128 = 128. Only two multiples exist that matter: 0 and 128. 0 is the closest to the IP address value in that same octet (3) without going over, making the subnet ID 10.77.0.0.

5. The third octet is the interesting octet, with magic number 256 – 254 = 2. The multiples of 2 include 0, 2, 4, 6, 8, and so on—essentially all even numbers. 54 is closest to the IP address value in that same octet (55) without going over, making the subnet ID 172.22.54.0.

6. The fourth octet is the interesting octet, with magic number 256 – 248 = 8. The multiples of 8 include 0, 8, 16, 24, ..., 64, 72, and 80. 72 is closest to the IP address value in that same octet (76) without going over, making the subnet ID 1.99.53.72.

Table 14-17   Answers to Problems in the Section "Subnet Broadcast Address Practice Problems"

	Subnet ID	Mask	Broadcast Address
1	10.72.0.0	255.248.0.0	10.79.255.255
2	172.30.64.0	255.255.192.0	172.30.127.255
3	192.168.6.52	255.255.255.252	192.168.6.55
4	10.77.0.0	255.255.128.0	10.77.127.255
5	172.22.54.0	255.255.254.0	172.22.55.255
6	1.99.53.72	255.255.255.248	1.99.53.79

The following list explains the answers for Table 14-17:

1. The second octet is the interesting octet. Completing the three easy octets means that the broadcast address in the interesting octet will be 10.___.255.255. With magic number 256 − 248 = 8, the second octet will be 72 (from the subnet ID), plus 8, minus 1, or 79.

2. The third octet is the interesting octet. Completing the three easy octets means that the broadcast address in the interesting octet will be 172.30.___.255. With magic number 256 − 192 = 64, the interesting octet will be 64 (from the subnet ID), plus 64 (the magic number), minus 1, for 127.

3. The fourth octet is the interesting octet. Completing the three easy octets means that the broadcast address in the interesting octet will be 192.168.6.___. With magic number 256 − 252 = 4, the interesting octet will be 52 (the subnet ID value), plus 4 (the magic number), minus 1, or 55.

4. The third octet is the interesting octet. Completing the three easy octets means that the broadcast address will be 10.77.___.255. With magic number 256 − 128 = 128, the interesting octet will be 0 (the subnet ID value), plus 128 (the magic number), minus 1, or 127.

5. The third octet is the interesting octet. Completing the three easy octets means that the broadcast address will be 172.22.___.255. With magic number 256 − 254 = 2, the broadcast address in the interesting octet will be 54 (the subnet ID value), plus 2 (the magic number), minus 1, or 55.

6. The fourth octet is the interesting octet. Completing the three easy octets means that the broadcast address will be 1.99.53.___. With magic number 256 − 248 = 8, the broadcast address in the interesting octet will be 72 (the subnet ID value), plus 8 (the magic number), minus 1, or 79.

Part IV Review

Keep track of your part review progress with the checklist in Table P4-1. Details on each task follow the table.

Table P4-1 Part IV Part Review Checklist

Activity	1st Date Completed	2nd Date Completed
Repeat All DIKTA Questions		
Answer Part Review Questions		
Review Key Topics		
Subnetting Exercises in Appendices on Companion Website		
Videos on Companion Website		
Subnetting Exercises on Author's Blog		
Subnetting Exercises in IP Subnetting Practice Question Kit		
Subnetting Labs in Pearson Network Simulator		

Repeat All DIKTA Questions

For this task, use the PCPT software to answer the "Do I Know This Already?" questions again for the chapters in this part of the book.

Answer Part Review Questions

For this task, use PCPT to answer the Part Review questions for this part of the book.

Review Key Topics

Review all key topics in all chapters in this part, either by browsing the chapters or by using the Key Topics application on the companion website.

Watch Videos

Chapter 14 recommends several videos as listed on this book's companion website. These videos help you understand how to use the process in the book to find facts about subnets, like the range of usable addresses in the subnet.

Subnetting Exercises

Chapters 12, 13, and 14 list some subnetting exercises, along with time and accuracy goals. Now is a good time to work on those goals. Some options include the following:

Practice from this book's appendices or web applications: The Chapter Review sections of Chapters 12, 13, and 14 mention addressing and subnetting exercises included with this book. Find all the related applications in the Part IV Review section of the companion website:

Appendix D, "Practice for Chapter 12: Analyzing Classful IPv4 Networks"

Appendix E, "Practice for Chapter 13: Analyzing Subnet Masks"

Appendix F, "Practice for Chapter 14: Analyzing Existing Subnets"

Pearson Network Simulator: The full Pearson ICND1 or CCNA simulator has subnetting math exercises that you can do by using CLI commands. Look for the labs with "IP Address Rejection" and "Subnet ID Calculation" in their names.

Author's blog: I've written a few dozen subnetting exercises on the blog over the years. Just look at the Questions menu item at the top of the page, and you will see a variety of IPv4 addressing and subnetting question types. Start at http://blog.certskills.com.

Parts V and VI work together to reveal the details of how to implement IPv4 routing in Cisco routers. To that end, Part V focuses on the most common features for Cisco routers, including IP address configuration, connected routes, and static routes. Part VI then goes into some detail about the one IP routing protocol discussed in this book: OSPF Version 2 (OSPFv2).

Part V follows a progression of topics. First, Chapter 15 examines the fundamentals of routers—the physical components, how to access the router command-line interface (CLI), and the configuration process. Chapter 15 makes a close comparison of the switch CLI and its basic administrative commands so that you have to learn only new commands that apply to routers but not to switches.

Chapter 16 then moves on to discuss how to configure routers to route IPv4 packets in the most basic designs. Those designs require a simple IP address/mask configuration on each interface, with the addition of a static route command—a command that directly configures a route into the IP routing table—for each destination subnet.

By the end of Chapter 16, you should have a solid understanding of how to enable IP addressing and routing in a Cisco router, so Chapter 17 continues the progression into more challenging but more realistic configurations related to routing between subnets in a LAN environment. Most LANs use many VLANs, with one subnet per VLAN. Cisco routers and switches can be configured to route packets between those subnets, with more than a few twists in the configuration.

Finally, Part V closes with a chapter about troubleshooting IPv4 routing. The chapter features the **ping** and **traceroute** commands, two commands that can help you discover not only whether a routing problem exists but also where the problem exists. Chapters 15, 16, and 17 show how to confirm whether a route has been added to one router's routing table, while the commands discussed in Chapter 18 teach you how to test the end-to-end routes from sending host to receiving host.

Part V

IPv4 Routing

CHAPTER 15

Operating Cisco Routers

This chapter covers the following exam topics:

1.0 Network Fundamentals

1.1 Explain the role and function of network components

    1.1.a Routers

1.2 Describe characteristics of network topology architectures

    1.2.e Small office/home office (SOHO)

1.6 Configure and verify IPv4 addressing and subnetting

Getting an IPv4 network up and working requires some basic steps: installing routers, installing cables, and ordering WAN services. The installation also requires some router configuration because routers often use defaults so that the router does not route IP packets until
configuration has been added. You will need to configure IPv4 addresses, enable interfaces,
and add IP routes—either through static configuration or by enabling some dynamic routing
protocol. This chapter focuses on the first steps to creating a small working network: how to
install an enterprise-class Cisco router and configure interfaces and IP addresses.

This chapter breaks the topics into two major headings. The first discusses the physical
installation of an enterprise-class Cisco router. The second section looks at the command-
line interface (CLI) on a Cisco router, which has the same look and feel as the Cisco switch
CLI. This section first lists the similarities between a switch and router CLI and then
introduces the configuration required to make the router start forwarding IP packets on its
interfaces.

"Do I Know This Already?" Quiz

Take the quiz (either here or use the PTP software) if you want to use the score to help you
decide how much time to spend on this chapter. The letter answers are listed at the bottom
of the page following the quiz. Appendix C, found both at the end of the book as well as on
the companion website, includes both the answers and explanations. You can also find both
answers and explanations in the PTP testing software.

Table 15-1 "Do I Know This Already?" Foundation Topics Section-to-Question Mapping

Foundation Topics Section	Questions
Installing Cisco Routers	1
Enabling IPv4 Support on Cisco Routers	2–6

1. Which of the following installation steps are more likely required on a Cisco router, but not typically required on a Cisco switch? (Choose two answers.)

   a. Connect Ethernet cables

   b. Connect serial cables

   c. Connect to the console port

   d. Connect the power cable

   e. Turn the on/off switch to "on"

2. Which of the following commands might you see associated with a router CLI, but not with a switch CLI?

   a. The **show mac address-table** command

   b. The **show ip route** command

   c. The **show running-config** command

   d. The **show interfaces status** command

3. Which answers list a task that could be helpful in making a router interface G0/0 ready to route packets? (Choose two answers.)

   a. Configuring the **ip address** *address mask* command in G0/0 configuration mode

   b. Configuring the **ip address** *address* and **ip mask** *mask* commands in G0/0 configuration mode

   c. Configuring the **no shutdown** command in G0/0 configuration mode

   d. Setting the interface **description** in G0/0 configuration mode

4. The output of the **show ip interface brief** command on R1 lists interface status codes of "down" and "down" for interface GigabitEthernet 0/0. The interface connects to a LAN switch with a UTP straight-through cable. Which of the following could be true?

   a. The **shutdown** command is currently configured for router interface G0/0.

   b. The **shutdown** command is currently configured for the switch interface on the other end of the cable.

   c. The router was never configured with an **ip address** command on the interface.

   d. The router was configured with the **no ip address** command.

5. Which of the following commands do not list the IP address and mask of at least one interface? (Choose two answers.)

   a. show running-config

   b. show protocols *type number*

   c. show ip interface brief

   d. show interfaces

   e. show version

6. Which of the following is different on the Cisco switch CLI for a Layer 2 switch as compared with the Cisco router CLI?

    a. The commands used to configure simple password checking for the console

    b. The number of IP addresses configured

    c. The configuration of the device's hostname

    d. The configuration of an interface description

Foundation Topics

Installing Cisco Routers

Routers collectively provide the main feature of the network layer—the capability to forward packets end to end through a network. As introduced in Chapter 3, "Fundamentals of WANs and IP Routing," routers forward packets by connecting to various physical network links, like Ethernet LAN, Ethernet WAN, and serial WAN links, then using Layer 3 routing logic to choose where to forward each packet. As a reminder, Chapter 2, "Fundamentals of Ethernet LANs," covered the details of making those physical connections to Ethernet networks, while Chapter 3 covered the basics of cabling with WAN links.

This section examines some of the details of router installation and cabling, first from the enterprise perspective and then from the perspective of connecting a typical small office/ home office (SOHO) to an ISP using high-speed Internet.

Installing Enterprise Routers

A typical enterprise network has a few centralized sites as well as lots of smaller remote sites. To support devices at each site (the computers, IP phones, printers, and other devices), the network includes at least one LAN switch at each site. In addition, each site has a router, which connects to the LAN switch and to some WAN link. The WAN link provides connectivity from each remote site, back to the central site, and to other sites through the connection to the central site.

Figures 15-1 and 15-2 show a couple of different kinds of network diagrams that might be used to represent an enterprise network. The style of Figure 15-1 supports discussions about Layer 3 topics, showing the subnet IDs, masks, and interface IP addresses in shorthand. The figure also keeps the physical and data-link details to a minimum with these conventions:

    Ethernet LAN: Simple straight lines with one or more LAN switches implied but not shown.

    Ethernet WAN: Shown as a straight line, often with a cloud over it, with some kind of Ethernet interface identifier shown by the router (in this case, G0/1/0 and G0/0/0, which refers to GigabitEthernet interfaces).

    Serial WAN: A line with a crooked part in the middle (a "lightning bolt") represents a typical point-to-point serial link as introduced in Chapter 3.

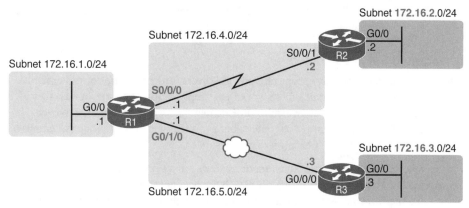

Figure 15-1 *Generic Enterprise Network Diagram*

In comparison, Figure 15-2 shows more detail about the physical cabling with less detail about the IP subnets and addresses. First, if the diagram needs to show physical details in the LAN, the diagram could show the LAN switches and related devices to the outside of the figure. The router Ethernet interfaces have an RJ-45 connector; just connect the appropriate UTP cable to both the router and the nearby LAN switch.

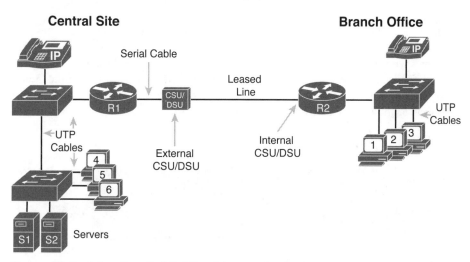

Figure 15-2 *More Detailed Cabling Diagram for the Same Enterprise Network*

Next, consider the hardware on the ends of the serial link, in particular where the channel service unit/data service unit (CSU/DSU) hardware resides on each end of the serial link. In a real serial link that runs through a service provider, the link terminates at a CSU/DSU. The CSU/DSU can either sit outside the router as a separate device (as shown on the left at router R1) or integrated into the router's serial interface hardware (as shown on the right).

As for cabling, the service provider will run the cable into the enterprise's wiring closet and often put an RJ-48 connector (same size as an RJ-45 connector) on the end of the cable. That cable should connect to the CSU/DSU. With an internal CSU/DSU (as with router R1 in Figure 15-2), the router serial port has an RJ-48 port to which the serial cable should connect. With an external CSU/DSU, the CSU/DSU must be connected to the router's serial card via a short serial cable.

Cisco Integrated Services Routers

Product vendors, including Cisco, typically provide several different types of router hardware. Today, routers often do much more work than simply routing packets; in fact, they serve as a device or platform from which to provide many network services. Cisco even brands its enterprise routers not just as routers, but as "integrated services routers," emphasizing the multipurpose nature of the products.

As an example, consider the networking functions needed at a typical branch office. A typical enterprise branch office needs a router for WAN/LAN connectivity, and a LAN switch to provide a high-performance local network and connectivity into the router and WAN. Many branches also need voice-over-IP (VoIP) services to support IP phones, and several security services as well. Plus, it is hard to imagine a site with users that does not have Wi-Fi access today. So, rather than require multiple separate devices at one site, as shown in Figure 15-2, Cisco offers single devices that act as both router and switch and provide other functions as well.

For the sake of learning and understanding the different functions, this book focuses on using a separate switch and separate router, which provides a much cleaner path for learning the basics.

Figure 15-3 shows a photo of the Cisco 4321 ISR, with some of the more important features highlighted. The top part of the figure shows a full view of the back of the router. This model comes with two built-in Gigabit Ethernet interfaces and two modular slots that allow you to add small cards called Network Interface Modules (NIMs). The bottom of the figure shows one example NIM (a NIM that provides two serial interfaces). The router has other items as well, including both an RJ-45 and USB console port.

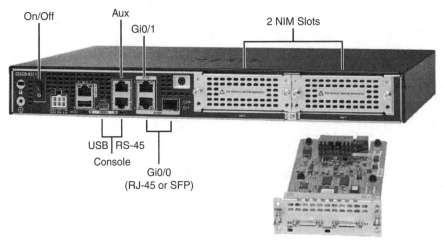

Figure 15-3 *Photos of a Model 4321 Cisco Integrated Services Router (ISR)*

The figure shows an important feature for using routers to connect to both Ethernet LANs and Ethernet WAN services. Look closely at Figure 15-3's Gigabit interfaces. Gi0/1 refers to interface GigabitEthernet0/1 and is an RJ-45 port that supports UTP cabling only. However, interface Gi0/0 (short for GigabitEthernet0/0) has some interesting features:

- The router has two ports for one interface (Gi0/0).
- You can use one or the other at any point in time, but not both.
- One physical port is an RJ-45 port that supports copper cabling (implying that it is used to connect to a LAN).
- The other Gi0/0 physical port is a Small Form Pluggable (SFP) port that would support various fiber Ethernet standards, allowing the port to be used for Ethernet WAN purposes.

Cisco commonly makes one or more of the Ethernet ports on its Enterprise class routers support SFPs so that the engineer can choose an SFP that supports the type of Ethernet cabling provided by the Ethernet WAN service provider.

NOTE   When building a lab network to study for CCNA or CCNP, because your devices will be in the same place, you can create Ethernet WAN links by using the RJ-45 ports and a UTP cable without the need to purchase an SFP for each router.

Physical Installation

Armed with the cabling details in images like Figure 15-2 and the router hardware details in photos like Figure 15-3, you can physically install a router. To install a router, follow these steps:

Step 1.   For any Ethernet LAN interface, connect the RJ-45 connector of an appropriate copper Ethernet cable between the RJ-45 Ethernet port on the router and one of the LAN switch ports.

Step 2.   For any serial WAN ports:

   A. If using an external CSU/DSU, connect the router's serial interface to the CSU/DSU and the CSU/DSU to the line from the telco.

   B. If using an internal CSU/DSU, connect the router's serial interface to the line from the telco.

Step 3.   For any Ethernet WAN ports:

   A. When ordering the Ethernet WAN service, confirm the required Ethernet standard and SFP type required to connect to the link, and order the SFPs.

   B. Install the SFPs into the routers, and connect the Ethernet cable for the Ethernet WAN link to the SFP on each end of the link.

Step 4.   Connect the router's console port to a PC (as discussed in Chapter 4, "Using the Command-Line Interface"), as needed, to configure the router.

Step 5.   Connect a power cable from a power outlet to the power port on the router.

Step 6.   Power on the router.

Note that Cisco enterprise routers typically have an on/off switch, while switches do not.

Installing SOHO Routers

The terms *enterprise router* and *small office/home office (SOHO) router* act as a pair of contrasting categories for routers, both in terms of how vendors like Cisco provide to the market, and how enterprises use and configure those devices. The term *enterprise router* typically refers to a router that a company would use in a permanent business location, while a *SOHO router* would reside at an employee's home or at a small permanent site with just a few people. However, as you might guess, the line between a router acting as an enterprise router and a SOHO router is blurry, so use these terms as general categories.

Even with that general comparison, SOHO routers typically have two features that an enterprise router would be less likely to have:

■ SOHO routers almost always use the Internet and virtual private network (VPN) technology for their WAN connections to send data back and forth to the rest of the Enterprise.

■ SOHO routers almost always use a multifunction device that does routing, LAN switching, VPN, wireless, and maybe other features.

For instance, at an enterprise business location, the building may contain enterprise routers, separate Ethernet switches, and separate wireless access points (AP), all connected together. At a permanent business site with four employees and 10 total devices in the network, one SOHO router could provide all those same features in one device.

For instance, Figure 15-4 shows a typical SOHO site. The three icons that represent a router, switch, and access point actually all exist inside one box; the figure just shows them separately to emphasize the fact that the one SOHO router provides several functions. On the left, the SOHO router provides wired and wireless LAN servers, and on the right, it provides WAN access through a cable Internet connection.

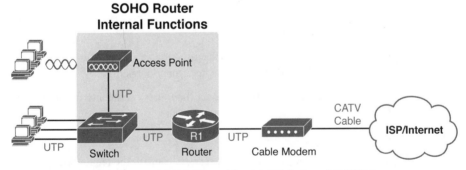

Figure 15-4 *Devices in a SOHO Network with High-Speed CATV Internet*

Figure 15-4 does not reflect the physical reality of a SOHO router, so Figure 15-5 shows one cabling example. The figure shows user devices on the left, connecting to the router via wireless or via Ethernet UTP cabling. On the right in this case, the router uses an external cable modem to connect to the coaxial cable provided by the ISP. Then the router must use a normal UTP Ethernet port to connect a short Ethernet cable between the SOHO router and the cable modem.

SOHO

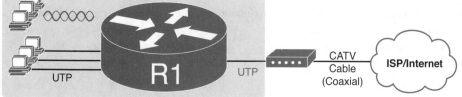

Figure 15-5 *SOHO Network, Using Cable Internet and an Integrated Device*

Enabling IPv4 Support on Cisco Router Interfaces

Routers support a relatively large number of features, with a large number of configuration and EXEC commands to support those features. You will learn about many of these features throughout the rest of this book.

> **NOTE**   For perspective, the Cisco router documentation includes a command reference, with an index to every single router command. A quick informal count of a recent IOS version listed around 5000 CLI commands.

This second section of the chapter focuses on commands related to router interfaces. To make routers work—that is, to route IPv4 packets—the interfaces must be configured. This section introduces the most common commands that configure interfaces, make them work, and give the interfaces IP addresses and masks.

Accessing the Router CLI

Accessing a router's command-line interface (CLI) works much like a switch. In fact, it works so much like accessing a Cisco switch CLI that this book relies on Chapter 4 instead of repeating the same details here. If the details from Chapter 4 are not fresh in your memory, it might be worthwhile to spend a few minutes briefly reviewing that chapter as well as Chapter 7, "Configuring and Verifying Switch Interfaces," before reading further.

Cisco switches and routers share many of the same CLI navigation features and many of the same configuration commands for management features. The following list mentions the highlights:

- User and Enable (privileged) mode
- Entering and exiting configuration mode, using the **configure terminal**, **end**, and **exit** commands and the Ctrl+Z key sequence
- Configuration of console, Telnet (vty), and enable secret passwords
- Configuration of Secure Shell (SSH) encryption keys and username/password login credentials
- Configuration of the hostname and interface description
- Configuration of Ethernet interfaces that can negotiate speed using the **speed** and **duplex** commands

■ Configuration of an interface to be administratively disabled (**shutdown**) and administratively enabled (**no shutdown**)

■ Navigation through different configuration mode contexts using commands like **line console 0** and **interface** *type number*

■ CLI help, command editing, and command recall features

■ The meaning and use of the startup-config (in NVRAM), running-config (in RAM), and external servers (like TFTP), along with how to use the **copy** command to copy the configuration files and IOS images

At first glance, this list seems to cover most everything you have read so far in this book about the switch CLI. However, a couple of topics do work differently with the router CLI as compared to the switch CLI, as follows:

■ The configuration of IP addresses differs in some ways, with switches using a VLAN interface and routers using an IP address configured on each working interface.

■ Many Cisco router models have an auxiliary (Aux) port, intended to be connected to an external modem and phone line to allow remote users to dial in to the router, and access the CLI, by making a phone call. Cisco switches do not have auxiliary ports.

■ Router IOS defaults to disallow both Telnet and SSH into the router because of the typical router default setting of **transport input none** in vty configuration mode. (Cisco Catalyst LAN switches typically default to allow both Telnet and SSH.) Chapter 6, "Configuring Basic Switch Management," already discussed the various options on this command to enable Telnet (**transport input telnet**), SSH (**transport input ssh**), or both (**transport input all** or **transport input telnet ssh**).

The router CLI also differs from a switch CLI just because switches and routers do different things. For example:

■ Cisco Layer 2 switches support the **show mac address-table** command, while Cisco routers do not.

■ Cisco routers support the **show ip route** command, while Cisco Layer 2 switches do not.

■ Cisco Layer 2 switches use the **show interfaces status** command to list one line of output per interface (and routers do not), while routers use the **show ip interface brief** command to list similar information (but switches do not).

Note also that some Cisco devices perform both Layer 2 switching and Layer 3 routing, and those devices support both router and switch commands. Chapter 17, "IP Routing in the LAN," discusses one such device, a Layer 3 switch, in more detail.

Router Interfaces

One minor difference between Cisco switches and routers is that routers support a much wider variety of interfaces. Today, LAN switches support Ethernet LAN interfaces of various speeds. Routers support a variety of other types of interfaces, including serial interfaces, cable TV, DSL, 3G/4G wireless, and others not mentioned in this book.

Most Cisco routers have at least one Ethernet interface of some type. Many of those Ethernet interfaces support multiple speeds and use autonegotiation, so for consistency, the router IOS refers to these interfaces based on the fastest speed. For example, a 10-Mbps-only Ethernet interface would be configured with the **interface ethernet** *number* configuration command, a 10/100 interface with the **interface fastethernet** *number* command, and a 10/100/1000 interface with the **interface gigabitethernet** *number* command. However, when discussing these interfaces all together, engineers would simply call them *ethernet interfaces*, regardless of the maximum speed.

Some Cisco routers have serial interfaces. As you might recall from Chapter 3, Cisco routers use serial interfaces to connect to a serial link. Each point-to-point serial link can then use High-Level Data Link Control (HDLC, the default) or Point-to-Point Protocol (PPP).

Routers refer to interfaces in many commands, first by the type of interface (Ethernet, Fast Ethernet, Gigabit Ethernet, Serial, and so on) and then with a unique number of that router. Depending on the router model, the interface numbers might be a single number, two numbers separated by a slash, or three numbers separated by slashes. For example, all three of the following configuration commands are correct on at least one model of Cisco router:

```
interface ethernet 0
interface fastethernet 0/1
interface gigabitethernet 0/0
interface gigabitethernet 0/1/0
interface serial 1/0/1
```

Two of the most common commands to display the interfaces, and their status, are the **show ip interface brief** and **show interfaces** commands. The first of these commands displays a list with one line per interface, with some basic information, including the interface IP address and interface status. The second command lists the interfaces, but with a large amount of information per interface. Example 15-1 shows a sample of each command. The output comes from a 2900-series ISR router, used in many examples in this book; note that it has both a Gi0/0 interface and a Gi0/1/0 interface, showing a case with both two-digit and three-digit interface identifiers.

Example 15-1 *Listing the Interfaces in a Router*

```
R1# show ip interface brief
Interface                    IP-Address      OK? Method Status                Protocol
Embedded-Service-Engine0/0   unassigned      YES NVRAM  administratively down down
GigabitEthernet0/0           172.16.1.1      YES NVRAM  up                    up
GigabitEthernet0/1           unassigned      YES NVRAM  administratively down down
Serial0/0/0                  172.16.4.1      YES manual up                    up
Serial0/0/1                  unassigned      YES unset  administratively down down
GigabitEthernet0/1/0         172.16.5.1      YES NVRAM  up                    up

R1# show interfaces gigabitEthernet 0/1/0
GigabitEthernet0/1/0 is up, line protocol is up
  Hardware is EHWIC-1GE-SFP-CU, address is 0201.a010.0001 (bia 30f7.0d29.8570)
  Description: Link in lab to R3's G0/0/0
  Internet address is 172.16.5.1/24
```

```
MTU 1500 bytes, BW 1000000 Kbit/sec, DLY 10 usec,
    reliability 255/255, txload 1/255, rxload 1/255
Encapsulation ARPA, loopback not set
Keepalive set (10 sec)
Full Duplex, 1Gbps, media type is RJ45
output flow-control is XON, input flow-control is XON
ARP type: ARPA, ARP Timeout 04:00:00
Last input 00:00:29, output 00:00:08, output hang never
Last clearing of "show interface" counters never
Input queue: 0/75/0/0 (size/max/drops/flushes); Total output drops: 0
Queueing strategy: fifo
Output queue: 0/40 (size/max)
5 minute input rate 0 bits/sec, 0 packets/sec
5 minute output rate 0 bits/sec, 0 packets/sec
    12 packets input, 4251 bytes, 0 no buffer
    Received 12 broadcasts (0 IP multicasts)
    0 runts, 0 giants, 0 throttles
    0 input errors, 0 CRC, 0 frame, 0 overrun, 0 ignored
    0 watchdog, 0 multicast, 0 pause input
    55 packets output, 8098 bytes, 0 underruns
    0 output errors, 0 collisions, 0 interface resets
    0 unknown protocol drops
    0 babbles, 0 late collision, 0 deferred
    0 lost carrier, 0 no carrier, 0 pause output
    0 output buffer failures, 0 output buffers swapped out
```

NOTE Commands that refer to router interfaces can be significantly shortened by truncating the words. For example, **sh int gi0/0** or **sh int g0/0** can be used instead of **show interfaces gigabitethernet 0/0**. In fact, many network engineers, when looking over someone's shoulder, would say something like "just do a show int G-i-oh-oh command" in this case, rather than speaking the long version of the command.

Also, note that the **show interfaces** command lists a text interface description on about the third line, if configured. In this case, interface G0/1/0 had been previously configured with the **description Link in lab to R3's G0/0/0** command in interface configuration mode for interface G0/1/0. The **description** interface subcommand provides an easy way to keep small notes about what router interfaces connect to which neighboring devices, with the **show interfaces** command listing that information.

Interface Status Codes

Each interface has two *interface status codes*. To be usable, the two interface status codes must be in an "up" state. The first status code refers essentially to whether Layer 1 is working, and the second status code mainly (but not always) refers to whether the data-link layer protocol is working. Table 15-2 summarizes these two status codes.

Table 15-2 Interface Status Codes and Their Meanings

Name	Location	General Meaning
Line status	First status code	Refers to the Layer 1 status. (For example, is the cable installed, is it the right/wrong cable, is the device on the other end powered on?)
Protocol status	Second status code	Refers generally to the Layer 2 status. It is always down if the line status is down. If the line status is up, a protocol status of down is usually caused by a mismatched data-link layer configuration.

Several combinations of interface status codes exist, as summarized in Table 15-3. The table lists the status codes in order, from being disabled on purpose by the configuration to a fully working state.

Table 15-3 Typical Combinations of Interface Status Codes

Line Status	Protocol Status	Typical Reasons
Administratively down	Down	The interface has a **shutdown** command configured on it.
Down	Down	The interface is not **shutdown**, but the physical layer has a problem. For example, no cable has been attached to the interface, or with Ethernet, the switch interface on the other end of the cable is shut down, or the switch is powered off, or the devices on the ends of the cable use a different transmission speed.
Up	Down	Almost always refers to data-link layer problems, most often configuration problems. For example, serial links have this combination when one router was configured to use PPP and the other defaults to use HDLC.
Up	Up	Layer 1 and Layer 2 of this interface are functioning.

For some examples, look back at Example 15-1's **show ip interface brief** command, to the three interfaces in the following list. The interfaces in this list each have a different combination of interface status codes; the list details the specific reasons for this status code in the lab used to create this example for the book.

G0/0: The interface is down/down, in this case because no cable was connected to the interface.

G0/1: The interface is administratively down/down, because the configuration includes the **shutdown** command under the G0/1 interface.

S0/0/0: The interface is up/up because a serial cable is installed, is connected to another router in a lab, and is working.

Router Interface IP Addresses

Cisco enterprise routers require at least some configuration beyond the default configuration before they will do their primary job: routing IP packets. The following facts tell us that to make a router ready to route IPv4 packets on an interface, you need to enable the interface and assign it an IPv4 address:

- Most Cisco router interfaces default to a disabled (**shutdown**) state and should be enabled with the **no shutdown** interface subcommand.

- Cisco routers do not route IP packets in or out an interface until an IP address and mask have been configured; by default, no interfaces have an IP address and mask.

- Cisco routers attempt to route IP packets for any interfaces that are in an up/up state and that have an IP address/mask assigned.

To configure the address and mask, simply use the **ip address** *address mask* interface subcommand. Figure 15-6 shows a simple IPv4 network with IPv4 addresses on Router R1, with Example 15-2 showing the matching configuration.

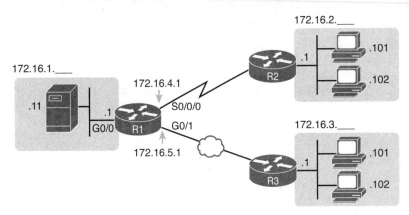

Figure 15-6 *IPv4 Addresses Used in Example 15-2*

Example 15-2 *Configuring IP Addresses on Cisco Routers*

```
R1# configure terminal
Enter configuration commands, one per line. End with CNTL/Z.
R1config)# interface G0/0
R1(config-if)# ip address 172.16.1.1 255.255.255.0
R1(config-if)# no shutdown
R1(config-if)# interface S0/0/0
R1(config-if)# ip address 172.16.4.1 255.255.255.0
R1(config-if)# no shutdown
R1(config-if)# interface G0/1/0
R1(config-if)# ip address 172.16.5.1 255.255.255.0
R1(config-if)# no shutdown
R1(config-if)# ^Z
R1#
```

Example 15-3 shows the output of the **show protocols** command. This command confirms the state of each of the three R1 interfaces in Figure 15-6 and the IP address and mask configured on those same interfaces.

Example 15-3 *Verifying IP Addresses on Cisco Routers*

```
R1# show protocols
Global values:
    Internet Protocol routing is enabled
Embedded-Service-Engine0/0 is administratively down, line protocol is down
GigabitEthernet0/0 is up, line protocol is up
    Internet address is 172.16.1.1/24
GigabitEthernet0/1 is administratively down, line protocol is down
Serial0/0/0 is up, line protocol is up
    Internet address is 172.16.4.1/24
Serial0/0/1 is administratively down, line protocol is down
GigabitEthernet0/1/0 is up, line protocol is up
    Internet address is 172.16.1.1/24
```

One of the first actions to take when verifying whether a router is working is to find the interfaces, check the interface status, and check to see whether the correct IP addresses and masks are used. Examples 15-1 and 15-3 showed samples of the key **show** commands, while Table 15-4 summarizes those commands and the types of information they display.

Table 15-4   Key Commands to List Router Interface Status

Command	Lines of Output per Interface	IP Configuration Listed	Interface Status Listed?
show ip interface brief	1	Address	Yes
show protocols [*type number*]	1 or 2	Address/mask	Yes
show interfaces [*type number*]	Many	Address/mask	Yes

Bandwidth and Clock Rate on Serial Interfaces

Cisco has included serial WAN topics in the CCNA exam topic list since its inception in 1998 until the CCNA 200-301 release in the year 2019. Because the CCNA 200-301 exam is the first to not mention serial technologies at all, this book includes some examples that show serial links. The exam might show them with the expectation that you at least understand basics, such as the fact that two routers can send data over a serial link if the router interfaces on both ends are up/up and the routers have IP addresses in the same subnet.

However, some of you will want to make serial links work in a lab because you have some serial interface cards in your lab. If so, take the time to look at a few pages in the section titled "Bandwidth and Clock Rate on Serial Interfaces," in Appendix J, "Topics from Previous Editions," which shows how to cable and configure a WAN serial link in the lab.

Router Auxiliary Port

Both routers and switches have a console port to allow administrative access, but most Cisco routers have an extra physical port called an auxiliary (Aux) port. The Aux port typically serves as a means to make a phone call to connect into the router to issue commands from the CLI.

The Aux port works like the console port, except that the Aux port is typically connected through a cable to an external analog modem, which in turn connects to a phone line. Then, the engineer uses a PC, terminal emulator, and modem to call the remote router. After being connected, the engineer can use the terminal emulator to access the router CLI, starting in user mode as usual.

Aux ports can be configured beginning with the **line aux 0** command to reach aux line configuration mode. From there, all the commands for the console line, covered mostly in Chapter 6, can be used. For example, the **login** and **password** *password* subcommands on the aux line could be used to set up simple password checking when a user dials in.

Chapter Review

One key to doing well on the exams is to perform repetitive spaced review sessions. Review this chapter's material using either the tools in the book or interactive tools for the same material found on the book's companion website. Refer to the "Your Study Plan" element for more details. Table 15-5 outlines the key review elements and where you can find them. To better track your study progress, record when you completed these activities in the second column.

Table 15-5   Chapter Review Tracking

Review Element	Review Date(s)	Resource Used
Review key topics		Book, website
Review key terms		Book, website
Answer DIKTA questions		Book, PTP
Review command tables		Book
Review memory tables		Website
Do labs		Blog
Watch video		Website

Review All the Key Topics

Table 15-6   Key Topics for Chapter 15

Key Topic	Description	Page Number
List	Steps required to install a router	353
List	Similarities between a router CLI and a switch CLI	355
List	Items covered for switches in Chapters 4 and 6 that differ in some way on routers	356
Table 15-2	Router interface status codes and their meanings	359
Table 15-3	Combinations of the two interface status codes and the likely reasons for each combination	359
Table 15-4	Commands useful to display interface IPv4 addresses, masks, and interface status	361

Key Terms You Should Know

enterprise router, SOHO router, Integrated Services Router (ISR)

Command References

Tables 15-7 and 15-8 list configuration and verification commands used in this chapter. As an easy review exercise, cover the left column in a table, read the right column, and try to recall the command without looking. Then repeat the exercise, covering the right column, and try to recall what the command does.

Table 15-7   Chapter 15 Configuration Command Reference

Command	Description
interface *type number*	Global command that moves the user into configuration mode of the named interface.
ip address *address mask*	Interface subcommand that sets the router's IPv4 address and mask.
[no] shutdown	Interface subcommand that enables (**no shutdown**) or disables (**shutdown**) the interface.
duplex {full | half | auto}	Interface command that sets the duplex, or sets the use of IEEE autonegotiation, for router LAN interfaces that support multiple speeds.
speed {10 | 100 | 1000}	Interface command for router Gigabit (10/100/1000) interfaces that sets the speed at which the router interface sends and receives data.
description *text*	An interface subcommand with which you can type a string of text to document information about that particular interface.

Table 15-8   Chapter 15 EXEC Command Reference

Command	Purpose
show interfaces [*type number*]	Lists a large set of informational messages about each interface, or about the one specifically listed interface.
show ip interface brief	Lists a single line of information about each interface, including the IP address, line and protocol status, and the method with which the address was configured (manual or Dynamic Host Configuration Protocol [DHCP]).
show protocols [*type number*]	Lists information about the listed interface (or all interfaces if the interface is omitted), including the IP address, mask, and line/protocol status.

CHAPTER 16

Configuring IPv4 Addresses and Static Routes

This chapter covers the following exam topics:

1.0 Network Fundamentals

1.6 Configure and verify IPv4 addressing and subnetting

3.0 IP Connectivity

3.1 Interpret the components of routing table

3.1.a Routing protocol code

3.1.b Prefix

3.1.c Network mask

3.1.d Next hop

3.1.e Administrative distance

3.1.f Metric

3.1.g Gateway of last resort

3.2 Determine how a router makes a forwarding decision by default

3.2.a Longest match

3.2.b Administrative distance

3.3 Configure and verify IPv4 and IPv6 static routing

3.3.a Default route

3.3.b Network route

3.3.c Host route

3.3.d Floating static

Routers route IPv4 packets. That simple statement actually carries a lot of hidden meaning. For routers to route packets, routers follow a routing process. That routing process relies on information called IP routes. Each IP route lists a destination—an IP network, IP subnet, or some other group of IP addresses. Each route also lists instructions that tell the router where to forward packets sent to addresses in that IP network or subnet. For routers to do a good job of routing packets, routers need to have a detailed, accurate list of IP routes.

Routers use three methods to add IPv4 routes to their IPv4 routing tables. Routers first learn *connected routes*, which are routes for subnets attached to a router interface. Routers can also use *static routes*, which are routes created through a configuration command (**ip route**) that tells the router what route to put in the IPv4 routing table. And routers can use a routing protocol, in which routers tell each other about all their known routes, so that all routers can learn and build routes to all networks and subnets.

This chapter examines IP routing in depth with the most straightforward routes that can be added to a router's routing table. The router starts with a detailed look at the IP packet routing (forwarding process)—a process that relies on each router having useful IP routes in their routing tables. The second section then examines connected routes, which are routes to subnets that exist on the interfaces connected to the local router. The third section then examines static routes, which are routes the network engineer configures directly. The chapter ends with a section that looks more specifically at the IP routing process in a router, how it matches packets to the routing table, and how to interpret all the details in the output of the **show ip route** command.

"Do I Know This Already?" Quiz

Take the quiz (either here or use the PTP software) if you want to use the score to help you decide how much time to spend on this chapter. The letter answers are listed at the bottom of the page following the quiz. Appendix C, found both at the end of the book as well as on the companion website, includes both the answers and explanations. You can also find both answers and explanations in the PTP testing software.

Table 16-1 "Do I Know This Already?" Foundation Topics Section-to-Question Mapping

Foundation Topics Section	Questions
IP Routing	1
Configuring Connected Routes	2
Configuring Static Routes	3–5
IP Forwarding with the Longest Prefix Match	6

1. Router R1 lists a route in its routing table. Which of the following answers list a fact from a route that the router uses when matching the packet's destination address? (Choose two answers.)

   a. Mask

   b. Next-hop router

   c. Subnet ID

   d. Outgoing interface

2. After configuring a working router interface with IP address/mask 10.1.1.100/26, which of the following routes would you expect to see in the output of the **show ip route** command? (Choose two answers.)

   a. A connected route for subnet 10.1.1.64 255.255.255.192

   b. A connected route for subnet 10.1.1.0 255.255.255.0

   c. A local route for host 10.1.1.100 255.255.255.192

   d. A local route for host 10.1.1.100 255.255.255.255

   e. A local route for host 10.1.1.64 255.255.255.255

3. An engineer configures a static IPv4 route on Router R1. Which of the following pieces of information should not be listed as a parameter in the configuration command that creates this static IPv4 route?

   a. The destination subnet's subnet ID

   b. The next-hop router's IP address

   c. The next-hop router's neighboring interface

   d. The subnet mask

4. Which of the following commands correctly configures a static route?

   a. ip route 10.1.3.0 255.255.255.0 10.1.130.253

   b. ip route 10.1.3.0 serial 0

   c. ip route 10.1.3.0 /24 10.1.130.253

   d. ip route 10.1.3.0 /24 serial 0

5. A network engineer configures the **ip route 10.1.1.0 255.255.255.0 s0/0/0** command on a router and then issues a **show ip route** command from enable mode. No routes for subnet 10.1.1.0/24 appear in the output. Which of the following could be true?

   a. The **ip route** command has incorrect syntax and was rejected in config mode.

   b. Interface s0/0/0 is down.

   c. The router has no up/up interfaces in Class A network 10.0.0.0.

   d. The **ip route** command is missing a next-hop router IP address.

6. A router lists the following partial output from the **show ip route** command. Out which interface will the router route packets destined to IP address 10.1.15.122?

   ```
          10.0.0.0/8 is variably subnetted, 8 subnets, 5 masks
   O         10.1.15.100/32 [110/50] via 172.16.25.2, 00:00:04, GigabitEthernet0/0/0
   O         10.1.15.64/26 [110/100] via 172.16.25.129, 00:00:09, GigabitEthernet0/1/0
   O         10.1.14.0/23 [110/65] via 172.16.24.2, 00:00:04, GigabitEthernet0/2/0
   O         10.1.15.96/27 [110/65] via 172.16.24.129, 00:00:09, GigabitEthernet0/3/0
   O         0.0.0.0/0 [110/129] via 172.16.25.129, 00:00:09, GigabitEthernet0/0/0
   ```

   a. G0/0/0

   b. G0/1/0

   c. G0/2/0

   d. G0/3/0

Foundation Topics

IP Routing

IP routing—the process of forwarding IP packets—delivers packets across entire TCP/IP networks, from the device that originally builds the IP packet to the device that is supposed to receive the packet. In other words, IP routing delivers IP packets from the sending host to the destination host.

The complete end-to-end routing process relies on network layer logic on hosts and on routers. The sending host uses Layer 3 concepts to create an IP packet, forwarding the IP packet to the host's default gateway (default router). The process requires Layer 3 logic on the routers as well, by which the routers compare the destination address in the packet to their routing tables, to decide where to forward the IP packet next.

The routing process also relies on data-link and physical details at each link. IP routing relies on serial WAN links, Ethernet WAN links, Ethernet LANs, wireless LANs, and many other networks that implement data-link and physical layer standards. These lower-layer devices and protocols move the IP packets around the TCP/IP network by encapsulating and transmitting the packets inside data-link layer frames.

The previous two paragraphs summarize the key concepts about IP routing as introduced back in Chapter 3, "Fundamentals of WANs and IP Routing." Next, this section reviews IP routing, while taking the discussion another step or two deeper, taking advantage of the additional depth of knowledge discussed in all the earlier chapters in this book.

IPv4 Routing Process Reference

Because you already saw the basics back in Chapter 3, this section collects the routing process into steps for reference. The steps use many specific Ethernet LAN terms discussed in Parts II and III of this book and some IP addressing terms discussed in Part IV. The upcoming descriptions and example then discuss these summaries of routing logic to make sure that each step is clear.

The routing process starts with the host that creates the IP packet. First, the host asks the question: Is the destination IP address of this new packet in my local subnet? The host uses its own IP address/mask to determine the range of addresses in the local subnet. Based on its own opinion of the range of addresses in the local subnet, a LAN-based host acts as follows:

Step 1. If the destination is local, send directly:

    A. Find the destination host's MAC address. Use the already-known Address Resolution Protocol (ARP) table entry, or use ARP messages to learn the information.

    B. Encapsulate the IP packet in a data-link frame, with the destination data-link address of the destination host.

Step 2. If the destination is not local, send to the default gateway:

    A. Find the default gateway's MAC address. Use the already-known Address Resolution Protocol (ARP) table entry, or use ARP messages to learn the information.

    B. Encapsulate the IP packet in a data-link frame, with the destination data-link address of the default gateway.

Figure 16-1 summarizes these same concepts. In the figure, host A sends a local packet directly to host D. However, for packets to host B, on the other side of a router and therefore in a different subnet, host A sends the packet to its default router (R1). (As a reminder, the terms *default gateway* and *default router* are synonyms.)

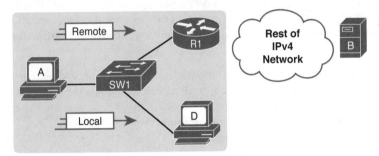

Figure 16-1 *Host Routing Logic Summary*

Routers have a little more routing work to do as compared with hosts. While the host logic began with an IP packet sitting in memory, a router has some work to do before getting to that point. With the following five-step summary of a router's routing logic, the router takes the first two steps just to receive the frame and extract the IP packet, before thinking about the packet's destination address at Step 3. The steps are as follows:

1. For each received data-link frame, choose whether or not to process the frame. Process it if

    A. The frame has no errors (per the data-link trailer Frame Check Sequence [FCS] field).

    B. The frame's destination data-link address is the router's address (or an appropriate multicast or broadcast address).

2. If choosing to process the frame at Step 1, de-encapsulate the packet from inside the data-link frame.

3. Make a routing decision. To do so, compare the packet's destination IP address to the routing table and find the route that matches the destination address. This route identifies the outgoing interface of the router and possibly the next-hop router.

4. Encapsulate the packet into a data-link frame appropriate for the outgoing interface. When forwarding out LAN interfaces, use ARP as needed to find the next device's MAC address.

5. Transmit the frame out the outgoing interface, as listed in the matched IP route.

This routing process summary lists many details, but sometimes you can think about the routing process in simpler terms. For example, leaving out some details, this paraphrase of the step list details the same big concepts:

> The router receives a frame, removes the packet from inside the frame, decides where to forward the packet, puts the packet into another frame, and sends the frame.

Answers to the "Do I Know This Already?" quiz:

1 A, C **2** A, D **3** C **4** A **5** B **6** D

To give you a little more perspective on these steps, Figure 16-2 breaks down the same five-step routing process as a diagram. The figure shows a packet arriving from the left, entering a router Ethernet interface, with an IP destination of host C. The figure shows the packet arriving, encapsulated inside an Ethernet frame (both header and trailer).

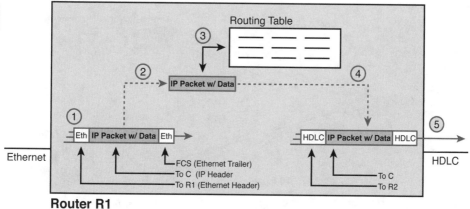

Figure 16-2 *Router Routing Logic Summary*

Router R1 processes the frame and packet as shown with the numbers in the figure, matching the same five-step process described just before the figure, as follows:

1. Router R1 notes that the received Ethernet frame passes the FCS check and that the destination Ethernet MAC address is R1's MAC address, so R1 processes the frame.
2. R1 de-encapsulates the IP packet from inside the Ethernet frame's header and trailer.
3. R1 compares the IP packet's destination IP address to R1's IP routing table.
4. R1 encapsulates the IP packet inside a new data-link frame, in this case, inside a High-Level Data Link Control (HDLC) header and trailer.
5. R1 transmits the IP packet, inside the new HDLC frame, out the serial link on the right.

NOTE This chapter uses several figures that show an IP packet encapsulated inside a data-link layer frame. These figures often show both the data-link header as well as the data-link trailer, with the IP packet in the middle. The IP packets all include the IP header, plus any encapsulated data.

An Example of IP Routing

The next several pages walk you through an example that discusses each routing step, in order, through multiple devices. The example uses a case in which host A (172.16.1.9) sends a packet to host B (172.16.2.9), with host routing logic and the five steps showing how R1 forwards the packet.

Figure 16-3 shows a typical IP addressing diagram for an IPv4 network with typical address abbreviations. The diagram can get a little too messy if it lists the full IP address for every router interface. When possible, these diagrams usually list the subnet and then the last octet or two of the individual IP addresses—just enough so that you know the IP address but with less clutter. For example, host A uses IP address 172.16.1.9, taking from subnet 172.16.1.0/24 (in which all addresses begin 172.16.1) and the .9 beside the host A icon. As another example, R1 uses address 172.16.1.1 on its LAN interface, 172.16.4.1 on one serial interface, and 172.16.5.1 on an Ethernet WAN interface.

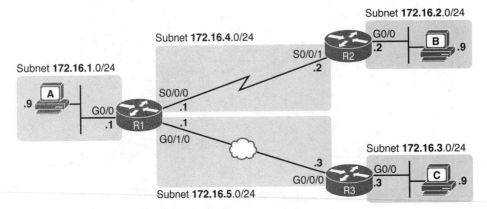

Figure 16-3 *IPv4 Network Used to Show Five-Step Routing Example*

Now on to the example, with host A (172.16.1.9) sending a packet to host B (172.16.2.9).

Host Forwards the IP Packet to the Default Router (Gateway)

In this example, host A uses some application that sends data to host B (172.16.2.9). After host A has the IP packet sitting in memory, host A's logic reduces to the following:

- My IP address/mask is 172.16.1.9/24, so my local subnet contains numbers 172.16.1.0– 172.16.1.255 (including the subnet ID and subnet broadcast address).

- The destination address is 172.16.2.9, which is clearly not in my local subnet.

- Send the packet to my default gateway, which is set to 172.16.1.1.

- To send the packet, encapsulate it in an Ethernet frame. Make the destination MAC address be R1's G0/0 MAC address (host A's default gateway).

Figure 16-4 pulls these concepts together, showing the destination IP address and destination MAC address in the frame and packet sent by host A in this case. Note that the figure uses a common drawing convention in networking, showing an Ethernet as a few lines, hiding all the detail of the Layer 2 switches.

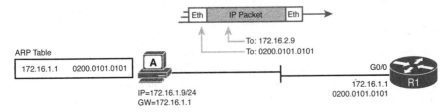

Figure 16-4 *Host A Sends Packet to Host B*

Routing Step 1: Decide Whether to Process the Incoming Frame

Routers receive many frames in an interface, particularly LAN interfaces. However, a router can and should ignore some of those frames. So, the first step in the routing process begins with a decision of whether a router should process the frame or silently discard (ignore) the frame.

First, the router does a simple but important check (Step 1A in the process summary) so that the router ignores all frames that had bit errors during transmission. The router uses the data-link trailer's FCS field to check the frame, and if errors occurred in transmission, the router discards the frame. (The router makes no attempt at error recovery; that is, the router does not ask the sender to retransmit the data.)

The router also checks the destination data-link address (Step 1B in the summary) to decide whether the frame is intended for the router. For example, frames sent to the router's unicast MAC address for that interface are clearly sent to that router. However, a router can actually receive a frame sent to some other unicast MAC address, and routers should ignore these frames.

For example, routers will receive some unicast frames sent to other devices in the VLAN just because of how LAN switches work. Think back to how LAN switches forward unknown unicast frames—frames for which the switch does not list the destination MAC address in the MAC address table. The LAN switch floods those frames. The result? Routers sometimes receive frames destined for some other device, with some other device's MAC address listed as the destination MAC address. Routers should ignore those frames.

In this example, host A sends a frame destined for R1's MAC address. So, after the frame is received, and after R1 confirms with the FCS that no errors occurred, R1 confirms that the frame is destined for R1's MAC address (0200.0101.0101 in this case). All checks have been passed, so R1 will process the frame, as shown in Figure 16-5. (Note that the large rectangle in the figure represents the internals of Router R1.)

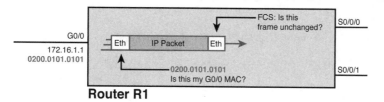

Figure 16-5 *Routing Step 1, on Router R1: Checking FCS and Destination MAC*

Routing Step 2: De-encapsulation of the IP Packet

After the router knows that it ought to process the received frame (per Step 1), the next step is relatively simple: de-encapsulating the packet. In router memory, the router no longer needs the original frame's data-link header and trailer, so the router removes and discards them, leaving the IP packet, as shown in Figure 16-6. Note that the destination IP address remains unchanged (172.16.2.9).

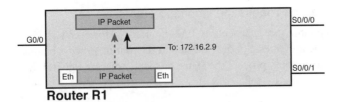

Router R1

Figure 16-6 *Routing Step 2 on Router R1: De-encapsulating the Packet*

Routing Step 3: Choosing Where to Forward the Packet

While routing Step 2 required little thought, Step 3 requires the most thought of all the steps. At this point, the router needs to make a choice about where to forward the packet next. That process uses the router's IP routing table, with some matching logic to compare the packet's destination address with the table.

First, an IP routing table lists multiple routes. Each individual route contains several facts, which in turn can be grouped as shown in Figure 16-7. Part of each route is used to match the destination address of the packet, while the rest of the route lists forwarding instructions: where to send the packet next.

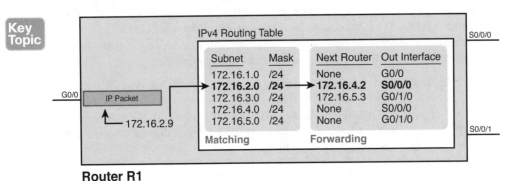

Router R1

Figure 16-7 *Routing Step 3 on Router R1: Matching the Routing Table*

Focus on the entire routing table for a moment, and notice the fact that it lists five routes. Earlier, Figure 16-3 showed the entire example network, with five subnets, so R1 has a route for each of the five subnets.

Next, look at the part of the five routes that Router R1 will use to match packets. To fully define each subnet, each route lists both the subnet ID and the subnet mask. When matching the IP packet's destination with the routing table, the router looks at the packet's destination IP address (172.16.2.9) and compares it to the range of addresses defined by each subnet. Specifically, the router looks at the subnet and mask information; with a little math, the router can figure out in which of these subnets 172.16.2.9 resides (the route for subnet 172.16.2.0/24).

Finally, look to the right side of the figure, to the forwarding instructions for these five routes. After the router matches a specific route, the router uses the forwarding information in the route to tell the router where to send the packet next. In this case, the router matched the route for subnet 172.16.2.0/24, so R1 will forward the packet out its own interface S0/0/0, to Router R2 next, listed with its next-hop router IP address of 172.16.4.2.

> **NOTE**   Routes for remote subnets typically list both an outgoing interface and next-hop router IP address. Routes for subnets that connect directly to the router list only the outgoing interface because packets to these destinations do not need to be sent to another router.

Routing Step 4: Encapsulating the Packet in a New Frame

At this point, the router knows how it will forward the packet. However, routers cannot forward a packet without first wrapping a data-link header and trailer around it (encapsulation).

Encapsulating packets for serial links does not require a lot of thought, but the current CCNA 200-301 exam does not require a lot from us. Point-to-point serial WAN links use either HDLC (the default) or PPP as the data-link protocol. However, we can ignore any data-link logic, even ignoring data-link addressing, because serial links have only two devices on the link: the sender and the then-obvious receiver; the data-link addressing does not matter. In this example, R1 forwards the packet out S0/0/0, after encapsulating the packet inside an HDLC frame, as shown in Figure 16-8.

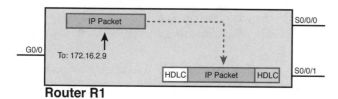

Router R1

Figure 16-8   *Routing Step 4 on Router R1: Encapsulating the Packet*

Note that with some other types of data links, the router has a little more work to do at this routing step. For example, sometimes a router forwards packets out an Ethernet interface. To encapsulate the IP packet, the router would need to build an Ethernet header, and that Ethernet header's destination MAC address would need to list the correct value.

For example, consider a packet sent by that same PC A (172.16.1.19) in Figure 16-3 but with a destination of PC C (172.16.3.9). When R1 processes the packet, R1 matches a route that tells R1 to forward the packet out R1's G0/1/0 Ethernet interface to 172.16.5.3 (R3) next. R1 needs to put R3's MAC address in the header, and to do that, R1 uses its IP ARP table information, as shown in Figure 16-9. If R1 did not have an ARP table entry for 172.16.5.3, R1 would first have to use ARP to learn the matching MAC address.

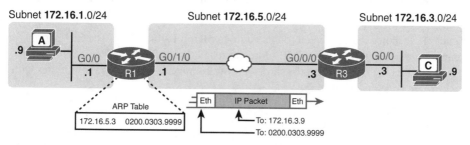

Figure 16-9   *Routing Step 4 on Router R1 with a LAN Outgoing Interface*

Routing Step 5: Transmitting the Frame

After the frame has been prepared, the router simply needs to transmit the frame. The router might have to wait, particularly if other frames are already waiting their turn to exit the interface.

Configuring IP Addresses and Connected Routes

Cisco routers enable IPv4 routing globally, by default. Then, to make the router be ready to route packets on a particular interface, the interface must be configured with an IP address and the interface must be configured such that it comes up, reaching a "line status up, line protocol up" state. Only at that point can routers route IP packets in and out a particular interface.

After a router can route IP packets out one or more interfaces, the router needs some routes. Routers can add routes to their routing tables through three methods:

Connected routes: Added because of the configuration of the **ip address** interface sub-command on the local router

Static routes: Added because of the configuration of the **ip route** global command on the local router

Routing protocols: Added as a function by configuration on all routers, resulting in a process by which routers dynamically tell each other about the network so that they all learn routes

This second of three sections discusses several variations on how to configure connected routes, while the next major section discusses static routes.

Connected Routes and the ip address Command

A Cisco router automatically adds a route to its routing table for the subnet connected to each interface, assuming that the following two facts are true:

■ The interface is in a working state. In other words, the interface status in the **show interfaces** command lists a line status of up and a protocol status of up.

■ The interface has an IP address assigned through the **ip address** interface subcommand.

The concept of connected routes is relatively basic. The router, of course, needs to know the subnet number connected to each of its interfaces, so the router can route packets to that subnet. The router does the math, taking the interface IP address and mask and calculating the subnet ID. However, the router only needs that route when the interface is up and working, so the router includes a connected route in the routing table only when the interface is working.

Example 16-1 shows the connected routes on Router R1 in Figure 16-10. The first part of the example shows the configuration of IP addresses on all three of R1's interfaces. The end of the example lists the output from the **show ip route** command, which lists these routes with a *c* as the route code, meaning *connected*.

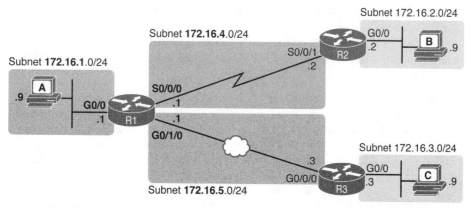

Figure 16-10 *Sample Network to Show Connected Routes*

Example 16-1 *Connected and Local Routes on Router R1*

```
! Excerpt from show running-config follows...
!
interface GigabitEthernet0/0
 ip address 172.16.1.1 255.255.255.0
!
interface Serial0/0/0
 ip address 172.16.4.1 255.255.255.0
!
interface GigabitEthernet0/1/0
 ip address 172.16.5.1 255.255.255.0

R1# show ip route
Codes: L - local, C - connected, S - static, R - RIP, M - mobile, B - BGP
       D - EIGRP, EX - EIGRP external, O - OSPF, IA - OSPF inter area
       N1 - OSPF NSSA external type 1, N2 - OSPF NSSA external type 2
       E1 - OSPF external type 1, E2 - OSPF external type 2
       i - IS-IS, su - IS-IS summary, L1 - IS-IS level-1, L2 - IS-IS level-2
       ia - IS-IS inter area, * - candidate default, U - per-user static route
       o - ODR, P - periodic downloaded static route, H - NHRP, l - LISP
       a - application route
       + - replicated route, % - next hop override, p - overrides from PfR

Gateway of last resort is not set

      172.16.0.0/16 is variably subnetted, 6 subnets, 2 masks
C        172.16.1.0/24 is directly connected, GigabitEthernet0/0
L        172.16.1.1/32 is directly connected, GigabitEthernet0/0
C        172.16.4.0/24 is directly connected, Serial0/0/0
L        172.16.4.1/32 is directly connected, Serial0/0/0
C        172.16.5.0/24 is directly connected, GigabitEthernet0/1/0
L        172.16.5.1/32 is directly connected, GigabitEthernet0/1/0
```

Take a moment to look closely at each of the three highlighted routes in the output of **show ip route**. Each lists a C in the first column, and each has text that says "directly connected"; both identify the route as connected to the router. The early part of each route lists the matching parameters (subnet ID and mask), as shown in the earlier example in Figure 16-7. The end of each of these routes lists the outgoing interface.

Note that the router also automatically produces a different kind of route, called a *local route*. The local routes define a route for the one specific IP address configured on the router interface. Each local route has a /32 prefix length, defining a *host route*, which defines a route just for that one IP address. For example, the last local route, for 172.16.5.1/32, defines a route that matches only the IP address of 172.16.5.1. Routers use these local routes that list their own local IP addresses to more efficiently forward packets sent to the router itself.

For the CCNA 200-301 exam, note that this example of the **show ip route** command reveals a few of the specific subitems within exam topic 3.1, with later examples revealing even more details. This section shows details related to the following terms from the exam topics:

- **Routing Protocol Code:** The legend at the top of the **show ip route** output (about nine lines) lists all the routing protocol codes (exam topic 3.1.a). This book references the codes for connected routes (C), local (L), static (S), and OSPF (O).
- **Prefix:** The word *prefix* (exam topic 3.1.b) is just another name for subnet ID.
- **Mask:** Each route lists a prefix (subnet ID) and network mask (exam topic 3.1.c) in prefix format, for example, /24.

The ARP Table on a Cisco Router

After a router has added these connected routes, the router can route IPv4 packets between those subnets. To do so, the router makes use of its IP ARP table.

The IPv4 ARP table lists the IPv4 address and matching MAC address of hosts connected to the same subnet as the router. When forwarding a packet to a host on the same subnet, the router encapsulates the packet, with a destination MAC address as found in the ARP table. If the router wants to forward a packet to an IP address on the same subnet as the router but does not find an ARP table entry for that IP address, the router will use ARP messages to learn that device's MAC address.

Example 16-2 shows R1's ARP table based on the previous example. The output lists R1's own IP address of 172.16.1.1, with an age of -, meaning that this entry does not time out. Dynamically learned ARP table entries have an upward counter, like the 35-minute value for the ARP table entry for IP address 172.16.1.9. By default, IOS will time out (remove) an ARP table entry after 240 minutes in which the entry is not used. (IOS resets the timer to 0 when an ARP table entry is used.) Note that to experiment in the lab, you might want to empty all dynamic entries (or a single entry for one IP address) using the **clear ip arp** [*ip-address*] EXEC command.

Example 16-2 *Displaying a Router's IP ARP Table*

```
R2# show ip arp
Protocol  Address         Age (min)  Hardware Addr   Type   Interface
Internet  172.16.1.1             -   0200.2222.2222  ARPA   GigabitEthernet0/0
Internet  172.16.1.9            35   0200.3333.3333  ARPA   GigabitEthernet0/0
```

Thinking about how Router R1 forwards a packet to host A (172.16.1.9), over that final subnet, R1 does the following:

1. R1 looks in its ARP table for an entry for 172.16.1.9.
2. R1 encapsulates the IP packet in an Ethernet frame, adding destination 0200.3333.3333 to the Ethernet header (as taken from the ARP table).
3. R1 transmits the frame out interface G0/0.

Configuring Static Routes

All routers add connected routes, as discussed in the previous section. Then, most networks use dynamic routing protocols to cause each router to learn the rest of the routes in an internetwork. Networks use static routes—routes added to a routing table through direct configuration—much less often than dynamic routing. However, static routes can be useful at times, and they happen to be useful learning tools as well. This next major section in the chapter discusses static routes.

> **NOTE** The CCNA 200-301 exam topic 3.2 breaks IPv4 (and IPv6) static routes into four subtopics: network routes, host routes, floating static routes, and default routes. This section explains all four types as noted in the upcoming headings.

Static Network Routes

IOS allows the definition of individual static routes using the **ip route** global configuration command. Every **ip route** command defines a destination that can be matched, usually with a subnet ID and mask. The command also lists the forwarding instructions, typically listing either the outgoing interface or the next-hop router's IP address. IOS then takes that information and adds that route to the IP routing table.

The static route is considered a *network route* when the destination listed in the **ip route** command defines a subnet, or an entire Class A, B, or C network. In contrast, a *default route* matches all destination IP addresses, while a *host route* matches a single IP address (that is, an address of one host.)

As an example of a network route, Figure 16-11 shows a subset of the figure used throughout this chapter so far, with some unrelated details removed. The figure shows only the details related to a static network route on R1, for destination subnet 172.16.2.0/24, which sits on the far right. To create that static network route on R1, R1 will configure the subnet ID and mask, and either R1's outgoing interface (S0/0/0) or R2 as the next-hop router IP address (172.16.4.2).

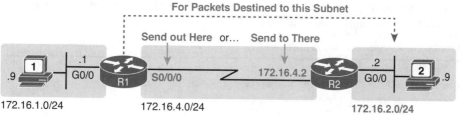

Figure 16-11 *Static Route Configuration Concept*

Example 16-3 shows the configuration of a couple of sample static routes. In particular, it shows routes on Router R1 in Figure 16-12, for the two subnets on the right side of the figure.

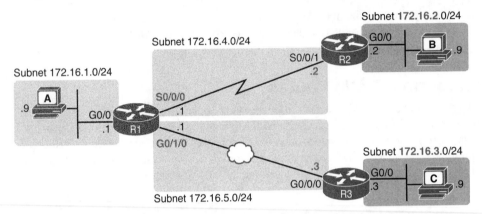

Figure 16-12   *Sample Network Used in Static Route Configuration Examples*

Example 16-3   *Static Routes Added to R1*

```
ip route 172.16.2.0 255.255.255.0 S0/0/0
ip route 172.16.3.0 255.255.255.0 172.16.5.3
```

The two example **ip route** commands show the two different styles of forwarding instructions. The first command shows subnet 172.16.2.0, mask 255.255.255.0, which sits on a LAN near Router R2. That same first command lists R1's S0/0/0 interface as the outgoing interface. This route basically states: To send packets to the subnet off Router R2, send them out my own local S0/0/0 interface (which happens to connect to R2).

The second route has the same kind of logic, except for using different forwarding instructions. Instead of referencing R1's outgoing interface, it instead lists the neighboring router's IP address on the WAN link as the next-hop router. This route basically says this: To send packets to the subnet off Router R3, send them to R3—specifically, R3's WAN IP address next.

The routes created by these two **ip route** commands actually look a little different in the IP routing table compared to each other. Both are static routes. However, the route that used the outgoing interface configuration is also noted as a connected route; this is just a quirk of the output of the **show ip route** command.

Example 16-4 lists these two routes using the **show ip route static** command. This command lists the details of static routes only, but it also lists a few statistics about all IPv4 routes. For example, the example shows two lines, for the two static routes configured in Example 16-4, but statistics state that this router has routes for eight subnets.

Example 16-4   *Static Routes Added to R1*

```
R1# show ip route static
Codes: L - local, C - connected, S - static, R - RIP, M - mobile, B - BGP
! lines omitted for brevity

Gateway of last resort is not set
```

```
      172.16.0.0/16 is variably subnetted, 8 subnets, 2 masks
S        172.16.2.0/24 is directly connected, Serial0/0/0
S        172.16.3.0/24 [1/0] via 172.16.5.3
```

IOS adds and removes these static routes dynamically over time, based on whether the outgoing interface is working or not. For example, in this case, if R1's S0/0/0 interface fails, R1 removes the static route to 172.16.2.0/24 from the IPv4 routing table. Later, when the interface comes up again, IOS adds the route back to the routing table.

Note that most sites use a dynamic routing protocol to learn all the routes to remote subnets rather than using static routes. However, when not using a dynamic routing protocol, the engineer would need to configure static routes to each subnet on each router. For example, if the routers had only the configuration shown in the examples so far, PC A (from Figure 16-12) would not be able to receive packets back from PC B because Router R2 does not have a route for PC A's subnet. R2 would need static routes for other subnets, as would R3.

Finally, note that static routes that will send packets out an Ethernet interface—LAN or WAN—should use the next-hop IP address option on the **ip address** command, as shown in Example 16-4. Routers expect their Ethernet interfaces to be able to reach any number of other IP addresses in the connected subnet. Referencing the next-hop router identifies the specific device in the connected subnet, while referencing the local router's outgoing interface does not identify the specific neighboring router.

Static Host Routes

Earlier, this chapter defined a host route as a route to a single host address. To configure such a static route, the **ip route** command uses an IP address plus a mask of 255.255.255.255 so that the matching logic matches just that one address.

An engineer might use host routes to direct packets sent to one host over one path, with all other traffic to that host's subnet over some other path. For instance, you could define these two static routes for subnet 10.1.1.0/24 and host 10.1.1.9, with two different next-hop addresses, as follows:

```
ip route 10.1.1.0 255.255.255.0 10.2.2.2
ip route 10.1.1.9 255.255.255.255 10.9.9.9
```

Note that these two routes overlap: a packet sent to 10.1.1.9 that arrives at the router would match both routes. When that happens, routers use the most specific route (that is, the route with the longest prefix length). So, a packet sent to 10.1.1.9 would be forwarded to next-hop router 10.9.9.9, and packets sent to other destinations in subnet 10.1.1.0/24 would be sent to next-hop router 10.2.2.2.

Note that the section "IP Forwarding with the Longest Prefix Match" later in this chapter gets into this topic in more detail.

Floating Static Routes

Next, consider the case in which a static route competes with other static routes or routes learned by a routing protocol. That is, the **ip route** command defines a route to a subnet, but the router also knows of other static or dynamically learned routes to reach that same subnet. In these cases, the router must first decide which routing source has the better *administrative distance*, with lower being better, and then use the route learned from the better source.

To see how that works, consider the example illustrated in Figure 16-13, which shows a different design than in the previous examples, this time with a branch office with two WAN links: one very fast Gigabit Ethernet link and one rather slow (but cheap) T1. In this design, the network uses Open Shortest Path First Version 2 (OSPFv2) over the primary link, learning a route for subnet 172.16.2.0/24. R1 also defines a static route over the backup link to that exact same subnet, so R1 must choose whether to use the static route or the OSPF-learned route.

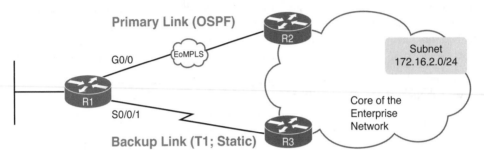

Figure 16-13   *Using a Floating Static Route to Key Subnet 172.16.2.0/24*

By default, IOS considers static routes better than OSPF-learned routes. By default, IOS gives static routes an administrative distance of 1 and OSPF routes an administrative distance of 110. Using these defaults in Figure 16-13, R1 would use the T1 to reach subnet 172.16.2.0/24 in this case, which is not the intended design. Instead, the engineer prefers to use the OSPF-learned routes over the much-faster primary link and use the static route over the backup link only as needed when the primary link fails.

To instead prefer the OSPF routes, the configuration would need to change the administrative distance settings and use what many networkers call a floating static route. A *floating static* route floats or moves into and out of the IP routing table depending on whether the better (lower) administrative distance route learned by the routing protocol happens to exist currently. Basically, the router ignores the static route during times when the better routing protocol route is known.

To implement a floating static route, you need to use a parameter on the **ip route** command that sets the administrative distance for just that route, making the value larger than the default administrative distance of the routing protocol. For example, the **ip route 172.16.2.0 255.255.255.0 172.16.5.3 130** command on R1 would do exactly that—setting the static route's administrative distance to 130. As long as the primary link stays up, and OSPF on R1 learns a route for 172.16.2.0/24, with a default administrative distance of 110, R1 ignores the static route.

Finally, note that while the **show ip route** command lists the administrative distance of most routes, as the first of two numbers inside two brackets, the **show ip route** *subnet* command plainly lists the administrative distance. Example 16-5 shows a sample, matching this most recent example.

Example 16-5 *Displaying the Administrative Distance of the Static Route*

```
R1# show ip route static
! Legend omitted for brevity
        172.16.0.0/16 is variably subnetted, 6 subnets, 2 masks
S          172.16.2.0/24 is directly connected, Serial0/0/1

R1# show ip route 172.16.2.0
Routing entry for 172.16.2.0/24
  Known via "static", distance 130, metric 0 (connected)
  Routing Descriptor Blocks:
  * directly connected, via Serial0/0/1
      Route metric is 0, traffic share count is 1
```

Static Default Routes

When a router tries to route a packet, the router might not match the packet's destination IP address with any route. When that happens, the router normally just discards the packet.

Routers can be configured so that they use either a statically configured or dynamically learned default route. The *default route* matches all packets, so that if a packet does not match any other more specific route in the routing table, the router can at least forward the packet based on the default route.

One classic example in which companies might use static default routes in their enterprise TCP/IP networks is when the company has many remote sites, each with a single, relatively slow WAN connection. Each remote site has only one possible physical route to use to send packets to the rest of the network. So, rather than use a routing protocol, which sends messages over the WAN and uses precious WAN bandwidth, each remote router might use a default route that sends all traffic to the central site, as shown in Figure 16-14.

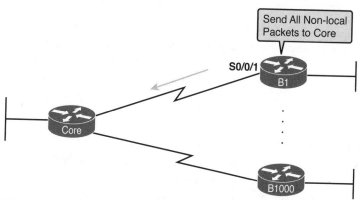

Figure 16-14 *Example Use of Static Default Routes at 1000 Low-Speed Remote Sites*

IOS allows the configuration of a static default route by using special values for the subnet and mask fields in the **ip route** command: 0.0.0.0 and 0.0.0.0. For example, the command **ip route 0.0.0.0 0.0.0.0 S0/0/1** creates a static default route on Router B1—a route that matches all IP packets—and sends those packets out interface S0/0/1.

Example 16-6 shows an example of a static default route, using Router R2 from Figure 16-13. Earlier, that figure, along with Example 16-5, showed R1 with static routes to the two subnets on the right side of the figure. Example 16-6 completes the configuration of static IP routes by configuring R2, on the right side of Figure 16-13, with a static default route to route packets back to the routers on the left side of the figure.

Example 16-6   *Adding a Static Default Route on R2 (Figure 16-13)*

```
R2# configure terminal
Enter configuration commands, one per line. End with CNTL/Z.
R2(config)# ip route 0.0.0.0 0.0.0.0 s0/0/1
R2(config)# ^Z
R2# show ip route
Codes: L - local, C - connected, S - static, R - RIP, M - mobile, B - BGP
       D - EIGRP, EX - EIGRP external, O - OSPF, IA - OSPF inter area
       N1 - OSPF NSSA external type 1, N2 - OSPF NSSA external type 2
       E1 - OSPF external type 1, E2 - OSPF external type 2
       i - IS-IS, su - IS-IS summary, L1 - IS-IS level-1, L2 - IS-IS level-2
       ia - IS-IS inter area, * - candidate default, U - per-user static route
       o - ODR, P - periodic downloaded static route, H - NHRP, l - LISP
       + - replicated route, % - next hop override

Gateway of last resort is 0.0.0.0 to network 0.0.0.0

S*   0.0.0.0/0 is directly connected, Serial0/0/1
       172.16.0.0/16 is variably subnetted, 4 subnets, 2 masks
C          172.16.2.0/24 is directly connected, GigabitEthernet0/0
L          172.16.2.2/32 is directly connected, GigabitEthernet0/0
C          172.16.4.0/24 is directly connected, Serial0/0/1
L          172.16.4.2/32 is directly connected, Serial0/0/1
```

The output of the **show ip route** command lists a few new and interesting facts. First, it lists the route with a code of S, meaning static, but also with a *, meaning it is a *candidate default route*. A router can learn about more than one default route, and the router then has to choose which one to use; the * means that it is at least a candidate to become the default route. Just above, the "Gateway of Last Resort" refers to the chosen default route, which in this case is the just-configured static route with outgoing interface S0/0/1.

Troubleshooting Static Routes

These final few pages about IPv4 static routes examine some issues that can occur with static routes, both reviewing some reasons mentioned over the last few pages, while adding more detail. This topic breaks static route troubleshooting into three perspectives:

■ The route is in the routing table but is incorrect.

■ The route is not in the routing table.

■ The route is in the routing table and is correct, but the packets do not arrive at the destination host.

Troubleshooting Incorrect Static Routes That Appear in the IP Routing Table

This first troubleshooting item can be obvious, but it is worth pausing to think about. A static route is only as good as the input typed into the **ip route** command. IOS checks the syntax, and as mentioned earlier, makes a few other checks that this section reviews in the next heading. But once those checks are passed, IOS puts the route into the IP routing table, even if the route had poorly chosen parameters.

For instance, the route might use a subnet and mask that implies a different range of addresses than the addresses in the destination subnet. Or, for a router sitting in the middle of a diagram, the next-hop address might be a router to the left, while the destination subnet is to the right. Or the next-hop address could be an IP address in a connected subnet, but it might be a typo and be an address of a PC or even a currently unused IP address.

When you see an exam question that has static routes, and you see them in the output of **show ip route**, remember to check on these items:

- Is there a subnetting math error in the subnet ID and mask?
- Is the next-hop IP address correct and referencing an IP address on a neighboring router?
- Does the next-hop IP address identify the correct router?
- Is the outgoing interface correct, and referencing an interface on the local router (that is, the same router where the static route is configured)?

The Static Route Does Not Appear in the IP Routing Table

After configuring an **ip route** command, IOS might or might not add the route to the IP routing table. IOS also considers the following before adding the route to its routing table:

- For **ip route** commands that list an outgoing interface, that interface must be in an up/up state.
- For **ip route** commands that list a next-hop IP address, the local router must have a route to reach that next-hop address.

For example, earlier in Example 16-3, R1's command **ip route 172.16.3.0 255.255.255.0 172.16.5.3** defines a static route. Before adding the route to the IP routing table, R1 looks for an existing IP route to reach 172.16.5.3. In that case, R1 will find a connected route for subnet 172.16.5.0/24 as long as its Ethernet WAN link is up. As a result, R1 adds the static route to subnet 172.16.3.0/24. Later, if R1's G0/1/0 were to fail, R1 would remove its connected route to 172.16.5.0/24 from the IP routing table—an action that would also then cause R1 to remove its static route to 172.16.3.0/24.

You can configure a static route so that IOS ignores these basic checks, always putting the IP route in the routing table. To do so, just use the **permanent** keyword on the **ip route** command. For example, by adding the **permanent** keyword to the end of the two commands as demonstrated in Example 16-7, R1 would now add these routes, regardless of whether the two WAN links were up.

Example 16-7 *Permanently Adding Static Routes to the IP Routing Table (Router R1)*

```
ip route 172.16.2.0 255.255.255.0 S0/0/0 permanent
ip route 172.16.3.0 255.255.255.0 172.16.5.3 permanent
```

Note that although the **permanent** keyword lets the router keep the route in the routing table without checking the outgoing interface or route to the next-hop address, it does not magically fix a broken route. For example, if the outgoing interface fails, the route will remain in the routing table, but the router cannot forward packets because the outgoing interface is down.

The Correct Static Route Appears but Works Poorly

This last section is a place to make two points—one mainstream and one point to review a bit of trivia.

First, on the mainstream point, the static route can be perfect, but the packets from one host to the next still might not arrive because of other problems. An incorrect static route is just one of many items to check when you're troubleshooting problems like "host A cannot connect to server B." The root cause may be the static route, or it may be something else. Chapter 18, "Troubleshooting IPv4 Routing," goes into some depth about troubleshooting these types of problems.

On the more specific point, be wary of any **ip route** command with the **permanent** keyword. IOS puts these routes in the routing table with no checks for accuracy. You should check whether the outgoing interface is down and/or whether the router has a route to reach the next-hop address.

IP Forwarding with the Longest Prefix Match

A router's IP routing process requires that the router compare the destination IP address of each packet with the existing contents of that router's IP routing table. Often, only one route matches a particular destination address. When only one route matches the packet's destination, the action is obvious: forward the packet based on the details listed in that route.

In some cases, a particular destination address matches more than one of the router's routes. For instance, one route might list subnet 10.1.0.0/16, another 10.1.1.0/25, and another 10.1.1.1/32. All would match packets sent to IP address 10.1.1.1. Many legitimate router features can cause these multiple routes to appear in a router's routing table, including

- Static routes
- Route autosummarization
- Manual route summarization

This fourth of four major sections of this chapter explains how a router makes its routing decisions when a packet matches multiple routes. When more than one route matches a packet's destination address, the router uses the "best" route, defined as follows:

When a particular destination IP address matches more than one route in a router's IPv4 routing table, the router uses the most specific route—in other words, the route with the longest prefix length mask.

Using show ip route to Find the Best Route

We humans have a couple of ways to figure out what choice a router makes for choosing the best route. One way uses the **show ip route** command, plus some subnetting math, to decide the route the router will choose. To let you see how to use this option, Example 16-8 shows a series of overlapping routes, all created with OSPF, so the output lists only OSPF-learned routes.

Example 16-8 show ip route *Command with Overlapping Routes*

```
R1# show ip route ospf
Codes: L - local, C - connected, S - static, R - RIP, M - mobile, B - BGP
       D - EIGRP, EX - EIGRP external, O - OSPF, IA - OSPF inter area
       N1 - OSPF NSSA external type 1, N2 - OSPF NSSA external type 2
       E1 - OSPF external type 1, E2 - OSPF external type 2
       i - IS-IS, su - IS-IS summary, L1 - IS-IS level-1, L2 - IS-IS level-2
       ia - IS-IS inter area, * - candidate default, U - per-user static route
       o - ODR, P - periodic downloaded static route, H - NHRP, l - LISP
       + - replicated route, % - next hop override


Gateway of last resort is 172.16.25.129 to network 0.0.0.0

      172.16.0.0/16 is variably subnetted, 9 subnets, 5 masks
O        172.16.1.1/32 [110/50] via 172.16.25.2, 00:00:04, GigabitEthernet0/0/0
O        172.16.1.0/24 [110/100] via 172.16.25.129, 00:00:09, GigabitEthernet0/1/0
O        172.16.0.0/22 [110/65] via 172.16.24.2, 00:00:04, GigabitEthernet0/2/0
O        172.16.0.0/16 [110/65] via 172.16.24.129, 00:00:09, GigabitEthernet0/3/0
O        0.0.0.0/0 [110/129] via 172.16.25.129, 00:00:09, GigabitEthernet0/0/0
```

To predict which of its routes a router will match, two pieces of information are required: the destination IP address of the packet and the contents of the router's routing table. The subnet ID and mask listed for a route define the range of addresses matched by that route. With a little subnetting math, a network engineer can find the range of addresses matched by each route. For instance, Table 16-2 lists the five subnets listed in Example 16-8 and the address ranges implied by each.

Table 16-2 Analysis of Address Ranges for the Subnets in Example 16-8

Subnet/Prefix	Address Range
172.16.1.1/32	172.16.1.1 (just this one address)
172.16.1.0/24	172.16.1.0 – 172.16.1.255
172.16.0.0/22	172.16.0.0 – 172.16.3.255
172.16.0.0/16	172.16.0.0 – 172.16.255.255
0.0.0.0/0	0.0.0.0 – 255.255.255.255 (all addresses)

NOTE The route listed as 0.0.0.0/0 is the default route.

As you can see from these ranges, several of the routes' address ranges overlap. When matching more than one route, the route with the longer prefix length is used. That is, a route with /16 is better than a route with /10; a route with a /25 prefix is better than a route with a /20 prefix; and so on.

For example, a packet sent to 172.16.1.1 actually matches all five routes listed in the routing table in Example 16-8. The various prefix lengths range from /0 to /32. The longest prefix (largest /P value, meaning the best and most specific route) is /32. So, a packet sent to 172.16.1.1 uses the route to 172.16.1.1/32, and not the other routes.

The following list gives some examples of destination IP addresses. For each address, the list describes the routes from Table 16-2 that the router would match, and which specific route the router would use.

172.16.1.1: Matches all five routes; the longest prefix is /32, the route to 172.16.1.1/32.

172.16.1.2: Matches the last four routes; the longest prefix is /24, the route to 172.16.1.0/24.

172.16.2.3: Matches the last three routes; the longest prefix is /22, the route to 172.16.0.0/22.

172.16.4.3: Matches the last two routes; the longest prefix is /16, the route to 172.16.0.0/16.

Using show ip route *address* to Find the Best Route

A second way to identify the route a router will use, one that does not require any subnetting math, is the **show ip route** *address* command. The last parameter on this command is the IP address of an assumed IP packet. The router replies by listing the route it would use to route a packet sent to that address.

For example, Example 16-9 lists the output of the **show ip route 172.16.4.3** command on the same router used in Example 24-4. The first line of (highlighted) output lists the matched route: the route to 172.16.0.0/16. The rest of the output lists the details of that particular route, like the outgoing interface of GigabitEthernet0/1/0 and the next-hop router of 172.16.25.129.

Example 16-9   show ip route *Command with Overlapping Routes*

```
R1# show ip route 172.16.4.3
Routing entry for 172.16.0.0/16
  Known via "ospf 1", distance 110, metric 65, type intra area
  Last update from 10.2.2.5 on GigabitEthernet0/2/0, 14:22:06 ago
  Routing Descriptor Blocks:
  * 172.16.25.129, from 172.16.25.129, 14:22:05 ago, via GigabitEthernet0/1/0
      Route metric is 65, traffic share count is 1
```

Certainly, if you have an option, just using a command to check what the router actually chooses is a much quicker option than doing the subnetting math.

Interpreting the IP Routing Table

The **show ip route** command plays a huge role in verifying and troubleshooting IP routing and addressing. This final topic of the chapter pulls the concepts together in one place for easier reference and study.

Figure 16-15 shows the output of a sample **show ip route** command. The figure numbers various parts of the command output for easier reference, with Table 16-3 describing the output noted by each number.

```
          ①                                    ②        ③
     10.0.0.0/8 is variably subnetted, 13 subnets, 5 masks
C       10.1.3.0/26 is directly connected, GigabitEthernet0/1
L       10.1.3.3/32 is directly connected, GigabitEthernet0/1
O       10.1.4.64/26 [110/65] via 10.2.2.10, 14:31:52, Serial0/1/0
O       10.2.2.0/30 [110/128] via 10.2.2.5, 14:31:52, Serial0/0/1
④         ⑤     ⑥ ⑦ ⑧           ⑨           ⑩          ⑪
```

Figure 16-15   show ip route *Command Output Reference*

Table 16-3   Descriptions of the **show ip route** Command Output

Item	Idea	Value in the Figure	Description
1	Classful network	10.0.0.0/8	The routing table is organized by classful network. This line is the heading line for classful network 10.0.0.0; it lists the default mask for Class A networks (/8).
2	Number of subnets	13 subnets	The number of routes for subnets of the classful network known to this router, from all sources, including local routes—the /32 routes that match each router interface IP address.
3	Number of masks	5 masks	The number of different masks used in all routes known to this router inside this classful network.
4	Legend code	C, L, O	A short code that identifies the source of the routing information. *O* is for OSPF, *D* for EIGRP, *C* for Connected, *S* for static, and *L* for local. (See Example 16-8 for a sample of the legend.)
5	Prefix (Subnet ID)	10.2.2.0	The subnet number of this particular route.
6	Prefix length (Mask)	/30	The prefix mask used with this subnet.
7	Administrative distance	110	If a router learns routes for the listed subnet from more than one source of routing information, the router uses the source with the lowest administrative distance (AD).
8	Metric	128	The metric for this route.
9	Next-hop router	10.2.2.5	For packets matching this route, the IP address of the next router to which the packet should be forwarded.
10	Timer	14:31:52	For OSPF and EIGRP routes, this is the time since the route was first learned.
11	Outgoing interface	Serial0/0/1	For packets matching this route, the interface out which the packet should be forwarded.

16

Chapter Review

One key to doing well on the exams is to perform repetitive spaced review sessions. Review this chapter's material using either the tools in the book or interactive tools for the same material found on the book's companion website. Refer to the "Your Study Plan" element for more details. Table 16-4 outlines the key review elements and where you can find them. To better track your study progress, record when you completed these activities in the second column.

Table 16-4 Chapter Review Tracking

Review Element	Review Date(s)	Resource Used
Review key topics		Book, website
Review key terms		Book, website
Answer DIKTA questions		Book, PTP
Review command tables		Book
Do labs		Blog

Review All the Key Topics

Table 16-5 Key Topics for Chapter 16

Key Topic Element	Description	Page Number
List	Steps taken by a host when forwarding IP packets	369
List	Steps taken by a router when forwarding IP packets	370
Figure 16-2	Diagram of five routing steps taken by a router	371
Figure 16-7	Breakdown of IP routing table with matching and forwarding details	374
List	Three common sources from which routers build IP routes	376
List	Rules regarding when a router creates a connected route	376
Figure 16-11	Static route configuration concept	379
List	Troubleshooting checklist for routes that do appear in the IP routing table	385
List	Troubleshooting checklist for static routes that do not appear in the IP routing table	385
Paragraph	A description of how a router makes a longest prefix decision to match the routing table	386
Table 16-3	List of items found in a Cisco router IP routing table	389

Key Terms You Should Know

ARP table, routing table, next-hop router, outgoing interface, connected route, static route, default route, host route, floating static route, network route, administrative distance

Command References

Tables 16-6 and 16-7 list configuration and verification commands used in this chapter. As an easy review exercise, cover the left column in a table, read the right column, and try to recall the command without looking. Then repeat the exercise, covering the right column, and try to recall what the command does.

Table 16-6   Chapter 16 Configuration Command Reference

Command	Description
ip address *ip-address mask*	Interface subcommand that assigns the interface's IP address
interface *type number.subint*	Global command to create a subinterface and to enter configuration mode for that subinterface
[no] ip routing	Global command that enables (**ip routing**) or disables (**no ip routing**) the routing of IPv4 packets on a router or Layer 3 switch
ip route *prefix mask* {*ip-address* | *interface-type interface-number*} [*distance*] [**permanent**]	Global configuration command that creates a static route

Table 16-7   Chapter 16 EXEC Command Reference

Command	Description
show ip route	Lists the router's entire routing table
show ip route [connected | static | ospf]	Lists a subset of the IP routing table
show ip route *ip-address*	Lists detailed information about the route that a router matches for the listed IP address
show arp, show ip arp	Lists the router's IPv4 ARP table
clear ip arp [ip-address]	Removes all dynamically learned ARP table entries, or if the command lists an IP address, removes the entry for that IP address only

CHAPTER 17

IP Routing in the LAN

This chapter covers the following exam topics:

1.0 Network Fundamentals

1.6 Configure and verify IPv4 addressing and subnetting

2.0 Network Access

2.4 Configure and verify (Layer 2/Layer 3) EtherChannel (LACP)

The preceding two chapters showed how to configure an IP address and mask on a router interface, making the router ready to route packets to/from the subnet implied by that address/mask combination. While true and useful, all the examples so far ignored the LAN switches and the possibility of VLANs. In fact, the examples so far show the simplest possible cases: the attached switches as Layer 2 switches, using only one VLAN, with the router configured with one **ip address** command on its physical interface. This chapter takes a detailed look at how to configure routers so that they route packets to/from the subnets that exist on each and every VLAN.

Because Layer 2 switches do not forward Layer 2 frames between VLANs, a network must use routers to route IP packets between subnets to allow those devices in different VLANs/subnets to communicate. To review, Ethernet defines the concept of a VLAN, while IP defines the concept of an IP subnet, so a VLAN is not equivalent to a subnet. However, the set of devices in one VLAN are typically also in one subnet. By the same reasoning, devices in two different VLANs are normally in two different subnets. For two devices in different VLANs to communicate with each other, routers must connect to the subnets that exist on each VLAN, and then the routers forward IP packets between the devices in those subnets.

This chapter discusses the configuration and verification steps related to three methods of routing between VLANs with three major sections:

- **VLAN Routing with Router 802.1Q Trunks:** The first section discusses how to configure a router to use VLAN trunking as connected to a Layer 2 switch. The router does the routing, with the switch creating the VLANs. The link between the router and switch use trunking so that the router has an interface connected to each VLAN/subnet. This feature is known as routing over a VLAN trunk and also known as router-on-a-stick (ROAS).

- **VLAN Routing with Layer 3 Switch SVIs:** The second section discusses using a LAN switch that supports both Layer 2 switching and Layer 3 routing (called a Layer 3 switch or multilayer switch). To route, the Layer 3 switch configuration uses interfaces called switched virtual interfaces (SVI), which are also called VLAN interfaces.

- **VLAN Routing with Layer 3 Switch Routed Ports:** The third major section of the chapter discusses an alternative to SVIs called routed ports, in which the physical switch ports are made to act like interfaces on a router. This third section also introduces the concept of an EtherChannel as used as a routed port in a feature called Layer 3 EtherChannel.

"Do I Know This Already?" Quiz

Take the quiz (either here or use the PTP software) if you want to use the score to help you decide how much time to spend on this chapter. The letter answers are listed at the bottom of the page following the quiz. Appendix C, found both at the end of the book as well as on the companion website, includes both the answers and explanations. You can also find both answers and explanations in the PTP testing software.

Table 17-1 "Do I Know This Already?" Foundation Topics Section-to-Question Mapping

Foundation Topics Section	Questions
VLAN Routing with Router 802.1Q Trunks	1, 2
VLAN Routing with Layer 3 Switch SVIs	3, 4
VLAN Routing with Layer 3 Switch Routed Ports	5, 6

1. Router 1 has a Fast Ethernet interface 0/0 with IP address 10.1.1.1. The interface is connected to a switch. This connection is then migrated to use 802.1Q trunking. Which of the following commands could be part of a valid configuration for Router 1's Fa0/0 interface? (Choose two answers.)

   a. interface fastethernet 0/0.4

   b. dot1q enable

   c. dot1q enable 4

   d. trunking enable

   e. trunking enable 4

   f. encapsulation dot1q 4

2. Router R1 has a router-on-a-stick (ROAS) configuration with two subinterfaces of interface G0/1: G0/1.1 and G0/1.2. Physical interface G0/1 is currently in a down/down state. The network engineer then configures a **shutdown** command when in interface configuration mode for G0/1.1 and a **no shutdown** command when in interface configuration mode for G0/1.2. Which answers are correct about the interface state for the subinterfaces? (Choose two answers.)

   a. G0/1.1 will be in a down/down state.

   b. G0/1.2 will be in a down/down state.

   c. G0/1.1 will be in an administratively down state.

   d. G0/1.2 will be in an up/up state.

3. A Layer 3 switch has been configured to route IP packets between VLANs 1, 2, and 3 using SVIs, which connect to subnets 172.20.1.0/25, 172.20.2.0/25, and 172.20.3.0/25, respectively. The engineer issues a **show ip route connected** command on the Layer 3 switch, listing the connected routes. Which of the following answers lists a piece of information that should be in at least one of the routes?

   a. Interface Gigabit Ethernet 0/0.3

   b. Next-hop router 172.20.2.1

   c. Interface VLAN 2

   d. Mask 255.255.255.0

4. An engineer has successfully configured a Layer 3 switch with SVIs for VLANs 2 and 3. Hosts in the subnets using VLANs 2 and 3 can ping each other with the Layer 3 switch routing the packets. The next week, the network engineer receives a call that those same users can no longer ping each other. If the problem is with the Layer 3 switching function, which of the following could have caused the problem? (Choose two answers.)

   a. Six (or more) out of 10 working VLAN 2 access ports failing due to physical problems

   b. A **shutdown** command issued from interface VLAN 4 configuration mode

   c. VTP on the switch removing VLAN 3 from the switch's VLAN list

   d. A **shutdown** command issued from VLAN 2 configuration mode

5. A LAN design uses a Layer 3 EtherChannel between two switches SW1 and SW2, with port-channel interface 1 used on both switches. SW1 uses ports G0/1, G0/2, and G0/3 in the channel. Which of the following are true about SW1's configuration to make the channel be able to route IPv4 packets correctly? (Choose two answers.)

   a. The **ip address** command must be on the port-channel 1 interface.

   b. The **ip address** command must be on interface G0/1 (lowest numbered port).

   c. The port-channel 1 interface must be configured with the **no switchport** command.

   d. Interface G0/1 must be configured with the **routedport** command.

6. A LAN design uses a Layer 3 EtherChannel between two switches SW1 and SW2, with port-channel interface 1 used on both switches. SW1 uses ports G0/1 and G0/2 in the channel. However, only interface G0/1 is bundled into the channel and working. Think about the configuration settings on port G0/2 that could have existed before adding G0/2 to the EtherChannel. Which answers identify a setting that could prevent IOS from adding G0/2 to the Layer 3 EtherChannel? (Choose two answers.)

   a. A different STP cost (**spanning-tree cost** *value*)

   b. A different speed (**speed** *value*)

   c. A default setting for switchport (**switchport**)

   d. A different access VLAN (**switchport access vlan** *vlan-id*)

Foundation Topics

VLAN Routing with Router 802.1Q Trunks

Almost all enterprise networks use VLANs. To route IP packets in and out of those VLANs, some devices (either routers or Layer 3 switches) need to have an IP address in each subnet and have a connected route to each of those subnets. Then the IP addresses on those routers or Layer 3 switches can serve as the default gateways in those subnets.

This chapter breaks down the LAN routing options into four categories:

■ Use a router, with one router LAN interface and cable connected to the switch for each and every VLAN (typically not used)

■ Use a router, with a VLAN trunk connecting to a LAN switch (known as router-on-a-stick, or ROAS)

■ Use a Layer 3 switch with switched virtual interfaces (SVI)

■ Use a Layer 3 switch with routed interfaces (which may or may not be Layer 3 EtherChannels)

Of the items in the list, the first option works, but to be practical, it requires far too many interfaces. It is mentioned here only to make the list complete.

As for the other three options, this chapter discusses each in turn as the main focus of one of the three major sections in this chapter. Each feature is used in real networks today, with the choice to use one or the other driven by the design and needs for a particular part of the network. Figure 17-1 shows cases in which these options could be used.

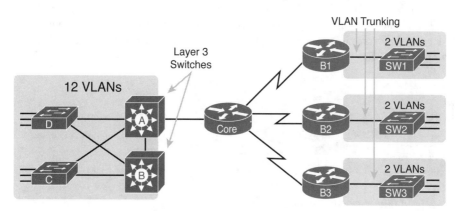

Figure 17-1 *Layer 3 Switching at the Central Site*

Figure 17-1 shows two switches, labeled A and B, which could act as Layer 3 switches—both with SVIs and routed interfaces. The figure shows a central site campus LAN on the left, with 12 VLANs. Switches A and B act as Layer 3 switches, combining the functions of a router and a switch, routing between all 12 subnets/VLANs, as well as routing to/from the Core router. Those Layer 3 switches could use SVIs, routed interfaces, or both.

Figure 17-1 also shows a classic case for using a router with a VLAN trunk. Sites like the remote sites on the right side of the figure may have a WAN-connected router and a LAN switch. These sites might use ROAS to take advantage of the router's ability to route over an 802.1Q trunk.

Note that Figure 17-1 just shows an example. The engineer could use Layer 3 switching at each site or routers with VLAN trunking at each site.

Configuring ROAS

This next topic discusses how routers route packets to subnets associated with VLANs connected to a router 802.1Q trunk. That long description can be a bit of a chore to repeat each time someone wants to discuss this feature, so over time, the networking world has instead settled on a shorter and more interesting name for this feature: router-on-a-stick (ROAS).

ROAS uses router VLAN trunking configuration to give the router a logical router interface connected to each VLAN. Because the router then has an interface connected to each VLAN, the router can also be configured with an IP address in the subnet that exists on each VLAN.

Routers use subinterfaces as the means to have an interface connected to a VLAN. The router needs to have an IP address/mask associated with each VLAN on the trunk. However, the router has only one physical interface for the link connected to the trunk. Cisco solves this problem by creating multiple virtual router interfaces, one associated with each VLAN on that trunk (at least for each VLAN that you want the trunk to support). Cisco calls these virtual interfaces *subinterfaces*. The configuration can then include an **ip address** command for each subinterface.

Figure 17-2 shows the concept with Router B1, one of the branch routers from Figure 17-1. Because this router needs to route between only two VLANs, the figure also shows two subinterfaces, named G0/0.10 and G0/0.20, which create a new place in the configuration where the per-VLAN configuration settings can be made. The router treats frames tagged with VLAN 10 as if they came in or out of G0/0.10 and frames tagged with VLAN 20 as if they came in or out G0/0.20.

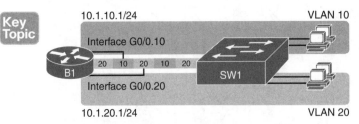

Figure 17-2 *Subinterfaces on Router B1*

In addition, note that most Cisco routers do not attempt to negotiate trunking, so both the router and switch need to manually configure trunking. This chapter discusses the router side of that trunking configuration; the matching switch interface would need to be configured with the **switchport mode trunk** command.

Answers to the "Do I Know This Already?" quiz:

1 A, F **2** B, C **3** C **4** C, D **5** A, C **6** B, C

Example 17-1 shows a full example of the 802.1Q trunking configuration required on Router B1 in Figure 17-2. More generally, these steps detail how to configure 802.1Q trunking on a router:

Step 1. Use the **interface** *type number.subint* command in global configuration mode to create a unique subinterface for each VLAN that needs to be routed.

Step 2. Use the **encapsulation dot1q** *vlan_id* command in subinterface configuration mode to enable 802.1Q and associate one specific VLAN with the subinterface.

Step 3. Use the **ip address** *address mask* command in subinterface configuration mode to configure IP settings (address and mask).

Example 17-1 *Router Configuration for the 802.1Q Encapsulation Shown in Figure 17-2*

```
B1# show running-config
! Only pertinent lines shown
interface gigabitethernet 0/0
! No IP address up here! No encapsulation up here!
!
interface gigabitethernet 0/0.10
 encapsulation dot1q 10
 ip address 10.1.10.1 255.255.255.0
!
interface gigabitethernet 0/0.20
 encapsulation dot1q 20
 ip address 10.1.20.1 255.255.255.0
```

First, look at the subinterface numbers. The subinterface number begins with the period, like .10 and .20 in this case. These numbers can be any number from 1 up through a very large number (over 4 billion). The number just needs to be unique among all subinterfaces associated with this one physical interface. In fact, the subinterface number does not even have to match the associated VLAN ID. (The **encapsulation** command, and not the subinterface number, defines the VLAN ID associated with the subinterface.)

NOTE Although not required, most sites do choose to make the subinterface number match the VLAN ID, as shown in Example 17-1, just to avoid confusion.

Each subinterface configuration lists two subcommands. One command (**encapsulation**) enables trunking and defines the VLAN whose frames are considered to be coming in and out of the subinterface. The **ip address** command works the same way it does on any other interface. Note that if the physical Ethernet interface reaches an up/up state, the subinterface should as well, which would then let the router add the connected routes shown at the bottom of the example.

Now that the router has a working interface, with IPv4 addresses configured, the router can route IPv4 packets on these subinterfaces. That is, the router treats these subinterfaces like any physical interface in terms of adding connected routes, matching those routes, and forwarding packets to/from those connected subnets.

The configuration and use of the native VLAN on the trunk require a little extra thought. The native VLAN can be configured on a subinterface, or on the physical interface, or ignored as in Example 17-1. Each 802.1Q trunk has one native VLAN, and if the router needs to route packets for a subnet that exists in the native VLAN, then the router needs some configuration to support that subnet. The two options to define a router interface for the native VLAN are

- Configure the **ip address** command on the physical interface, but without an **encapsulation** command; the router considers this physical interface to be using the native VLAN.

- Configure the **ip address** command on a subinterface and use the **encapsulation dot1q** *vlan-id* **native** subcommand to tell the router both the VLAN ID and the fact that it is the native VLAN.

Example 17-2 shows both native VLAN configuration options with a small change to the same configuration in Example 17-1. In this case, VLAN 10 becomes the native VLAN. The top part of the example shows the option to configure the router physical interface to use native VLAN 10. The second half of the example shows how to configure that same native VLAN on a subinterface. In both cases, the switch configuration also needs to be changed to make VLAN 10 the native VLAN.

Example 17-2 *Router Configuration Using Native VLAN 10 on Router B1*

```
! First option: put the native VLAN IP address on the physical interface
interface gigabitethernet 0/0
 ip address 10.1.10.1 255.255.255.0
!
interface gigabitethernet 0/0.20
 encapsulation dot1q 20
 ip address 10.1.20.1 255.255.255.0
! Second option: like Example 17-1, but add the native keyword
interface gigabitethernet 0/0.10
 encapsulation dot1q 10 native
 ip address 10.1.10.1 255.255.255.0
!
interface gigabitethernet 0/0.20
 encapsulation dot1q 20
 ip address 10.1.20.1 255.255.255.0
```

Verifying ROAS

Beyond using the **show running-config** command, ROAS configuration on a router can be best verified with two commands: **show ip route [connected]** and **show vlans**. As with any router interface, as long as the interface is in an up/up state and has an IPv4 address configured, IOS will put a connected (and local) route in the IPv4 routing table. So, a first and obvious check would be to see if all the expected connected routes exist. Example 17-3 lists the connected routes per the configuration shown in Example 17-1.

Example 17-3 *Connected Routes Based on Example 17-1 Configuration*

```
B1# show ip route connected
Codes: L - local, C - connected, S - static, R - RIP, M - mobile, B - BGP
! Legend omitted for brevity

      10.0.0.0/8 is variably subnetted, 4 subnets, 2 masks
C        10.1.10.0/24 is directly connected, GigabitEthernet0/0.10
L        10.1.10.1/32 is directly connected, GigabitEthernet0/0.10
C        10.1.20.0/24 is directly connected, GigabitEthernet0/0.20
L        10.1.20.1/32 is directly connected, GigabitEthernet0/0.20
```

As for interface and subinterface state, note that the ROAS subinterface state does depend to some degree on the physical interface state. In particular, the subinterface state cannot be better than the state of the matching physical interface. For instance, on Router B1 in the examples so far, physical interface G0/0 is in an up/up state, and the subinterfaces are in an up/up state. But if you unplugged the cable from that port, the physical port would fail to a down/down state, and the subinterfaces would also fail to a down/down state. Example 17-4 shows another example, with the physical interface being shut down, with the subinterfaces then automatically changed to an administratively down state as a result.

Example 17-4 *Subinterface State Tied to Physical Interface State*

```
B1# configure terminal
Enter configuration commands, one per line. End with CNTL/Z.
B1(config)# interface g0/0
B1(config-if)# shutdown
B1(config-if)# ^Z
B1# show ip interface brief | include 0/0
GigabitEthernet0/0           unassigned     YES manual administratively down down
GigabitEthernet0/0.10        10.1.10.1      YES manual administratively down down
GigabitEthernet0/0.20        10.1.20.1      YES manual administratively down down
```

Additionally, the subinterface state can also be enabled and disabled independently from the physical interface, using the **no shutdown** and **shutdown** commands in subinterface configuration mode.

Another useful ROAS verification command, **show vlans**, spells out which router trunk interfaces use which VLANs, which VLAN is the native VLAN, plus some packet statistics. The fact that the packet counters are increasing can be useful when verifying whether traffic is happening or not. Example 17-5 shows a sample, based on the Router B1 configuration in Example 17-2 (bottom half), in which native VLAN 10 is configured on subinterface G0/0.10. Note that the output identifies VLAN 1 associated with the physical interface, VLAN 10 as the native VLAN associated with G0/0.10, and VLAN 20 associated with G0/0.20. It also lists the IP addresses assigned to each interface/subinterface.

17

Example 17-5 *Sample* **show vlans** *Command to Match Sample Router Trunking Configuration*

```
R1# show vlans
Virtual LAN ID: 1 (IEEE 802.1Q Encapsulation)

   vLAN Trunk Interface: GigabitEthernet0/0

   Protocols Configured:   Address:        Received:     Transmitted:
      Other                                    0               83


   69 packets, 20914 bytes input
   147 packets, 11841 bytes output


Virtual LAN ID:   10 (IEEE 802.1Q Encapsulation)

   vLAN Trunk Interface:   GigabitEthernet0/0.10


This is configured as native Vlan for the following interface(s) :
GigabitEthernet0/0      Native-vlan Tx-type: Untagged

       Protocols Configured:   Address:      Received:     Transmitted:
          IP               10.1.10.1            2               3
             Other                              0               1


   3 packets, 722 bytes input
   4 packets, 264 bytes output

Virtual LAN ID:   20 (IEEE 802.1Q Encapsulation)

   vLAN Trunk Interface:   GigabitEthernet0/0.20

   Protocols Configured:   Address:        Received:   Transmitted:
      IP               10.1.20.1              0             134
         Other                                0             1


   0 packets, 0 bytes input
   135 packets, 10498 bytes output
```

Troubleshooting ROAS

The biggest challenge when troubleshooting ROAS has to do with the fact that if you mis-configure only the router or misconfigure only the switch, the other device on the trunk has no way to know that the other side is misconfigured. That is, if you check the **show ip route** and **show vlans** commands on a router, and the output looks like it matches the intended configuration, and the connected routes for the correct subinterfaces show up, routing may still fail because of problems on the attached switch. So, troubleshooting ROAS often begins with checking the configuration on both the router and switch because there is no status output on either device that tells you where the problem might be.

First, to check ROAS on the router, you need to start with the intended configuration and ask questions about the configuration:

1. Is each non-native VLAN configured on the router with an **encapsulation dot1q** *vlan-id* command on a subinterface?

2. Do those same VLANs exist on the trunk on the neighboring switch (**show interfaces trunk**), and are they in the allowed list, not VTP pruned, and not STP blocked?

3. Does each router ROAS subinterface have an IP address/mask configured per the planned configuration?

4. If using the native VLAN, is it configured correctly on the router either on a subinterface (with an **encapsulation dot1q** *vlan-id* **native** command) or implied on the physical interface?

5. Is the same native VLAN configured on the neighboring switch's trunk in comparison to the native VLAN configured on the router?

6. Are the router physical or ROAS subinterfaces configured with a **shutdown** command?

For some of these steps, you need to be ready to investigate possible VLAN trunking issues on the LAN switch. The reason is that on many Cisco routers, router interfaces do not negotiate trunking. As a result, ROAS relies on static trunk configuration on both the router and switch. If the switch has any problems with VLANs or the VLAN trunking configuration on its side of the trunk, the router has no way to realize that the problem exists.

For example, imagine you configured ROAS on a router just like in Example 17-1 or Example 17-2. However, the switch on the other end of the link had no matching configuration. For instance, maybe the switch did not even define VLANs 10 and 20. Maybe the switch did not configure trunking on the port connected to the router. Even with blatant misconfiguration or missing configuration on the switch, the router still shows up/up ROAS interfaces and subinterfaces, IP routes in the output of **show ip route**, and meaningful configuration information in the output of the **show vlans** command.

VLAN Routing with Layer 3 Switch SVIs

Using a router with ROAS to route packets makes sense in some cases, particularly at small remote sites. In sites with a larger LAN, network designers choose to use Layer 3 switches for most inter-VLAN routing.

A Layer 3 switch (also called a multilayer switch) is one device, but it executes logic at two layers: Layer 2 LAN switching and Layer 3 IP routing. The Layer 2 switch function forwards frames inside each VLAN, but it will not forward frames between VLANs. The Layer 3 forwarding (routing) logic forwards IP packets between VLANs.

Layer 3 switches typically support two configuration options to enable IPv4 routing inside the switch, specifically to enable IPv4 on switch interfaces. This section explains one option, an option that uses switched virtual interfaces (SVI). The final major section of the chapter deals with the other option for configuring IPv4 addresses on Layer 3 switches: routed interfaces.

Configuring Routing Using Switch SVIs

The configuration of a Layer 3 switch mostly looks like the Layer 2 switching configuration shown back in Parts II and III of this book, with a small bit of configuration added for the Layer 3 functions. The Layer 3 switching function needs a virtual interface connected to each VLAN internal to the switch. These *VLAN interfaces* act like router interfaces, with an IP address and mask. The Layer 3 switch has an IP routing table, with connected routes off each of these VLAN interfaces. (These interfaces are also referred to as *switched virtual interfaces* [SVI].)

To show the concept of Layer 3 switching with SVIs, the following example uses the same branch office with two VLANs shown in the earlier examples, but now the design will use Layer 3 switching in the LAN switch. Figure 17-3 shows the design changes and configuration concept for the Layer 3 switch function with a router icon inside the switch, to emphasize that the switch routes the packets.

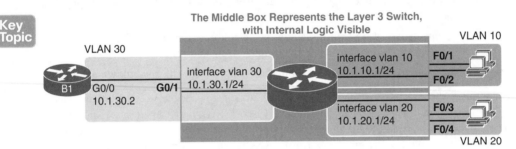

Figure 17-3 *Routing on VLAN Interfaces in a Layer 3 Switch*

Note that the figure represents the internals of the Layer 3 switch within the box in the middle of the figure. The branch still has two user VLANs (10 and 20), so the Layer 3 switch needs one VLAN interface for each VLAN. The figure shows a router icon inside the gray box to represent the Layer 3 switching function, with two VLAN interfaces on the right side of that icon. In addition, the traffic still needs to get to router B1 (a physical router) to access the WAN, so the switch uses a third VLAN (VLAN 30 in this case) for the link to Router B1. The physical link between the Layer 3 switch and router B1 would not be a trunk, but instead be an access link.

The following steps show how to configure Layer 3 switching using SVIs. Note that on some switches, like the 2960 and 2960-XR switches used for the examples in this book, the ability to route IPv4 packets must be enabled first, with a **reload** of the switch required to enable the feature. The steps that occur after the reload would apply to all models of Cisco switches that are capable of doing Layer 3 switching.

Step 1.   Enable IP routing on the switch, as needed:

   A. Use the **sdm prefer lanbase-routing** command (or similar) in global configuration mode to change the switch forwarding ASIC settings to make space for IPv4 routes at the next reload of the switch.

   B. Use the **reload** EXEC command in enable mode to reload (reboot) the switch to pick up the new **sdm prefer** command setting.

   C. Once reloaded, use the **ip routing** command in global configuration mode to enable the IPv4 routing function in IOS software and to enable key commands like **show ip route**.

Step 2. Configure each SVI interface, one per VLAN for which routing should be done by this Layer 3 switch:

    A. Use the **interface vlan** *vlan_id* command in global configuration mode to create a VLAN interface and to give the switch's routing logic a Layer 3 interface connected into the VLAN of the same number.

    B. Use the **ip address** *address mask* command in VLAN interface configuration mode to configure an IP address and mask on the VLAN interface, enabling IPv4 routing on that VLAN interface.

    C. (As needed) Use the **no shutdown** command in interface configuration mode to enable the VLAN interface (if it is currently in a shutdown state).

Example 17-6 shows the configuration to match Figure 17-3. In this case, switch SW1 has already used the **sdm prefer** global command to change to a setting that supports IPv4 routing, and the switch has been reloaded. The example shows the related configuration on all three VLAN interfaces.

Example 17-6 *VLAN Interface Configuration for Layer 3 Switching*

```
ip routing
!
interface vlan 10
 ip address 10.1.10.1 255.255.255.0
!
interface vlan 20
 ip address 10.1.20.1 255.255.255.0
!
interface vlan 30
 ip address 10.1.30.1 255.255.255.0
```

Verifying Routing with SVIs

With the VLAN configuration shown in the previous section, the switch is ready to route packets between the VLANs as shown in Figure 17-3. To support the routing of packets, the switch adds connected IP routes as shown in Example 17-7; note that each route is listed as being connected to a different VLAN interface.

Example 17-7 *Connected Routes on a Layer 3 Switch*

```
SW1# show ip route
! legend omitted for brevity


      10.0.0.0/8 is variably subnetted, 6 subnets, 2 masks
C        10.1.10.0/24 is directly connected, Vlan10
L        10.1.10.1/32 is directly connected, Vlan10
C        10.1.20.0/24 is directly connected, Vlan20
L        10.1.20.1/32 is directly connected, Vlan20
C        10.1.30.0/24 is directly connected, Vlan30
L        10.1.30.1/32 is directly connected, Vlan30
```

The switch would also need additional routes to the rest of the network (not shown in the figures in this chapter). The Layer 3 switch could use static routes or a routing protocol, depending on the capabilities of the switch. For instance, if you then enabled OSPF on the Layer 3 switch, the configuration and verification would work the same as it does on a router, as discussed in Chapter 20, "Implementing OSPF." The routes that IOS adds to the Layer 3 switch's IP routing table would list the VLAN interfaces as outgoing interfaces.

NOTE Some models of Cisco enterprise switches, based on model, IOS version, and IOS feature set, support different capabilities for IP routing and routing protocols, so for real networks, check the capabilities of the switch model by browsing at Cisco.com. In particular, check the Cisco Feature Navigator (CFN) tool at http://www.cisco.com/go/cfn.

Troubleshooting Routing with SVIs

There are two big topics to investigate when troubleshooting routing over LANs with SVIs. First, you have to make sure the switch has been enabled to support IP routing. Second, the VLAN associated with each VLAN interface must be known and active on the local switch; otherwise, the VLAN interfaces do not come up.

First, about enabling IP routing, note that some models of Cisco switches default to enable Layer 3 switching, and some do not. So, to make sure your switch supports Layer 3 routing, look to those first few configuration commands listed in the configuration checklist found in the earlier section "Configuring Routing Using Switch SVIs." Those commands are **sdm prefer** (followed by a **reload**) and then **ip routing** (after the **reload**).

The **sdm prefer** command changes how the switch forwarding chips allocate memory for different forwarding tables, and changes to those tables require a reload of the switch. By default, many access switches that support Layer 3 switching still have an SDM default that does not allocate space for an IP routing table. Once changed and reloaded, the **ip routing** command then enables IPv4 routing in IOS software. Both are necessary before some Cisco switches will act as a Layer 3 switch.

Example 17-8 shows some symptoms on a router for which Layer 3 switching had not yet been enabled by the **sdm prefer** command. As you can see, both the **show ip route** EXEC command and the **ip routing** config command are rejected because they do not exist to IOS until the **sdm prefer** command has been used (followed by a **reload** of the switch).

Example 17-8 *Evidence That a Switch Has Not Yet Enabled IPv4 Routing*

```
SW1# show ip route
         ^
% Invalid input detected at '^' marker.


SW3# configure terminal
Enter configuration commands, one per line. End with CNTL/Z.
SW3(config)# ip routing
            ^
% Invalid input detected at '^' marker.
```

The second big area to investigate when troubleshooting SVIs relates to the SVI state, a state that ties to the state of the associated VLANs. Each VLAN interface has a matching VLAN of the same number, and the VLAN interface's state is tied to the state of the VLAN in certain ways. In particular, for a VLAN interface to be in an up/up state:

Step 1.   The VLAN must be defined on the local switch (either explicitly or learned with VTP).

Step 2.   The switch must have at least one up/up interface using the VLAN, either/both:

   A. An up/up access interface assigned to that VLAN

   B. A trunk interface for which the VLAN is in the allowed list, is STP forwarding, and is not VTP pruned

Step 3.   The VLAN (not the VLAN interface) must be administratively enabled (that is, not **shutdown**).

Step 4.   The VLAN interface (not the VLAN) must be administratively enabled (that is, not **shutdown**).

When working through the steps in the list, keep in mind that the VLAN and the VLAN interface are related but separate ideas, and the configuration items are separate in the CLI. The VLAN interface is a switch's Layer 3 interface connected to the VLAN. If you want to route packets for the subnets on VLANs 11, 12, and 13, the matching VLAN interfaces must be numbered 11, 12, and 13. And both the VLANs and the VLAN interfaces can be disabled and enabled with the **shutdown** and **no shutdown** commands (as mentioned in Steps 3 and 4 in the previous list), so you have to check for both.

Example 17-9 shows three scenarios, each of which leads to one of the VLAN interfaces in the previous configuration example (Figure 17-3, Example 17-6) to fail. At the beginning of the example, all three VLAN interfaces are up/up. VLANs 10, 20, and 30 each have at least one access interface up and working. The example works through three scenarios:

- **Scenario 1:** The last access interface in VLAN 10 is shut down (F0/1), so IOS shuts down the VLAN 10 interface.

- **Scenario 2:** VLAN 20 (not VLAN interface 20, but VLAN 20) is deleted, which results in IOS then bringing down (not shutting down) the VLAN 20 interface.

- **Scenario 3:** VLAN 30 (not VLAN interface 30, but VLAN 30) is shut down, which results in IOS then bringing down (not shutting down) the VLAN 30 interface.

Example 17-9   *Three Examples That Cause VLAN Interfaces to Fail*

```
SW1# show interfaces status
! Only ports related to the example are shown
Port      Name           Status       Vlan    Duplex  Speed Type
Fa0/1                    connected    10       a-full  a-100 10/100BaseTX
Fa0/2                    notconnect   10        auto    auto 10/100BaseTX
Fa0/3                    connected    20       a-full  a-100 10/100BaseTX
Fa0/4                    connected    20       a-full  a-100 10/100BaseTX
Gi0/1                    connected    30       a-full a-1000 10/100/1000BaseTX
```

```
SW1# configure terminal
Enter configuration commands, one per line. End with CNTL/Z.


! Case 1: Interface F0/1, the last up/up access interface in VLAN 10, is shutdown
SW1(config)# interface fastEthernet 0/1
SW1(config-if)# shutdown
SW1(config-if)#
*Apr 2 19:54:08.784: %LINEPROTO-5-UPDOWN: Line protocol on Interface Vlan10, changed
state to down
SW1(config-if)#
*Apr 2 19:54:10.772: %LINK-5-CHANGED: Interface FastEthernet0/1, changed state to
administratively down
*Apr 2 19:54:11.779: %LINEPROTO-5-UPDOWN: Line protocol on Interface FastEthernet0/1,
changed state to down


! Case 2: VLAN 20 is deleted
SW1(config)# no vlan 20
SW1(config)#
*Apr 2 19:54:39.688: %LINEPROTO-5-UPDOWN: Line protocol on Interface Vlan20, changed
state to down


! Case 3: VLAN 30, the VLAN from the switch to the router, is shutdown
SW1(config)# vlan 30
SW1(config-vlan)# shutdown
SW1(config-vlan)# exit
SW1(config)#
*Apr 2 19:55:25.204: %LINEPROTO-5-UPDOWN: Line protocol on Interface Vlan30, changed
state to down


! Final status of all three VLAN interfaces are below
SW1# show ip interface brief | include Vlan
Vlan1            unassigned     YES manual administratively down down
Vlan10           10.1.10.1      YES manual up                   down
Vlan20           10.1.20.1      YES manual up                   down
Vlan30           10.1.30.1      YES manual up                   down
```

Note that the example ends with the three VLAN interfaces in an up/down state per the
show ip interface brief command.

VLAN Routing with Layer 3 Switch Routed Ports

When Layer 3 switches use SVIs, the physical interfaces on the switches act like they always
have: as Layer 2 interfaces. That is, the physical interfaces receive Ethernet frames. The
switch learns the source MAC address of the frame, and the switch forwards the frame based
on the destination MAC address. To perform routing, any Ethernet frames destined for any
of the SVI interface MAC addresses trigger the processing of the Layer 2 switching logic,
resulting in normal routing actions like stripping data-link headers, making a routing decision, and so on.

Alternately, the Layer 3 switch configuration can make a physical port act like a router interface instead of a switch interface. To do so, the switch configuration makes that port a routed port. On a *routed* port, the switch does not perform Layer 2 switching logic on that frame. Instead, frames arriving in a routed port trigger the Layer 3 routing logic, including

1. Stripping off the incoming frame's Ethernet data-link header/trailer
2. Making a Layer 3 forwarding decision by comparing the destination IP address to the IP routing table
3. Adding a new Ethernet data-link header/trailer to the packet
4. Forwarding the packet, encapsulated in a new frame

This third major section of the chapter examines routed interfaces as configured on Cisco Layer 3 switches, but with a particular goal in mind: to also discuss Layer 3 EtherChannels. The exam topics do not mention routed interfaces specifically, but the exam topics do mention L3 EtherChannels, meaning Layer 3 EtherChannels.

You might recall that Chapter 10, "RSTP and EtherChannel Configuration," discussed Layer 2 EtherChannels. Like Layer 2 EtherChannels, Layer 3 EtherChannels also treat multiple links as one link. Unlike Layer 2 EtherChannels, however, Layer 3 EtherChannels treat the channel as a *routed* port instead of *switched* port. So this section first looks at routed ports on Cisco Layer 3 switches and then discusses Layer 3 EtherChannels.

Implementing Routed Interfaces on Switches

When a Layer 3 switch needs a Layer 3 interface connected to a subnet, and only one physical interface connects to that subnet, the network engineer can choose to use a routed port instead of an SVI. Conversely, when the Layer 3 switch needs a Layer 3 interface connected to a subnet, and many physical interfaces on the switch connect to that subnet, an SVI needs to be used. (SVIs forward traffic internally into the VLAN, so that then the Layer 2 logic can forward the frame out any of the ports in the VLAN. Routed ports cannot.)

To see why, consider the design in Figure 17-4, which repeats the same design from Figure 17-3 (used in the SVI examples). In that design, the gray rectangle on the right represents the switch and its internals. On the right of the switch, at least two access ports sit in both VLAN 10 and VLAN 20. However, that figure shows a single link from the switch to Router B1. The switch could configure the port as an access port in a separate VLAN, as shown with VLAN 30 in Examples 17-6 and 17-7. However, with only one switch port needed, the switch could configure that link as a routed port, as shown in the figure.

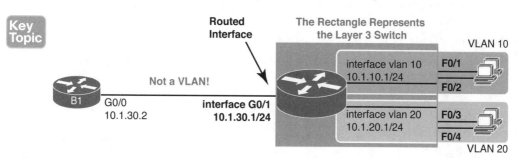

Figure 17-4 *Routing on a Routed Interface on a Switch*

Enabling a switch interface to be a routed interface instead of a switched interface is simple: just use the **no switchport** subcommand on the physical interface. Cisco switches capable of being a Layer 3 switch use a default of the **switchport** command to each switch physical interface. Think about the word *switchport* for a moment. With that term, Cisco tells the switch to treat the port like it is a port on a switch—that is, a Layer 2 port on a switch. To make the port stop acting like a switch port and instead act like a router port, use the **no switchport** command on the interface.

Once the port is acting as a routed port, think of it like a router interface. That is, configure the IP address on the physical port, as implied in Figure 17-4. Example 17-10 shows a completed configuration for the interfaces configured on the switch in Figure 17-4. Note that the design uses the exact same IP subnets as the example that showed SVI configuration in Example 17-6, but now, the port connected to subnet 10.1.30.0 has been converted to a routed port. All you have to do is add the **no switchport** command to the physical interface and configure the IP address on the physical interface.

Example 17-10   *Configuring Interface G0/1 on Switch SW1 as a Routed Port*

```
ip routing
!
interface vlan 10
 ip address 10.1.10.1 255.255.255.0
!
interface vlan 20
 ip address 10.1.20.1 255.255.255.0
!
interface gigabitethernet 0/1
 no switchport
 ip address 10.1.30.1 255.255.255.0
```

Once configured, the routed interface will show up differently in command output in the switch. In particular, for an interface configured as a routed port with an IP address, like interface GigabitEthernet0/1 in the previous example:

show interfaces: Similar to the same command on a router, the output will display the IP address of the interface. (Conversely, for switch ports, this command does not list an IP address.)

show interfaces status: Under the "VLAN" heading, instead of listing the access VLAN or the word *trunk*, the output lists the word *routed*, meaning that it is a routed port.

show ip route: Lists the routed port as an outgoing interface in routes.

show interfaces *type number* **switchport:** If a routed port, the output is short and confirms that the port is not a switch port. (If the port is a Layer 2 port, this command lists many configuration and status details.)

Example 17-11 shows samples of all four of these commands as taken from the switch as configured in Example 17-10.

Example 17-11   *Verification Commands for Routed Ports on Switches*

```
SW11# show interfaces g0/1
GigabitEthernet0/1 is up, line protocol is up (connected)
 Hardware is Gigabit Ethernet, address is bcc4.938b.e541 (bia bcc4.938b.e541)
 Internet address is 10.1.30.1/24
 ! lines omitted for brevity


SW1# show interfaces status
! Only ports related to the example are shown; the command lists physical only
Port      Name              Status       Vlan      Duplex  Speed Type
Fa0/1                       connected    10         a-full  a-100 10/100BaseTX
Fa0/2                       notconnect   10          auto    auto 10/100BaseTX
Fa0/3                       connected    20         a-full  a-100 10/100BaseTX
Fa0/4                       connected    20         a-full  a-100 10/100BaseTX
Gi0/1                       connected    routed     a-full a-1000 10/100/1000BaseTX


SW1# show ip route
! legend omitted for brevity


      10.0.0.0/8 is variably subnetted, 6 subnets, 2 masks
C        10.1.10.0/24 is directly connected, Vlan10
L        10.1.10.1/32 is directly connected, Vlan10
C        10.1.20.0/24 is directly connected, Vlan20
L        10.1.20.1/32 is directly connected, Vlan20
C        10.1.30.0/24 is directly connected, GigabitEthernet0/1
L        10.1.30.1/32 is directly connected, GigabitEthernet0/1


SW1# show interfaces g0/1 switchport
Name: Gi0/1
Switchport: Disabled
```

So, with two options—SVI and routed ports—where should you use each?

For any topologies with a point-to-point link between two devices that do routing, a routed interface works well.

Figure 17-5 shows an example of where to use SVIs and where to use routed ports in a typical core/distribution/access design. In this design, the core (Core1, Core2) and distribution (D11 through D14) switches perform Layer 3 switching. All the ports that are links directly between the Layer 3 switches can be routed interfaces. For VLANs for which many interfaces (access and trunk) connect to the VLAN, SVIs make sense because the SVIs can send and receive traffic out multiple ports on the same switch. In this design, all the ports on Core1 and Core2 will be routed ports, while the four distribution switches will use some routed ports and some SVIs.

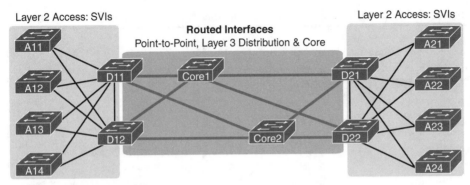

Figure 17-5   *Using Routed Interfaces for Core and Distribution Layer 3 Links*

Implementing Layer 3 EtherChannels

So far, this section has stated that routed interfaces can be used with a single point-to-point link between pairs of Layer 3 switches, or between a Layer 3 switch and a router. However, in most designs, the network engineers use at least two links between each pair of distribution and core switches, as shown in Figure 17-6.

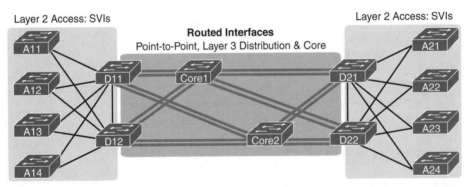

Figure 17-6   *Two Links Between Each Distribution and Core Switch*

While each individual port in the distribution and core could be treated as a separate routed port, it is better to combine each pair of parallel links into a Layer 3 EtherChannel. Without using EtherChannel, you can still make each port on each switch in the center of the figure be a routed port. It works. However, once you enable a routing protocol but don't use EtherChannels, each Layer 3 switch will now learn two IP routes with the same neighboring switch as the next hop—one route over one link, another route over the other link.

Using a Layer 3 EtherChannel makes more sense with multiple parallel links between two switches. By doing so, each pair of links acts as one Layer 3 link. So, each pair of switches has one routing protocol neighbor relationship with the neighbor, and not two. Each switch learns one route per destination per pair of links, and not two. IOS then balances the traffic, often with better balancing than the balancing that occurs with the use of multiple IP routes to the same subnet. Overall, the Layer 3 EtherChannel approach works much better than leaving each link as a separate routed port and using Layer 3 balancing.

Compared to what you have already learned, configuring a Layer 3 EtherChannel takes only a little more work. Chapter 10 already showed you how to configure an EtherChannel. This chapter has already shown how to make a port a Layer 3 routed port. Next, you have to combine the two ideas by combining both the EtherChannel and routed port configuration. The following checklist shows the steps, assuming a static definition.

Step 1.   Configure the physical interfaces as follows, in interface configuration mode:

A.   Add the **channel-group** *number* **mode on** command to add it to the channel. Use the same number for all physical interfaces on the same switch, but the number used (the channel-group number) can differ on the two neighboring switches.

B.   Add the **no switchport** command to make each physical port a routed port.

Step 2.   Configure the PortChannel interface:

A.   Use the **interface port-channel** *number* command to move to port-channel configuration mode for the same channel number configured on the physical interfaces.

B.   Add the **no switchport** command to make sure that the port-channel interface acts as a routed port. (IOS may have already added this command.)

C.   Use the **ip address** *address mask* command to configure the address and mask.

> **NOTE**   Cisco uses the term *EtherChannel* in concepts discussed in this section and then uses the term *PortChannel*, with command keyword **port-channel**, when verifying and configuring EtherChannels. For the purposes of understanding the technology, you may treat these terms as synonyms. However, it helps to pay close attention to the use of the terms *PortChannel* and *EtherChannel* as you work through the examples in this section because IOS uses both.

Example 17-12 shows an example of the configuration for a Layer 3 EtherChannel for switch SW1 in Figure 17-7. The EtherChannel defines port-channel interface 12 and uses subnet 10.1.12.0/24.

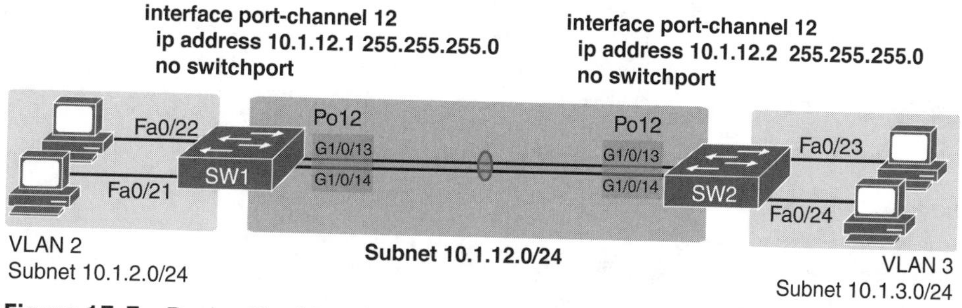

Figure 17-7   *Design Used in EtherChannel Configuration Examples*

Example 17-12 *Layer 3 EtherChannel Configuration on Switch SW1*

```
interface GigabitEthernet1/0/13
 no switchport
 no ip address
 channel-group 12 mode on
!
interface GigabitEthernet1/0/14
 no switchport
 no ip address
 channel-group 12 mode on
!
interface Port-channel12
 no switchport
 ip address 10.1.12.1 255.255.255.0
```

Of particular importance, note that although the physical interfaces and PortChannel interface are all routed ports, the IP address should be placed on the PortChannel interface only. In fact, when the **no switchport** command is configured on an interface, IOS adds the **no ip address** command to the interface. Then configure the IP address on the PortChannel interface only.

Once configured, the PortChannel interface appears in several commands, as shown in Example 17-13. The commands that list IP addresses and routes refer to the PortChannel interface. Also, note that the **show interfaces status** command lists the fact that the physical ports and the port-channel 12 interface are all routed ports.

Example 17-13 *Verification Commands Listing Interface Port-Channel 12 from Switch SW1*

```
SW1# show interfaces port-channel 12
Port-channel12 is up, line protocol is up (connected)
  Hardware is EtherChannel, address is bcc4.938b.e543 (bia bcc4.938b.e543)
  Internet address is 10.1.12.1/24
! lines omitted for brevity


SW1# show interfaces status
! Only ports related to the example are shown.
Port      Name               Status       Vlan       Duplex  Speed Type
Gi1/0/13                     connected    routed     a-full a-1000 10/100/1000BaseTX
Gi1/0/14                     connected    routed     a-full a-1000 10/100/1000BaseTX
Po12                         connected    routed     a-full a-1000


SW1# show ip route
! legend omitted for brevity
      10.0.0.0/8 is variably subnetted, 4 subnets, 2 masks
C         10.1.2.0/24 is directly connected, Vlan2
L         10.1.2.1/32 is directly connected, Vlan2
C         10.1.12.0/24 is directly connected, Port-channel12
L         10.1.12.1/32 is directly connected, Port-channel12
```

For a final bit of verification, you can examine the EtherChannel directly with the **show etherchannel summary** command as listed in Example 17-14. Note in particular that it lists a flag legend for characters that identify key operational states, such as whether a port is bundled (included) in the PortChannel (P) and whether it is acting as a routed (R) or switched (S) port.

Example 17-14 *Verifying the EtherChannel*

```
SW1# show etherchannel 12 summary
Flags: D - down         P - bundled in port-channel
       I - stand-alone s - suspended
       H - Hot-standby (LACP only)
       R - Layer3       S - Layer2
       U - in use       f - failed to allocate aggregator

       M - not in use, minimum links not met
       u - unsuitable for bundling
       w - waiting to be aggregated
       d - default port


Number of channel-groups in use: 1
Number of aggregators:           1


Group  Port-channel  Protocol    Ports
------+-------------+-----------+-----------------------------------------------
12     Po12(RU)         -        Gi1/0/13(P) Gi1/0/14(P)
```

Troubleshooting Layer 3 EtherChannels

When you are troubleshooting a Layer 3 EtherChannel, there are two main areas to consider. First, you need to look at the configuration of the **channel-group** command, which enables an interface for an EtherChannel. Second, you should check a list of settings that must match on the interfaces for a Layer 3 EtherChannel to work correctly.

As for the **channel-group** interface subcommand, this command can enable EtherChannel statically or dynamically. If dynamic, this command's keywords imply either Port Aggregation Protocol (PaGP) or Link Aggregation Control Protocol (LACP) as the protocol to negotiate between the neighboring switches whether they put the link into the EtherChannel.

If all this sounds vaguely familiar, it is the exact same configuration covered way back in the Chapter 10 section "Configuring Dynamic EtherChannels." The configuration of the **channel-group** subcommand is exactly the same, with the same requirements, whether configuring Layer 2 or Layer 3 EtherChannels. So, it might be a good time to review those EtherChannel configuration details from Chapter 10. However, regardless of when you review and master those commands, note that the configuration of the EtherChannel (with the **channel-group** subcommand) is the same, whether Layer 2 or Layer 3.

Additionally, you must do more than just configure the **channel-group** command correctly for all the physical ports to be bundled into the EtherChannel. Layer 2 EtherChannels have a longer list of requirements, but Layer 3 EtherChannels also require a few consistency checks between the ports before they can be added to the EtherChannel. The following is the list of requirements for Layer 3 EtherChannels:

no switchport: The PortChannel interface must be configured with the **no switchport** command, and so must the physical interfaces. If a physical interface is not also configured with the **no switchport** command, it will not become operational in the EtherChannel.

Speed: The physical ports in the channel must use the same speed.

duplex: The physical ports in the channel must use the same duplex.

Chapter Review

One key to doing well on the exams is to perform repetitive spaced review sessions. Review this chapter's material using either the tools in the book or interactive tools for the same material found on the book's companion website. Refer to the "Your Study Plan" element for more details. Table 17-2 outlines the key review elements and where you can find them. To better track your study progress, record when you completed these activities in the second column.

Table 17-2   Chapter Review Tracking

Review Element	Review Date(s)	Resource Used
Review key topics		Book, website
Review key terms		Book, website
Repeat DIKTA questions		Book, PTP
Review config checklists		Book, website
Review command tables		Book
Do labs		Blog
Watch video		Website

Review All the Key Topics

Table 17-3   Key Topics for Chapter 17

Key Topic Element	Description	Page Number
Figure 17-2	Concept of VLAN subinterfaces on a router	396
List	Two alternative methods to configure the native VLAN in a ROAS configuration	398
List	Troubleshooting suggestions for ROAS configuration	401
Figure 17-3	Layer 3 switching with SVIs concept and configuration	402

Key Topic Element	Description	Page Number
List	Troubleshooting suggestions for correct operation of a Layer 3 switch that uses SVIs	405
Figure 17-4	Layer 3 switching with routed ports concept and configuration	407
List	**show** commands that list Layer 3 routed ports in their output	408
Figure 17-7	Layer 3 EtherChannel concept and configuration	411
List	List of configuration settings that must be consistent before IOS will bundle a link with an existing Layer 3 EtherChannel	414

17

Key Terms You Should Know

router-on-a-stick (ROAS), switched virtual interface (SVI), VLAN interface, Layer 3 EtherChannel (L3 EtherChannel), routed port, Layer 3 switch, multilayer switch, subinterfaces

Command References

Tables 17-4 and 17-5 list configuration and verification commands used in this chapter. As an easy review exercise, cover the left column in a table, read the right column, and try to recall the command without looking. Then repeat the exercise, covering the right column, and try to recall what the command does.

Table 17-4   Chapter 17 Configuration Command Reference

Command	Description
interface *type number.subint*	Router global command to create a subinterface and to enter configuration mode for that subinterface
encapsulation dot1q *vlan-id* [**native**]	Router subinterface subcommand that tells the router to use 802.1Q trunking, for a particular VLAN, and with the **native** keyword, to not encapsulate in a trunking header
[**no**] **ip routing**	Global command that enables (**ip routing**) or disables (**no ip routing**) the routing of IPv4 packets on a router or Layer 3 switch
interface vlan *vlan-id*	A switch global command on a Layer 3 switch to create a VLAN interface and to enter configuration mode for that VLAN interface
sdm prefer lanbase-routing	Command on some Cisco switches that reallocates forwarding chip memory to allow for an IPv4 routing table
[**no**] **switchport**	Layer 3 switch subcommand that makes the port act as a Layer 2 port (**switchport**) or Layer 3 routed port (**no switchport**)

Command	Description
interface port-channel *channel-number*	A switch command to enter PortChannel configuration mode and also to create the PortChannel if not already created
channel-group *channel-number* **mode {auto	desirable	active	passive	on}**	Interface subcommand that enables EtherChannel on the interface

Table 17-5   Chapter 17 EXEC Command Reference

Command	Description
show ip route	Lists the router's entire routing table
show ip route [connected]	Lists a subset of the IP routing table
show vlans	Lists VLAN configuration and statistics for VLAN trunks configured on routers
show interfaces [interface *type number*]	Lists detailed status and statistical information, including IP address and mask, about all interfaces (or the listed interface only)
show interfaces [interface *type number*] **status**	Among other facts, for switch ports, lists the access VLAN or the fact that the interface is a trunk; or, for routed ports, lists "routed"
show interfaces *interface-id* **switchport**	For switch ports, lists information about any interface regarding administrative settings and operational state; for routed ports, the output simply confirms the port is a routed (not switched) port
show interfaces vlan *number*	Lists the interface status, the switch's IPv4 address and mask, and much more
show etherchannel [*channel-group-number*] **summary**	Lists information about the state of EtherChannels on this switch, including whether the channel is a Layer 2 or Layer 3 EtherChannel

CHAPTER 18

Troubleshooting IPv4 Routing

This chapter covers the following exam topics:

1.0 Network Fundamentals

1.6 Configure and verify IPv4 addressing and subnetting

3.0 IP Connectivity

3.3 Configure and verify IPv4 and IPv6 static routing

3.3.a Default route

3.3.b Network route

3.3.c Host route

3.3.d Floating static

The first three chapters in this part of the book took you from a starting point of understanding IP addressing and subnetting to the details of implementing IP addressing, routing between connected subnets, and configuring static routes. All those steps include the idea of configuring a command and seeing a route show up in the IP routing table on that same router.

This chapter turns our attention to routing from end-to-end across an entire enterprise network. How do you troubleshoot an IPv4 network? How do you verify correct operation, identify root causes, and fix those for various IP routing features? How do you do that in the presence of an IP addressing and subnetting plan, requiring you to apply all that subnetting math from Part IV of this book and the basic address/mask and static route configuration from the other chapters here in Part V? This chapter answers some of those questions.

In particular, this chapter focuses on two tools and how to use them: ping and traceroute. Both tools test the IPv4 data plane; that is, the ability of each networking device to route or forward IPv4 packets. This chapter devotes a major section each to **ping** and **traceroute**. The chapter then ends with a short discussion of two other router tools that can also be useful for troubleshooting: Telnet and Secure Shell (SSH).

"Do I Know This Already?" Quiz

I put DIKTA quizzes in most of the chapters as a tool to help you decide how to approach reading a chapter. However, this chapter does not have a DIKTA quiz because I think you should read it regardless of your prior knowledge. As with all chapters in this book, this chapter introduces new concepts, but it also acts as a tool to review and deepen your understanding of IP routing. I hope you enjoy the perspectives on using ping and traceroute in this chapter.

Problem Isolation Using the ping Command

Someone sends you an email or text, or a phone message, asking you to look into a user's network problem. You Secure Shell (SSH) to a router and issue a **ping** command that works. What does that result rule out as a possible reason for the problem? What does it rule in as still being a possible root cause?

Then you issue another **ping** to another address, and this time the ping fails. Again, what does the failure of that **ping** command tell you? What parts of IPv4 routing may still be a problem, and what parts do you now know are not a problem?

The **ping** command gives us one of the most common network troubleshooting tools. When the **ping** command succeeds, it confirms many individual parts of how IP routing works, ruling out some possible causes of the current problem. When a **ping** command fails, it often helps narrow down where in the internetwork the root cause of the problem may be happening, further isolating the problem.

This section begins with a brief explanation of how ping works. It then moves on to some suggestions and analysis of how to use the **ping** command to isolate problems by removing some items from consideration.

Ping Command Basics

The **ping** command tests connectivity by sending packets to an IP address, expecting the device at that address to send packets back. The command sends packets that mean "if you receive this packet, and it is addressed to you, send a reply back." Each time the **ping** command sends one of these packets and receives the message sent back by the other host, the **ping** command knows a packet made it from the source host to the destination and back.

More formally, the **ping** command uses the Internet Control Message Protocol (ICMP), specifically the ICMP echo request and ICMP echo reply messages. ICMP defines many other messages as well, but these two messages were made specifically for connectivity testing by commands like ping. As a protocol, ICMP does not rely on TCP or UDP, and it does not use any application layer protocol. It functions as part of Layer 3, as a control protocol to assist IP by helping manage the IP network functions.

Figure 18-1 shows the ICMP messages, with IP headers, in an example. In this case, the user at host A opens a command prompt and issues the **ping 172.16.2.101** command, testing connectivity to host B. The command sends one echo request and waits (Step 1); host B receives the messages and sends back an echo reply (Step 2).

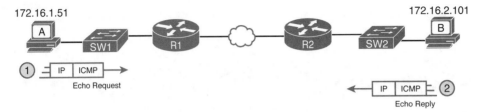

172.16.1.51   172.16.2.101

Figure 18-1 *Concept Behind* **ping** *172.16.2.101 on Host A*

The **ping** command is supported on many different devices and many common operating systems. The command has many options: the name or IP address of the destination, how many times the command should send an echo request, how long the command should wait (timeout) for an echo reply, how big to make the packets, and many other options. Example 18-1 shows a sample from host A, with the same command that matches the concept in Figure 18-1: a **ping** **172.16.2.101** command on host A.

Example 18-1 *Sample Output from Host A's* **ping** *172.16.2.101 Command*

```
Wendell-Odoms-iMac:~ wendellodom$ ping 172.16.2.101
PING 172.16.2.101 (172.16.2.101): 56 data bytes
64 bytes from 172.16.2.101: icmp_seq=0 ttl=64 time=1.112 ms
64 bytes from 172.16.2.101: icmp_seq=1 ttl=64 time=0.673 ms
64 bytes from 172.16.2.101: icmp_seq=2 ttl=64 time=0.631 ms
64 bytes from 172.16.2.101: icmp_seq=3 ttl=64 time=0.674 ms
64 bytes from 172.16.2.101: icmp_seq=4 ttl=64 time=0.642 ms
64 bytes from 172.16.2.101: icmp_seq=5 ttl=64 time=0.656 ms
^C
--- 172.16.2.101 ping statistics ---
6 packets transmitted, 6 packets received, 0.0% packet loss
round-trip min/avg/max/stddev = 0.631/0.731/1.112/0.171 ms
```

Strategies and Results When Testing with the ping Command

Often, the person handling initial calls from users about problems (often called a customer support rep, or CSR) cannot issue **ping** commands from the user's device. In some cases, talking users through typing the right commands and making the right clicks on their machines can be a problem. Or, the user just might not be available. As an alternative, using different **ping** commands from different routers can help isolate the problem.

The problem with using **ping** commands from routers, instead of from the host that has the problem, is that no single router **ping** command can exactly replicate a **ping** command done from the user's device. However, each different **ping** command can help isolate a problem further. The rest of this section of **ping** commands discusses troubleshooting IPv4 routing by using various **ping** commands from the command-line interface (CLI) of a router.

Testing Longer Routes from Near the Source of the Problem

Most problems begin with some idea like "host X cannot communicate with host Y." A great first troubleshooting step is to issue a **ping** command from X for host Y's IP address. However, assuming the engineer does not have access to host X, the engineer can instead issue the **ping** from the router nearest X, typically the router acting as host X's default gateway.

For instance, in Figure 18-1, imagine that the user of host A had called IT support with a problem related to sending packets to host B. A **ping 172.16.2.101** command on host A would be a great first troubleshooting step, but the CSR cannot access host A or get in touch with the user of host A. So, the CSR telnets to Router R1 and pings host B from there, as shown in Example 18-2.

Example 18-2   *Router R2 Pings Host B (Two Commands)*

```
R1# ping 172.16.2.101
Type escape sequence to abort.
Sending 5, 100-byte ICMP Echos to 172.16.2.101, timeout is 2 seconds:
.!!!!
Success rate is 80 percent (4/5), round-trip min/avg/max = 1/2/4 ms
R1# ping 172.16.2.101
Type escape sequence to abort.
Sending 5, 100-byte ICMP Echos to 172.16.2.101, timeout is 2 seconds:
!!!!!
Success rate is 100 percent (5/5), round-trip min/avg/max = 1/2/4 ms
```

First, take a moment to review the output of the first IOS **ping** command. By default, the Cisco IOS **ping** command sends five echo messages, with a timeout of 2 seconds. If the command does not receive an echo reply within 2 seconds, the command considers that message to be a failure, and the command lists a period. If a successful reply is received within 2 seconds, the command displays an exclamation point. So, in this first command, the first echo reply timed out, whereas the other four received a matching echo reply within 2 seconds.

As a quick aside, the example shows a common and normal behavior with **ping** commands: the first **ping** command shows one failure to start, but then the rest of the messages work. This usually happens because some device in the end-to-end route is missing an ARP table entry.

Now think about troubleshooting and what a working **ping** command tells us about the current behavior of this internetwork. First, focus on the big picture for a moment:

- R1 can send ICMP echo request messages to host B (172.16.2.101).

- R1 sends these messages from its outgoing interface's IP address (by default), 172.16.4.1 in this case.

- Host B can send ICMP echo reply messages to R1's 172.16.4.1 IP address (hosts send echo reply messages to the IP address from which the echo request was received).

Figure 18-2 shows the packet flow.

18

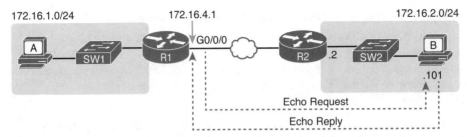

Figure 18-2   *Standard* **ping 172.6.2.101** *Command Using the Source Interface IP Address*

Next, think about IPv4 routing. In the forward direction, R1 must have a route that matches host B's address (172.16.2.101); this route will be either a static route or one learned with a routing protocol. R2 also needs a route for host B's address, in this case a connected route to B's subnet (172.16.2.0/24), as shown in the top arrow lines in Figure 18-3.

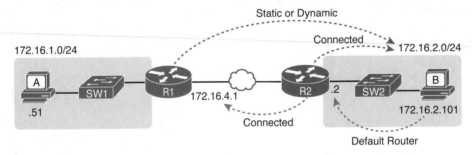

Figure 18-3   *Layer 3 Routes Needed for R1's Ping 172.16.2.101 to Work*

The arrow lines on the bottom of Figure 18-3 show the routes needed to forward the ICMP echo reply message back to Router R1's 172.16.4.1 interface. First, host B must have a valid default router setting because 172.16.4.1 sits in a different subnet than host B. R2 must also have a route that matches destination 172.16.4.1 (in this case, likely to be a connected route).

The working **ping** commands in Example 18-2 also require the data-link and physical layer details to be working. The WAN link must be working: The router interfaces must be up/up, which typically indicates that the link can pass data. On the LAN, R2's LAN interface must be in an up/up state. In addition, everything discussed about Ethernet LANs must be working because the **ping** confirmed that the packets went all the way from R1 to host B and back. In particular

■ The switch interfaces in use are in a connected (up/up) state.

■ Port security (discussed in the *CCNA 200-301 Official Cert Guide, Volume 2*) does not filter frames sent by R2 or host B.

■ STP has placed the right ports into a forwarding state.

The **ping 172.16.2.101** command in Example 18-2 also confirms that IP access control lists (ACL) did not filter the ICMP messages. One ACL contains a set of matching rules and actions: some matched packets are filtered (discarded), while others can continue on their path as normal. ACLs can examine packets as they enter or exit a router interface, so Figure 18-4 shows the various locations on routers R1 and R2 where an ACL could have filtered (discarded) the ICMP messages. (Note that an outbound ACL on router R1 would not filter packets created on R1, so there is no rightward-facing arrow over R1.)

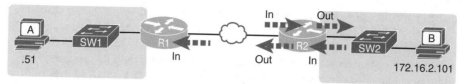

Figure 18-4 *Locations Where IP ACLs Could Have Filtered the Ping Messages*

Finally, the working **ping 172.16.2.101** command on R1 can also be used to reasonably predict that ARP worked and that switch SW2 learned MAC addresses for its MAC address table. R2 and host B need to know each other's MAC addresses so that they can encapsulate the IP packet inside an Ethernet frame, which means both must have a matching ARP table entry. The switch learns the MAC address used by R2 and by host B when it sends the ARP messages or when it sends the frames that hold the IP packets. Figure 18-5 shows the type of information expected in those tables.

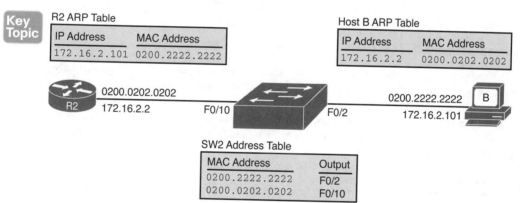

Figure 18-5 *Router and Host ARP Tables, with the Switch MAC Address Table*

As you can see from the last few pages, a strategy of using a **ping** command from near the source of the problem can rule out a lot of possible root causes of any problems between two hosts—assuming the **ping** command succeeds. However, this **ping** command does not act exactly like the same **ping** command on the actual host. To overcome some of what is missing in the **ping** command from a nearby router, the next several examples show some strategies for testing other parts of the path between the two hosts that might have a current problem.

Using Extended Ping to Test the Reverse Route

Pinging from the default router, as discussed in the past few pages, misses an opportunity to test IP routes more fully. In particular, it does not test the reverse route back toward the original host.

For instance, referring to the internetwork in Figure 18-2 again, note that the reverse routes do not point to an address in host A's subnet. When R1 processes the **ping 172.16.2.101** command, R1 has to pick a source IP address to use for the echo request, and routers choose the *IP address of the outgoing interface*. The echo request from R1 to host B flows with source IP address 172.16.4.1 (R1's G0/0/0 IP address). The echo reply flows back to that same address (172.16.4.1).

A standard ping often does not test the reverse route that you need to test. In this case, the standard **ping 172.16.2.101** command on R1 does not test whether the routers can route back to subnet 172.16.1.0/24, instead testing their routes for subnet172.16.4.0. A better ping test would test the route back to host A's subnet; an extended ping from R1 can cause that test to happen. Extended ping allows R1's **ping** command to use R1's LAN IP address from within subnet 172.16.1.0/24. Then, the echo reply messages would flow to host A's subnet, as shown in Figure 18-6.

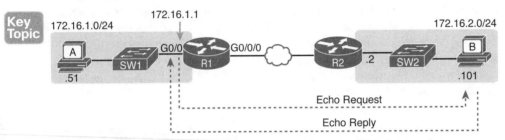

Figure 18-6 *Extended Ping Command Tests the Route to 172.16.1.51 (Host A)*

The extended **ping** command does allow the user to type all the parameters on a potentially long command, but it also allows users to simply issue the **ping** command, press **Enter**, with IOS then asking the user to answer questions to complete the command, as shown in Example 18-3. The example shows the **ping** command on R1 that matches the logic in Figure 18-6. This same command could have been issued from the command line as **ping 172.16.2.101 source 172.16.1.1**.

Example 18-3 *Testing the Reverse Route Using the Extended Ping*

```
R1# ping
Protocol [ip]:
Target IP address: 172.16.2.101
Repeat count [5]:
Datagram size [100]:
Timeout in seconds [2]:
Extended commands [n]: y
Source address or interface: 172.16.1.1
Type of service [0]:
Set DF bit in IP header? [no]:
Validate reply data? [no]:
Data pattern [0xABCD]:
Loose, Strict, Record, Timestamp, Verbose[none]:
Sweep range of sizes [n]:
Type escape sequence to abort.
Sending 5, 100-byte ICMP Echos to 172.16.2.101, timeout is 2 seconds:
Packet sent with a source address of 172.16.1.1
!!!!!
Success rate is 100 percent (5/5), round-trip min/avg/max = 1/2/4 ms
```

This particular extended **ping** command tests the same routes for the echo request going to the right, but it forces a better test of routes pointing back to the left for the ICMP echo reply. For that direction, R2 needs a route that matches address 172.16.1.1, which is likely to be a route for subnet 172.16.1.0/24—the same subnet in which host A resides.

From a troubleshooting perspective, using both standard and extended **ping** commands can be useful. However, neither can exactly mimic a **ping** command created on the host itself because the routers cannot send packets with the host's IP address. For instance, the extended **ping** in Example 18-3 uses source IP address 172.16.1.1, which is not host A's IP address. As a result, neither the standard or extended **ping** commands in these two examples so far in this chapter can test for some kinds of problems, such as the following:

- IP ACLs that discard packets based on host A's IP address but allow packets that match the router's IP address
- LAN switch port security that filters A's frames (based on A's MAC address)
- IP routes on routers that happen to match host A's 172.16.1.51 address, with different routes that match R1's 172.16.1.1 address
- Problems with host A's default router setting

> **NOTE** IP ACLs and LAN switch port security are covered in *CCNA 200-301 Official Cert Guide, Volume 2*. For now, know that IP ACLs can filter packets on routers, focusing on the Layer 3 and 4 headers. Port security can be enabled on Layer 2 switches to filter based on source MAC addresses.

Testing LAN Neighbors with Standard Ping

Testing using a **ping** of another device on the LAN can quickly confirm whether the LAN can pass packets and frames. Specifically, a working **ping** rules out many possible root causes of a problem. For instance, Figure 18-7 shows the ICMP messages that occur if R1 issues the command **ping 172.16.1.51**, pinging host A, which sits on the same VLAN as R1.

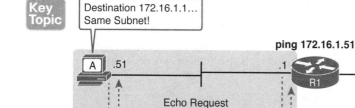

Figure 18-7 *Standard **ping** Command Confirms That the LAN Works*

If the ping works, it confirms the following, which rules out some potential issues:

- The host with address 172.16.1.51 replied.
- The LAN can pass unicast frames from R1 to host 172.16.1.51 and vice versa.

- You can reasonably assume that the switches learned the MAC addresses of the router and the host, adding those to the MAC address tables.

- Host A and Router R1 completed the ARP process and list each other in their respective Address Resolution Protocol (ARP) tables.

The failure of a ping, even with two devices on the same subnet, can point to a variety of problems, like those mentioned in this list. For instance, if the **ping 172.16.1.51** on R1 fails (Figure 18-7), that result points to this list of potential root causes:

- **IP addressing problem:** Host A could be statically configured with the wrong IP address.

- **DHCP problems:** If you are using Dynamic Host Configuration Protocol (DHCP), many problems could exist. Chapter 7, "Implementing DHCP" in *CCNA 200-301 Official Cert Guide, Volume 2*, discusses those possibilities in some depth.

- **VLAN trunking problems:** The router could be configured for 802.1Q trunking, when the switch is not (or vice versa).

- **LAN problems:** A wide variety of issues could exist with the Layer 2 switches, preventing any frames from flowing between host A and the router.

So, whether the ping works or fails, simply pinging a LAN host from a router can help further isolate the problem.

Testing LAN Neighbors with Extended Ping

A standard ping of a LAN host from a router does not test that host's default router setting. However, an extended ping can test the host's default router setting. Both tests can be useful, especially for problem isolation, because

- If a standard ping of a local LAN host works...

- But an extended ping of the same LAN host fails...

- The problem likely relates somehow to the host's default router setting.

First, to understand why the standard and extended ping results have different effects, consider first the standard **ping 172.16.1.51** command on R1, as shown previously in Figure 18-7. As a standard **ping** command, R1 used its LAN interface IP address (172.16.1.1) as the source of the ICMP Echo. So, when the host (A) sent back its ICMP echo reply, host A considered the destination of 172.16.1.1 as being on the same subnet. Host A's ICMP echo reply message, sent back to 172.16.1.1, would work even if host A did not have a default router setting at all!

In comparison, Figure 18-8 shows the difference when using an extended ping on Router R1. An extended ping from local Router R1, using R1's S0/0/0 IP address of 172.16.4.1 as the source of the ICMP echo request, means that host A's ICMP echo reply will flow to an address in another subnet, which makes host A use its default router setting.

The comparison between the previous two figures shows one of the most classic mistakes when troubleshooting networks. Sometimes, the temptation is to connect to a router and ping the host on the attached LAN, and it works. So, the engineer moves on, thinking that the network layer issues between the router and host work fine, when the problem still exists with the host's default router setting.

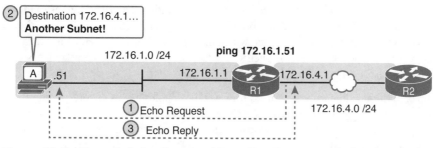

Figure 18-8 *Extended **ping** Command Does Test Host A's Default Router Setting*

Testing WAN Neighbors with Standard Ping

As with a standard ping test across a LAN, a standard ping test between routers over a serial or Ethernet WAN link tests whether the link can pass IPv4 packets. With a properly designed IPv4 addressing plan, two routers on the same serial or Ethernet WAN link should have IP addresses in the same subnet. A ping from one router to the IP address of the other router confirms that an IP packet can be sent over the link and back, as shown in the **ping 172.16.4.2** command on R1 in Figure 18-9.

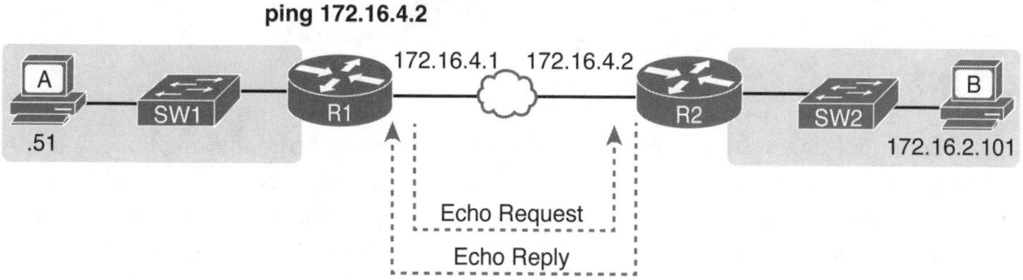

ping 172.16.4.2

172.16.4.1   172.16.4.2

Echo Request
Echo Reply

.51   172.16.2.101

Figure 18-9 *Pinging Across a WAN Link*

A successful ping of the IP address on the other end of an Ethernet WAN link that sits between two routers confirms several specific facts, such as the following:

- Both routers' WAN interfaces are in an up/up state.
- The Layer 1 and 2 features of the link work.
- The routers believe that the neighboring router's IP address is in the same subnet.
- Inbound ACLs on both routers do not filter the incoming packets, respectively.
- The remote router is configured with the expected IP address (172.16.4.2 in this case).

Testing by pinging the other neighboring router does not test many other features. However, although the test is limited in scope, it does let you rule out WAN links as having a Layer 1 or 2 problem, and it rules out some basic Layer 3 addressing problems.

Using Ping with Names and with IP Addresses

All the ping examples so far in this chapter show a ping of an IP address. However, the **ping** command can use hostnames, and pinging a hostname allows the network engineer to further test whether the Domain Name System (DNS) process works.

First, most every TCP/IP application today uses hostnames rather than IP addresses to identify the other device. No one opens a web browser and types in 72.163.4.185. Instead, they type in a web address, like www.cisco.com, which includes the hostname www.cisco.com. Then, before a host can send data to a specific IP address, the host must first ask a DNS server to resolve that hostname into the matching IP address.

For example, in the small internetwork used for several examples in this chapter, a **ping B** command on host A tests A's DNS settings, as shown in Figure 18-10. When host A sees the use of a hostname (B), it first looks in its local DNS name cache to find out whether it has already resolved the name B. If not, host A first asks the DNS to supply (resolve) the name into its matching IP address (Step 1 in the figure). Only then does host A send a packet to 172.16.2.101, host B's IP address (Step 2).

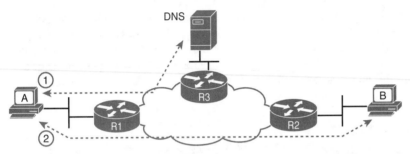

Figure 18-10 *DNS Name Resolution by Host A*

When troubleshooting, testing from the host by pinging using a hostname can be very helpful. The command, of course, tests the host's own DNS client settings. For instance, a classic comparison is to first ping the destination host using the hostname, which requires a DNS request. Then, repeat the same test, but use the destination host's IP address instead of its name, which does not require the DNS request. If the ping of the hostname fails but the ping of the IP address works, the problem usually has something to do with DNS.

Problem Isolation Using the traceroute Command

Like **ping**, the **traceroute** command helps network engineers isolate problems. Here is a comparison of the two:

- Both send messages in the network to test connectivity.
- Both rely on other devices to send back a reply.
- Both have wide support on many different operating systems.
- Both can use a hostname or an IP address to identify the destination.
- On routers, both have a standard and extended version, allowing better testing of the reverse route.

The biggest differences relate to the more detailed results in the output of the **traceroute** command and the extra time and effort it takes **traceroute** to build that output. This second major section examines how **traceroute** works; plus it provides some suggestions on how to use this more detailed information to more quickly isolate IP routing problems.

traceroute Basics

Imagine some network engineer or CSR starts to troubleshoot some problem. The engineer pings from the user's host, pings from a nearby router, and after a few commands, convinces herself that the host can indeed send and receive IP packets. The problem might not be solved yet, but the problem does not appear to be a network problem.

Now imagine the next problem comes along, and this time the **ping** command fails. It appears that some problem does exist in the IP network. Where is the problem? Where should the engineer look more closely? Although the **ping** command can prove helpful in isolating the source of the problem, the **traceroute** command may be a better option. The **traceroute** command systematically helps pinpoint routing problems by showing how far a packet goes through an IP network before being discarded.

The **traceroute** command identifies the routers in the path from source host to destination host. Specifically, it lists the next-hop IP address of each router that would be in each of the individual routes. For instance, a **traceroute 172.16.2.101** command on host A in Figure 18-11 would identify an IP address on Router R1, another on Router R2, and then host B, as shown in the figure. Example 18-4, which follows, lists the output of the command, taken from host A.

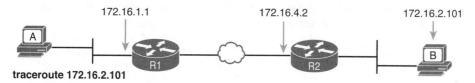

Figure 18-11 *IP Addresses Identified by a Successful* **traceroute 172.16.2.101** *Command*

Example 18-4 *Output from* **traceroute 172.16.2.101** *on Host A*

```
Wendell-Odoms-iMac:~ wendellodom$ traceroute 172.16.2.101
traceroute to 172.16.2.101, 64 hops max, 52 byte packets
 1 172.16.1.1 (172.16.1.1) 0.870 ms 0.520 ms 0.496 ms
 2 172.16.4.2 (172.16.4.2) 8.263 ms 7.518 ms 9.319 ms
 3 172.16.2.101 (172.16.2.101) 16.770 ms 9.819 ms 9.830 ms
```

How the traceroute Command Works

The **traceroute** command gathers information by generating packets that trigger error messages from routers; these messages identify the routers, letting the **traceroute** command list the routers' IP addresses in the output of the command. That error message is the ICMP Time-to-Live Exceeded (TTL Exceeded) message, originally meant to notify hosts when a packet had been looping around a network.

Ignoring traceroute for a moment and instead focusing on IP routing, IPv4 routers defeat routing loops in part by discarding looping IP packets. To do so, the IPv4 header holds a field called Time To Live (TTL). The original host that creates the packet sets an initial TTL value. Then each router that forwards the packet decrements the TTL value by 1. When a router decrements the TTL to 0, the router perceives the packet is looping, and the router discards the packet. The router also notifies the host that sent the discarded packet by sending an ICMP TTL Exceeded message.

Now back to traceroute. Traceroute sends messages with low TTL values to make the routers send back a TTL Exceeded message. Specifically, a **traceroute** command begins by sending several packets (usually three), each with the header TTL field equal to 1. When that packet arrives at the next router—host A's default Router R1 in the example of Figure 18-12—the router decrements TTL to 0 and discards the packet. The router then sends host A the TTL Exceeded message, which identifies the router's IP address to the **traceroute** command.

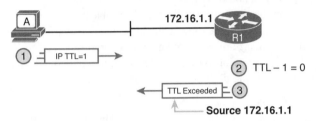

Figure 18-12 *How* traceroute *Identifies the First Router in the Route*

The **traceroute** command sends several TTL=1 packets, checking them to see whether the TTL Exceeded messages flow from the same router, based on the source IP address of the TTL Exceeded message. Assuming the messages come from the same router, the **traceroute** command lists that IP address as the next line of output on the command.

To find all the routers in the path, and finally confirm that packets flow all the way to the destination host, the **traceroute** command sends a small set of packets with TTL=1, then a small set with TTL=2, then 3, 4, and so on, until the destination host replies. Figure 18-13 shows the packet from the second set with TTL=2. In this case, one router (R1) actually forwards the packet, while another router (R2) happens to decrement the TTL to 0, causing a TTL Exceeded message to be sent back to host A.

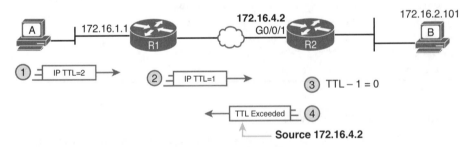

Figure 18-13 *TTL=2 Message Sent by* traceroute

The figure shows these four steps:

1. The traceroute command sends a packet from the second set with TTL=2.
2. Router R1 processes the packet and decrements TTL to 1. R1 forwards the packet.
3. Router R2 processes the packet and decrements TTL to 0. R2 discards the packet.
4. R2 notifies the sending host of the discarded packet by sending a TTL Exceeded ICMP message. The source IP address of that message is 172.16.4.2.

Finally, the choice of source IP address to use on the time-exceeded message returned by routers has a big impact on the output of the **traceroute** command. Most routers use simpler logic that also makes command output like **traceroute** more consistent and meaningful. That logic: choose the TTL Exceeded message's source IP address based on the source interface of the original message that was discarded due to TTL. In the example in Figure 18-13, the original message at Step 2 arrived on R2's G0/0/1 interface, so at Step 3, R2 uses G0/0/1's IP address as the source IP address of the TTL Exceeded message, and as the interface out which to send the message.

Standard and Extended traceroute

The standard and extended options for the **traceroute** command give you many of the same options as the **ping** command. For instance, Example 18-5 lists the output of a standard **traceroute** command on Router R1. Like the standard **ping** command, a standard **traceroute** command chooses an IP address based on the outgoing interface for the packet sent by the command. So, in this example, the packets sent by R1 come from source IP address 172.16.4.1, R1's G0/0/0 IP address.

Example 18-5 *Standard* **traceroute** *Command on R1*

```
R1# traceroute 172.16.2.101
Type escape sequence to abort.
Tracing the route to 172.16.2.101
VRF info: (vrf in name/id, vrf out name/id)
  1 172.16.4.2 0 msec 0 msec 0 msec
  2 172.16.2.101 0 msec 0 msec *
```

The extended **traceroute** command, as shown in Example 18-6, follows the same basic command structure as the extended **ping** command. The user can type all the parameters on one command line, but it is much easier to just type **traceroute**, press **Enter**, and let IOS prompt for all the parameters, including the source IP address of the packets (172.16.1.1 in this example).

Example 18-6 *Extended* **traceroute** *Command on R1*

```
R1# traceroute
Protocol [ip]:
Target IP address: 172.16.2.101
Source address: 172.16.1.1
Numeric display [n]:
Timeout in seconds [3]:
Probe count [3]:
Minimum Time to Live [1]:
Maximum Time to Live [30]:
Port Number [33434]:
Loose, Strict, Record, Timestamp, Verbose[none]:
Type escape sequence to abort.
Tracing the route to 172.16.2.101
VRF info: (vrf in name/id, vrf out name/id)
  1 172.16.4.2 0 msec 0 msec 0 msec
  2 172.16.2.101 0 msec 0 msec *
```

18

Both the **ping** and **traceroute** commands exist on most operating systems, including Cisco IOS. However, some operating systems use a slightly different syntax for **traceroute**. For example, most Windows operating systems support **tracert** and **pathping**, and not **traceroute**. Linux and OS X support the **traceroute** command.

> **NOTE** Host OS **traceroute** commands usually create ICMP echo requests. The Cisco IOS **traceroute** command instead creates IP packets with a UDP header. This bit of information may seem trivial at this point. However, note that an ACL may actually filter the traffic from a host's **traceroute** messages but not the router **traceroute** command, or vice versa.

Telnet and SSH

The **ping** and **traceroute** commands do give networkers two great tools to begin isolating the cause of an IP routing problem. However, these two commands tell us nothing about the operation state inside the various network devices. Once you begin to get an idea of the kinds of problems and the possible locations of the problems using **ping** and **traceroute**, the next step is to look at the status of various router and switch features. One way to do that is to use Telnet or Secure Shell (SSH) to log in to the devices.

Common Reasons to Use the IOS Telnet and SSH Client

Normally, a network engineer would log in to the remote device using a Telnet or SSH client on a PC, tablet, or any other user device. In fact, often, the same software package does both Telnet and SSH. However, in some cases, you may want to take advantage of the Telnet and SSH client built in to IOS on the routers and switches to Telnet/SSH from one Cisco device to the next.

To understand why, consider the example shown in Figure 18-14. The figure shows arrowed lines to three separate IP addresses on three separate Cisco routers. PC1 has attempted to Telnet to each address from a different tab in PC1's Telnet/SSH client. However, R2 happens to have an error in its routing protocol configuration, so R1, R2, and R3 fail to learn any routes from each other. As a result, PC1's Telnet attempt to both 10.1.2.2 (R2) and 10.1.3.3 (R3) fails.

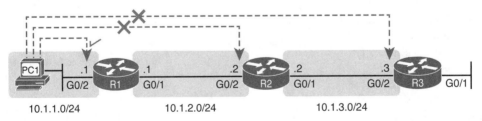

Figure 18-14 *Telnet Works from PC1 to R1 but Not to R2 or R3*

In some cases, like this one, a Telnet or SSH login from the network engineer's device can fail, while you could still find a way to log in using the **telnet** and **ssh** commands to use the Telnet and SSH clients on the routers or switches. With this particular scenario, all the individual data links work; the problem is with the routing protocol exchanging routes. PC1 can ping R1's 10.1.1.1 IP address, R1 can ping R2's 10.1.2.2 address, and R2 can ping R3's 10.1.3.3 address. Because each link works, and each router can send and receive packets with its neighbor on the shared data link, you could Telnet/SSH to each successive device.

Figure 18-15 shows the idea. On the left, PC1 begins with either a Telnet/SSH or a console connection into Router R1, as shown on the left. Then the user issues the **telnet 10.1.2.2** command from R1 to Telnet to R2. Once logged in to R2, the user can issue commands on R2. Then from R2, the user could issue the **telnet 10.1.3.3** command to Telnet to R3, from which the user could issue commands on R3.

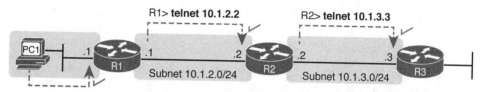

Figure 18-15   *Successive Telnet Connections: PC1 to R1, R1 to R2, and R2 to R3*

The Telnet connections shown in Figure 18-15 work because each Telnet in this case uses source and destination addresses in the same subnet. For example, R1's **telnet 10.1.2.2** command uses 10.1.2.2 as the destination, of course. R1 uses the outgoing interface IP address used to send packets to 10.1.2.2, 10.1.2.1 in this case. Because each of these **telnet** commands connects to an IP address in a connected subnet, the routing protocol could be completely misconfigured, and you could still Telnet/SSH to each successive device to troubleshoot and fix the problem.

Network engineers also use the IOS Telnet and SSH client just for preference. For instance, if you need to log in to several Cisco devices, you could open several windows and tabs on your PC, and log in from your PC (assuming the network was not having problems). Or, you could log in from your PC to some nearby Cisco router or switch, and from there Telnet or SSH to other Cisco devices.

IOS Telnet and SSH Examples

Using the IOS Telnet client via the **telnet** *host* command is pretty simple. Just use the IP address or hostname to identify the host to which you want to connect, and press **Enter**. Example 18-7 shows an example based on Figure 18-15, with R1 using Telnet to connect to 10.1.2.2 (R2).

Example 18-7   *Telnet from R1 to R2 to View Interface Status on R2*

```
R1# telnet 10.1.2.2
Trying 10.1.2.2 ... Open


User Access Verification


Username: wendell
Password:
R2>
R2> show ip interface brief
```

```
Interface              IP-Address      OK? Method Status                Protocol
GigabitEthernet0/0     unassigned      YES unset  administratively down down
GigabitEthernet0/1     10.1.3.2        YES manual up                    up
GigabitEthernet0/2     10.1.2.2        YES manual up                    up
GigabitEthernet0/3     unassigned      YES unset  administratively down down
```

Take the time to pay close attention to the command prompts. The example begins with the user logged in to Router R1, with the R1# command prompt. After issuing the **telnet 10.1.2.2** command, R2 asks the user for both a username and password because Router R2 uses local username authentication, which requires those credentials. The **show ip interfaces brief** command at the end of the output shows Router R2's interfaces and IP addresses again per Example 18-7 and Figure 18-15.

The **ssh -l** *username host* command in Example 18-8 follows the same basic ideas as the **telnet** *host* command, but with an SSH client. The **-l** flag means that the next parameter is the login username. In this case, the user begins logged in to Router R1 and then uses the **ssh -l wendell 10.1.2.2** command to SSH to Router R2. R2 expects a username/password of wendell/odom, with wendell supplied in the command and odom supplied when R2 prompts the user.

Example 18-8 *SSH Client from R1 to R2 to View Interface Status on R2*

```
R1# ssh -l wendell 10.1.2.2

Password:

R2>
Interface              IP-Address      OK? Method Status                Protocol
GigabitEthernet0/0     unassigned      YES unset  administratively down down
GigabitEthernet0/1     10.1.3.2        YES manual up                    up
GigabitEthernet0/2     10.1.2.2        YES manual up                    up
GigabitEthernet0/3     unassigned      YES unset  administratively down down
```

When you have finished using the other router, you can log out from your Telnet or SSH connection using the **exit** or **quit** command.

Finally, note that IOS supports a mechanism to use hotkeys to move between multiple Telnet or SSH sessions from the CLI. Basically, starting at one router, you could telnet or SSH to a router, do some commands, and instead of using the exit command to end your connection, you could keep the connection open while still moving back to the command prompt of the original router. For instance, if starting at Router R1, you could Telnet to R2, R3, and R4, suspending but not exiting those Telnet connections. Then you could easily move between the sessions to issue new commands with a few keystrokes.

Chapter Review

One key to doing well on the exams is to perform repetitive spaced review sessions. Review this chapter's material using either the tools in the book or interactive tools for the same material found on the book's companion website. Refer to the "Your Study Plan" element for more details. Table 18-1 outlines the key review elements and where you can find them. To better track your study progress, record when you completed these activities in the second column.

Table 18-1   Chapter Review Tracking

Review Element	Review Date(s)	Resource Used
Review key topics		Book, website
Review key terms		Book, website
Watch video		Website

Review All the Key Topics

Table 18-2   Key Topics for Chapter 18

Key Topic Element	Description	Page Number
Figure 18-5	ARP tables on Layer 3 hosts, with MAC address tables on Layer 2 switch	423
Figure 18-6	How extended ping in IOS performs a better test of the reverse route	424
Figure 18-7	Why a standard ping over a LAN does not exercise a host's default router logic	425
List	Network layer problems that could cause a ping to fail between a router and host on the same LAN subnet	426
List	Testing a host's default router setting using extended ping	426
List	Comparisons between the **ping** and **traceroute** commands	428

Key Terms You Should Know

ping, traceroute, ICMP echo request, ICMP echo reply, extended ping, forward route, reverse route, DNS

Part V Review

Keep track of your part review progress with the checklist in Table P5-1. Details on each task follow the table.

Table P5-1   Part V Part Review Checklist

Activity	1st Date Completed	2nd Date Completed
Repeat All DIKTA Questions		
Answer Part Review Questions		
Review Key Topics		
Do Labs		
Review Videos		

Repeat All DIKTA Questions

For this task, answer the "Do I Know This Already?" questions again for the chapters in this part of the book, using the PTP software.

Answer Part Review Questions

For this task, use PTP to answer the Part Review questions for this part of the book.

Review Key Topics

Review all key topics in all chapters in this part, either by browsing the chapters or by using the Key Topics application on the companion website.

Labs

Depending on your chosen lab tool, here are some suggestions for what to do in lab:

Pearson Network Simulator: If you use the full Pearson ICND1 or CCNA simulator, focus more on the configuration scenario and troubleshooting scenario labs associated with the topics in this part of the book. These types of labs include a larger set of topics and work well as Part Review activities. (See the Introduction for some details about how to find which labs are about topics in this part of the book.)

Blog Config Labs: The author's blog includes a series of configuration-focused labs that you can do on paper, each in 10–15 minutes. Review and perform the labs for this part of the book, as found at http://blog.certskills.com. Then navigate to the Hands-on Config labs.

Other: If using other lab tools, here are a few suggestions: Make sure to experiment heavily with IPv4 addressing, static routing, and Layer 3 switching. In each case, test all your routes using **ping** and **traceroute**.

Watch Videos

Chapters 15, 17, and 18 each list a video to be found on the companion website, on topics ranging from how to use the router CLI, how to configure ROAS, and how to troubleshoot using Extended **ping**.

Part IV began the story in this book about IP Version 4 (IPv4) addressing. Part V continued that story with how to implement addressing in Cisco routers, along with a variety of methods to route packets between local interfaces. But those topics delayed the discussion of one of the most important topics in TCP/IP, namely IP routing protocols.

Routers use IP routing protocols to learn about the subnets in an internetwork, choose the current best routes to reach each subnet, and to add those routes to each router's IP routing table. Cisco chose to include one and only one IP routing protocol in the CCNA 200-301 exam: the Open Shortest Path First (OSPF) routing protocol. This entire part focuses on OSPF as an example of how routing protocols work.

Part VI

OSPF

CHAPTER 19

Understanding OSPF Concepts

This chapter covers the following exam topics:

3.0 IP Connectivity

3.2 Determine how a router makes a forwarding decision by default

3.2.b Administrative distance

3.2.c Routing protocol metric

3.4 Configure and verify single area OSPFv2

3.4.a Neighbor adjacencies

3.4.b Point-to-point

3.4.c Broadcast (DR/BR selection)

3.4.d Router ID

This chapter takes a long look at Open Shortest Path First Version 2 (OSPFv2) concepts. OSPF runs on each router, sending and receiving OSPF messages with neighboring (nearby) routers. These messages give OSPF the means to exchange data about the network and to learn and add IP Version 4 (IPv4) routes to the IPv4 routing table on each router.

Most enterprises over the last 25 years have used either OSPF or the Enhanced Interior Gateway Routing Protocol (EIGRP) for their primary IPv4 routing protocol. For perspective, both OSPF and EIGRP have been part of CCNA throughout most of its 20+ year history. For the CCNA 200-301 exam blueprint, Cisco has included OSPFv2 as the only IPv4 routing protocol. (Note that Cisco does include EIGRP in the CCNP Enterprise certification.)

This chapter breaks the content into three major sections. The first section sets the context about routing protocols in general, defining interior and exterior routing protocols and basic routing protocol features and terms. The second major section presents the nuts and bolts of how OSPFv2 works, using OSPF neighbor relationships, database exchange, and then route calculation. The third section wraps up the discussion by looking at OSPF areas and LSAs.

"Do I Know This Already?" Quiz

Take the quiz (either here or use the PTP software) if you want to use the score to help you decide how much time to spend on this chapter. The letter answers are listed at the bottom of the page following the quiz. Appendix C, found both at the end of the book as well as on the companion website, includes both the answers and explanations. You can also find both answers and explanations in the PTP testing software.

Table 19-1 "Do I Know This Already?" Foundation Topics Section-to-Question Mapping

Foundation Topics Section	Questions
Comparing Dynamic Routing Protocol Features	1–3
OSPF Concepts and Operation	4, 5
OSPF Areas and LSAs	6

1. Which of the following routing protocols is considered to use link-state logic?

   a. RIPv1

   b. RIPv2

   c. EIGRP

   d. OSPF

2. Which of the following routing protocols use a metric that is, by default, at least partially affected by link bandwidth? (Choose two answers.)

   a. RIPv1

   b. RIPv2

   c. EIGRP

   d. OSPF

3. Which of the following interior routing protocols support VLSM? (Choose three answers.)

   a. RIPv1

   b. RIPv2

   c. EIGRP

   d. OSPF

4. Two routers using OSPFv2 have become neighbors and exchanged all LSAs. As a result, Router R1 now lists some OSPF-learned routes in its routing table. Which of the following best describes how R1 uses those recently learned LSAs to choose which IP routes to add to its IP routing table?

   a. Each LSA lists a route to be copied to the routing table.

   b. Some LSAs list a route that can be copied to the routing table.

   c. Run some SPF math against the LSAs to calculate the routes.

   d. R1 does not use the LSAs at all when choosing what routes to add.

5. Which of the following OSPF neighbor states is expected when the exchange of topology information is complete between two OSPF neighbors?

   a. 2-way

   b. Full

   c. Up/up

   d. Final

6. A company has a small/medium-sized network with 15 routers and 40 subnets and uses OSPFv2. Which of the following is considered an advantage of using a single-area design as opposed to a multiarea design?

   a. It reduces the processing overhead on most routers.

   b. Status changes to one link may not require SPF to run on all other routers.

   c. It allows for simpler planning and operations.

   d. It allows for route summarization, reducing the size of IP routing tables.

Foundation Topics

Comparing Dynamic Routing Protocol Features

Routers add IP routes to their routing tables using three methods: connected routes, static routes, and routes learned by using dynamic routing protocols. Before we get too far into the discussion, however, it is important to define a few related terms and clear up any misconceptions about the terms *routing protocol*, *routed protocol*, and *routable protocol*. The concepts behind these terms are not that difficult, but because the terms are so similar, and because many documents pay poor attention to when each of these terms is used, they can be a bit confusing. These terms are generally defined as follows:

- **Routing protocol:** A set of messages, rules, and algorithms used by routers for the overall purpose of learning routes. This process includes the exchange and analysis of routing information. Each router chooses the best route to each subnet (path selection) and finally places those best routes in its IP routing table. Examples include RIP, EIGRP, OSPF, and BGP.

- **Routed protocol and routable protocol:** Both terms refer to a protocol that defines a packet structure and logical addressing, allowing routers to forward or route the packets. Routers forward packets defined by routed and routable protocols. Examples include IP Version 4 (IPv4) and IP Version 6 (IPv6).

> **NOTE**   The term *path selection* sometimes refers to part of the job of a routing protocol, in which the routing protocol chooses the best route.

Even though routing protocols (such as OSPF) are different from routed protocols (such as IP), they do work together very closely. The routing process forwards IP packets, but if a router does not have any routes in its IP routing table that match a packet's destination address, the router discards the packet. Routers need routing protocols so that the routers can learn all the possible routes and add them to the routing table so that the routing process can forward (route) routable protocols such as IP.

Routing Protocol Functions

Cisco IOS software supports several IP routing protocols, performing the same general functions:

1. Learn routing information about IP subnets from neighboring routers.

2. Advertise routing information about IP subnets to neighboring routers.

3. If more than one possible route exists to reach one subnet, pick the best route based on a metric.

4. If the network topology changes—for example, a link fails—react by advertising that some routes have failed and pick a new currently best route. (This process is called convergence.)

> **NOTE** A neighboring router connects to the same link as another router, such as the same WAN link or the same Ethernet LAN.

19

Figure 19-1 shows an example of three of the four functions in the list. Router R1, in the lower left of the figure, must make a decision about the best route to reach the subnet connected off router R2, on the bottom right of the figure. Following the steps in the figure:

Step 1.   R2 advertises a route to the lower right subnet—172.16.3.0/24—to both router R1 and R3.

Step 2.   After R3 learns about the route to 172.16.3.0/24 from R2, R3 advertises that route to R1.

Step 3.   R1 must make a decision about the two routes it learned about for reaching subnet 172.16.3.0/24—one with metric 1 from R2 and one with metric 2 from R3. R1 chooses the lower metric route through R2 (function 3).

The other routing protocol function, *convergence*, occurs when the topology changes—that is, when either a router or link fails or comes back up again. When something changes, the best routes available in the network can change. Convergence simply refers to the process by which all the routers collectively realize something has changed, advertise the information about the changes to all the other routers, and all the routers then choose the currently best routes for each subnet. The ability to converge quickly, without causing loops, is one of the most important considerations when choosing which IP routing protocol to use.

In Figure 19-1, convergence might occur if the link between R1 and R2 failed. In that case, R1 should stop using its old route for subnet 172.16.3.0/24 (directly through R2) and begin sending packets to R3.

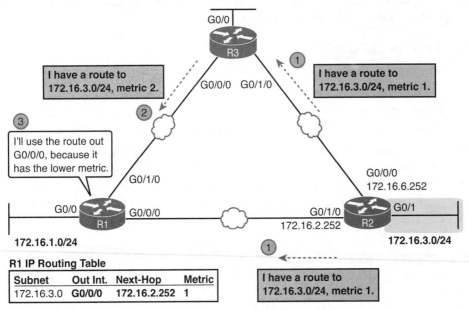

Figure 19-1   *Three of the Four Basic Functions of Routing Protocols*

Interior and Exterior Routing Protocols

IP routing protocols fall into one of two major categories: *interior gateway protocols* (IGP) or *exterior gateway protocols* (EGP). The definitions of each are as follows:

- **IGP:** A routing protocol that was designed and intended for use inside a single autonomous system (AS)

- **EGP:** A routing protocol that was designed and intended for use between different autonomous systems

> **NOTE**   The terms *IGP* and *EGP* include the word *gateway* because routers used to be called gateways.

These definitions use another new term: *autonomous system* (AS). An AS is a network under the administrative control of a single organization. For example, a network created and paid for by a single company is probably a single AS, and a network created by a single school system is probably a single AS. Other examples include large divisions of a state or national government, where different government agencies might be able to build their own networks. Each ISP is also typically a single different AS.

Some routing protocols work best inside a single AS by design, so these routing protocols are called IGPs. Conversely, routing protocols designed to exchange routes between routers

---

Answers to the "Do I Know This Already?" quiz:

1 D **2** C, D **3** B, C, D **4** C **5** B **6** C

in different autonomous systems are called EGPs. Today, Border Gateway Protocol (BGP) is the only EGP used.

Each AS can be assigned a number called (unsurprisingly) an *AS number* (ASN). Like public IP addresses, the Internet Assigned Numbers Authority (IANA, www.iana.org) controls the worldwide rights to assigning ASNs. It delegates that authority to other organizations around the world, typically to the same organizations that assign public IP addresses. For example, in North America, the American Registry for Internet Numbers (ARIN, www.arin.net) assigns public IP address ranges and ASNs.

Figure 19-2 shows a small view of the worldwide Internet. The figure shows two enterprises and three ISPs using IGPs (OSPF and EIGRP) inside their own networks and with BGP being used between the ASNs.

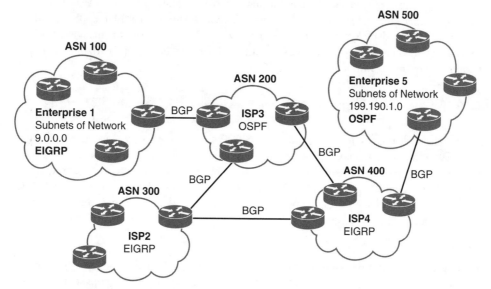

Figure 19-2 *Comparing Locations for Using IGPs and EGPs*

Comparing IGPs

Organizations have several options when choosing an IGP for their enterprise network, but most companies today use either OSPF or EIGRP. This book discusses OSPFv2, with the CCNP Enterprise certification adding EIGRP. Before getting into detail on these two protocols, the next section first discusses some of the main goals of every IGP, comparing OSPF, EIGRP, plus a few other IPv4 routing protocols.

IGP Routing Protocol Algorithms

A routing protocol's underlying algorithm determines how the routing protocol does its job. The term *routing protocol algorithm* simply refers to the logic and processes used by different routing protocols to solve the problem of learning all routes, choosing the best route to each subnet, and converging in reaction to changes in the internetwork. Three main branches of routing protocol algorithms exist for IGP routing protocols:

- Distance vector (sometimes called Bellman-Ford after its creators)
- Advanced distance vector (sometimes called "balanced hybrid")
- Link-state

Historically speaking, distance vector protocols were invented first, mainly in the early 1980s. Routing Information Protocol (RIP) was the first popularly used IP distance vector protocol, with the Cisco-proprietary Interior Gateway Routing Protocol (IGRP) being introduced a little later.

By the early 1990s, distance vector protocols' somewhat slow convergence and potential for routing loops drove the development of new alternative routing protocols that used new algorithms. Link-state protocols—in particular, Open Shortest Path First (OSPF) and Integrated Intermediate System to Intermediate System (IS-IS)—solved the main issues. They also came with a price: they required extra CPU and memory on routers, with more planning required from the network engineers.

> **NOTE**   All references to OSPF in this chapter refer to OSPFv2 unless otherwise stated.

Around the same time as the introduction of OSPF, Cisco created a proprietary routing protocol called Enhanced Interior Gateway Routing Protocol (EIGRP), which used some features of the earlier IGRP protocol. EIGRP solved the same problems as did link-state routing protocols, but EIGRP required less planning when implementing the network. As time went on, EIGRP was classified as a unique type of routing protocol. However, it used more distance vector features than link-state, so it is more commonly classified as an advanced distance vector protocol.

Metrics

Routing protocols choose the best route to reach a subnet by choosing the route with the lowest metric. For example, RIP uses a counter of the number of routers (hops) between a router and the destination subnet, as shown in the example of Figure 19-1. OSPF totals the cost associated with each interface in the end-to-end route, with the cost based on link bandwidth. Table 19-2 lists the most common IP routing protocols and some details about the metric in each case.

Table 19-2   IP IGP Metrics

IGP	Metric	Description
RIPv2	Hop count	The number of routers (hops) between a router and the destination subnet
OSPF	Cost	The sum of all interface cost settings for all links in a route, with the cost defaulting to be based on interface bandwidth
EIGRP	Calculation based on bandwidth and delay	Calculated based on the route's slowest link and the cumulative delay associated with each interface in the route

A brief comparison of the metric used by the older RIP versus the metric used by OSPF shows some insight into why OSPF and EIGRP surpassed RIP. Figure 19-3 shows an example in which Router B has two possible routes to subnet 10.1.1.0 on the left side of the network: a shorter route over a very slow serial link at 1544 Kbps, or a longer route over two Gigabit Ethernet WAN links.

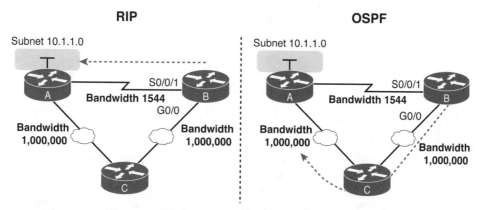

Figure 19-3 *RIP and OSPF Metrics Compared*

The left side of the figure shows the results of RIP in this network. Using hop count, Router B learns of a one-hop route directly to Router A through B's S0/0/1 interface. B also learns of a two-hop route through Router C, through B's G0/0 interface. Router B chooses the lower hop count route, which happens to go over the slow-speed serial link.

The right side of the figure shows the better choice made by OSPF based on its better metric. To cause OSPF to make the right choice, the engineer could use default settings based on the correct interface bandwidth to match the actual link speeds, thereby allowing OSPF to choose the faster route. (The **bandwidth** interface subcommand does not change the actual physical speed of the interface. It just tells IOS what speed to assume the interface is using.)

Other IGP Comparisons

Routing protocols can be compared based on many features, some of which matter to the current CCNA exam, whereas some do not. Table 19-3 introduces a few more points and lists the comparison points mentioned in this book for easier study, with a few supporting comments following the table.

Table 19-3 Interior IP Routing Protocols Compared

Feature	RIPv2	EIGRP	OSPF
Classless/sends mask in updates/supports VLSM	Yes	Yes	Yes
Algorithm (DV, advanced DV, LS)	DV	Advanced DV	LS
Supports manual summarization	Yes	Yes	Yes
Cisco-proprietary	No	Yes[1]	No
Routing updates are sent to a multicast IP address	Yes	Yes	Yes
Convergence	Slow	Fast	Fast

[1] Although Cisco created EIGRP and has kept it as a proprietary protocol for many years, Cisco chose to publish EIGRP as an informational RFC in 2013. This allows other vendors to implement EIGRP, while Cisco retains the rights to the protocol.

Regarding the top row of the table, routing protocols can be considered to be a classless routing protocol or a classful routing protocol. Classless routing protocols support variable-length subnet masks (VLSM) as well as manual route summarization by sending routing protocol messages that include the subnet masks in the message. The older RIPv1 and IGRP routing protocols—both classful routing protocols—do not.

Also, note that the older routing protocols (RIPv1, IGRP) sent routing protocol messages as IP broadcast addresses, while the newer routing protocols in the table all use IP multicast destination addresses. The use of multicasts makes the protocol more efficient and causes less overhead and fewer issues with the devices in the subnet that are not running the routing protocol.

Administrative Distance

Many companies and organizations use a single routing protocol. However, in some cases, a company needs to use multiple routing protocols. For example, if two companies connect their networks so that they can exchange information, they need to exchange some routing information. If one company uses OSPF and the other uses EIGRP on at least one router, both OSPF and EIGRP must be used. Then that router can take routes learned by OSPF and advertise them into EIGRP, and vice versa, through a process called *route redistribution*.

Depending on the network topology, the two routing protocols might learn routes to the same subnets. When a single routing protocol learns multiple routes to the same subnet, the metric tells it which route is best. However, when two different routing protocols learn routes to the same subnet, because each routing protocol's metric is based on different information, IOS cannot compare the metrics. For example, OSPF might learn a route to subnet 10.1.1.0 with metric 101, and EIGRP might learn a route to 10.1.1.0 with metric 2,195,416, but the EIGRP-learned route might be the better route—or it might not. There is simply no basis for comparison between the two metrics.

When IOS must choose between routes learned using different routing protocols, IOS uses a concept called *administrative distance*. Administrative distance is a number that denotes how believable an entire routing protocol is on a single router. The lower the number, the better, or more believable, the routing protocol. For example, RIP has a default administrative distance of 120, OSPF uses a default of 110, and EIGRP defaults to 90. When using OSPF and EIGRP, the router will believe the EIGRP route instead of the OSPF route (at least by default). The administrative distance values are configured on a single router and are not exchanged with other routers. Table 19-4 lists the various sources of routing information, along with the default administrative distances.

Table 19-4 Default Administrative Distances

Route Type	Administrative Distance
Connected	0
Static	1
BGP (external routes [eBGP])	20
EIGRP (internal routes)	90
IGRP	100
OSPF	110

Route Type	Administrative Distance
IS-IS	115
RIP	120
EIGRP (external routes)	170
BGP (internal routes [iBGP])	200
DHCP default route	254
Unusable	255

NOTE   The **show ip route** command lists each route's administrative distance as the first of the two numbers inside the brackets. The second number in brackets is the metric.

The table shows the default administrative distance values, but IOS can be configured to change the administrative distance of a particular routing protocol, a particular route, or even a static route. For example, the command **ip route 10.1.3.0 255.255.255.0 10.1.130.253** defines a static route with a default administrative distance of 1, but the command **ip route 10.1.3.0 255.255.255.0 10.1.130.253 210** defines the same static route with an administrative distance of 210. So, you can actually create a static route that is only used when the routing protocol does not find a route, just by giving the static route a higher administrative distance.

OSPF Concepts and Operation

Routing protocols basically exchange information so routers can learn routes. The routers learn information about subnets, routes to those subnets, and metric information about how good each route is compared to others. The routing protocol can then choose the currently best route to each subnet, building the IP routing table.

Link-state protocols like OSPF take a little different approach to the particulars of what information they exchange and what the routers do with that information once learned. This next (second) major section narrows the focus to only link-state protocols, specifically OSPFv2.

This section begins with an overview of what OSPF does by exchanging data about the network in data structures called *link-state advertisements* (LSA). Then the discussion backs up a bit to provide more details about each of three fundamental parts of how OSPF operates: how OSPF routers use neighbor relationships, how routers exchange LSAs with neighbors, and then how routers calculate the best routes once they learn all the LSAs.

OSPF Overview

Link-state protocols build IP routes with a couple of major steps. First, the routers together build a lot of information about the network: routers, links, IP addresses, status information, and so on. Then the routers flood the information, so all routers know the same information. At that point, each router can calculate routes to all subnets, but from each router's own perspective.

Topology Information and LSAs

Routers using link-state routing protocols need to collectively advertise practically every detail about the internetwork to all the other routers. At the end of the process of *flooding* the information to all routers, every router in the internetwork has the exact same information about the internetwork. Flooding a lot of detailed information to every router sounds like a lot of work, and relative to distance vector routing protocols, it is.

Open Shortest Path First (OSPF), the most popular link-state IP routing protocol, organizes topology information using LSAs and the link-state database (LSDB). Figure 19-4 represents the ideas. Each LSA is a data structure with some specific information about the network topology; the LSDB is simply the collection of all the LSAs known to a router.

Link State Database (LSDB)

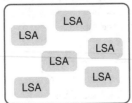

Figure 19-4 *LSA and LSDB Relationship*

Figure 19-5 shows the general idea of the flooding process, with R8 creating and flooding its *router LSA*. The router LSA for Router R8 describes the router itself, including the existence of subnet 172.16.3.0/24, as seen on the right side of the figure. (Note that Figure 19-5 actually shows only a subset of the information in R8's router LSA.)

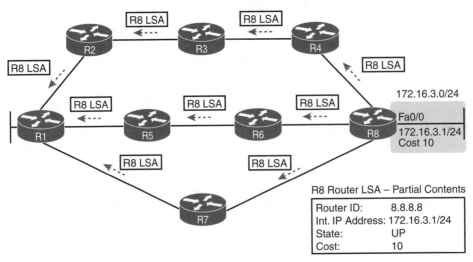

Figure 19-5 *Flooding LSAs Using a Link-State Routing Protocol*

Figure 19-5 shows the rather basic flooding process, with R8 sending the original LSA for itself, and the other routers flooding the LSA by forwarding it until every router has a copy. The flooding process causes every router to learn the contents of the LSA while preventing the LSA from being flooded around in circles. Basically, before sending an LSA to yet another neighbor, routers communicate, asking "Do you already have this LSA?," and then sending the LSA to the next neighbor only if the neighbor has not yet learned about the LSA.

Once flooded, routers do occasionally reflood each LSA. Routers reflood an LSA when some information changes (for example, when a link goes up or comes down). They also reflood each LSA based on each LSA's separate aging timer (default 30 minutes).

Applying Dijkstra SPF Math to Find the Best Routes

The link-state flooding process results in every router having an identical copy of the LSDB in memory, but the flooding process alone does not cause a router to learn what routes to add to the IP routing table. Although incredibly detailed and useful, the information in the LSDB does not explicitly state each router's best route to reach a destination.

To build routes, link-state routers have to do some math. Thankfully, you and I do not have to know the math! However, all link-state protocols use a type of math algorithm, called the Dijkstra Shortest Path First (SPF) algorithm, to process the LSDB. That algorithm analyzes (with math) the LSDB and builds the routes that the local router should add to the IP routing table—routes that list a subnet number and mask, an outgoing interface, and a next-hop router IP address.

Now that you have the big ideas down, the next several topics walk through the three main phases of how OSPF routers accomplish the work of exchanging LSAs and calculating routes. Those three phases are

Becoming neighbors: A relationship between two routers that connect to the same data link, created so that the neighboring routers have a means to exchange their LSDBs.

Exchanging databases: The process of sending LSAs to neighbors so that all routers learn the same LSAs.

Adding the best routes: The process of each router independently running SPF, on their local copy of the LSDB, calculating the best routes, and adding those to the IPv4 routing table.

Becoming OSPF Neighbors

Of everything you learn about OSPF in this chapter, OSPF neighbor concepts have the most to do with how you will configure and troubleshoot OSPF in Cisco routers. You configure OSPF to cause routers to run OSPF and become neighbors with other routers. Once that happens, OSPF does the rest of the work to exchange LSAs and calculate routers in the background, with no additional configuration required. This section discusses the fundamental concepts of OSPF neighbors.

The Basics of OSPF Neighbors

OSPF neighbors are routers that both use OSPF and both sit on the same data link. Two routers can become OSPF neighbors if connected to the same VLAN, or same serial link, or same Ethernet WAN link.

Two routers need to do more than simply exist on the same link to become OSPF neighbors; they must send OSPF messages and agree to become OSPF neighbors. To do so, the routers send OSPF Hello messages, introducing themselves to the potential neighbor. Assuming the two potential neighbors have compatible OSPF parameters, the two form an OSPF neighbor relationship, and would be displayed in the output of the **show ip ospf neighbor** command.

The OSPF neighbor relationship also lets OSPF know when a neighbor might not be a good option for routing packets right now. Imagine R1 and R2 form a neighbor relationship, learn LSAs, and calculate routes that send packets through the other router. Months later, R1 notices that the neighbor relationship with R2 fails. That failed neighbor connection to R2 makes R1 react: R1 refloods LSAs impacted by the failed link, and R1 runs SPF to recalculate its own routes.

Finally, the OSPF neighbor model allows new routers to be dynamically discovered. That means new routers can be added to a network without requiring every router to be reconfigured. Instead, OSPF routers listen for OSPF Hello messages from new routers and react to those messages, attempting to become neighbors and exchange LSDBs.

Meeting Neighbors and Learning Their Router ID

The OSPF Hello process, by which new neighbor relationships are formed, works somewhat like when you move to a new house and meet your various neighbors. When you see each other outside, you might walk over, say hello, and learn each other's name. After talking a bit, you form a first impression, particularly as to whether you think you'll enjoy chatting with this neighbor occasionally, or whether you can just wave and not take the time to talk the next time you see him outside.

Similarly, with OSPF, the process starts with messages called OSPF *Hello* messages. The Hellos in turn list each router's *router ID* (RID), which serves as each router's unique name or identifier for OSPF. Finally, OSPF does several checks of the information in the Hello messages to ensure that the two routers should become neighbors.

OSPF RIDs are 32-bit numbers. As a result, most command output lists these as dotted-decimal numbers (DDN). By default, IOS chooses one of the router's interface IPv4 addresses to use as its OSPF RID. However, the OSPF RID can be directly configured, as covered in the section "Configuring the OSPF Router ID" in Chapter 20, "Implementing OSPF."

As soon as a router has chosen its OSPF RID and some interfaces come up, the router is ready to meet its OSPF neighbors. OSPF routers can become neighbors if they are connected to the same subnet. To discover other OSPF-speaking routers, a router sends multicast OSPF Hello packets to each interface and hopes to receive OSPF Hello packets from other routers connected to those interfaces. Figure 19-6 outlines the basic concept.

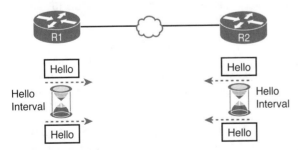

Figure 19-6 *OSPF Hello Packets*

Routers R1 and R2 both send Hello messages onto the link. They continue to send Hellos at a regular interval based on their Hello timer settings. The Hello messages themselves have the following features:

- The Hello message follows the IP packet header, with IP protocol type 89.

- Hello packets are sent to multicast IP address 224.0.0.5, a multicast IP address intended for all OSPF-speaking routers.

- OSPF routers listen for packets sent to IP multicast address 224.0.0.5, in part hoping to receive Hello packets and learn about new neighbors.

Taking a closer look, Figure 19-7 shows several of the neighbor states used by the early formation of an OSPF neighbor relationship. The figure shows the Hello messages in the center and the resulting neighbor states on the left and right edges of the figure. Each router keeps an OSPF state variable for how it views the neighbor.

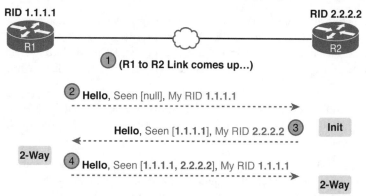

19

Figure 19-7 *Early Neighbor States*

Following the steps in the figure, the scenario begins with the link down, so the routers have no knowledge of each other as OSPF neighbors. As a result, they have no state (status) information about each other as neighbors, and they would not list each other in the output of the **show ip ospf neighbor** command. At Step 2, R1 sends the first Hello, so R2 learns of the existence of R1 as an OSPF router. At that point, R2 lists R1 as a neighbor, with an interim beginning state of init.

The process continues at Step 3, with R2 sending back a Hello. This message tells R1 that R2 exists, and it allows R1 to move through the init state and quickly to a 2-way state. At Step 4, R2 receives the next Hello from R1, and R2 can also move to a 2-way state.

The 2-way state is a particularly important OSPF state. At that point, the following major facts are true:

- The router received a Hello from the neighbor, with that router's own RID listed as being seen by the neighbor.

- The router has checked all the parameters in the Hello received from the neighbor, with no problems. The router is willing to become an OSPF neighbor.

- If both routers reach a 2-way state with each other, it means that both routers meet all OSPF configuration requirements to become neighbors. Effectively, at that point, they are neighbors and ready to exchange their LSDB with each other.

Exchanging the LSDB Between Neighbors

One purpose of forming OSPF neighbor relationships is to allow the two neighbors to exchange their databases. This next topic works through some of the details of OSPF database exchange.

Fully Exchanging LSAs with Neighbors

The OSPF neighbor state 2-way means that the router is available to exchange its LSDB with the neighbor. In other words, it is ready to begin a 2-way exchange of the LSDB. So, once two routers on a link reach the 2-way state, they can immediately move on to the process of database exchange.

The database exchange process can be quite involved, with several OSPF messages and several interim neighbor states. This chapter is more concerned with a few of the messages and the final state when database exchange has completed: the full state.

After two routers decide to exchange databases, they do not simply send the contents of the entire database. First, they tell each other a list of LSAs in their respective databases—not all the details of the LSAs, just a list. (Think of these lists as checklists.) Then each router can check which LSAs it already has and then ask the other router for only the LSAs that are not known yet.

For instance, R1 might send R2 a checklist that lists 10 LSAs (using an OSPF Database Description, or DD, packet). R2 then checks its LSDB and finds six of those 10 LSAs. So, R2 asks R1 (using a Link-State Request packet) to send the four additional LSAs.

Thankfully, most OSPFv2 work does not require detailed knowledge of these specific protocol steps. However, a few of the terms are used quite a bit and should be remembered. In particular, the OSPF messages that actually send the LSAs between neighbors are called Link-State Update (LSU) packets. That is, the LSU packet holds data structures called link-state advertisements (LSA). The LSAs are not packets, but rather data structures that sit inside the LSDB and describe the topology.

Figure 19-8 pulls some of these terms and processes together, with a general example. The story picks up the example shown in Figure 19-7, with Figure 19-8 showing an example of the database exchange process between Routers R1 and R2. The center shows the protocol messages, and the outer items show the neighbor states at different points in the process. Focus on two items in particular:

- The routers exchange the LSAs inside LSU packets.
- When finished, the routers reach a full state, meaning they have fully exchanged the contents of their LSDBs.

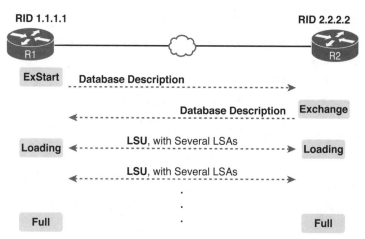

Figure 19-8 *Database Exchange Example, Ending in a Full State*

Maintaining Neighbors and the LSDB

Once two neighbors reach a full state, they have done all the initial work to exchange OSPF information between them. However, neighbors still have to do some small ongoing tasks to maintain the neighbor relationship.

First, routers monitor each neighbor relationship using Hello messages and two related timers: the *Hello Interval* and the *Dead Interval*. Routers send Hellos every Hello Interval to each neighbor. Each router expects to receive a Hello from each neighbor based on the Hello Interval, so if a neighbor is silent for the length of the Dead Interval (by default, four times as long as the Hello Interval), the loss of Hellos means that the neighbor has failed.

Next, routers must react when the topology changes as well, and neighbors play a key role in that process. When something changes, one or more routers change one or more LSAs. Then the routers must flood the changed LSAs to each neighbor so that the neighbor can change its LSDB.

For example, imagine a LAN switch loses power, so a router's G0/0 interface fails from up/up to down/down. That router updates an LSA that shows the router's G0/0 as being down. That router then sends the LSA to its neighbors, and that neighbor in turn sends it to its neighbors, until all routers again have an identical copy of the LSDB. Each router's LSDB now reflects the fact that the original router's G0/0 interface failed, so each router will then use SPF to recalculate any routes affected by the failed interface.

A third maintenance task done by neighbors is to reflood each LSA occasionally, even when the network is completely stable. By default, each router that creates an LSA also has the responsibility to reflood the LSA every 30 minutes (the default), even if no changes occur. (Note that each LSA has a separate timer, based on when the LSA was created, so there is no single big event where the network is overloaded with flooding LSAs.)

The following list summarizes these three maintenance tasks for easier review:

- Maintain neighbor state by sending Hello messages based on the Hello Interval and listening for Hellos before the Dead Interval expires
- Flood any changed LSAs to each neighbor
- Reflood unchanged LSAs as their lifetime expires (default 30 minutes)

Using Designated Routers on Ethernet Links

OSPF behaves differently on some types of interfaces based on a per-interface setting called the OSPF *network type*. On Ethernet links, OSPF defaults to use a network type of *broadcast*, which causes OSPF to elect one of the routers on the same subnet to act as the *designated router* (DR). The DR plays a key role in how the database exchange process works, with different rules than with point-to-point links.

To see how, consider the example that begins with Figure 19-9. The figure shows five OSPFv2 routers on the same Ethernet VLAN. These five OSPF routers elect one router to act as the DR and one router to be a backup DR (BDR). The figure shows A and B as DR and BDR, for no other reason than the Ethernet must have one of each.

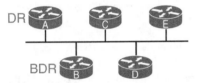

Figure 19-9   *Routers A and B Elected as DR and BDR*

The database exchange process on an Ethernet link does not happen between every pair of routers on the same VLAN/subnet. Instead, it happens between the DR and each of the other routers, with the DR making sure that all the other routers get a copy of each LSA. In other words, the database exchange happens over the flows shown in Figure 19-10.

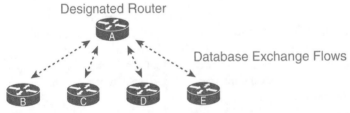

Figure 19-10   *Database Exchange to and from the DR on an Ethernet*

OSPF uses the BDR concept because the DR is so important to the database exchange process. The BDR watches the status of the DR and takes over for the DR if it fails. (When the DR fails, the BDR takes over, and then a new BDR is elected.)

The use of a DR/BDR, along with the use of multicast IP addresses, makes the exchange of OSPF LSDBs more efficient on networks that allow more than two routers on the same link. The DR can send a packet to all OSPF routers in the subnet by using multicast IP address 224.0.0.5. IANA reserves this address as the "All SPF Routers" multicast address just for this purpose. For instance, in Figure 19-10, the DR can send one set of messages to all the OSPF routers rather than sending one message to each router.

Similarly, any OSPF router needing to send a message to the DR and also to the BDR (so it remains ready to take over for the DR) can send those messages to the "All SPF DRs" multicast address 224.0.0.6. So, instead of having to send one set of messages to the DR and another set to the BDR, an OSPF router can send one set of messages, making the exchange more efficient.

At this point, you might be getting a little tired of some of the theory, but finally, the theory actually shows something that you may see in **show** commands on a router. Because the DR and BDR both do full database exchange with all the other OSPF routers in the LAN, they reach a full state with all neighbors. However, routers that are neither a DR nor a BDR—called *DROthers* by OSPF—never reach a full state because they do not exchange LSDBs directly with each other. As a result, the **show ip ospf neighbor** command on these DROther routers lists some neighbors in a 2-way state, remaining in that state under normal operation.

For instance, with OSPF working normally on the Ethernet LAN in Figure 19-10, a **show ip ospf neighbor** command on router C (which is a DROther router) would show the following:

- Two neighbors (A and B, the DR and BDR, respectively) with a full state (called *fully adjacent neighbors*)
- Two neighbors (D and E, which are DROthers) with a 2-way state (called *neighbors*)

OSPF requires some terms to describe all neighbors versus the subset of all neighbors that reach the full state. First, all OSPF routers on the same link that reach the 2-way state—that is, they send Hello messages and the parameters match—are called *neighbors*. The subset of neighbors for which the neighbor relationship continues on and reaches the full state are called *adjacent neighbors*. Additionally, OSPFv2 RFC 2328 emphasizes the connection between the full state and the term *adjacent neighbor* by using the synonyms of *fully adjacent* and *fully adjacent neighbor*. Finally, while the terms so far refer to the neighbor, two other terms refer to the relationship: *neighbor relationship* refers to any OSPF neighbor relationship, while the term *adjacency* refers to neighbor relationships that reach a full state. Table 19-5 details the terms.

Table 19-5   Stable OSPF Neighbor States and Their Meanings

Neighbor State	Term for Neighbor	Term for Relationship
2-way	Neighbor	Neighbor Relationship
Full	Adjacent Neighbor Fully Adjacent Neighbor	Adjacency

Calculating the Best Routes with SPF

OSPF LSAs contain useful information, but they do not contain the specific information that a router needs to add to its IPv4 routing table. In other words, a router cannot just copy information from the LSDB into a route in the IPv4 routing table. The LSAs individually are more like pieces of a jigsaw puzzle. So, to know what routes to add to the routing table, each router must do some SPF math to choose the best routes from that router's perspective. The router then adds each route to its routing table: a route with a subnet number and mask, an outgoing interface, and a next-hop router IP address.

Although engineers do not need to know the details of how SPF does the math, they do need to know how to predict which routes SPF will choose as the best route. The SPF algorithm calculates all the routes for a subnet—that is, all possible routes from the router to the destination subnet. If more than one route exists, the router compares the metrics, picking the best (lowest) metric route to add to the routing table. Although the SPF math can be complex, engineers with a network diagram, router status information, and simple addition can calculate the metric for each route, predicting what SPF will choose.

Once SPF has identified a route, OSPF calculates the metric for a route as follows:

Key Topic

The sum of the OSPF interface costs for all outgoing interfaces in the route.

Figure 19-11 shows an example with three possible routes from R1 to Subnet X (172.16.3.0/24) at the bottom of the figure.

Key Topic

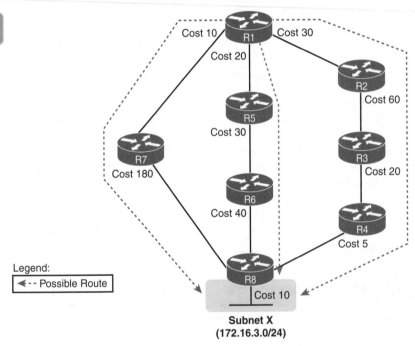

Figure 19-11 *SPF Tree to Find R1's Route to 172.16.3.0/24*

> **NOTE** OSPF considers the costs of the outgoing interfaces (only) in each route. It does not add the cost for incoming interfaces in the route.

Table 19-6 lists the three routes shown in Figure 19-11, with their cumulative costs, showing that R1's best route to 172.16.3.0/24 starts by going through R5.

Table 19-6 Comparing R1's Three Alternatives for the Route to 172.16.3.0/24

Route	Location in Figure 19-11	Cumulative Cost
R1–R7–R8	Left	10 + 180 + 10 = 200
R1–R5–R6–R8	Middle	20 + 30 + 40 + 10 = 100
R1–R2–R3–R4–R8	Right	30 + 60 + 20 + 5 + 10 = 125

As a result of the SPF algorithm's analysis of the LSDB, R1 adds a route to subnet 172.16.3.0/24 to its routing table, with the next-hop router of R5.

In real OSPF networks, an engineer can do the same process by knowing the OSPF cost for each interface. Armed with a network diagram, the engineer can examine all routes, add the costs, and predict the metric for each route.

OSPF Areas and LSAs

OSPF can be used in some networks with very little thought about design issues. You just turn on OSPF in all the routers, put all interfaces into the same area (usually area 0), and it works! Figure 19-12 shows one such network example, with 11 routers and all interfaces in area 0.

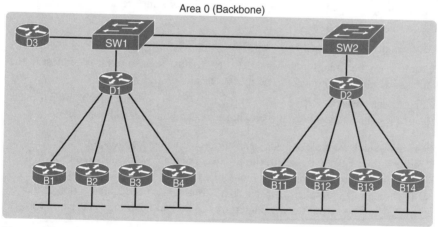

Figure 19-12   *Single-Area OSPF*

Larger OSPFv2 networks suffer with a single-area design. For instance, now imagine an enterprise network with 900 routers, rather than only 11, and several thousand subnets. As it turns out, the CPU time to run the SPF algorithm on all that topology data just takes time. As a result, OSPFv2 convergence time—the time required to react to changes in the network—can be slow. The routers might run low on RAM as well. Additional problems with a single area design include the following:

- A larger topology database requires more memory on each router.

- The SPF algorithm requires processing power that grows exponentially compared to the size of the topology database.

- A single interface status change anywhere in the internetwork (up to down, or down to up) forces *every router* to run SPF again!

The solution is to take the one large LSDB and break it into several smaller LSDBs by using OSPF areas. With areas, each link is placed into one area. SPF does its complicated math on the topology inside the area, and that area's topology only. For instance, an internetwork with 1000 routers and 2000 subnets, broken in 100 areas, would average 10 routers and 20 subnets per area. The SPF calculation on a router would have to only process topology about 10 routers and 20 links, rather than 1000 routers and 2000 links.

So, how large does a network have to be before OSPF needs to use areas? Well, there is no set answer because the behavior of the SPF process depends largely on CPU processing speed, the amount of RAM, the size of the LSDB, and so on. Generally, networks larger than a few dozen routers benefit from areas, and some documents over the years have listed 50 routers as the dividing line at which a network really should use multiple OSPF areas.

The next few pages look at how OSPF area design works, with more reasons as to why areas help make larger OSPF networks work better.

OSPF Areas

OSPF area design follows a couple of basic rules. To apply the rules, start with a clean drawing of the internetwork, with routers, and all interfaces. Then choose the area for each router interface, as follows:

- Put all interfaces connected to the same subnet inside the same area.
- An area should be contiguous.
- Some routers may be internal to an area, with all interfaces assigned to that single area.
- Some routers may be Area Border Routers (ABR) because some interfaces connect to the backbone area, and some connect to nonbackbone areas.
- All nonbackbone areas must have a path to reach the backbone area (area 0) by having at least one ABR connected to both the backbone area and the nonbackbone area.

Figure 19-13 shows one example. An engineer started with a network diagram that showed all 11 routers and their links. On the left, the engineer put four WAN links and the LANs connected to branch routers B1 through B4 into area 1. Similarly, he placed the links to branches B11 through B14 and their LANs in area 2. Both areas need a connection to the backbone area, area 0, so he put the LAN interfaces of D1 and D2 into area 0, along with D3, creating the backbone area.

The figure also shows a few important OSPF area design terms. Table 19-7 summarizes the meaning of these terms, plus some other related terms, but pay closest attention to the terms from the figure.

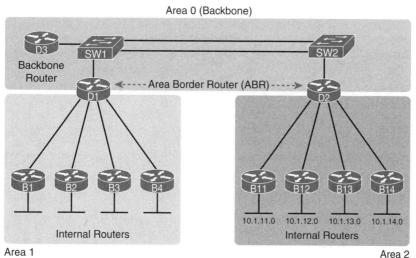

Figure 19-13 *Three-Area OSPF with D1 and D2 as ABRs*

Table 19-7 OSPF Design Terminology

Term	Description
Area Border Router (ABR)	An OSPF router with interfaces connected to the backbone area and to at least one other area
Backbone router	A router connected to the backbone area (includes ABRs)
Internal router	A router in one area (not the backbone area)
Area	A set of routers and links that shares the same detailed LSDB information, but not with routers in other areas, for better efficiency
Backbone area	A special OSPF area to which all other areas must connect—area 0
Intra-area route	A route to a subnet inside the same area as the router
Interarea route	A route to a subnet in an area of which the router is not a part

How Areas Reduce SPF Calculation Time

Figure 19-13 shows a sample area design and some terminology related to areas, but it does not show the power and benefit of the areas. To understand how areas reduce the work SPF has to do, you need to understand what changes about the LSDB inside an area, as a result of the area design.

SPF spends most of its processing time working through all the topology details, namely routers and the links that connect routers. Areas reduce SPF's workload because, for a given area, the LSDB lists only routers and links inside that area, as shown on the left side of Figure 19-14.

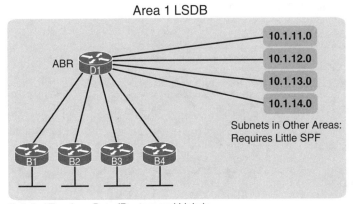

Figure 19-14 *Smaller Area 1 LSDB Concept*

While the LSDB has less topology information, it still has to have information about all subnets in all areas, so that each router can create IPv4 routes for all subnets. So, with an area design, OSPFv2 uses very brief summary information about the subnets in other areas. These summary LSAs do not include topology information about the other areas; however, each summary LSA *does* list a subnet ID and mask of a subnet in some other area. Summary LSAs do not require much SPF processing at all. Instead, these subnets all appear like subnets connected to the ABR (in Figure 19-14, ABR D1).

Using multiple areas improves OSPF operations in many ways for larger networks. The following list summarizes some of the key points arguing for the use of multiple areas in larger OSPF networks:

■ Routers require fewer CPU cycles to process the smaller per-area LSDB with the SPF algorithm, reducing CPU overhead and improving convergence time.

■ The smaller per-area LSDB requires less memory.

■ Changes in the network (for example, links failing and recovering) require SPF calculations only on routers in the area where the link changed state, reducing the number of routers that must rerun SPF.

■ Less information must be advertised between areas, reducing the bandwidth required to send LSAs.

(OSPFv2) Link-State Advertisements

Many people tend to get a little intimidated by OSPF LSAs when first learning about them. Commands that list a summary of the LSDB's contents, like the **show ip ospf database** command, actually list a lot of information. Commands that list the details of the LSDB can list overwhelming amounts of information, and those details appear to be in some kind of code, using lots of numbers. It can seem like a bit of a mess.

However, if you examine LSAs while thinking about OSPF areas and area design, some of the most common LSA types will make a lot more sense. For instance, think about the LSDB in one area. The topology in one area includes routers and the links between the routers. As it turns out, OSPF defines the first two types of LSAs to define those exact details, as follows:

- One *router LSA* for each router in the area
- One *network LSA* for each network that has a DR plus one neighbor of the DR

Next, think about the subnets in the other areas. The ABR creates summary information about each subnet in one area to advertise into other areas—basically just the subnet IDs and masks—as a third type of LSA:

- One *summary* LSA for each subnet ID that exists in a different area

The next few pages discuss these three LSA types in a little more detail; Table 19-8 lists some information about all three for easier reference and study.

Table 19-8   The Three OSPFv2 LSA Types Seen with a Multiarea OSPF Design

LSA Name	LSA Type	Primary Purpose	Contents of LSA
Router	1	Describe a router	RID, interfaces, IP address/mask, current interface state (status)
Network	2	Describe a network that has a DR	DR and BDR IP addresses, subnet ID, mask
Summary	3	Describe a subnet in another area	Subnet ID, mask, RID of ABR that advertises the LSA

Router LSAs Build Most of the Intra-Area Topology

OSPF needs very detailed topology information inside each area. The routers inside area X need to know all the details about the topology inside area X. And the mechanism to give routers all these details is for the routers to create and flood router (Type 1) and network (Type 2) LSAs about the routers and links in the area.

Router LSAs, also known as Type 1 LSAs, describe the router in detail. Each lists a router's RID, its interfaces, its IPv4 addresses and masks, its interface state, and notes about what neighbors the router knows about via each of its interfaces.

To see a specific instance, first review Figure 19-15. It lists internetwork topology, with subnets listed. Because it's a small internetwork, the engineer chose a single-area design, with all interfaces in backbone area 0.

With the single-area design planned for this small internetwork, the LSDB will contain four router LSAs. Each router creates a router LSA for itself, with its own RID as the LSA identifier. The LSA lists that router's own interfaces, IP address/mask, with pointers to neighbors.

19

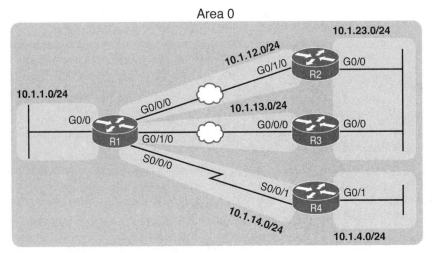

Figure 19-15   *Enterprise Network with Seven IPv4 Subnets*

Once all four routers have copies of all four router LSAs, SPF can mathematically analyze the LSAs to create a model. The model looks a lot like the concept drawing in Figure 19-16. Note that the drawing shows each router with an obvious RID value. Each router has pointers that represent each of its interfaces, and because the LSAs identify neighbors, SPF can figure out which interfaces connect to which other routers.

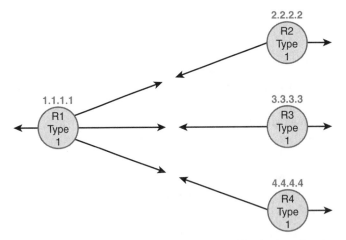

Figure 19-16   *Type 1 LSAs, Assuming a Single-Area Design*

Network LSAs Complete the Intra-Area Topology

Whereas router LSAs define most of the intra-area topology, network LSAs define the rest. As it turns out, when OSPF elects a DR on some subnet *and* that DR has at least one neighbor, OSPF treats that subnet as another node in its mathematical model of the network. To represent that network, the DR creates and floods a network (Type 2) LSA for that network (subnet).

For instance, back in Figure 19-15, one Ethernet LAN and two Ethernet WANs exist. The Ethernet LAN between R2 and R3 will elect a DR, and the two routers will become neighbors; so, whichever router is the DR will create a network LSA. Similarly, R1 and R2 connect with an Ethernet WAN, so the DR on that link will create a network LSA. Likewise, the DR on the Ethernet WAN link between R1 and R3 will also create a network LSA.

Figure 19-17 shows the completed version of the intra-area LSAs in area 0 with this design. Note that the router LSAs actually point to the network LSAs when they exist, which lets the SPF processes connect the pieces together.

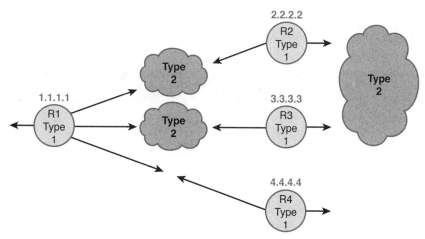

Figure 19-17   *Type 1 and Type 2 LSAs in Area 0, Assuming a Single-Area Design*

Finally, note that in this single-area design example no summary (Type 3) LSAs exist at all. These LSAs represent subnets in other areas, and there are no other areas. Given that the CCNA 200-301 exam topics refer specifically to single-area OSPF designs, this section stops at showing the details of the intra-area LSAs (Types 1 and 2).

Chapter Review

One key to doing well on the exams is to perform repetitive spaced review sessions. Review this chapter's material using either the tools in the book or interactive tools for the same material found on the book's companion website. Refer to the "Your Study Plan" element for more details. Table 19-9 outlines the key review elements and where you can find them. To better track your study progress, record when you completed these activities in the second column.

Table 19-9   Chapter Review Tracking

Review Element	Review Date(s)	Resource Used:
Review key topics		Book, website
Review key terms		Book, website
Answer DIKTA questions		Book, PTP
Review memory tables		Website

Review All the Key Topics

Table 19-10   Key Topics for Chapter 19

Key Topic Element	Description	Page Number
List	Functions of IP routing protocols	443
List	Definitions of IGP and EGP	444
List	Types of IGP routing protocols	446
Table 19-2	IGP metrics	446
List	Key facts about the OSPF 2-way state	453
Table 19-5	Key OSPF neighbor states	457
Item	Definition of how OSPF calculates the cost for a route	458
Figure 19-11	Example of calculating the cost for multiple competing routes	458
List	OSPF area design rules	460
Figure 19-13	Sample OSPF multiarea design with terminology	461
Table 19-7	OSPF design terms and definitions	461

Key Terms You Should Know

convergence, Shortest Path First (SPF) algorithm, distance vector, Interior Gateway Protocol (IGP), link-state, link-state advertisement (LSA), link-state database (LSDB), metric, 2-way state, full state, Area Border Router (ABR), designated router (DR), backup designated router (BDR), fully adjacent, Hello Interval, Dead Interval, link-state update, neighbor, router ID (RID), topology database, internal router, backbone area

CHAPTER 20

Implementing OSPF

This chapter covers the following exam topics:

3.0 IP Connectivity

3.2 Determine how a router makes a forwarding decision by default

3.2.b Administrative distance

3.2.c Routing protocol metric

3.4 Configure and verify single area OSPFv2

3.4.a Neighbor adjacencies

3.4.b Point-to-point

3.4.c Broadcast (DR/BR selection)

3.4.d Router ID

OSPFv2 requires only a few configuration commands if you rely on default settings. To use OSPF, all you need to do is enable OSPF on each interface you intend to use in the network, and OSPF uses messages to discover neighbors and learn routes through those neighbors. However, the complexity of OSPFv2 results in a large number of show commands, many of which reveal those default settings. So while you can make OSPFv2 work in a lab with all default settings, to become comfortable working with it, you need to know the most common optional features as well. This chapter begins that process.

The first major section of this chapter focuses on traditional OSPFv2 configuration using the **network** command, along with the large variety of associated show commands. This section teaches you how to make OSPFv2 operate with default settings and convince yourself that it really is working through use of those show commands.

The second major section shows an alternative configuration option called OSPF interface mode, in contrast with the traditional OSPF configuration shown in the first section of the chapter. This mode uses the **ip ospf** *process-id* **area** *area-number* configuration command instead of the **network** command.

The final section then moves on to discuss a variety of optional but popular configuration topics. The features include topics such as how to use passive interfaces, how to change OSPF costs (which influences the routes OSPF chooses), and how to create a default route advertised by OSPF.

"Do I Know This Already?" Quiz

Take the quiz (either here or use the PTP software) if you want to use the score to help you decide how much time to spend on this chapter. The letter answers are listed at the bottom of the page following the quiz. Appendix C, found both at the end of the book as well as on the companion website, includes both the answers and explanations. You can also find both answers and explanations in the PTP testing software.

Table 20-1 "Do I Know This Already?" Foundation Topics Section-to-Question Mapping

Foundation Topics Section	Questions
Implementing Single-Area OSPFv2	1–3
OSPFv2 Interface Configuration	4
Additional OSPFv2 Features	5, 6

1. Which of the following **network** commands, following the command **router ospf 1**, tells this router to start using OSPF on interfaces whose IP addresses are 10.1.1.1, 10.1.100.1, and 10.1.120.1?

   a. network 10.0.0.0 255.0.0.0 area 0

   b. network 10.0.0.0 0.255.255.255 area 0

   c. network 10.0.0.1 0.0.0.255 area 0

   d. network 10.0.0.1 0.0.255.255 area 0

2. Which of the following **network** commands, following the command **router ospf 1**, tells this router to start using OSPF on interfaces whose IP addresses are 10.1.1.1, 10.1.100.1, and 10.1.120.1?

   a. network 10.1.0.0 0.0.255.255 area 0

   b. network 10.0.0.0 0.255.255.0 area 0

   c. network 10.1.1.0 0.x.1x.0 area 0

   d. network 10.1.1.0 255.0.0.0 area 0

   e. network 10.0.0.0 255.0.0.0 area 0

3. Which of the following commands list the OSPF neighbors off interface serial 0/0? (Choose two answers.)

   a. show ip ospf neighbor

   b. show ip ospf interface brief

   c. show ip neighbor

   d. show ip interface

   e. show ip ospf neighbor serial 0/0

4. An engineer migrates from a more traditional OSPFv2 configuration that uses **network** commands in OSPF configuration mode to instead use OSPFv2 interface configuration. Which of the following commands configures the area number assigned to an interface in this new configuration?

    a. The **area** command in interface configuration mode

    b. The **ip ospf** command in interface configuration mode

    c. The **router ospf** command in interface configuration mode

    d. The **network** command in interface configuration mode

5. Which of the following configuration settings on a router does not influence which IPv4 route a router chooses to add to its IPv4 routing table when using OSPFv2?

    a. auto-cost reference-bandwidth

    b. delay

    c. bandwidth

    d. ip ospf cost

6. OSPF interface configuration uses the **ip ospf** *process-id* **area** *area-number* configuration command. In which modes do you configure the following settings when using this command?

    a. The router ID is configured explicitly in router mode.

    b. The router ID is configured explicitly in interface mode.

    c. An interface's area number is configured in router mode.

    d. An interface's area number is configured in interface mode.

Foundation Topics

Implementing Single-Area OSPFv2

After an OSPF design has been chosen—a task that can be complex in larger IP internetworks—the configuration can be as simple as enabling OSPF on each router interface and placing that interface in the correct OSPF area. This first major section of the chapter focuses on the required configuration using the traditional OSPFv2 **network** command along with one optional configuration setting: how to set the OSPF router-id. Additionally, this section works through how to show the various lists and tables that confirm how OSPF is working.

For reference and study, the following list outlines the configuration steps covered in this first major section of the chapter:

Step 1.   Use the **router ospf** *process-id* global command to enter OSPF configuration mode for a particular OSPF process.

Step 2.   (Optional) Configure the OSPF router ID by doing the following:

   A. Use the **router-id** *id-value* router subcommand to define the router ID, or

   B. Use the **interface loopback** *number* global command, along with an **ip address** *address mask* command, to configure an IP address on a loopback interface (chooses the highest IP address of all working loopbacks), or

C. Rely on an interface IP address (chooses the highest IP address of all working nonloopbacks).

Step 3. Use one or more **network** *ip-address wildcard-mask* **area** *area-id* router subcommands to enable OSPFv2 on any interfaces matched by the configured address and mask, enabling OSPF on the interface for the listed area.

Figure 20-1 shows the relationship between the OSPF configuration commands, with the idea that the configuration creates a routing process in one part of the configuration, and then indirectly enables OSPF on each interface. The configuration does not name the interfaces on which OSPF is enabled, instead requiring IOS to apply some logic by comparing the OSPF **network** command to the interface **ip address** commands. The upcoming example discusses more about this logic.

Configuration

```
OSPF Mode:
  router ospf 1           ◄────────────  Define Process ID
    router-id 1.1.1.1  ◄────────────  Set Router ID (Optional)
                                          (Indirectly) Enable OSPF Process
                                          on the Interface
    network 10.0.0.0 0.255.255.255  area 0
                                          Define Area Number

Interface Mode:        Indirect!
  interface S0/0/0
    ip address 10.1.1.1 255.255.255.0
```

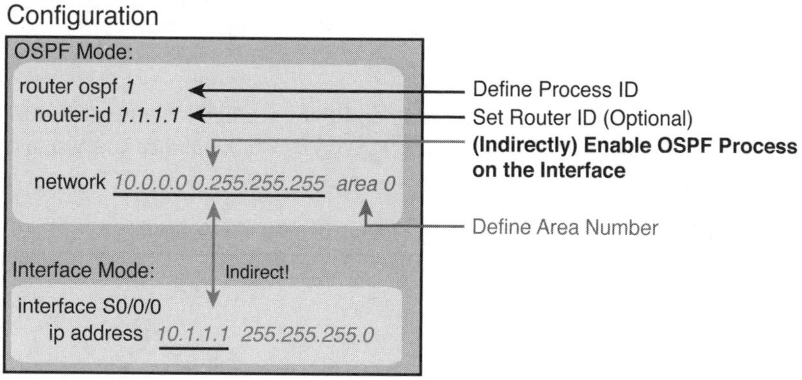

Figure 20-1 *Organization of OSPFv2 Configuration with the* **network** *Command*

OSPF Single-Area Configuration

Figure 20-2 shows a sample network that will be used for most examples throughout this chapter. All links reside in area 0, making the area design a single-area design, with four routers. You can think of Router R1 as a router at a central site, with WAN links to each remote site, and using router-on-a-stick (ROAS) to connect to two LAN subnets on the left. Routers R2 and R3 might be at one large remote site that needs two WAN links and two routers for WAN redundancy, with both routers connected to the LAN at that remote site. Router R4 might be a typical smaller remote site with a single router needed for that site.

NOTE The interface numbering on Router R1, with interfaces G0/0 and G0/0/0, may seem a bit strange. However, real routers, like the Cisco 2901 used in the example, use this numbering. That model includes a built-in Gi0/0 and Gi0/1 port. Additionally, if you add one-port Gigabit WAN Interface Cards (WICs), the router numbers them G0/0/0, G0/1/0, and so on. This is just one example of how router hardware may use two-digit interface numbering, or three-digit, or both.

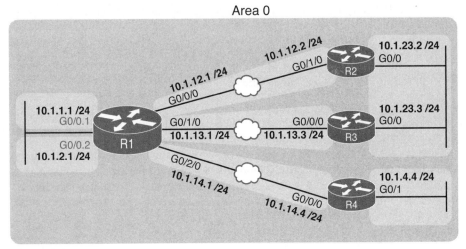

Figure 20-2   *Sample Network for OSPF Single-Area Configuration*

Example 20-1 shows the IPv4 addressing configuration on Router R1, before getting into the OSPF detail. Note that R1 enables 802.1Q trunking (ROAS) on its G0/0 interface and assigns an IP address to each subinterface.

Example 20-1   *IPv4 Address Configuration on R1 (Including VLAN Trunking)*

```
interface GigabitEthernet0/0.1
 encapsulation dot1q 1 native
 ip address 10.1.1.1 255.255.255.0
!
interface GigabitEthernet0/0.2
 encapsulation dot1q 2
 ip address 10.1.2.1 255.255.255.0
!
interface GigabitEthernet0/0/0
 ip address 10.1.12.1 255.255.255.0
!
interface GigabitEthernet0/1/0
 ip address 10.1.13.1 255.255.255.0
!
interface GigabitEthernet0/2/0
 ip address 10.1.14.1 255.255.255.0
```

The OSPF configuration begins with the **router ospf** *process-id* global command, which puts the user in OSPF configuration mode, and sets the OSPF *process-id* value. The *process-id* number just needs to be unique on the local router, allowing the router to support multiple OSPF processes in a single router by using different process IDs. (The

router command uses the *process-id* to distinguish between the processes.) The *process-id* does not have to match on each router, and it can be any integer between 1 and 65,535.

Second, the configuration needs one or more **network** commands in OSPF mode. These commands tell the router to find its local interfaces that match the first two parameters on the **network** command. Then, for each matched interface, the router enables OSPF on those interfaces, discovers neighbors, creates neighbor relationships, and assigns the interface to the area listed in the **network** command. (Note that the area can be configured as either an integer or a dotted-decimal number, but this book makes a habit of configuring the area number as an integer. The integer area numbers range from 0 through 4,294,967,295.)

Example 20-2 shows an example configuration on router R2 from Figure 20-2. The **router ospf 1** command enables OSPF process 1, and the single **network** command enables OSPF on all interfaces shown in the figure.

Example 20-2 *OSPF Single-Area Configuration on R2 Using One* **network** *Command*

```
router ospf 1
 network 10.0.0.0 0.255.255.255 area 0
```

For the specific **network** command in Example 20-2, any matched interfaces are assigned to area 0. However, the first two parameters—the *ip_address* and *wildcard_mask* parameter values of 10.0.0.0 and 0.255.255.255—need some explaining. In this case, the command matches both interfaces shown for Router R2; the next topic explains why.

Wildcard Matching with the network Command

The key to understanding the traditional OSPFv2 configuration shown in this first example is to understand the OSPF **network** command. The OSPF **network** command compares the first parameter in the command to each interface IP address on the local router, trying to find a match. However, rather than comparing the entire number in the **network** command to the entire IPv4 address on the interface, the router can compare a subset of the octets, based on the wildcard mask, as follows:

Wildcard 0.0.0.0: Compare all four octets. In other words, the numbers must exactly match.

Wildcard 0.0.0.255: Compare the first three octets only. Ignore the last octet when comparing the numbers.

Wildcard 0.0.255.255: Compare the first two octets only. Ignore the last two octets when comparing the numbers.

Wildcard 0.255.255.255: Compare the first octet only. Ignore the last three octets when comparing the numbers.

Wildcard 255.255.255.255: Compare nothing; this wildcard mask means that all addresses will match the **network** command.

Basically, a wildcard mask value of decimal 0 in an octet tells IOS to compare to see if the numbers match, and a value of 255 tells IOS to ignore that octet when comparing the numbers.

The **network** command provides many flexible options because of the wildcard mask. For example, in Router R1, many **network** commands could be used, with some matching all interfaces, and some matching a subset of interfaces. Table 20-2 shows a sampling of options, with notes.

Table 20-2 Example OSPF **network** Commands on R3, with Expected Results

Command	Logic in Command	Matched Interfaces
network 10.1.0.0 0.0.255.255	Match addresses that begin with 10.1	G0/0.1
		G0/0.2
		G0/0/0
		G0/1/0
		G0/2/0
network 10.0.0.0 0.255.255.255	Match addresses that begin with 10	G0/0.1
		G0/0.2
		G0/0/0
		G0/1/0
		G0/2/0
network 0.0.0.0 255.255.255.255	Match all addresses	G0/0.1
		G0/0.2
		G0/0/0
		G0/1/0
		G0/2/0
network 10.1.13.0 0.0.0.255	Match addresses that begin with 10.1.13	G0/1/0
network 10.1.13.1 0.0.0.0	Match one address: 10.1.13.1	G0/1/0

The wildcard mask gives the local router its rules for matching its own interfaces. To show examples of the different options, Example 20-3 shows the configuration on routers R2, R3, and R4, each using different wildcard masks. Note that all three routers (R2, R3, and R4) enable OSPF on all the interfaces shown in Figure 20-2.

Example 20-3 *OSPF Configuration on Routers R2, R3, and R4*

```
! R2 configuration next - one network command enables OSPF on both interfaces
interface GigabitEthernet0/0
 ip address 10.1.23.2 255.255.255.0
!
interface GigabitEthernet0/1/0
 ip address 10.1.12.2 255.255.255.0
!
router ospf 1
 network 10.0.0.0 0.255.255.255 area 0
! R3 configuration next - One network command per interface
interface GigabitEthernet0/0
 ip address 10.1.23.3 255.255.255.0
```

```
!
interface GigabitEthernet0/0/0
 ip address 10.1.13.3 255.255.255.0
!
router ospf 1
 network 10.1.13.3 0.0.0.0 area 0
 network 10.1.23.3 0.0.0.0 area 0
```

```
! R4 configuration next - One network command per interface with wildcard 0.0.0.255
interface GigabitEthernet0/1
 ip address 10.1.4.4 255.255.255.0
!
interface GigabitEthernet0/0/0
 ip address 10.1.14.4 255.255.255.0
!
router ospf 1
 network 10.1.14.0 0.0.0.255 area 0
 network 10.1.4.0 0.0.0.255 area 0
```

Finally, note that OSPF uses the same wildcard mask logic as defined by Cisco IOS access control lists. The section titled "Finding the Right Wildcard Mask to Match a Subnet" section in Chapter 2 of the *CCNA 200-301 Official Cert Guide*, *Volume 2*, provides more detail about wildcard masks.

NOTE IOS will change a **network** command if it does not follow a particular rule: by convention, if the wildcard mask octet is 255, the matching address octet should be configured as a 0. Interestingly, IOS will actually accept a **network** command that breaks this rule, but then IOS will change that octet of the address to a 0 before putting it into the running configuration file. For example, IOS will change a typed command that begins with **network 1.2.3.4 0.0.255.255** to **network 1.2.0.0 0.0.255.255**.

Verifying OSPF Operation

As mentioned in Chapter 19, "Understanding OSPF Concepts," OSPF routers use a three-step process to eventually add OSPF-learned routes to the IP routing table. First, they create neighbor relationships. Then they build and flood LSAs between those neighbors so each router in the same area has a copy of the same LSDB. Finally, each router independently computes its own IP routes using the SPF algorithm and adds them to its routing table. This next topic works through how to display the results of each of those steps, which lets you confirm whether OSPF has worked correctly or not.

The **show ip ospf neighbor**, **show ip ospf database**, and **show ip route** commands display information to match each of these three steps, respectively. Figure 20-3 summarizes the commands you can use (and others) when verifying OSPF.

20

Many engineers begin OSPF verification by looking at the output of the **show ip ospf neighbor** command. For instance, Example 20-4 shows a sample from Router R1, which should have one neighbor relationship each with routers R2, R3, and R4. Example 20-4 shows all three.

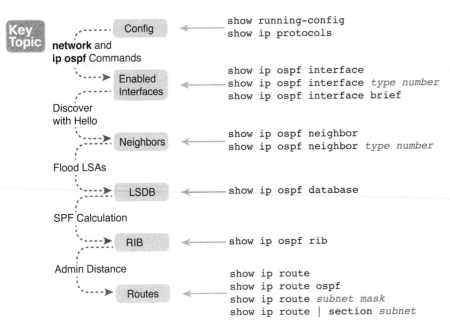

Figure 20-3 *OSPF Verification Commands*

Example 20-4 *OSPF Neighbors on Router R1 from Figure 20-2*

```
R1# show ip ospf neighbor
Neighbor ID     Pri   State       Dead Time   Address     Interface
2.2.2.2         1     FULL/DR     00:00:37    10.1.12.2   GigabitEthernet0/0/0
3.3.3.3         1     FULL/DR     00:00:37    10.1.13.3   GigabitEthernet0/1/0
4.4.4.4         1     FULL/BDR    00:00:34    10.1.14.4   GigabitEthernet0/2/0
```

The detail in the output mentions several important facts, and for most people, working right to left works best in this case. For example, look at the headings:

Interface: This is the local router's interface connected to the neighbor. For example, the first neighbor in the list is reachable through R1's G0/0/0 interface.

Address: This is the neighbor's IP address on that link. Again, for this first neighbor, which is R1, uses IP address 10.1.13.1.

State: While many possible states exist, for the details discussed in this chapter, FULL is the correct and fully working state in this case.

Neighbor ID: This is the router ID of the neighbor.

Once OSPF convergence has completed, a router should list each neighbor. On links that use a designated router (DR), the state will also list the role of the neighboring router after the / (DR, BDR, or DROTHER. As a result, the normal working states will be:

FULL/ -: The neighbor state is full, with the "-" instead of letters meaning that the link does not use a DR/BDR.

FULL/DR: The neighbor state is full, and the neighbor is the DR.

FULL/BDR: The neighbor state is full, and the neighbor is the backup DR (BDR).

FULL/DROTHER: The neighbor state is full, and the neighbor is neither the DR nor BDR. (It also implies that the local router is a DR or BDR because the state is FULL.)

2WAY/DROTHER: The neighbor state is 2-way, and the neighbor is neither the DR nor BDR—that is, a DROther router. (It also implies that the local router is also a DROther router because otherwise the state would reach a full state.)

Once a router's OSPF process forms a working neighbor relationship, the routers exchange the contents of their LSDBs, either directly or through the DR on the subnet. Example 20-5 shows the contents of the LSDB on Router R1. Interestingly, with a single-area design, all the routers will have the same LSDB contents once all neighbors are up and all LSAs have been exchanged. So, the **show ip ospf database** command in Example 20-5 should list the same exact information, no matter on which of the four routers it is issued.

Example 20-5 *OSPF Database on Router R1 from Figure 20-2*

```
R1# show ip ospf database

            OSPF Router with ID (1.1.1.1) (Process ID 1)

                Router Link States (Area 0)

Link ID        ADV Router      Age       Seq#        Checksum Link count
1.1.1.1        1.1.1.1         431       0x8000008F 0x00DCCA 5
2.2.2.2        2.2.2.2         1167      0x8000007F 0x009DA1 2
3.3.3.3        3.3.3.3         441       0x80000005 0x002FB1 1
4.4.4.4        4.4.4.4         530       0x80000004 0x007F39 2


                Net Link States (Area 0)

Link ID        ADV Router      Age       Seq#        Checksum
10.1.12.2      2.2.2.2         1167      0x8000007C 0x00BBD5
10.1.13.3      3.3.3.3         453       0x80000001 0x00A161
10.1.14.1      1.1.1.1         745       0x8000007B 0x004449
10.1.23.3      3.3.3.3         8         0x80000001 0x00658F
```

For the purposes of this book, do not be concerned about the specifics in the output of this command. However, for perspective, note that the LSDB should list one "Router Link State" (Type 1 Router LSA) for each of the routers in the same area, so with the design based on Figure 20-2, the output lists four Type 1 LSAs. Also, with all default settings in this design, the routers will create a total of four Type 2 Network LSAs as shown, one each for the subnets that have a DR and contain at least two routers in that subnet.

Next, Example 20-6 shows R4's IPv4 routing table with the **show ip route** command. As configured, with all links working, the design in Figure 20-2 includes seven subnets. R4 has connected routes to two of those subnets and should learn OSPF routes to the other five subnets.

Example 20-6 *IPv4 Routes Added by OSPF on Router R1 from Figure 20-2*

```
R4# show ip route
Codes: L - local, C - connected, S - static, R - RIP, M - mobile, B - BGP
       D - EIGRP, EX - EIGRP external, O - OSPF, IA - OSPF inter area
       N1 - OSPF NSSA external type 1, N2 - OSPF NSSA external type 2
       E1 - OSPF external type 1, E2 - OSPF external type 2
! Additional legend lines omitted for brevity

Gateway of last resort is not set

      10.0.0.0/8 is variably subnetted, 9 subnets, 2 masks
O        10.1.1.0/24 [110/2] via 10.1.14.1, 00:27:24, GigabitEthernet0/0/0
O        10.1.2.0/24 [110/2] via 10.1.14.1, 00:27:24, GigabitEthernet0/0/0
C        10.1.4.0/24 is directly connected, Vlan4
L        10.1.4.4/32 is directly connected, Vlan4
O        10.1.12.0/24 [110/2] via 10.1.14.1, 00:27:24, GigabitEthernet0/0/0
O        10.1.13.0/24 [110/2] via 10.1.14.1, 00:25:15, GigabitEthernet0/0/0
C        10.1.14.0/24 is directly connected, GigabitEthernet0/0/0
L        10.1.14.4/32 is directly connected, GigabitEthernet0/0/0
O        10.1.23.0/24 [110/3] via 10.1.14.1, 00:27:24, GigabitEthernet0/0/0
```

Any time you want to check OSPF on a router in a small design like the ones in the book, you can count all the subnets, then count the subnets connected to the local router, and know that OSPF should learn routes to the rest of the subnets. Then just use the **show ip route** command and add up how many connected and OSPF routes exist as a quick check of whether all the routes have been learned or not.

In this case, router R4 has two connected subnets, but seven subnets exist per the figure, so router R4 should learn five OSPF routes. Next look for the code of "O" on the left, which identifies a route as being learned by OSPF. The output lists five such IP routes: two for the LAN subnets off Router R1, one for the LAN subnets connected to both R2 and R3, and one each for the WAN subnets from R1 to R2 and R1 to R3.

Next, take a look at the first route (to subnet 10.1.1.0/24). It lists the subnet ID and mask, identifying the subnet. It also lists two numbers in brackets. The first, 110, is the administrative distance of the route. All the OSPF routes in this example use the default of 110 (see Chapter 19's Table 19-4 for the list of administrative distance values). The second number, 2, is the OSPF metric for this route. The route also lists the forwarding instructions: the next-hop IP address (10.1.14.1) and R4's outgoing interface (G0/0/0).

Verifying OSPF Configuration

Once you can configure OSPF with confidence, you will likely verify OSPF focusing on OSPF neighbors and the IP routing table as just discussed. However, if OSPF does not work immediately, you may need to circle back and check the configuration. To do so, you can use these steps:

- If you have enable mode access, use the **show running-config** command to examine the configuration.

- If you have only user mode access, use the **show ip protocols** command to re-create the OSPF configuration.

- Use the **show ip ospf interface [brief]** command to determine whether the router enabled OSPF on the correct interfaces or not based on the configuration.

NOTE The exam's Sim and Simlet questions can restrict access to enable mode, so knowing how to extract the configuration from show commands other than **show running-config** can be particularly helpful for any configuration topic.

The best way to verify the configuration begins with the **show running-config** command, of course. However, the **show ip protocols** command repeats the details of the OSPFv2 configuration and does not require enable mode access. To see how, consider Example 20-7, which lists the output of the **show ip protocols** command on router R3.

Example 20-7 *Router R3 Configuration and the* **show ip protocols** *Command*

```
! First, a reminder of R3's configuration per Example 20-3:
router ospf 1
 network 10.1.13.3 0.0.0.0 area 0
 network 10.1.23.3 0.0.0.0 area 0
!
! The output from router R3:
R3# show ip protocols
*** IP Routing is NSF aware ***

Routing Protocol is "ospf 1"
  Outgoing update filter list for all interfaces is not set
  Incoming update filter list for all interfaces is not set
  Router ID 3.3.3.3
  Number of areas in this router is 1. 1 normal 0 stub 0 nssa
  Maximum path: 4
  Routing for Networks:
    10.1.13.3 0.0.0.0 area 0
    10.1.23.3 0.0.0.0 area 0
  Routing Information Sources:
    Gateway         Distance      Last Update
    1.1.1.1              110      02:05:26
    4.4.4.4              110      02:05:26
    2.2.2.2              110      01:51:16
  Distance: (default is 110)
```

20

The highlighted output emphasizes some of the configuration. The first highlighted line repeats the parameters on the **router ospf 1** global configuration command. (The second highlighted item points out each router's router ID, which will be discussed in the next section.) The third set of highlighted lines begins with a heading of "Routing for Networks:" followed by two lines that closely resemble the parameters on the configured **network** commands. In fact, closely compare those last two highlighted lines with the **network** configuration commands at the top of the example, and you will see that they mirror each other, but the **show** command just leaves out the word *network*. For instance:

Configuration: network 10.1.13.3 0.0.0.0 area 0

Show Command: 10.1.13.3 0.0.0.0 area 0

IOS interprets the **network** commands to choose interfaces on which to run OSPF, so it could be that IOS chooses a different set of interfaces than you predicted. To check the list of interfaces chosen by IOS, use the **show ip ospf interface brief** command, which lists all interfaces that have been enabled for OSPF processing. Verifying the interfaces can be a useful step if you have issues with OSPF neighbors because OSPF must first be enabled on an interface before a router will attempt to discover neighbors on that interface. Example 20-8 shows a sample from Router R1.

Example 20-8   *Router R1* show ip ospf interface brief *Command*

```
R1# show ip ospf interface brief
Interface       PID   Area          IP Address/Mask      Cost  State  Nbrs F/C
Gi0/0/0         1     0             10.1.12.1/24         1     BDR    1/1
Gi0/1/0         1     0             10.1.13.1/24         1     BDR    1/1
Gi0/2/0         1     0             10.1.14.1/24         1     DR     1/1
Gi0/0.2         1     0             10.1.2.1/24          1     DR     0/0
Gi0/0.1         1     0             10.1.1.1/24          1     DR     0/0
```

First, consider the **show ip ospf interface brief** command shown here. It lists one line per interface, with the list showing all the interfaces on which OSPF has been enabled. Each item in the list identifies the OSPF process ID (per the **router ospf** *process-id* command), the area, the interface IP address, and the number of neighbors found via each interface.

More generally, note that the **show ip ospf interface** command with the **brief** keyword at the end lists a single line of output per interface, but the **show ip ospf interface** command (without the **brief** keyword) displays about 20 lines of output per interface, with much more information about various OSPF per-interface settings.

Configuring the OSPF Router ID

While OSPF has many other optional features, most enterprise networks that use OSPF choose to configure each router's OSPF router ID. OSPF-speaking routers must have a router ID (RID) for proper operation. By default, routers will choose an interface IP address to use as the RID. However, many network engineers prefer to choose each router's router ID, so command output from commands like **show ip ospf neighbor** lists more recognizable router IDs.

To choose its RID, a Cisco router uses the following process when the router reloads and brings up the OSPF process. Note that the router stops looking for a router ID to use once one of the steps identifies a value to use.

1. If the **router-id** *rid* OSPF subcommand is configured, this value is used as the RID.

2. If any loopback interfaces have an IP address configured, and the interface has an interface status of up, the router picks the highest numeric IP address among these loopback interfaces.

3. The router picks the highest numeric IP address from all other interfaces whose interface status code (first status code) is up. (In other words, an interface in up/down state will be included by OSPF when choosing its router ID.)

The first and third criteria should make some sense right away: the RID is either configured or is taken from a working interface's IP address. However, this book has not yet explained the concept of a *loopback interface*, as mentioned in Step 2.

A loopback interface is a virtual interface that can be configured with the **interface loopback** *interface-number* command, where *interface-number* is an integer. Loopback interfaces are always in an "up and up" state unless administratively placed in a shutdown state. For example, a simple configuration of the command **interface loopback 0**, followed by **ip address 2.2.2.2 255.255.255.0**, would create a loopback interface and assign it an IP address. Because loopback interfaces do not rely on any hardware, these interfaces can be up/up whenever IOS is running, making them good interfaces on which to base an OSPF RID.

Example 20-9 shows the configuration that existed in Routers R1 and R2 before the creation of the **show** command output earlier in this chapter. R1 set its router ID using the direct method, while R2 used a loopback IP address.

Example 20-9 *OSPF Router ID Configuration Examples*

```
! R1 Configuration first
router ospf 1
 router-id 1.1.1.1
 network 10.1.0.0 0.0.255.255 area 0


! R2 Configuration next
!
interface Loopback2
 ip address 2.2.2.2 255.255.255.255
```

Each router chooses its OSPF RID when OSPF is initialized, which happens when the router boots or when a CLI user stops and restarts the OSPF process (with the **clear ip ospf process** command). So, if OSPF comes up, and later the configuration changes in a way that would impact the OSPF RID, OSPF does not change the RID immediately. Instead, IOS waits until the next time the OSPF process is restarted.

Example 20-10 shows the output of the **show ip ospf** command on R1, which identifies the OSPF RID used by R1.

Example 20-10 *Confirming the Current OSPF Router ID*

```
R1# show ip ospf
Routing Process "ospf 1" with ID 1.1.1.1
! lines omitted for brevity
```

Implementing Multiarea OSPF

Even though the current CCNA 200-301 exam blueprint mentions single-area OSPF and does not mention multiarea OSPF, you only need to learn one more idea to know how to configure multiarea OSPF. So, this chapter takes a brief page to show how.

For example, consider a multiarea OSPF design as shown in Figure 20-4. It uses the same routers and IP addresses as shown earlier in Figure 20-2, on which all the examples in this chapter have been based so far. However, the design shows three areas instead of the single-area design shown in Figure 20-2.

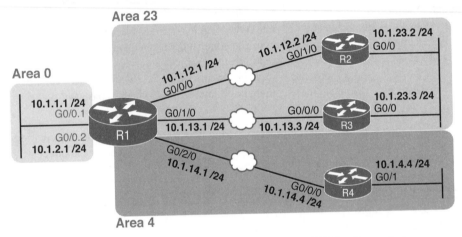

Figure 20-4 *Area Design for an Example Multiarea OSPF Configuration*

Configuring the routers in a multiarea design is almost like configuring OSPFv2 for a single area. To configure multiarea OSPF, all you need is a valid OSPF area design (for instance, like Figure 20-4) and a configuration that places each router interface into the correct area per that design. For example, both of R4's interfaces connect to links in area 4, making R4 an internal router, so any **network** commands on router R4 will list area 4.

Example 20-11 shows a sample configuration for Router R1. To make the configuration clear, it uses **network** commands with a wildcard mask of 0.0.0.0, meaning each **network** command matches a single interface. Each interface will be placed into either area 0, 23, or 4 to match the figure.

Example 20-11 *OSPF Configuration on R1, Placing Interfaces into Different Areas*

```
router ospf 1
 network 10.1.1.1 0.0.0.0 area 0
 network 10.1.2.1 0.0.0.0 area 0
 network 10.1.12.1 0.0.0.0 area 23
 network 10.1.13.1 0.0.0.0 area 23
 network 10.1.14.1 0.0.0.0 area 4
```

Using OSPFv2 Interface Subcommands

From the earliest days of OSPFv2 support in Cisco routers, the configuration used the OSPF **network** command as discussed in this chapter. However, that configuration style can be confusing, and it does require some interpretation of the **network** commands and interface IP addresses to decide on which interfaces IOS will enable OSPF. As a result, Cisco added another option for OSPFv2 configuration called OSPF interface configuration.

The newer interface-style OSPF configuration still enables OSPF on interfaces, but it does so directly with the **ip ospf** interface subcommand instead of using the **network** command in router configuration mode. Basically, instead of matching interfaces with indirect logic using **network** commands, you directly enable OSPFv2 on interfaces by configuring an interface subcommand on each interface.

OSPF Interface Configuration Example

To show how OSPF interface configuration works, this example basically repeats the example shown earlier in the book using the traditional OSPFv2 configuration with **network** commands. So, before looking at the OSPFv2 interface configuration, take a moment to look back to review traditional OSPFv2 configuration with Figure 20-2 and Examples 20-2 and 20-3.

After reviewing the traditional configuration, consider this checklist, which details how to convert from the old-style configuration in Examples 20-2 and 20-3 to use interface configuration:

Step 1.   Use the **no network** *network-id* **area** *area-id* subcommands in OSPF configuration mode to remove the **network** commands.

Step 2.   Add one **ip ospf** *process-id* **area** *area-id* command in interface configuration mode under each interface on which OSPF should operate, with the correct OSPF process (*process-id*) and the correct OSPF area number.

Figure 20-5 repeats the design for both the original examples in this chapter and for this upcoming interface configuration example.

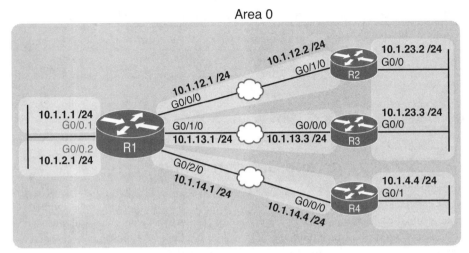

Figure 20-5 *Area Design Used in the Upcoming OSPF Interface Config Example*

Example 20-2 shows a single **network** command: **network 10.0.0.0 0.255.255.255 area 0**.
Example 20-12 follows the steps in the migration checklist, beginning with the removal of
the previous configuration using the **no network 10.0.0.0 0.255.255.255 area 0** command.
The example then shows the addition of the **ip ospf 1 area 0** command on each of the five
interfaces on Router R1, enabling OSPF process 1 on the interface and placing each interface
into area 0.

Example 20-12 *OSPF Single-Area Configuration on R1 Using One **network** Command*

```
R1# configure terminal
Enter configuration commands, one per line.  End with CNTL/Z.
R1(config)# router ospf 1
R1(config-router)# no network 10.0.0.0 0.255.255.255 area 0
R1(config-router)#
*Apr  8 19:35:24.994: %OSPF-5-ADJCHG: Process 1, Nbr 2.2.2.2 on GigabitEthernet0/0/0
   from FULL to DOWN, Neighbor Down: Interface down or detached
*Apr  8 19:35:24.994: %OSPF-5-ADJCHG: Process 1, Nbr 3.3.3.3 on GigabitEthernet0/1/0
   from FULL to DOWN, Neighbor Down: Interface down or detached
*Apr  8 19:35:24.994: %OSPF-5-ADJCHG: Process 1, Nbr 4.4.4.4 on GigabitEthernet0/2/0
   from FULL to DOWN, Neighbor Down: Interface down or detached
R1(config-router)# interface g0/0.1
R1(config-subif)# ip ospf 1 area 0
R1(config-subif)# interface g0/0.2
R1(config-subif)# ip ospf 1 area 0
R1(config-subif)# interface g0/0/0
R1(config-if)# ip ospf 1 area 0
R1(config-if)#
*Apr  8 19:35:52.970: %OSPF-5-ADJCHG: Process 1, Nbr 2.2.2.2 on GigabitEthernet0/0/0
   from LOADING to FULL, Loading Done
R1(config-if)# interface g0/1/0
R1(config-if)# ip ospf 1 area 0
```

```
R1(config-if)#
*Apr  8 19:36:13.362: %OSPF-5-ADJCHG: Process 1, Nbr 3.3.3.3 on GigabitEthernet0/1/0
  from LOADING to FULL, Loading Done
R1(config-if)# interface g0/2/0
R1(config-if)# ip ospf 1 area 0
R1(config-if)#
*Apr  8 19:37:05.398: %OSPF-5-ADJCHG: Process 1, Nbr 4.4.4.4 on GigabitEthernet0/2/0
  from LOADING to FULL, Loading Done
R1(config-if)#
```

When reading the example, read from top to bottom, and also consider the details about the failed and recovered neighbor relationships shown in the log messages. Removing the **network** command disabled OSPF on all interfaces on Router R1, causing all three neighbor relationships to fail. The example then shows the addition of the **ip ospf 1 area 0** command on the two LAN subinterfaces, which enables OSPF. Then the example shows the same command added to each of the WAN links in succession, and in each case, the OSPF neighbor available over that WAN link comes up (as noted in the log messages.)

Verifying OSPF Interface Configuration

OSPF operates the same way whether you use the new style or old style of configuration. The OSPF area design works the same, neighbor relationships form the same way, routers negotiate to become the DR and BDR the same way, and so on. However, you can see a few small differences in show command output when using the newer OSPFv2 configuration if you look closely.

The **show ip protocols** command relists most of the routing protocol configuration, so it does list some different details if you use interface configuration versus the **network** command. With the newer-style configuration, the output lists the phrase "Interfaces Configured Explicitly," with the list of interfaces configured with the new **ip ospf** *process-id* **area** *area-id* commands, as highlighted in Example 20-13. The example first shows the relevant parts of the **show ip protocols** command when using interface configuration on Router R1, and then lists the same portions of the command from when R1 used **network** commands.

Example 20-13 *Differences in* **show ip protocols** *Output: Old- and New-Style OSPFv2 Configuration*

```
! First, with the new interface configuration
R1# show ip protocols
! … beginning lines omitted for brevity
 Routing for Networks:
 Routing on Interfaces Configured Explicitly (Area 0):
    GigabitEthernet0/2/0
    GigabitEthernet0/1/0
    GigabitEthernet0/0/0
    GigabitEthernet0/0.2
    GigabitEthernet0/0.1
 Routing Information Sources:
   Gateway         Distance      Last Update
```

```
   4.4.4.4                110       00:09:30
   2.2.2.2                110       00:10:49
   3.3.3.3                110       05:20:07
 Distance: (default is 110)
```

```
! For comparison, the old results with the use of the OSPF network command
R1# show ip protocols
! … beginning lines omitted for brevity
  Routing for Networks:
    10.1.0.0 0.0.255.255 area 0
! … ending line omitted for brevity
```

Another small piece of different output exists in the **show ip ospf interface** [*interface*] command. The command lists details about OSPF settings for the interface(s) on which OSPF is enabled. The output also makes a subtle reference to whether that interface was enabled for OSPF with the old or new configuration style. Example 20-14 also begins with output based on interface configuration on Router R1, followed by the output that would exist if R1 still used the old-style **network** command.

Example 20-14   *Differences in* **show ip ospf interface** *Output with OSPFv2 Interface Configuration*

```
! First, with the new interface configuration
R1# show ip ospf interface g0/0/0
GigabitEthernet0/0/0 is up, line protocol is up
  Internet Address 10.1.12.1/24, Area 0, Attached via Interface Enable
! Lines omitted for brevity
```

```
! For comparison, the old results with the use of the OSPF network command
R1# show ip ospf interface g0/0/0
GigabitEthernet0/0/0 is up, line protocol is up
  Internet Address 10.1.12.1/24, Area 0, Attached via Network Statement
! … ending line omitted for brevity
```

Other than these small differences in a few show commands, the rest of the commands show nothing different depending on the style of configuration. For instance, the **show ip ospf interface brief** command does not change depending on the configuration style, nor do the **show ip ospf database**, **show ip ospf neighbor**, or **show ip route** commands.

Additional OSPFv2 Features

This final major section of the chapter discusses some very popular but optional OSPFv2 configuration features, as listed here in their order of appearance:

■ Passive interfaces

■ Default routes

■ Metrics

■ Load balancing

OSPF Passive Interfaces

Once OSPF has been enabled on an interface, the router tries to discover neighboring OSPF routers and form a neighbor relationship. To do so, the router sends OSPF Hello messages on a regular time interval (called the Hello Interval). The router also listens for incoming Hello messages from potential neighbors.

Sometimes, a router does not need to form neighbor relationships with neighbors on an interface. Often, no other routers exist on a particular link, so the router has no need to keep sending those repetitive OSPF Hello messages. In such cases, an engineer can make the interface passive, which means

- OSPF continues to advertise about the subnet that is connected to the interface.
- OSPF no longer sends OSPF Hellos on the interface.
- OSPF no longer processes any received Hellos on the interface.

The result of enabling OSPF on an interface but then making it passive is that OSPF still advertises about the connected subnet, but OSPF also does not form neighbor relationships over the interface.

To configure an interface as passive, two options exist. First, you can add the following command to the configuration of the OSPF process, in router configuration mode:

passive-interface *type number*

Alternately, the configuration can change the default setting so that all interfaces are passive by default and then add a **no passive-interface** command for all interfaces that need to not be passive:

passive-interface default

no passive-interface *type number*

For example, in the sample internetwork in Figure 20-2 (and in Figure 20-5), Router R1, on the left side of the figure, has a LAN interface configured for VLAN trunking. The only router connected to both VLANs is Router R1, so R1 will never discover an OSPF neighbor on these subnets. Example 20-15 shows two alternative configurations to make the two LAN subinterfaces passive to OSPF.

Example 20-15 *Configuring Passive Interfaces on R1 from Figure 20-5*

```
! First, make each subinterface passive directly
router ospf 1
 passive-interface GigabitEthernet0/0.1
 passive-interface GigabitEthernet0/0.2


! Or, change the default to passive, and make the other interfaces not be passive
router ospf 1
 passive-interface default
 no passive-interface GigabitEthernet0/0/0
 no passive-interface GigabitEthernet0/1/0
 no passive-interface GigabitEthernet0/2/0
```

In real internetworks, the choice of configuration style reduces to which option requires the least number of commands. For example, a router with 20 interfaces, 18 of which are passive to OSPF, has far fewer configuration commands when using the **passive-interface default** command to change the default to passive. If only two of those 20 interfaces need to be passive, use the default setting, in which all interfaces are not passive, to keep the configuration shorter.

Interestingly, OSPF makes it a bit of a challenge to use **show** commands to find whether or not an interface is passive. The **show running-config** command lists the configuration directly, but if you cannot get into enable mode to use this command, note these two facts:

The **show ip ospf interface brief** command lists all interfaces on which OSPF is enabled, *including passive interfaces.*

The **show ip ospf interface** command lists a single line that mentions that the interface is passive.

Example 20-16 shows these two commands on Router R1, based on the configuration shown in the top of Example 20-15. Note that subinterfaces G0/0.1 and G0/0.2 both show up in the output of **show ip ospf interface brief**.

Example 20-16   *Displaying Passive Interfaces*

```
R1# show ip ospf interface brief
Interface               IP-Address      OK? Method Status                 Protocol
GigabitEthernet0/0      unassigned      YES manual up                     up
GigabitEthernet0/0.1    10.1.1.1        YES manual up                     up
GigabitEthernet0/0.2    10.1.2.1        YES manual up                     up
GigabitEthernet0/1      unassigned      YES manual administratively down  down
GigabitEthernet0/0/0    10.1.12.1       YES manual up                     up
GigabitEthernet0/1/0    10.1.13.1       YES manual up                     up
GigabitEthernet0/2/0    10.1.14.1       YES manual up                     up


R1# show ip ospf interface g0/0.1
GigabitEthernet0/0.1 is up, line protocol is up
  Internet Address 10.1.1.1/24, Area 0, Attached via Network Statement
  Process ID 1, Router ID 1.1.1.1, Network Type BROADCAST, Cost: 1
  Topology-MTID    Cost    Disabled    Shutdown     Topology Name
      0             1         no          no           Base
  Transmit Delay is 1 sec, State DR, Priority 1
  Designated Router (ID) 1.1.1.1, Interface address 10.1.1.1
  No backup designated router on this network
  Timer intervals configured, Hello 10, Dead 40, Wait 40, Retransmit 5
    oob-resync timeout 40
    No Hellos (Passive interface)
! Lines omitted for brevity
```

OSPF Default Routes

Chapter 16, "Configuring IPv4 Addressing and Static Routes," showed some of the uses and benefits of default routes, with examples of static default routes. For those exact same reasons, networks can use OSPF to advertise default routes.

The most classic case for using a routing protocol to advertise a default route has to do with an enterprise's connection to the Internet. As a strategy, the enterprise engineer uses these design goals:

- All routers learn specific (nondefault) routes for subnets inside the company; a default route is not needed when forwarding packets to these destinations.

- One router connects to the Internet, and it has a default route that points toward the Internet.

- All routers should dynamically learn a default route, used for all traffic going to the Internet, so that all packets destined to locations in the Internet go to the one router connected to the Internet.

Figure 20-6 shows the idea of how OSPF advertises the default route, with the specific OSPF configuration. In this case, a company connects to an ISP with its Router R1. That router has a static default route (destination 0.0.0.0, mask 0.0.0.0) with a next-hop address of the ISP router. Then the use of the OSPF **default-information originate** command (Step 2) makes the router advertise a default route using OSPF to the remote routers (B1 and B2).

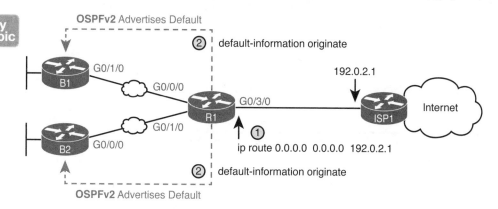

Figure 20-6 *Using OSPF to Create and Flood a Default Route*

Figure 20-7 shows the default routes that result from OSPF's advertisements in Figure 20-6. On the far left, the branch routers all have OSPF-learned default routes, pointing to R1. R1 itself also needs a default route, pointing to the ISP router, so that R1 can forward all Internet-bound traffic to the ISP.

Finally, this feature gives the engineer control over when the router originates this default route. First, R1 needs a default route, either defined as a static default route, learned from the ISP with DHCP or learned from the ISP with a routing protocol like eBGP. The OSPF subcommand **default-information originate** then tells OSPF on R1 to advertise a default route when its own default route is working and to advertise the default route as down when its own default route fails.

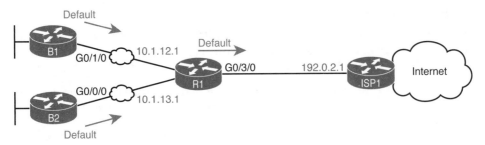

Figure 20-7   *Default Routes Resulting from the* **default-information originate** *Command*

> **NOTE**   Interestingly, the **default-information originate always** router subcommand tells the router to always advertise the default route, no matter whether the router's default route is working or not.

Example 20-17 shows details of the default route on both R1 and branch router B1 from Figure 20-7. R1 then creates a static default route with the ISP router's IP address of 192.0.2.1 as the next-hop address, as highlighted in the output of the **show ip route static** command output.

Example 20-17   *Default Routes on Routers R1 and B1*

```
! The next command is from Router R1. Note the static code for the default route
R1# show ip route static
Codes: L - local, C - connected, S - static, R - RIP, M - mobile, B - BGP
! Rest of the legend omitted for brevity


Gateway of last resort is 192.0.2.1 to network 0.0.0.0


S*     0.0.0.0/0 [254/0] via 192.0.2.1
! The next command is from router B01; notice the External route code for the default
B1# show ip route ospf
Codes: L - local, C - connected, S - static, R - RIP, M - mobile, B - BGP
       D - EIGRP, EX - EIGRP external, O - OSPF, IA - OSPF inter area
       N1 - OSPF NSSA external type 1, N2 - OSPF NSSA external type 2
       E1 - OSPF external type 1, E2 - OSPF external type 2
! Rest of the legend omitted for brevity


Gateway of last resort is 10.1.12.1 to network 0.0.0.0


O*E2   0.0.0.0/0 [110/1] via 10.1.12.1, 00:20:51, GigabitEthernet0/1/0
          10.0.0.0/8 is variably subnetted, 6 subnets, 2 masks
O         10.1.3.0/24 [110/3] via 10.1.12.1, 00:20:51, GigabitEthernet0/1/0
O         10.1.13.0/24 [110/2] via 10.1.12.1, 00:20:51, GigabitEthernet0/1/0
```

Keeping the focus on the command on Router R1, note that R1 indeed has a default route—that is, a route to 0.0.0.0/0. The "Gateway of last resort," which refers to the default route currently used by the router, points to next-hop IP address 192.0.2.1, which is the ISP router's IP address. (Refer to Figure 20-7 for the particulars.)

Next look to the bottom half of the example and router B1's OSPF-learned default route. B1 lists a route for 0.0.0.0/0 as well. The next-hop router in this case is 10.1.12.1, which is Router R1's IP address on the WAN link. The code on the far left is O*E2, meaning an OSPF-learned route, which is a default route, and is specifically an external OSPF route. Finally, B1's gateway of last resort setting uses that one OSPF-learned default route, with next-hop router 10.1.12.1.

OSPF Metrics (Cost)

The section "Calculating the Best Routes with SPF" in Chapter 19 discussed how SPF calculates the metric for each route, choosing the route with the best metric for each destination subnet. OSPF routers can influence that choice by changing the OSPF interface cost on any and all interfaces.

Cisco routers allow three different ways to change the OSPF interface cost:

- Directly, using the interface subcommand **ip ospf cost** *x*.

- Using the default calculation per interface, and changing the *interface bandwidth* setting, which changes the calculated value.

- Using the default calculation per interface, and changing the OSPF *reference bandwidth* setting, which changes the calculated value.

Setting the Cost Directly

Setting the cost directly requires a simple configuration command, as shown in Example 20-18. The example sets the cost of two interfaces on Router R1. (This example uses the Figure 20-2 design, as configured in Examples 20-2 and 20-3.) The **show ip ospf interface brief** command that follows details the cost of each interface. Note that the show command confirms the cost settings.

Example 20-18 *Confirming OSPF Interface Costs*

```
R1# conf t
Enter configuration commands, one per line.  End with CNTL/Z.
R1(config)# interface g0/0/0
R1(config-if)# ip ospf cost 4
R1(config-if)# interface g0/1/0
R1(config-if)# ip ospf cost 5
R1(config-if)# ^Z
R1#
R1# show ip ospf interface brief
Interface    PID   Area        IP Address/Mask   Cost  State Nbrs F/C
Gi0/0.2      1     0           10.1.2.1/24       1     DR    0/0
Gi0/0.1      1     0           10.1.1.1/24       1     DR    0/0
```

```
Gi0/0/0      1      0                  10.1.12.1/24      4      DR    1/1
Gi0/1/0      1      0                  10.1.13.1/24      5      BDR   1/1
Gi0/2/0      1      0                  10.1.14.1/24      1      DR    1/1
```

The output also shows a cost value of 1 for the other Gigabit interfaces, which is the default OSPF cost for any interface faster than 100 Mbps. The next topic discusses how IOS determines the default cost values.

Setting the Cost Based on Interface and Reference Bandwidth

Routers use a per-interface bandwidth setting to describe the speed of the interface. Note that the interface bandwidth setting does not influence the actual transmission speed. Instead, the interface bandwidth acts as a configurable setting to represent the speed of the interface, with the option to configure the bandwidth to match the actual transmission speed...or not. To support this logic, IOS sets a default interface bandwidth value that matches the physical transmission speed when possible, but also allows the configuration of the interface bandwidth using **bandwidth** *speed* interface subcommand.

OSPF (as well as other IOS features) uses the interface bandwidth to make decisions, with OSPF using the interface bandwidth in its calculation of the default OSPF cost for each interface. IOS uses the following formula to choose an interface's OSPF cost if the cost for cases in which the **ip ospf cost** command is not configured on the interface. IOS puts the interface's bandwidth in the denominator and an OSPF setting called the *reference bandwidth* in the numerator:

Reference_bandwidth / Interface_bandwidth

Note that while you can change both the interface bandwidth and reference bandwidth via configuration, because several IOS features make use of the bandwidth setting, you should avoid changing the interface bandwidth as a means to influence the default OSPF cost.

That being said, many enterprises do use default cost settings while influencing the default by changing the OSPF reference bandwidth while leaving the interface bandwidth as an accurate representation of link speed. Cisco chose the IOS default reference bandwidth setting decades ago in an era with much slower links. As a result, any interface with an interface bandwidth of 100 Mbps or faster ties with a calculated OSPF cost of 1 when using the default reference bandwidth. So, when relying on the default OSPF cost calculation, it helps to configure the reference bandwidth to another value.

To see the issue, consider Table 20-3, which lists several types of interfaces, the default interface bandwidth on those interfaces, and the OSPF cost calculated with the default OSPF reference bandwidth of 100 MBps (that is, 100,000 Kbps). (OSPF rounds up for these calculations, resulting in a lowest possible OSPF interface cost of 1.)

Table 20-3 Faster Interfaces with Equal OSPF Costs

Interface	Interface Default Bandwidth (Kbps)	Formula (Kbps)	OSPF Cost
Serial	1544 Kbps	100,000 / 1544	64
Ethernet	10,000 Kbps	100,000 / 10,000	10
Fast Ethernet	100,000 Kbps	100,000/100,000	1
Gigabit Ethernet	1,000,000 Kbps	100,000/1,000,000	1
10 Gigabit Ethernet	10,000,000 Kbps	100,000/10,000,000	1
100 Gigabit Ethernet	100,000,000 Kbps	100,000/100,000,000	1

As you can see from the table, with a default reference bandwidth, all interfaces from Fast Ethernet's 100 Mbps and faster tie with their default OSPF cost. As a result, OSPF would treat a 100-Mbps link as having the same cost as a 10- or 100-Gbps link, which is probably not the right basis for choosing routes.

You can still use OSPF's default cost calculation (and many do) just by changing the reference bandwidth with the **auto-cost reference-bandwidth** *speed* OSPF mode subcommand. This command sets a value in a unit of megabits per second (Mbps). Set the reference bandwidth value to a value at least as much as the fastest link speed in the network, but preferably higher, in anticipation of adding even faster links in the future.

For instance, in an enterprise whose fastest links are 10 Gbps (10,000 Mbps), you could set all routers to use **auto-cost reference-bandwidth 10000**, meaning 10,000 Mbps or 10 Gbps. In that case, by default, a 10-Gbps link would have an OSPF cost of 1, while a 1-Gbps link would have a cost of 10, and a 100-MBps link a cost of 100.

Better still, in that same enterprise, use a reference bandwidth of a faster speed than the fastest interface in the network, to allow room for higher speeds. For instance, in that same enterprise, whose fastest link is 10 Gbps, set the reference bandwidth to 40 Gbps or even 100 Gbps to be ready for future upgrades to use 40-Gbps links, or even 100-Gbps links. (For example, use the **auto-cost reference-bandwidth 100000** command, meaning 100,000 Mbps or 100 Gbps.) That causes 100-Gbps links to have an OSPF cost of 1, 40-Gbps links to have a cost of 4, 10-Gbps links to have a cost of 10, and 1-Gbps links to have a cost of 100.

> **NOTE** Cisco recommends making the OSPF reference bandwidth setting the same on all OSPF routers in an enterprise network.

For convenient study, the following list summarizes the rules for how a router sets its OSPF interface costs:

1. Set the cost explicitly, using the **ip ospf cost** *x* interface subcommand, to a value between 1 and 65,535, inclusive.

2. Although it should be avoided, change the interface bandwidth with the **bandwidth** *speed* command, with *speed* being a number in kilobits per second (Kbps).

3. Change the reference bandwidth, using router OSPF subcommand **auto-cost reference-bandwidth** *ref-bw*, with a unit of megabits per second (Mbps).

OSPF Load Balancing

When a router uses SPF to calculate the metric for each of several routes to reach one subnet, one route may have the lowest metric, so OSPF puts that route in the routing table. However, when the metrics tie for multiple routes to the same subnet, the router can put multiple equal-cost routes in the routing table (the default is four different routes) based on the setting of the **maximum-paths** *number* router subcommand. For example, if an internetwork has six possible paths between some parts of the network, and the engineer wants all routes to be used, the routers can be configured with the **maximum-paths 6** subcommand under **router ospf**.

The more challenging concept relates to how the routers use those multiple routes. A router could load balance the packets on a per-packet basis. For example, if the router has three equal-cost OSPF routes for the same subnet in the routing table, the router could send the one packet over the first route, the next packet over the second route, the next packet over the third route, and then start over with the first route for the next packet. Note that per-packet load balancing is generally a poor choice because it causes the most overhead work on the router. Alternatively, using the default (and better) method, the load balancing could be on a per-destination IP address basis.

Note that the default setting of **maximum-paths** varies by router platform.

Chapter Review

One key to doing well on the exams is to perform repetitive spaced review sessions. Review this chapter's material using either the tools in the book or interactive tools for the same material found on the book's companion website. Refer to the "Your Study Plan" element for more details. Table 20-4 outlines the key review elements and where you can find them. To better track your study progress, record when you completed these activities in the second column.

Table 20-4   Chapter Review Tracking

Review Element	Review Date(s)	Resource Used:
Review key topics		Book, website
Review key terms		Book, website
Answer DIKTA questions		Book, PTP
Review Config Checklists		Book, website
Review command tables		Book
Do labs		Blog

Review All the Key Topics

Table 20-5   Key Topics for Chapter 20

Key Topic Element	Description	Page Number
Figure 20-1	Organization of OSPFv2 configuration with the **network** command	471
List	Example OSPF wildcard masks and their meaning	473
Figure 20-3	OSPF verification commands	476
Example 20-4	Example of the **show ip ospf neighbor** command	476
List	Neighbor states and their meanings	477
List	Rules for setting the router ID	481
Example 20-14	Differences in **show ip ospf interface** output with OSPF interface configuration	486
List	Actions IOS takes when an OSPF interface is passive	487
Figure 20-6	Actions taken by the OSPF **default-information originate** command	489
List	Rules for setting OSPF interface cost	493

20

Key Terms You Should Know

reference bandwidth, interface bandwidth, maximum paths

Command References

Tables 20-6 and 20-7 list configuration and verification commands used in this chapter. As an easy review exercise, cover the left column in a table, read the right column, and try to recall the command without looking. Then repeat the exercise, covering the right column, and try to recall what the command does.

Table 20-6   Chapter 20 Configuration Command Reference

Command	Description
router ospf *process-id*	Router subcommand that enters OSPF configuration mode for the listed process.
network *ip-address wildcard-mask* **area** *area-id*	Router subcommand that enables OSPF on interfaces matching the address/wildcard combination and sets the OSPF area.
ip ospf *process-id* **area** *area-number*	Interface subcommand to enable OSPF on the interface and to assign the interface to a specific OSPF area.

Command	Description
ip ospf cost *interface-cost*	Interface subcommand that sets the OSPF cost associated with the interface.
bandwidth *bandwidth*	Interface subcommand that directly sets the interface bandwidth (Kbps).
auto-cost reference-bandwidth *number*	Router subcommand that tells OSPF the numerator in the Reference_bandwidth / Interface_bandwidth formula used to calculate the OSPF cost based on the interface bandwidth.
router-id *id*	OSPF command that statically sets the router ID.
interface loopback *number*	Global command to create a loopback interface and to navigate to interface configuration mode for that interface.
maximum-paths *number-of-paths*	Router subcommand that defines the maximum number of equal-cost routes that can be added to the routing table.
passive-interface *type number*	Router subcommand that makes the interface passive to OSPF, meaning that the OSPF process will not form neighbor relationships with neighbors reachable on that interface.
passive-interface *default*	OSPF subcommand that changes the OSPF default for interfaces to be passive instead of active (not passive).
no passive-interface *type number*	OSPF subcommand that tells OSPF to be active (not passive) on that interface or subinterface.
default-information originate [always]	OSPF subcommand to tell OSPF to create and advertise an OSPF default route, as long as the router has some default route (or to always advertise a default, if the **always** option is configured).

Table 20-7   Chapter 20 EXEC Command Reference

Command	Description
show ip ospf	Lists information about the OSPF process running on the router, including the OSPF router ID, areas to which the router connects, and the number of interfaces in each area.
show ip ospf interface brief	Lists the interfaces on which the OSPF protocol is enabled (based on the **network** commands), including passive interfaces.
show ip ospf interface [*type number*]	Lists a long section of settings, status, and counters for OSPF operation on all interfaces, or on the listed interface, including the Hello and Dead Timers.
show ip protocols	Shows routing protocol parameters and current timer values.

Command	Description
show ip ospf neighbor [*type number*]	Lists brief output about neighbors, identified by neighbor router ID, including current state, with one line per neighbor; optionally, limits the output to neighbors on the listed interface.
show ip ospf neighbor *neighbor-ID*	Lists the same output as the **show ip ospf neighbor** detail command, but only for the listed neighbor (by neighbor RID).
show ip ospf database	Lists a summary of the LSAs in the database, with one line of output per LSA. It is organized by LSA type (first type 1, then type 2, and so on).
show ip route	Lists all IPv4 routes.
show ip route ospf	Lists routes in the routing table learned by OSPF.
show ip route *ip-address mask*	Shows a detailed description of the route for the listed subnet/mask.
clear ip ospf process	Resets the OSPF process, resetting all neighbor relationships and also causing the process to make a choice of OSPF RID.

20

CHAPTER 21

OSPF Network Types and Neighbors

This chapter covers the following exam topics:

3.0 IP Connectivity

3.4 Configure and verify single area OSPFv2

3.4.a Neighbor adjacencies

3.4.b Point-to-point

3.4.c Broadcast (DR/BDR selection)

3.4.d Router ID

Chapter 20, "Implementing OSPF," discussed the required and most common optional OSPF configuration settings, along with the many verification commands to show how OSPF works with those settings. This chapter continues with more OSPF implementation topics, both to round out the discussion of OSPF and to focus even more on the specific CCNA 200-301 exam topics.

The first of two major sections of this chapter focuses on OSPF network types, specifically types point-to-point and broadcast. The CCNA 200-301 exam topics mention those by name. Chapter 20 showed how OSPF operates on Ethernet interfaces when using their default network type (broadcast). This first section of the chapter discusses the meaning of OSPF network types, default settings, how to configure to use other settings, and how OSPF works differently with different settings.

The second major section then focuses on neighbors and neighbor adjacencies as mentioned in yet another of the OSPF exam topics. OSPF routers cannot exchange LSAs with another router unless they first become neighbors. This second section discusses the various OSPF features that can prevent OSPF routers from becoming neighbors and how you can go about discovering if those bad conditions exist—even if you do not have access to the running configuration.

"Do I Know This Already?" Quiz

Take the quiz (either here or use the PTP software) if you want to use the score to help you decide how much time to spend on this chapter. The letter answers are listed at the bottom of the page following the quiz. Appendix C, found both at the end of the book as well as on the companion website, includes both the answers and explanations. You can also find both answers and explanations in the PTP testing software.

Table 21-1 "Do I Know This Already?" Foundation Topics Section-to-Question Mapping

Foundation Topics Section	Questions
OSPF Network Types	1–3
OSPF Neighbor Relationships	4–6

1. Routers R1 and R2, with router IDs 1.1.1.1 and 2.2.2.2, connect over an Ethernet WAN link. If using all default OSPF settings, if the WAN link initializes for both routers at the same time, which of the following answers are true? (Choose two answers.)

   a. Router R1 will become the DR.

   b. Router R1 will dynamically discover the existence of router R2.

   c. Router R2 will be neither the DR nor the BDR.

   d. Router R1's **show ip ospf neighbor** command will list R2 with a state of "FULL/DR."

2. Routers R1 and R2, with router IDs 1.1.1.1 and 2.2.2.2, connect over an Ethernet WAN link. The configuration uses all defaults, except giving R1 an interface priority of 11 and changing both routers to use OSPF network type point-to-point. If the WAN link initializes for both routers at the same time, which of the following answers are true? (Choose two answers.)

   a. Router R1 will become the DR.

   b. Router R1 will dynamically discover the existence of router R2.

   c. Router R2 will be neither the DR nor the BDR.

   d. Router R2's **show ip ospf neighbor** command will list R1 with a state of "FULL/DR."

3. Per the command output, with how many routers is router R9 full adjacent over its Gi0/0 interface?

   ```
   R9# show ip ospf interface brief
   Interface    PID   Area            IP Address/Mask    Cost   State Nbrs F/C
   Gi0/0        1     0               10.1.1.1/24        1      DROTH 2/5
   ```

   a. 7

   b. 0

   c. 5

   d. 2

4. An engineer connects routers R11 and R12 to the same Ethernet LAN and configures them to use OSPFv2. Which answers describe a combination of settings that would prevent the two routers from becoming OSPF neighbors? (Choose two answers.)

   a. R11's interface uses area 11 while R12's interface uses area 12.

   b. R11's OSPF process uses process ID 11 while R12 uses process ID 12.

   c. R11's interface uses OSPF priority 11 while R12's uses OSPF priority 12.

   d. R11's interface uses an OSPF Hello timer value of 11 while R12's uses 12.

5. An engineer connects routers R13 and R14 to the same Ethernet LAN and configures them to use OSPFv2. Which answers describe a combination of settings that would prevent the two routers from becoming OSPF neighbors?

   a. Both routers' interface IP addresses reside in the same subnet.

   b. Both routers' OSPF process uses process ID 13.

   c. Both routers' OSPF process uses router ID 13.13.13.13.

   d. Both routers' interfaces use an OSPF Dead interval of 40.

6. Router R15 has been a working part of a network that uses OSPFv2. An engineer then issues the **shutdown** command in OSPF configuration mode on R15. Which of the following occurs?

   a. R15 empties its IP routing table of all OSPF routes but keeps its LSDB intact.

   b. R15 empties its LSDB but keeps OSPF neighbor relationships active.

   c. R15 keeps OSPF neighbors open but does not accept new OSPF neighbors.

   d. R15 keeps all OSPF configuration but ceases all OSPF activities (routes, LSDB, neighbors).

Foundation Topics

OSPF Network Types

Two CCNA 200-301 exam topics might be completely misunderstood without taking a closer look at yet more default OSPF settings. In particular, the following exam topics refer to a specific per-interface OSPF setting called the *network type*—even listing the keywords used to configure the setting in the exam topics:

   3.4.b: **point-to-point**

   3.4.c: **broadcast** (DR/BDR selection)

OSPF includes a small number of network types as a setting on each OSPF-enabled interface. The setting tells the router whether or not to dynamically discover OSPF neighbors (versus requiring the static configuration of the neighboring router's IP address) and whether or not the router should attempt to use a designated router (DR) and backup DR (BDR) in the subnet. Of the two OSPF network types included in the CCNA exam topics, both cause routers to dynamically discover neighbors, but one calls for the use of a DR while the other does not. Table 21-2 summarizes the features of the two OSPF network types mentioned in the exam topics.

Table 21-2   Two OSPF Network Types and Key Behaviors

Network Type Keyword	Dynamically Discovers Neighbors	Uses a DR/BDR
broadcast	Yes	Yes
point-to-point	Yes	No

The rest of this first major section of the chapter explores each type.

The OSPF Broadcast Network Type

OSPF defaults to use a *broadcast* network type on all types of Ethernet interfaces. Note that all the Ethernet interfaces in examples in Chapter 20 relied on that default setting.

To see all the details of how the OSPF broadcast network type works, this chapter begins with a different design than the examples in Chapter 20, instead using a single area design that connects four routers to the same subnet, as shown in Figure 21-1. All links reside in area 0, making the design a single area design.

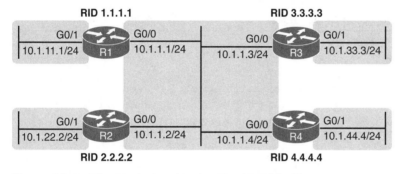

Figure 21-1   *The Single Area Design Used in This Chapter*

To get a sense for how OSPF operates with the broadcast network type, imagine that all four routers use a straightforward OSPF interface configuration like the router R1 configuration shown in Example 21-1. Both GigabitEthernet interfaces on all four routers default to use network type broadcast. Note that the configuration on routers R2, R3, and R4 mirrors R1's configuration except that they use router IDs 2.2.2.2, 3.3.3.3, and 4.4.4.4, respectively, and they use the IP addresses shown in the figure.

Example 21-1   *R1 OSPF Configuration to Match Figure 21-1*

```
router ospf 1
 router-id 1.1.1.1
 !
interface gigabitEthernet0/0
 ip ospf 1 area 0
 !
interface gigabitEthernet0/1
 ip ospf 1 area 0
```

This simple design gives us a great backdrop from which to observe the results of the broadcast network type on each router. Both interfaces (G0/0 and G0/1) on each router use the broadcast network type and perform the following actions:

- Attempt to discover neighbors by sending OSPF Hellos to the 224.0.0.5 multicast address (an address reserved for sending packets to all OSPF routers in the subnet)

- Attempt to elect a DR and BDR on each subnet

- On the interface with no other routers on the subnet (G0/1), become the DR

- On the interface with three other routers on the subnet (G0/0), be either DR, BDR, or a DROther router

- When sending OSPF messages to the DR or BDR, send the messages to the all-OSPF-DRs multicast address 224.0.0.6

Example 21-2 shows some of the results using the **show ip ospf neighbor** command. Note that R1 lists R2, R3, and R4 as neighbors (based on their 2.2.2.2, 3.3.3.3, and 4.4.4.4 router IDs), confirming that R1 dynamically discovered the other routers. Also, note that the output lists 4.4.4.4 as the DR and 3.3.3.3 as the BDR.

Example 21-2 *R1's List of Neighbors*

```
R1# show ip ospf neighbor


Neighbor ID    Pri   State          Dead Time   Address     Interface
2.2.2.2          1   2WAY/DROTHER   00:00:35    10.1.1.2    GigabitEthernet0/0
3.3.3.3          1   FULL/BDR       00:00:33    10.1.1.3    GigabitEthernet0/0
4.4.4.4          1   FULL/DR        00:00:35    10.1.1.4    GigabitEthernet0/0
```

Verifying Operations with Network Type Broadcast

As discussed in the section "Using Designated Routers on Ethernet Links" in Chapter 19, "Understanding OSPF Concepts," all discovered routers on the link should become neighbors and at least reach the *2-way* state. For all neighbor relationships that include the DR and/or BDR, the neighbor relationship should further reach the *full* state. That section defined the term *fully adjacent* as a special term that refers to neighbors that reach this full state.

The design in Figure 21-1, with four routers on the same LAN, provides just enough routers so that one neighbor relationship will remain in a 2-way state and not reach the full state, as a perfectly normal way for OSPF to operate. Figure 21-2 shows the current conditions when the **show** commands in this chapter were gathered, with R4 as the DR, R3 as the BDR, and with R1 and R2 as DROther routers.

Now consider router R1's neighbors as listed in Example 21-2. R1 has three neighbors, all reachable out its G0/0 interface. However, R1's **show ip ospf neighbor** command refers to the state of R1's relationship with the neighbor: 2-way with router 2.2.2.2. Because both R1 and R2 currently serve as DROther routers—that is, they wait ready to become the BDR if either the DR or BDR fails—their neighbor relationship remains in a 2-way state.

Answers to the "Do I Know This Already?" quiz:

1 B, D **2** B, C **3** D **4** A, D **5** C **6** D

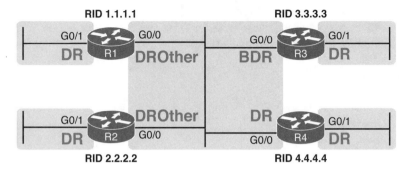

Figure 21-2 *OSPF DR/BDR/DROther Roles in the Network*

Examining Example 21-2 one last time, R1, as a DROther router itself, has two neighbor relationships that reach a full state: R1's neighbor adjacency with DR R4 and R1's neighbor adjacency with BDR R3. But R1 has a total of three neighbors, all reachable off R1's G0/0 interface.

The idea that R1 has three neighbors off its G0/0 interface, with two being fully adjacent, is reflected on the far right of the output of the **show ip ospf interface brief** command output in Example 21-3. It shows "2/3," meaning two neighbors in the full state off port G0/0, with three total neighbors on that interface. Also, note that this command's "State" column differs from the **show ip ospf neighbor** commands, in that the **show ip ospf interface brief** command lists the local router's role on the interface (as shown in Figure 21-2), with R1's G0/1 acting as DR and R1's G0/0 acting as a DROther router.

Example 21-3 *Router R1 OSPF Interfaces: Local Role and Neighbor Counts*

```
R1# show ip ospf interface brief
Interface     PID    Area           IP Address/Mask    Cost   State  Nbrs F/C
Gi0/1         1      0              10.1.11.1/24       1      DR     0/0
Gi0/0         1      0              10.1.1.1/24        1      DROTH  2/3
```

So far, this topic has described the effect of the OSPF broadcast network type by taking advantage of the default setting on Ethernet interfaces. To see the setting, use the **show ip ospf interface** command, as shown in Example 21-4. The first highlighted item identifies the network type. However, this command's output restates many of the facts seen in both the **show ip ospf neighbor** and **show ip ospf interface brief** commands in Examples 21-2 and 21-3, so take the time to browse through all of Example 21-4 and focus on the additional highlights to see those familiar items.

Example 21-4 *Displaying OSPF Network Type Broadcast*

```
R1# show ip ospf interface g0/0
GigabitEthernet0/0 is up, line protocol is up
  Internet Address 10.1.1.1/24, Area 0, Attached via Interface Enable
  Process ID 1, Router ID 1.1.1.1, Network Type BROADCAST, Cost: 1
  Topology-MTID    Cost    Disabled    Shutdown    Topology Name
      0             1        no          no           Base
  Enabled by interface config, including secondary ip addresses
```

```
Transmit Delay is 1 sec, State DROTHER, Priority 1
Designated Router (ID) 4.4.4.4, Interface address 10.1.1.4
Backup Designated router (ID) 3.3.3.3, Interface address 10.1.1.3
Timer intervals configured, Hello 10, Dead 40, Wait 40, Retransmit 5
  oob-resync timeout 40
  Hello due in 00:00:00
Supports Link-local Signaling (LLS)
Cisco NSF helper support enabled
IETF NSF helper support enabled
Index 1/1/1, flood queue length 0
Next 0x0(0)/0x0(0)/0x0(0)
Last flood scan length is 0, maximum is 1
Last flood scan time is 0 msec, maximum is 0 msec
Neighbor Count is 3, Adjacent neighbor count is 2
  Adjacent with neighbor 3.3.3.3  (Backup Designated Router)
  Adjacent with neighbor 4.4.4.4  (Designated Router)
Suppress hello for 0 neighbor(s)
```

Although you would not need to configure an Ethernet interface to use the broadcast network type, some older types of interfaces over the years have used different defaults and with the option to use the broadcast network type. In those cases, the **ip ospf network broadcast** interface subcommand would configure the setting.

Configuring to Influence the DR/BDR Election

In some cases, you may want to influence the OSPF DR election. However, before deciding that makes sense in every case, note that OSPF DR/BDR election rules will not result in a specific router always being the DR, and another always being the BDR, assuming that each is up and working. In short, here are the rules once a DR and BDR have been elected:

- If the DR fails, the BDR becomes the DR, and a new BDR is elected.
- When a better router enters the subnet, no preemption of the existing DR or BDR occurs.

As a result of these rules, while you can configure a router to be the best (highest priority) router to become the DR in an election, doing so only increases that router's statistical chances of being the DR at a given point in time. If the router fails, other routers will become DR and BDR, and the best router will not be DR again until the current DR and BDR fail.

NOTE If you have begun to think about STP elections, note that the rules are similar, but with two key differences. STP uses a lowest-is-best approach and allows new switches to preempt the existing root switch to become the root. OSPF uses a highest-is-best approach and does not preempt the DR as just noted.

In some cases, you may want to influence the DR/BDR election with two configurable settings, listed here in order of precedence:

- **The highest OSPF interface priority:** The highest value wins during an election, with values ranging from 0 to 255.
- **The highest OSPF Router ID:** If the priority ties, the election chooses the router with the highest OSPF RID.

For example, imagine all four routers in the design shown in Figure 21-1 trying to elect the DR and BDR at the same time—for instance, after a power hit in which all four routers power off and back on again. They all participate in the election. They all tie with default priority values of 1 (see Example 21-4 for R1's priority in the **show ip ospf interface** command output.) In this case, R4, with the numerically highest RID of 4.4.4.4, wins the election, and R3, with the next highest RID of 3.3.3.3, becomes the BDR.

To influence the election, you could set the various RIDs with your preferred router with the highest RID value. However, many networks choose OSPF router IDs to help identify the router easily. Instead, using the OSPF priority setting makes better sense. For instance, if an engineer preferred that R1 be the DR, the engineer could add the configuration in Example 21-5 to set R1's interface priority to 99.

Example 21-5 *Influencing DR/BDR Election Using OSPF Priority*

```
R1# configure terminal
Configuring from terminal, memory, or network [terminal]?
Enter configuration commands, one per line.  End with CNTL/Z.
R1(config)# interface g0/0
R1(config-if)# ip ospf priority 99
R1(config-if)# ^Z
R1#
R1# show ip ospf interface g0/0 | include Priority
  Transmit Delay is 1 sec, State DROTHER, Priority 99

R1# show ip ospf neighbor
Neighbor ID     Pri   State           Dead Time   Address         Interface
2.2.2.2           1   2WAY/DROTHER    00:00:36    10.1.1.2        GigabitEthernet0/0
3.3.3.3           1   FULL/BDR        00:00:30    10.1.1.3        GigabitEthernet0/0
4.4.4.4           1   FULL/DR         00:00:37    10.1.1.4        GigabitEthernet0/0

R1# show ip ospf interface brief
Interface   PID   Area          IP Address/Mask   Cost  State Nbrs F/C
Gi0/1       1     0             10.1.11.1/24      1     DR    0/0
Gi0/0       1     0             10.1.1.1/24       1     DROTH 2/3
```

The configuration shows R1's interface priority value now as 99, and the **show ip ospf interface G0/0** command that follows confirms the setting. However, the last two commands in the example seem to show that the DR and BDR have not changed at all—and that output is indeed correct. In the example, note that the **show ip ospf neighbor** command still lists R4's state as DR, meaning R4 still acts as the DR, while the **show ip ospf interface brief** command lists R1's State (role) as DROTH.

21

Just to complete the process, Example 21-6 shows the results after forcing a free election (by failing the LAN switch that sits between the four routers). As expected, R1 wins and becomes DR due to its higher priority, with the other three routers tying based on priority. R4 wins between R2, R3, and R4 due to its higher RID to become the BDR.

Example 21-6 *Results of a Completely New DR/BDR Election*

```
! Not shown: LAN fails, and then recovers, causing a new OSPF Election
R1# show ip ospf neighbor

Neighbor ID    Pri   State         Dead Time   Address      Interface
2.2.2.2         1    FULL/DROTHER  00:00:37    10.1.1.2     GigabitEthernet0/0
3.3.3.3         1    FULL/DROTHER  00:00:38    10.1.1.3     GigabitEthernet0/0
4.4.4.4         1    FULL/BDR      00:00:38    10.1.1.4     GigabitEthernet0/0

R1# show ip ospf interface brief
Interface   PID   Area       IP Address/Mask    Cost  State Nbrs F/C
Gi0/1        1     0         10.1.11.1/24       1     DR    0/0
Gi0/0        1     0         10.1.1.1/24        1     DR    3/3
```

The OSPF Point-to-Point Network Type

The other OSPF network type mentioned in the CCNA 200-301 exam topics, point-to-point, works well for data links that by their nature have just two routers on the link. For example, consider the topology in Figure 21-3, which shows router R1 with three WAN links—two Ethernet WAN links and one serial link.

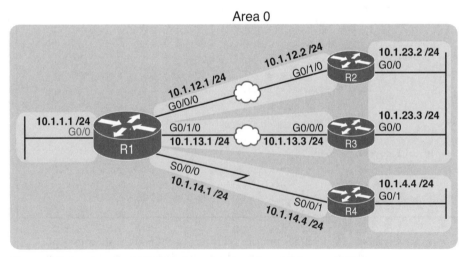

Figure 21-3 *Sample OSPF Design with Serial and Ethernet WAN*

First, focus on the serial link itself. To review, the jagged line represents a physical link that can at most have two devices using the link, specifically R1 and R4 in this case. The link does not support the ability to add a third router to the link. As you might guess, the data-link protocols to control a link with at most two devices can work differently than Ethernet.

For instance, the data-link protocols most often used on the link (HDLC and PPP) do not support data-link broadcasts.

Next, consider the OSPF point-to-point network type: it exists for serial links and other links that use a point-to-point topology. These links often do not support data-link broadcasts. Additionally, with only two devices on the link, using a DR/BDR is not a help, and it actually adds a little extra convergence time. Using a network type of point-to-point tells the router to not use a DR/BDR on the link.

While you may see some serial links in networks today, the CCNA and CCNP Enterprise exams make no specific mention of serial technology at this point. However, you will see other point-to-point links—like some Ethernet WAN links.

To connect the thoughts, note that all the Ethernet WAN links used in this book happen to use a point-to-point Ethernet WAN service called an Ethernet Private Wire Service or simply an Ethernet Line (E-Line). For that service, the service provider will send Ethernet frames between two devices (routers) connected to the service, but only those two devices. In other words, an E-line is a point-to-point service in concept. So while the Ethernet data-link protocol supports broadcast frames, only two devices can exist on the link, and there is no advantage to using a DR/BDR. As a result, many engineers prefer to instead use an OSPF point-to-point network type on Ethernet WAN links that in effect act as a point-to-point link.

Example 21-7 shows the configuration of router R1's G0/0/0 interface in Figure 21-3 to use OSPF network type point-to-point. R2, on the other end of the WAN link, would need the same configuration command on its matching interface.

Example 21-7   *OSPF Network Type Point-to-Point on an Ethernet WAN Interface on R1*

```
R1# configure terminal
Enter configuration commands, one per line.  End with CNTL/Z.
R1(config)# interface g0/0/0
R1(config-if)# ip ospf network point-to-point
R1(config-if)#

R1# show ip ospf interface g0/0/0
GigabitEthernet0/0/0 is up, line protocol is up
  Internet Address 10.1.12.1/24, Area 0, Attached via Interface Enable
  Process ID 1, Router ID 1.1.1.1, Network Type POINT_TO_POINT, Cost: 1
  Topology-MTID    Cost    Disabled    Shutdown       Topology Name
        0            4        no          no            Base
  Enabled by interface config, including secondary ip addresses
  Transmit Delay is 1 sec, State POINT_TO_POINT
  Timer intervals configured, Hello 10, Dead 40, Wait 40, Retransmit 5
    oob-resync timeout 40
    Hello due in 00:00:01
  Supports Link-local Signaling (LLS)
  Cisco NSF helper support enabled
  IETF NSF helper support enabled
  Index 1/3/3, flood queue length 0
  Next 0x0(0)/0x0(0)/0x0(0)
```

21

```
Last flood scan length is 1, maximum is 3
Last flood scan time is 0 msec, maximum is 0 msec
Neighbor Count is 1, Adjacent neighbor count is 1
   Adjacent with neighbor 2.2.2.2
Suppress hello for 0 neighbor(s)
```

Note the highlighted portions of the **show** command in Example 21-6. The first two highlights note the network type. The final highlight with two lines notes that R1 has one neighbor on the interface, a neighbor with which it has become fully adjacent per the output.

Example 21-8 closes this section with a confirmation of some of those facts with two more commands. Note that the **show ip ospf neighbor** command on R1 lists router R2 (RID 2.2.2.2) with a full state, but with no DR nor BDR designation, instead listing a -. The - acts as a reminder that the link does not use a DR/BDR. The second command, **show ip ospf interface brief**, shows the state (the local router's role) as P2P, which is short for point-to-point, with a counter of 1 for the number of fully adjacent neighbors and total number of neighbors.

Example 21-8 *OSPF Network Type Point-to-Point on an Ethernet WAN Interface on R1*

```
R1# show ip ospf neighbor

Neighbor ID     Pri    State          Dead Time    Address       Interface
2.2.2.2           0    FULL/  -       00:00:39     10.1.12.2     GigabitEthernet0/0/0
! lines omitted for brevity


R1# show ip ospf interface brief
Interface    PID    Area           IP Address/Mask    Cost    State   Nbrs F/C
Gi0/0/0       1      0             10.1.12.1/24         4     P2P     1/1
! lines omitted for brevity
```

When using Ethernet WAN links that behave as a point-to-point link, consider using OSPF network type point-to-point rather than using the default broadcast type.

OSPF Neighbor Relationships

A router's OSPF configuration enables OSPF on a set of interfaces. IOS then attempts to discover other neighbors on those interfaces by sending and listening for OSPF Hello messages. However, once discovered, two routers may not become neighbors. They must have compatible values for several settings as listed in the Hellos exchanged between the two routers. This second major section of the chapter examines those reasons.

OSPF Neighbor Requirements

After an OSPF router hears a Hello from a new neighbor, the routing protocol examines the information in the Hello and compares that information with the local router's own settings. If the settings match, great. If not, the routers do not become neighbors. Because there is no formal term for all these items that a routing protocol considers, this book just calls them *neighbor requirements*. Table 21-3 lists the neighbor requirements for OSPF, with some comments about the various issues following the table.

Table 21-3   Neighbor Requirements for OSPF

Requirement	Required for OSPF	Neighbor Missing if Incorrect
Interfaces must be in an up/up state.	Yes	Yes
Access control lists (ACL) must not filter routing protocol messages.	Yes	Yes
Interfaces must be in the same subnet.	Yes	Yes
They must pass routing protocol neighbor authentication (if configured).	Yes	Yes
Hello and hold/dead timers must match.	Yes	Yes
Router IDs (RID) must be unique.	Yes	Yes
They must be in the same area.	Yes	Yes
OSPF process must not be shut down.	Yes	Yes
Neighboring interfaces must use same MTU setting.	Yes	No
Neighboring interfaces must use same OSPF network type.	Yes	No

First, consider the meaning of the two rightmost columns. The column labeled "Required for OSPF" means that the item must be working correctly for the neighbor relationship to work correctly. Note that all the items in this column list a "yes," meaning that all must be correct for the neighbor relationship to work correctly. The last column heading states "Neighbor Missing if Incorrect." For items listing a "yes" in this column, if that item is configured incorrectly, the neighbor will not appear in lists of OSPF neighbors—for instance, with the **show ip ospf neighbor** command.

Next, focus on the shaded items at the top of the table. The symptom that occurs if either of these is a problem is that the **show ip ospf neighbor** command would not list the other router. For instance, the first item states that the router interfaces must be up and working. If the router interface is not working, the router cannot send any OSPF messages and discover any OSPF neighbors on that interface.

The middle section of the table (the unshaded rows) focuses on some OSPF settings. These items must be correct, but if not, they also result in the neighbor not being listed in the output of the **show ip ospf neighbor** command.

As you can see, using the **show ip ospf neighbor** command can give you a good starting point to troubleshoot OSPF on the exam and in real life. If you see the neighbor you expect to see, great! If not, the table gives you a good list to use for items to investigate.

Finally, the last section (shaded) lists a couple of OSPF settings that give a different symptom when incorrect. Again, those two items must be correct for OSPF neighbors to work. However, for these two items, when incorrect, a router can list the other router as a neighbor, but the neighbor relationship does not work properly in that the routers do not exchange LSAs as they should.

For reference, Table 21-4 relists some of the requirements from Table 21-3, along with the most useful commands with which to find the answers.

21

Table 21-4   OSPF Neighbor Requirements and the Best **show/debug** Commands

Requirement	Best show Command
Hello and dead timers must match.	show ip ospf interface
They must be in the same area.	show ip ospf interface brief
RIDs must be unique.	show ip ospf
They must pass any neighbor authentication.	show ip ospf interface
OSPF process must not be shut down.	show ip ospf, show ip ospf interface

The rest of this section looks at some of the items from Table 21-3 in a little more detail.

NOTE   One configuration choice that people sometimes think is an issue, but is not, is the process ID as defined by the **router ospf** *process-id* command. Neighboring routers can use the same process ID values, or different process ID values, with no impact on whether two routers become OSPF neighbors.

Issues That Prevent Neighbor Adjacencies

The next few pages look at three of the topics from Table 21-3 for which, if a problem exists, the router does not become a neighbor (that is, the unshaded parts of the table.). To show the issues, this section uses the same topology shown earlier in Figure 21-1 but now with some incorrect configuration introduced. In other words, the configuration matches Example 21-1 that began this chapter, but with the following errors introduced:

- R2 has been configured with both LAN interfaces in area 1, whereas the other three routers' G0/0 interfaces are assigned to area 0.

- R3 is using the same RID (1.1.1.1) as R1.

- R4 has been configured with a Hello/dead timer of 5/20 on its G0/0 interface, instead of the 10/40 used (by default) on R1, R2, and R3.

Figure 21-4 shows these same problems for reference.

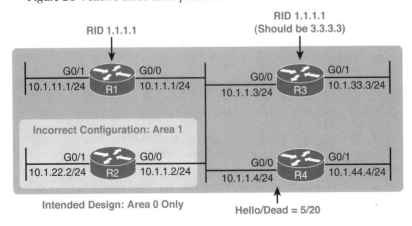

Figure 21-4   *Summary of Problems That Prevent OSPF Neighbors on the Central LAN*

Finding Area Mismatches

To create an area mismatch, the configuration on some router must place the interface into the wrong area per the design. As shown in Figure 21-4, router R2 was configured incorrectly, placing both its interfaces into area 1 instead of area 0. Example 21-9 shows the configuration, which uses the correct syntax (and is therefore accepted by the router) but sets the wrong area number.

Example 21-9 *Setting Area 1 on R2's Interfaces, When They Should Be in Area 0*

```
router ospf 1
 router-id 2.2.2.2
!
interface gigabitEthernet0/0
 ip ospf 1 area 1
!
interface gigabitEthernet0/1
 ip ospf 1 area 1
```

With an area mismatch error, the **show ip ospf neighbor** command will not list the neighbor. Because you see nothing in the OSPF neighbor table, to troubleshoot this problem, you need to find the area configuration on each interface on potentially neighboring routers. To do so:

- Check the output of **show running-config** to look for
  - **ip ospf** *process-id* **area** *area-number* interface subcommands
  - **network** commands in OSPF configuration mode
- Use the **show ip ospf interface [brief]** command to list the area number

Finding Duplicate OSPF Router IDs

Next, Example 21-10 shows R1 and R3 both trying to use RID 1.1.1.1. Interestingly, both routers automatically generate a log message for the duplicate OSPF RID problem between R1 and R3; the end of Example 21-10 shows one such message. For the exams, just use the **show ip ospf** commands on both R3 and R1 to easily list the RID on each router, noting that they both use the same value.

Example 21-10 *Comparing OSPF Router IDs on R1 and R3*

```
! Next, on R3: R3 lists the RID of 1.1.1.1
!
R3# show ip ospf
Routing Process "ospf 1" with ID 1.1.1.1
Start time: 00:00:37.136, Time elapsed: 02:20:37.200
! lines omitted for brevity

! Back to R1: R1 also uses RID 1.1.1.1
R1# show ip ospf
Routing Process "ospf 1" with ID 1.1.1.1
```

21

```
Start time: 00:01:51.864, Time elapsed: 12:13:50.904
! lines omitted for brevity


*May 29 00:01:25.679: %OSPF-4-DUP_RTRID_NBR: OSPF detected duplicate router-id
1.1.1.1 from 10.1.1.3 on interface GigabitEthernet0/0
```

First, focus on the problem: the duplicate RIDs. The first line of the **show ip ospf** command on the two routers quickly shows the duplicate use of 1.1.1.1. To solve the problem, assuming R1 should use 1.1.1.1 and R3 should use another RID (maybe 3.3.3.3), change the RID on R3 and restart the OSPF process. To do so, use the **router-id 3.3.3.3** OSPF subcommand and use the EXEC mode command **clear ip ospf process**. (OSPF will not begin using a new RID value until the process restarts, either via command or reload.)

Finding OSPF Hello and Dead Timer Mismatches

First, as a reminder from chapters past:

- **Hello interval/timer:** The per-interface timer that tells a router how often to send OSPF Hello messages on an interface.

- **Dead interval/timer:** The per-interface timer that tells the router how long to wait without having received a Hello from a neighbor before believing that neighbor has failed. (Defaults to four times the Hello timer.)

Next, consider the problem created on R4, with the configuration of a different Hello timer and dead timer (5 and 20, respectively) as compared with the default settings on R1, R2, and R3 (10 and 40, respectively). A Hello or Dead interval mismatch prevents R4 from becoming neighbors with any of the other three OSPF routers. Routers list their Hello and Dead interval settings in their Hello messages and choose to not become neighbors if the values do not match. As a result, none of the routers become neighbors with router R4 in this case.

Example 21-11 shows the easiest way to find the mismatch using the **show ip ospf interface** command on both R1 and R4. This command lists the Hello and dead timers for each interface, as highlighted in the example. Note that R1 uses 10 and 40 (Hello and dead), whereas R4 uses 5 and 20.

Example 21-11 *Finding Mismatched Hello/Dead Timers*

```
R1# show ip ospf interface G0/0
GigabitEthernet0/0 is up, line protocol is up
  Internet Address 10.1.1.1/24, Area 0, Attached via Network Statement
  Process ID 1, Router ID 1.1.1.1, Network Type BROADCAST, Cost: 1
  Topology-MTID   Cost   Disabled   Shutdown   Topology Name
        0          1       no         no         Base
  Transmit Delay is 1 sec, State DR, Priority 1
  Designated Router (ID) 1.1.1.1, Interface address 10.1.1.1
  No backup designated router on this network
```

```
   Timer intervals configured, Hello 10, Dead 40, Wait 40, Retransmit 5
! lines omitted for brevity
```

```
! Moving on to R4 next
!
R4# show ip ospf interface Gi0/0
GigabitEthernet0/0 is up, line protocol is up
   Internet Address 10.1.1.4/24, Area 0, Attached via Network Statement
   Process ID 4, Router ID 10.1.44.4, Network Type BROADCAST, Cost: 1
   Topology-MTID  Cost  Disabled  Shutdown   Topology Name
        0          1       no       no          Base
   Transmit Delay is 1 sec, State DR, Priority 1
   Transmit Delay is 1 sec, State DR, Priority 1
   Designated Router (ID) 10.1.44.4, Interface address 10.1.1.4
   No backup designated router on this network
   Timer intervals configured, Hello 5, Dead 20, Wait 20, Retransmit 5
! lines omitted for brevity
```

Shutting Down the OSPF Process

Similar to administratively disabling and enabling an interface, IOS also allows the OSPFv2 routing protocol process to be disabled and enabled with the **shutdown** and **no shutdown** router mode subcommands, respectively. When a routing protocol process is shut down, IOS does the following:

- Brings down all neighbor relationships and clears the OSPF neighbor table
- Clears the LSDB
- Clears the IP routing table of any OSPF-learned routes

At the same time, shutting down OSPF does retain some important details about OSPF, in particular:

- IOS retains all OSPF configuration.
- IOS still lists all OSPF-enabled interfaces in the OSPF interface list (**show ip ospf interface**) but in a DOWN state.

Basically, shutting down the OSPF routing protocol process gives the network engineer a way to stop using the routing protocol on that router without having to remove all the configuration. Once shut down, the **show ip ospf interface [brief]** command should still list some output, as will the **show ip ospf** command, but the rest of the commands will list nothing.

Example 21-12 shows an example on Router R5, as shown in Figure 21-5. R5 is a different router than the one used in earlier examples, but it begins the example with two OSPF neighbors, R2 and R3, with router IDs 2.2.2.2 and 3.3.3.3. The example shows the OSPF process being shut down, the neighbors failing, and those two key OSPF **show** commands: **show ip ospf neighbor** and **show ip ospf interface brief**.

21

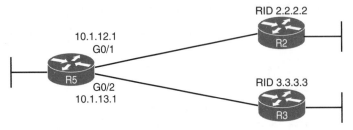

Figure 21-5 *Example Network to Demonstrate OSPF Process Shutdown*

Example 21-12 *Shutting Down an OSPF Process, and the Resulting Neighbor States*

```
R5# show ip ospf neighbor
Neighbor ID   Pri   State      Dead Time   Address      Interface
2.2.2.2         1   FULL/DR    00:00:35    10.1.12.2    GigabitEthernet0/1
3.3.3.3         1   FULL/DR    00:00:33    10.1.13.3    GigabitEthernet0/2
R5# configure terminal
Enter configuration commands, one per line. End with CNTL/Z.
R5(config)# router ospf 1
R5(config-router)# shutdown
R5(config-router)# ^Z
*Mar 23 12:43:30.634: %OSPF-5-ADJCHG: Process 1, Nbr 2.2.2.2 on GigabitEthernet0/1
  from FULL to DOWN, Neighbor Down: Interface down or detached
*Mar 23 12:43:30.635: %OSPF-5-ADJCHG: Process 1, Nbr 3.3.3.3 on GigabitEthernet0/2
  from FULL to DOWN, Neighbor Down: Interface down or detached
R5# show ip ospf interface brief
Interface   PID   Area      IP Address/Mask   Cost   State  Nbrs F/C
Gi0/1         1   0         10.1.12.1/24      1      DOWN   0/0
Gi0/2         1   0         10.1.13.1/24      1      DOWN   0/0


R5# show ip ospf
 Routing Process "ospf 1" with ID 5.5.5.5
 Start time: 5d23h, Time elapsed: 1d04h
 Routing Process is shutdown
! lines omitted for brevity


R5# show ip ospf neighbor
R5#
R5# show ip ospf database
          OSPF Router with ID (3.3.3.3) (Process ID 1)
R5#
```

First, before the **shutdown**, the **show ip ospf neighbor** command lists two neighbors.
After the **shutdown**, the same command lists no neighbors at all. Second, the **show ip ospf
interface brief** command does list the interfaces on which OSPF is enabled, on the local
router's own IP addresses. However, it lists a state of DOWN, which is a reference to the
local router's state. Also, note that the **show ip ospf** command positively states that the

OSPF process is in a shutdown state, while the **show ip ospf database** command output lists only a heading line, with no LSAs.

Issues That Allow Adjacencies but Prevent IP Routes

The last two issues to discuss in this section have a symptom in which the **show ip ospf neighbor** command does list a neighbor, but some other problem exists that prevents the eventual addition of OSPF routes to the routing table. The two issues: a mismatched MTU setting and a mismatched OSPF network type.

Mismatched MTU Settings

The MTU size defines a per-interface setting used by the router for its Layer 3 forwarding logic, defining the largest network layer packet that the router will forward out each interface. For instance, the IPv4 MTU size of an interface defines the maximum size IPv4 packet that the router can forward out an interface.

Routers often use a default MTU size of 1500 bytes, with the ability to set the value as well. The **ip mtu** *size* interface subcommand defines the IPv4 MTU setting, and the **ipv6 mtu** *size* command sets the equivalent for IPv6 packets.

In an odd twist, two OSPFv2 routers can actually become OSPF neighbors, be listed in the output of the **show ip ospf neighbor** command, and reach 2-way state, even if they happen to use different IPv4 MTU settings on their interfaces. However, they fail to exchange their LSDBs. Eventually, after trying and failing to exchange their LSDBs, the neighbor relationship also fails. So also keep a watch for MTU mismatches, although they may be unusual and obscure, by looking at the running-config and by using the **show interfaces** command (which lists the IP MTU).

Mismatched OSPF Network Types

Earlier in this chapter you read about the OSPF broadcast network type, which uses a DR/BDR, and the OSPF point-to-point network type, which does not. Interestingly, if you misconfigure network type settings such that one router uses broadcast, and the other uses point-to-point, the following occurs:

- The two routers become fully adjacent neighbors (that is, they reach a full state).
- They exchange their LSDBs.
- They do not add IP routes to the IP routing table.

The reason for not adding the routes has to do with the details of LSAs and how the use of a DR (or not) changes those LSAs. Basically, the two routers expect different details in the LSAs, and the SPF algorithm notices those differences and cannot trust the LSAs because of those differences.

For instance, earlier in Example 21-7, the configuration showed router R1 using network type point-to-point on its G0/0/0 interface, with the expectation that router R2 would also use point-to-point on its matching G0/1/0 interface. Example 21-13 shows some of the results if the engineer neglected to configure R2, leaving it with the default setting of broadcast.

Example 21-13 *Shutting Down an OSPF Process, and the Resulting Neighbor States*

```
*Apr 10 16:31:01.951: %OSPF-4-NET_TYPE_MISMATCH: Received Hello from 2.2.2.2 on
 GigabitEthernet0/0/0 indicating a potential network type mismatch
R1# show ip ospf neighbor

Neighbor ID     Pri   State         Dead Time   Address      Interface
2.2.2.2           0   FULL/  -      00:00:38    10.1.12.2    GigabitEthernet0/0/0
R1#
R2# show ip ospf neighbor

Neighbor ID     Pri   State         Dead Time   Address      Interface
1.1.1.1           1   FULL/BDR      00:00:30    10.1.12.1    GigabitEthernet0/1/0
```

As you can see, both routers list the other as an OSPF neighbor in the full state. However, R1, with network type point-to-point, does not list a DR or BDR role in the output, while R2 does, which is one clue for this type of problem. The other comes with noticing that the expected routes are not in the IP routing table.

Chapter Review

One key to doing well on the exams is to perform repetitive spaced review sessions. Review this chapter's material using either the tools in the book or interactive tools for the same material found on the book's companion website. Refer to the "Your Study Plan" element for more details. Table 21-5 outlines the key review elements and where you can find them. To better track your study progress, record when you completed these activities in the second column.

Table 21-5 Chapter Review Tracking

Review Element	Review Date(s)	Resource Used:
Review key topics		Book, website
Review command tables		Book
Review memory tables		Website
Watch video		Website

Review All the Key Topics

Table 21-6 Key Topics for Chapter 21

Key Topic Element	Description	Page Number
Table 21-2	Two OSPF Network Types and Key Behaviors	501
Example 21-3	OSPF interfaces, local roles, and neighbor counts	503
List	Rules for electing an OSPF DR/BDR	505
Example 21-8	Evidences of OSPF network type point-to-point	508

Key Topic Element	Description	Page Number
Table 21-3	Neighbor requirements for OSPF	509
Table 21-4	Useful commands to discover OSPF neighbor issues	510
List	Symptoms of an OSPF network type mismatch	515

Command References

Tables 21-7 and 21-8 list configuration and verification commands used in this chapter. As an easy review exercise, cover the left column in a table, read the right column, and try to recall the command without looking. Then repeat the exercise, covering the right column, and try to recall what the command does.

Table 21-7 Chapter 21 Configuration Command Reference

Command	Description
ip ospf hello-interval *seconds*	Interface subcommand that sets the interval for periodic Hellos
ip ospf dead-interval *number*	Interface subcommand that sets the OSPF dead timer
passive-interface *type number*	Router subcommand, for both OSPF and EIGRP, that tells the routing protocol to stop sending Hellos and stop trying to discover neighbors on that interface
ip ospf priority *value*	Interface subcommand that sets the OSPF priority, used when electing a new DR or BDR
ip ospf network {broadcast | point-to-point}	Interface subcommand used to set the OSPF network type on the interface
[no] shutdown	An OSPF configuration mode command to disable (**shutdown**) or enable (**no shutdown**) the OSPF process

Table 21-8 Chapter 21 **show** Command Reference

Command	Description
show ip protocols	Shows routing protocol parameters and current timer values, including an effective copy of the routing protocols' **network** commands and a list of passive interfaces
show ip ospf interface brief	Lists the interfaces on which the OSPF protocol is enabled (based on the **network** commands), including passive interfaces
show ip ospf interface [*type number*]	Lists detailed OSPF settings for all interfaces, or the listed interface, including Hello and dead timers and OSPF area
show ip ospf neighbor	Lists neighbors and current status with neighbors, per interface
show ip ospf	Lists a group of messages about the OSPF process itself, listing the OSPF Router ID in the first line
show interfaces	Lists a long set of messages, per interface, that lists configuration, state, and counter information

21

Part VI Review

Keep track of your part review progress with the checklist in Table P6-1. Details about each task follow the table.

Table P6-1 Part VI Part Review Checklist

Activity	1st Date Completed	2nd Date Completed
Repeat All DIKTA Questions		
Answer Part Review Questions		
Review Key Topics		
Do Labs		
Watch Videos		

Repeat All DIKTA Questions

For this task, answer the "Do I Know This Already?" questions again for the chapters in this part of the book using the PTP software. See the section "How to View Only DIKTA Questions by Chapter or Part" in the Introduction to this book to learn how to make the PTP software show you DIKTA questions for this part only.

Answer Part Review Questions

For this task, answer the Part Review questions for this part of the book using the PTP software. See the section "How to View Part Review Questions" in the Introduction to this book to learn how to make the PTP software show you Part Review questions for this part only.

Review Key Topics

Review all Key Topics in all chapters in this part, either by browsing the chapters or by using the Key Topics application on the companion website.

Do Labs

Depending on your chosen lab tool, here are some suggestions for what to do in lab:

Pearson Network Simulator: If you use the full Pearson ICND1 or CCNA simulator, focus more on the configuration scenario and troubleshooting scenario labs associated with the topics in this part of the book. These types of labs include a larger set of topics and work well as Part Review activities. (See the Introduction for some details about how to find which labs are about topics in this part of the book.)

Blog: Config Labs: The author's blog includes a series of configuration-focused labs that you can do on paper, each in 10–15 minutes. Review and perform the labs for this part of the book, as found at http://blog.certskills.com. Then navigate to the Hands-on Config labs.

Other: If using other lab tools, here are a few suggestions: Make sure to experiment heavily with VLAN configuration and VLAN trunking configuration.

Watch Videos

Chapter 21 recommends one video from the companion website about troubleshooting OSPF neighbors. Take a few minutes to watch the video if you haven't done so already.

So far, this book has mostly ignored IP version 6 (IPv6). This part reverses the trend, collecting all the specific IPv6 topics into four chapters.

The chapters in Part VII walk you through the same topics discussed throughout this book for IPv4, often using IPv4 as a point of comparison. Certainly, many details differ when comparing IPv4 and IPv6. However, many core concepts about IP addressing, subnetting, routing, and routing protocols remain the same. The chapters in this part build on those foundational concepts, adding the specific details about how IPv6 forwards IPv6 packets from one host to another.

Part VII

IP Version 6

CHAPTER 22

Fundamentals of IP Version 6

This chapter covers the following exam topics:

1.0 Network Fundamentals

1.8 Configure and verify IPv6 addressing and prefix

IPv4 has been a solid and highly useful part of the growth of TCP/IP and the Internet. For most of the long history of the Internet, and for most corporate networks that use TCP/IP, IPv4 is the core protocol that defines addressing and routing. However, even though IPv4 has many great qualities, it does have some shortcomings, creating the need for a replacement protocol: IP version 6 (IPv6).

IPv6 defines the same general functions as IPv4, but with different methods of implementing those functions. For example, both IPv4 and IPv6 define addressing, the concepts of subnetting larger groups of addresses into smaller groups, headers used to create an IPv4 or IPv6 packet, and the rules for routing those packets. At the same time, IPv6 handles the details differently; for example, using a 128-bit IPv6 address rather than the 32-bit IPv4 address.

This chapter focuses on the core network layer functions of addressing and routing. The first section of this chapter looks at the big concepts, while the second section looks at the specifics of how to write and type IPv6 addresses.

"Do I Know This Already?" Quiz

Take the quiz (either here or use the PTP software) if you want to use the score to help you decide how much time to spend on this chapter. The letter answers are listed at the bottom of the page following the quiz. Appendix C, found both at the end of the book as well as on the companion website, includes both the answers and explanations. You can also find both answers and explanations in the PTP testing software.

Table 22-1 "Do I Know This Already?" Foundation Topics Section-to-Question Mapping

Foundation Topics Section	Questions
Introduction to IPv6	1–2
IPv6 Addressing Formats and Conventions	3–6

1. Which of the following was a short-term solution to the IPv4 address exhaustion problem?

    a. IP version 6

    b. IP version 5

    c. NAT/PAT

    d. ARP

2. A router receives an Ethernet frame that holds an IPv6 packet. The router then makes a decision to route the packet out a serial link. Which of the following statements is true about how a router forwards an IPv6 packet?

    a. The router discards the Ethernet data-link header and trailer of the received frame.

    b. The router makes the forwarding decision based on the packet's source IPv6 address.

    c. The router keeps the Ethernet header, encapsulating the entire frame inside a new IPv6 packet before sending it over the serial link.

    d. The router uses the IPv4 routing table when choosing where to forward the packet.

3. Which of the following is the shortest valid abbreviation for FE80:0000:0000:0100: 0000:0000:0000:0123?

    a. FE80::100::123

    b. FE8::1::123

    c. FE80::100:0:0:0:123:4567

    d. FE80:0:0:100::123

4. Which of the following is the shortest valid abbreviation for 2000:0300:0040:0005: 6000:0700:0080:0009?

    a. 2:3:4:5:6:7:8:9

    b. 2000:300:40:5:6000:700:80:9

    c. 2000:300:4:5:6000:700:8:9

    d. 2000:3:4:5:6:7:8:9

5. Which of the following is the unabbreviated version of IPv6 address 2001:DB8::200:28?

    a. 2001:0DB8:0000:0000:0000:0000:0200:0028

    b. 2001:0DB8::0200:0028

    c. 2001:0DB8:0:0:0:0:0200:0028

    d. 2001:0DB8:0000:0000:0000:0000:200:0028

6. Which of the following is the prefix for address 2000:0000:0000:0005:6000:0700: 0080:0009, assuming a mask of /64?

    a. 2000::5::/64

    b. 2000::5:0:0:0:0/64

    c. 2000:0:0:5::/64

    d. 2000:0:0:5:0:0:0:0/64

Foundation Topics

Introduction to IPv6

IP version 6 (IPv6) serves as the replacement protocol for IP version 4 (IPv4).

Unfortunately, that one bold statement creates more questions than it answers. Why does IPv4 need to be replaced? If IPv4 needs to be replaced, when will that happen—and will it happen quickly? What exactly happens when a company or the Internet replaces IPv4 with IPv6? And the list goes on.

While this introductory chapter cannot get into every detail of why IPv4 needs to eventually be replaced by IPv6, the clearest and most obvious reason for migrating TCP/IP networks to use IPv6 is growth. IPv4 uses a 32-bit address, which totals to a few billion addresses. Interestingly, that seemingly large number of addresses is too small. IPv6 increases the address to 128 bits in length. For perspective, IPv6 supplies more than 10,000,000,000,000,000,000,000,000,000,000 times as many addresses as IPv4.

The fact that IPv6 uses a different size address field, with some different addressing rules, means that many other protocols and functions change as well. For example, IPv4 routing—in other words, the packet-forwarding process—relies on an understanding of IPv4 addresses. To support IPv6 routing, routers must understand IPv6 addresses and routing. To dynamically learn routes for IPv6 subnets, routing protocols must support these different IPv6 addressing rules, including rules about how IPv6 creates subnets. As a result, the migration from IPv4 to IPv6 is much more than changing one protocol (IP), but it impacts many protocols.

This first section of the chapter discusses some of the reasons for the change from IPv4 to IPv6, along with the protocols that must change as a result.

The Historical Reasons for IPv6

In the last 40+ years, the Internet has gone from its infancy to being a huge influence in the world. It first grew through research at universities, from the ARPANET beginnings of the Internet in the late 1960s into the 1970s. The Internet kept growing fast in the 1980s, with the Internet's fast growth still primarily driven by research and the universities that joined in that research. By the early 1990s, the Internet began to transform to allow commerce, allowing people to sell services and products over the Internet, which drove yet another steep spike upward in the growth of the Internet. Eventually, fixed Internet access (primarily through dial, digital subscriber line [DSL], and cable) became common, followed by the pervasive use of the Internet from mobile devices like smartphones. Figure 22-1 shows some of these major milestones with general dates.

The incredible growth of the Internet over a fairly long time created a big problem for public IPv4 addresses: the world was running out of addresses. For instance, in 2011, IANA allocated the final /8 address blocks (the same size as a Class A network), allocating one final /8 block to each of the five Regional Internet Registries (RIR). At that point, RIRs could no

---

Answers to the "Do I Know This Already?" quiz:
1 C **2** A **3** D **4** B **5** A **6** C

longer receive new allocations of public addresses from IANA to then turn around and assign smaller address blocks to companies or ISPs.

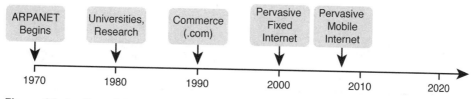

Figure 22-1   *Some Major Events in the Growth of the Internet*

At that point in 2011, each of the five RIRs still had public addresses to allocate or assign. However, that same year, APNIC (Asia Pacific) became the first RIR to exhaust its available IPv4 address allocation. In late 2015, ARIN (North America) announced that it had exhausted its supply. When we were revising this chapter in 2019, IANA considered all RIRs except AFRINIC to have exhausted their supply of IPv4 addresses, with AFRINIC expected to run out of IPv4 address during the year 2019.

These events are significant in that the day has finally come in which new companies can attempt to connect to the Internet, but they can no longer simply use IPv4, ignoring IPv6. Their only option will be IPv6 because IPv4 has no public addresses left.

NOTE   You can track ARIN's progress through this interesting transition in the history of the Internet at its IPv4 address depletion site: http://teamarin.net/category/ipv4-depletion/. You can also see a summary report at http://ipv4.potaroo.net.

Even though the press has rightfully made a big deal about running out of IPv4 addresses, those who care about the Internet knew about this potential problem since the late 1980s. The problem, generally called the *IPv4 address exhaustion* problem, could literally have caused the huge growth of the Internet in the 1990s to have come to a screeching halt! Something had to be done.

The IETF came up with several short-term solutions to make IPv4 addresses last longer, and one long-term solution: IPv6. However, several other tools like Network Address Translation (NAT) and classless interdomain routing (CIDR) helped extend IPv4's life another couple of decades. IPv6 creates a more permanent and long-lasting solution, replacing IPv4, with a new IPv6 header and new IPv6 addresses. The address size supports a huge number of addresses, solving the address shortage problem for generations (we hope). Figure 22-2 shows some of the major address exhaustion timing.

The rest of this first section examines IPv6, comparing it to IPv4, focusing on the common features of the two protocols. In particular, this section compares the protocols (including addresses), routing, routing protocols, and miscellaneous other related topics.

NOTE   You might wonder why the next version of IP is not called IP version 5. There was an earlier effort to create a new version of IP, and it was numbered version 5. IPv5 did not progress to the standards stage. However, to prevent any issues, because version 5 had been used in some documents, the next effort to update IP was numbered as version 6.

22

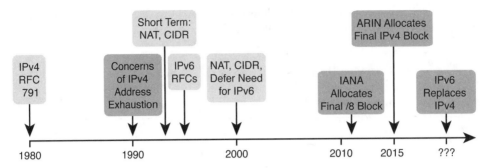

Figure 22-2 *Timeline for IPv4 Address Exhaustion and Short-/Long-Term Solutions*

The IPv6 Protocols

The primary purpose of the core IPv6 protocol mirrors the same purpose of the IPv4 protocol. That core IPv6 protocol, as defined in RFC 2460, defines a packet concept, addresses for those packets, and the role of hosts and routers. These rules allow the devices to forward packets sourced by hosts, through multiple routers, so that they arrive at the correct destination host. (IPv4 defines those same concepts for IPv4 back in RFC 791.)

However, because IPv6 impacts so many other functions in a TCP/IP network, many more RFCs must define details of IPv6. Some other RFCs define how to migrate from IPv4 to IPv6. Others define new versions of familiar protocols or replace old protocols with new ones. For example:

Older OSPF Version 2 Upgraded to OSPF Version 3: The older Open Shortest Path First (OSPF) version 2 works for IPv4, but not for IPv6, so a newer version, OSPF version 3, was created to support IPv6. (Note: OSPFv3 was later upgraded to support advertising both IPv4 and IPv6 routes.)

ICMP Upgraded to ICMP Version 6: Internet Control Message Protocol (ICMP) worked well with IPv4 but needed to be changed to support IPv6. The new name is ICMPv6.

ARP Replaced by Neighbor Discovery Protocol: For IPv4, Address Resolution Protocol (ARP) discovers the MAC address used by neighbors. IPv6 replaces ARP with a more general Neighbor Discovery Protocol (NDP).

NOTE If you go to any website that lists the RFCs, like http://www.rfc-editor.org, you can find almost 300 RFCs that have IPv6 in the title.

Although the term IPv6, when used broadly, includes many protocols, the one specific protocol called IPv6 defines the new 128-bit IPv6 address. Of course, writing these addresses in binary would be a problem—they probably would not even fit on the width of a piece of paper! IPv6 defines a shorter hexadecimal format, requiring at most 32 hexadecimal digits (one hex digit per 4 bits), with methods to abbreviate the hexadecimal addresses as well.

For example, all of the following are IPv6 addresses, each with 32 or fewer hex digits:

```
2345:1111:2222:3333:4444:5555:6666:AAAA
2000:1:2:3:4:5:6:A
FE80::1
```

The upcoming section "IPv6 Addressing Formats and Conventions" discusses the specifics of how to represent IPv6 addresses, including how to legally abbreviate the hex address values.

Like IPv4, IPv6 defines a header, with places to hold both the source and destination address fields. Compared to IPv4, the IPv6 header does make some other changes besides simply making the address fields larger. However, even though the IPv6 header is larger than an IPv4 header, the IPv6 header is actually simpler (on purpose), to reduce the work done each time a router must route an IPv6 packet. Figure 22-3 shows the required 40-byte part of the IPv6 header.

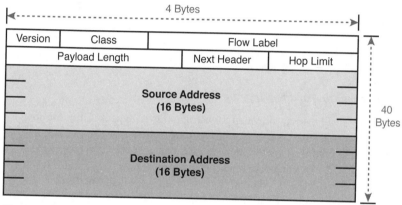

Figure 22-3 *IPv6 Header*

IPv6 Routing

As with many functions of IPv6, IPv6 routing looks just like IPv4 routing from a general perspective, with the differences being clear only once you look at the specifics. Keeping the discussion general for now, IPv6 uses these ideas the same way as IPv4:

■ To be able to build and send IPv6 packets out an interface, end-user devices need an IPv6 address on that interface.

■ End-user hosts need to know the IPv6 address of a default router, to which the host sends IPv6 packets if the host is in a different subnet.

■ IPv6 routers de-encapsulate and re-encapsulate each IPv6 packet when routing the packet.

■ IPv6 routers make routing decisions by comparing the IPv6 packet's destination address to the router's IPv6 routing table; the matched route lists directions of where to send the IPv6 packet next.

NOTE You could take the preceding list and replace every instance of IPv6 with IPv4, and all the statements would be true of IPv4 as well.

While the list shows some concepts that should be familiar from IPv4, the next few figures show the concepts with an example. First, Figure 22-4 shows a few settings on a host.

The host (PC1) has an address of 2345::1. PC1 also knows its default gateway of 2345::2. (Both values are valid abbreviations for real IPv6 addresses.) To send an IPv6 packet to host PC2, on another IPv6 subnet, PC1 creates an IPv6 packet and sends it to R1, PC1's default gateway.

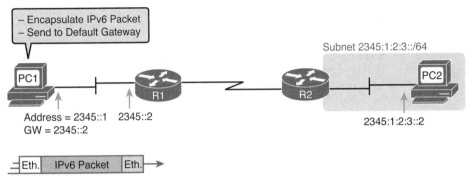

Figure 22-4 *IPv6 Host Building and Sending an IPv6 Packet*

The router (R1) has many small tasks to do when forwarding this IPv6 packet, but for now, focus on the work R1 does related to encapsulation. As seen in Step 1 of Figure 22-5, R1 receives the incoming data-link frame and extracts (de-encapsulates) the IPv6 packet from inside the frame, discarding the original data-link header and trailer. At Step 2, once R1 knows to forward the IPv6 packet to R2, R1 adds a correct outgoing data-link header and trailer to the IPv6 packet, encapsulating the IPv6 packet.

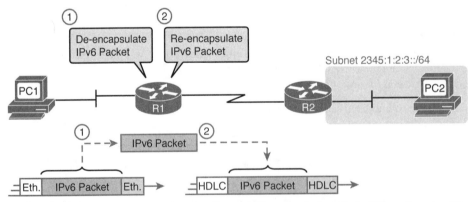

Figure 22-5 *IPv6 Router Performing Routine Encapsulation Tasks When Routing IPv6*

When a router like R1 de-encapsulates the packet from the data-link frame, it must also decide what type of packet sits inside the frame. To do so, the router must look at a protocol type field in the data-link header, which identifies the type of packet inside the data-link frame. Today, most data-link frames carry either an IPv4 packet or an IPv6 packet.

To route an IPv6 packet, a router must use its IPv6 routing table instead of the IPv4 routing table. The router must look at the packet's destination IPv6 address and compare that address to the router's current IPv6 routing table. The router uses the forwarding instructions in the matched IPv6 route to forward the IPv6 packet. Figure 22-6 shows the overall process.

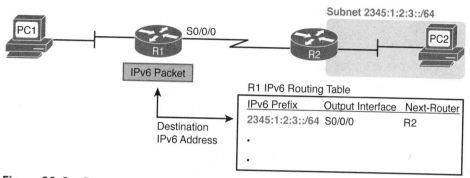

Figure 22-6 *Comparing an IPv6 Packet to R1's IPv6 Routing Table*

Note that again, the process works like IPv4, except that the IPv6 packet lists IPv6 addresses, and the IPv6 routing table lists routing information for IPv6 subnets (called prefixes).

Finally, in most enterprise networks, the routers will route both IPv4 and IPv6 packets at the same time. That is, your company will not decide to adopt IPv6, and then late one weekend night turn off all IPv4 and enable IPv6 on every device. Instead, IPv6 allows for a slow migration, during which some or all routers forward both IPv4 and IPv6 packets. (The migration strategy of running both IPv4 and IPv6 is called *dual stack*.) All you have to do is configure the router to route IPv6 packets, in addition to the existing configuration for routing IPv4 packets.

IPv6 Routing Protocols

IPv6 routers need to learn routes for all the possible IPv6 prefixes (subnets). Just like with IPv4, IPv6 routers use routing protocols, with familiar names, and generally speaking, with familiar functions.

None of the IPv4 routing protocols could be used to advertise IPv6 routes originally. They all required some kind of update to add messages, protocols, and rules to support IPv6. Over time, Routing Information Protocol (RIP), Open Shortest Path First (OSPF), Enhanced Interior Gateway Routing Protocol (EIGRP), and Border Gateway Protocol (BGP) were all updated to support IPv6. Table 22-2 lists the names of these routing protocols, with a few comments.

Table 22-2   IPv6 Routing Protocols

Routing Protocol	Defined By	Notes
RIPng (RIP next generation)	RFC	The "next generation" is a reference to a TV series, *Star Trek: the Next Generation*.
OSPFv3 (OSPF version 3)	RFC	The OSPF you have worked with for IPv4 is actually OSPF version 2, so the new version for IPv6 is OSPFv3.
EIGRPv6 (EIGRP for IPv6)	Cisco	Cisco owns the rights to the EIGRP protocol, but Cisco also now publishes EIGRP as an informational RFC.
MP BGP-4 (Multiprotocol BGP version 4)	RFC	BGP version 4 was created to be highly extendable; IPv6 support was added to BGP version 4 through one such enhancement, MP BGP-4.

22

In addition, these routing protocols also follow the same interior gateway protocol (IGP) and exterior gateway protocol (EGP) conventions as their IPv4 cousins. RIPng, EIGRPv6, and OSPFv3 act as interior gateway protocols, advertising IPv6 routes inside an enterprise.

As you can see from this introduction, IPv6 uses many of the same big ideas as IPv4. Both define headers with a source and destination address. Both define the routing of packets, with the routing process discarding old data-link headers and trailers when forwarding the packets. And routers use the same general process to make a routing decision, comparing the packet's destination IP address to the routing table.

The big differences between IPv4 and IPv6 revolve around the bigger IPv6 addresses. The next topic begins looking at the specifics of these IPv6 addresses.

IPv6 Addressing Formats and Conventions

The CCNA exam requires some fundamental skills in working with IPv4 addresses. For example, you need to be able to interpret IPv4 addresses, like 172.21.73.14. You need to be able to work with prefix-style masks, like /25, and interpret what that means when used with a particular IPv4 address. And you need to be able to take an address and mask, like 172.21.73.14/25, and find the subnet ID.

This second major section of this chapter discusses these same ideas for IPv6 addresses. In particular, this section looks at

- How to write and interpret unabbreviated 32-digit IPv6 addresses
- How to abbreviate IPv6 addresses and how to interpret abbreviated addresses
- How to interpret the IPv6 prefix length mask
- How to find the IPv6 prefix (subnet ID), based on an address and prefix length mask

The biggest challenge with these tasks lies in the sheer size of the numbers. Thankfully, the math to find the subnet ID—often a challenge for IPv4—is easier for IPv6, at least to the depth discussed in this book.

Representing Full (Unabbreviated) IPv6 Addresses

IPv6 uses a convenient hexadecimal (hex) format for addresses. To make it more readable, IPv6 uses a format with eight sets of four hex digits, with each set of four digits separated by a colon. For example:

```
2340:1111:AAAA:0001:1234:5678:9ABC:1234
```

> **NOTE**   For convenience, the author uses the term *quartet* for one set of four hex digits, with eight quartets in each IPv6 address. Note that the IPv6 RFCs do not use the term *quartet*.

IPv6 addresses also have a binary format as well, but thankfully, most of the time you do not need to look at the binary version of the addresses. However, in those cases, converting from hex to binary is relatively easy. Just change each hex digit to the equivalent 4-bit value listed in Table 22-3.

Table 22-3   Hexadecimal/Binary Conversion Chart

Hex	Binary	Hex	Binary
0	0000	8	1000
1	0001	9	1001
2	0010	A	1010
3	0011	B	1011
4	0100	C	1100
5	0101	D	1101
6	0110	E	1110
7	0111	F	1111

Abbreviating and Expanding IPv6 Addresses

IPv6 also defines ways to abbreviate or shorten how you write or type an IPv6 address. Why? Although using a 32-digit hex number works much better than working with a 128-bit binary number, 32 hex digits are still a lot of digits to remember, recognize in command output, and type on a command line. The IPv6 address abbreviation rules let you shorten these numbers.

Computers and routers typically use the shortest abbreviation, even if you type all 32 hex digits of the address. So even if you would prefer to use the longer unabbreviated version of the IPv6 address, you need to be ready to interpret the meaning of an abbreviated IPv6 address as listed by a router or host. This section first looks at abbreviating addresses and then at expanding addresses.

Abbreviating IPv6 Addresses

Two basic rules let you, or any computer, shorten or abbreviate an IPv6 address:

1. Inside each quartet of four hex digits, remove the leading 0s (0s on the left side of the quartet) in the three positions on the left. (Note: at this step, a quartet of 0000 will leave a single 0.)

2. Find any string of two or more consecutive quartets of all hex 0s, and replace that set of quartets with a double colon (::). The :: means "two or more quartets of all 0s." However, you can use :: only once in a single address because otherwise the exact IPv6 might not be clear.

For example, consider the following IPv6 address. The bold digits represent digits in which the address could be abbreviated.

`FE00:0000:0000:0001:0000:0000:0000:0056`

Applying the first rule, you would look at all eight quartets independently. In each, remove all the leading 0s. Note that five of the quartets have four 0s, so for these, remove only three 0s, leaving the following value:

`FE00:0:0:1:0:0:0:56`

While this abbreviation is valid, the address can be abbreviated more, using the second rule. In this case, two instances exist where more than one quartet in a row has only a 0. Pick the longest such sequence, and replace it with ::, giving you the shortest legal abbreviation:

```
FE00:0:0:1::56
```

While FE00:0:0:1::56 is indeed the shortest abbreviation, this example happens to make it easier to see the two most common mistakes when abbreviating IPv6 addresses. First, never remove trailing 0s in a quartet (0s on the right side of the quartet). In this case, the first quartet of FE00 cannot be shortened at all because the two 0s trail. So, the following address, which begins now with only FE in the first quartet, is not a correct abbreviation of the original IPv6 address:

```
FE:0:0:1::56
```

The second common mistake is to replace all series of all 0 quartets with a double colon. For example, the following abbreviation would be incorrect for the original IPv6 address listed in this topic:

```
FE00::1::56
```

The reason this abbreviation is incorrect is that now you do not know how many quartets of all 0s to substitute into each :: to find the original unabbreviated address.

Expanding Abbreviated IPv6 Addresses

To expand an IPv6 address back into its full unabbreviated 32-digit number, use two similar rules. The rules basically reverse the logic of the previous two rules:

1. In each quartet, add leading 0s as needed until the quartet has four hex digits.

2. If a double colon (::) exists, count the quartets currently shown; the total should be less than 8. Replace the :: with multiple quartets of 0000 so that eight total quartets exist.

The best way to get comfortable with these addresses and abbreviations is to do some yourself. Table 22-4 lists some practice problems, with the full 32-digit IPv6 address on the left and the best abbreviation on the right. The table gives you either the expanded or abbreviated address, and you need to supply the opposite value. The answers sit at the end of the chapter, in the section "Answers to Earlier Practice Problems."

Table 22-4   IPv6 Address Abbreviation and Expansion Practice

Full	Abbreviation
2340:0000:0010:0100:1000:ABCD:0101:1010	
	30A0:ABCD:EF12:3456:ABC:B0B0:9999:9009
2222:3333:4444:5555:0000:0000:6060:0707	
	3210::
210F:0000:0000:0000:CCCC:0000:0000:000D	
	34BA:B:B::20
FE80:0000:0000:0000:DEAD:BEFF:FEEF:CAFE	
	FE80::FACE:BAFF:FEBE:CAFE

Representing the Prefix Length of an Address

IPv6 uses a mask concept, called the *prefix length*, similar to IPv4 subnet masks. Similar to the IPv4 prefix-style mask, the IPv6 prefix length is written as a /, followed by a decimal number. The prefix length defines how many bits of the IPv6 address define the IPv6 prefix, which is basically the same concept as the IPv4 subnet ID.

When writing an IPv6 address and prefix length in documentation, you can choose to leave a space before the /, or not, as shown in the next two examples.

```
2222:1111:0:1:A:B:C:D/64
2222:1111:0:1:A:B:C:D /64
```

Finally, note that the prefix length is a number of bits, so with IPv6, the legal value range is from 0 through 128, inclusive.

Calculating the IPv6 Prefix (Subnet ID)

With IPv4, you can take an IP address and the associated subnet mask, and calculate the subnet ID. With IPv6 subnetting, you can take an IPv6 address and the associated prefix length, and calculate the IPv6 equivalent of the subnet ID: an *IPv6 prefix*.

Like with different IPv4 subnet masks, some IPv6 prefix lengths make for an easy math problem to find the IPv6 prefix, while some prefix lengths make the math more difficult. This section looks at the easier cases, mainly because the size of the IPv6 address space lets us all choose to use IPv6 prefix lengths that make the math much easier.

Finding the IPv6 Prefix

In IPv6, a prefix represents a group of IPv6 addresses. For now, this section focuses on the math, and only the math, for finding the number that represents that prefix. Chapter 23, "IPv6 Addressing and Subnetting," then starts putting more meaning behind the actual numbers.

Each IPv6 prefix, or subnet if you prefer, has a number that represents the group. Per the IPv6 RFCs, the number itself is also called the *prefix*, but many people just call it a subnet number or subnet ID, using the same terms as IPv4.

As with IPv4, you can start with an IPv6 address and prefix length, and find the prefix, with the same general rules that you use in IPv4. If the prefix length is /P, use these rules:

1. Copy the first P bits.

2. Change the rest of the bits to 0.

When using a prefix length that happens to be a multiple of 4, you do not have to think in terms of bits, but in terms of hex digits. A prefix length that is a multiple of 4 means that each hex digit is either copied or changed to hex 0. Just for completeness, if the prefix length is indeed a multiple of 4, the process becomes

1. Identify the number of hex digits in the prefix by dividing the prefix length (which is in bits) by 4.

2. Copy the hex digits determined to be in the prefix per the first step.

3. Change the rest of the hex digits to 0.

Figure 22-7 shows an example, with a prefix length of 64. In this case, Step 1 looks at the /64 prefix length and calculates that the prefix has 16 hex digits. Step 2 copies the first 16 digits of the IPv6 address, while Step 3 records hex 0s for the rest of the digits.

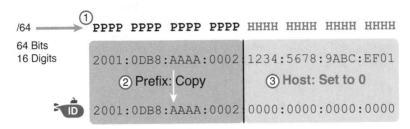

Legend:

ID Subnet ID

Figure 22-7 *Creating the IPv6 Prefix from an Address/Length*

After you find the IPv6 prefix, you should also be ready to abbreviate the IPv6 prefix using the same rules you use to abbreviate IPv6 addresses. However, you should pay extra attention to the end of the prefix because it often has several octets of all 0 values. As a result, the abbreviation typically ends with two colons (::).

For example, consider the following IPv6 address that is assigned to a host on a LAN:

`2000:1234:5678:9ABC:1234:5678:9ABC:1111/64`

This example shows an IPv6 address that itself cannot be abbreviated. After you calculate the prefix for the subnet in which the address resides, by zeroing out the last 64 bits (16 digits) of the address, you find the following prefix value:

`2000:1234:5678:9ABC:`**`0000:0000:0000:0000`**`/64`

This value can be abbreviated, with four quartets of all 0s at the end, as follows:

`2000:1234:5678:9ABC::/64`

To get better at the math, take some time to work through finding the prefix for several practice problems, as listed in Table 22-5. The answers sit at the end of the chapter, in the section "Answers to Earlier Practice Problems."

Table 22-5 Finding the IPv6 Prefix from an Address/Length Value

Address/Length	Prefix
`2340:0:10:100:1000:ABCD:101:1010/64`	
`30A0:ABCD:EF12:3456:ABC:B0B0:9999:9009/64`	
`2222:3333:4444:5555::6060:707/64`	
`3210::ABCD:101:1010/64`	

Address/Length	Prefix
210F::CCCC:B0B0:9999:9009/64	
34BA:B:B:0:5555:0:6060:707/64	
3124::DEAD:CAFE:FF:FE00:1/64	
2BCD::FACE:BEFF:FEBE:CAFE/64	

Working with More-Difficult IPv6 Prefix Lengths

Some prefix lengths make the math to find the prefix very easy, some mostly easy, and some require you to work in binary. If the prefix length is a multiple of 16, the process of copying part of the address copies entire quartets. If the prefix length is not a multiple of 16 but is a multiple of 4, at least the boundary sits at the edge of a hex digit, so you can avoid working in binary.

Although the /64 prefix length is by far the most common prefix length, you should be ready to find the prefix when using a prefix length that is any multiple of 4. For example, consider the following IPv6 address and prefix length:

2000:1234:5678:9ABC:1234:5678:9ABC:1111/56

Because this example uses a /56 prefix length, the prefix includes the first 56 bits, or first 14 complete hex digits, of the address. The rest of the hex digits will be 0, resulting in the following prefix:

2000:1234:5678:9A00:0000:0000:0000:0000/56

This value can be abbreviated, with four quartets of all 0s at the end, as follows:

2000:1234:5678:9A00::/56

This example shows an easy place to make a mistake. Sometimes, people look at the /56 and think of that as the first 14 hex digits, which is correct. However, they then copy the first 14 hex digits and add a double colon, showing the following:

2000:1234:5678:9A::/56

This abbreviation is not correct because it removed the trailing "00" at the end of the fourth quartet. If you expanded the abbreviated value, it would begin with 2000:1234:5678:009A, not 2000:1234:5678:9A00. So, be careful when abbreviating when the boundary is not at the edge of a quartet.

Once again, some extra practice can help. Table 22-6 uses examples that have a prefix length that is a multiple of 4, but is not on a quartet boundary, just to get some extra practice. The answers sit at the end of the chapter, in the section "Answers to Earlier Practice Problems."

22

Table 22-6   Finding the IPv6 Prefix from an Address/Length Value

Address/Length	Prefix
`34BA:B:B:0:5555:0:6060:707/80`	
`3124::DEAD:CAFE:FF:FE00:1/80`	
`2BCD::FACE:BEFF:FEBE:CAFE/48`	
`3FED:F:E0:D00:FACE:BAFF:FE00:0/48`	
`210F:A:B:C:CCCC:B0B0:9999:9009/40`	
`34BA:B:B:0:5555:0:6060:707/36`	
`3124::DEAD:CAFE:FF:FE00:1/60`	
`2BCD::FACE:1:BEFF:FEBE:CAFE/56`	

Chapter Review

One key to doing well on the exams is to perform repetitive spaced review sessions. Review this chapter's material using either the tools in the book or interactive tools for the same material found on the book's companion website. Refer to the "Your Study Plan" element for more details. Table 22-7 outlines the key review elements and where you can find them. To better track your study progress, record when you completed these activities in the second column.

Table 22-7   Chapter Review Tracking

Review Element	Review Date(s)	Resource Used
Review key topics		Book, website
Review key terms		Book, website
Repeat DIKTA questions		Book, PTP
Review command tables		Book
Review memory table		Book, website

Review All the Key Topics

Table 22-8   Key Topics for Chapter 22

Key Topic Element	Description	Page Number
List	Similarities between IPv4 and IPv6	527
List	Rules for abbreviating IPv6 addresses	531
List	Rules for expanding an abbreviated IPv6 address	532
List	Process steps to find an IPv6 prefix, based on the IPv6 address and prefix length	533

Key Terms You Should Know

IPv4 address exhaustion, IP version 6 (IPv6), OSPF version 3 (OSPFv3), EIGRP version 6 (EIGRPv6), prefix, prefix length, quartet

Additional Practice for This Chapter's Processes

For additional practice with IPv6 abbreviations, you may do the same set of practice problems based on Appendix G, "Practice for Chapter 22: Fundamentals of IP Version 6." You have two options to use:

PDF: Navigate to the companion website and open the PDF for Appendix G.

Application: Navigate to the companion website and use these applications:

"Practice Exercise: Abbreviating and Expanding Addresses"

"Practice Exercise: Calculating the IPv6 Prefix"

"Practice Exercise: Calculating the IPv6 Prefix Round 2"

Answers to Earlier Practice Problems

This chapter includes practice problems spread around different locations in the chapter. The answers are located in Tables 22-9, 22-10, and 22-11.

Table 22-9   Answers to Questions in the Earlier Table 22-4

Full	Abbreviation
2340:0000:0010:0100:1000:ABCD:0101:1010	2340:0:10:100:1000:ABCD:101:1010
30A0:ABCD:EF12:3456:0ABC:B0B0:9999:9009	30A0:ABCD:EF12:3456:ABC:B0B0:9999:9009
2222:3333:4444:5555:0000:0000:6060:0707	2222:3333:4444:5555::6060:707
3210:0000:0000:0000:0000:0000:0000:0000	3210::
210F:0000:0000:0000:CCCC:0000:0000:000D	210F::CCCC:0:0:D
34BA:000B:000B:0000:0000:0000:0000:0020	34BA:B:B::20
FE80:0000:0000:0000:DEAD:BEFF:FEEF:CAFE	FE80::DEAD:BEFF:FEEF:CAFE
FE80:0000:0000:0000:FACE:BAFF:FEBE:CAFE	FE80::FACE:BAFF:FEBE:CAFE

Table 22-10   Answers to Questions in the Earlier Table 22-5

Address/Length	Prefix
2340:0:10:100:1000:ABCD:101:1010/64	2340:0:10:100::/64
30A0:ABCD:EF12:3456:ABC:B0B0:9999:9009/64	30A0:ABCD:EF12:3456::/64
2222:3333:4444:5555::6060:707/64	2222:3333:4444:5555::/64
3210::ABCD:101:1010/64	3210::/64
210F::CCCC:B0B0:9999:9009/64	210F::/64
34BA:B:B:0:5555:0:6060:707/64	34BA:B:B::/64
3124::DEAD:CAFE:FF:FE00:1/64	3124:0:0:DEAD::/64
2BCD::FACE:BEFF:FEBE:CAFE/64	2BCD::/64

22

Table 22-11 Answers to Questions in the Earlier Table 22-6

Address/Length	Prefix
34BA:B:B:0:5555:0:6060:707/80	34BA:B:B:0:5555::/80
3124::DEAD:CAFE:FF:FE00:1/80	3124:0:0:DEAD:CAFE::/80
2BCD::FACE:BEFF:FEBE:CAFE/48	2BCD::/48
3FED:F:E0:D00:FACE:BAFF:FE00:0/48	3FED:F:E0::/48
210F:A:B:C:CCCC:B0B0:9999:9009/40	210F:A::/40
34BA:B:B:0:5555:0:6060:707/36	34BA:B::/36
3124::DEAD:CAFE:FF:FE00:1/60	3124:0:0:DEA0::/60
2BCD::FACE:1:BEFF:FEBE:CAFE/56	2BCD:0:0:FA00::/56

CHAPTER 23

IPv6 Addressing and Subnetting

This chapter covers the following exam topics:

1.0 Network Fundamentals

1.8 Configure and verify IPv6 addressing and prefix

1.9 Compare and contrast IPv6 address types

1.9.a Global unicast

1.9.b Unique local

IPv4 organizes the address space in a couple of ways. First, IPv4 splits addresses by class, with Classes A, B, and C defining unicast IPv4 addresses. (The term *unicast* refers to the fact that each address is used by only one interface.) Then, within the Class A, B, and C address range, the Internet Assigned Numbers Authority (IANA) and the Internet Corporation for Assigned Names and Numbers (ICANN) reserve most of the addresses as public IPv4 addresses, with a few reserved as private IPv4 addresses.

IPv6 does not use any concept like the classful network concept used by IPv4. However, IANA does still reserve some IPv6 address ranges for specific purposes, even with some address ranges that serve as both public IPv6 addresses and private IPv6 addresses. IANA also attempts to take a practical approach to reserving ranges of the entire IPv6 address space for different purposes, using the wisdom gained from several decades of fast growth in the IPv4 Internet.

This chapter has two major sections. The first examines *global unicast addresses*, which serve as public IPv6 addresses. The second major section looks at *unique local addresses*, which serve as private IPv6 addresses.

"Do I Know This Already?" Quiz

Take the quiz (either here or use the PTP software) if you want to use the score to help you decide how much time to spend on this chapter. The letter answers are listed at the bottom of the page following the quiz. Appendix C, found both at the end of the book as well as on the companion website, includes both the answers and explanations. You can also find both answers and explanations in the PTP testing software.

Table 23-1 "Do I Know This Already?" Foundation Topics Section-to-Question Mapping

Foundation Topics Section	Questions
Global Unicast Addressing Concepts	1–4
Unique Local Unicast Addresses	5

1. Which of the following IPv6 addresses appears to be a unique local unicast address, based on its first few hex digits?

   a. 3123:1:3:5::1

   b. FE80::1234:56FF:FE78:9ABC

   c. FDAD::1

   d. FF00::5

2. Which of the following IPv6 addresses appears to be a global unicast address, based on its first few hex digits?

   a. 3123:1:3:5::1

   b. FE80::1234:56FF:FE78:9ABC

   c. FDAD::1

   d. FF00::5

3. When subnetting an IPv6 address block, an engineer shows a drawing that breaks the address structure into three pieces. Comparing this concept to a three-part IPv4 address structure, which part of the IPv6 address structure is most like the IPv4 network part of the address?

   a. Subnet

   b. Interface ID

   c. Network

   d. Global routing prefix

   e. Subnet router anycast

4. When subnetting an IPv6 address block, an engineer shows a drawing that breaks the address structure into three pieces. Assuming that all subnets use the same prefix length, which of the following answers lists the name of the field on the far right side of the address?

   a. Subnet

   b. Interface ID

   c. Network

   d. Global routing prefix

   e. Subnet router anycast

5. For the IPv6 address FD00:1234:5678:9ABC:DEF1:2345:6789:ABCD, which part of the address is considered the global ID of the unique local address?

   a. None; this address has no global ID.

   b. 00:1234:5678:9ABC

   c. DEF1:2345:6789:ABCD

   d. 00:1234:5678

   e. FD00

Foundation Topics

Global Unicast Addressing Concepts

This first major section of the chapter focuses on one type of unicast IPv6 addresses: global unicast addresses. As it turns out, many of the general concepts and processes behind these global unicast IPv6 addresses follow the original intent for public IPv4 addresses. So, this section begins with a review of some IPv4 concepts, followed by the details of how a company can use global unicast addresses.

This first section also discusses IPv6 subnetting and the entire process of taking a block of global unicast addresses and creating subnets for one company. This process takes a globally unique global routing prefix, creates IPv6 subnets, and assigns IPv6 addresses from within each subnet, much like with IPv4.

Public and Private IPv6 Addresses

In the history of IPv4 addressing, the world started out with a plan that gave every single host a globally unique public IPv4 address. However, as discussed in several places already, the IPv4 address space had too few addresses. So, in the 1990s, companies started using addresses from the private IPv4 address range, as defined in RFC 1918. These companies either simply did not connect to the Internet, or to connect to the Internet, they used Network Address Translation (NAT), sharing a few public globally unique IPv4 addresses for all host connections into the Internet.

IPv6 allows two similar options of public and private unicast addressing, beginning with *global unicast* addresses as the public IPv6 address space. Similar to public IPv4 addresses, IPv6 global unicast addresses rely on an administrative process that assigns each company a unique IPv6 address block. Each company then subnets this IPv6 address block and only uses addresses from within that block. The result: that company uses addresses that are unique across the globe as well.

The second IPv6 option uses *unique local* IPv6 addresses, which work more like the IPv4 private addresses. Companies that do not plan to connect to the Internet and companies that plan to use IPv6 NAT can use these private unique local addresses. The process also works similarly to IPv4: The engineer can read the details in an RFC, pick some numbers, and start assigning IPv6 addresses without having to register with IANA or any other authority.

The following lists summarizes the comparisons between global unicast addresses and unique local addresses:

Global unicast: Addresses that work like public IPv4 addresses. The organization that needs IPv6 addresses asks for a registered IPv6 address block, which is assigned as a global routing prefix. After that, only that organization uses the addresses inside that block of addresses—that is, the addresses that begin with the assigned prefix.

Unique local: Works somewhat like private IPv4 addresses, with the possibility that multiple organizations use the exact same addresses, and with no requirement for registering with any numbering authority.

Answers to the "Do I Know This Already?" quiz:
1 C **2** A **3** D **4** B **5** D

The rest of this first major section of the chapter examines global unicast addresses in more detail, while the second major section of the chapter examines unique local addresses.

The IPv6 Global Routing Prefix

IPv6 global unicast addresses allow IPv6 to work more like the original design of the IPv4 Internet. Each organization asks for a block of IPv6 addresses, which no one else can use. That organization further subdivides the address block into smaller chunks, called *subnets*. Finally, to choose what IPv6 address to use for any host, the engineer chooses an address from the right subnet.

That reserved block of IPv6 addresses—a set of addresses that only one company can use—is called a *global routing prefix*. Each organization that wants to connect to the Internet and use IPv6 global unicast addresses should ask for and receive a global routing prefix. Very generally, you can think of the global routing prefix like an IPv4 Class A, B, or C network number from the range of public IPv4 addresses.

The term *global routing prefix* might not make you think of a block of IPv6 addresses at first. The term actually refers to the idea that Internet routers can have one route that refers to all the addresses inside the address block, without a need to have routes for smaller parts of that block. For example, Figure 23-1 shows three companies, with three different IPv6 global routing prefixes; the router on the right (R4) has one IPv6 route for each global routing prefix.

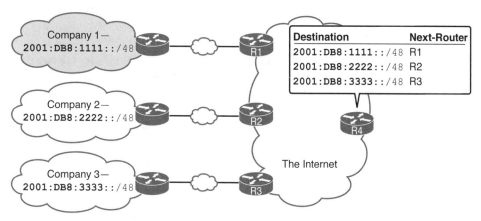

Figure 23-1   *Three Global Routing Prefixes, with One Route per Prefix*

The global routing prefix sets those IPv6 addresses apart for use by that one company, just like a public IPv4 network or CIDR address block does in IPv4. All IPv6 addresses inside that company should begin with that global routing prefix, to avoid using other companies' IPv6 addresses. No other companies should use IPv6 addresses with that same prefix. And thankfully, IPv6 has plenty of space to allow all companies to have a global routing prefix, with plenty of addresses.

Both the IPv6 and IPv4 address assignment processes rely on the same organizations: IANA (along with ICANN), the Regional Internet Registries (RIR), and ISPs. For example, an imaginary company, Company1, received the assignment of a global routing prefix. The prefix means "All addresses whose first 12 hex digits are 2001:0DB8:1111," as represented by prefix 2001:0DB8:1111::/48. To receive that assignment, the process shown in Figure 23-2 happened.

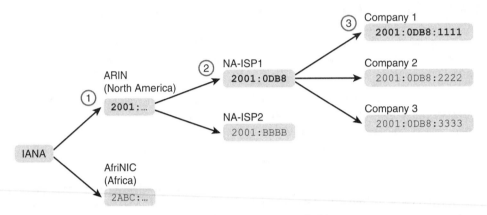

Figure 23-2 *Prefix Assignment with IANA, RIRs, and ISPs*

The event timeline in the figure uses a left-to-right flow; in other words, the event on the far left must happen first. Following the flow from left to right in the figure:

1. **IANA allocates ARIN prefix 2001::/16:** ARIN (the RIR for North America) asks IANA for the allocation of a large block of addresses. In this imaginary example, IANA gives ARIN a prefix of "all addresses that begin 2001," or 2001::/16.

2. **ARIN allocates NA-ISP1 prefix 2001:0DB8::/32:** NA-ISP1, an imaginary ISP based in North America, asks ARIN for a new IPv6 prefix. ARIN takes a subset of its 2001::/16 prefix, specifically all addresses that begin with the 32 bits (8 hex digits) 2001:0DB8, and allocates it to the ISP.

3. **NA-ISP1 assigns Company 1 2001:0DB8:1111::/48:** Company 1 decides to start supporting IPv6, so it goes to its ISP, NA-ISP1, to ask for a block of global unicast addresses. NA-ISP1 assigns Company 1 a "small" piece of NA-ISP1's address block, in this case the addresses that begin with the 48 bits (12 hex digits) of 2001:0DB8:1111 (2001:0DB8:1111::/48).

> **NOTE** If you do not plan to connect to the Internet using IPv6 for a while and just want to experiment, you do not need to ask for an IPv6 global routing prefix to be assigned. Just make up IPv6 addresses and configure your devices, or use unique local addresses as discussed toward the end of this chapter.

Address Ranges for Global Unicast Addresses

Global unicast addresses make up the majority of the IPv6 address space. However, unlike IPv4, the rules for which IPv6 addresses fall into which category are purposefully more flexible than they were with IPv4 and the rules for IPv4 Classes A, B, C, D, and E.

Originally, IANA reserved all IPv6 addresses that begin with hex 2 or 3 as global unicast addresses. (This address range can be written succinctly as prefix 2000::/3.)

Later IANA made the global unicast address range wider, basically to include all IPv6 addresses not otherwise allocated for other purposes. For example, the unique local unicast addresses, discussed later in this chapter, all start with hex FD. So, while global unicast addresses would not include any addresses that begin with FD, any address ranges that are not specifically reserved, for now, are considered to be global unicast addresses.

Finally, just because an amazingly enormous number of addresses sit within the global unicast address range, IANA does not assign prefixes from all over the address range. IPv4 has survived well for more than 30 years with an admittedly too-small address size because IANA has adopted good practices to conserve the IPv4 address space. By making smart and practical choices in assigning IPv6 addresses, the IPv6 address space could last much longer than IPv4.

Table 23-2 lists the address prefixes discussed in this book and their purpose.

Table 23-2   Some Types of IPv6 Addresses and Their First Hex Digit(s)

Address Type	First Hex Digits
Global unicast	2 or 3 (originally); all not otherwise reserved (today)
Unique local	FD
Multicast	FF
Link local	FE80

IPv6 Subnetting Using Global Unicast Addresses

After an enterprise has a block of reserved global unicast addresses—in other words, a global routing prefix—the company needs to subdivide that large address block into subnets.

Subnetting IPv6 addresses works generally like IPv4, but with mostly simpler math (hoorah!). Because of the absolutely large number of addresses available, most everyone uses the easiest possible IPv6 prefix length: /64. Using /64 as the prefix length for all subnets makes the IPv6 subnetting math just as easy as using a /24 mask for all IPv4 subnets. In addition, the dynamic IPv6 address assignment process works better with a /64 prefix length as well; so in practice, and in this book, expect IPv6 designs to use a /64 prefix length.

This section does walk you through the different parts of IPv6 subnetting, while mostly using examples that use a /64 prefix length. The discussion defines the rules about which addresses should be in the same subnet and which addresses need to be in different subnets. Plus this section looks at how to analyze the global routing prefix and associated prefix length to find all the IPv6 prefixes (subnet IDs) and the addresses in each subnet.

NOTE   If the IPv4 subnetting concepts are a little vague, you might want to reread Chapter 11, "Perspectives on IPv4 Subnetting," which discusses the subnetting concepts for IPv4.

23

Deciding Where IPv6 Subnets Are Needed

First, IPv6 and IPv4 both use the same concepts about where a subnet is needed: one for each VLAN and one for each point-to-point WAN connection (serial and Ethernet). Figure 23-3 shows an example of the idea, using the small enterprise internetwork of Company 1. Company 1 has two LANs, with a point-to-point serial link connecting the sites. It also has an Ethernet WAN link connected to an ISP. Using the same logic you would use for IPv4, Company 1 needs four IPv6 subnets.

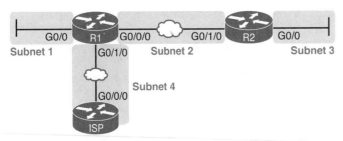

Figure 23-3 *Locations for IPv6 Subnets*

The Mechanics of Subnetting IPv6 Global Unicast Addresses

To understand how to subnet your one large block of IPv6 addresses, you need to understand some of the theory and mechanisms IPv6 uses. To learn those details, it can help to compare IPv6 with some similar concepts from IPv4.

With IPv4, without subnetting, an address has two parts: a network part and a host part. Class A, B, and C rules define the length of the network part, with the host part making up the rest of the 32-bit IPv4 address, as shown in Figure 23-4.

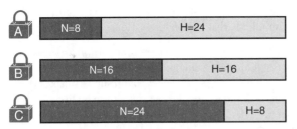

Figure 23-4 *Classful View of Unsubnetted IPv4 Networks*

To subnet an IPv4 Class A, B, or C network, the network engineer for the enterprise makes some choices. Conceptually, the engineer creates a three-part view of the addresses, adding a subnet field in the center while shortening the host field. (Many people call this "borrowing host bits.") The size of the network part stays locked per the Class A, B, and C rules, with the line between the subnet and host part being flexible, based on the choice of subnet mask. Figure 23-5 shows the idea for a subnetted Class B network.

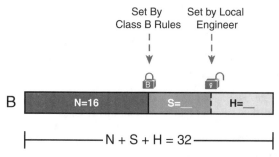

Figure 23-5 *Classful View of Subnetted IPv4 Networks*

IPv6 uses a similar concept, with the details in Figure 23-6. The structure shows three major parts, beginning with the global routing prefix, which is the initial value that must be the same in all IPv6 addresses inside the enterprise. The address ends with the interface ID, which acts like the IPv4 host field. The subnet field sits between the two other fields, used as a way to number and identify subnets, much like the subnet field in IPv4 addresses.

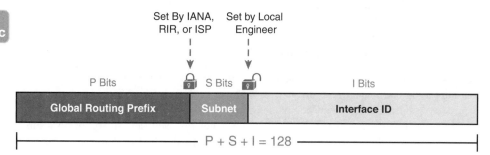

Figure 23-6 *Structure of Subnetted IPv6 Global Unicast Addresses*

First, just think about the general idea with IPv6, comparing Figure 23-6 to Figure 23-5. The IPv6 global routing prefix (the prefix/length assigned by the RIR or ISP) acts like the IPv4 network part of the address structure. The IPv6 subnet part acts like the IPv4 subnet part. And the right side of the IPv6, formally called the *interface ID* (short for interface identifier), acts like the IPv4 host field.

Now focus on the IPv6 global routing prefix and its prefix length. Unlike IPv4, IPv6 has no concept of address classes, so no preset rules determine the prefix length of the global routing prefix. However, when a company applies to an ISP, RIR, or any other organization that can assign a global routing prefix, that assignment includes both the prefix and the prefix length. After a company receives a global routing prefix and that prefix length, the length of the prefix typically does not change over time and is basically locked. (Note that the prefix length of the global routing prefix is often between /32 and /48, or possibly as long as /56.)

Next, look to the right side of Figure 23-6 to the interface ID field. For several reasons that become more obvious the more you learn about IPv6, this field is often 64 bits long. Does it have to be 64 bits long? No. However, using a 64-bit interface ID field works well in real networks, and there are no reasons to avoid using a 64-bit interface ID field.

Finally, look to the subnet field in the center of Figure 23-6. Similar to IPv4, this field creates a place with which to number IPv6 subnets. The length of the subnet field is based on the other two facts: the length of the global routing prefix and the length of the interface ID. And with the commonly used 64-bit interface ID field, the subnet field is typically 64–P bits, with P being the length of the global routing prefix.

Next, consider the structure of a specific global unicast IPv6 address, 2001:0DB8:1111:0001:0000:0000:0000:0001, as seen in Figure 23-7. In this case:

- The company was assigned prefix 2001:0DB8:1111, with prefix length /48.

- The company uses the usual 64-bit interface ID.

- The company has a subnet field of 16 bits, allowing for 2^{16} IPv6 subnets.

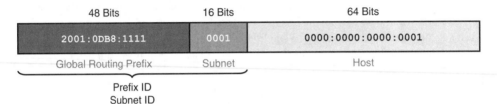

Figure 23-7 *Address Structure for Company 1 Example*

The example in Figure 23-7, along with a little math, shows one reason why so many companies use a /64 prefix length for all subnets. With this structure, Company 1 can support 2^{16} possible subnets (65,536). Few companies need that many subnets. Then, each subnet supports over 10^{18} addresses per subnet (2^{64}, minus some reserved values). So, for both subnets and hosts, the address structure supports far more than are needed. Plus, the /64 prefix length for all subnets makes the math simple because it cuts the 128-bit IPv6 address in half.

Listing the IPv6 Subnet Identifier

Like with IPv4, IPv6 needs to identify each IPv6 subnet with some kind of a subnet identifier, or subnet ID. Figure 23-7 lists the informal names for this number (subnet ID) and the more formal name (prefix ID). Routers then list the IPv6 subnet ID in routing tables, along with the prefix length.

Chapter 22, "Fundamentals of IP Version 6," already discussed how to find the subnet ID, given an IPv6 address and prefix length. The math works the same way when working with global unicast addresses, as well as the unique local addresses discussed later in the chapter. Chapter 28, "Securing Wireless Networks," has already discussed the math, but for completeness, note that the subnet ID shown in Figure 23-7 would be

```
2001:DB8:1111:1::/64
```

List All IPv6 Subnets

With IPv4, if you choose to use a single subnet mask for all subnets, you can sit and write down all the subnets of a Class A, B, or C network using that one subnet mask. With IPv6, the same ideas apply. If you plan to use a single prefix length for all subnets, you can start with the global routing prefix and write down all the IPv6 subnet IDs as well.

To find all the subnet IDs, you simply need to find all the unique values that will fit inside the subnet part of the IPv6 address, basically following these rules:

- All subnet IDs begin with the global routing prefix.

- Use a different value in the subnet field to identify each different subnet.

- All subnet IDs have all 0s in the interface ID.

As an example, take the IPv6 design shown in Figure 23-7, and think about all the subnet IDs. First, all subnets will use the commonly used /64 prefix length. This company uses a global routing prefix of 2001:0DB8:1111::/48, which defines the first 12 hex digits of all the subnet IDs. To find all the possible IPv6 subnet IDs, think of all the combinations of unique values in the fourth quartet and then represent the last four quartets of all 0s with a :: symbol. Figure 23-8 shows the beginning of just such a list.

```
   2001:0DB8:1111:0000::       2001:0DB8:1111:0008::
 ✓ 2001:0DB8:1111:0001::       2001:0DB8:1111:0009::
 ✓ 2001:0DB8:1111:0002::       2001:0DB8:1111:000A::
 ✓ 2001:0DB8:1111:0003::       2001:0DB8:1111:000B::
 ✓ 2001:0DB8:1111:0004::       2001:0DB8:1111:000C::
   2001:0DB8:1111:0005::       2001:0DB8:1111:000D::
   2001:0DB8:1111:0006::       2001:0DB8:1111:000E::
   2001:0DB8:1111:0007::       2001:0DB8:1111:000F::
```

Global Routing Prefix   Subnet   Global Routing Prefix   Subnet

Figure 23-8 *First 16 Possible Subnets with a 16-bit Subnet Field in This Example*

The example allows for 65,536 subnets, so clearly the example will not list all the possible subnets. However, in that fourth quartet, all combinations of hex values would be allowed.

NOTE The IPv6 subnet ID, more formally called the *subnet router anycast address*, is reserved and should not be used as an IPv6 address for any host.

23

Assign Subnets to the Internetwork Topology

After an engineer lists all the possible subnet IDs (based on the subnet design), the next step is to choose which subnet ID to use for each link that needs an IPv6 subnet. Just like with IPv4, each VLAN, each serial link, each Ethernet WAN link, and many other data-link instances need an IPv6 subnet.

Figure 23-9 shows an example using Company 1 again. The figure uses the four subnets from Figure 23-8 that have check marks beside them. The check marks are just a reminder to not use those four subnets in other locations.

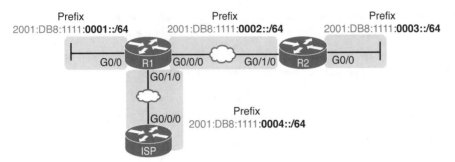

Figure 23-9 *Subnets in Company 1, with Global Routing Prefix of 2001:0DB8:1111::/48*

Assigning Addresses to Hosts in a Subnet

Now that the engineer has planned which IPv6 subnet will be used in each location, the individual IPv6 addressing can be planned and implemented. Each address must be unique, in that no other host interface uses the same IPv6 address. Also, the hosts cannot use the subnet ID itself.

The process of assigning IPv6 addresses to interfaces works similarly to IPv4. Addresses can be configured statically, along with the prefix length, default router, and Domain Name System (DNS) IPv6 addresses. Alternatively, hosts can learn these same settings dynamically, using either Dynamic Host Configuration Protocol (DHCP) or a built-in IPv6 mechanism called Stateless Address Autoconfiguration (SLAAC).

For example, Figure 23-10 shows some static IP addresses that could be chosen for the router interfaces based on the subnet choices shown in Figure 23-9. In each case, the router interfaces use an interface ID that is a relatively low number, easily remembered.

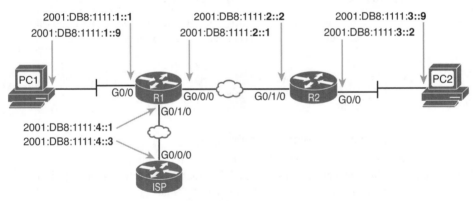

Figure 23-10 *Example Static IPv6 Addresses Based on the Subnet Design of Figure 23-9*

This chapter puts off the details of how to configure the IPv6 addresses until Chapter 24, "Implementing IPv6 Addressing on Routers."

Unique Local Unicast Addresses

Unique local unicast addresses act as private IPv6 addresses. These addresses have many similarities with global unicast addresses, particularly in how to subnet. The biggest difference lies in the literal number (unique local addresses begin with hex FD) and with the administrative process: the unique local prefixes are not registered with any numbering authority and can be used by multiple organizations.

Although the network engineer creates unique local addresses without any registration or assignment process, the addresses still need to follow some rules, as follows:

- Use FD as the first two hex digits.
- Choose a unique 40-bit global ID.
- Append the global ID to FD to create a 48-bit prefix, used as the prefix for all your addresses.
- Use the next 16 bits as a subnet field.
- Note that the structure leaves a convenient 64-bit interface ID field.

Figure 23-11 shows the format of these unique local unicast addresses.

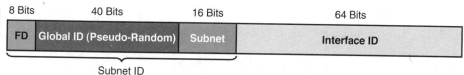

Figure 23-11   *IPv6 Unique Local Unicast Address Format*

> **NOTE**   Just to be completely exact, IANA actually reserves prefix FC00::/7, and not FD00::/8, for these addresses. FC00::/7 includes all addresses that begin with hex FC and FD. However, an RFC (4193) requires the eighth bit of these addresses to be set to 1, which means that in practice today, the unique local addresses all begin with their first two digits as FD.

23

Subnetting with Unique Local IPv6 Addresses

Subnetting using unique local addresses works just like subnetting with global unicast addresses with a 48-bit global routing prefix. The only difference is that with global unicasts, you start by asking for a global routing prefix to be assigned to your company, and that global routing prefix might or might not have a /48 prefix length. With unique local, you create that prefix locally, and the prefix begins with /48, with the first 8 bits set and the next 40 bits randomly chosen.

The process can be as simple as choosing a 40-bit value as your global ID. These 40 bits require 10 hex digits, so you can even avoid thinking in binary and just make up a unique 10-hex-digit value and add hex FD to the front. For example, imagine you chose a 10-hex-digit value of hex 00 0001 0001, prepend a hex FD, making the entire prefix be FD00:0001:0001::/48, or FD00:1:1::/48 when abbreviated.

To create subnets, just as you did in the earlier examples with a 48-bit global routing prefix, treat the entire fourth quartet as a subnet field, as shown in Figure 23-11.

Figure 23-12 shows an example subnetting plan using unique local addresses. The example repeats the same topology shown earlier in Figure 23-9; that figure showed subnetting with a global unicast prefix. This example uses the exact same numbers for the fourth quartet's subnet field, simply replacing the 48-bit global unicast prefix with this new local unique prefix of FD00:1:1.

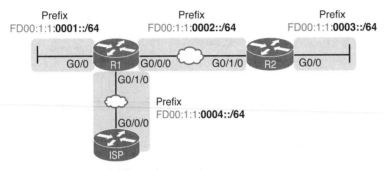

Figure 23-12 *Subnetting Using Unique Local Addresses*

The Need for Globally Unique Local Addresses

The example in Figure 23-12 shows an easy-to-remember prefix of FD00:1:1::/48. Clearly, I made up the easy-to-remember global ID in this example. What global ID would you choose for your company? Would you pick a number that you could not abbreviate and make it shorter? If you had to pick the IPv6 prefix for your unique local addresses from the options in the following list, which would you pick for your company?

- `FDE9:81BE:A059::/48`
- `FDF0:E1D2:C3B4::/48`
- `FD00:1:1::/48`

Given freedom to choose, most people would pick an easy-to-remember, short-to-type prefix, like FD00:1:1::/48. And in a lab or other small network used for testing, making up an easy-to-use number is reasonable. However, for use in real corporate networks, you should not just make up any global ID you like; you should try to follow the unique local address rules that strive to help make your addresses unique in the universe—even without registering a prefix with an ISP or RIR.

RFC 4193 defines unique local addresses, and that RFC stresses the importance of choosing your global ID in a way to make it statistically unlikely to be used by other companies. What is the result of unique global IDs at every company? Making all these unique local addresses unique across the globe. So, if you do plan on using unique local addresses in a real network, plan on using the random number generator logic listed in RFC 4193 to create your prefix.

One of the big reasons to attempt to use a unique prefix, rather than everyone using the same easy-to-remember prefixes, is to be ready for the day that your company merges with or buys another company. Today, with IPv4, a high percentage of companies use private IPv4 network 10.0.0.0. When they merge their networks, the fact that both use network 10.0.0.0 makes the network merger more painful than if the companies had used different private IPv4 networks. With IPv6 unique local addresses, if both companies did the right thing and randomly chose a prefix, they will most likely be using completely different prefixes, making the merger much simpler. However, companies that take the seemingly easy way out and choose an easy-to-remember prefix like FD00:1:1 greatly increase their risk of requiring extra effort when merging with another company that also chose to use that same prefix.

Chapter Review

One key to doing well on the exams is to perform repetitive spaced review sessions. Review this chapter's material using either the tools in the book or interactive tools for the same material found on the book's companion website. Refer to the "Your Study Plan" element for more details. Table 23-3 outlines the key review elements and where you can find them. To better track your study progress, record when you completed these activities in the second column.

Table 23-3   Chapter Review Tracking

Review Element	Review Date(s)	Resource Used
Review key topics		Book, website
Review key terms		Book, website
Answer DIKTA questions		Book, PTP
Review memory table		Website

Review All the Key Topics

Table 23-4   Key Topics for Chapter 23

Key Topic Element	Description	Page Number
List	Two types of IPv6 unicast addresses	542
Table 23-2	Values of the initial hex digits of IPv6 addresses, and the address type implied by each	545
Figure 23-6	Subnetting concepts for IPv6 global unicast addresses	547
List	Rules for how to find all IPv6 subnet IDs, given the global routing prefix, and prefix length used for all subnets	548
List	Rules for building unique local unicast addresses	551
Figure 23-11	Subnetting concepts for IPv6 unique local addresses	551

Key Terms You Should Know

global unicast address, global routing prefix, unique local address, subnet ID (prefix ID), subnet router anycast address

CHAPTER 24

Implementing IPv6 Addressing on Routers

This chapter covers the following exam topics:

1.0 Network Fundamentals

1.9 Compare and contrast IPv6 address types

1.9.a Global unicast

1.9.b Unique local

1.9.c Link local

1.9.d Anycast

1.9.e Multicast

1.9.f Modified EUI 64

With IPv4 addressing, some devices, like servers and routers, typically use static predefined IPv4 addresses. End-user devices do not mind if their address changes from time to time, and they typically learn an IPv4 address dynamically using DHCP. IPv6 uses the same approach, with servers, routers, and other devices in the control of the IT group often using predefined IPv6 addresses, and with end-user devices using dynamically learned IPv6 addresses.

This chapter focuses on IPv6 address configuration on routers. The chapter begins with the more obvious IPv6 addressing configuration, with features that mirror IPv4 features, showing how to configure interfaces with IPv6 addresses and view that configuration with **show** commands. The second half of the chapter introduces new IPv6 addressing concepts, showing some other addresses used by routers when doing different tasks.

"Do I Know This Already?" Quiz

Take the quiz (either here or use the PTP software) if you want to use the score to help you decide how much time to spend on this chapter. The letter answers are listed at the bottom of the page following the quiz. Appendix C, found both at the end of the book as well as on the companion website, includes both the answers and explanations. You can also find both answers and explanations in the PTP testing software.

Table 24-1 "Do I Know This Already?" Foundation Topics Section-to-Question Mapping

Foundation Topics Section	Questions
Implementing Unicast IPv6 Addresses on Routers	1–3
Special Addresses Used by Routers	4–5

1. Router R1 has an interface named Gigabit Ethernet 0/1, whose MAC address has been set to 0200.0001.000A. Which of the following commands, added in R1's Gigabit Ethernet 0/1 configuration mode, gives this router's G0/1 interface a unicast IPv6 address of 2001:1:1:1:1:200:1:A, with a /64 prefix length?

   a. ipv6 address 2001:1:1:1:1:200:1:A/64

   b. ipv6 address 2001:1:1:1:1:200:1:A/64 eui-64

   c. ipv6 address 2001:1:1:1:1:200:1:A /64 eui-64

   d. ipv6 address 2001:1:1:1:1:200:1:A /64

   e. None of the other answers are correct.

2. Router R1 has an interface named Gigabit Ethernet 0/1, whose MAC address has been set to 5055.4444.3333. This interface has been configured with the **ipv6 address 2000:1:1:1::/64 eui-64** subcommand. What unicast address will this interface use?

   a. 2000:1:1:1:52FF:FE55:4444:3333

   b. 2000:1:1:1:5255:44FF:FE44:3333

   c. 2000:1:1:1:5255:4444:33FF:FE33

   d. 2000:1:1:1:200:FF:FE00:0

3. Router R1 currently supports IPv4, routing packets in and out all its interfaces. R1's configuration needs to be migrated to support dual-stack operation, routing both IPv4 and IPv6. Which of the following tasks must be performed before the router can also support routing IPv6 packets? (Choose two answers.)

   a. Enable IPv6 on each interface using an **ipv6 address** interface subcommand.

   b. Enable support for both versions with the **ip versions 4 6** global command.

   c. Additionally enable IPv6 routing using the **ipv6 unicast-routing** global command.

   d. Migrate to dual-stack routing using the **ip routing dual-stack** global command.

4. Router R1 has an interface named Gigabit Ethernet 0/1, whose MAC address has been set to 0200.0001.000A. The interface is then configured with the **ipv6 address 2001:1:1:1:200:FF:FE01:B/64** interface subcommand; no other **ipv6 address** commands are configured on the interface. Which of the following answers lists the link-local address used on the interface?

   a. FE80::FF:FE01:A

   b. FE80::FF:FE01:B

   c. FE80::200:FF:FE01:A

   d. FE80::200:FF:FE01:B

5. Which of the following multicast addresses is defined as the address for sending packets to only the IPv6 routers on the local link?

    a. FF02::1

    b. FF02::2

    c. FF02::5

    d. FF02::A

Foundation Topics

Implementing Unicast IPv6 Addresses on Routers

Every company bases its enterprise network on one or more protocol models, or protocol stacks. In the earlier days of networking, enterprise networks used one or more protocol stacks from different vendors, as shown on the left of Figure 24-1. Over time, companies added TCP/IP (based on IPv4) to the mix. Eventually, companies migrated fully to TCP/IP as the only protocol stack in use.

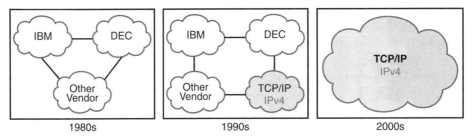

Figure 24-1 *Migration of Enterprise Networks to Use TCP/IP Stack Only, IPv4*

The emergence of IPv6 requires that IPv6 be implemented in end-user hosts, servers, routers, and other devices. However, corporations cannot just migrate all devices from IPv4 to IPv6 over one weekend. Instead, what will likely occur is some kind of long-term migration and coexistence, in which for a large number of years, most corporate networks again use multiple protocol stacks—one based on IPv4 and one based on IPv6.

Eventually, over time, we might all see the day when enterprise networks run only IPv6, without any IPv4 remaining, but that day might take awhile. Figure 24-2 shows the progression, just to make the point, but who knows how long it will take?

One way to add IPv6 support to an established IPv4-based enterprise internetwork is to implement a *dual-stack* strategy. To do so, the routers can be configured to route IPv6 packets, with IPv6 addresses on their interfaces, with a similar model to how routers support IPv4. Then hosts can implement IPv6 when ready, running both IPv4 and IPv6 (dual stacks). The first major section of this chapter shows how to configure and verify unicast IPv6 addresses on routers.

Answers to the "Do I Know This Already?" quiz:

1 A **2** B **3** A, C **4** A **5** B

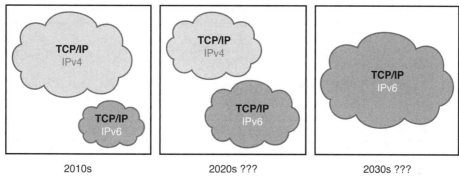

Figure 24-2 *Possible Path Through Dual-Stack (IPv4 and IPv6) over a Long Period*

Static Unicast Address Configuration

Cisco routers give us two options for static configuration of IPv6 addresses. In one case, you configure the full 128-bit address, while in the other, you configure a 64-bit prefix and let the router derive the second half of the address (the interface ID). The next few pages show how to configure both options and how the router chooses the second half of the IPv6 address.

Configuring the Full 128-Bit Address

To statically configure the full 128-bit unicast address—either global unicast or unique local—the router needs an **ipv6 address** *address/prefix-length* interface subcommand on each interface. The address can be an abbreviated IPv6 address or the full 32-digit hex address. The command includes the prefix length value, at the end, with no space between the address and prefix length.

The configuration of the router interface IPv6 address really is that simple. Figure 24-3, along with Examples 24-1 and 24-2, shows a basic example. The figure shows the global unicast IPv6 address used by two different routers, on two interfaces each. As usual, all subnets use a /64 prefix length.

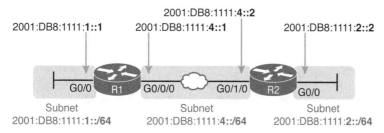

Figure 24-3 *Sample 128-bit IPv6 Addresses to Be Configured on Cisco Router Interfaces*

24

Example 24-1 *Configuring Static IPv6 Addresses on R1*

```
ipv6 unicast-routing
!
interface GigabitEthernet0/0
 ipv6 address 2001:DB8:1111:1::1/64
!
interface GigabitEthernet0/0/0
 ipv6 address 2001:0db8:1111:0004:0000:0000:0000:0001/64
```

Example 24-2 *Configuring Static IPv6 Addresses on R2*

```
ipv6 unicast-routing
!
interface GigabitEthernet0/0
 ipv6 address 2001:DB8:1111:2::2/64
!
interface GigabitEthernet0/1/0
 ipv6 address 2001:db8:1111:4::2/64
```

NOTE The configuration on R1 in Example 24-1 uses both abbreviated and unabbreviated addresses, and both lowercase and uppercase hex digits, showing that all are allowed. Router **show** commands list the abbreviated value with uppercase hex digits.

Enabling IPv6 Routing

While the configurations shown in Examples 24-1 and 24-2 focus on the IPv6 address configuration, they also include an important but often overlooked step when configuring IPv6 on Cisco routers: IPv6 routing needs to be enabled. On Cisco routers, IPv4 routing is enabled by default, but IPv6 routing is not enabled by default. The solution takes only a single command—**ipv6 unicast-routing**—which enables IPv6 routing on the router.

A router must enable IPv6 globally (**ipv6 unicast-routing**) and enable IPv6 on the interface (**ipv6 address**) before the router will attempt to route IPv6 packets in and out an interface. If you omit the **ipv6 unicast-routing** command but configure interface IPv6 addresses, the router will not route any received IPv6 packets, but the router will act as an IPv6 host. If you include the **ipv6 unicast-routing** command but omit all the interface IPv6 addresses, the router will be ready to route IPv6 packets but have no interfaces that have IPv6 enabled, effectively disabling IPv6 routing.

Verifying the IPv6 Address Configuration

IPv6 uses many **show** commands that mimic the syntax of IPv4 **show** commands. For example:

- The **show ipv6 interface brief** command gives you interface IPv6 address info, but not prefix length info, similar to the IPv4 **show ip interface brief** command.
- The **show ipv6 interface** command gives the details of IPv6 interface settings, much like the **show ip interface** command does for IPv4.

The one notable difference in the most common commands is that the **show interfaces** command still lists the IPv4 address and mask but tells us nothing about IPv6. So, to see IPv6 interface addresses, use commands that begin with **show ipv6**. Example 24-3 lists a few samples from Router R1, with the explanations following.

Example 24-3 *Verifying Static IPv6 Addresses on Router R1*

```
! The first interface is in subnet 1
R1# show ipv6 interface GigabitEthernet 0/0
GigabitEthernet0/0 is up, line protocol is up
  IPv6 is enabled, link-local address is FE80::1:AAFF:FE00:1
  No Virtual link-local address(es):
  Global unicast address(es):
    2001:DB8:1111:1::1, subnet is 2001:DB8:1111:1::/64
  Joined group address(es):
    FF02::1
    FF02::2
    FF02::1:FF00:1
  MTU is 1500 bytes
  ICMP error messages limited to one every 100 milliseconds
  ICMP redirects are enabled
  ICMP unreachables are sent
  ND DAD is enabled, number of DAD attempts: 1
  ND reachable time is 30000 milliseconds (using 30000)
  ND advertised reachable time is 0 (unspecified)
  ND advertised retransmit interval is 0 (unspecified)
  ND router advertisements are sent every 200 seconds
  ND router advertisements live for 1800 seconds
  ND advertised default router preference is Medium
  Hosts use stateless autoconfig for addresses.


R1# show ipv6 interface brief
GigabitEthernet0/0     [up/up]
    FE80::1:AAFF:FE00:1
    2001:DB8:1111:1::1
GigabitEthernet0/1     [administratively down/down]
    unassigned
GigabitEthernet0/0/0   [up/up]
    FE80::32F7:DFF:FE29:8568
    2001:DB8:1111:4::1
GigabitEthernet0/1/0   [administratively down/down]
    unassigned
```

First, focus on the output of the two **show ipv6 interface** commands at the top of the example, which lists interface G0/0, showing output about that interface only. Note that the output lists the configured IPv6 address and prefix length, as well as the IPv6 subnet (2001:DB8:1111:1::/64), which the router calculated based on the IPv6 address.

The end of the example lists the output of the **show ipv6 interface brief** command. Similar to the IPv4-focused **show ip interface brief** command, this command lists IPv6 addresses, but not the prefix length or prefixes. This command also lists all interfaces on the router, whether or not IPv6 is enabled on the interfaces. For example, in this case, the only two interfaces on R1 that have an IPv6 address are G0/0 and G0/0/0, as configured earlier in Example 24-1.

Beyond the IPv6 addresses on the interfaces, the router also adds IPv6 connected routes to the IPv6 routing table off each interface. Just as with IPv4, the router keeps these connected routes in the IPv6 routing table only when the interface is in a working (up/up) state. But if the interface has an IPv6 unicast address configured, and the interface is working, the router adds the connected routes. Example 24-4 shows the connected IPv6 on Router R1 from Figure 24-3.

Example 24-4 *Displaying Connected IPv6 Routes on Router R1*

```
R1# show ipv6 route connected
IPv6 Routing Table - default - 5 entries
Codes: C - Connected, L - Local, S - Static, U - Per-user Static route
       B - BGP, HA - Home Agent, MR - Mobile Router, R - RIP
       H - NHRP, I1 - ISIS L1, I2 - ISIS L2, IA - ISIS interarea
       IS - ISIS summary, D - EIGRP, EX - EIGRP external, NM - NEMO
       ND - ND Default, NDp - ND Prefix, DCE - Destination, NDr - Redirect
       RL - RPL, O - OSPF Intra, OI - OSPF Inter, OE1 - OSPF ext 1
       OE2 - OSPF ext 2, ON1 - OSPF NSSA ext 1, ON2 - OSPF NSSA ext 2
       la - LISP alt, lr - LISP site-registrations, ld - LISP dyn-eid
       lA - LISP away, a - Application
C    2001:DB8:1111:1::/64 [0/0]
     via GigabitEthernet0/0, directly connected
C    2001:DB8:1111:4::/64 [0/0]
     via GigabitEthernet0/0/0, directly connected
```

Generating a Unique Interface ID Using Modified EUI-64

IPv6 follows the same general model as IPv4 regarding which types of devices typically use static, predefined addresses and which use dynamically learned address. For example, routers inside an enterprise use static IPv4 addresses, while end-user devices typically learn their IPv4 address using DHCP. With IPv6, routers also typically use static IPv6 addresses, while user devices use DHCP or Stateless Address Auto Configuration (SLAAC) to dynamically learn their IPv6 address.

Even though engineers typically choose to use stable and predictable IPv6 interface addresses, IOS supports two different methods to configure a stable address. One method uses the **ipv6 address** command to define the entire 128-bit address, as shown in Examples 24-1 and 24-2. The other method uses this same **ipv6 address** command, but the command configures only the 64-bit IPv6 prefix for the interface and lets the router automatically generate a unique interface ID.

This second method uses rules called *modified EUI-64* (extended unique identifier). Often, in the context of IPv6 addressing, people refer to modified EUI-64 as just EUI-64; there is no other term or concept about EUI-64 that you need to know for IPv6. The configuration that uses EUI-64 includes a keyword to tell the router to use EUI-64 rules, along with the 64-bit prefix. The router then uses EUI-64 rules to create the interface ID part of the address, as follows:

1. Split the 6-byte (12-hex-digit) MAC address in two halves (6 hex digits each).

2. Insert FFFE in between the two, making the interface ID now have a total of 16 hex digits (64 bits).

3. Invert the seventh bit of the interface ID.

Figure 24-4 shows the major pieces of how the address is formed.

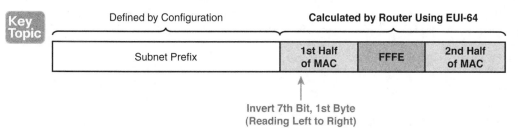

Figure 24-4   *IPv6 Address Format with Interface ID and EUI-64*

> **NOTE**   You can find a video about the EUI-64 process on the companion website, in the Chapter Review section for this chapter.

Although this process might seem a bit convoluted, it works. Also, with a little practice, you can look at an IPv6 address and quickly notice the FFFE in the middle of the interface ID and then easily find the two halves of the corresponding interface's MAC address. But you need to be ready to do the same math, in this case to predict the EUI-64 formatted IPv6 address on an interface.

For example, if you ignore the final step of inverting the seventh bit, the rest of the steps just require that you move the pieces around. Figure 24-5 shows two examples, just so you see the process.

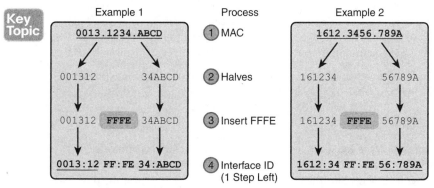

Figure 24-5   *Two Examples of Most of the EUI-64 Interface ID Process*

Both examples follow the same process. Each starts with the MAC address, breaking it into two halves (Step 2). The third step inserts FFFE in the middle, and the fourth step inserts a colon every four hex digits, keeping with IPv6 conventions.

While the examples in Figure 24-5 show most of the steps, they omit the final step. The final step requires that you convert the first byte (first two hex digits) from hex to binary, invert the seventh of the 8 bits, and convert the bits back to hex. Inverting a bit means that if the bit is a 0, make it a 1; if it is a 1, make it a 0. Most of the time, with IPv6 addresses, the original bit will be 0 and will be inverted to a 1.

For example, Figure 24-6 completes the two examples from Figure 24-5, focusing only on the first two hex digits. The examples show each pair of hex digits (Step 1) and the binary equivalent (Step 2). Step 3 shows a copy of those same 8 bits, except the seventh bit is inverted; the example on the left inverts from 0 to 1, and the example on the right inverts from 1 to 0. Finally, the bits are converted back to hex at Step 4.

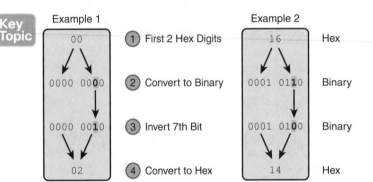

Figure 24-6   *Inverting the Seventh Bit of an EUI-64 Interface ID Field*

NOTE   If you do not remember how to do hex-to-binary conversions, take a few moments to review the process. If you memorize the 16 hex values for digits 0 through F, with the corresponding binary values, the conversion can be easy. If you do not have those handy in your memory, take a few moments to look at Table A-2 in Appendix A, "Numeric Reference Tables."

For those of you who prefer the decimal shortcuts, with a little memorization you can do the bit-flip math without doing any hex-binary conversions. First, note that the process to invert the seventh bit, when working with a hexadecimal IPv6 address, flips the third of 4 bits in a single hex digit. With only 16 single hex digits, you could memorize what each hex digit becomes if its third bit is inverted, and you can easily memorize those values with a visual process.

If you want to try to memorize the values, it helps to work through the following process a few times, so grab a piece of scratch paper. Then write the 16 single hex digits as shown on the left side of Figure 24-7. That is, write them in eight rows of two numbers each, with the spacing as directed in the figure.

Next, start at the top of the lists and draw arrow lines between two numbers in the same column on the top left (0 and 2). Then move down the left-side column, connecting the next two digits (4 and 6) with an arrow line, then 8 and A, and then C and E. Repeat the process on the right, re-creating the right side of Figure 24-7.

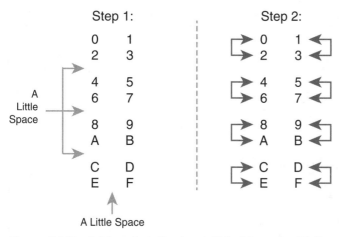

Figure 24-7   *A Mnemonic Device to Help Memorize Bit Inversion Shortcut*

The figure you drew (and the right side of Figure 24-7) shows the hex digits which, when you invert their third bit, convert to the other. That is, 0 converts to 2; 2 converts to 0; 1 converts to 3; 3 converts to 1; 4 converts to 6; 6 converts to 4; and so on. So, on the exam, if you can remember the pattern to redraw Figure 24-7, you could avoid doing binary/hexadecimal conversion. Use whichever approach makes you more comfortable.

As usual, the best way to get comfortable with forming these EUI-64 interface IDs is to calculate some yourself. Table 24-2 lists some practice problems, with an IPv6 64-bit prefix in the first column and the MAC address in the second column. Your job is to calculate the full (unabbreviated) IPv6 address using EUI-64 rules. The answers are at the end of the chapter, in the section "Answers to Earlier Practice Problems."

Table 24-2   IPv6 EUI-64 Address Creation Practice

Prefix	MAC Address	Unabbreviated IPv6 Address
2001:DB8:1:1::/64	0013.ABAB.1001	
2001:DB8:1:1::/64	AA13.ABAB.1001	
2001:DB8:1:1::/64	000C.BEEF.CAFE	
2001:DB8:1:1::/64	B80C.BEEF.CAFE	
2001:DB8:FE:FE::/64	0C0C.ABAC.CABA	
2001:DB8:FE:FE::/64	0A0C.ABAC.CABA	

Configuring a router interface to use the EUI-64 format uses the **ipv6 address** *address/prefix-length* **eui-64** interface subcommand. The **eui-64** keyword tells the router to find the interface MAC address and do the EUI-64 conversion math to find the interface ID.

Example 24-5 shows a revised configuration on Router R1, as compared to the earlier Example 24-1. In this case, R1 uses EUI-64 formatting for its IPv6 addresses.

Example 24-5 *Configuring R1's IPv6 Interfaces Using EUI-64*

```
ipv6 unicast-routing
!
! The ipv6 address command now lists a prefix, not the full address
interface GigabitEthernet0/0
 mac-address 0201.aa00.0001
 ipv6 address 2001:DB8:1111:1::/64 eui-64
!
interface GigabitEthernet0/0/0
 ipv6 address 2001:DB8:1111:4::/64 eui-64

R1# show ipv6 interface brief
GigabitEthernet0/0      [up/up]
    FE80::1:AAFF:FE00:1
    2001:DB8:1111:1:1:AAFF:FE00:1
GigabitEthernet0/1      [administratively down/down]
    unassigned
GigabitEthernet0/0/0    [up/up]
    FE80::32F7:DFF:FE29:8568
    2001:DB8:1111:4:32F7:DFF:FE29:8568
GigabitEthernet0/0/1    [administratively down/down]
    unassigned
```

The example uses only Ethernet interfaces, all of which have a universal MAC address to use to create their EUI-64 interface IDs. However, in this case, the configuration includes the **mac-address** command under R1's G0/0 interface, which causes IOS to use the configured MAC address instead of the universal (burned-in) MAC address. Interface G0/0/0 defaults to use its universal MAC address. Following that math:

G0/0 – MAC `0201.AA00.0001` – Interface ID `0001.AAFF.FE00.0001`

G0/0 – MAC `30F7.0D29.8568` – Interface ID `32F7.0DFF.FE29.8568`

Also, be aware that for interfaces that do not have a MAC address, like serial interfaces, the router uses the MAC of the lowest-numbered router interface that does have a MAC.

> **NOTE** When you use EUI-64, the address value in the **ipv6 address** command should be the prefix, not the full 128-bit IPv6 address. However, if you mistakenly type the full address and still use the **eui-64** keyword, IOS accepts the command and converts the address to the matching prefix before putting the command into the running config file. For example, IOS converts **ipv6 address 2000:1:1:1::1/64 eui-64** to **ipv6 address 2000:1:1:1::/64 eui-64**.

Dynamic Unicast Address Configuration

In most cases, network engineers will configure the IPv6 addresses of router interfaces so that the addresses do not change until the engineer changes the router configuration. However, routers can be configured to use dynamically learned IPv6 addresses. These can be useful for routers connecting to the Internet through some types of Internet access technologies, like DSL and cable modems.

Cisco routers support two ways for the router interface to dynamically learn an IPv6 address to use:

- Stateful DHCP
- Stateless Address Autoconfiguration (SLAAC)

Both methods use the familiar **ipv6 address** command. Of course, neither option configures the actual IPv6 address; instead, the commands configure a keyword that tells the router which method to use to learn its IPv6 address. Example 24-6 shows the configuration, with one interface using stateful DHCP and one using SLAAC.

Example 24-6 *Router Configuration to Learn IPv6 Addresses with DHCP and SLAAC*

```
! This interface uses DHCP to learn its IPv6 address
interface FastEthernet0/0
 ipv6 address dhcp
!
! This interface uses SLAAC to learn its IPv6 address
interface FastEthernet0/1
 ipv6 address autoconfig
```

Special Addresses Used by Routers

IPv6 configuration on a router begins with the simple steps discussed in the first part of this chapter. After you configure the **ipv6 unicast-routing** global configuration command, to enable the function of IPv6 routing, the addition of a unicast IPv6 address on an interface causes the router to do the following:

- Gives the interface a unicast IPv6 address
- Enables the routing of IPv6 packets in/out that interface
- Defines the IPv6 prefix (subnet) that exists off that interface
- Tells the router to add a connected IPv6 route for that prefix, to the IPv6 routing table, when that interface is up/up

NOTE In fact, if you pause and look at the list again, the same ideas happen for IPv4 when you configure an IPv4 address on a router interface.

While all the IPv6 features in this list work much like similar features in IPv4, IPv6 also has a number of additional functions not seen in IPv4. Often, these additional functions use other IPv6 addresses, many of which are multicast addresses. This second major section of the chapter examines the additional IPv6 addresses seen on routers, with a brief description of how they are used.

24

Link-Local Addresses

IPv6 uses link-local addresses as a special kind of unicast IPv6 address. These addresses are not used for normal IPv6 packet flows that contain data for applications. Instead, these addresses are used by some overhead protocols and for routing. This next topic first looks at how IPv6 uses link-local addresses and then how routers create link-local addresses.

Link-Local Address Concepts

IPv6 defines rules so that packets sent to any link-local address should not be forwarded by any router to another subnet. As a result, several IPv6 protocols make use of link-local addresses when the protocol's messages need to stay within the local LAN. For example, Neighbor Discovery Protocol (NDP), which replaces the functions of IPv4's ARP, uses link-local addresses.

Routers also use link-local addresses as the next-hop IP addresses in IPv6 routes, as shown in Figure 24-8. IPv6 hosts also use a default router (default gateway) concept, like IPv4, but instead of the router address being in the same subnet, hosts refer to the router's link-local address. The **show ipv6 route** command lists the link-local address of the neighboring router, rather than the global unicast or unique local unicast address.

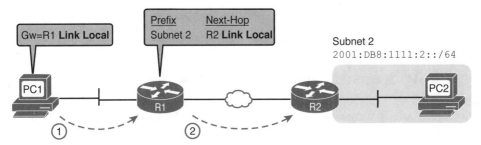

Figure 24-8   *IPv6 Using Link-Local Addresses as the Next-Hop Address*

Following are some key facts about link-local addresses:

Unicast (not multicast): Link-local addresses represent a single host, and packets sent to a link-local address should be processed by only that one IPv6 host.

Forwarding scope is the local link only: Packets sent to a link-local address do not leave the local data link because routers do not forward packets with link-local destination addresses.

Automatically generated: Every IPv6 host interface (and router interface) can create its own link-local address automatically, solving some initialization problems for hosts before they learn a dynamically learned global unicast address.

Common uses: Link-local addresses are used for some overhead protocols that stay local to one subnet and as the next-hop address for IPv6 routes.

Creating Link-Local Addresses on Routers

IPv6 hosts and routers can calculate their own link-local address, for each interface, using some basic rules. First, all link-local addresses start with the same prefix, as shown on the left side of Figure 24-9. By definition, the first 10 bits must match prefix FE80::/10, meaning that the first three hex digits will be either FE8, FE9, FEA, or FEB. However, when following the RFC, the next 54 bits should be binary 0, so the link-local address should always start with FE80:0000:0000:0000 as the first four unabbreviated quartets.

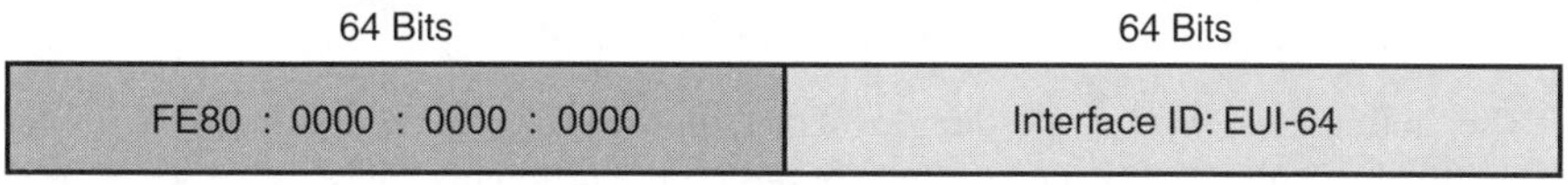

64 Bits	64 Bits
FE80 : 0000 : 0000 : 0000	Interface ID: EUI-64

Figure 24-9 *Link-Local Address Format*

The second half of the link-local address, in practice, can be formed using EUI-64 rules, can be randomly generated, or even configured. Cisco routers use the EUI-64 format to create the interface ID (see the earlier section "Generating a Unique Interface ID Using Modified EUI-64"). As a result, a router's complete link-local address should be unique because the MAC address that feeds into the EUI-64 process should be unique.

Alternately, some OSs create their link-local addresses by randomly generating the interface ID. For example, Microsoft OSs use a somewhat random process to choose the interface ID and change it over time in an attempt to prevent some forms of attacks.

IOS creates a link-local address for any interface that has configured at least one other unicast address using the **ipv6 address** command (global unicast or unique local). To see the link-local address, just use the usual commands that also list the unicast IPv6 address: **show ipv6 interface** and **show ipv6 interface brief**. Note that Example 24-7 shows an example from Router R1 just after it was configured as shown in Example 24-5 (with the **eui-64** keyword on the **ipv6 address** commands).

Example 24-7 *Comparing Link-Local Addresses with EUI-Generated Unicast Addresses*

```
R1# show ipv6 interface brief
GigabitEthernet0/0     [up/up]
   FE80::1:AAFF:FE00:1
   2001:DB8:1111:1:1:AAFF:FE00:1
GigabitEthernet0/1     [administratively down/down]
   unassigned
GigabitEthernet0/0/0   [up/up]
   FE80::32F7:DFF:FE29:8568
   2001:DB8:1111:4:32F7:DFF:FE29:8568
GigabitEthernet0/0/1   [administratively down/down]
   unassigned
```

First, examine the two pairs of highlighted entries in the example. For each of the two interfaces that have a global unicast address (G0/0 and G0/0/0), the output lists the global unicast, which happens to begin with 2001 in this case. At the same time, the output also lists the link-local address for each interface, beginning with FE80.

Next, focus on the two addresses listed under interface G0/0. If you look closely at the second half of the two addresses listed for interface G0/0, you will see that both addresses have the same interface ID value. The global unicast address was configured in this case with the

24

ipv6 address 2001:DB8:1111:1::/64 eui-64 command, so the router used EUI-64 logic to form both the global unicast address and the link-local address. The interface MAC address in this case is 0201.AA00.0001, so the router calculates an interface ID portion of both addresses as 0001:AAFF:FE00:0001 (unabbreviated). After abbreviation, Router R1's link-local address on interface G0/0 becomes FE80::AAFF:FE00:1.

IOS can either automatically create the link-local address, or it can be configured. IOS chooses the link-local address for the interface based on the following rules:

■ If configured, the router uses the value in the **ipv6 address** *address* **link-local** interface subcommand. Note that the configured link-local address must be from the correct address range for link-local addresses; that is, an address from prefix FE80::/10. In other words, the address must begin with FE8, FE9, FEA, or FEB.

■ If not configured, the IOS calculates the link-local address using EUI-64 rules, as discussed and demonstrated in and around Example 24-7. The calculation uses EUI-64 rules even if the interface unicast address does not use EUI-64.

Routing IPv6 with Only Link-Local Addresses on an Interface

This chapter has shown four variations on the **ipv6 address** command so far. To review:

ipv6 address *address/prefix-length*: Static configuration of a specific address

ipv6 address *prefix/prefix-length* **eui-64**: Static configuration of a specific prefix and prefix length, with the router calculating the interface ID using EUI-64 rules

ipv6 address dhcp: Dynamic learning on the address and prefix length using DHCP

ipv6 address autoconfig: Dynamic learning of the prefix and prefix length, with the router calculating the interface ID using EUI-64 rules (SLAAC)

This next short topic completes the list with the following command:

ipv6 enable: Enables IPv6 processing and adds a link-local address, but adds no other unicast IPv6 addresses.

The purpose of the **ipv6 enable** command will not make sense until you realize that some links, particularly WAN links, do not need a global unicast address. Using the backdrop of Figure 24-10, think about the destination of packets sent by hosts like PC1 and PC2. When PC1 sends PC2 an IPv6 packet, the packet holds PC1's and PC2's IPv6 addresses and never contains the WAN link's IPv6 addresses. PC1 and PC2 may need to know the routers' LAN IPv6 addresses, to use as their default gateway, but the hosts do not need to know the routers' WAN interface addresses.

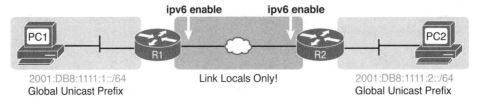

Figure 24-10 *Typical Use of the* **ipv6 enable** *Command*

Additionally, the routers do not need to have global unicast (or unique local) addresses on the WAN links for routing to work. IPv6 routing protocols use link-local addresses as the next-hop address when dynamically building IPv6 routes. Additionally, static routes, as discussed in Chapter 25, "Implementing IPv6 Routing," can use link-local addresses for the next-hop address.

In short, creating a WAN link with no global unicast (or unique local) addresses works. As a result, you would not even need to assign an IPv6 subnet to each WAN link. Then to configure the WAN interfaces, use the **ipv6 enable** command, enabling IPv6 and giving each interface a generated link-local IPv6 address.

To use the command, just configure the **ipv6 enable** command on the interfaces on both ends of the WAN link.

IPv6 Multicast Addresses

IPv6 uses multicast IPv6 addresses for several purposes. Like IPv4, IPv6 includes a range of multicast addresses that can be used by multicast applications, with many of the same fundamental concepts as IPv4 multicasts. For instance, IANA defines the range FF30::/12 (all IPv6 addresses that begin with FF3) as the range of addresses to be used for some types of multicast applications.

Additionally, different IPv6 RFCs reserve multicast addresses for specific purposes. For instance, OSPFv3 uses FF02::5 and FF02::6 as the all-OSPF-routers and all-DR-Routers multicast addresses, respectively, similar to how OSPFv2 uses IPv4 addresses 224.0.0.5 and 224.0.0.6 for the equivalent purposes.

This next section focuses on IPv6 multicast addresses reserved for use with different protocols. The first, link-local multicast addresses, are multicast addresses useful for communicating over a single link. The other type is a special overhead multicast address calculated for each host, called the solicited-node multicast address.

Reserved Multicast Addresses

Stop for a moment and think about some of the control plane protocols discussed throughout this book so far. Some of those IPv4 control plane protocols used IPv4 broadcasts, meaning that the packet destination address was either 255.255.255.255 (the address for all hosts in the local LAN) or the subnet broadcast address (the address for all hosts in that specific subnet). Those broadcast packets were then sent as Ethernet broadcast frames, destined to the Ethernet broadcast address of FFFF.FFFF.FFFF.

While useful, the IPv4 approach of IPv4 broadcast and LAN broadcast requires every host in the VLAN to process the broadcast frame, even if only one other device needed to think about the message. Also, each host has to process the frame, then packet, read the type of message, and so on, before ignoring the task. For example, an IPv4 ARP Request—an IPv4 and LAN broadcast—requires a host to process the Ethernet, IP, and ARP details of the message before deciding whether to reply or not.

24

IPv6, instead of using Layer 3 and Layer 2 broadcasts, instead uses Layer 3 multicast addresses, which in turn cause Ethernet frames to use Ethernet multicast addresses. As a result:

- All the hosts that should receive the message receive the message, which is necessary for the protocols to work. However...
- ...Hosts that do not need to process the message can make that choice with much less processing as compared to IPv4.

For instance, OSPFv3 uses IPv6 multicast addresses FF02::5 and FF02::6. In a subnet, the OSPFv3 routers will listen for packets sent to those addresses. However, all the endpoint hosts do not use OSPFv3 and should ignore those OSPFv3 messages. If a host receives a packet with FF02::5 as the destination IPv6 address, the host can ignore the packet because the host knows it does not care about packets sent to that multicast address. That check takes much less time than the equivalent checks with IPv4.

Table 24-3 lists the most common reserved IPv6 multicast addresses.

Table 24-3   Key IPv6 Local-Scope Multicast Addresses

Short Name	Multicast Address	Meaning	IPv4 Equivalent
All-nodes	FF02::1	All-nodes (all interfaces that use IPv6 that are on the link)	224.0.0.1
All-routers	FF02::2	All-routers (all IPv6 router interfaces on the link)	224.0.0.2
All-OSPF, All-OSPF-DR	FF02::5, FF02::6	All OSPF routers and all OSPF-designated routers, respectively	224.0.0.5, 224.0.0.6
RIPng Routers	FF02::9	All RIPng routers	224.0.0.9
EIGRPv6 Routers	FF02::A	All routers using EIGRP for IPv6 (EIGRPv6)	224.0.0.10
DHCP Relay Agent	FF02::1:2	All routers acting as a DHCPv6 relay agent	None

NOTE An Internet search of "IPv6 Multicast Address Space Registry" will show the IANA page that lists all the reserved values and the RFC that defines the use of each address.

Example 24-8 repeats the output of the **show ipv6 interface** command to show the multicast addresses used by Router R1 on its G0/0 interface. In this case, the highlighted lines show the all-nodes address (FF02::1), all-routers (FF02::2), and two for OSPFv3 (FF02::5 and FF02::6). Note that the IPv6 multicast addresses that the router interface is listening for and processing are listed under the heading "Joined group address(es):" at the top of the highlighted section of the output.

Example 24-8   *Verifying Static IPv6 Addresses on Router R1*

```
R1# show ipv6 interface GigabitEthernet 0/0
GigabitEthernet0/0 is up, line protocol is up
  IPv6 is enabled, link-local address is FE80::1
  No Virtual link-local address(es):
  Global unicast address(es):
    2001:DB8:1111:1::1, subnet is 2001:DB8:1111:1::/64 [EUI]
  Joined group address(es):
    FF02::1
    FF02::2
    FF02::5
    FF02::6
    FF02::1:FF00:1
! Lines omitted for brevity
```

Multicast Address Scopes

IPv6 RFC 4291 defines IPv6 addressing including the ideas of IPv6 address scope. Each scope defines a different set of rules about whether routers should or should not forward a packet, and how far routers should forward packets, based on those scopes.

For instance, you read earlier in this chapter about the link-local address on an interface—a unicast IPv6 address—but with a link-local scope. The scope definition called "link-local" dictates that packets sent to a link-local unicast address should remain on the link and not be forwarded by any router.

Most of the scope discussion in RFC 4291 applies to multicast addresses, using the term *multicast scope*. Per that RFC, the fourth digit of the multicast address identifies the scope, as noted in Table 24-4.

Table 24-4   IPv6 Multicast Scope Terms

Scope Name	First Quartet	Scope Defined by...	Meaning
Interface-Local	FF01	Derived by Device	Packet remains within the device. Useful for internally sending packets to services running on that same host.
Link-Local	FF02	Derived by Device	Host that creates the packet can send it onto the link, but no routers forward the packet.
Site-Local	FF05	Configuration on Routers	Intended to be more than Link-Local, so routers forward, but must be less than Organization-Local; generally meant to limit packets so they do not cross WAN links.
Organization-Local	FF08	Configuration on Routers	Intended to be broad, probably for an entire company or organization. Must be broader than Site-Local.
Global	FF0E	No Boundaries	No boundaries.

24

Breaking down the concepts a little further, packets sent to a multicast address with a link-local scope should stay on the local link, that is, the local subnet. Hosts know they can process a link-local packet if received, as do routers. However, routers know to not route the packet to other subnets because of the scope. Packets with an organization-local scope should be routed inside the organization but not out to the Internet or over a link to another company. (Note that routers can predict the boundaries of some scopes, like link-local, but they need configuration to know the boundaries of other scopes, for instance, organization-local.)

Comparing a few of the scopes in terms of where the packets can flow, the higher the value in the fourth hex digit, the further away from the sending host the scope allows the packet to be forwarded. Table 24-4 shows that progression top to bottom, while Figure 24-11 shows an example with three scopes: link-local, site-local, and organization-local. In the figure, site-local messages do not cross the WAN, and organization-local messages do not leave the organization over the link to the Internet.

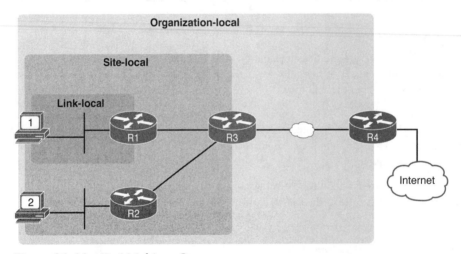

Figure 24-11 *IPv6 Multicast Scopes*

Finally, the term *link-local* has a couple of common uses in IPv6 and can be confusing as a result. The following descriptions should clarify the different uses of the term:

Link-local address: An IPv6 address that begins FE80. This serves as a unicast address for an interface to which devices apply a link-local scope. Devices often create their own link-local addresses using EUI-64 rules. A more complete term for comparison would be *link-local unicast address*.

Link-local multicast address: An IPv6 address that begins with FF02. This serves as a reserved multicast address to which devices apply a link-local scope.

Link-local scope: A reference to the scope itself, rather than an address. This scope defines that routers should not forward packets sent to an address in this scope.

Solicited-Node Multicast Addresses

IPv6 Neighbor Discovery Protocol (NDP) replaces IPv4 ARP, as discussed in Chapter 25. NDP improves the MAC-discovery process by sending IPv6 multicast packets that can be processed by the correct host but discarded with less processing by the rest of the hosts in the subnet. The process uses the solicited-node multicast address associated with the unicast IPv6 address.

Figure 24-12 shows how to determine the solicited node multicast address associated with a unicast address. Start with the predefined /104 prefix (26 hex digits) shown in Figure 24-12. In other words, all the solicited-node multicast addresses begin with the abbreviated FF02::1:FF. In the last 24 bits (6 hex digits), copy the last 6 hex digits of the unicast address into the solicited-node address.

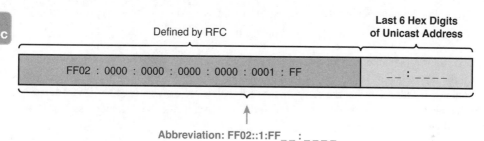

Figure 24-12 *Solicited-Node Multicast Address Format*

Note that a host or router calculates a matching solicited node multicast address for every unicast address on an interface. Example 24-9 shows an example, in which the router interface has a unicast address of 2001:DB8:1111:1::1/64, and a link-local address of FE80::AA:AAAA. As a result, the interface has two solicited node multicast addresses, shown at the end of the output.

Example 24-9 *Verifying Static IPv6 Addresses on Router R1*

```
R1# show ipv6 interface GigabitEthernet 0/0
GigabitEthernet0/0 is up, line protocol is up
  IPv6 is enabled, link-local address is FE80::AA:AAAA
  No Virtual link-local address(es):
  Global unicast address(es):
    2001:DB8:1111:1::1, subnet is 2001:DB8:1111:1::/64 [TEN]
  Joined group address(es):
    FF02::1
    FF02::2
    FF02::5
    FF02::1:FF00:1
    FF02::1:FFAA:AAAA
! Lines omitted for brevity
```

24

Note that in this case, R1's global unicast address ends with 00:0001 (unabbreviated), resulting in an unabbreviated solicited node multicast address of FF02:0000:0000:0000:0000:0001:FF00:00001. This value begins with the 26-hex-digit prefix shown in Figure 24-12, followed by 00:0001. The solicited node multicast address corresponding to link-local address FE80::AA:AAAA ends in AA:AAAA and is shown in the last line of the example.

Miscellaneous IPv6 Addresses

Together, this chapter and the preceding chapter have introduced most of the IPv6 addressing concepts included in this book. This short topic mentions a few remaining IPv6 addressing ideas and summarizes the topics for easy study.

First, all IPv6 hosts can use two additional special addresses:

- The unknown (unspecified) IPv6 address, ::, or all 0s
- The loopback IPv6 address, ::1, or 127 binary 0s with a single 1

A host can use the unknown address (::) when its own IPv6 address is not yet known or when the host wonders if its own IPv6 address might have problems. For example, hosts use the unknown address during the early stages of dynamically discovering their IPv6 address. When a host does not yet know what IPv6 address to use, it can use the :: address as its source IPv6 address.

The IPv6 loopback address gives each IPv6 host a way to test its own protocol stack. Just like the IPv4 127.0.0.1 loopback address, packets sent to ::1 do not leave the host but are instead simply delivered down the stack to IPv6 and back up the stack to the application on the local host.

Anycast Addresses

Imagine that routers collectively need to implement some service. Rather than have one router supply that service, that service works best when implemented on several routers. But the hosts that use the service need to contact only the nearest such service, and the network wants to hide all these details from the hosts. Hosts can send just one packet to an IPv6 address, and the routers will forward the packet to the nearest router that supports that service by virtue of supporting that destination IPv6 address.

IPv6 anycast addresses provide that exact function. The *any* part of the name refers to the fact that any instances of the service can be used. Figure 24-13 shows this big concept, with two major steps:

Step 1. Two routers configure the exact same IPv6 address, designated as an anycast address, to support some service.

Step 2. In the future, when any router receives a packet for that anycast address, the other routers simply route the packet to the nearest router that supports the address.

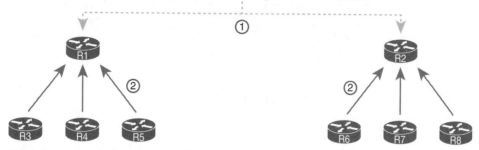

Figure 24-13 *IPv6 Anycast Addresses*

To make this anycast process work, the routers implementing the anycast address must be configured and then advertise a route for the anycast address. The addresses do not come from a special reserved range of addresses; instead, they are from the unicast address range. Often, the address is configured with a /128 prefix so that the routers advertise a host route for that one anycast address. At that point, the routing protocol advertises the route just like any other IPv6 route; the other routers cannot tell the difference.

Example 24-10 shows a sample configuration on a router. Note that the actual address (2001:1:1:2::99) looks like any other unicast address; the value can be chosen like any other IPv6 unicast addresses. However, note the different **anycast** keyword on the **ipv6 address** command, telling the local router that the address has a special purpose as an anycast address. Finally, note that the **show ipv6 interface** command does identify the address as an anycast address, but the **show ipv6 interface brief** command does not.

Example 24-10 *Configuring and Verifying IPv6 Anycast Addresses*

```
R1# configure terminal
Enter configuration commands, one per line. End with CNTL/Z.
R1(config)# interface gigabitEthernet 0/0
R1(config-if)# ipv6 address 2001:1:1:1::1/64
R1(config-if)# ipv6 address 2001:1:1:2::99/128 anycast
R1(config-if)# ^Z
R1#
R1# show ipv6 interface g0/0
GigabitEthernet0/0 is up, line protocol is up
    IPv6 is enabled, link-local address is FE80::11FF:FE11:1111
    No Virtual link-local address(es):
    Global unicast address(es):
        2001:1:1:1::1, subnet is 2001:1:1:1::/64
        2001:1:1:2::99, subnet is 2001:1:1:2::99/128 [ANY]
 ! Lines omitted for brevity
R1# show ipv6 interface brief g0/0
GigabitEthernet0/0 [up/up]
    FE80::11FF:FE11:1111
    2001:1:1:1::1
    2001:1:1:2::99
```

24

> **NOTE** The *subnet router anycast address* is one special anycast address in each subnet. It is reserved for use by routers as a way to send a packet to any router on the subnet. The address's value in each subnet is the same number as the subnet ID; that is, the address has the same prefix value as the other addresses and all binary 0s in the interface ID.

IPv6 Addressing Configuration Summary

This chapter completes the discussion of various IPv6 address types, while showing how to enable IPv6 on interfaces. Many implementations will use the **ipv6 address** command on each router LAN interface, and either that same command or the **ipv6 enable** command on the WAN interfaces. For exam prep, Table 24-5 summarizes the various commands and the automatically generated IPv6 addresses in one place for review and study.

Table 24-5   Summary of IPv6 Address Types and the Commands That Create Them

Type	Prefix/Address Notes	Enabled with What Interface Subcommand
Global unicast	Many prefixes	**ipv6 address** *address/prefix-length* **ipv6 address** *prefix/prefix-length* **eui-64**
Unique Local	FD00::/8	**ipv6 address** *prefix/prefix-length* **eui-64**
Link local	FE80::/10	**ipv6 address** *address* **link-local** Autogenerated by all **ipv6 address** commands Autogenerated by the **ipv6 enable** command
All hosts multicast	FF02::1	Autogenerated by all **ipv6 address** commands
All routers multicast	FF02::2	Autogenerated by all **ipv6 address** commands
Routing protocol multicasts	Various	Added to the interface when the corresponding routing protocol is enabled on the interface
Solicited-node multicast	FF02::1:FF /104	Autogenerated by all **ipv6 address** commands

Chapter Review

One key to doing well on the exams is to perform repetitive spaced review sessions. Review this chapter's material using either the tools in the book or interactive tools for the same material found on the book's companion website. Refer to the "Your Study Plan" element for more details. Table 24-6 outlines the key review elements and where you can find them. To better track your study progress, record when you completed these activities in the second column.

Table 24-6   Chapter Review Tracking

Review Element	Review Date(s)	Resource Used
Review key topics		Book, website
Review key terms		Book, website
Answer DIKTA questions		Book, PTP
Review command tables		Book
Review memory tables		Website
Do labs		Blog
Watch video		Website

Review All the Key Topics

Table 24-7   Key Topics for Chapter 24

Key Topic Element	Description	Page Number
Figure 24-2	Conceptual drawing about the need for dual stacks for the foreseeable future	557
List	Rules for creating an IPv6 address using EUI-64 rules	561
Figure 24-4	IPv6 EUI-64 Address Format and Rules	561
Figure 24-5	Conceptual drawing of how to create an IPv6 address using EUI-64 rules	561
Figure 24-6	Example of performing the bit inversion when using EUI-64	562
List	Functions IOS enables when an IPv6 is configured on a working interface	565
List	Key facts about IPv6 link-local addresses	566
Table 24-4	Link-local scope terms and meanings	571
List	Comparisons of the use of the term *link-local*	572
Figure 24-12	Conceptual drawing of how to make a solicited-node multicast address	573
List	Other special IPv6 addresses	574
Table 24-5	IPv6 address summary with the commands that enable each address type	576

24

Key Terms You Should Know

anycast address, dual stacks, EUI-64, link-local address, link-local scope, link-local multicast address, site-local scope, organization-local scope, interface-local scope, IPv6 address scope, solicited-node multicast address, all-nodes multicast address, all-routers multicast address, subnet-router anycast address

Additional Practice for This Chapter's Processes

For additional practice with IPv6 abbreviations, you may do the same set of practice problems using your choice of tools:

For additional practice with calculating IPv6 address using EUI-64 rules and finding the solicited-node multicast address based on a unicast address, use the exercises in Appendix H, "Practice for Chapter 24: Implementing IPv6 Addressing on Routers." You have two options to use:

PDF: Navigate to the companion website and open the PDF for Appendix H.

Application: Navigate to the companion website and open the application "Practice Exercise: EUI-64 and Solicited Node Multicast Problems"

Additionally, you can create your own problems using any real router or simulator: Get into the router CLI, into configuration mode, and configure the **mac-address** *address* and **ipv6 address** *prefix***/64 eui-64** command. Then predict the IPv6 unicast address, link-local address, and solicited-node multicast address; finally, check your predictions against the **show ipv6 interface** command.

Command References

Tables 24-8 and 24-9 list configuration and verification commands used in this chapter. As an easy review exercise, cover the left column in a table, read the right column, and try to recall the command without looking. Then repeat the exercise, covering the right column, and try to recall what the command does.

Table 24-8   Chapter 24 Configuration Command Reference

Command	Description
ipv6 unicast-routing	Global command that enables IPv6 routing on the router.
ipv6 address *ipv6-address/ prefix-length* [**eui-64**]	Interface subcommand that manually configures either the entire interface IP address or a /64 prefix with the router building the EUI-64 format interface ID automatically.
ipv6 address *ipv6-address/ prefix-length* [**anycast**]	Interface subcommand that manually configures an address to be used as an anycast address.
ipv6 enable	Command that enables IPv6 on an interface and generates a link-local address.
ipv6 address dhcp	Interface subcommand that enables IPv6 on an interface, causes the router to use DHCP client processes to try to lease an IPv6 address, and creates a link-local address for the interface.

Table 24-9   Chapter 24 EXEC Command Reference

Command	Description
show ipv6 route [connected] [local]	Lists IPv6 routes, or just the connected routes, or just the local routes.
show ipv6 interface [*type number*]	Lists IPv6 settings on an interface, including link-local and other unicast IP addresses (or for the listed interface).
show ipv6 interface brief [*type number*]	Lists interface status and IPv6 addresses for each interface (or for the listed interface).

Answers to Earlier Practice Problems

Table 24-2, earlier in this chapter, listed several practice problems in which you needed to calculate the IPv6 address based on EUI-64 rules. Table 24-10 lists the answers to those problems.

Table 24-10   Answers to IPv6 EUI-64 Address Creation Practice

Prefix	MAC Address	Unabbreviated IPv6 Address
2001:DB8:1:1::/64	0013.ABAB.1001	2001:DB8:1:1:0213:ABFF:FEAB:1001
2001:DB8:1:1::/64	AA13.ABAB.1001	2001:DB8:1:1:A813:ABFF:FEAB:1001
2001:DB8:1:1::/64	000C.BEEF.CAFE	2001:DB8:1:1:020C:BEFF:FEEF:CAFE
2001:DB8:1:1::/64	B80C.BEEF.CAFE	2001:DB8:1:1:BA0C:BEFF:FEEF:CAFE
2001:DB8:FE:FE::/64	0C0C.ABAC.CABA	2001:DB8:FE:FE:0E0C:ABFF:FEAC:CABA
2001:DB8:FE:FE::/64	0A0C.ABAC.CABA	2001:DB8:FE:FE:080C:ABFF:FEAC:CABA

24

CHAPTER 25

Implementing IPv6 Routing

3.0 IP Connectivity

3.3 Configure and verify IPv4 and IPv6 static routing

3.3.a Default route

3.3.b Network route

3.3.c Host route

3.3.d Floating static

This last chapter in Part VII of the book completes the materials about IPv6 by examining three major topics. The first section examines IPv6 connected and local routes, similar to IPv4, showing how a router adds both connected and local routes based on each interface IPv6 address. The second major section of this chapter then looks at how to configure static IPv6 routes by typing in commands, in this case using the **ipv6 route** command instead of IPv4's **ip route** command. The final major section examines the Neighbor Discovery Protocol (NDP).

"Do I Know This Already?" Quiz

Take the quiz (either here or use the PTP software) if you want to use the score to help you decide how much time to spend on this chapter. The letter answers are listed at the bottom of the page following the quiz. Appendix C, found both at the end of the book as well as on the companion website, includes both the answers and explanations. You can also find both answers and explanations in the PTP testing software.

Table 25-1 "Do I Know This Already?" Foundation Topics Section-to-Question Mapping

Foundation Topics Section	Questions
Connected and Local IPv6 Routes	1–2
Static IPv6 Routes	3–6
The Neighbor Discovery Protocol	7–8

Refer to the following figure for questions 1, 3, and 4.

1. A router has been configured with the **ipv6 address 2000:1:2:3::1/64** command on its G0/1 interface as shown in the figure. The router creates a link-local address of FE80::FF:FE00:1 as well. The interface is working. Which of the following routes will the router add to its IPv6 routing table? (Choose two answers.)

   a. A route for 2000:1:2:3::/64

   b. A route for FE80::FF:FE00:1/64

   c. A route for 2000:1:2:3::1/128

   d. A route for FE80::FF:FE00:1/128

2. A router has been configured with the **ipv6 address 3111:1:1:1::1/64** command on its G0/1 interface and **ipv6 address 3222:2:2:2::1/64** on its G0/2 interface. Both interfaces are working. Which of the following routes would you expect to see in the output of the **show ipv6 route connected** command? (Choose two answers.)

   a. A route for 3111:1:1:1::/64

   b. A route for 3111:1:1:1::1/64

   c. A route for 3222:2:2:2::/64

   d. A route for 3222:2:2:2::2/128

3. An engineer needs to add a static IPv6 route for prefix 2000:1:2:3::/64 to Router R5's configuration, in the figure shown with question 1. Which of the following answers shows a valid static IPv6 route for that subnet, on Router R5?

   a. **ipv6 route 2000:1:2:3::/64 S0/1/1**

   b. **ipv6 route 2000:1:2:3::/64 S0/1/0**

   c. **ip route 2000:1:2:3::/64 S0/1/1**

   d. **ip route 2000:1:2:3::/64 S0/1/0**

4. An engineer needs to add a static IPv6 route for prefix 2000:1:2:3::/64 to Router R5 in the figure shown with question 1. Which of the following answers shows a valid static IPv6 route for that subnet on Router R5?

   a. **ipv6 route 2000:1:2:3::/64 2000:1:2:56::5**

   b. **ipv6 route 2000:1:2:3::/64 2000:1:2:56::6**

   c. **ipv6 route 2000:1:2:3::/64 FE80::FF:FE00:5**

   d. **ipv6 route 2000:1:2:3::/64 FE80::FF:FE00:6**

5. An engineer types the command **ipv6 route 2001:DB8:8:8::/64 2001:DB8:9:9::9 129** in configuration mode of Router R1 and presses **Enter**. Later, a **show ipv6 route** command does not list any route for subnet 2001:DB8:8:8::/64. Which of the following could have caused the route to not be in the IPv6 routing table?

   a. The command should be using a next-hop link-local address instead of a global unicast.

   b. The command is missing an outgoing interface parameter, so IOS rejected the **ipv6 route** command.

   c. The router has no routes that match 2001:DB8:9:9::9.

   d. A route for 2001:DB8:8:8::/64 with administrative distance 110 already exists.

6. The command output shows two routes from the longer output of the **show ipv6 route** command. Which answers are true about the output? (Choose two answers.)

   ```
   R1# show ipv6 route static
   ! Legend omitted for brevity
   S 2001:DB8:2:2::/64 [1/0]
    via 2001:DB8:4:4::4
   S ::/0 [1/0]
    via Serial0/0/1, directly connected
   ```

   a. The route to ::/0 is added because of an **ipv6 route** global command.

   b. The administrative distance of the route to 2001:DB8:2:2::/64 is 1.

   c. The route to ::/0 is added because of an **ipv6 address** interface subcommand.

   d. The route to 2001:DB8:2:2::/64 is added because of an IPv6 routing protocol.

7. PC1, PC2, and Router R1 all connect to the same VLAN and IPv6 subnet. PC1 wants to send its first IPv6 packet to PC2. What protocol or message will PC1 use to discover the MAC address to which PC1 should send the Ethernet frame that encapsulates this IPv6 packet?

   a. ARP

   b. NDP NS

   c. NDP RS

   d. SLAAC

8. Which of the following pieces of information does a router supply in an NDP Router Advertisement (RA) message? (Choose two answers.)

   a. Router IPv6 address

   b. Host name of the router

   c. IPv6 prefix(es) on the link

   d. IPv6 address of DHCP server

Foundation Topics

Connected and Local IPv6 Routes

A Cisco router adds IPv6 routes to its IPv6 routing table for several reasons. Many of you could predict those reasons at this point in your reading, in part because the logic mirrors the logic routers use for IPv4. Specifically, a router adds IPv6 routes based on the following:

- The configuration of IPv6 addresses on working interfaces (connected and local routes)
- The direct configuration of a static route (static routes)
- The configuration of a routing protocol, like OSPFv3, on routers that share the same data link (dynamic routes)

The first two sections of this chapter examine the first of these two topics, with discussions of IPv6 routing protocols now residing in the CCNP Enterprise exams.

Rules for Connected and Local Routes

Routers add and remove connected routes and local routes, based on the interface configuration and the interface state. First, the router looks for any configured unicast addresses on any interfaces by looking for the **ipv6 address** command. Then, if the interface is working—if the interface has a "line status is up, protocol status is up" notice in the output of the **show interfaces** command—the router adds both a connected and local route.

> **NOTE**   Routers do not create connected or local IPv6 routes for link-local addresses.

The connected and local routes themselves follow the same general logic as with IPv4. The connected route represents the subnet connected to the interface, whereas the local route is a host route for only the specific IPv6 address configured on the interface.

As an example, consider a router, with a working interface, configured with the **ipv6 address 2000:1:1:1::1/64** command. The router will calculate the subnet ID based on this address and prefix length, and it will place a connected route for that subnet (2000:1:1:1::/64) into the routing table. The router also takes the listed IPv6 address and creates a host route for that address, with a /128 prefix length. (With IPv4, host routes have a /32 prefix length, while IPv6 uses a /128 prefix length, meaning "exactly this one address.")

The following list summarizes the rules about how routers create routes based on the configuration of an interface IPv6 unicast address, for easier review and study:

1. Routers create IPv6 routes based on each unicast IPv6 address on an interface, as configured with the **ipv6 address** command, as follows:
   A. The router creates a route for the subnet (a connected route).
   B. The router creates a host route (/128 prefix length) for the router IPv6 address (a local route).
2. Routers do not create routes based on the link-local addresses associated with the interface.
3. Routers remove the connected and local routes for an interface if the interface fails, and they re-add these routes when the interface is again in a working (up/up) state.

25

Example of Connected IPv6 Routes

While the concept of connected and local IPv6 routes works much like IPv4 routes, seeing a few examples can certainly help. To show some sample routes, Figure 25-1 gives the details of one sample internetwork used in this chapter. The figure shows the IPv6 subnet IDs. The upcoming examples focus on the connected and local routes on Router R1.

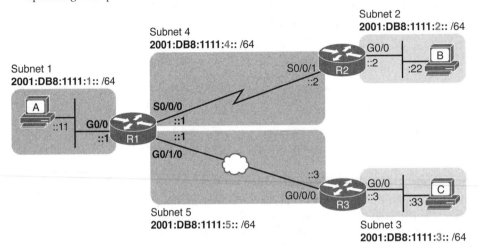

Figure 25-1   *Sample Network Used to Show Connected and Local Routes*

To clarify the notes in Figure 25-1, note that the figure shows IPv6 prefixes (subnets), with a shorthand notation for the interface IPv6 addresses. The figure shows only the abbreviated interface ID portion of each interface address near each interface. For example, R1's G0/0 interface address would begin with subnet ID value 2001:DB8:1111:1, added to ::1, for 2001:DB8:1111:1::1.

Now on to the example of connected routes. To begin, consider the configuration of Router R1 from Figure 25-1, as shown in Example 25-1. The excerpt from the **show running-config** command on R1 shows three interfaces, all of which are working. Also note that no static route or routing protocol configuration exists.

Example 25-1   *IPv6 Addressing Configuration on Router R1*

```
ipv6 unicast-routing
!
interface GigabitEthernet0/0
 ipv6 address 2001:DB8:1111:1::1/64
!
interface Serial0/0/0
 ipv6 address 2001:db8:1111:4::1/64
!
interface GigabitEthernet0/1/0
 ipv6 address 2001:db8:1111:5::1/64
```

Answers to the "Do I Know This Already?" quiz:

1 A, C **2** A, C **3** A **4** B **5** C **6** A, B **7** B **8** A, C

Based on Figure 25-1 and Example 25-1, R1 should have three connected IPv6 routes, as highlighted in Example 25-2.

Example 25-2   *Routes on Router R1 Before Adding Static Routes or Routing Protocols*

```
R1# show ipv6 route
IPv6 Routing Table - default - 7 entries
Codes: C - Connected, L - Local, S - Static, U - Per-user Static route
       B - BGP, HA - Home Agent, MR - Mobile Router, R - RIP
       H - NHRP, I1 - ISIS L1, I2 - ISIS L2, IA - ISIS interarea
       IS - ISIS summary, D - EIGRP, EX - EIGRP external, NM - NEMO
       ND - ND Default, NDp - ND Prefix, DCE - Destination, NDr - Redirect
       RL - RPL, O - OSPF Intra, OI - OSPF Inter, OE1 - OSPF ext 1
       OE2 - OSPF ext 2, ON1 - OSPF NSSA ext 1, ON2 - OSPF NSSA ext 2
       la - LISP alt, lr - LISP site-registrations, ld - LISP dyn-eid
       lA - LISP away, a - Application
C   2001:DB8:1111:1::/64 [0/0]
     via GigabitEthernet0/0, directly connected
L   2001:DB8:1111:1::1/128 [0/0]
     via GigabitEthernet0/0, receive
C   2001:DB8:1111:4::/64 [0/0]
     via Serial0/0/0, directly connected
L   2001:DB8:1111:4::1/128 [0/0]
     via GigabitEthernet0/0/0, receive
C   2001:DB8:1111:5::/64 [0/0]
     via GigabitEthernet0/1/0, directly connected
L   2001:DB8:1111:5::1/128 [0/0]
     via GigabitEthernet0/1/0, receive
L   FF00::/8 [0/0]
     via Null0, receive
```

All three highlighted routes show the same basic kinds of information, so for discussion, focus on the first pair of highlighted lines, which detail the connected route for subnet 2001:DB8:1111:1::/64. The first pair of highlighted lines state: The route is a "directly connected" route; the interface ID is GigabitEthernet0/0; and the prefix/length is 2001:DB8:1111:1::/64. At the far left, the code letter "C" identifies the route as a connected route (per the legend above). Also note that the numbers in brackets mirror the same ideas as IPv4's **show ip route** command: The first number represents the administrative distance, and the second is the metric.

Examples of Local IPv6 Routes

Continuing this same example, three local routes should exist on R1 for the same three interfaces as the connected routes. Indeed, that is the case, with one extra local route for other purposes. Example 25-3 shows only the local routes, as listed by the **show ipv6 route local** command, with highlights of one particular local route for discussion.

25

Example 25-3 *Local IPv6 Routes on Router R1*

```
R1# show ipv6 route local
! Legend omitted for brevity


L   2001:DB8:1111:1::1/128 [0/0]
      via GigabitEthernet0/0, receive
L   2001:DB8:1111:4::1/128 [0/0]
      via Serial0/0/0, receive
L   2001:DB8:1111:5::1/128 [0/0]
      via GigabitEthernet0/1/0, receive
L   FF00::/8 [0/0]
      via Null0, receive
```

For the highlighted local route, look for a couple of quick facts. First, look back to R1's configuration in Example 25-1, and note R1's IPv6 address on its G0/0 interface. This local route lists the exact same address. Also note the /128 prefix length, meaning this route matches packets sent to that address (2001:DB8:1111:1::1), and only that address.

NOTE   While the **show ipv6 route local** command shows all local IPv6 routes, the **show ipv6 route connected** command shows all connected routes.

Static IPv6 Routes

While routers automatically add connected and local routes based on the interface configuration, static routes require direct configuration with the **ipv6 route** command. Simply put, someone configures the command, and the router places the details from the command into a route in the IPv6 routing table.

The **ipv6 route** command follows the same general logic as does IPv4's **ip route** command, as discussed in Chapter 16, "Configuring IPv4 Addressing and Static Routes." For IPv4, the **ip route** command starts by listing the subnet ID and mask, so for IPv6, the **ipv6 route** command begins with the prefix and prefix length. Then the respective commands list the directions of how this router should forward packets toward that destination subnet or prefix by listing the outgoing interface or the address of the next-hop router.

Figure 25-2 shows the concepts behind a single **ipv6 route** command, demonstrating the concepts behind a static route on Router R1 for the subnet on the right (subnet 2, or 2001:DB8:1111:2::/64). A static route on R1, for this subnet, will begin with **ipv6 route 2001:DB8:1111:2::/64**, followed by either the outgoing interface (S0/0/0) or the next-hop IPv6 address, or both.

Now that you understand the big ideas with IPv6 static routes, the next few pages walk you through a series of examples. In particular, the examples look at configuring static routes with an outgoing interface, then with a next-hop global unicast address, and then with a next-hop link-local address. This section ends with a discussion of static IPv6 default routes.

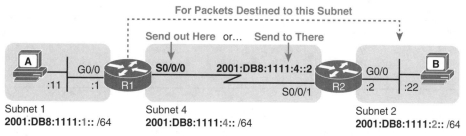

Figure 25-2 *Logic Behind IPv6 Static Route Commands (IPv6 Route)*

Static Routes Using the Outgoing Interface

This first IPv6 static route example uses the outgoing interface option. As a reminder, for both IPv4 and IPv6 static routes, when the command references an interface, the interface is a local interface. That is, it is an interface on the router where the command is added. In this case, as shown in Figure 25-2, R1's **ipv6 route** command would use interface S0/0/0, as shown in Example 25-4.

Example 25-4 *Static IPv6 Routes on Router R1*

```
! Static route on router R1
R1(config)# ipv6 route 2001:db8:1111:2::/64 S0/0/0
```

While Example 25-4 shows the correct syntax of the route, if using static routes throughout this internetwork, more static routes are needed. For example, to support traffic between hosts A and B, R1 is now prepared. Host A will forward all its IPv6 packets to its default router (R1), and R1 can now route those packets out S0/0/0 to R2 next. However, Router R2 does not yet have a route back to host A's subnet, subnet 1 (2001:DB8:1111:1::/64), so a complete solution requires more routes.

Example 25-5 solves this problem by giving Router R2 a static route for subnet 1 (2001:DB8:1111:1::/64). After this route is added, hosts A and B should be able to ping each other.

Example 25-5 *Static IPv6 Routes on Router R2*

```
! Static route on router R2
R2(config)# ipv6 route 2001:db8:1111:1::/64 s0/0/1
```

Many options exist for verifying the existence of the static route and testing whether hosts can use the route. **ping** and **traceroute** can test connectivity. From the router command line, the **show ipv6 route** command will list all the IPv6 routes. The shorter output of the **show ipv6 route static** command, which lists only static routes, could also be used; Example 25-6 shows that output, with the legend omitted.

25

Example 25-6 *Verification of Static Routes Only on R1*

```
R1# show ipv6 route static
! Legend omitted for brevity
S    2001:DB8:1111:2::/64 [1/0]
     via Serial0/0/0, directly connected
```

This command lists many facts about the one static route on R1. First, the code "S" in the left column does identify the route as a static route. (However, the later phrase "directly connected" might mislead you to think this is a connected route; trust the "S" code.) Note that the prefix (2001:DB8:1111:2::/64) matches the configuration (in Example 25-4), as does the outgoing interface (S0/0/0).

While this command lists basic information about each static route, it does not state whether this route would be used when forwarding packets to a particular destination. For example, if host A sent an IPv6 packet to host B (2001:DB8:1111:2::22), would R1 use this static route? As it turns out, R1 would use that route, as confirmed by the **show ipv6 route 2001:DB8:1111:2::22** command. This command asks the router to list the route that the router would use when forwarding packets to that particular address. Example 25-7 shows an example.

Example 25-7 *Displaying the Route R1 Uses to Forward to Host B*

```
R1# show ipv6 route 2001:db8:1111:2::22
Routing entry for 2001:DB8:1111:2::/64
  Known via "static", distance 1, metric 0
  Route count is 1/1, share count 0
  Routing paths:
    directly connected via Serial0/0/0
      Last updated 00:01:29 ago
```

Static Routes Using Next-Hop IPv6 Address

The previous example used a serial WAN link on purpose. With a point-to-point WAN link, the **ipv6 route** command can use the outgoing interface style of configuration Static IPv6 routes that refer to a next-hop address have two options: the unicast address on the neighboring router (global unicast or unique local) or the link-local address of that same neighboring router. Figure 25-3 spells out those two options with an updated version of Figure 25-2, this time showing Router R2's global unicast as well as R2's link-local address.

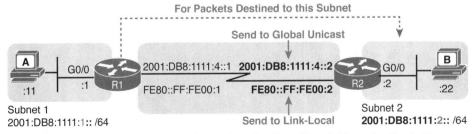

Figure 25-3 *Using Unicast or Link-Local as the Next-Hop Address for Static Routes*

The next few pages walk you through examples, first with a global unicast as a next-hop and then with a link-local as a next-hop.

Example Static Route with a Global Unicast Next-Hop Address

This example uses the internetwork shown in Figure 25-3, but with the earlier static routes removed. That is, both routers have only connected and local routes to begin the example.

In Example 25-8, both R1 and R2 add static routes that refer to the neighbor's global unicast address. R1 adds a route for subnet 2 (on the right), while R2 adds a route for subnet 1 (on the left). Note that the example shows routes in both directions so that the two hosts can send packets to each other.

Example 25-8 *Static IPv6 Routes Using Global Unicast Addresses*

```
! The first command is on router R1, listing R2's global unicast address
R1(config)# ipv6 route 2001:db8:1111:2::/64 2001:DB8:1111:4::2
```

```
! The next command is on router R2, listing R1's global unicast address
R2(config)# ipv6 route 2001:db8:1111:1::/64 2001:db8:1111:4::1
```

The **ipv6 route** command itself is relatively straightforward. Focus on R1's route, which matches the logic shown in Figure 25-3. The command lists subnet 2 (2001:DB8:1111:2::/64). It then lists R2's global unicast address (ending in 4::2).

The verification commands on R1, as shown in Example 25-9, list the usual information. Example 25-9 shows two commands, first listing R1's only static route (the one configured in Example 25-8). The end of the example lists the **show ipv6 route 2001:DB8:1111:2::22** command, which lists the route R1 uses when forwarding packets to Host B, proving that R1 uses this new static route when forwarding packets to that host.

Example 25-9 *Verification of Static Routes to a Next-Hop Global Unicast Address*

```
R1# show ipv6 route static
! Legend omitted for brevity
S    2001:DB8:1111:2::/64 [1/0]
      via 2001:DB8:1111:4::2


R1# show ipv6 route 2001:db8:1111:2::22/64
Routing entry for 2001:DB8:1111:2::/64
  Known via "static", distance 1, metric 0
  Backup from "ospf 1 [110]"
  Route count is 1/1, share count 0
  Routing paths:
    2001:DB8:1111:4::2
      Last updated 00:07:43 ago
```

Example Static Route with a Link-Local Next-Hop Address

Static routes that refer to a neighbor's link-local address work a little like both of the preceding two styles of static routes. First, the **ipv6 route** command refers to a next-hop address,

25

namely a link-local address. However, the command must also refer to the router's local outgoing interface. Why both? The **ipv6 route** command cannot simply refer to a link-local next-hop address by itself because the link-local address does not, by itself, tell the local router which outgoing interface to use.

Interestingly, when the **ipv6 route** command refers to a global unicast next-hop address, the router can deduce the outgoing interface. For example, the earlier example on R1, as shown in Example 25-8, shows R1 with a static IPv6 route with a next-hop IPv6 address of 2001:DB8:1111:4::2. R1 can look at its IPv6 routing table, see its connected route that includes this 2001:DB8:1111:4::2 address, and see a connected route off R1's S0/0/0. As a result, with a next-hop global unicast address, R1 can deduce the correct outgoing interface (R1's S0/0/0).

With a link-local next-hop address, a router cannot work through this same logic, so the outgoing interface must also be configured. Example 25-10 shows the configuration of static routes on R1 and R2, replacements for the two routes previously configured in Example 25-8.

Example 25-10 *Static IPv6 Routes Using Link-Local Neighbor Addresses*

```
! The first command is on router R1, listing R2's link-local address
R1(config)# ipv6 route 2001:db8:1111:2::/64 S0/0/0 FE80::FF:FE00:2

! The next command is on router R2, listing R1's link-local address
R2(config)# ipv6 route 2001:db8:1111:1::/64 S0/0/1 FE80::FF:FE00:1
```

Example 25-11 verifies the configuration in Example 25-10 by repeating the **show ipv6 route static** and **show ipv6 route 2001:DB8:1111:2::22** commands used in Example 25-9. Note that the output from both commands differs slightly in regard to the forwarding details. Because the new commands list both the next-hop address and outgoing interface, the **show** commands also list both the next-hop (link-local) address and the outgoing interface. If you refer back to Example 25-9, you will see only a next-hop address listed.

Example 25-11 *Verification of Static Routes to a Next-Hop Link-Local Address*

```
R1# show ipv6 route static
! Legend omitted for brevity


S    2001:DB8:1111:2::/64 [1/0]
        via FE80::FF:FE00:2, Serial0/0/0


R1# show ipv6 route 2001:db8:1111:2::22
Routing entry for 2001:DB8:1111:2::/64
  Known via "static", distance 1, metric 0
  Backup from "ospf 1 [110]"
  Route count is 1/1, share count 0
  Routing paths:
    FE80::FF:FE00:2, Serial0/0/0
      Last updated 00:08:10 ago
```

Static Routes over Ethernet Links

You might have wondered why the chapter shows examples with a serial link, knowing that most networks use fewer and fewer serial links today. Using serial links in the examples avoids one complication when defining static routes that use Ethernet interfaces (LAN or WAN). The next example discusses the issues and shows configuration options for static routes when the outgoing interface is an Ethernet interface.

To configure a static route that uses an Ethernet interface, the **ipv6 route** command's forwarding parameters should always include a next-hop IPv6 address. IOS allows you to configure the **ipv6 route** command using only the outgoing-interface parameter, without listing a next-hop address. The router will accept the command; however, if that outgoing interface happens to be an Ethernet interface, the router cannot successfully forward IPv6 packets using the route.

To configure the **ipv6 route** correctly when directing packets out an Ethernet interface, the configuration should use one of these styles:

- Refer to the next-hop global unicast address (or unique local address) only
- Refer to both the outgoing interface and next-hop global unicast address (or unique local address)
- Refer to both the outgoing interface and next-hop link-local address

Example 25-12 shows a sample configuration from routers R1 and R3 in Figure 25-4. The top part of the figure shows the details for R1's route to the subnet on the right side of the figure, with the details labeled with an "A." The bottom half shows the details for R3's route to the LAN subnet on the left of the figure, labeled with a "B."

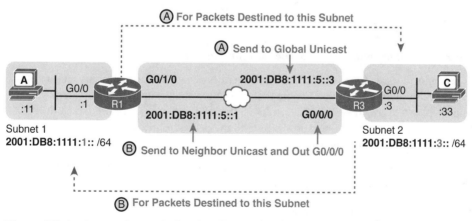

Figure 25-4 *Network Details for IPv6 Static Routes on an Ethernet Interface*

Example 25-12 *Static IPv6 Routes with an Ethernet WAN Interface*

```
! The first command is on router R1, listing R3's global unicast address
R1(config)# ipv6 route 2001:db8:1111:3::/64 2001:db8:1111:5::3

! The next command is on router R2, listing R1's link-local address
R2(config)# ipv6 route 2001:db8:1111:1::/64 G0/0/0 2001:db8:1111:5::1
```

25

Static Default Routes

IPv6 supports a default route concept, similar to IPv4. The default route tells the router what to do with an IPv6 packet when the packet matches no other IPv6 route. The logic is pretty basic:

■ With no default route, the router discards the IPv6 packet.

■ With a default route, the router forwards the IPv6 packet based on the default route.

Default routes can be particularly useful in a couple of network design cases. For example, with an enterprise network design that uses a single router at each branch office, with one WAN link to each branch, the branch routers have only one possible path over which to forward packets. In a large network, when using a routing protocol, the branch router could learn thousands of routes—all of which point back toward the core of the network over that one WAN link.

Branch routers could use default routes instead of a routing protocol. The branch router would forward all traffic to the core of the network. Figure 25-5 shows just such an example, with two sample branch routers on the right and a core site router on the left.

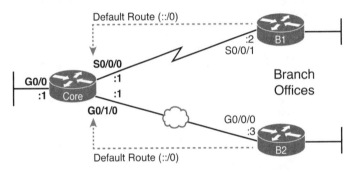

Figure 25-5   *Using Static Default Routes at Branches to Forward Back to the Core*

To configure a static default route, use the same rules already discussed in this section of the chapter, but use a specific value to note the route as a default route: ::/0. Taken literally, the double colon (::) is the IPv6 abbreviation for all 0s, and the /0 means the prefix length is 0. This idea mirrors the IPv4 convention to refer to the default route as 0.0.0.0/0. Otherwise, just configure the **ipv6 route** command as normal.

Example 25-13 shows one such sample static default route on Router B1 from Figure 25-5. This example uses the outgoing interface option.

Example 25-13   *Static Default Route for Branch Router B1*

```
!Forward out B1's S0/0/1 local interface...
B1(config)# ipv6 route ::/0 S0/0/1
```

With IPv6, the router displays the default a little more cleanly than with IPv4. The **show ipv6 route** command simply includes the route in the output of the command, along with the other routes. Example 25-14 shows an example, with "::/0" listed to denote this route as the default route.

Example 25-14 *Router B1's Static Default Route (Using Outgoing Interface)*

```
B1# show ipv6 route static
IPv6 Routing Table - default - 10 entries
Codes: C - Connected, L - Local, S - Static, U - Per-user Static route
       B - BGP, R - RIP, I1 - ISIS L1, I2 - ISIS L2
       IA - ISIS interarea, IS - ISIS summary, D - EIGRP, EX - EIGRP external
       ND - ND Default, NDp - ND Prefix, DCE - Destination, NDr - Redirect
       O - OSPF Intra, OI - OSPF Inter, OE1 - OSPF ext 1, OE2 - OSPF ext 2
       ON1 - OSPF NSSA ext 1, ON2 - OSPF NSSA ext 2
S   ::/0 [1/0]
     via Serial0/0/1, directly connected
```

Static IPv6 Host Routes

Both IPv4 and IPv6 allow the definition of static host routes—that is, a route to a single host IP address. With IPv4, those routes use a /32 mask, which identifies a single IPv4 address in the **ip route** command; with IPv6, a /128 mask identifies that single host in the **ipv6 route** command.

A host route follows the same rules as a route for any other IPv6 subnet. For instance, if you refer back to Figure 25-3, host B sits on the right side of the figure. Earlier examples showed R1's static routes for the subnet in which host B resides—for example, the routes for Router R1 in Examples 25-8 and 25-10. To create a host route on R1, referring to host B's specific IPv6 address, just change those commands to refer to host B's entire IPv6 address (2001:DB8:1111:2::22), with prefix length /128.

Example 25-15 shows two sample host routes on Router R1. Both define a host route to host B's IPv6 address as seen in Figure 25-3. One route uses Router R2's link-local address as the next-hop address, and one route uses R2's global unicast address as the next-hop address.

Example 25-15 *Static Host IPv6 Routes on R1, for Host B*

```
! The first command lists host B's address, prefix length /128,
! with R2's link-local address as next-hop, with an outgoing interface.
R1(config)# ipv6 route 2001:db8:1111:2::22/128 S0/0/0 FE80::FF:FE00:2
R1(config)#
! The next command also lists host B's address, prefix length /128,
! but with R2's global unicast address as next-hop, and no outgoing interface.
R1(config)# ipv6 route 2001:db8:1111:2::22/128 2001:DB8:1111:4::2
```

Floating Static IPv6 Routes

Next, consider the case in which a static route competes with other static routes or routes learned by a routing protocol. For example, consider the topology shown in Figure 25-6, which shows a branch office with two WAN links: one very fast Gigabit Ethernet link and one rather slow (but cheap) T1. In this design, the network uses OSPFv3 to learn IPv6 routes over the primary link, learning a route for subnet 2001:DB8:1111:7::/64. R1 also defines a static route over the backup link to that exact same subnet, so R1 must choose whether to use the static route or the OSPF-learned route.

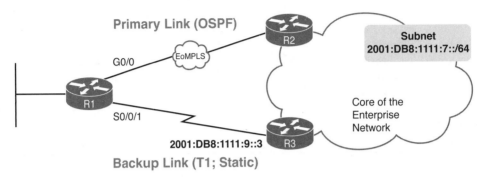

Figure 25-6   *Using a Floating Static Route to Key Subnet 2001:DB8:1111:7::/64*

IOS considers static routes better than OSPF-learned routes by default due to administrative distance. IOS uses the same administrative distance concept and default values for IPv6 as it does for IPv4. As a result, a static IPv6 route over the lower path would be given an administrative distance of 1, and an OSPFv3-learned route over the top path would be given an administrative distance of 110. R1 would use the lower path to reach subnet 2001:DB8:1111:7::/64 in this case, which is not the intended design. Instead, the engineer prefers to use the OSPF-learned routes over the much-faster primary link and use the static route over the backup link only as needed when the primary link fails.

To instead prefer the OSPF routes, the configuration would need to change the administrative distance settings and use what many networkers call a floating static route. Like an IPv4 floating static route, an IPv6 *floating static* route floats or moves into and out of the IPv6 routing table depending on whether the better (lower) administrative distance route learned by the routing protocol happens to exist currently. Basically, the router ignores the static route during times when the better routing protocol route is known.

To implement an IPv6 floating static route, just override the default administrative distance on the static route, making the value larger than the default administrative distance of the routing protocol. For example, the **ipv6 route 2001:db8:1111:7::/64 2001:db8:1111:9::3 130** command on R1 would do exactly that, setting the static route's administrative distance to 130. As long as the primary link (G0/0) stays up, and OSPFv3 on R1 learns a route for **2001:db8:1111:7::/64** with OSPF's default administrative distance of 110, R1 ignores the static route whose administrative distance is explicitly configured as 130.

Finally, note that both the **show ipv6 route** and **show ipv6 route 2001:db8:1111:7::/64** commands list the administrative distance. Example 25-16 shows a sample matching this most recent example. Note that in this case, the static route is in use in the IPv6 routing table.

Example 25-16 *Displaying the Administrative Distance of the Static Route*

```
R1# show ipv6 route static
! Legend omitted for brevity
S    2001:db8:1111:7::/64 [130/0]
        via 2001:db8:1111:9::3


R1# show ipv6 route 2001:db8:1111:7::/64
Routing entry for 2001:db8:1111:7::/64
  Known via "static", distance 130, metric 0
  Route count is 1/1, share count 0
  Routing paths:
    2001:db8:1111:9::3
      Last updated 00:00:58 ago
```

Table 25-2 lists some of the default administrative distance values used with IPv6.

Table 25-2 IOS Defaults for Administrative Distance

Route Source	Administrative Distance
Connected routes	0
Static routes	1
NDP	2
EIGRP	90
OSPF	110
RIP	120
Unknown or unbelievable	255

Troubleshooting Static IPv6 Routes

IPv6 static routes have the same potential issues and mistakes as do static IPv4 routes, as discussed in Chapter 16. However, IPv6 static routes do have a few small differences. This last part of the static route content in the chapter looks at troubleshooting IPv6 static routes, reviewing many of the same troubleshooting rules applied to IPv4 static routes, while focusing on the details specific to IPv6.

This topic breaks static route troubleshooting into two perspectives: cases in which the route is in the routing table but is incorrect, and cases in which the route is not in the routing table.

25

Troubleshooting Incorrect Static Routes That Appear in the IPv6 Routing Table

A static route is only as good as the input typed into the **ipv6 route** command. IOS checks the syntax of the command, of course. However, IOS cannot tell if you choose the incorrect outgoing interface, incorrect next-hop address, or incorrect prefix/prefix-length in a static route. If the parameters pass the syntax checks, IOS places the **ipv6 route** command into the running-config file. Then, if no other problem exists (as discussed at the next heading), IOS puts the route into the IP routing table—even though the route may not work because of the poorly chosen parameters.

For instance, an exam question might show a figure with Router R1 having an address of 2001:1:1:1::1 and neighboring Router R2 with an address of 2001:1:1:1::2. If R1 lists a static route with the command **ipv6 route 3333::/64 2001:1:1:1::1**, the command would be accepted by IOS with correct syntax, but it would not be effective as a route. Note that the command lists R1's address as the next-hop address, and R1 cannot use its own IPv6 address as a next-hop address. IOS does not prevent the configuration of the command, however; it allows the command and adds the route to the IPv6 routing table, but the route cannot possibly forward packets correctly.

When you see an exam question that has static routes, and you see them in the output of **show ipv6 route**, remember that the routes may have incorrect parameters. Check for these types of mistakes:

Step 1.   Prefix/Length: Does the **ipv6 route** command reference the correct subnet ID (prefix) and mask (prefix length)?

Step 2.   If using a next-hop IPv6 address that is a link-local address:

    A. Is the link-local address an address on the correct neighboring router? (It should be an address on another router on a shared link.)

    B. Does the **ipv6 route** command also refer to the correct outgoing interface on the local router?

Step 3.   If using a next-hop IPv6 address that is a global unicast or unique local address, is the address the correct unicast address of the neighboring router?

Step 4.   If referencing an outgoing interface, does the **ipv6 route** command reference the interface on the local router (that is, the same router where the static route is configured)?

This troubleshooting checklist works through the various cases in which IOS would accept the configuration of the static IPv6 route, but the route would not work because of the incorrect parameters in context. It helps to see a few examples. Figure 25-7 shows a sample network to use for the examples; all the examples focus on routes added to Router R1, for the subnet on the far right.

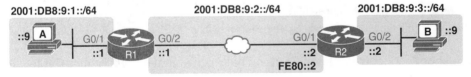

Figure 25-7   *Sample Topology for Incorrect IPv6 Route Examples*

Example 25-17 shows five **ipv6 route** commands. All have correct syntax, but all have one incorrect value; that is, the route will not work because of the types of problems in the troubleshooting checklist. Look for the short comment at the end of each configuration command to see why each is incorrect.

Example 25-17   ipv6 route *Commands with Correct Syntax but Incorrect Ideas*

```
ipv6 route 2001:DB8:9:33::/64 2001:DB8:9:2::2    ! Step 1: Wrong prefix
ipv6 route 2001:DB8:9:3::/64 G0/2 FE80::AAA9      ! Step 2A: Wrong neighbor link local
ipv6 route 2001:DB8:9:3::/64 FE80::2              ! Step 2B: Missing outgoing interface
ipv6 route 2001:DB8:9:3::/64 2001:DB8:9:2::1      ! Step 3: Wrong neighbor address
ipv6 route 2001:DB8:9:3::/64 G0/1 FE80::2         ! Step 4: Wrong interface on R1
```

All these incorrect examples have correct syntax and would be added to R1's IPv6 routing table if configured on R1. However, all have flaws. Working through the examples in order:

Step 1.   The prefix (2001:DB8:9:33::) has a typo in the fourth quartet (33 instead of 3).

Step 2A.   The figure shows R2's G0/1 with link-local address FE80::2, but the command uses FE80::AAA9.

Step 2B.   The command uses the correct link-local address on R2's address on the common link (FE80::2 per the figure), but it omits the outgoing interface of R1's G0/2 interface. (See the next example for more detail.)

Step 3.   The figure shows the subnet in the center as 2001:DB8:9:2::/64, with R1 using the ::1 address and R2 using ::2. For the fourth command, R1's command should use R2's address 2001:DB8:9:2::2, but it uses R1's own 2001:DB8:9:2::1 address instead.

Step 4.   As a command on R1, the outgoing interface references R1's own interfaces. R1's G0/1 is the interface on the left, whereas R1 should use its G0/2 interface on the right when forwarding packets to subnet 2001:DB8:9:3::/64.

The key takeaway for this section is to know that a route in the IPv6 routing table may be incorrect due to poor choices for the parameters. The parameters should always include the neighboring router's IPv6 addresses, but the local router's interface type/number, and in all cases, the correct prefix/length. The fact that a route is in the IPv6 routing table, particularly a static route, does not mean it is a correct route.

Note that of the five example commands in Example 25-17, IOS would accept all of them except the third one. IOS can notice the case of omitting the outgoing interface if the next-hop address is a link-local address. Example 25-18 shows a sample of the error message from IOS.

Example 25-18   *IOS Rejects the* ipv6 route *Command with Link-Local and No Outgoing Interface*

```
R1# configure terminal
Enter configuration commands, one per line. End with CNTL/Z.
R1(config)# ipv6 route 2001:DB8:9:3::/64 FE80::2
% Interface has to be specified for a link-local nexthop
```

25

```
R1(config)# ^Z
R1#
R1# show running-config | include ipv6 route
R1#
```

The Static Route Does Not Appear in the IPv6 Routing Table

The preceding few pages focused on IPv6 static routes that show up in the IPv6 routing table but unfortunately have incorrect parameters. The next page looks at IPv6 routes that have correct parameters, but IOS does not place them into the IPv6 routing table.

When you add an **ipv6 route** command to the configuration, and the syntax is correct, IOS considers that route to be added to the IPv6 routing table. IOS makes the following checks before adding the route; note that IOS uses this same kind of logic for IPv4 static routes:

- For **ipv6 route** commands that list an outgoing interface, that interface must be in an up/up state.
- For **ipv6 route** commands that list a global unicast or unique local next-hop IP address (that is, not a link-local address), the local router must have a route to reach that next-hop address.
- If another IPv6 route exists for that exact same prefix/prefix-length, the static route must have a better (lower) administrative distance.

The Neighbor Discovery Protocol

Similar to ICMP for IPv4, IPv6 defines the ICMP protocol for IPv6 (ICMPv6). However, ICMPv6 reaches further than ICMPv4, pulling in functions done by other miscellaneous protocols in IPv4. For instance, with IPv4, ARP works as a separate protocol; with IPv6, the Neighbor Discovery Protocol (NDP), a part of ICMPv6, performs the same functions.

As it turns out, routers play a key role in several NDP protocol functions, so this final major section of the chapter explains a few of the functions of the NDP protocol (RFC 4861). Some of those NDP functions are

Neighbor MAC Discovery: An IPv6 LAN-based host will need to learn the MAC address of other hosts in the same subnet. NDP replaces IPv4's ARP, providing messages that replace the ARP Request and Reply messages.

Router Discovery: Hosts learn the IPv6 addresses of the available IPv6 routers in the same subnet.

SLAAC: When using Stateless Address Auto Configuration (SLAAC), the host uses NDP messages to learn the subnet (prefix) used on the link plus the prefix length.

DAD: Before using an IPv6 address, hosts use NDP to perform a Duplicate Address Detection (DAD) process, to ensure no other host uses the same IPv6 address before attempting to use it.

Discovering Neighbor Link Addresses with NDP NS and NA

NDP replaces IPv4 ARP using a pair of matched solicitation and advertisement messages: the *Neighbor Solicitation* (NS) and *Neighbor Advertisement* (NA) messages. Basically, the NS acts like an IPv4 ARP request, asking the host with a particular unicast IPv6 address to send back a reply. The NA message acts like an IPv4 ARP Reply, listing that host's MAC address.

The process of sending the NS and NA messages follows the same general process with IPv4 ARP: the NS message asks for information, and the NA supplies the information, as summarized in this list:

Neighbor Solicitation (NS): This message asks the host with a particular IPv6 address (the target address) to reply with an NA message that lists its MAC address. The NS message is sent to the solicited-node multicast address associated with the target address, so the message is processed only by hosts whose last six hex digits match the address that is being queried.

Neighbor Advertisement (NA): This message lists the sender's IPv6 and MAC addresses. It can be sent in reply to an NS message, and if so, the packet is sent to the IPv6 unicast address of the host that sent the original NS message. A host can also send an unsolicited NA, announcing its IPv6 and MAC addresses, in which case the message is sent to the all-IPv6-hosts local-scope multicast address FF02::1.

> **NOTE**   With NDP, the word *neighbor* refers to the fact that the devices will be on the same data link—for example, the same VLAN.

Figure 25-8 shows an example of how a host (PC1) uses an NS message to learn the MAC address used by another host. The NS message lists a target IPv6 unicast address, with the implied question: "What is your link address?" The NA message, in this example sent back to the original host that asked the question, lists that link address.

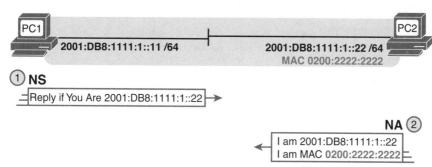

Figure 25-8   *Example NDP NS/NA Process to Find the Neighbor's Link Addresses*

At Step 1 of this particular example, PC1 sends the solicitation to find PC2's MAC address. PC1 first looks in its NDP neighbor table, the equivalent of the IPv4 ARP cache, and does not find the MAC address for IPv6 address 2001:DB8:1111:1::22. So, at Step 1, PC1 sends the NDP NS message to the matching solicited-node multicast address for 2001:DB8:1111:1::22 or FF02::1:FF00:22. Only IPv6 hosts whose address ends with 00:0022 will listen for this solicited-node multicast address. As a result, only a small subset of hosts on this link will process the received NDP NS message.

At Step 2, PC2 reacts to the received NS message. PC2 sends back an NA message in reply, listing PC2's MAC address. PC1 records PC2's MAC address in PC1's NDP neighbor table.

25

Example 25-19 shows an example of the IPv6 neighbor table on Router R3, as seen originally back in Figure 25-1. In this case, R3 has learned the MAC addresses of Router R1's WAN interface (G0/1/0)—both its global unicast address as well as the link-local address on that same interface.

Example 25-19 *IPv6 Neighbor Table on Router R3*

```
R3# show ipv6 neighbors
IPv6 Address                        Age Link-layer Addr State Interface
2001:DB8:1111:5::1                    0 0201.a010.0001  REACH Gi0/0/0
FE80::1:A0FF:FE10:1                   0 0201.a010.0001  REACH Gi0/0/0
```

NOTE To view a host's NDP neighbor table, use these commands: (Windows) **netsh interface ipv6 show neighbors**; (Linux) **ip -6 neighbor show**; (Mac OS) **ndp -an**.

Discovering Routers with NDP RS and RA

IPv4 hosts use the concept of an IPv4 default gateway or default router. When the host needs to send a packet to some IPv4 subnet other than the local subnet, the host sends the IPv4 packet to the default router, expecting the router to be able to route the packet to the destination. Note that hosts either statically set the IP address of their default gateway or learn it from a server called a Dynamic Host Configuration Protocol (DHCP) server.

IPv6 uses the same concept of a default gateway, but it improves the method for hosts to learn the identity of possible default gateways using NDP. NDP defines two messages that allow any host to discover all routers in the subnet:

Router Solicitation (RS): This message is sent to the "all-IPv6-routers" local-scope multicast address of FF02::2 so that the message asks all routers, on the local link only, to identify themselves.

Router Advertisement (RA): This message, sent by the router, lists many facts, including the link-local IPv6 address of the router. When sent in response to an RS message, it flows back to either the unicast address of the host that sent the RS or to the all-IPv6-hosts address FF02::1. Routers also send RA messages without being asked, sent to the all-IPv6-hosts local-scope multicast address of FF02::1.

For example, Figure 25-9 shows how host PC1 can learn R1's link-local address. The process is indeed simple, with PC1 first asking and R1 replying.

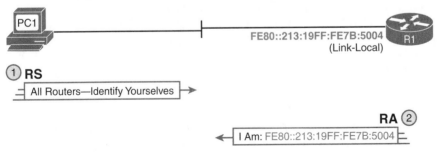

Figure 25-9 *Example NDP RS/RA Process to Find the Default Routers*

> **NOTE**   IPv6 allows multiple prefixes and multiple default routers to be listed in the RA message; Figure 25-9 just shows one of each for simplicity's sake.

IPv6 does not use broadcasts, but it does use multicasts. In this case, the RS message flows to the all-routers multicast address (FF02::2) so that all routers will receive the message. It has the same good effect as a broadcast with IPv4, without the negatives of a broadcast. In this case, only IPv6 routers will spend any CPU cycles processing the RS message, and IPv6 hosts will ignore the message. The RA message can flow either to the unicast IPv6 address of PC1 or to the all-nodes FF02::1 address.

Note that while Figure 25-9 shows how a host can ask to learn about any routers, routers also periodically send unsolicited RA messages, even without an incoming RS. When routers send these periodic RA messages, they basically advertise details about IPv6 on the link. In this case, the RA messages flow to the FF02::1 all-nodes IPv6 multicast address.

Using SLAAC with NDP RS and RA

Both IPv4 and IPv6 support the idea of dynamic address assignment for hosts via the Dynamic Host Configuration Protocol (DHCP). To find an address to use with DHCP, the DHCP client sends messages to a DHCP server, and the server assigns a currently unused address in the correct subnet for the endpoint host to use. The process relies on DHCP client functions in each device and a DHCP server configured and working in the network.

IPv6 supports an alternative method for IPv6 hosts to dynamically choose an unused IPv6 address to use—a process that does not require a server like a DHCP server. The process goes by the name *Stateless Address Autoconfiguration* (SLAAC). SLAAC uses a simple three-step process that begins by learning the prefix/length as shown in the figure. The steps are as follows:

1. Learn the IPv6 prefix used on the link, from any router, using NDP RS/RA messages.
2. Build an address from the prefix plus an interface ID, chosen either by using EUI-64 rules or as a random value.
3. Before using the address, first use DAD to make sure that no other host is already using the same address.

Figure 25-10 shows the structure of an IPv6 address created with SLACC using Steps 1 and 2 in the process, with the next topic detailing the third step (DAD).

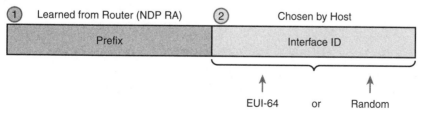

Figure 25-10   *Host IPv6 Address Formation Using SLAAC*

25

Discovering Duplicate Addresses Using NDP NS and NA

IPv6 uses the Duplicate Address Detection (DAD) process before using a unicast address to make sure that no other node on that link is already using the address. Hosts use DAD not only at the end of the SLAAC process, but also any time that a host interface initializes, no matter whether using SLAAC, DHCP, or static address configuration. When performing DAD, if another host already uses that address, the first host simply does not use the address until the problem is resolved.

The term *DAD* refers to the function, but the function uses NDP NS and NA messages. Basically, a host sends an NS message for its own IPv6 address. No other host should be using that address, so no other host should send an NDP NA in reply. However, if another host already uses that address, that host will reply with an NA, identifying a duplicate use of the address.

Figure 25-11 shows an example. PC1 initializes and does a DAD check, but PC2 happens to already be working and already be using the address. The figure shows the following steps:

1. PC1, before using address 2001:DB8:1111:1::11, must use DAD.

2. PC1 sends an NS message, listing the address PC1 now wants to use (2001:DB8:1111:1::11) as the target.

3. PC2 receives the NS, sees what PC2 already uses as its own address, and sends back an NA.

4. PC1, on receiving the NA message for its own IPv6 address, realizes a duplicate address exists.

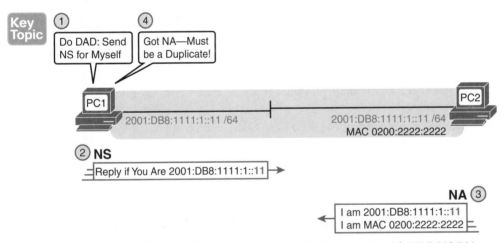

Figure 25-11 *Example Duplicate Address Detection (DAD) with NDP NS/NA*

Hosts do the DAD check for each of their unicast addresses, link-local addresses included, both when the address is first used and each time the host's interface comes up.

NDP Summary

This chapter explains some of the more important functions performed by NDP. NDP does more than what is listed in this chapter, and the protocol allows for addition of other functions, so NDP might continue to grow over time. For now, use Table 25-3 as a study reference for the four NDP features discussed here.

Table 25-3   NDP Function Summary

Function	Protocol Messages	Who Discovers Info	Who Supplies Info	Info Supplied
Router discovery	RS and RA	Any IPv6 host	Any IPv6 router	Link-local IPv6 address of router
Prefix/length discovery	RS and RA	Any IPv6 host	Any IPv6 router	Prefix(es) and associated prefix lengths used on local link
Neighbor discovery	NS and NA	Any IPv6 host	Any IPv6 host	Link-layer address (for example, MAC address) used by a neighbor
Duplicate Address Detection	NS and NA	Any IPv6 host	Any IPv6 host	Simple confirmation whether a unicast address is already in use

Chapter Review

One key to doing well on the exams is to perform repetitive spaced review sessions. Review this chapter's material using either the tools in the book or interactive tools for the same material found on the book's companion website. Refer to the "Your Study Plan" element for more details. Table 25-4 outlines the key review elements and where you can find them. To better track your study progress, record when you completed these activities in the second column.

Table 25-4   Chapter Review Tracking

Review Element	Review Date(s)	Resource Used
Review key topics		Book, website
Answer DIKTA questions		Book, PTP
Review command tables		Book
Review memory tables		Book, website
Do labs		Blog

25

Review All the Key Topics

Table 25-5 Key Topics for Chapter 25

Key Topic Element	Description	Page Number
List	Methods by which a router can build IPv6 routes	583
List	Rules for IPv6 connected and local routes	583
Figure 25-2	IPv6 static route concepts	587
Checklist	Items to check on **ipv6 route** command that cause problems with IPv6 static routes	596
Checklist	Items to check other than the **ipv6 route** command that cause problems with IPv6 static routes	598
List	Four functions that use NDP messages	598
List	NDP NS and NA messages and meanings	599
List	NDP RS and RA messages and meanings	600
Figure 25-11	Example DAD check	602
Table 25-3	NDP Function summary table	603

Key Terms You Should Know

IPv6 host route, local route, IPv6 local route, IPv6 administrative distance, IPv6 multicast scope

Command References

Tables 25-6 and 25-7 list configuration and verification commands used in this chapter. As an easy review exercise, cover the left column in a table, read the right column, and try to recall the command without looking. Then repeat the exercise, covering the right column, and try to recall what the command does.

Table 25-6 Chapter 25 Configuration Command Reference

Command	Description
ipv6 route *prefix/length next-hop-address*	Global command to define an IPv6 static route to a next-hop router IPv6 address.
ipv6 route *prefix/length outgoing-interface*	Global command to define an IPv6 static route, with packets forwarded out the local router interface listed in the command.
ipv6 route *prefix/length outgoing-interface next-hop-address*	Global command to define an IPv6 static route, with both the next-hop address and local router outgoing interface listed.

Command	Description
ipv6 route ::/0 *{[next-hop-address] [outgoing-interface]}*	Global command to define a default IPv6 static route.
ipv6 address autoconfig [default]	Interface subcommand that tells the router to use SLAAC to find/build its own interface IPv6 address, and with the **default** parameter, to add a default route with a next hop of the router that responds with the RA message.

Table 25-7   Chapter 25 EXEC Command Reference

Command	Description
show ipv6 route [connected | local | static]	Lists routes in the routing table.
show ipv6 route *address*	Displays detailed information about the route this router uses to forward packets to the IPv6 address listed in the command.
show ipv6 neighbors	Lists the contents of the IPv6 neighbor table, which lists the MAC address associated with IPv6 addresses on common subnets.

25

Part VII Review

Keep track of your part review progress with the checklist in Table P7-1. Details on each task follow the table.

Table P7-1 Part VII Part Review Checklist

Activity	1st Date Completed	2nd Date Completed
Repeat All DIKTA Questions		
Answer Part Review Questions		
Review Key Topics		
Do Labs		
Watch Videos		

Repeat All DIKTA Questions

For this task, use the PCPT software to answer the "Do I Know This Already?" questions again for the chapters in this part of the book.

Answer Part Review Questions

For this task, use PTP to answer the Part Review questions for this part of the book.

Review Key Topics

Review all key topics in all chapters in this part, either by browsing the chapters or using the Key Topics application on the companion website.

Do Labs

Depending on your chosen lab tool, here are some suggestions for what to do in lab:

Pearson Network Simulator: If you use the full Pearson simulator, focus more on the configuration scenario and troubleshooting scenario labs associated with the topics in this part of the book. These types of labs include a larger set of topics and work well as Part Review activities. (See the Introduction for some details about how to find which labs are about topics in this part of the book.)

Blog: Config Labs: The author's blog includes a series of configuration-focused labs that you can do on paper, each in 10–15 minutes. Review and perform the labs for this part of the book, as found at http://blog.certskills.com. Then navigate to the Hands-on Config labs.

Other: If using other lab tools, here are a few suggestions: Configure IPv6 addresses on interfaces, and before using any show commands, predict the connected and local routes that should be added to the IPv6 routing table, and predict the link-local (unicast) address and various multicast addresses you expect to see in the output of the **show ipv6 interfaces** command.

Watch Videos

Chapter 24 mentions that the companion website's section for Chapter 24 review includes a video about the EUI-64 address generation process, so consider using the video as a review.

This book began with an overview of the fundamentals of LANs, WANs, and IP routing. It then described Ethernet LANs (wired LANs) in some depth over the course of seven chapters. The book then meandered through many chapters exploring the many concepts of IPv4 and IPv6 addressing, routing, and how to implement those features in Cisco devices.

This final part of Volume 1 turns our attention back to the LAN, not to wired Ethernet LANs, but to IEEE 802.11 wireless LANs—in other words, Wi-Fi. The four chapters in this part of the book lay down the foundations of how wireless LANs work and then show how to implement wireless LANs using Cisco devices.

Building wireless LANs requires some thought because the endpoints that use the LAN do not sit in one place and connect via a known cable and known switch port. To explain those details, Chapter 26 begins with the basics of how a wireless client can connect to the wireless network through a wireless access point (AP). After you learn the foundations in Chapter 26, Chapter 27 takes an architectural view of wireless LANs to discuss how you might build a wireless LAN for an enterprise, which requires much different thinking than, for instance, building a wireless LAN for your home.

Chapter 28 completes the three concepts-focused wireless LAN chapters by working through the alphabet soup that is wireless LAN security. The fact that wireless LAN clients come and go means that the LAN may be under constant attack as an easy place for an attacker to gain access to the network, so wireless LANs must use effective security. Finally, Chapter 29 closes by showing how to configure an enterprise wireless LAN using Cisco APs and the Cisco Wireless LAN Controller (WLC) from the WLC's graphical interface.

Part VIII

Wireless LANs

CHAPTER 26

Fundamentals of Wireless Networks

This chapter covers the following exam topics:

1.0 Network Fundamentals

1.1 Explain the role and function of network components

1.1.d Access Points

1.11 Describe wireless principles

1.11.a Nonoverlapping Wi-Fi channels

1.11.b SSID

1.11.c RF

Wireless communication usually involves a data exchange between two devices. A wireless LAN goes even further; many devices can participate in sharing the medium for data exchanges. Wireless LANs must transmit a signal over radio frequencies (RF) to move data from one device to another. Transmitters and receivers can be fixed in consistent locations, or they can be mobile and free to move around. This chapter explains the topologies that can be used to control access to the wireless medium and provide data exchange between devices.

"Do I Know This Already?" Quiz

Take the quiz (either here or use the PTP software) if you want to use the score to help you decide how much time to spend on this chapter. The letter answers are listed at the bottom of the page following the quiz. Appendix C, found both at the end of the book as well as on the companion website, includes both the answers and explanations. You can also find both answers and explanations in the PTP testing software.

Table 26-1 "Do I Know This Already?" Foundation Topics Section-to-Question Mapping

Foundation Topics Section	Questions
Comparing Wired and Wireless Networks	1
Wireless LAN Topologies	2–4
Other Wireless Topologies	5–6
Wireless Bands and Channels	7–8

1. Wired Ethernet and Wi-Fi are based on which two IEEE standards, respectively?
   a. 802.1, 802.3
   b. 802.3, 802.1
   c. 802.3, 802.11
   d. 802.11, 802.3

2. Devices using a wireless LAN must operate in which one of the following modes?
   a. Round-robin access
   b. Half duplex
   c. Full duplex
   d. None of these answers

3. An access point is set up to offer wireless coverage in an office. Which one of the following is the correct 802.11 term for the resulting standalone network?
   a. BSA
   b. BSD
   c. BSS
   d. IBSS

4. Which one of the following is used to uniquely identify an AP and the basic service set it maintains with its associated wireless clients?
   a. SSID
   b. BSSID
   c. Ethernet MAC address
   d. Radio MAC address

5. Which one of the following can be used to provide wireless connectivity to a nonwireless device?
   a. Wireless repeater
   b. Workgroup bridge
   c. Transparent bridge
   d. Adaptive bridge

6. Which one of the following is not needed in a Cisco outdoor mesh network?
   a. A BSS function
   b. Ethernet cabling to each AP
   c. A workgroup bridge
   d. A backhaul network

7. Which of the following are frequency bands commonly used for Wi-Fi?

    a. 2.5 KHz

    b. 2.5 MHz

    c. 5 MHz

    d. 2.5 GHz

    e. 5 GHz

8. Which of the following are considered to be nonoverlapping channels?

    a. Channels 1, 2, and 3 in the 2.4-GHz band

    b. Channels 1, 5, and 10 in the 2.4-GHz band

    c. Channels 1, 6, and 11 in the 2.4-GHz band

    d. Channels 40, 44, and 48 in the 5-GHz band

Foundation Topics

Comparing Wired and Wireless Networks

In a wired network, any two devices that need to communicate with each other must be connected by a wire. (That was obvious!) The "wire" might contain strands of metal or fiber-optic material that run continuously from one end to the other. Data that passes over the wire is bounded by the physical properties of the wire. In fact, the IEEE 802.3 set of standards defines strict guidelines for the Ethernet wire itself, in addition to how devices may connect, send, and receive data over the wire.

Wired connections have been engineered with tight constraints and have few variables that might prevent successful communication. Even the type and size of the wire strands, the number of twists the strands must make around each other over a distance, and the maximum length of the wire must adhere to the standard.

Therefore, a wired network is essentially a bounded medium; data must travel over whatever path the wire or cable takes between two devices. If the cable goes around a corner or lies in a coil, the electrical signals used to carry the data must also go around a corner or around a coil. Because only two devices may connect to a wire, only those two devices may send or transmit data. Even better: the two devices may transmit data to each other simultaneously because they each have a private, direct path to each other.

Wired networks also have some shortcomings. When a device is connected by a wire, it cannot move around very easily or very far. Before a device can connect to a wired network, it must have a connector that is compatible with the one on the end of the wire. As devices get smaller and more mobile, it just is not practical to connect them to a wire.

As its name implies, a wireless network removes the need to be tethered to a wire or cable. Convenience and mobility become paramount, enabling users to move around at will while staying connected to the network. A user can (and often does) bring along many different wireless devices that can all connect to the network easily and seamlessly.

Wireless data must travel through free space, without the constraints and protection of a wire. In the free space environment, many variables can affect the data and its delivery. To minimize the variables, wireless engineering efforts must focus on two things:

- Wireless devices must adhere to a common standard (IEEE 802.11).
- Wireless coverage must exist in the area where devices are expected to use it.

As you study for the CCNA 200-301 exam, keep in mind that the exam is geared more toward a functional view of wireless technology. More detailed topics like RF characteristics, antenna performance, and so on are reserved for the Implementing Cisco Enterprise Network Core Technologies ENCOR 300-401 exam.

Wireless LAN Topologies

Wireless communication takes place over free space through the use of radio frequency (RF) signals. The theory behind RF signals can be complex, and is described further in the "RF Overview" section in this chapter. For now, just assume that one device, the transmitter, sends RF signals to another device, the receiver. As Figure 26-1 shows, the transmitter can contact the receiver at any and all times, as long as both devices are tuned to the same frequency (or channel) and use the same scheme to carry the data between them. That all sounds simple, except that it is not really practical.

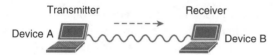

Figure 26-1   *Unidirectional Communication*

To fully leverage wireless communication, data should travel in *both* directions, as shown in Figure 26-2. Sometimes Device A needs to send data to Device B, while Device B would like to take a turn to send at other times.

Figure 26-2   *Bidirectional Communication*

Because the two devices are using the same channel, two phrases in the preceding sentence become vitally important: *take a turn* and *send at other times*. With wireless communication, if multiple signals are received at the same time, they can interfere with each other. The likelihood of interference increases as the number of wireless devices grows. For example, Figure 26-3 shows four devices tuned to the same channel and what might happen if some or all of them transmit at the same time.

Figure 26-3   *Interference from Simultaneous Transmissions*

All this talk about waiting turns and avoiding interference might remind you of a traditional (nonswitched) Ethernet LAN, where multiple hosts can connect to a shared media and share a common bandwidth. To use the media effectively, all the hosts must operate in half-duplex mode so that they try to avoid colliding with other transmissions already in progress. The side effect is that no host can transmit and receive at the same time on a shared medium.

A wireless LAN is similar. Because multiple hosts can share the same channel, they also share the "airtime" or access to that channel at any given time. Therefore, to keep everything clean, only one device should transmit at any given time. To contend for use of the channel, devices based on the 802.11 standard have to determine whether the channel is clear and available before transmitting anything.

NOTE   IEEE 802.11 WLANs are always half duplex because transmissions between stations use the same frequency or channel. Only one station can transmit at any time; otherwise, collisions occur. To achieve full-duplex mode, one station's transmission would have to occur on one frequency while it receives over a different frequency—much like full-duplex Ethernet links work. Although this is certainly possible and practical, the 802.11 standard does not permit full-duplex operation. Some amendments to the standard do provide a means for multiple devices to transmit on the same channel at the same time, but this is beyond the scope of this book.

At the most basic level, there is no inherent organization to a wireless medium or any inherent control over the number of devices that can transmit and receive frames. Any device that has a wireless network adapter can power up at any time and try to communicate. At a minimum, a wireless network should have a way to make sure that every device using a channel can support a common set of parameters. Beyond that, there should be a way to control which devices (and users) are allowed to use the wireless medium and the methods that are used to secure the wireless transmissions.

Basic Service Set

The solution is to make every wireless service area a closed group of mobile devices that forms around a fixed device; before a device can participate, it must advertise its capabilities and then be granted permission to join. The 802.11 standard calls this a *basic service set* (BSS). At the heart of every BSS is a wireless *access point* (AP), as shown in Figure 26-4. The AP operates in *infrastructure mode*, which means it offers the services that are necessary to form the infrastructure of a wireless network. The AP also establishes its BSS over a single wireless channel. The AP and the members of the BSS must all use the same channel to communicate properly.

Because the operation of a BSS hinges on the AP, the BSS is bounded by the area where the AP's signal is usable. This is known as the *basic service area* (BSA) or *cell*. In Figure 26-4, the cell is shown as a simple shaded circular area that centers around the AP itself. Cells can

Answers to the "Do I Know This Already?" quiz:

1 C **2** B **3** C **4** B **5** B **6** B **7** D, E **8** C, D

have other shapes too, depending on the antenna that is connected to the AP and on the physical surroundings that might affect the AP's signals.

The AP serves as a single point of contact for every device that wants to use the BSS. It advertises the existence of the BSS so that devices can find it and try to join. To do that, the AP uses a unique BSS identifier (BSSID) that is based on the AP's own radio MAC address.

> **NOTE**   Recall that wired Ethernet devices each have a unique MAC address to send frames from a source to a destination over a Layer 2 network. Wireless devices must also have unique MAC addresses to send wireless frames at Layer 2 over the air.

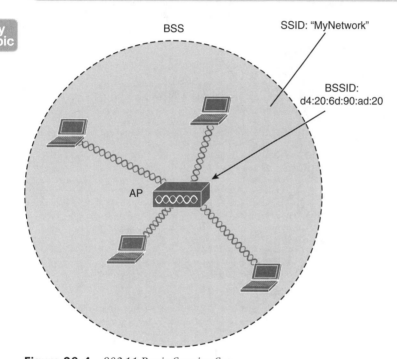

Figure 26-4   *802.11 Basic Service Set*

In addition, the AP advertises the wireless network with a Service Set Identifier (SSID), which is a text string containing a logical name. Think of the BSSID as a machine-readable name tag that uniquely identifies the BSS ambassador (the AP), and the SSID as a nonunique, human-readable name tag that identifies the wireless service.

Membership with the BSS is called an *association*. A wireless device must send an association request to the AP and the AP must either grant or deny the request. Once associated, a device becomes a client, or an 802.11 *station* (STA), of the BSS. What then? As long as a wireless client remains associated with a BSS, most communications to and from the client must pass *through* the AP, as indicated in Figure 26-5. By using the BSSID as a source or destination address, data frames can be relayed to or from the AP.

You might be wondering why all client traffic has to traverse the AP at all. Why can two clients not simply transmit data frames directly to each other and bypass the middleman? If clients

26

are allowed to communicate directly, then the whole idea of organizing and managing a BSS is moot. By sending data through the AP first, the BSS remains stable and under control.

NOTE Even though data frames are meant to pass through an AP, keep in mind that other devices in the same general area that are listening on the same channel can overhear the transmissions. After all, wireless frames are not contained within a wire that connects a device to an AP. Instead, the frames are freely available over the air to anyone that is within range to receive them. If the frames are unencrypted, then anyone may inspect their contents. Only the BSSID value contained within the frames indicates that the intended sender or recipient is the AP.

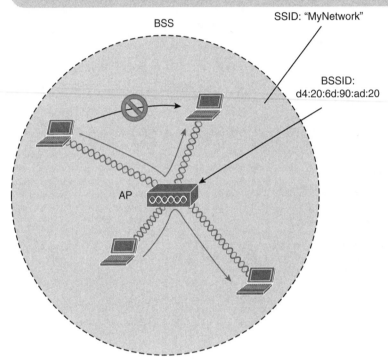

Figure 26-5 *Traffic Flows Within a BSS*

Distribution System

Notice that a BSS involves a single AP and no explicit connection into a regular Ethernet network. In that setting, the AP and its associated clients make up a standalone network. But the AP's role at the center of the BSS does not just stop with managing the BSS; sooner or later, wireless clients will need to communicate with other devices that are not members of the BSS. Fortunately, an AP can also uplink into an Ethernet network because it has both wireless and wired capabilities. The 802.11 standard refers to the upstream wired Ethernet as the *distribution system* (DS) for the wireless BSS, as shown in Figure 26-6.

You can think of an AP as a translational bridge, where frames from two dissimilar media (wireless and wired) are translated and then bridged at Layer 2. In simple terms, the AP is in charge of mapping a virtual local-area network (VLAN) to an SSID. In Figure 26-6, the AP maps VLAN 10 to the wireless LAN using SSID "MyNetwork." Clients associated with the "MyNetwork" SSID will appear to be connected to VLAN 10.

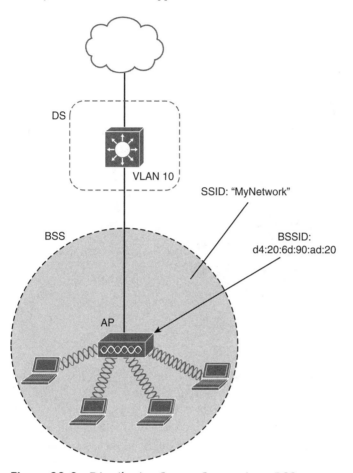

Figure 26-6   *Distribution System Supporting a BSS*

This concept can be extended so that multiple VLANs are mapped to multiple SSIDs. To do this, the AP must be connected to the switch by a trunk link that carries the VLANs. In Figure 26-7, VLANs 10, 20, and 30 are trunked to the AP over the DS. The AP uses the 802.1Q tag to map the VLAN numbers to the appropriate SSIDs. For example, VLAN 10 is mapped to SSID "MyNetwork," VLAN 20 is mapped to SSID "YourNetwork," and VLAN 30 to SSID "Guest."

In effect, when an AP uses multiple SSIDs, it is trunking VLANs over the air, and over the same channel, to wireless clients. The clients must use the appropriate SSID that has been mapped to the respective VLAN when the AP was configured. The AP then appears as multiple logical APs—one per BSS—with a unique BSSID for each. With Cisco APs, this is usually accomplished by incrementing the last digit of the radio's MAC address for each SSID.

Even though an AP can advertise and support multiple logical wireless networks, each of the SSIDs covers the same geographic area. The reason is that the AP uses the same transmitter, receiver, antennas, and channel for every SSID that it supports. Beware of one misconception though: multiple SSIDs can give an illusion of scale. Even though wireless clients can be

26

distributed across many SSIDs, all of those clients must share the same AP's hardware and must contend for airtime on the same channel.

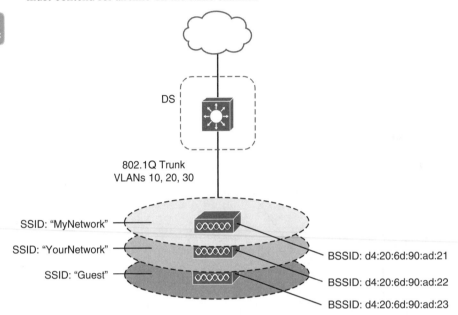

Figure 26-7   *Supporting Multiple SSIDs on One AP*

Extended Service Set

Normally, one AP cannot cover the entire area where clients might be located. For example, you might need wireless coverage throughout an entire floor of a business, hotel, hospital, or other large building. To cover more area than a single AP's cell can cover, you simply need to add more APs and spread them out geographically.

When APs are placed at different geographic locations, they can all be interconnected by a switched infrastructure. The 802.11 standard calls this an extended service set (ESS), as shown in Figure 26-8.

The idea is to make multiple APs cooperate so that the wireless service is consistent and seamless from the client's perspective. Ideally, any SSIDs that are defined on one AP should be defined on all the APs in an ESS; otherwise, it would be very cumbersome and inconvenient for a client to be reconfigured each time it moves into a different AP's cell.

Notice that each cell in Figure 26-8 has a unique BSSID, but both cells share one common SSID. Regardless of a client's location within the ESS, the SSID will remain the same but the client can always distinguish one AP from another.

In an ESS, a wireless client can associate with one AP while it is physically located near that AP. If the client later moves to a different location, it can associate with a different nearby AP automatically. Passing from one AP to another is called *roaming*. Keep in mind that each AP offers its own BSS on its own channel, to prevent interference between the APs. As a client device roams from one AP to another, it must scan the available channels to find a new AP (and BSS) to roam toward. In effect, the client is roaming from BSS to BSS, and from channel to channel.

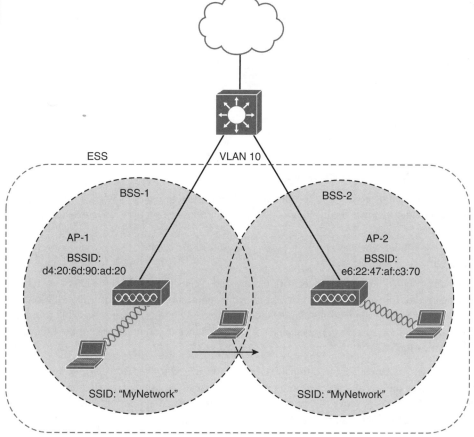

Figure 26-8   *Scaling Wireless Coverage with an 802.11 Extended Service Set*

Independent Basic Service Set

Usually a wireless network leverages APs for organization, control, and scalability. Sometimes that is not possible or convenient in an impromptu situation. For example, two people who want to exchange electronic documents at a meeting might not be able to find a BSS available or might want to avoid having to authenticate to a production network. In addition, many personal printers have the capability to print documents wirelessly, without relying on a regular BSS or AP.

The 802.11 standard allows two or more wireless clients to communicate directly with each other, with no other means of network connectivity. This is known as an *ad hoc* wireless network, or an *independent basic service set* (IBSS), as shown in Figure 26-9. For this to work, one of the devices must take the lead and begin advertising a network name and the necessary radio parameters, much like an AP would do. Any other device can then join as needed. IBSSs are meant to be organized in an impromptu, distributed fashion; therefore, they do not scale well beyond eight to ten devices.

26

IBSS

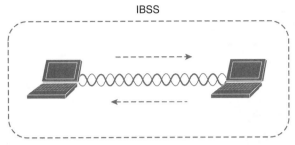

Figure 26-9 *802.11 Independent Basic Service Set*

Other Wireless Topologies

Wireless APs can be configured to operate in noninfrastructure modes when a normal BSS cannot provide the functionality that is needed. The following sections cover the most common modes.

Repeater

Normally, each AP in a wireless network has a wired connection back to the DS or switched infrastructure. To extend wireless coverage beyond a normal AP's cell footprint, additional APs and their wired connections can be added. In some scenarios, it is not possible to run a wired connection to a new AP because the cable distance is too great to support Ethernet communication.

In that case, you can add an additional AP that is configured for *repeater mode*. A wireless repeater takes the signal it receives and repeats or retransmits it in a new cell area around the repeater. The idea is to move the repeater out away from the AP so that it is still within range of both the AP and the distant client, as shown in Figure 26-10.

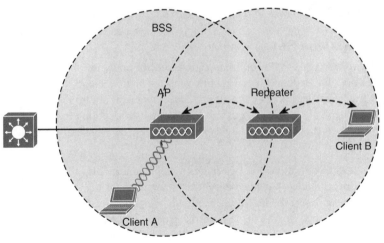

Figure 26-10 *Extending the Range of an AP with a Wireless Repeater*

If the repeater has a single transmitter and receiver, it must operate on the same channel that the AP is using. That can create the possibility that the AP's signal will be received and retransmitted by the repeater, only to be received again by the AP—halving the effective throughput because the channel will be kept busy twice as long as before. As a remedy, some repeaters can use two transmitters and receivers to keep the original and repeated signals isolated on different channels. One transmitter and receiver pair is dedicated to signals in the AP's cell, while the other pair is dedicated to signals in the repeater's own cell.

Workgroup Bridge

Suppose you have a device that supports a wired Ethernet link but is not capable of having a wireless connection. For example, some mobile medical devices might be designed with only a wired connection. While it is possible to plug the device into an Ethernet connection when needed, a wireless connection would be much more practical. You can use a workgroup bridge (WGB) to connect the device's wired network adapter to a wireless network.

Rather than providing a BSS for wireless service, a WGB becomes a wireless client of a BSS. In effect, the WGB acts as an external wireless network adapter for a device that has none. In Figure 26-11, an AP provides a BSS; Client A is a regular wireless client, while Client B is associated with the AP through a WGB.

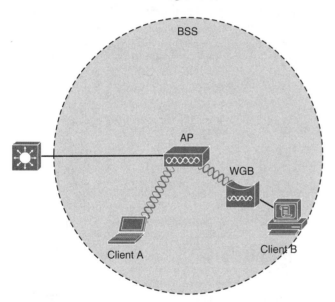

Figure 26-11 *Nonwireless Device Connecting Through a Workgroup Bridge*

You might encounter two types of workgroup bridges:

- **Universal workgroup bridge (uWGB):** A single wired device can be bridged to a wireless network.

- **Workgroup bridge (WGB):** A Cisco-proprietary implementation that allows multiple wired devices to be bridged to a wireless network.

Outdoor Bridge

An AP can be configured to act as a bridge to form a single wireless link from one LAN to another over a long distance. Outdoor bridged links are commonly used for connectivity between buildings or between cities.

26

If the LANs at two locations need to be bridged, a point-to-point bridged link can be used. One AP configured in bridge mode is needed on each end of the wireless link. Special purpose antennas are normally used with the bridges to focus their signals in one direction— toward the antenna of the AP at the far end of the link. This maximizes the link distance, as shown in Figure 26-12.

Figure 26-12   *Point-to-Point Outdoor Bridge*

Sometimes the LANs at multiple sites need to be bridged together. A point-to-multipoint bridged link allows a central site to be bridged to several other sites. The central site bridge is connected to an omnidirectional antenna, such that its signal is transmitted equally in all directions so that it can reach the other sites simultaneously. The bridges at each of the other sites can be connected to a directional antenna aimed at the central site. Figure 26-13 shows the point-to-multipoint scenario.

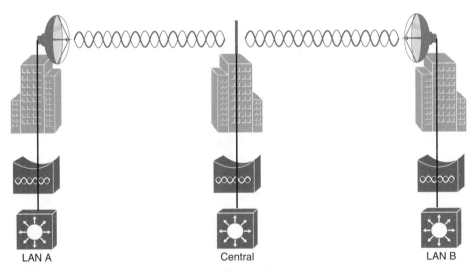

Figure 26-13   *Point-to-Multipoint Outdoor Bridge*

Mesh Network

To provide wireless coverage over a very large area, it is not always practical to run Ethernet cabling to every AP that would be needed. Instead, you could use multiple APs configured in mesh mode. In a mesh topology, wireless traffic is bridged from AP to AP, in a daisy-chain fashion, using another wireless channel.

Mesh APs can leverage dual radios—one using a channel in one range of frequencies and one a different range. Each mesh AP usually maintains a BSS on one channel, with which wireless clients can associate. Client traffic is then usually bridged from AP to AP over other channels as a backhaul network. At the edge of the mesh network, the backhaul traffic is bridged to the wired LAN infrastructure. Figure 26-14 shows a typical mesh network. With Cisco APs, you can build a mesh network indoors or outdoors. The mesh network runs its own dynamic routing protocol to work out the best path for backhaul traffic to take across the mesh APs.

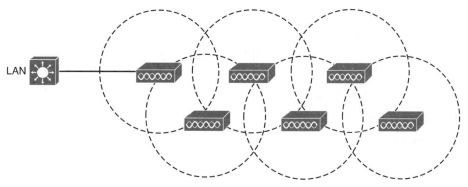

Figure 26-14   *Typical Wireless Mesh Network*

RF Overview

To send data across a wired link, an electrical signal is applied at one end and carried to the other end. The wire itself is continuous and conductive, so the signal can propagate rather easily. A wireless link has no physical strands of anything to carry the signal along.

How, then, can an electrical signal be sent across the air, or free space? Consider a simple analogy of two people standing far apart. One person wants to signal something to the other. They are connected by a long and somewhat loose rope; the rope represents free space. The sender at one end decides to lift his end of the rope high and hold it there so that the other end of the rope will also rise and notify the partner. After all, if the rope were a wire, he knows that he could apply a steady voltage at one end of the wire and it would appear at the other end. Figure 26-15 shows the end result; the rope falls back down after a tiny distance, and the receiver never notices a change.

Sender   Receiver

Figure 26-15   *Failed Attempt to Pass a Message Down a Rope*

The sender tries a different strategy. He cannot push the rope, but when he begins to wave it up and down in a steady, regular motion, a curious thing happens. A continuous wave pattern appears along the entire length of the rope, as shown in Figure 26-16. In fact, the waves (each representing one up and down cycle of the sender's arm) actually travel from the sender to the receiver.

26

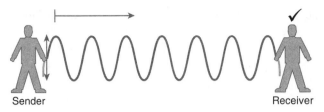

Figure 26-16   *Sending a Continuous Wave Down a Rope*

In free space, a similar principle occurs. The sender (a transmitter) can send an alternating current into a section of wire (an antenna), which sets up moving electric and magnetic fields that propagate out and away as traveling waves. The electric and magnetic fields travel along together and are always at right angles to each other, as shown in Figure 26-17. The signal must keep changing, or alternating, by cycling up and down, to keep the electric and magnetic fields cycling and pushing ever outward.

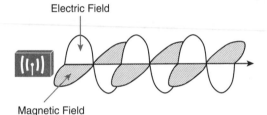

Figure 26-17   *Traveling Electric and Magnetic Waves*

Electromagnetic waves do not travel in a straight line. Instead, they travel by expanding in *all* directions away from the antenna. To get a visual image, think of dropping a pebble into a pond when the surface is still. Where it drops in, the pebble sets the water's surface into a cyclic motion. The waves that result begin small and expand outward, only to be replaced by new waves. In free space, the electromagnetic waves expand outward in all three dimensions.

Figure 26-18 shows a simple idealistic antenna that is a single point at the end of a wire. The waves produced expand outward in a spherical shape. The waves will eventually reach the receiver, in addition to many other locations in other directions.

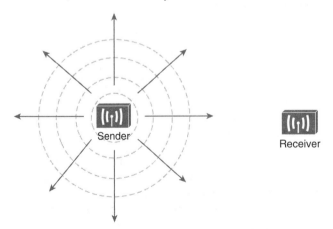

Figure 26-18   *Wave Propagation with an Idealistic Antenna*

At the receiving end of a wireless link, the process is reversed. As the electromagnetic waves reach the receiver's antenna, they induce an electrical signal. If everything works right, the received signal will be a reasonable copy of the original transmitted signal.

The electromagnetic waves involved in a wireless link can be measured and described in several ways. One fundamental property is the *frequency* of the wave, or the number of times the signal makes one complete up and down *cycle* in 1 second. Figure 26-19 shows how a cycle of a wave can be identified. A cycle can begin as the signal rises from the center line, falls through the center line, and rises again to meet the center line. A cycle can also be measured from the center of one peak to the center of the next peak. No matter where you start measuring a cycle, the signal must make a complete sequence back to its starting position where it is ready to repeat the same cyclic pattern.

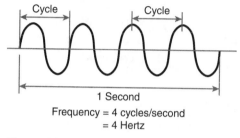

Figure 26-19   *Cycles Within a Wave*

In Figure 26-19, suppose that 1 second has elapsed, as shown. During that 1 second, the signal progressed through four complete cycles. Therefore, its frequency is 4 cycles/second or 4 hertz. A *hertz* (Hz) is the most commonly used frequency unit and is nothing other than one cycle per second.

Frequency can vary over a very wide range. As frequency increases by orders of magnitude, the numbers can become quite large. To keep things simple, the frequency unit name can be modified to denote an increasing number of zeros, as listed in Table 26-2.

Table 26-2   Frequency Unit Names

Unit	Abbreviation	Meaning
Hertz	Hz	Cycles per second
Kilohertz	kHz	1000 Hz
Megahertz	MHz	1,000,000 Hz
Gigahertz	GHz	1,000,000,000 Hz

Figure 26-20 shows a simple representation of the continuous frequency spectrum ranging from 0 Hz to 10^{22} (or 1 followed by 22 zeros) Hz. At the low end of the spectrum are frequencies that are too low to be heard by the human ear, followed by audible sounds. The highest range of frequencies contains light, followed by X, gamma, and cosmic rays.

26

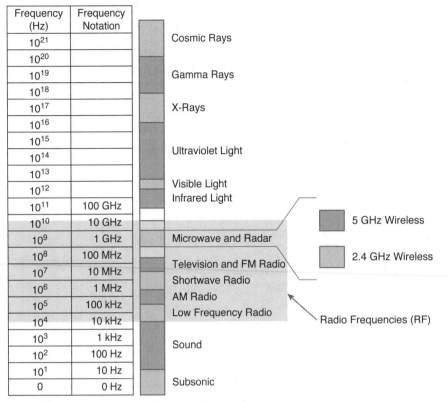

Figure 26-20 *Continuous Frequency Spectrum*

The frequency range from around 3 kHz to 300 GHz is commonly called *radio frequency* (RF). It includes many different types of radio communication, including low-frequency radio, AM radio, shortwave radio, television, FM radio, microwave, and radar. The microwave category also contains the two main frequency ranges that are used for wireless LAN communication: 2.4 and 5 GHz.

Wireless Bands and Channels

Because a range of frequencies might be used for the same purpose, it is customary to refer to the range as a *band* of frequencies. For example, the range from 530 kHz to around 1710 kHz is used by AM radio stations; therefore, it is commonly called the AM band or the AM broadcast band.

One of the two main frequency ranges used for wireless LAN communication lies between 2.400 and 2.4835 GHz. This is usually called the *2.4-GHz band*, even though it does not encompass the entire range between 2.4 and 2.5 GHz. It is much more convenient to refer to the band name instead of the specific range of frequencies included.

The other wireless LAN range is usually called the *5-GHz band* because it lies between 5.150 and 5.825 GHz. The 5-GHz band actually contains the following four separate and distinct bands:

5.150 to 5.250 GHz

5.250 to 5.350 GHz

5.470 to 5.725 GHz

5.725 to 5.825 GHz

> **TIP**   You might have noticed that most of the 5-GHz bands are contiguous except for a gap between 5.350 and 5.470. At the time of this writing, this gap exists and cannot be used for wireless LANs. However, some governmental agencies have moved to reclaim the frequencies and repurpose them for wireless LANs. Efforts are also underway to add 5.825 through 5.925 GHz.

It is interesting that the 5-GHz band can contain several smaller bands. Remember that the term *band* is simply a relative term that is used for convenience. Do not worry about memorizing the band names or exact frequency ranges; just be aware of the two main bands at 2.4 and 5 GHz.

A frequency band contains a continuous range of frequencies. If two devices require a single frequency for a wireless link between them, which frequency can they use? Beyond that, how many unique frequencies can be used within a band? To keep everything orderly and compatible, bands are usually divided into a number of distinct *channels*. Each channel is known by a channel number and is assigned to a specific frequency. As long as the channels are defined by a national or international standards body, they can be used consistently in all locations. Figures 26-21 and 26-22 show the channel layout for the 2.4 and 5 GHz bands, respectively.

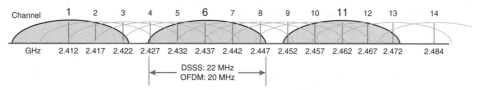

Figure 26-21   *Channel Layout in the 2.4-GHz Band*

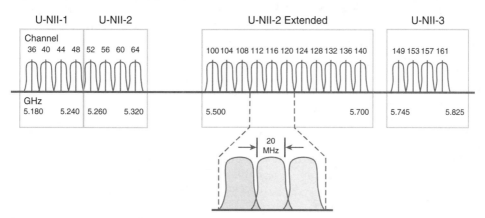

Figure 26-22   *Channel Layout in the 5-GHz Band*

26

You might assume that an AP can use any channel number without affecting any APs that use other channel numbers. In the 5-GHz band, this is the case because each channel is allocated a frequency range that does not encroach on or overlap the frequencies allocated for any other channel. In other words, the 5-GHz band consists of *nonoverlapping channels*.

The same is *not* true of the 2.4-GHz band. Each of its channels is much too wide to avoid overlapping the next lower or upper channel number. In fact, each channel covers the frequency range that is allocated to more than four consecutive channels! Notice the width of the channel spacing in Figure 26-21 as compared to the width of one of the shaded signals centered on channels 1, 6, and 11. The only way to avoid any overlap between adjacent channels is to configure APs to use only channels 1, 6, and 11. Even though there are 14 channels available to use, you should always strive for nonoverlapping channels in your network.

APs and Wireless Standards

It might be obvious that wireless devices and APs should all be capable of operating on the same band. For example, a 5-GHz wireless phone can communicate only with an AP that offers Wi-Fi service on 5-GHz channels. In addition, the devices and APs must also share a compatibility with the parts of the 802.11 standard they support.

As the IEEE 802.11 Wi-Fi standard evolves and develops, new amendments with new functionality get proposed. These amendments are known by "802.11" followed by a one- or two-letter suffix until they are accepted and rolled up into the next generation of the complete 802.11 standard. Even then, it is common to see the amendment suffixes still used to distinguish specific functions.

You should be aware of several amendments that define important characteristics such as data rates, methods used to transmit and receive data, and so on. For the CCNA 200-301 exam, you should know which band each of the amendments listed in Table 26-3 uses. The ENCOR 300-401 exam goes further into the data rates and modulation and coding schemes used by each.

Table 26-3   Basic Characteristics of Some IEEE 802.11 Amendments

Amendment	2.4 GHz	5 GHz	Max Data Rate	Notes
802.11-1997	Yes	No	2 Mbps	The original 802.11 standard ratified in 1997
802.11b	Yes	No	11 Mbps	Introduced in 1999
802.11g	Yes	No	54 Mbps	Introduced in 2003
802.11a	No	Yes	54 Mbps	Introduced in 1999
802.11n	Yes	Yes	600 Mbps	HT (high throughput), introduced in 2009
802.11ac	No	Yes	6.93 Gbps	VHT (very high throughput), introduced in 2013
802.11ax	Yes	Yes	4x 802.11ac	High Efficiency Wireless, Wi-Fi6; expected late 2019; will operate on other bands too, as they become available

The 802.11 amendments are not mutually exclusive. Wireless client devices and APs can be compatible with one or more amendments; however, a client and an AP can communicate only if they both support and agree to use the same amendment. When you look at the specifications for a wireless device, you may find supported amendments listed in a single string, separated by slashes. For example, a device that supports 802.11b/g will support both 802.11b and 802.11g. One that supports b/g/a/n/ac will support 802.11b, 802.11g, 802.11n, and 802.11ac. You should become familiar with Table 26-3 so that you can know which bands a device can use based on its 802.11 amendment support.

If a device can operate on both bands, how does it decide which band to use? APs can usually operate on both bands simultaneously to support any clients that might be present on each band. However, wireless clients typically associate with an AP on one band at a time, while scanning for potential APs on both bands. The band used to connect to an AP is chosen according to the operating system, wireless adapter driver, and other internal configuration. A wireless client can initiate an association with an AP on one band and then switch to the other band if the signal conditions are better there.

> **NOTE** Cisco APs have dual radios (sets of transmitters and receivers) to support BSSs on one 2.4-GHz channel and other BSSs on one 5-GHz channel simultaneously. Some models also have two 5-GHz radios that can be configured to operate BSSs on two different channels at the same time, providing wireless coverage to higher densities of users that are located in the same vicinity.
>
> You can configure a Cisco AP to operate on a specific channel number. As the number of APs grows, manual channel assignment can become a difficult task. Fortunately, Cisco wireless architectures can automatically and dynamically assign each AP to an appropriate channel. The architecture is covered in Chapter 27, "Analyzing Cisco Wireless Architectures," while dynamic channel assignment is covered on the ENCOR 300-401 exam.

In open space, RF signals propagate or reach further on the 2.4-GHz band than on the 5-GHz band. They also tend to penetrate indoor walls and objects easier at 2.4 GHz than 5 GHz. However, the 2.4-GHz band is commonly more crowded with wireless devices. Remember that only three nonoverlapping channels are available, so the chances of other neighboring APs using the same channels is greater. In contrast, the 5-GHz band has many more channels available to use, making channels less crowded and experiencing less interference.

Chapter Review

Review this chapter's material using either the tools in the book or the interactive tools for the same material found on the book's companion website. Table 26-4 outlines the key review elements and where you can find them. To better track your study progress, record when you completed these activities in the second column.

Table 26-4   Chapter Review Tracking

Review Element	Review Date(s)	Resource Used
Review key topics		Book, website
Review key terms		Book, website
Answer DIKTA questions		Book, PTP
Review memory tables		Website

Review All the Key Topics

Table 26-5   Key Topics for Chapter 26

Key Topic Element	Description	Page Number
Figure 26-4	Basic service set	615
Figure 26-7	Multiple SSIDs	618
Figure 26-8	Extended service set	619
Paragraph	Nonoverlapping channels and bands	628
Table 26-3	Basic Characteristics of Some 802.11 Amendments	628

Key Terms You Should Know

access point (AP), ad hoc network, Band, basic service set (BSS), Basic Service Set Identifier (BSSID), channel, cell, distribution system (DS), extended service set (ESS), independent basic service set (IBSS), infrastructure mode, mesh network, nonoverlapping channels, point-to-point bridge, repeater, roaming, Service Set Identifier (SSID), station (STA), workgroup bridge (WGB)

CHAPTER 27

Analyzing Cisco Wireless Architectures

This chapter covers the following exam topics:

2.0 Network Access

2.6 Compare Cisco Wireless Architectures and AP modes

In Chapter 26, "Fundamentals of Wireless Networks," you learned about how a single access point (AP) can provide a basic service set (BSS) for a cell area and how multiple APs can be connected to form an extended service set (ESS) for a larger network. In this chapter, you learn more about different approaches or architectures that allow APs to be networked together for an enterprise. You also learn how some architectures are more scalable than others and how to manage each type of wireless network architecture.

As you work through this chapter, think about how each architecture can be applied to specific environments—how easy it would be to manage, deploy, and troubleshoot the network, how the APs can be controlled, and how data would move through the network.

"Do I Know This Already?" Quiz

Take the quiz (either here or use the PTP software) if you want to use the score to help you decide how much time to spend on this chapter. The letter answers are listed at the bottom of the page following the quiz. Appendix C, found both at the end of the book as well as on the companion website, includes both the answers and explanations. You can also find both answers and explanations in the PTP testing software.

Table 27-1 "Do I Know This Already?" Section-to-Question Mapping

Foundation Topics Section	Questions
Autonomous AP Architectures	1
Cloud-based AP Architecture	2
Split-MAC Architectures	3–5
Comparing Wireless LAN Controller Deployments	6
Cisco AP Modes	7–8

1. Which one of the following terms best describes a Cisco wireless access point that operates in a standalone, independent manner?

   a. Autonomous AP

   b. Independent AP

   c. Lightweight AP

   d. Embedded AP

2. The Cisco Meraki cloud-based APs are most accurately described by which one of the following statements?

    a. Autonomous APs joined to a WLC

    b. Autonomous APs centrally managed

    c. Lightweight APs joined to a WLC

    d. Lightweight APs centrally managed

3. A lightweight access point is said to participate in which one of the following architectures?

    a. Light-MAC

    b. Tunnel-MAC

    c. Split-MAC

    d. Big-MAC

4. How does a lightweight access point communicate with a wireless LAN controller?

    a. Through an IPsec tunnel

    b. Through a CAPWAP tunnel

    c. Through a GRE tunnel

    d. Directly over Layer 2

5. Which one of the following is not needed for a lightweight AP in default local mode to be able to support three SSIDs that are bound to three VLANs?

    a. A trunk link carrying three VLANs

    b. An access link bound to a single VLAN

    c. A WLC connected to three VLANs

    d. A CAPWAP tunnel to a WLC

6. Which one of the following WLC deployment models would be best for a large enterprise with around 3000 lightweight APs?

    a. Cisco Mobility Express

    b. Embedded

    c. Unified

    d. Cloud-based

7. If a lightweight AP provides at least one BSS for wireless clients, which one of the following modes does it use?

    a. Local

    b. Normal

    c. Monitor

    d. Client

8. Regarding lightweight AP modes, which one of the following is true?

    a. An AP can operate in multiple modes at the same time.

    b. An AP only has one possible mode of operation.

    c. The Run mode is the default mode.

    d. The SE-Connect mode is used for spectrum analysis.

Foundation Topics

Autonomous AP Architecture

An access point's primary function is to bridge wireless data from the air to a normal wired network. An AP can accept "connections" from a number of wireless clients so that they become members of the LAN, as if the same clients were using wired connections.

APs act as the central point of access (hence the AP name), controlling client access to the wireless LAN. An *autonomous AP* is self-contained; it is equipped with both wired and wireless hardware so that the wireless client associations can be terminated onto a wired connection locally at the AP. The APs and their data connections must be distributed across the coverage area and across the network.

Autonomous APs offer one or more fully functional, standalone basic service sets (BSSs). They are also a natural extension of a switched network, connecting wireless service set identifiers (SSIDs) to wired virtual LANs (VLANs) at the access layer. Figure 27-1 shows the basic architecture; even though only four APs are shown across the bottom, a typical enterprise network could consist of hundreds or thousands of APs.

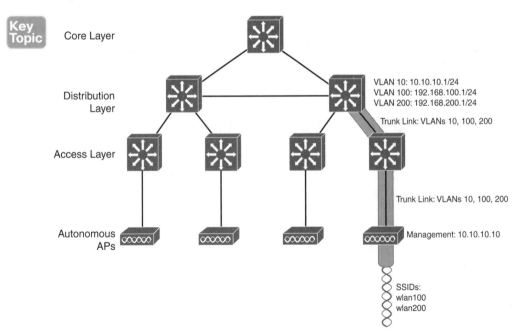

Figure 27-1 *Wireless Network Architecture with Autonomous APs*

What exactly does an autonomous AP need to become a part of the network? The wireless network in Figure 27-1 consists of two SSIDs: wlan100 and wlan200. These correspond to wired VLANs 100 and 200, respectively. As shown by the shaded links, the VLANs must be trunked from the distribution layer switch (where routing commonly takes place) to the access layer, where they are extended further over a trunk link to the AP.

An autonomous AP offers a short and simple path for data to travel between the wireless and wired networks. Data has to travel only through the AP to reach the network on the other side. Two wireless users that are associated to the same autonomous AP can reach each other through the AP without having to pass up into the wired network. As you work through the wireless architectures discussed in the rest of the chapter, notice the data path that is required for each.

An autonomous AP must also be configured with a management IP address (10.10.10.10 in Figure 27-1) so that you can remotely manage it. After all, you will want to configure SSIDs, VLANs, and many RF parameters like the channel and transmit power to be used. The management address is not normally part of any of the data VLANs, so a dedicated management VLAN (i.e., VLAN 10) must be added to the trunk links to reach the AP. Each AP must be configured and maintained individually unless you leverage a management platform such as Cisco Prime Infrastructure or Cisco DNA Center.

Because the data and management VLANs may need to reach every autonomous AP, the network configuration and efficiency can become cumbersome as the network scales. For example, you will likely want to offer the same SSID on many APs so that wireless clients can associate with that SSID in most any location or while roaming between any two APs. You might also want to extend the corresponding VLAN (and IP subnet) to each and every AP so that clients do not have to request a new IP address for each new association.

Because SSIDs and their VLANs must be extended at Layer 2, you should consider how they are extended throughout the switched network. The shaded links in Figure 27-2 show an example of a single VLAN's extent in the data plane. Working top to bottom, follow VLAN 100 as it reaches through the network. VLAN 100 is routed within the distribution layer and must be carried over trunk links to the access layer switches and then to each autonomous AP. In effect, VLAN 100 must extend end to end across the whole infrastructure—something that is usually considered to be a bad practice.

That might sound straightforward until you have to add a new VLAN and configure every switch and AP in your network to carry and support it. Even worse, suppose your network has redundant links between each layer of switches. The Spanning Tree Protocol (STP) running on each switch becomes a vital ingredient to prevent bridging loops from forming and corrupting the network. For these reasons, client roaming across autonomous APs is typically limited to the Layer 2 domain, or the extent of a single VLAN. As the wireless network expands, the infrastructure becomes more difficult to configure correctly and becomes less efficient.

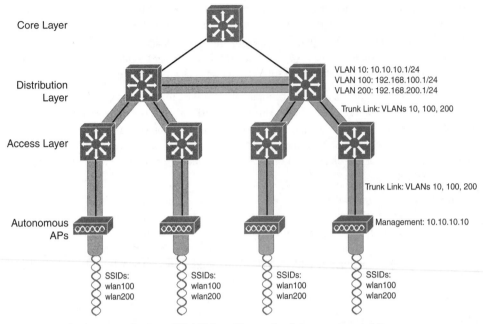

Figure 27-2   *Extent of a Data VLAN in a Network of Autonomous APs*

Cloud-based AP Architecture

Recall that an autonomous AP needs quite a bit of configuration and management. To help manage more and more autonomous APs as the wireless network grows, you could place an AP management platform such as Cisco Prime Infrastructure in a central location within the enterprise. The management platform would need to be purchased, configured, and maintained too.

A simpler approach is a *cloud-based AP* architecture, where the AP management function is pushed out of the enterprise and into the Internet cloud. Cisco Meraki is cloud-based and offers centralized management of wireless, switched, and security networks built from Meraki products. For example, through the cloud networking service, you can configure and manage APs, monitor wireless performance and activity, generate reports, and so on.

Cisco Meraki APs can be deployed automatically, once you register with the Meraki cloud. Each AP will contact the cloud when it powers up and will self-configure. From that point on, you can manage the AP through the Meraki cloud dashboard.

Figure 27-3 illustrates the basic cloud-based architecture. Notice that the network is arranged identically to that of the autonomous AP network. The reason is that the APs in a cloud-based network are all autonomous, too. The most visible difference is that all of the APs are managed, controlled, and monitored centrally from the cloud.

Answers to the "Do I Know This Already?" quiz:

1 A **2** B **3** C **4** B **5** A **6** C **7** A **8** D

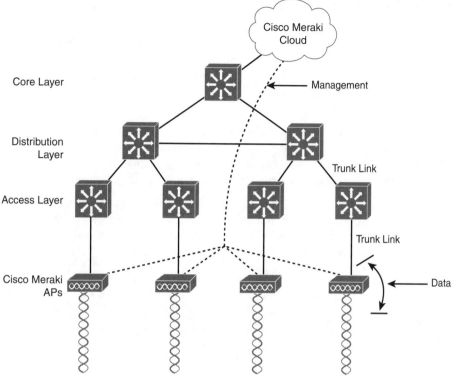

Figure 27-3 *Cisco Meraki Cloud-Based Wireless Network Architecture*

From the cloud, you can push out code upgrades and configuration changes to the APs in the enterprise. The Cisco Meraki cloud also adds the intelligence needed to automatically instruct each AP on which channel and transmit power level to use. It can also collect information from all of the APs about things such as RF interference, rogue or unexpected wireless devices that were overheard, and wireless usage statistics.

Finally, there are a couple of things you should observe about the cloud-based architecture. The data path from the wireless network to the wired network is very short; the autonomous AP links the two networks. Data to and from wireless clients does not have to travel up into the cloud and back; the cloud is used to bring management functions into the data plane.

Also, notice that the network in Figure 27-3 consists of two distinct paths—one for data traffic and another for management traffic, corresponding to the following two functions:

- **A control plane:** Traffic used to control, configure, manage, and monitor the AP itself
- **A data plane:** End-user traffic passing through the AP

This division will become important in the following sections as other types of architecture are discussed.

Split-MAC Architectures

Because autonomous APs are...well, autonomous, managing their RF operation can be quite difficult. As a network administrator, you are in charge of selecting and configuring the channel used by each AP and detecting and dealing with any rogue APs that might be interfering. You must also manage things such as the transmit power level to make sure that the wireless coverage is sufficient, it does not overlap too much, and there aren't any coverage holes—even when an AP's radio fails.

Managing wireless network security can also be difficult. Each autonomous AP handles its own security policies, with no central point of entry between the wireless and wired networks. That means there is no convenient place to monitor traffic for things such as intrusion detection and prevention, quality of service, bandwidth policing, and so on.

To overcome the limitations of distributed autonomous APs, many of the functions found within autonomous APs have to be shifted toward some central location. In Figure 27-4, most of the activities performed by an autonomous AP on the left are broken up into two groups—management functions on the top and real-time processes on the bottom.

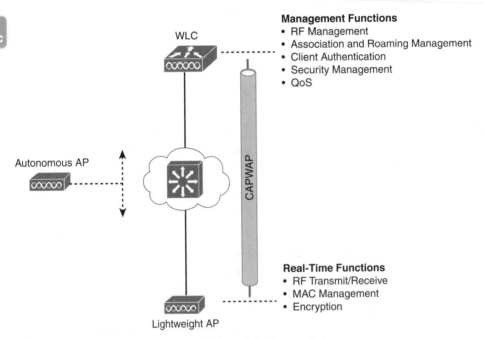

Figure 27-4 *Autonomous Versus Lightweight Access Point*

The real-time processes involve sending and receiving 802.11 frames, beacons, and probe messages. 802.11 data encryption is also handled in real time, on a per-packet basis. The AP must interact with wireless clients on some low level, known as the *Media Access Control* (MAC) layer. These functions must stay with the AP hardware, closest to the clients.

The management functions are not integral to handling frames over the RF channels, but are things that should be centrally administered. Therefore, those functions can be moved to a centrally located platform away from the AP.

When the functions of an autonomous AP are divided, the AP hardware is known as a *lightweight access point*, and performs only the real-time 802.11 operation. The lightweight AP gets its name because the code image and the local intelligence are stripped down, or lightweight, compared to the traditional autonomous AP.

The management functions are usually performed on a *wireless LAN controller* (WLC), which controls many lightweight APs. This is shown in the bottom right portion of Figure 27-4. Notice that the AP is left with duties in Layers 1 and 2, where frames are moved into and out of the RF domain. The AP becomes totally dependent on the WLC for every other WLAN function, such as authenticating users, managing security policies, and even selecting RF channels and output power.

> **NOTE**   Remember that a lightweight AP cannot normally operate on its own; it is very dependent on a WLC somewhere in the network. The only exception is the FlexConnect architecture, which is discussed later in this chapter.

The lightweight AP-WLC division of labor is known as a *split-MAC architecture*, where the normal MAC operations are pulled apart into two distinct locations. This occurs for every AP in the network; each one must boot and bind itself to a WLC to support wireless clients. The WLC becomes the central hub that supports a number of APs scattered about in the network.

How does a lightweight AP bind with a WLC to form a complete working access point? The two devices must use a tunneling protocol between them, to carry 802.11-related messages and also client data. Remember that the AP and WLC can be located on the same VLAN or IP subnet, but they do not have to be. Instead, they can be located on two entirely different IP subnets in two entirely different locations.

The Control and Provisioning of Wireless Access Points (*CAPWAP*) tunneling protocol makes this all possible by encapsulating the data between the LAP and WLC within new IP packets. The tunneled data can then be switched or routed across the campus network. As Figure 27-5 shows, the CAPWAP relationship actually consists of two separate tunnels, as follows:

- **CAPWAP control messages:** Carries exchanges that are used to configure the AP and manage its operation. The control messages are authenticated and encrypted, so the AP is securely controlled by only the appropriate WLC, then transported over the control tunnel.

- **CAPWAP data:** Used for packets traveling to and from wireless clients that are associated with the AP. Data packets are transported over the data tunnel but are not encrypted by default. When data encryption is enabled for an AP, packets are protected with Datagram Transport Layer Security (DTLS).

> **NOTE**   CAPWAP is defined in RFCs 5415, 5416, 5417, and 5418. CAPWAP is based on the Lightweight Access Point Protocol (LWAPP), which was a legacy Cisco proprietary solution.

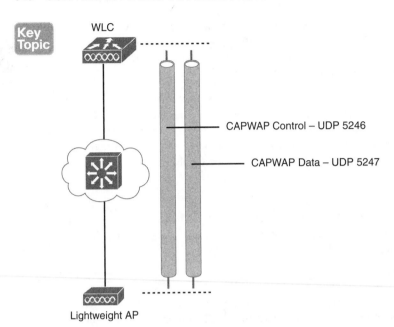

Figure 27-5 *Linking a Lightweight AP and WLC with CAPWAP*

Every AP and WLC must also authenticate each other with digital certificates. An X.509 certificate is preinstalled in each device when it is purchased. By using certificates behind the scenes, every device is properly authenticated before becoming part of the wireless network. This process helps assure that no one can add an unauthorized AP to your network.

The CAPWAP tunneling allows the AP and WLC to be separated geographically and logically. It also breaks the dependence on Layer 2 connectivity between them. For example, Figure 27-6 uses shaded areas to show the extent of VLAN 100. Notice how VLAN 100 exists at the WLC and in the air as SSID 100, near the wireless clients—but not in between the AP and the WLC. Instead, traffic to and from clients associated with SSID 100 is transported across the network infrastructure encapsulated inside the CAPWAP data tunnel. The tunnel exists between the IP address of the WLC and the IP address of the AP, which allows all of the tunneled packets to be routed at Layer 3.

Also, notice how the AP is known by only a single IP address: 10.10.10.10. Because the AP sits on the access layer where its CAPWAP tunnels terminate, it can use one IP address for both management and tunneling. No trunk link is needed because all of the VLANs it supports are encapsulated and tunneled as Layer 3 IP packets, rather than individual Layer 2 VLANs.

As the wireless network grows, the WLC simply builds more CAPWAP tunnels to reach more APs. Figure 27-7 depicts a network with four APs. Each AP has a control and a data tunnel back to the centralized WLC. SSID 100 can exist on every AP, and VLAN 100 can reach every AP through the network of tunnels.

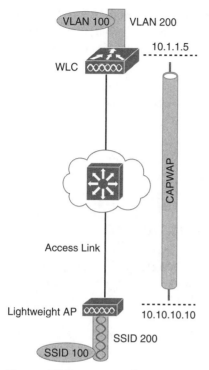

Figure 27-6 *Extent of VLAN 100 in a Cisco Wireless Network*

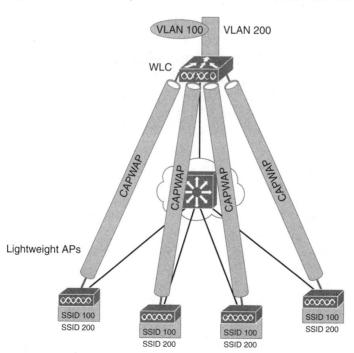

Figure 27-7 *Using CAPWAP Tunnels to Connect APs to One Central WLC*

Once CAPWAP tunnels are built from a WLC to one or more lightweight APs, the WLC can begin offering a variety of additional functions. Think of all the puzzles and shortcomings that were discussed for the traditional autonomous WLAN architecture as you read over the following list of WLC activities:

■ **Dynamic channel assignment:** The WLC can automatically choose and configure the RF channel used by each AP, based on other active access points in the area.

■ **Transmit power optimization:** The WLC can automatically set the transmit power of each AP based on the coverage area needed.

■ **Self-healing wireless coverage:** If an AP radio dies, the coverage hole can be "healed" by turning up the transmit power of surrounding APs automatically.

■ **Flexible client roaming:** Clients can roam between APs with very fast roaming times.

■ **Dynamic client load balancing:** If two or more APs are positioned to cover the same geographic area, the WLC can associate clients with the least used AP. This distributes the client load across the APs.

■ **RF monitoring:** The WLC manages each AP so that it scans channels to monitor the RF usage. By listening to a channel, the WLC can remotely gather information about RF interference, noise, signals from neighboring APs, and signals from rogue APs or ad hoc clients.

■ **Security management:** The WLC can authenticate clients from a central service and can require wireless clients to obtain an IP address from a trusted DHCP server before allowing them to associate and access the WLAN.

■ **Wireless intrusion protection system:** Leveraging its central location, the WLC can monitor client data to detect and prevent malicious activity.

Comparing Wireless LAN Controller Deployments

Suppose you want to deploy a WLC to support multiple lightweight APs in your network. Where should you put the WLC? The split-MAC concept can be applied to several different network architectures. Each architecture places the WLC in a different location within the network—a choice that also affects how many WLCs might be needed to support the number of APs required.

One approach is to locate the WLC in a central location so that you can maximize the number of APs joined to it. This is usually called a *unified* or *centralized WLC deployment*, which tends to follow the concept that most of the resources users need to reach are located in a central location such as a data center or the Internet. Traffic to and from wireless users would travel over CAPWAP tunnels that reach into the center of the network, near the core, as shown in Figure 27-8. A centralized WLC also provides a convenient place to enforce security policies that affect all wireless users.

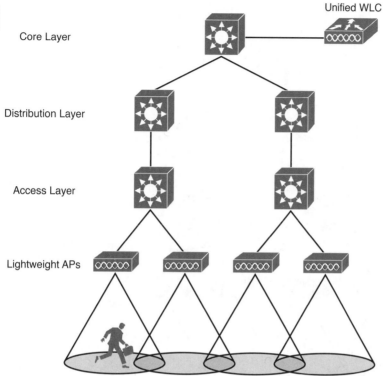

Figure 27-8 *WLC Location in a Unified Deployment*

Figure 27-8 shows four APs joined to a single WLC. Your network might have more APs—many, many more. A large enterprise network might have thousands of APs connected to its access layer. Scalability then becomes an important factor in the centralized design. Typical unified WLCs can support a maximum of 6000 APs. If you have more APs than the maximum, you will need to add more WLCs to the design, each located centrally.

A WLC can also be located in a central position in the network, inside a data center in a private cloud, as shown in Figure 27-9. This is known as a *cloud-based WLC deployment*, where the WLC exists as a virtual machine rather than a physical device. If the cloud computing platform already exists, then deploying a cloud-based WLC becomes straightforward. Such a controller can typically support up to 3000 APs. If your wireless network scales beyond that, then additional WLCs can be added as more virtual machines.

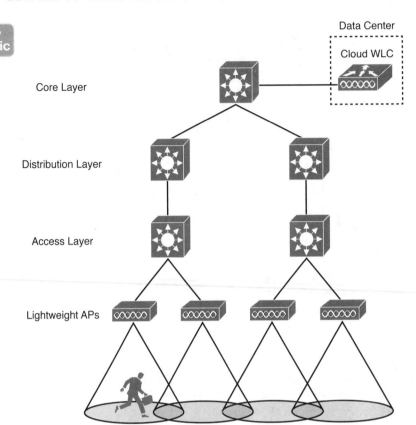

Figure 27-9 *WLC Location in a Cloud-based Deployment*

For small campuses or distributed branch locations, where the number of APs is relatively small in each, the WLC can be co-located with a stack of switches, as shown in Figure 27-10. This is known as an *embedded WLC deployment* because the controller is embedded within the switching hardware. Typical Cisco embedded WLCs can support up to 200 APs. The APs do not necessarily have to be connected to the switches that host the WLC; APs connected to other switches in other locations can join the embedded WLC too. As the number of APs grows, additional WLCs can be added by embedding them in other switch stacks at the site.

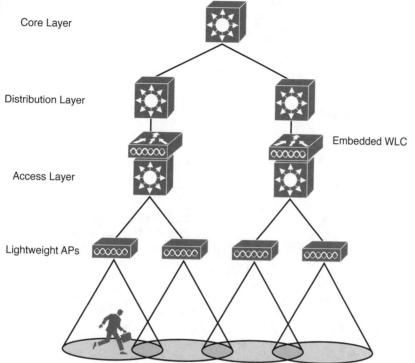

27

Figure 27-10 *WLC Location in an Embedded Deployment*

Finally, in small-scale environments, such as small, midsize, or multisite branch locations, you might not want to invest in dedicated WLCs at all. In this case, the WLC function can be co-located with an AP that is installed at the branch site. This is known as a Cisco *Mobility Express WLC deployment*, as shown in Figure 27-11. The AP that hosts the WLC forms a CAPWAP tunnel with the WLC, along with any other APs at the same location. A Mobility Express WLC can support up to 100 APs.

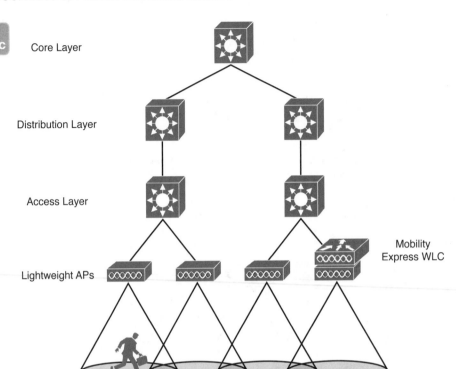

Core Layer

Distribution Layer

Access Layer

Mobility Express WLC

Lightweight APs

Figure 27-11   *WLC Location in a Mobility Express Deployment*

See Table 27-2 for a summary of WLC deployment models, WLC locations, and a typical maximum number of APs and clients that each one supports.

Table 27-2   Summary of WLC Deployment Models

Deployment Model	WLC Location (DC, Access, Central, AP)	APs Supported	Clients Supported	Typical Use
Unified	Central	6000	64,000	Large enterprise
Cloud	DC	3000	32,000	Private cloud
Embedded	Access	200	4000	Small campus
Mobility Express	Other	100	2000	Branch location
Autonomous	N/A	N/A	N/A	N/A

Cisco AP Modes

Many Cisco APs can operate in either autonomous or lightweight mode, depending on which code image is loaded and run. From the WLC, you can also configure a lightweight AP to operate in one of the following special-purpose modes:

- **Local:** The default lightweight mode that offers one or more functioning BSSs on a specific channel. During times that it is not transmitting, the AP will scan the other channels to measure the level of noise, measure interference, discover rogue devices, and match against intrusion detection system (IDS) events.

- **Monitor:** The AP does not transmit at all, but its receiver is enabled to act as a dedicated sensor. The AP checks for IDS events, detects rogue access points, and determines the position of stations through location-based services.

- **FlexConnect:** An AP at a remote site can locally switch traffic between an SSID and a VLAN if its CAPWAP tunnel to the WLC is down and if it is configured to do so.

- **Sniffer:** An AP dedicates its radios to receiving 802.11 traffic from other sources, much like a sniffer or packet capture device. The captured traffic is then forwarded to a PC running network analyzer software such as Wildpackets OmniPeek or WireShark, where it can be analyzed further.

- **Rogue detector:** An AP dedicates itself to detecting rogue devices by correlating MAC addresses heard on the wired network with those heard over the air. Rogue devices are those that appear on both networks.

- **Bridge:** An AP becomes a dedicated bridge (point-to-point or point-to-multipoint) between two networks. Two APs in bridge mode can be used to link two locations separated by a distance. Multiple APs in bridge mode can form an indoor or outdoor mesh network.

- **Flex+Bridge:** FlexConnect operation is enabled on a mesh AP.

- **SE-Connect:** The AP dedicates its radios to spectrum analysis on all wireless channels. You can remotely connect a PC running software such as MetaGeek Chanalyzer or Cisco Spectrum Expert to the AP to collect and analyze the spectrum analysis data to discover sources of interference.

> **NOTE**   Remember that a lightweight AP is normally in local mode when it is providing BSSs and allowing client devices to associate to wireless LANs. When an AP is configured to operate in one of the other modes, local mode (and the BSSs) is disabled.

Chapter Review

Review this chapter's material using either the tools in the book or the interactive tools for the same material found on the book's companion website. Table 27-3 outlines the key review elements and where you can find them. To better track your study progress, record when you completed these activities in the second column.

Table 27-3 Chapter Review Tracking

Review Element	Review Date(s)	Resource Used
Review key topics		Book, website
Review key terms		Book, website
Answer DIKTA questions		Book, PTP
Review memory tables		Website

Review All the Key Topics

Review the most important topics in this chapter, noted with the Key Topic icon in the outer margin of the page. Table 27-4 lists a reference of these key topics and the page numbers on which each is found.

Table 27-4 Key Topics for Chapter 28

Key Topic Element	Description	Page Number
Figure 27-1	Autonomous AP architecture	634
Figure 27-3	Cloud-based AP architecture	637
Figure 27-4	Split-MAC architecture	638
Figure 27-5	CAPWAP tunnels	640
Figure 27-8	Unified WLC deployment	643
Figure 27-9	Cloud-based WLC deployment	644
Figure 27-10	Embedded WLC deployment	645
Figure 27-11	Mobility Express WLC deployment	646
List	Cisco lightweight AP modes	647

Key Terms You Should Know

autonomous AP, CAPWAP, centralized WLC deployment, cloud-based AP, cloud-based WLC deployment, embedded WLC deployment, lightweight AP, local mode, Media Access Control (MAC) layer, Mobility Express WLC deployment, split-MAC architecture, unified WLC deployment, wireless LAN controller (WLC)

CHAPTER 28

Securing Wireless Networks

This chapter covers the following exam topics:

1.0 Network Fundamentals

1.11 Describe wireless principles

1.11.d Encryption

5.0 Security Fundamentals

5.9 Describe wireless security protocols (WPA, WPA2, and WPA3)

As you know by now, wireless networks are complex. Many technologies and protocols work behind the scenes to give end users a stable, yet mobile, connection to a wired network infrastructure. From the user's perspective, a wireless connection should seem no different than a wired connection. A wired connection can give users a sense of security; data traveling over a wire is probably not going to be overheard by others. A wireless connection is inherently different; data traveling over the air can be overheard by anyone within range.

Therefore, securing a wireless network becomes just as important as any other aspect. A comprehensive approach to wireless security focuses on the following areas:

■ Identifying the endpoints of a wireless connection

■ Identifying the end user

■ Protecting the wireless data from eavesdroppers

■ Protecting the wireless data from tampering

The identification process is performed through various authentication schemes. Protecting wireless data involves security functions like encryption and frame authentication.

This chapter covers many of the methods you can use to secure a wireless network. Be warned: wireless security can be a confusing topic because it is filled with many acronyms. Some of the acronyms rhyme like words from a children's book. In fact, this chapter is a story about WEP, PSK, TKIP, MIC, AES, EAP, EAP-FAST, EAP-TLS, LEAP, PEAP, WPA, WPA2, WPA3, CCMP, GCMP, and on and on it goes. When you finish with this chapter, though, you will come away with a clearer view of what these terms mean and how they all fit together. You might even be ready to configure a wireless LAN with effective security.

"Do I Know This Already?" Quiz

Take the quiz (either here or use the PTP software) if you want to use the score to help you decide how much time to spend on this chapter. The letter answers are listed at the bottom of the page following the quiz. Appendix C, found both at the end of the book as well as on the companion website, includes both the answers and explanations. You can also find both answers and explanations in the PTP testing software.

Table 28-1 "Do I Know This Already?" Section-to-Question Mapping

Foundation Topics Section	Questions
Anatomy of a Secure Connection	1–2
Wireless Client Authentication Methods	3–4
Wireless Privacy and Integrity Methods	5–6
WPA, WPA2, and WPA3	7–8

1. Which of the following are necessary components of a secure wireless connection? (Choose all that apply.)

    a. Encryption

    b. MIC

    c. Authentication

    d. All of these answers are correct.

2. Which one of the following is used to protect the integrity of data in a wireless frame?

    a. WIPS

    b. WEP

    c. MIC

    d. EAP

3. Which one of the following is a wireless encryption method that has been found to be vulnerable and is not recommended for use?

    a. AES

    b. WPA

    c. EAP

    d. WEP

4. Which one of the following is used as the authentication framework when 802.1x is used on a WLAN?

    a. Open authentication

    b. WEP

    c. EAP

    d. WPA

5. Suppose you would like to select a method to protect the privacy and integrity of wireless data. Which one of the following methods should you avoid because it has been deprecated ?

   a. TKIP

   b. CCMP

   c. GCMP

   d. EAP

6. Which one of the following is the data encryption and integrity method used by WPA2?

   a. WEP

   b. TKIP

   c. CCMP

   d. WPA

7. The Wi-Fi Alliance offers which of the following certifications for wireless devices that correctly implement security standards? (Choose all that apply.)

   a. WEP

   b. WPA2

   c. 802.11

   d. AES

8. A pre-shared key is used in which of the following wireless security configurations? (Choose all that apply.)

   a. WPA2 personal mode

   b. WPA2 enterprise mode

   c. WPA3 personal mode

   d. WPA3 enterprise mode

Foundation Topics

Anatomy of a Secure Connection

In the previous chapters of this book, you learned about wireless clients forming associations with wireless access points (APs) and passing data back and forth across the air.

As long as all clients and APs conform to the 802.11 standard, they can all coexist—even on the same channel. Not every 802.11 device is friendly and trustworthy, however. Sometimes it is easy to forget that transmitted frames do not just go directly from the sender to the receiver, as in a wired or switched connection. Instead, they travel according to the transmitter's antenna pattern, potentially reaching any receiver that is within range.

Consider the scenario in Figure 28-1. The wireless client opens a session with some remote entity and shares a confidential password. Because two untrusted users are also located within range of the client's signal, they may also learn the password by capturing frames that have been sent on the channel. The convenience of wireless communication also makes it easy for transmissions to be overheard and exploited by malicious users.

If data is sent through open space, how can it be secured so that it stays private and intact? The 802.11 standard offers a framework of wireless security mechanisms that can be used to add trust, privacy, and integrity to a wireless network. The following sections give an overview of the wireless security framework.

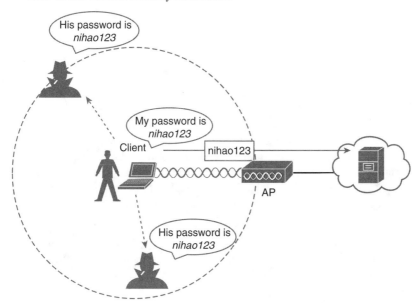

Figure 28-1   *Wireless Transmissions Reaching Unintended Recipients*

Authentication

To use a wireless network, clients must first discover a basic service set (BSS) and then request permission to associate with it. Clients should be authenticated by some means before they can become functioning members of the wireless LAN. Why?

Suppose that your wireless network connects to corporate resources where confidential information can be accessed. In that case, only devices known to be trusted and expected should be given access. Guest users, if they are permitted at all, should be allowed to join a different guest WLAN where they can access nonconfidential or public resources. Rogue clients, which are not expected or welcomed, should not be permitted to associate at all. After all, they are not affiliated with the corporate network and are likely to be unknown devices that happen to be within range of your network.

To control access, wireless networks can authenticate the client devices before they are allowed to associate. Potential clients must identify themselves by presenting some form of credentials to the APs. Figure 28-2 shows the basic client authentication process.

Wireless authentication can take many forms. Some methods require only a static text string that is common across all trusted clients and APs. The text string is stored on the client device and presented directly to the AP when needed. What might happen if the device was stolen or lost? Most likely, any user who possessed the device could still authenticate to the network. Other more stringent authentication methods require interaction with a corporate user database. In those cases, the end user must enter a valid username and password—something that would not be known to a thief or an imposter.

Figure 28-2 *Authenticating a Wireless Client*

If you have ever joined a wireless network, you might have focused on authenticating your device or yourself, while implicitly trusting the nearest AP. For example, if you turn on your wireless device and find a wireless network that is available at your workplace, you probably join it without hesitating. The same is true for wireless networks in an airport, a hotel, a hot spot, or in your home—you expect the AP that is advertising the SSID to be owned and operated by the entity where you are located. But how can you be sure?

Normally, the only piece of information you have is the SSID being broadcast or advertised by an AP. If the SSID looks familiar, you will likely choose to join it. Perhaps your computer is configured to automatically connect to a known SSID so that it associates without your intervention. Either way, you might unwittingly join the same SSID even if it was being advertised by an imposter.

Some common attacks focus on a malicious user pretending to be an AP. The fake AP can send beacons, answer probes, and associate clients just like the real AP it is impersonating. Once a client associates with the fake AP, the attacker can easily intercept all communication to and from the client from its central position. A fake AP could also send spoofed management frames to disassociate or deauthenticate legitimate and active clients, just to disrupt normal network operation.

To prevent this type of man-in-the-middle attack, the client should authenticate the AP before the client itself is authenticated. Figure 28-3 shows a simple scenario. Even further, any management frames received by a client should be authenticated too, as proof that they were sent by a legitimate and expected AP.

Figure 28-3 *Authenticating a Wireless AP*

Answers to the "Do I Know This Already?" quiz:

1 D **2** C **3** D **4** C **5** A **6** C **7** B **8** A, C

Message Privacy

Suppose that the client in Figure 28-3 must authenticate before joining the wireless network. It might also authenticate the AP and its management frames after it associates but before it is itself authenticated. The client's relationship with the AP might become much more trusted, but data passing to and from the client is still available to eavesdroppers on the same channel.

To protect data privacy on a wireless network, the data should be encrypted for its journey through free space. This is accomplished by encrypting the data payload in each wireless frame just prior to being transmitted, then decrypting it as it is received. The idea is to use an encryption method that the transmitter and receiver share, so the data can be encrypted and decrypted successfully.

In wireless networks, each WLAN may support only one authentication and encryption scheme, so all clients must use the same encryption method when they associate. You might think that having one encryption method in common would allow every client to eavesdrop on every other client. That is not necessarily the case because the AP should securely negotiate a unique encryption key to use for each associated client.

Ideally, the AP and a client are the only two devices that have the encryption keys in common so that they can understand each other's data. No other device should know about or be able to use the same keys to eavesdrop and decrypt the data. In Figure 28-4, the client's confidential password information has been encrypted before being transmitted. The AP can decrypt it successfully before forwarding it onto the wired network, but other wireless devices cannot.

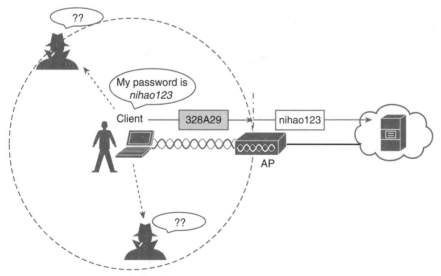

Figure 28-4 *Encrypting Wireless Data to Protect Data Privacy*

The AP also maintains a "group key" that it uses when it needs to send encrypted data to all clients in its cell at one time. Each of the associated clients uses the same group key to decrypt the data.

Message Integrity

Encrypting data obscures it from view while it is traveling over a public or untrusted network. The intended recipient should be able to decrypt the message and recover the original contents, but what if someone managed to alter the contents along the way? The recipient would have a very difficult time discovering that the original data had been modified.

A message integrity check (MIC) is a security tool that can protect against data tampering. You can think of a MIC as a way for the sender to add a secret stamp inside the encrypted data frame. The stamp is based on the contents of the data bits to be transmitted. Once the recipient decrypts the frame, it can compare the secret stamp to its own idea of what the stamp should be, based on the data bits that were received. If the two stamps are identical, the recipient can safely assume that the data has not been tampered with. Figure 28-5 shows the MIC process.

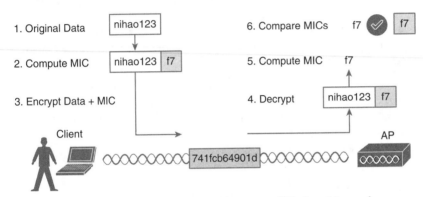

Figure 28-5   *Checking Message Integrity over a Wireless Network*

Wireless Client Authentication Methods

You can use many different methods to authenticate wireless clients as they try to associate with the network. The methods have been introduced over time and have evolved as security weaknesses have been exposed and wireless hardware has advanced. This section covers the most common authentication methods you might encounter.

Open Authentication

The original 802.11 standard offered only two choices to authenticate a client: open authentication and WEP.

Open authentication is true to its name; it offers open access to a WLAN. The only requirement is that a client must use an 802.11 authentication request before it attempts to associate with an AP. No other credentials are needed.

When would you want to use open authentication? After all, it does not sound very secure because it is not. With no challenge, any 802.11 client may authenticate to access the network. That is, in fact, the whole purpose of open authentication—to validate that a client is a valid 802.11 device by authenticating the wireless hardware and the protocol. Authenticating the user's identity is handled as a true security process through other means.

You have probably seen a WLAN with open authentication when you have visited a public location. If any client screening is used at all, it comes in the form of web authentication. A client can associate right away but must open a web browser to see and accept the terms for use and enter basic credentials. From that point, network access is opened up for the client. Most client operating systems flag such networks to warn you that your wireless data will not be secured in any way if you join.

WEP

As you might expect, open authentication offers nothing that can obscure or encrypt the data being sent between a client and an AP. As an alternative, the 802.11 standard has traditionally defined Wired Equivalent Privacy (WEP) as a method to make a wireless link more like or equivalent to a wired connection.

WEP uses the RC4 cipher algorithm to make every wireless data frame private and hidden from eavesdroppers. The same algorithm encrypts data at the sender and decrypts it at the receiver. The algorithm uses a string of bits as a key, commonly called a WEP key, to derive other encryption keys—one per wireless frame. As long as the sender and receiver have an identical key, one can decrypt what the other encrypts.

WEP is known as a shared-key security method. The same key must be shared between the sender and receiver ahead of time, so that each can derive other mutually agreeable encryption keys. In fact, every potential client and AP must share the same key ahead of time so that any client can associate with the AP.

The WEP key can also be used as an optional authentication method as well as an encryption tool. Unless a client can use the correct WEP key, it cannot associate with an AP. The AP tests the client's knowledge of the WEP key by sending it a random challenge phrase. The client encrypts the challenge phrase with WEP and returns the result to the AP. The AP can compare the client's encryption with its own to see whether the two WEP keys yield identical results.

WEP keys can be either 40 or 104 bits long, represented by a string of 10 or 26 hex digits. As a rule of thumb, longer keys offer more unique bits for the algorithm, resulting in more robust encryption. Except in WEP's case, that is. Because WEP was defined in the original 802.11 standard in 1999, every wireless adapter was built with encryption hardware specific to WEP. In 2001, a number of weaknesses were discovered and revealed, so work began to find better wireless security methods. By 2004, the 802.11i amendment was ratified and WEP was officially deprecated. Both WEP encryption and WEP shared-key authentication are widely considered to be weak methods to secure a wireless LAN.

802.1x/EAP

With only open authentication and WEP available in the original 802.11 standard, a more secure authentication method was needed. Client authentication generally involves some sort of challenge, a response, and then a decision to grant access. Behind the scenes, it can also involve an exchange of session or encryption keys, in addition to other parameters needed for client access. Each authentication method might have unique requirements as a unique way to pass information between the client and the AP.

Rather than build additional authentication methods into the 802.11 standard, a more flexible and scalable authentication framework, the Extensible Authentication Protocol (EAP), was chosen. As its name implies, EAP is extensible and does not consist of any one authentication method. Instead, EAP defines a set of common functions that actual authentication methods can use to authenticate users. As you read through this section, notice how many authentication methods have *EAP* in their names. Each method is unique and different, but each one follows the EAP framework.

EAP has another interesting quality: it can integrate with the IEEE 802.1x port-based access control standard. When 802.1x is enabled, it limits access to a network media until a client authenticates. This means that a wireless client might be able to associate with an AP but will not be able to pass data to any other part of the network until it successfully authenticates.

With open and WEP authentication, wireless clients are authenticated locally at the AP without further intervention. The scenario changes with 802.1x; the client uses open authentication to associate with the AP, and then the actual client authentication process occurs at a dedicated authentication server. Figure 28-6 shows the three-party 802.1x arrangement that consists of the following entities:

- **Supplicant:** The client device that is requesting access
- **Authenticator:** The network device that provides access to the network (usually a wireless LAN controller [WLC])
- **Authentication server (AS):** The device that takes user or client credentials and permits or denies network access based on a user database and policies (usually a RADIUS server)

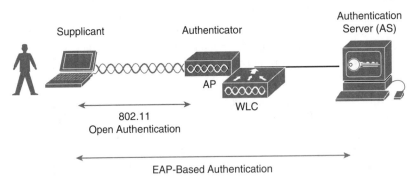

Figure 28-6 *802.1x Client Authentication Roles*

The wireless LAN controller becomes a middleman in the client authentication process, controlling user access with 802.1x and communicating with the authentication server using the EAP framework.

The following sections provide an overview of several common EAP-based authentication methods. The goal here is to become aware of the many methods without trying to memorize them all. In fact, even when you configure user authentication on a wireless LAN, you will not have to select a specific method. Instead, you select 802.1x on the WLC so that it is ready to handle a variety of EAP methods. It is then up to the client and the authentication server to use a compatible method. You will learn more about configuring security on a wireless LAN in Chapter 29, "Building a Wireless LAN."

LEAP

As an early attempt to address the weaknesses in WEP, Cisco developed a proprietary wireless authentication method called Lightweight EAP (LEAP). To authenticate, the client must supply username and password credentials. Both the authentication server and the client exchange challenge messages that are then encrypted and returned. This provides mutual authentication; as long as the messages can be decrypted successfully, the client and the AS have essentially authenticated each other.

At the time, WEP-based hardware was still widely used. Therefore, LEAP attempted to overcome WEP weaknesses by using dynamic WEP keys that changed frequently. Nevertheless, the method used to encrypt the challenge messages was found to be vulnerable, so LEAP has since been deprecated. Even though wireless clients and controllers still offer LEAP, you should not use it.

EAP-FAST

Cisco developed a more secure method called EAP Flexible Authentication by Secure Tunneling (EAP-FAST). Authentication credentials are protected by passing a protected access credential (PAC) between the AS and the supplicant. The PAC is a form of shared secret that is generated by the AS and used for mutual authentication. EAP-FAST is a sequence of three phases:

- **Phase 0:** The PAC is generated or provisioned and installed on the client.
- **Phase 1:** After the supplicant and AS have authenticated each other, they negotiate a Transport Layer Security (TLS) tunnel.
- **Phase 2:** The end user can then be authenticated through the TLS tunnel for additional security.

Notice that two separate authentication processes occur in EAP-FAST—one between the AS and the supplicant and another with the end user. These occur in a nested fashion, as an outer authentication (outside the TLS tunnel) and an inner authentication (inside the TLS tunnel).

Like other EAP-based methods, a RADIUS server is required. However, the RADIUS server must also operate as an EAP-FAST server to be able to generate PACs, one per user.

PEAP

Like EAP-FAST, the Protected EAP (PEAP) method uses an inner and outer authentication; however, the AS presents a digital certificate to authenticate itself with the supplicant in the outer authentication. If the supplicant is satisfied with the identity of the AS, the two will build a TLS tunnel to be used for the inner client authentication and encryption key exchange.

The digital certificate of the AS consists of data in a standard format that identifies the owner and is "signed" or validated by a third party. The third party is known as a certificate authority (CA) and is known and trusted by both the AS and the supplicants. The supplicant must also possess the CA certificate just so that it can validate the one it receives from the AS. The certificate is also used to pass a public key, in plain view, which can be used to help decrypt messages from the AS.

Notice that only the AS has a certificate for PEAP. That means the supplicant can readily authenticate the AS. The client does not have or use a certificate of its own, so it must be authenticated within the TLS tunnel using one of the following two methods:

- **MSCHAPv2:** Microsoft Challenge Authentication Protocol version 2
- **GTC:** Generic Token Card; a hardware device that generates one-time passwords for the user or a manually generated password

EAP-TLS

PEAP leverages a digital certificate on the AS as a robust method to authenticate the RADIUS server. It is easy to obtain and install a certificate on a single server, but the clients are left to identify themselves through other means. EAP Transport Layer Security (EAP-TLS) goes one step further by requiring certificates on the AS and on every client device.

With EAP-TLS, the AS and the supplicant exchange certificates and can authenticate each other. A TLS tunnel is built afterward so that encryption key material can be securely exchanged.

EAP-TLS is considered to be the most secure wireless authentication method available; however, implementing it can sometimes be complex. Along with the AS, each wireless client must obtain and install a certificate. Manually installing certificates on hundreds or thousands of clients can be impractical. Instead, you would need to implement a Public Key Infrastructure (PKI) that could supply certificates securely and efficiently and revoke them when a client or user should no longer have access to the network. This usually involves setting up your own CA or building a trust relationship with a third-party CA that can supply certificates to your clients.

NOTE   EAP-TLS is practical only if the wireless clients can accept and use digital certificates. Many wireless devices, such as communicators, medical devices, and RFID tags, have an underlying operating system that cannot interface with a CA or use certificates.

Wireless Privacy and Integrity Methods

The original 802.11 standard supported only one method to secure wireless data from eavesdroppers: WEP. As you have learned in this chapter, WEP has been compromised, deprecated, and can no longer be recommended. What other options are available to encrypt data and protect its integrity as it travels through free space?

TKIP

During the time when WEP was embedded in wireless client and AP hardware, yet was known to be vulnerable, the Temporal Key Integrity Protocol (TKIP) was developed.

TKIP adds the following security features using legacy hardware and the underlying WEP encryption:

- **MIC:** This efficient algorithm adds a hash value to each frame as a message integrity check to prevent tampering; commonly called "Michael" as an informal reference to MIC.

- **Time stamp:** A time stamp is added into the MIC to prevent replay attacks that attempt to reuse or replay frames that have already been sent.

- **Sender's MAC address:** The MIC also includes the sender's MAC address as evidence of the frame source.

- **TKIP sequence counter:** This feature provides a record of frames sent by a unique MAC address, to prevent frames from being replayed as an attack.

- **Key mixing algorithm:** This algorithm computes a unique 128-bit WEP key for each frame.

- **Longer initialization vector (IV):** The IV size is doubled from 24 to 48 bits, making it virtually impossible to exhaust all WEP keys by brute-force calculation.

TKIP became a reasonably secure stopgap security method, buying time until the 802.11i standard could be ratified. Some attacks have been created against TKIP, so it, too, should be avoided if a better method is available. In fact, TKIP was deprecated in the 802.11-2012 standard.

CCMP

The Counter/CBC-MAC Protocol (CCMP) is considered to be more secure than TKIP. CCMP consists of two algorithms:

- AES counter mode encryption
- Cipher Block Chaining Message Authentication Code (CBC-MAC) used as a message integrity check (MIC)

The Advanced Encryption Standard (AES) is the current encryption algorithm adopted by U.S. National Institute of Standards and Technology (NIST) and the U.S. government, and widely used around the world. In other words, AES is open, publicly accessible, and represents the most secure encryption method available today.

Before CCMP can be used to secure a wireless network, the client devices and APs must support the AES counter mode and CBC-MAC in hardware. CCMP cannot be used on legacy devices that support only WEP or TKIP. How can you know if a device supports CCMP? Look for the WPA2 designation, which is described in the following section.

GCMP

The Galois/Counter Mode Protocol (GCMP) is a robust authenticated encryption suite that is more secure and more efficient than CCMP. GCMP consists of two algorithms:

- AES counter mode encryption
- Galois Message Authentication Code (GMAC) used as a message integrity check (MIC)

GCMP is used in WPA3, which is described in the following section.

WPA, WPA2, and WPA3

This chapter covers a variety of authentication methods and encryption and message integrity algorithms. When it comes time to configure a WLAN with wireless security, should you try to select some combination of schemes based on which one is best or which one is not deprecated? Which authentication methods are compatible with which encryption algorithms?

The Wi-Fi Alliance (http://wi-fi.org), a nonprofit wireless industry association, has worked out straightforward ways to do that through its Wi-Fi Protected Access (WPA) industry certifications. To date, there are three different versions: WPA, WPA2, and WPA3. Wireless products are tested in authorized testing labs against stringent criteria that represent correct implementation of a standard. As long as the Wi-Fi Alliance has certified a wireless client device and an AP and its associated WLC for the same WPA version, they should be compatible and offer the same security components.

The Wi-Fi Alliance introduced its first generation WPA certification (known simply as WPA and not WPA1) while the IEEE 802.11i amendment for best practice security methods was still being developed. WPA was based on parts of 802.11i and included 802.1x authentication, TKIP, and a method for dynamic encryption key management.

Once 802.11i was ratified and published, the Wi-Fi Alliance included it in full in its WPA Version 2 (WPA2) certification. WPA2 is based around the superior AES CCMP algorithms, rather than the deprecated TKIP from WPA. It should be obvious that WPA2 was meant as a replacement for WPA.

In 2018, the Wi-Fi Alliance introduced WPA Version 3 (WPA3) as a future replacement for WPA2, adding several important and superior security mechanisms. WPA3 leverages stronger encryption by AES with the Galois/Counter Mode Protocol (GCMP). It also uses Protected Management Frames (PMF) to secure important 802.11 management frames between APs and clients, to prevent malicious activity that might spoof or tamper with a BSS's operation.

Table 28-2 summarizes the basic differences between WPA, WPA2, and WPA3. Each successive version is meant to replace prior versions by offering better security features. You should avoid using WPA and use WPA2 instead—at least until WPA3 becomes widely available on wireless client devices, APs, and WLCs.

Table 28-2   Comparing WPA, WPA2, and WPA3

Authentication and Encryption Feature Support	WPA	WPA2	WPA3*
Authentication with **Pre-Shared Keys?**	Yes	Yes	Yes
Authentication with **802.1x?**	Yes	Yes	Yes
Encryption and MIC with **TKIP?**	Yes	No	No
Encryption and MIC with **AES and CCMP?**	Yes	Yes	No
Encryption and MIC with **AES and GCMP?**	No	No	Yes

* WPA3 includes other features beyond WPA and WPA2, such as Simultaneous Authentication of Equals (SAE), Forward secrecy, and Protected management frames (PMF).

Notice that all three WPA versions support two client authentication modes: a pre-shared key (PSK) or 802.1x, based on the scale of the deployment. These are also known as *personal mode* and *enterprise mode*, respectively. With personal mode, a key string must be shared or configured on every client and AP before the clients can connect to the wireless network. The pre-shared key is normally kept confidential so that unauthorized users have no knowledge of it. The key string is never sent over the air. Instead, clients and APs work through a four-way handshake procedure that uses the pre-shared key string to construct and exchange encryption key material that can be openly exchanged. Once that process is successful, the AP can authenticate the client and the two can secure data frames that are sent over the air.

With WPA-Personal and WPA2-Personal modes, a malicious user can eavesdrop and capture the four-way handshake between a client and an AP. That user can then use a dictionary attack to automate guessing the pre-shared key. If he is successful, he can then decrypt the wireless data or even join the network posing as a legitimate user.

WPA3-Personal avoids such an attack by strengthening the key exchange between clients and APs through a method known as Simultaneous Authentication of Equals (SAE). Rather than a client authenticating against a server or AP, the client and AP can initiate the authentication process equally and even simultaneously.

Even if a password or key is compromised, WPA3-Personal offers forward secrecy, which prevents attackers from being able to use a key to unencrypt data that has already been transmitted over the air.

NOTE   The Personal mode of any WPA version is usually easy to deploy in a small environment or with clients that are embedded in certain devices because a simple text key string is all that is needed to authenticate the clients. Be aware that every device using the WLAN must be configured with an identical pre-shared key. If you ever need to update or change the key, you must touch every device to do so. As well, the pre-shared key should remain a well kept secret; you should never divulge the pre-shared key to any unauthorized person.

Notice from Table 28-2 that WPA, WPA2, and WPA3 also support 802.1x or enterprise authentication. This implies EAP-based authentication, but the WPA versions do not require any specific EAP method. Instead, the Wi-Fi Alliance certifies interoperability with well-known EAP methods like EAP-TLS, PEAP, EAP-TTLS, and EAP-SIM. Enterprise authentication is more complex to deploy than personal mode because authentication servers must be set up and configured as a critical enterprise resource.

NOTE   The Wi-Fi Alliance has made wireless security configuration straightforward and consistent through its WPA, WPA2, and WPA3 certifications. Each version is meant to replace its predecessors because of improved security mechanisms. You should always select the highest WPA version that the clients and wireless infrastructure in your environment will support.

Chapter Review

At this point in the chapter, you might still be a little overwhelmed with the number of acronyms and security terms to learn and keep straight in your mind. Spend some time reviewing Table 28-3, which lists all of the topics described in this chapter. The table is organized in a way that should help you remember how the acronyms and functions are grouped together. Remember that an effective wireless security strategy includes a method to authenticate clients and a method to provide data privacy and integrity. These two types of methods are listed in the leftmost column. Work your way to the right to remember what types of authentication and privacy/integrity are available. The table also expands the name of each acronym as a memory tool.

Also remember that WPA, WPA2, and WPA3 simplify wireless network configuration and compatibility because they limit which authentication and privacy/integrity methods can be used.

Table 28-3   Review of Wireless Security Mechanisms and Options

Security Mechanism	Type		Type Expansion	Credentials Used
Authentication Methods	Open		Open Authentication	None, other than 802.11 protocol
	WEP		Wired Equivalent Privacy	Static WEP keys
	802.1x/EAP (Extensible Authentication Protocol)	LEAP	Lightweight EAP	Deprecated; uses dynamic WEP keys
		EAP-FAST	EAP Flexible Authentication by Secure Tunneling	Uses protected access credential (PAC)
		PEAP	Protected EAP	AS authenticated by digital certificate
		EAP-TLS	EAP Transport Layer Security	Client and AS authenticated by digital certificate
Privacy & Integrity Methods	TKIP		Temporal Key Integrity Protocol	N/A
	CCMP		Counter/CBC-MAC Protocol	N/A
	GCMP		Galois/Counter Mode Protocol	N/A

You should also review this chapter's material using either the tools in the book or the interactive tools for the same material found on the book's companion website. Table 28-4 outlines the key review elements and where you can find them. To better track your study progress, record when you completed these activities in the second column.

Table 28-4   Chapter Review Tracking

Review Element	Review Date(s)	Resource Used
Review key topics		Book, website
Review key terms		Book, website
Answer DIKTA questions		Book, PTP
Review memory tables		Website

Review All the Key Topics

Review the most important topics in this chapter, noted with the Key Topic icon in the outer margin of the page. Table 28-5 lists a reference of these key topics and the page numbers on which each is found.

Table 28-5   Key Topics for Chapter 28

Key Topic Element	Description	Page Number
List	802.1x entities	658
Table 28-2	WPA, WPA2, and WPA3 comparison	662
Table 28-3	Wireless security mechanism review	664

Key Terms You Should Know

802.1x, authentication server (AS), authenticator, certificate authority (CA), Counter/CBC-MAC Protocol (CCMP), EAP Flexible Authentication by Secure Tunneling (EAP-FAST), EAP Transport Layer Security (EAP-TLS), enterprise mode, Extensible Authentication Protocol (EAP), forward secrecy, Galois/Counter Mode Protocol (GCMP), Lightweight EAP (LEAP), message integrity check (MIC), open authentication, personal mode, protected access credential (PAC), Protected EAP (PEAP), Protected Management Frame (PMF), Public Key Infrastructure (PKI), RADIUS server, Simultaneous Authentication of Equals (SAE), supplicant, Temporal Key Integrity Protocol (TKIP), Wired Equivalent Privacy (WEP), Wi-Fi Protected Access (WPA), WPA Version 2 (WPA2), WPA Version 3 (WPA3)

Building a Wireless LAN

This chapter covers the following exam topics:

2.0 Network Access

2.7 Describe physical infrastructure connections of WLAN components (AP, WLC, access/trunk ports, and LAG)

2.8 Describe AP and WLC management access connections (Telnet, SSH, HTTP, HTTPS, console, and TACACS+/RADIUS)

2.9 Configure the components of a wireless LAN access for client connectivity using GUI only, such as WLAN creation, security settings, QoS profiles, and advanced WLAN settings

5.0 Security Fundamentals

5.10 Configure WLAN using WPA2 PSK using the GUI

In Chapters 26 through 28, you learned about the fundamentals of wireless networks. As a CCNA, you will also need to know how to apply that knowledge toward building a functioning network with APs and a WLC.

In addition, based on the concepts you learned in Chapter 28, "Securing Wireless Networks," you will be able to configure the WLAN to use WPA2-Personal.

"Do I Know This Already?" Quiz

Take the quiz (either here or use the PTP software) if you want to use the score to help you decide how much time to spend on this chapter. The letter answers are listed at the bottom of the page following the quiz. Appendix C, found both at the end of the book as well as on the companion website, includes both the answers and explanations. You can also find both answers and explanations in the PTP testing software.

Table 29-1 "Do I Know This Already?" Section-to-Question Mapping

Foundation Topics Section	Questions
Connecting a Cisco AP	1–2
Accessing a Cisco WLC	3
Connecting a Cisco WLC	4–5
Configuring a WLAN	6–8

1. Suppose you need to connect a lightweight AP to a network. Which one of the following link types would be necessary?

   a. Access mode link

   b. Trunk mode link

   c. LAG mode link

   d. EtherChannel link

2. An autonomous AP will be configured to support three WLANs that correspond to three VLANs. The AP will connect to the network over which one of the following?

   a. Access mode link

   b. Trunk mode link

   c. LAG mode link

   d. EtherChannel link

3. Suppose you would like to connect to a WLC to configure a new WLAN on it. Which one of the following is a valid method to use?

   a. SSH

   b. HTTPS

   c. HTTP

   d. All of these answers are correct.

4. Which one of the following correctly describes the single logical link formed by bundling all of a controller's distribution system ports together?

   a. PHY

   b. DSP

   c. LAG

   d. GEC

5. Which one of the following controller interfaces maps a WLAN to a VLAN?

   a. Bridge interface

   b. Virtual interface

   c. WLAN interface

   d. Dynamic interface

6. Which two of the following things are bound together when a new WLAN is created?

   a. VLAN

   b. AP

   c. Controller interface

   d. SSID

7. What is the maximum number of WLANs you can configure on a Cisco wireless controller?

   a. 8

   b. 16

   c. 512

   d. 1024

8. Which of the following parameters are necessary when creating a new WLAN with the controller GUI? (Choose all that apply.)

   a. SSID

   b. VLAN number

   c. Interface

   d. BSSID

   e. IP subnet

Foundation Topics

Connecting a Cisco AP

A Cisco wireless network can consist of autonomous APs or lightweight APs that are coupled with one or more wireless LAN controllers. Both types of APs are covered in Chapter 27, "Analyzing Cisco Wireless Architectures," from a functional perspective. You should also understand how to connect the wired side of each type of AP so that it can pass traffic between the appropriate VLANs and WLANs.

Recall that an autonomous AP is a standalone device; nothing else is needed to forward Ethernet frames from a wired VLAN to a wireless LAN, and vice versa. In effect, the AP maps each VLAN to a WLAN and BSS. The autonomous AP has a single wired Ethernet interface, as shown in the left portion of Figure 29-1, which means that multiple VLANs must be brought to it over a trunk link.

> **NOTE**   A switch port providing a wired connection to an AP must be configured to support either access or trunk mode. In trunk mode, 802.1Q encapsulation tags each frame according to the VLAN number it came from. The wireless side of an AP inherently trunks 802.11 frames by marking them with the BSSID of the WLAN where they belong.

A lightweight AP also has a single wired Ethernet interface; however, it must be paired with a WLC to be fully functional. Wired VLANs that terminate at the WLC can be mapped to WLANs that emerge at the AP. Even though multiple VLANs are being extended from the WLC to the AP, they are all carried over the CAPWAP tunnel between the two. That means the AP needs only an access link to connect to the network infrastructure and terminate its end of the tunnel, as shown in the right portion of Figure 29-1.

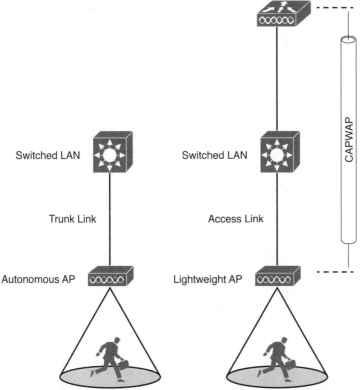

29

Figure 29-1   *Comparing Connections to Autonomous and Lightweight APs*

To configure and manage Cisco APs, you can connect a serial console cable from your PC to the console port on the AP. Once the AP is operational and has an IP address, you can also use Telnet or SSH to connect to its CLI over the wired network. Autonomous APs support browser-based management sessions via HTTP and HTTPS. You can manage lightweight APs from a browser session to the WLC.

Accessing a Cisco WLC

To connect and configure a WLC, you will need to open a web browser to the WLC's management address with either HTTP or HTTPS. This can be done only after the WLC has an initial configuration and a management IP address assigned to its management interface. The web-based GUI provides an effective way to monitor, configure, and troubleshoot a wireless network. You can also connect to a WLC with an SSH session, where you can use its CLI to monitor, configure, and debug activity.

Both the web-based GUI and the CLI require management users to log in. Users can be authenticated against an internal list of local usernames or against an authentication, authorization, and accounting (AAA) server, such as TACACS+ or RADIUS.

When you first open a web browser to the management address, you will see the initial login screen. Click on the **Login** button, as shown in Figure 29-2; then enter your user credentials as you are prompted for them.

Figure 29-2 *Accessing a WLC with a Web Browser*

NOTE The CCNA exam objectives focus on using the WLC GUI to configure a WLAN and a security suite. Therefore, the examples in this section assume that someone has already entered an initial configuration to give the WLC a working IP address for management.

When you are successfully logged in, the WLC will display a monitoring dashboard similar to the one shown in Figure 29-3. You will not be able to make any configuration changes there, so you must click on the **Advanced** link in the upper-right corner. This will bring up the full WLC GUI, as shown in Figure 29-4.

Notice the tabs across the top of the screen in Figure 29-4. You can select categories of functions from among Monitor, WLANs, Controller, Wireless, Security, and so on. As you select one of these categories, the vertical list of functions at the left side of the screen will change accordingly. You can expand the list entries if needed and select one to work on. The main screen area will display all of the relevant fields and options you can edit as you make configuration changes. You will get a feel for which tabs and list items you should use as you work through the remainder of the chapter.

Answers to the "Do I Know This Already?" quiz:
1 A **2** B **3** D **4** C **5** D **6** C, D **7** C **8** A, C

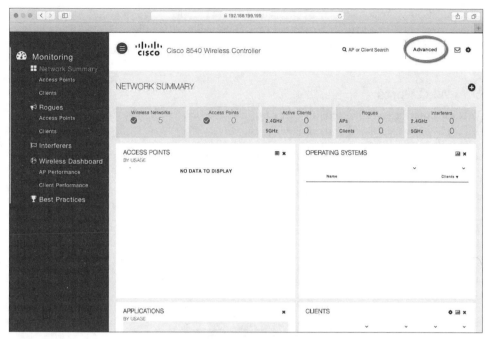

Figure 29-3 *Accessing the Advanced Configuration Interface*

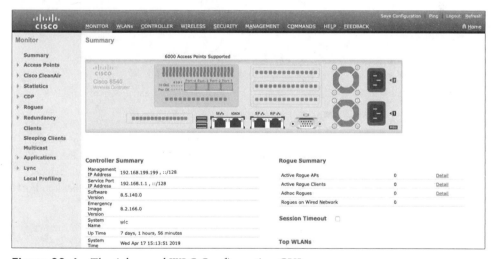

Figure 29-4 *The Advanced WLC Configuration GUI*

Connecting a Cisco WLC

Connecting a Cisco wireless LAN controller to the network is not quite as straightforward because it has several different types of connections. From your work with Cisco routers and switches, you probably know that the terms *interface* and *port* are usually interchangeable. For example, switches can come in 48-port models, and you apply configuration changes to the corresponding interfaces. Cisco wireless controllers differ a bit; ports and interfaces refer to different concepts.

Controller ports are physical connections made to an external wired or switched network, whereas interfaces are logical connections made internally within the controller. The following sections explain each connection type in more detail. You will learn more about configuring ports and interfaces in the "Configuring a WLAN" section later in the chapter.

Using WLC Ports

You can connect several different types of controller ports to your network, as shown in Figure 29-5 and discussed in the following list:

- **Service port:** Used for out-of-band management, system recovery, and initial boot functions; always connects to a switch port in access mode

- **Distribution system port:** Used for all normal AP and management traffic; usually connects to a switch port in 802.1Q trunk mode

- **Console port:** Used for out-of-band management, system recovery, and initial boot functions; asynchronous connection to a terminal emulator (9600 baud, 8 data bits, 1 stop bit, by default)

- **Redundancy port:** Used to connect to a peer controller for high availability (HA) operation

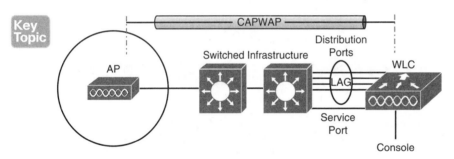

Figure 29-5   *Cisco Wireless LAN Controller Ports*

Controllers can have a single service port that must be connected to a switched network. Usually, the service port is assigned to a management VLAN so that you can access the controller with SSH or a web browser to perform initial configuration or for maintenance. Notice that the service port supports only a single VLAN, so the corresponding switch port must be configured for access mode only.

Controllers also have multiple distribution system ports that you must connect to the network. These ports carry most of the data coming to and going from the controller. For example, the CAPWAP tunnels (control and data) that extend to each of a controller's APs pass across the distribution system ports. Client data also passes from wireless LANs to wired VLANs over the ports. In addition, any management traffic using a web browser, SSH, Simple Network Management Protocol (SNMP), Trivial File Transfer Protocol (TFTP), and so on, normally reaches the controller in-band through the ports.

NOTE   You might be thinking that *distribution system ports* is an odd name for what appear to be regular data ports. Recall from the section titled "Wireless LAN Topologies" in Chapter 26, "Fundamentals of Wireless Networks," that the wired network that connects APs together is called the distribution system (DS). With the split MAC architecture, the point where APs touch the DS is moved upstream to the WLC instead.

Because the distribution system ports must carry data that is associated with many different VLANs, VLAN tags and numbers become very important. For that reason, the distribution system ports always operate in 802.1Q trunking mode. When you connect the ports to a switch, you should also configure the switch ports for unconditional 802.1Q trunk mode.

The distribution system ports can operate independently, each one transporting multiple VLANs to a unique group of internal controller interfaces. For resiliency, you can configure distribution system ports in redundant pairs. One port is primarily used; if it fails, a backup port is used instead.

To get the most use out of each distribution system port, you can configure all of them to operate as a single logical group, much like an EtherChannel or port-channel on a switch. Controller distribution system ports can be configured as a link aggregation group (LAG) such that they are bundled together to act as one larger link. In Figure 29-5, the four distribution system ports are configured as a LAG. With a LAG configuration, traffic can be load-balanced across the individual ports that make up the LAG. In addition, LAG offers resiliency; if one individual port fails, traffic will be redirected to the remaining working ports instead.

NOTE   Be aware that even though the LAG acts as a traditional EtherChannel, Cisco WLCs do not support any link aggregation negotiation protocol, like LACP or PaGP, at all. Therefore, you must configure the switch ports as an unconditional or always-on EtherChannel.

Using WLC Interfaces

Through its distribution system ports, a controller can connect to multiple VLANs on the switched network. Internally, the controller must somehow map those wired VLANs to equivalent logical wireless networks. For example, suppose that VLAN 10 is set aside for wireless users in the Engineering division of a company. That VLAN must be connected to a unique wireless LAN that exists on a controller and its associated APs. The wireless LAN must then be extended to every client that associates with the Service Set Identifier (SSID) "Engineering."

Cisco wireless controllers provide the necessary connectivity through internal logical interfaces, which must be configured with an IP address, subnet mask, default gateway, and a Dynamic Host Configuration Protocol (DHCP) server. Each interface is then assigned to a physical port and a VLAN ID. You can think of an interface as a Layer 3 termination on a VLAN.

Cisco controllers support the following interface types, also shown in Figure 29-6.

- **Management interface:** Used for normal management traffic, such as RADIUS user authentication, WLC-to-WLC communication, web-based and SSH sessions, SNMP, Network Time Protocol (NTP), syslog, and so on. The management interface is also used to terminate CAPWAP tunnels between the controller and its APs.

- **Redundancy management:** The management IP address of a redundant WLC that is part of a high availability pair of controllers. The active WLC uses the management interface address, while the standby WLC uses the redundancy management address.

- **Virtual interface:** IP address facing wireless clients when the controller is relaying client DHCP requests, performing client web authentication, and supporting client mobility.

- **Service port interface:** Bound to the service port and used for out-of-band management.

- **Dynamic interface:** Used to connect a VLAN to a WLAN.

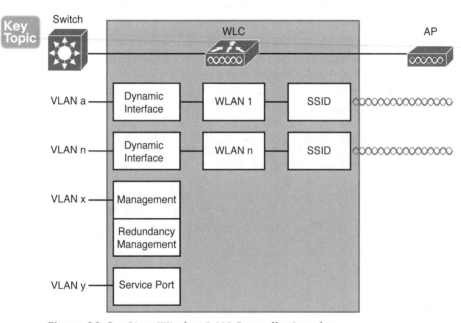

Figure 29-6 *Cisco Wireless LAN Controller Interfaces*

The management interface faces the switched network, where management users and APs are located. Management traffic will usually consist of protocols like HTTPS, SSH, SNMP, NTP, TFTP, and so on. In addition, management interface traffic consists of CAPWAP packets that carry control and data tunnels to and from the APs.

The virtual interface is used only for certain client-facing operations. For example, when a wireless client issues a request to obtain an IP address, the controller can relay the request on to an actual DHCP server that can provide the appropriate IP address. From the client's perspective, the DHCP server appears to be the controller's virtual interface address. Clients may see the virtual interface's address, but that address is never used when the controller communicates with other devices on the switched network.

Because the virtual interface is used only for some client management functions, you should configure it with a unique, nonroutable address. For example, you might use 10.1.1.1 because it is within a private address space defined in RFC 1918.

> **NOTE**   Traditionally, many people have assigned IP address 1.1.1.1 to the virtual interface. Although it is a unique address, it is routable and already in use elsewhere on the Internet. A better practice is to use an IP address from the RFC 1918 private address space that is unused or reserved, such as 192.168.1.1. You could also use a reserved address from RFC 5737 (192.0.2.0/24) that is set aside for documentation purposes and is never used.

The virtual interface address is also used to support client mobility. For that reason, every controller that exists in the same mobility group should be configured with a virtual address that is identical to the others. By using one common virtual address, all the controllers will appear to operate as a cluster as clients roam from controller to controller.

Dynamic interfaces map WLANs to VLANs, making the logical connections between wireless and wired networks. You will configure one dynamic interface for each wireless LAN that is offered by the controller's APs and then map the interface to the WLAN. Each dynamic interface must also be configured with its own IP address and can act as a DHCP relay for wireless clients. To filter traffic passing through a dynamic interface, you can configure an optional access list.

Configuring a WLAN

A wireless LAN controller and an access point work in concert to provide network connectivity to wireless clients. From a wireless perspective, the AP advertises a Service Set Identifier (SSID) for the client to join. From a wired perspective, the controller connects to a virtual LAN (VLAN) through one of its dynamic interfaces. To complete the path between the SSID and the VLAN, as illustrated in Figure 29-7, you must first define a WLAN on the controller.

> **NOTE**   Two of the CCNA exam objectives involve configuring a WLAN for client connectivity with WPA2 and a PSK using only the controller GUI. As you work through this section, you will find that it presents a complete WLAN example that is based on the topology shown in Figure 29-7 using the WPA2-Personal (PSK) security model.

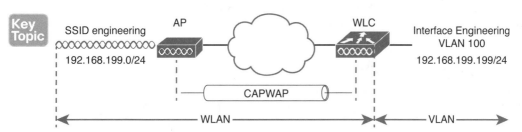

Figure 29-7   *Connecting Wired and Wireless Networks with a WLAN*

The controller will bind the WLAN to one of its interfaces and then push the WLAN configuration out to all of its APs by default. From that point on, wireless clients will be able to learn about the new WLAN by receiving its beacons and will be able to probe and join the new BSS.

Like VLANs, you can use WLANs to segregate wireless users and their traffic into logical networks. Users associated with one WLAN cannot cross over into another one unless their traffic is bridged or routed from one VLAN to another through the wired network infrastructure.

Before you begin to create new WLANs, it is usually wise to plan your wireless network first. In a large enterprise, you might have to support a wide variety of wireless devices, user communities, security policies, and so on. You might be tempted to create a new WLAN for every occasion, just to keep groups of users isolated from each other or to support different types of devices. Although that is an appealing strategy, you should be aware of two limitations:

- Cisco controllers support a maximum of 512 WLANs, but only 16 of them can be actively configured on an AP.
- Advertising each WLAN to potential wireless clients uses up valuable airtime.

Every AP must broadcast beacon management frames at regular intervals to advertise the existence of a BSS. Because each WLAN is bound to a BSS, each WLAN must be advertised with its own beacons. Beacons are normally sent 10 times per second, or once every 100 ms, at the lowest mandatory data rate. The more WLANs you have created, the more beacons you will need to announce them.

Even further, the lower the mandatory data rate, the more time each beacon will take to be transmitted. The end result is this: if you create too many WLANs, a channel can be starved of any usable airtime. Clients will have a hard time transmitting their own data because the channel is overly busy with beacon transmissions coming from the AP. As a rule of thumb, always limit the number of WLANs to five or fewer; a maximum of three WLANs is best.

By default, a controller has a limited initial configuration, so no WLANs are defined. Before you create a new WLAN, think about the following parameters it will need to have:

- SSID string
- Controller interface and VLAN number
- Type of wireless security needed

As you work through this section, you will create the appropriate dynamic controller interface to support the new WLAN; then you will enter the necessary WLAN parameters. Each configuration step is performed using a web browser session that is connected to the WLC's management IP address.

Step 1. Configure a RADIUS Server

If your new WLAN will use a security scheme that requires a RADIUS server, such as WPA2-Enterprise or WPA3-Enterprise, you will need to define the server first. Select **Security > AAA > RADIUS > Authentication** to see a list of servers that have already been configured, as shown in Figure 29-8. If multiple servers are defined, the controller will try them in sequential order. Click **New** to create a new server.

Next, enter the server's IP address, shared secret key, and port number, as shown in Figure 29-9. Because the controller already had two other RADIUS servers configured, the server at 192.168.200.30 will be index number 3. Be sure to set the server status to **Enabled** so that the controller can begin using it. At the bottom of the page, you can select the type of user that will be authenticated with the server. Check **Network User** to authenticate wireless clients or **Management** to authenticate wireless administrators that will access the controller's management functions. Click **Apply** to complete the server configuration.

Figure 29-8 *Displaying the List of RADIUS Authentication Servers*

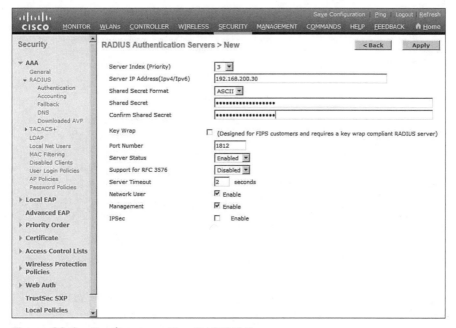

Figure 29-9 *Configuring a New RADIUS Server*

Step 2. Create a Dynamic Interface

In the "Using WLC Interfaces" section of this chapter, you learned about the different types of controller interfaces. A dynamic interface is used to connect the controller to a VLAN on the wired network. When you create a WLAN, you will bind the dynamic interface (and VLAN) to a wireless network.

To create a new dynamic interface, navigate to **Controller > Interfaces**. You should see a list of all the controller interfaces that are currently configured. In Figure 29-10, two interfaces named "management" and "virtual" already exist. Click the **New** button to define a new interface. Enter a name for the interface and the VLAN number it will be bound to. In Figure 29-11, the interface named Engineering is mapped to wired VLAN 100. Click the **Apply** button.

Figure 29-10 *Displaying a List of Dynamic Interfaces*

Figure 29-11 *Defining a Dynamic Interface Name and VLAN ID*

Next, enter the IP address, subnet mask, and gateway address for the interface. You should also define primary and secondary DHCP server addresses that the controller will use when it relays DHCP requests from clients that are bound to the interface. Figure 29-12 shows how the interface named Engineering has been configured with IP address 192.168.100.10, subnet mask 255.255.255.0, gateway 192.168.100.1, and DHCP servers 192.168.1.17 and 192.168.1.18. Click the **Apply** button to complete the interface configuration and return to the list of interfaces.

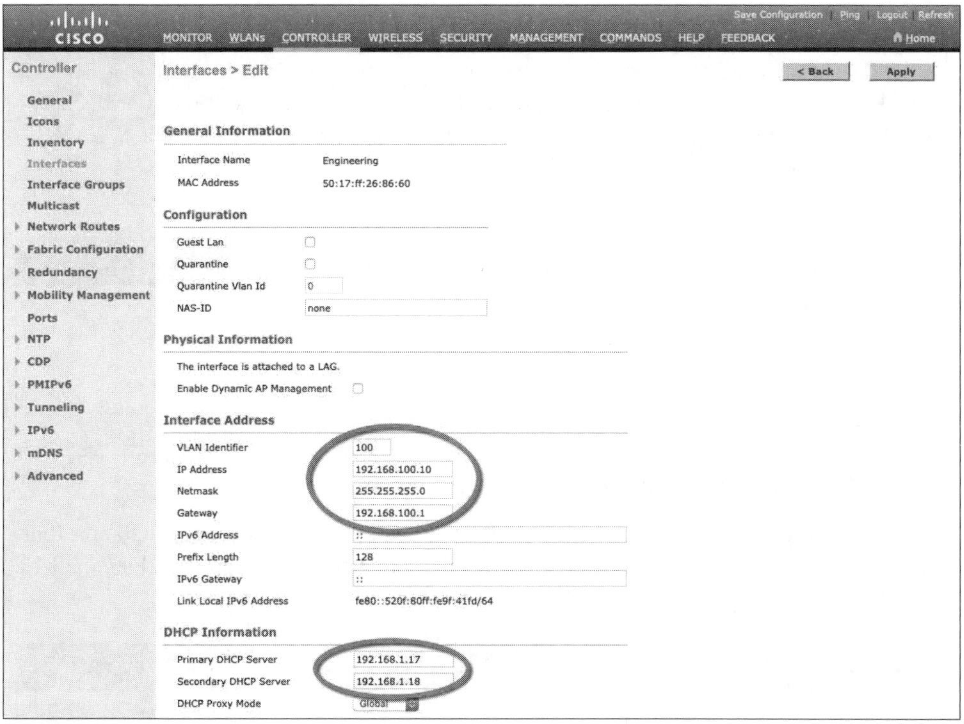

Figure 29-12   *Editing the Dynamic Interface Parameters*

Step 3. Create a New WLAN

You can display a list of the currently defined WLANs by selecting **WLANs** from the top menu bar. In Figure 29-13, the controller does not have any WLANs already defined. You can create a new WLAN by selecting **Create New** from the drop-down menu and then clicking the **Go** button.

Figure 29-13   *Displaying a List of WLANs*

Next, enter a descriptive name as the profile name and the SSID text string. In Figure 29-14, the profile name and SSID are identical, just to keep things straightforward. The ID number is used as an index into the list of WLANs that are defined on the controller. The ID number becomes useful when you use templates in Prime Infrastructure (PI) to configure WLANs on multiple controllers at the same time.

NOTE WLAN templates are applied to specific WLAN ID numbers on controllers. The WLAN ID is only locally significant and is not passed between controllers. As a rule, you should keep the sequence of WLAN names and IDs consistent across multiple controllers so that any configuration templates you use in the future will be applied to the same WLANs on each controller.

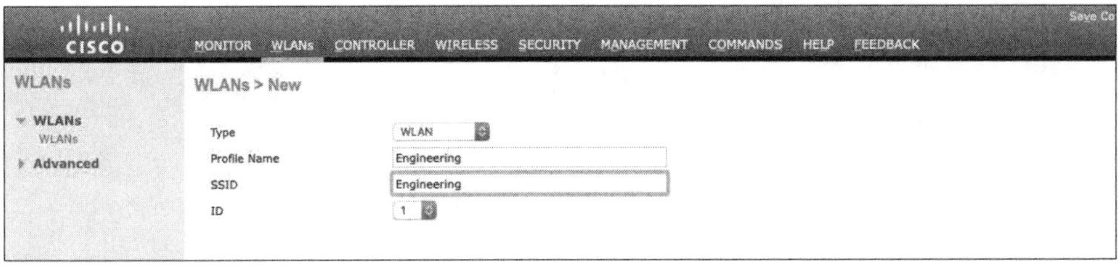

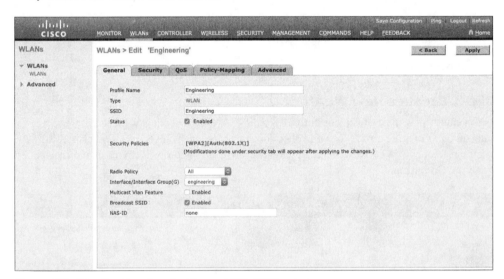

Figure 29-14 *Creating a New WLAN*

Click the **Apply** button to create the new WLAN. The next page will allow you to edit four categories of parameters, corresponding to the tabs across the top as shown in Figure 29-15. By default, the General tab is selected.

Figure 29-15 *Configuring the General WLAN Parameters*

You can control whether the WLAN is enabled or disabled with the Status check box. Even though the General page shows a specific security policy for the WLAN (the default WPA2 with 802.1x), you can make changes in a later step through the Security tab.

Under Radio Policy, select the type of radio that will offer the WLAN. By default, the WLAN will be offered on all radios that are joined with the controller. You can select a more specific policy with 802.11a only, 802.11a/g only, 802.11g only, or 802.11b/g only. For example, if you are creating a new WLAN for devices that have only a 2.4-GHz radio, it probably does not make sense to advertise the WLAN on both 2.4- and 5-GHz AP radios.

Next, select which of the controller's dynamic interfaces will be bound to the WLAN. By default, the management interface is selected. The drop-down list contains all the interface names that are available. In Figure 29-15, the new engineering WLAN will be bound to the Engineering interface.

Finally, use the Broadcast SSID check box to select whether the APs should broadcast the SSID name in the beacons they transmit. Broadcasting SSIDs is usually more convenient for users because their devices can learn and display the SSID names automatically. In fact, most devices actually need the SSID in the beacons to understand that the AP is still available for that SSID. Hiding the SSID name, by not broadcasting it, does not really provide any worthwhile security. Instead, it just prevents user devices from discovering an SSID and trying to use it as a default network.

Configuring WLAN Security

Select the Security tab to configure the security settings. By default, the Layer 2 Security tab is selected. From the Layer 2 Security drop-down menu, select the appropriate security scheme to use. Table 29-2 lists the types that are available.

Table 29-2   Layer 2 WLAN Security Type

Option	Description
None	Open authentication
WPA+WPA2	Wi-Fi protected access WPA or WPA2
802.1x	EAP authentication with dynamic WEP
Static WEP	WEP key security
Static WEP + 802.1x	EAP authentication or static WEP
CKIP	Cisco Key Integrity Protocol
None + EAP Passthrough	Open authentication with remote EAP authentication

As you select a security type, be sure to remember which choices are types that have been deprecated or proven to be weak, and avoid them if possible. Further down the screen, you can select which specific WPA, WPA2, and WPA3 methods to support on the WLAN. You can select more than one, if you need to support different types of wireless clients that require several security methods.

In Figure 29-16, WPA+WPA2 has been selected from the pull-down menu; then only WPA2 and AES encryption have been selected. WPA and TKIP have been avoided because they are legacy, deprecated methods. Under the Authentication Key Management section, you can select the authentication methods the WLAN will use. Only PSK has been selected in the figure, so the WLAN will allow only WPA2-Personal with pre-shared key authentication.

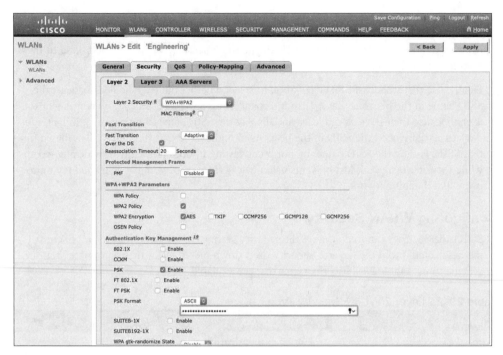

Figure 29-16 *Configuring Layer 2 WLAN Security*

To use WPA2-Enterprise, the 802.1X option would be selected. In that case, 802.1x and EAP would be used to authenticate wireless clients against one or more RADIUS servers. The controller would use servers from the global list you have defined under **Security > AAA > RADIUS > Authentication**, as described in the "Step 1. Configure a RADIUS Server" section in this chapter. To specify which servers the WLAN should use, you would select the Security tab and then the AAA Servers tab in the WLAN edit screen. You can identify up to six specific RADIUS servers in the WLAN configuration. Beside each server, select a specific server IP address from the drop-down menu of globally defined servers. The servers are tried in sequential order until one of them responds. Although the example in this chapter uses WPA2-Personal, Figure 29-17 shows what a WLAN configured for WPA2-Enterprise might look like, with servers 1 through 3 being set to 192.168.200.28, 192.168.200.29, and 192.168.200.30, respectively.

By default, a controller will contact a RADIUS server from its management interface. You can override this behavior by checking the box next to Radius Server Overwrite Interface so that the controller sources RADIUS requests from the dynamic interface that is associated with the WLAN.

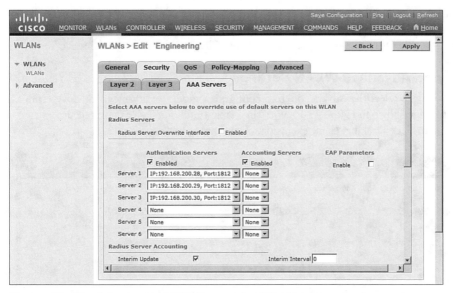

Figure 29-17 *Selecting RADIUS Servers for WLAN Authentication*

Configuring WLAN QoS

Select the **QoS** tab to configure quality of service settings for the WLAN, as shown in Figure 29-18. By default, the controller will consider all frames in the WLAN to be normal data, to be handled in a "best effort" manner. You can set the Quality of Service (QoS) drop-down menu to classify all frames in one of the following ways:

- Platinum (voice)
- Gold (video)
- Silver (best effort)
- Bronze (background)

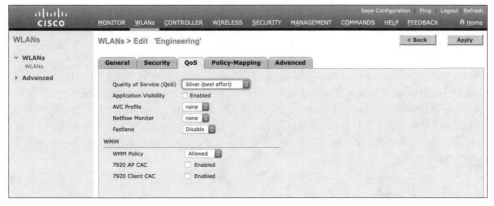

Figure 29-18 *Configuring QoS Settings*

You can also set the Wi-Fi Multimedia (WMM) policy, call admission control (CAC) policies, and bandwidth parameters on the QoS page. You can learn more about QoS in the *CCNA 200-301 Official Cert Guide, Volume 2*, in Chapter 11, "Quality of Service."

Configuring Advanced WLAN Settings

Finally, you can select the Advanced tab to configure a variety of advanced WLAN settings. From the page shown in Figure 29-19, you can enable functions such as coverage hole detection, peer-to-peer blocking, client exclusion, client load limits, and so on.

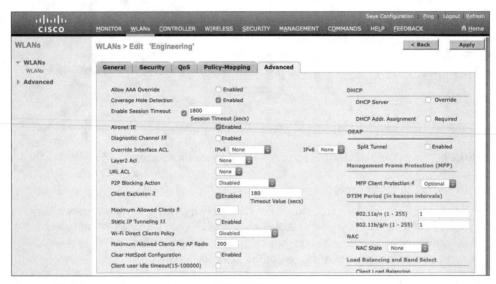

Figure 29-19   *Configuring Advanced WLAN Settings*

Although most of the advanced settings are beyond the scope of the CCNA objectives, you should be aware of a few defaults that might affect your wireless clients.

By default, client sessions with the WLAN are limited to 1800 seconds (30 minutes). Once that session time expires, a client will be required to reauthenticate. This setting is controlled by the Enable Session Timeout check box and the Timeout field.

A controller maintains a set of security policies that are used to detect potentially malicious wireless clients. If a client exhibits a certain behavior, the controller can exclude it from the WLAN for a period of time. By default, all clients are subject to the policies configured under **Security > Wireless Protection Policies > Client Exclusion Policies**. These policies include excessive 802.11 association failures, 802.11 authentication failures, 802.1x authentication failures, web authentication failures, and IP address theft or reuse. Offending clients will be automatically excluded or blocked for 60 seconds, as a deterrent to attacks on the wireless network.

> **NOTE**   Is 60 seconds really enough time to deter an attack coming from a wireless client? In the case of a brute-force attack, where passwords are guessed from a dictionary of possibilities, 60 seconds is enough to disrupt and delay an attacker's progress. What might have taken 2 minutes to find a matching password without an exclusion policy would take 15 years with one.

Finalizing WLAN Configuration

When you are satisfied with the settings in each of the WLAN configuration tabs, click the Apply button in the upper-right corner of the WLAN Edit screen. The WLAN will be created and added to the controller configuration. In Figure 29-20, the Engineering WLAN has been added as WLAN ID 1 and is enabled for use.

Figure 29-20   *Displaying WLANs Configured on a Controller*

Be aware that, by default, a controller will not allow management traffic that is initiated from a WLAN. That means you (or anybody else) cannot access the controller GUI or CLI from a wireless device that is associated to the WLAN. This is considered to be a good security practice because the controller is kept isolated from networks that might be easily accessible or where someone might eavesdrop on the management session traffic. Instead, you can access the controller through its wired interfaces.

You can change the default behavior on a global basis (all WLANs) by selecting the Management tab and then selecting Mgmt Via Wireless, as shown in Figure 29-21. Check the box to allow management sessions from any WLAN that is configured on the controller.

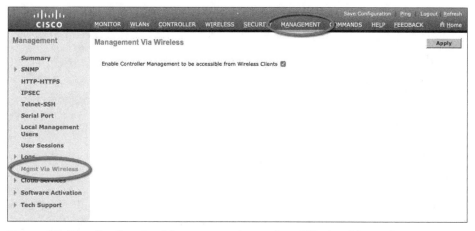

Figure 29-21   *Configuring Management Access from Wireless Networks*

Chapter Review

Review this chapter's material using either the tools in the book or the interactive tools for the same material found on the book's companion website. Table 29-3 outlines the key review elements and where you can find them. To better track your study progress, record when you completed these activities in the second column.

Table 29-3   Chapter Review Tracking

Review Element	Review Date(s)	Resource Used
Review key topics		Book, website
Review key terms		Book, website
Answer DIKTA questions		Book, PTP

Review All the Key Topics

Review the most important topics in this chapter, noted with the Key Topic icon in the outer margin of the page. Table 29-4 lists a reference of these key topics and the page numbers on which each is found.

Table 29-4   Key Topics for Chapter 29

Key Topic Element	Description	Page Number
Figure 29-1	Physical connections to an AP	669
Figure 29-5	Wireless LAN controller ports	672
Figure 29-6	Wireless LAN controller interfaces	674
Figure 29-7	Creating a WLAN	675
Table 29-2	Configuring WLAN security	681

Part VIII Review

Keep track of your part review progress with the checklist in Table P8-1. Details on each task follow the table.

Table P8-1 Part VIII Part Review Checklist

Activity	1st Date Completed	2nd Date Completed
Repeat All DIKTA Questions		
Answer Part Review Questions		
Review Key Topics		

Repeat All DIKTA Questions

For this task, use the PCPT software to answer the "Do I Know This Already?" questions again for the chapters in this part of the book.

Answer Part Review Questions

For this task, use PTP to answer the Part Review questions for this part of the book.

Review Key Topics

Review all key topics in all chapters in this part, either by browsing the chapters or using the Key Topics application on the companion website.

Part IX

Appendixes

Glossary

Appendix A Numeric Reference Tables

Appendix B Exam Updates

Appendix C Answers to the "Do I Know This Already?" Quizzes

Numeric Reference Tables

This appendix provides several useful reference tables that list numbers used throughout this book. Specifically:

Table A-1: A decimal-binary cross reference, useful when converting from decimal to binary and vice versa.

Table A-1   Decimal-Binary Cross Reference, Decimal Values 0–255

Decimal Value	Binary Value	Decimal Value	Binary Value	Decimal Value	Binary Value	Decimal Value	Binary Value
0	00000000	32	00100000	64	01000000	96	01100000
1	00000001	33	00100001	65	01000001	97	01100001
2	00000010	34	00100010	66	01000010	98	01100010
3	00000011	35	00100011	67	01000011	99	01100011
4	00000100	36	00100100	68	01000100	100	01100100
5	00000101	37	00100101	69	01000101	101	01100101
6	00000110	38	00100110	70	01000110	102	01100110
7	00000111	39	00100111	71	01000111	103	01100111
8	00001000	40	00101000	72	01001000	104	01101000
9	00001001	41	00101001	73	01001001	105	01101001
10	00001010	42	00101010	74	01001010	106	01101010
11	00001011	43	00101011	75	01001011	107	01101011
12	00001100	44	00101100	76	01001100	108	01101100
13	00001101	45	00101101	77	01001101	109	01101101
14	00001110	46	00101110	78	01001110	110	01101110
15	00001111	47	00101111	79	01001111	111	01101111
16	00010000	48	00110000	80	01010000	112	01110000
17	00010001	49	00110001	81	01010001	113	01110001
18	00010010	50	00110010	82	01010010	114	01110010
19	00010011	51	00110011	83	01010011	115	01110011
20	00010100	52	00110100	84	01010100	116	01110100
21	00010101	53	00110101	85	01010101	117	01110101
22	00010110	54	00110110	86	01010110	118	01110110
23	00010111	55	00110111	87	01010111	119	01110111
24	00011000	56	00111000	88	01011000	120	01111000
25	00011001	57	00111001	89	01011001	121	01111001
26	00011010	58	00111010	90	01011010	122	01111010
27	00011011	59	00111011	91	01011011	123	01111011
28	00011100	60	00111100	92	01011100	124	01111100
29	00011101	61	00111101	93	01011101	125	01111101
30	00011110	62	00111110	94	01011110	126	01111110
31	00011111	63	00111111	95	01011111	127	01111111

Decimal Value	Binary Value	Decimal Value	Binary Value	Decimal Value	Binary Value	Decimal Value	Binary Value
128	10000000	160	10100000	192	11000000	224	11100000
129	10000001	161	10100001	193	11000001	225	11100001
130	10000010	162	10100010	194	11000010	226	11100010
131	10000011	163	10100011	195	11000011	227	11100011
132	10000100	164	10100100	196	11000100	228	11100100
133	10000101	165	10100101	197	11000101	229	11100101
134	10000110	166	10100110	198	11000110	230	11100110
135	10000111	167	10100111	199	11000111	231	11100111
136	10001000	168	10101000	200	11001000	232	11101000
137	10001001	169	10101001	201	11001001	233	11101001
138	10001010	170	10101010	202	11001010	234	11101010
139	10001011	171	10101011	203	11001011	235	11101011
140	10001100	172	10101100	204	11001100	236	11101100
141	10001101	173	10101101	205	11001101	237	11101101
142	10001110	174	10101110	206	11001110	238	11101110
143	10001111	175	10101111	207	11001111	239	11101111
144	10010000	176	10110000	208	11010000	240	11110000
145	10010001	177	10110001	209	11010001	241	11110001
146	10010010	178	10110010	210	11010010	242	11110010
147	10010011	179	10110011	211	11010011	243	11110011
148	10010100	180	10110100	212	11010100	244	11110100
149	10010101	181	10110101	213	11010101	245	11110101
150	10010110	182	10110110	214	11010110	246	11110110
151	10010111	183	10110111	215	11010111	247	11110111
152	10011000	184	10111000	216	11011000	248	11111000
153	10011001	185	10111001	217	11011001	249	11111001
154	10011010	186	10111010	218	11011010	250	11111010
155	10011011	187	10111011	219	11011011	251	11111011
156	10011100	188	10111100	220	11011100	252	11111100
157	10011101	189	10111101	221	11011101	253	11111101
158	10011110	190	10111110	222	11011110	254	11111110
159	10011111	191	10111111	223	11011111	255	11111111

A

Table A-2: A hexadecimal-binary cross reference, useful when converting from hex to binary and vice versa.

Table A-2   Hex-Binary Cross Reference

Hex	4-Bit Binary
0	0000
1	0001
2	0010
3	0011
4	0100
5	0101
6	0110
7	0111
8	1000
9	1001
A	1010
B	1011
C	1100
D	1101
E	1110
F	1111

Table A-3: Powers of 2, from 2^1 through 2^{32}.

Table A-3 Powers of 2

X	2^x	X	2^x
1	2	17	131,072
2	4	18	262,144
3	8	19	524,288
4	16	20	1,048,576
5	32	21	2,097,152
6	64	22	4,194,304
7	128	23	8,388,608
8	256	24	16,777,216
9	512	25	33,554,432
10	1024	26	67,108,864
11	2048	27	134,217,728
12	4096	28	268,435,456
13	8192	29	536,870,912
14	16,384	30	1,073,741,824
15	32,768	31	2,147,483,648
16	65,536	32	4,294,967,296

A

Table A-4: Table of all 33 possible subnet masks, in all three formats.

Table A-4   All Subnet Masks

Decimal	Prefix	Binary
0.0.0.0	/0	00000000 00000000 00000000 00000000
128.0.0.0	/1	10000000 00000000 00000000 00000000
192.0.0.0	/2	11000000 00000000 00000000 00000000
224.0.0.0	/3	11100000 00000000 00000000 00000000
240.0.0.0	/4	11110000 00000000 00000000 00000000
248.0.0.0	/5	11111000 00000000 00000000 00000000
252.0.0.0	/6	11111100 00000000 00000000 00000000
254.0.0.0	/7	11111110 00000000 00000000 00000000
255.0.0.0	/8	11111111 00000000 00000000 00000000
255.128.0.0	/9	11111111 10000000 00000000 00000000
255.192.0.0	/10	11111111 11000000 00000000 00000000
255.224.0.0	/11	11111111 11100000 00000000 00000000
255.240.0.0	/12	11111111 11110000 00000000 00000000
255.248.0.0	/13	11111111 11111000 00000000 00000000
255.252.0.0	/14	11111111 11111100 00000000 00000000
255.254.0.0	/15	11111111 11111110 00000000 00000000
255.255.0.0	/16	11111111 11111111 00000000 00000000
255.255.128.0	/17	11111111 11111111 10000000 00000000
255.255.192.0	/18	11111111 11111111 11000000 00000000
255.255.224.0	/19	11111111 11111111 11100000 00000000
255.255.240.0	/20	11111111 11111111 11110000 00000000
255.255.248.0	/21	11111111 11111111 11111000 00000000
255.255.252.0	/22	11111111 11111111 11111100 00000000
255.255.254.0	/23	11111111 11111111 11111110 00000000
255.255.255.0	/24	11111111 11111111 11111111 00000000
255.255.255.128	/25	11111111 11111111 11111111 10000000
255.255.255.192	/26	11111111 11111111 11111111 11000000
255.255.255.224	/27	11111111 11111111 11111111 11100000
255.255.255.240	/28	11111111 11111111 11111111 11110000
255.255.255.248	/29	11111111 11111111 11111111 11111000
255.255.255.252	/30	11111111 11111111 11111111 11111100
255.255.255.254	/31	11111111 11111111 11111111 11111110
255.255.255.255	/32	11111111 11111111 11111111 11111111

CCNA 200-301, Volume 1 Exam Updates

Over time, reader feedback allows Pearson to gauge which topics give our readers the most problems when taking the exams. To assist readers with those topics, the authors create new materials clarifying and expanding on those troublesome exam topics. As mentioned in the Introduction, the additional content about the exam is contained in a PDF on this book's companion website, at http://www.ciscopress.com/title/9780135792735.

This appendix provides you with updated information if Cisco makes minor modifications to the exam topics during the life of the 200-301 exam. In particular, this appendix does the following:

- Mentions technical items that might not have been mentioned elsewhere in the book

- Covers new topics if Cisco adds new content to the exam over time

- Provides a way to get up-to-the-minute current information about content for the exam

Note that this appendix shows updated information related to the subset of CCNA 200-301 exam topics covered in this book. Refer also to the *CCNA 200-301 Official Cert Guide, Volume 2*, for more details about the rest of the exam topics and for an Appendix B similar to that of this book.

Always Get the Latest at the Book's Product Page

Many of you are reading the version of this appendix that was available when your book was printed or when you downloaded the e-book. However, given that the main purpose of this appendix is to be a living, changing document, it is important that you look for the latest version online at the book's companion website. To do so, follow these steps:

Step 1. Browse to www.ciscopress.com/title/9780135792735.

Step 2. Click the **Updates** tab.

Step 3. If there is a new Appendix B document on the page, download the latest Appendix B document.

> **NOTE**   The downloaded document has a version number. Comparing the version of the print Appendix B (**Version 1.0**) with the latest downloadable version of this appendix, you should do the following:
>
> ■   **Same version:** Ignore the PDF that you downloaded from the companion website.
>
> ■   **Website has a later version:** Ignore this Appendix B in your book and read only the latest version that you downloaded from the companion website.

Technical Content

The current **Version 1.0** of this appendix does not contain additional technical coverage.

Answers to the "Do I Know This Already?" Quizzes

Chapter 1

1. D and F. Of the remaining answers, Ethernet defines both physical and data-link protocols, PPP is a data-link protocol, IP is a network layer protocol, and SMTP and HTTP are application layer protocols.

2. A and G. Of the remaining answers, IP is a network layer protocol, TCP and UDP are transport layer protocols, and SMTP and HTTP are application layer protocols.

3. B. Adjacent-layer interaction occurs on one computer, with two adjacent layers in the model. The higher layer requests services from the next lower layer, and the lower layer provides the services to the next higher layer.

4. B. Same-layer interaction occurs on multiple computers. The functions defined by that layer typically need to be accomplished by multiple computers—for example, the sender setting a sequence number for a segment and the receiver acknowledging receipt of that segment. A single layer defines that process, but the implementation of that layer on multiple devices is required to accomplish the function.

5. A. Encapsulation is defined as the process of adding a header in front of data supplied by a higher layer (and possibly adding a trailer as well).

6. D. By convention, the term *frame* refers to the part of a network message that includes the data-link header and trailer, with encapsulated data. The term *packet* omits the data-link header and trailer, leaving the network layer header with its encapsulated data. The term *segment* omits the network layer header, leaving the transport layer header and its encapsulated data.

7. B. The term frame refers to the data-link (that is, Layer 2) data structure created by a Layer 2 protocol. As a result, the matching OSI term for protocol data units (PDUs) mentions that same layer, that is, Layer 2 PDU, or L2PDU.

Chapter 2

1. A. The IEEE defines Ethernet LAN standards, with standard names that begin with 802.3, all of which happen to use cabling. The IEEE also defines wireless LAN standards, with standard names that begin with 802.11, which are separate standards from Ethernet.

2. C. The number before the word *BASE* defines the speed, in megabits per second (Mbps). 1000 Mbps equals 1 gigabit per second (1 Gbps). The *T* in the suffix implies twisted-pair or UTP cabling, so 1000BASE-T is the UTP-based Gigabit Ethernet standard name.

3.   B. Crossover cables cross the wire at one node's transmit pin pair to the different pins used as the receive pins on the other device. For 10- and 100-Mbps Ethernet, the specific crossover cable wiring connects the pair at pins 1 and 2 on each end of the cable to pins 3 and 6 on the other end of the cable, respectively.

4.   B, D, and E. Routers, wireless access point Ethernet ports, and PC NICs all send using pins 1 and 2, whereas hubs and LAN switches transmit on pins 3 and 6. Straight-through cables connect devices that use opposite pin pairs for sending, because the cable does not need to cross the pairs.

5.   B. Multimode fiber works with LED-based transmitters rather than laser-based transmitters. Two answers mention the type of transmitters, making one of those answers correct and one incorrect.

   Two answers mention distance. The answer that mentions the longest distance possible is incorrect because single-mode cables, not multimode cables, provide the longest distances. The other (correct) answer mentions the tradeoff of multimode being used for distances just longer than UTP's 100 meter limit, while happening to use less expensive hardware than single mode.

6.   B. NICs (and switch ports) use the carrier sense multiple access with collision detection (CSMA/CD) algorithm to implement half-duplex logic. CSMA/CD attempts to avoid collisions, but it also notices when collisions do occur, with rules about how the Ethernet nodes should stop sending, wait, and try again later.

7.   C. The 4-byte Ethernet FCS field, found in the Ethernet trailer, allows the receiving node to see what the sending node computed with a math formula that is a key part of the error-detection process. Note that Ethernet defines the process of detecting errors (error detection), but not error recovery.

8.   B, C, and E. The pre-assigned universal MAC address, given to each Ethernet port when manufactured, breaks the address into two 3-byte halves. The first half is called the organizationally unique identifier (OUI), which the IEEE assigns to the company that builds the product as a unique hex number to be used only by that company.

9.   C and D. Ethernet supports unicast addresses, which identify a single Ethernet node, and group addresses, which can be used to send one frame to multiple Ethernet nodes. The two types of group addresses are the *broadcast address* and *multicast address.*

Chapter 3

1.   B. The standard HDLC header does not include a Type field, which identifies the type of packet encapsulated inside the HDLC frame.

2.   B and D. The physical installation uses a model in which each router uses a physical Ethernet link to connect to some SP device in an SP facility called a point of presence (PoP). The Ethernet link does not span from each customer device to the other. From a data-link perspective, both routers use the same Ethernet standard header and trailer used on LANs; HDLC does not matter on these Ethernet WAN links.

3.   A. PC1 will send an Ethernet frame to Router 1, with PC1's MAC address as the source address and Router 1's MAC address as the destination address. Router 1 will remove the encapsulated IP packet from that Ethernet frame, discarding the frame header and trailer. Router 1 will forward the IP packet by first encapsulating it inside an HDLC frame, but Router 1 will not encapsulate the Ethernet frame in the HDLC frame but rather the IP packet. Router 2 will de-encapsulate the IP packet from the HDLC frame and forward it onto the Ethernet LAN, adding a new Ethernet header and trailer, but this header will differ. It will list Router 2's MAC address as the source address and PC2's MAC address as the destination address.

4. C. Routers compare the packet's destination IP address to the router's IP routing table, making a match and using the forwarding instructions in the matched route to forward the IP packet.

5. C. IPv4 hosts generally use basic two-branch logic. To send an IP packet to another host on the same IP network or subnet that is on the same LAN, the sender sends the IP packet directly to that host. Otherwise, the sender sends the packet to its default router (also called the default gateway).

6. A and C. Routers do all the actions listed in all four answers; however, the routing protocol does the functions in the two listed answers. Independent of the routing protocol, a router learns routes for IP subnets and IP networks directly connected to its interfaces. Routers also forward (route) IP packets, but that process is called IP routing, or IP forwarding, and is an independent process compared to the work of a routing protocol.

7. C. Address Resolution Protocol (ARP) does allow PC1 to learn information, but the information is not stored on a server. The **ping** command does let the user at PC1 learn whether packets can flow in the network, but it again does not use a server. With the Domain Name System (DNS), PC1 acts as a DNS client, relying on a DNS server to respond with information about the IP addresses that match a given hostname.

Chapter 4

1. A and B. The command in the question is an EXEC command that happens to require only user mode access. As such, you can use this command in both user mode and enable mode. Because it is an EXEC command, you cannot use the command (as shown in the question) in configuration mode. Note that you can put the word **do** in front of the EXEC command while in configuration mode (for example, **do show mac address-table**) to issue the command from inside any configuration mode.

2. B. The command referenced in the question, the **reload** command, is an EXEC command that happens to require privileged mode, also known as enable mode. This command is not available in user mode. Note that you can put the word **do** in front of the EXEC command while in configuration mode (for example, **do reload**) to issue the command from inside any configuration mode.

3. B. SSH provides a secure remote login option, encrypting all data flows, including password exchanges. Telnet sends all data (including passwords) as clear text.

4. A. Switches (and routers) keep the currently used configuration in RAM, using NVRAM to store the configuration file that is loaded when the switch (or router) next loads the IOS.

5. F. The startup-config file is in NVRAM, and the running-config file is in RAM.

6. B and C. The **exit** command moves the user one config mode backward, toward global configuration mode, or if already in global configuration mode, it moves the user back to enable mode. From console mode, it moves the user back to global configuration mode. The **end** command and the Ctrl+Z key sequence both move the user back to enable mode regardless of the current configuration submode.

Chapter 5

1. A. A switch compares the destination MAC address to the MAC address table. If a matching entry is found, the switch forwards the frame out the appropriate interface. If no matching entry is found, the switch floods the frame.

2. C. A switch floods broadcast frames, multicast frames (if no multicast optimizations are enabled), and unknown unicast destination frames (frames whose destination MAC address is not in the MAC address table).

3. A. A switch floods broadcast frames, multicast frames (if no multicast optimizations are enabled), and unknown unicast destination frames (frames whose destination MAC address is not in the MAC address table).

4. B. Switches need to learn the location of each MAC address used in the LAN relative to that local switch. When a switch receives a frame, the source MAC identifies the sender. The interface in which the frame arrives identifies the local switch interface closest to that node in the LAN topology.

5. C. The **show interfaces status** command lists one line of output per interface. Cisco Catalyst switches name the type of interface based on the fastest speed of the interface, so 10/100 interfaces would be Fast Ethernet. With a working connection, ports from FastEthernet 0/1 through 0/10 would be listed in a connected state, while the rest would be listed in a notconnected state.

6. D. For the correct answer, each entry lists the learned MAC address. By definition, dynamically learned MAC addresses are learned by looking at the source MAC address of received frames. (That fact rules out one of the incorrect answers as well.)

    The **show mac address-table dynamic** command lists the current list of MAC table entries, with three known entries at the point at which the command output was gathered. The counter in the last line of output lists the number of current entries, not the total number of learned MAC addresses since the last reboot. For instance, the switch could have learned other MAC addresses whose entries timed out from the MAC address table.

    Finally, the answer that claims that port Gi0/2 connects directly to a device with a particular MAC address may or may not be true. That port could connect to another switch, and another, and so on, with one of those switches connecting to the device that uses the listed MAC address.

Chapter 6

1. B. If both commands are configured, IOS accepts only the password as configured in the **enable secret** command.

2. A. To answer this question, it might be best to first think of the complete configuration and then find any answers that match the configuration. The commands, in vty line configuration mode, would be **password** *password* and **login**. Only one answer lists a vty subcommand that is one of these two commands.

    Of note in the incorrect answers:

    One answer mentions console subcommands. The console does not define what happens when remote users log in; those details sit in the vty line configuration.

    One answer mentions the **login local** command; this command means that the switch should use the local list of configured usernames/passwords. The question stated that the engineer wanted to use passwords only, with no usernames.

    One answer mentions the **transport input ssh** command, which, by omitting the **telnet** keyword, disables Telnet. While that command can be useful, SSH does not work when using passwords only; SSH requires both a username and a password. So, by disabling Telnet (and allowing SSH only), the configuration would allow no one to remotely log in to the switch.

3. B and C. SSH requires the use of usernames in addition to a password. Using the **username** global command would be one way to define usernames (and matching passwords) to support SSH. The vty lines would also need to be configured to require the use of usernames, with the **login local** vty subcommand being one such option.

    The **transport input ssh** command could be part of a meaningful configuration, but it is not a global configuration command (as claimed in one wrong answer). Likewise, one answer refers to the **username** command as a command in vty config mode, which is also the wrong mode.

4. A, D, and F. To allow access through Telnet, the switch must have password security enabled, at a minimum using the **password** vty line configuration subcommand. In addition, the switch needs an IP address (configured under one VLAN interface) and a default gateway when the switch needs to communicate with hosts in a different subnet.

5. B and C. To allow SSH or Telnet access, a switch must have a correct IP configuration. That includes the configuration of a correct IP address and mask on a VLAN interface. That VLAN interface then must have a path out of the switch via ports assigned to that VLAN. In this case, with all ports assigned to VLAN 2, the switch must use interface VLAN 2 (using the **interface vlan 2** configuration command).

    To meet the requirement to support login from hosts outside the local subnet, the switch must configure a correct default gateway setting with the **ip default-gateway 172.16.2.254** global command in this case.

6. A. The **logging synchronous** line subcommand synchronizes the log message display with other command output so the log message does not interrupt a **show** command's output. The **no ip domain-lookup** command is not a line subcommand. The other two incorrect answers are line subcommands but do not configure the function listed in the question.

Chapter 7

1. F. Cisco switches do not have a command to disable autonegotiation of speed and duplex. Instead, a switch port that has both **speed** and **duplex** configured disables autonegotiation.

2. E. Cisco switches can be configured for speed (with the **speed** command) and duplex (with the **duplex** command) in interface configuration mode.

3. A and D. The IEEE autonegotiation rules dictate that if a device attempts autonegotiation but the other side does not participate, use the slowest speed it supports. However, Cisco switches override that logic, instead sampling the electrical signal to detect the speed used by the connected device, so the switch will operate at 1000 Mbps. The switch uses the IEEE default setting for duplex based on the speed, and the IEEE default for duplex when using 1000 Mbps is to use full duplex. So in this case, the switch will match both the speed and the duplex setting made on the PC.

4. A, B, and D. The disabled state in the **show interfaces status** command is the same as an "administratively down and down" state shown in the **show interfaces** command. The interface must be in a connected state (per the **show interfaces status** command) before the switch can send frames out the interface.

5. A and D. SW2 has effectively disabled IEEE standard autonegotiation by configuring both speed and duplex. However, Cisco switches can detect the speed used by the other device, even with autonegotiation turned off. Also, at 1 Gbps, the IEEE autonegotiation standard says to use full duplex. If the duplex setting cannot be negotiated, both ends use 1 Gbps, full duplex.

6. D. For the two answers about a duplex mismatch, that condition does cause collisions, particularly late collisions, but only the side using CSMA/CD logic (the half-duplex side) has any concept of collisions. So, if switch SW1 was using half duplex, and switch SW2 using full duplex, SW1 would likely see late collisions and see that counter increment over time.

   If switch SW2 had shut down its interface, switch SW1's interface would be in a down/down state, and none of the counters would increment. Also, if both switch ports had been configured with different speeds, again the ports would be in a down/down state, and none of the interface counters would increment.

Chapter 8

1. B. A VLAN is a set of devices in the same Layer 2 broadcast domain. A subnet often includes the exact same set of devices, but it is a Layer 3 concept. A collision domain refers to a set of Ethernet devices, but with different rules than VLAN rules for determining which devices are in the same collision domain.

2. D. Although a subnet and a VLAN are not equivalent concepts, the devices in one VLAN are typically in the same IP subnet and vice versa.

3. B. 802.1Q defines a 4-byte header, inserted after the original frame's destination and source MAC address fields. The insertion of this header does not change the original frame's source or destination address. The header itself holds a 12-bit VLAN ID field, which identifies the VLAN associated with the frame.

4.   A and C. The **dynamic auto** setting means that the switch can negotiate trunking, but it can only respond to negotiation messages, and it cannot initiate the negotiation process. So, the other switch must be configured to trunk or to initiate the negotiation process (based on being configured with the **dynamic desirable** option).

5.   A and B. The configured VTP setting of VTP transparent mode means that the switch can configure VLANs, so the VLAN is configured. In addition, the VLAN configuration details, including the VLAN name, show up as part of the running-config file.

6.   B and C. The **show interfaces switchport** command lists both the administrative and operational status of each port. When a switch considers a port to be trunking, this command lists an operational trunking state of "trunk." The **show interfaces trunk** command lists a set of interfaces—the interfaces that are currently operating as trunks. So, both of these commands identify interfaces that are operational trunks.

7.   A and B. On switches that do not use VTP (by using VTP modes off or transparent), the switch lists all VLAN configuration in the configuration file (making one answer correct). Also, the **show vlan brief** command lists all defined VLANs, regardless of VTP mode and regardless of shutdown state. As a result, the two answers that mention commands are correct.

The two incorrect answers are incorrect because VLAN 30 has been shut down, which means the switch will not forward frames in that VLAN, regardless of whether they arrive on access or trunk ports.

8.   B. The first list of VLAN IDs includes all VLANs (1–4094) except those overtly removed per the details in any **switchport trunk allowed vlan** interface subcommands on the trunk interface. If no such commands are configured, the first list in the output will include 1–4094. The two incorrect answers that mention VLAN 30 both list conditions that change the second of two lists of VLANs in the command output, while STP's choice to block an interface would impact the third list.

Chapter 9

1.   A and B. Listening and learning are transitory port states, used only when moving from the blocking to the forwarding state. Discarding is not an STP port state.

2.   C. The smallest numeric bridge ID wins the election.

3.   C and D. Listening and learning are transitory port states used only when moving from the blocking to the forwarding state. Discarding is not an STP port state. Forwarding and blocking are stable states.

4.   B. Nonroot switches forward Hellos received from the root; the root sends these Hellos based on the root's configured Hello timer.

5.   B and D. RSTP uses port state forwarding, learning, and discarding. Forwarding and learning perform the same functions as the port states used by traditional STP.

6.   A and D. With RSTP, an alternate port is an alternate to the root port when a switch's root port fails. A backup port takes over for a designated port if the designated port fails.

7. D. The PortFast feature allows STP to move a port from blocking to forwarding without going through the interim listening and learning states. STP allows this exception when the link is known to have no switch on the other end of the link, removing the risk of a switching loop. BPDU Guard is a common feature to use at the same time as PortFast because it watches for incoming bridge protocol data units (BPDU), which should not happen on an access port, and prevents the loops from a rogue switch by disabling the port.

Chapter 10

1. A. Of the four answers, only **pvst** and **rapid-pvst** are valid options on the command. Of those, the **rapid-pvst** option enables Rapid Per VLAN Spanning Tree (RPVST+), which uses RSTP. The **pvst** option enables Per VLAN Spanning Tree (PVST) which uses STP, not RSTP. The other two options, if attempted, would cause the command to be rejected because the option does not exist.

2. A and C. The system ID extension (or extended system ID) part of a bridge ID contains 12 bits and sits after the 4-bit priority field and before the 48-bit system ID. Switches use this field to store the VLAN ID when using STP or RSTP to build spanning trees per VLAN. So of the two answers that mention the system ID extension, the one that lists the VLAN ID, in this case 5, is correct.

    The output also lists a priority of 32773. However, that output lists the decimal equivalent of the 16-bit priority value. In reality, this decimal value is the sum of the configured decimal priority plus the VLAN ID: 32768 + 5 = 32773. So in this case, the root's configured priority is 32,768.

3. A, B, and D. The Cisco Rapid Per VLAN Spanning Tree (RPVST+) creates one spanning tree instance per VLAN. To do so, it sends BPDUs per-VLAN. Each switch identifies itself with a unique Bridge ID (BID) per VLAN, made unique per-VLAN by adding the VLAN ID to the system ID extension 12-bit field of the BID. RVPST also adds a new Type-Length Value (TLV) to the BPDU itself, which includes a place to list the VLAN ID. Finally, when transmitting the BPDUs over VLAN trunks, the switch uses a trunking header that lists the VLAN ID (a practice sometimes called tunneling in 802.1Q.) The receiving switch can check all three locations that list the VLAN ID to ensure that they all agree about what VLAN the BPDU is describing. Of the four answers, the three correct answers describe the three actual locations in which RPVST+ lists the VLAN ID.

4. D. IOS uses the **channel-group** configuration command to create an EtherChannel. Then the term *etherchannel* is used in the **show etherchannel** command, which displays the status of the channel. The output of this **show** command then names the channel a *PortChannel*. The only answer that is not used somewhere in IOS to describe this multilink channel is *Ethernet-Channel*.

5. B and D. The channel-group command will direct the switch to use LACP to dynamically negotiate to add a link to an EtherChannel when the command uses the **active** and **passive** keywords, respectively. The **desirable** and **passive** keywords direct the switch to use PaGP instead of LACP. Of the four answers, the two correct answers use two LACP values, while the two incorrect answers use at least one value that would cause the switch to use PaGP, making the answer incorrect.

Of the two correct answers, both combinations result in the switches attempting to add the link to an EtherChannel using LACP as the negotiation protocol. If both switches used the **passive** keyword, they would both sit and wait for the other switch to begin sending LACP messages and therefore never attempt to add the link to the channel.

6. C. EtherChannel load distribution, or load balancing, on Cisco Catalyst switches uses an algorithm. The algorithm examines some fields in the various headers, so messages that have the same values in those fields always flow over the same link in a particular EtherChannel. Note that it does not break the frames into smaller fragments nor use a round-robin approach that ignores the header values, and it does not examine link utilization when making the choice.

Chapter 11

1. B and D. The general rule to determine whether two devices' interfaces should be in the same subnet is whether the two interfaces are separated from each other by a router. To provide a way for hosts in one VLAN to send data to hosts outside that VLAN, a local router must connect its LAN interface to the same VLAN as the hosts and have an address in the same subnet as the hosts. All the hosts in that same VLAN on the same switch would not be separated from each other by a router, so these hosts would also be in the same subnet. However, another PC, connected to the same switch but in a different VLAN, will require its packets to flow through a router to reach Host A, so Host A's IP address would need to be in a different subnet compared to this new host.

2. D. By definition, two address values in every IPv4 subnet cannot be used as host IPv4 addresses: the first (lowest) numeric value in the subnet for the subnet ID and the last (highest) numeric value in the subnet for the subnet broadcast address.

3. B and C. At least 7 subnet bits are needed because 2^6 = 64, so 6 subnet bits could not number 100 different subnets. Seven subnet bits could because 2^7 = 128 >= 100. Similarly, 6 host bits is not enough because 2^6 – 2 = 62, but 7 host bits is enough because 2^7 – 2 = 126 >= 100.

The number of network, subnet, and host bits must total 32 bits, making one of the answers incorrect. The answer with 8 network bits cannot be correct because the question states that a Class B network is used, so the number of network bits must always be 16. The two correct answers have 16 network bits (required because the question states the use of a Class B network) and at least 7 subnet and host bits each.

4. A and C. The private IPv4 networks, defined by RFC 1918, are Class A network 10.0.0.0, the 16 Class B networks from 172.16.0.0 to 172.31.0.0, and the 256 Class C networks that begin with 192.168.

5. A, D, and E. The private IPv4 networks, defined by RFC 1918, are Class A network 10.0.0.0, the 16 Class B networks from 172.16.0.0 to 172.31.0.0, and the 256 Class C networks that begin with 192.168. The three correct answers are from the public IP network range, and none are reserved values.

6. A and C. An unsubnetted Class A, B, or C network has two parts: the network and host parts.

C

7.   B. An unsubnetted Class A, B, or C network has two parts: the network and host parts. To perform subnetting, the engineer creates a new subnet part by borrowing host bits, shrinking the number of host bits. The subnet part of the address structure exists only after the engineer chooses a nondefault mask. The network part remains a constant size.

Chapter 12

1.   B and C. Class A networks have a first octet in the range of 1–126, inclusive, and their network IDs have a 0 in the last three octets. 130.0.0.0 is actually a Class B network (first octet range 128–191, inclusive). All addresses that begin with 127 are reserved, so 127.0.0.0 is not a Class A network.

2.   E. All Class B networks begin with values between 128 and 191, inclusive, in their first octets. The network ID has any value in the 128–191 range in the first octet, and any value from 0 to 255 inclusive in the second octet, with decimal 0s in the final two octets. Two of the answers show a 255 in the second octet, which is acceptable. Two of the answers show a 0 in the second octet, which is also acceptable.

3.   B and D. The first octet (172) is in the range of values for Class B addresses (128–191). As a result, the network ID can be formed by copying the first two octets (172.16) and writing 0s for the last two octets (172.16.0.0). The default mask for all Class B networks is 255.255.0.0, and the number of host bits in all unsubnetted Class B networks is 16.

4.   A and C. The first octet (192) is in the range of values for Class C addresses (192–223). As a result, the network ID can be formed by copying the first three octets (192.168.6) and writing 0 for the last octet (192.168.6.0). The default mask for all Class C networks is 255.255.255.0, and the number of host bits in all unsubnetted Class C networks is 8.

5.   D. To find the network broadcast address, first determine the class, and then determine the number of host octets. At that point, convert the host octets to 255 to create the network broadcast address. In this case, 10.1.255.255 is in a Class A network, with the last three octets as host octets, for a network broadcast address of 10.255.255.255. For 192.168.255.1, it is a Class C address, with the last octet as the host part, for a network broadcast address of 192.168.255.255. Address 224.1.1.255 is a Class D address, so it is not in any unicast IP network and the question does not apply. For 172.30.255.255, it is a Class B address, with the last two octets as host octets, so the network broadcast address is 172.30.255.255.

Chapter 13

1.   C. If you think about the conversion one octet at a time, the first two octets each convert to 8 binary 1s. 254 converts to 8-bit binary 11111110, and decimal 0 converts to 8-bit binary 00000000. So, the total number of binary 1s (which defines the prefix length) is 8 + 8 + 7 + 0 = /23.

2.   B. If you think about the conversion one octet at a time, the first three octets each convert to 8 binary 1s. 240 converts to 8-bit binary 11110000, so the total number of binary 1s (which defines the prefix length) is 8 + 8 + 8 + 4 = /28.

3. B. /30 is the equivalent of the mask that in binary has 30 binary 1s. To convert that to DDN format, write down all the binary 1s (30 in this case), followed by binary 0s for the remainder of the 32-bit mask. Then take 8 bits at a time and convert from binary to decimal (or memorize the nine possible DDN mask octet values and their binary equivalents). Using the /30 mask in this question, the binary mask is 11111111 11111111 11111111 11111100. Each of the first three octets is all binary 1s, so each converts to 255. The last octet, 11111100, converts to 252, for a DDN mask of 255.255.255.252. See Appendix A, "Numeric Reference Tables," for a decimal/binary conversion table.

4. C. The size of the network part is always either 8, 16, or 24 bits, based on whether it is Class A, B, or C, respectively. As a Class A address, N=8. The mask 255.255.255.0, converted to prefix format, is /24. The number of subnet bits is the difference between the prefix length (24) and N, so S=16 in this case. The size of the host part is a number that, when added to the prefix length (24), gives you 32, so H=8 in this case.

5. A. The size of the network part is always either 8, 16, or 24 bits, based on whether it is Class A, B, or C, respectively. As a Class C address, N=24. The number of subnet bits is the difference between the prefix length (27) and N, so S=3 in this case. The size of the host part is a number that, when added to the prefix length (27), gives you 32, so H=5 in this case.

6. D. Classless addressing rules define a two-part IP address structure: the prefix and the host part. This logic ignores Class A, B, and C rules, and can be applied to the 32-bit IPv4 addresses from any address class. By ignoring Class A, B, and C rules, classless addressing ignores any distinction as to the network part of an IPv4 address.

7. A and B. The masks in binary define a number of binary 1s, and the number of binary 1s defines the length of the prefix (network + subnet) part. With a Class B network, the network part is 16 bits. To support 100 subnets, the subnet part must be at least 7 bits long. Six subnet bits would supply only 2^6 = 64 subnets, while 7 subnet bits supply 2^7 = 128 subnets. The /24 answer supplies 8 subnet bits, and the 255.255.255.252 answer supplies 14 subnet bits.

Chapter 14

1. D. When using classful IP addressing concepts as described in Chapter 13, "Analyzing Subnet Masks," addresses have three parts: network, subnet, and host. For addresses in a single classful network, the network parts must be identical for the numbers to be in the same network. For addresses in the same subnet, both the network and subnet parts must have identical values. The host part differs when comparing different addresses in the same subnet.

2. B and D. In any subnet, the subnet ID is the smallest number in the range, the subnet broadcast address is the largest number, and the usable IP addresses sit between them. All numbers in a subnet have identical binary values in the prefix part (classless view) and network + subnet part (classful view). To be the lowest number, the subnet ID must have the lowest possible binary value (all 0s) in the host part. To be the largest number, the broadcast address must have the highest possible binary value (all binary 1s) in the host part. The usable addresses do not include the subnet ID and subnet broadcast address, so the addresses in the range of usable IP addresses never have a value of all 0s or 1s in their host parts.

C

3.   C. The mask converts to 255.255.255.0. To find the subnet ID, for each octet of the mask that is 255, you can copy the IP address's corresponding values. For mask octets of decimal 0, you can record a 0 in that octet of the subnet ID. As such, copy the 10.7.99 and write a 0 for the fourth octet, for a subnet ID of 10.7.99.0.

4.   C. First, the resident subnet (the subnet ID of the subnet in which the address resides) must be numerically smaller than the IP address, which rules out one of the answers. The mask converts to 255.255.255.252. As such, you can copy the first three octets of the IP address because of their value of 255. For the fourth octet, the subnet ID value must be a multiple of 4, because 256 – 252 (mask) = 4. Those multiples include 96 and 100, and the right choice is the multiple closest to the IP address value in that octet (97) without going over. So, the correct subnet ID is 192.168.44.96.

5.   C. The resident subnet ID in this case is 172.31.77.192. You can find the subnet broadcast address based on the subnet ID and mask using several methods. Following the decimal process in the book, the mask converts to 255.255.255.224, making the interesting octet be octet 4, with magic number 256 – 224 = 32. For the three octets where the mask = 255, copy the subnet ID (172.31.77). For the interesting octet, take the subnet ID value (192), add magic (32), and subtract 1, for 223. That makes the subnet broadcast address 172.31.77.223.

6.   C. To answer this question, you need to find the range of addresses in the subnet, which typically then means you need to calculate the subnet ID and subnet broadcast address. With a subnet ID/mask of 10.1.4.0/23, the mask converts to 255.255.254.0. To find the subnet broadcast address, following the decimal process described in this chapter, you can copy the subnet ID's first two octets because the mask's value is 255 in each octet. You write a 255 in the fourth octet because the mask has a 0 on the fourth octet. In octet 3, the interesting octet, add the magic number (2) to the subnet ID's value (4), minus 1, for a value of 2 + 4 – 1 = 5. (The magic number in this case is calculated as 256 – 254 = 2.) That makes the broadcast address 10.1.5.255. The last usable address is 1 less: 10.1.5.254. The range that includes the last 100 addresses is 10.1.5.155 – 10.1.5.254.

Chapter 15

1.   B and E. Cisco routers have an on/off switch, but Cisco switches generally do not.

2.   B. Cisco routers that do not also have any Layer 2 switch features support commands needed for Layer 3 routing as well as commands in common between Layer 2 switching and Layer 3 routing devices. In this case, the **show interfaces status** and **show mac address-table** commands happen to be commands supported on Layer 2 switches but not on routers. Both types of devices use the **show running-config** command. Of the answers, only the **show ip interface brief** command is unique to routers.

3.   A and C. To route packets on an interface, the router interface configuration must include an IP address and mask. One correct command shows the correct single command used to configure both values, while one incorrect command shows those settings as two separate commands. Also, to route packets, the interface must reach an "up/up" state; that is, the **show interfaces** and other commands list two status values, and both must be "up." The **no shutdown** command enables the interface.

4. C. If the first of the two status codes is "down," it typically means that a Layer 1 problem exists. In this case, the question states that the router connects to a switch with a UTP straight-through cable, which is the correct cable pinout. Of the two answers that mention the **shutdown** command, if the router interface were shut down, the first router status code would be "administratively down," so that answer is incorrect. However, if the neighboring device interface sits in a shutdown state, the router will sense no electrical signals over the cable, seeing that as a physical problem, and place the interface into a "down/down" state, making that answer correct.

    Second, the two answers that mention interface IP addresses have no impact on the status codes of the **show interfaces brief** command. Both answers imply that the interface does not have an IP address configured. However, both the first and second status codes are not related to whether IP addresses have been configured or not, making both answers incorrect.

5. C and E. The **show ip interface brief** command lists all the interface IPv4 addresses but none of the masks. The **show version** command lists none of the IP addresses and none of the masks. The other three commands list both the address and mask.

6. B. A router has one IPv4 address for each interface in use, whereas a LAN switch has a single IPv4 address that is just used for accessing the switch. The rest of the answers list configuration settings that use the same conventions on both routers and switches.

Chapter 16

1. A and C. The route defines the group of addresses represented by the route using the subnet ID and mask. The router can use those numbers to find the range of addresses that should be matched by this route. The other two answers list facts useful when forwarding packets that happen to match the route.

2. A and D. First, for the subnetting math, address 10.1.1.100, with mask /26, implies a subnet ID of 10.1.1.64. Also, mask /26 converts to a DDN mask of 255.255.255.192. For any working router interface, after adding the **ip address** command to configure an address and mask, the router adds a connected route for the subnet. In this case, that means the router adds a connected route for subnet 10.1.1.64 255.255.255.192. The router also adds a route called a local route, which is a route for the interface IP address with a 255.255.255.255 mask. In this case, that means the router adds a local route for address 10.1.1.100 with mask 255.255.255.255.

3. C. The **ip route** command can refer to the IP address of the next-hop router or to the local router's interface. It also refers to the subnet ID and matching subnet mask, defining the range of addresses matched by the route.

4. A. The correct syntax lists a subnet number, then a subnet mask in dotted-decimal form, and then either an outgoing interface or a next-hop IP address.

5. B. The **ip route** command can reference an outgoing interface or a next-hop IP address, and the command lists a next-hop IP address, which rules out one answer. The command does use the correct syntax, ruling out another answer. There is no requirement for a router to have any particular interface IP addresses in relation to the configuration of an **ip route** command, ruling out yet another answer.

The checks that IOS uses when looking at a new **ip route** command include whether the outgoing interface is up/up, whether the next-hop address is reachable, and, if there is a competing route from another source, whether the other route has a better administrative distance.

6. D. Destination address 10.1.15.122 matches all the routes listed except the host route to 10.1.15.100/32. In that case, the router will choose the matching route that has the longest prefix length, that is, the prefix-style mask with the highest number. In this case, that route lists subnet 10.1.15.96 and mask /27, which lists interface G0/3/0 as the outgoing interface.

Chapter 17

1. A and F. Of all the commands listed, only the two correct answers are syntactically correct router configuration commands. The command to enable 802.1Q trunking is **encapsulation dot1q** *vlan_id*.

2. B and C. Subinterface G0/1.1 must be in an administratively down state due to the **shutdown** command being issued on that subinterface. For subinterface G0/1.2, its status cannot be administratively down because of the **no shutdown** command. G0/1.2's state will then track to the state of the underlying physical interface. With a physical interface state of down/down, subinterface G0/1.2 will be in a down/down state in this case.

3. C. The configuration of the Layer 3 switch's routing feature uses VLAN interfaces. The VLAN interface numbers must match the associated VLAN ID, so with VLANs 1, 2, and 3 in use, the switch will configure **interface vlan 1**, **interface vlan 2** (which is the correct answer), and **interface vlan 3**. The matching connected routes, like all connected IP routes, will list the VLAN interfaces.

   As for the incorrect answers, a list of connected routes will not list any next-hop IP addresses. Each route will list an outgoing interface; the outgoing interface will not be a physical interface, but rather a VLAN interface, because the question states that the configuration uses SVIs. Finally, all the listed subnets have a /25 mask, which is 255.255.255.128, so none of the routes will list a 255.255.255.0 mask.

4. C and D. First, for the correct answers, a Layer 3 switch will not route packets on a VLAN interface unless it is in an up/up state. A VLAN interface will only be up/up if the matching VLAN (with the same VLAN number) exists on the switch. If VTP deletes the VLAN, then the VLAN interface moves to a down/down state, and routing in/out that interface stops. Also, disabling VLAN 2 with the **shutdown** command in VLAN configuration mode also causes the matching VLAN 2 interface to fail, which makes routing on interface VLAN 2 stop as well.

   As for the incorrect answers, a Layer 3 switch needs only one access port or trunk port forwarding for a VLAN to enable routing for that VLAN, so nine of the ten access ports in VLAN 2 could fail, leaving one working port, and the switch would keep routing for VLAN 2.

   A **shutdown** of VLAN 4 has no effect on routing for VLAN interfaces 2 and 3. Had that answer listed VLANs 2 or 3, it would definitely be a reason to make routing fail for that VLAN interface.

5. A and C. With a Layer 3 EtherChannel, the physical ports and the port-channel interface must disable the behavior of acting like a switch port, and therefore act like a routed port, through the configuration of the **no switchport** interface subcommand. (The **routedport** command is not an IOS command.) Once created, the physical interfaces should not have an IP address configured. The port-channel interface (the interface representing the EtherChannel) should be configured with the IP address.

6. B and C. With a Layer 3 EtherChannel, two configuration settings must be the same on all the physical ports, specifically the speed and duplex as set with the **speed** and **duplex** commands. Additionally, the physical ports and port-channel port must all have the **no switchport** command configured to make each act as a routed port. So, having a different speed setting, or being configured with **switchport** rather than **no switchport**, would prevent IOS from adding interface G0/2 to the Layer 3 EtherChannel.

   As for the wrong answers, both have to do with Layer 2 configuration settings. Once Layer 2 operations have been disabled because of the **no switchport** command, those settings related to Layer 2 that could cause problems on Layer 2 EtherChannels do not then cause problems for the Layer 3 EtherChannel. So, Layer 2 settings about access VLANs, trunking allowed lists, and STP settings, which must match before an interface can be added to a Layer 2 EtherChannel, do not matter for a Layer 3 EtherChannel.

Chapter 19

1. D. Both versions of RIP use distance vector logic, and EIGRP uses a different kind of logic, characterized either as advanced distance vector or a balanced hybrid.

2. C and D. Both versions of RIP use the same hop-count metric, neither of which is affected by link bandwidth. EIGRP's metric, by default, is calculated based on bandwidth and delay. OSPF's metric is a sum of outgoing interfaces costs, with those costs (by default) based on interface bandwidth.

3. B, C, and D. Of the listed routing protocols, only the old RIP Version 1 (RIP-1) protocol does not support variable-length subnet masks (VLSM).

4. C. LSAs contain topology information that is useful in calculating routes, but the LSAs do not directly list the route that a router should add to its routing table. In this case, R1 would run a calculation called the Shortest Path First (SPF) algorithm, against the LSAs, to determine what IP routes to add to the IP routing table.

5. B. Neighboring OSPF routers that complete the database exchange are considered fully adjacent and rest in a full neighbor state. The up/up and final states are not OSPF states at all. The 2-way state is either an interim state or a stable state between some routers on the same VLAN.

6. C. The correct answer is the one advantage of using a single-area design. The three wrong answers are advantages of using a multiarea design, with all reasons being much more important with a larger internetwork.

Chapter 20

1. B. The **network 10.0.0.0 0.255.255.255 area 0** command works because it matches all interfaces whose first octet is 10. The rest of the commands match as follows: all addresses that end with 0.0.0 (wildcard mask 255.0.0.0); all addresses that begin with 10.0.0 (wildcard mask 0.0.0.255); and all addresses that begin with 10.0 (wildcard mask 0.0.255.255).

2. A. The **network 10.1.0.0 0.0.255.255 area 0** command matches all IP addresses that begin with 10.1, enabling OSPF in area 0 on all interfaces. The answer with wildcard mask 0.255.255.0 is illegal because it represents more than one string of binary 0s separated by binary 1s. The answer with x's is syntactically incorrect. The answer with wildcard mask 255.0.0.0 means "Match all addresses whose last three octets are 0.0.0," so none of the three interfaces are matched.

3. A and E. Of the three wrong answers, two are real commands that simply do not list the OSPF neighbors. **show ip ospf interface brief** lists interfaces on which OSPF is enabled but does not list neighbors. **show ip interface** lists IPv4 details about interfaces, but none related to OSPF. One incorrect answer, **show ip neighbor**, is not a valid IOS command.

4. B. With OSPFv2 interface configuration mode, the configuration looks just like the traditional configuration, with a couple of exceptions. The **network** router subcommand is no longer required. Instead, each interface on which OSPF should be enabled is configured with an **ip ospf** *process-id* **area** *area-id* interface subcommand. This command refers to the OSPF routing process that should be enabled on the interface and specifies the OSPFv2 area.

5. B. SPF calculates the cost of a route as the sum of the OSPF interface costs for all outgoing interfaces in the route. The interface cost can be set directly (**ip ospf cost**), or IOS uses a default based on the reference bandwidth and the interface bandwidth. Of the listed answers, **delay** is the only setting that does not influence OSPFv2 metric calculations.

6. A and D. The configuration enables OSPF and identifies the area number to use with the interface using an interface subcommand in interface mode: the **ip ospf** *process-id* **area** *area-number* command. However, to explicitly configure the router ID, the configuration must use the **router-id** *router-id-value* command, which is a command issued in OSPF router mode.

Chapter 21

1. B and D. By default, IOS assigns Ethernet interfaces an OSPF network type of broadcast, with an OSPF interface priority of 1. As a result, both routers attempt to discover the other routers on the link (which identifies one correct answer).

   The broadcast network type means that the routers also attempt to elect a DR and BDR. With a tie-in priority, the routers choose the DR based on the highest router ID (RID) values, meaning that R2 will become the DR and R1 will become the BDR. These facts combine to show why the two incorrect answers are incorrect. The other correct answer is correct because the **show ip ospf neighbor** command lists the local router's neighbor relationship state (FULL) and the role filled by that neighbor (DR), which would be the output shown on R1 when R2 is acting as DR.

2. B and C. First, the OSPF point-to-point network type causes the two routers to dynamically discover neighbors, making one answer correct.

Next, IOS assigns a default OSPF interface priority of 1, so R1's configured priority of 11 would be better in a DR/BDR election. However, the point-to-point network type causes the router to not use a DR/BDR on the interface. As a result, the answer about R1 becoming the DR is incorrect (because no DR exists at all), and the answer listing a state of "FULL/DR" is incorrect for the same reason. However, the answer that claims that R2 will be neither DR nor BDR is true because no DR or BDR is elected.

3. D. The **show ip ospf interface brief** command lists a pair of counters under the heading "Nbrs F/C" on the far right of the output. The first of the two numbers represents the number of fully adjacent neighbors (2 in this case), and the second number represents the total number of neighbors.

4. A and D. As worded, the correct answers list a scenario that would prevent the neighbor relationship. One correct answer mentions the use of two different OSPF areas on the potential OSPF neighbors; to become neighbors, the two routers must use the same area number. The other correct answer mentions the use of two different Hello timers, a mismatch that causes two routers to reject each other and to not become neighbors.

   The two incorrect answers list scenarios that do not cause issues, making them incorrect answers. One mentions mismatched OSPF process IDs; OSPF process IDs do not need to match for two routers to become neighbors. The other incorrect answer (that is, a scenario that does not cause a problem) mentions the use of two different priority values. The priority values give OSPF a means to prefer one router over the other when electing a DR/BDR, so the setting is intended to be set to different values on different routers and does not cause a problem.

5. C. As worded, the correct answers should be a scenario that would prevent the neighbor relationship. The answers all list values that are identical or similar on the two routers. Of those, the use of an identical OSPF router ID (RID) on the two routers prevents them from becoming neighbors, making that one answer correct.

   Of the incorrect answers, both routers must have the same Dead interval, so both using a Dead interval of 40 causes no issues. The two routers can use any OSPF process ID (the same or different value, it does not matter), making that answer incorrect. Finally, the two routers' IP addresses must be in the same subnet, so again that scenario does not prevent R13 and R14 from becoming neighbors.

6. D. The OSPF **shutdown** command tells the OSPF process to stop operating. That process includes removing any OSPF-learned routes from the IP routing table, clearing the router's LSDB, and closing existing OSPF neighbor relationships. In effect, it causes OSPF to stop working on the router, but it does retain the configuration so that a **no shutdown** command will cause the router to start using OSPF again with no changes to the configuration.

Chapter 22

1. C. NAT, specifically the PAT feature that allows many hosts to use private IPv4 addresses while being supported by a single public IPv4 address, was one short-term solution to the IPv4 address exhaustion problem. IP version 5 existed briefly as an experimental protocol and had nothing to do with IPv4 address exhaustion. IPv6 directly addresses the IPv4 address exhaustion problem, but it is a long-term solution. ARP has no impact on the number of IPv4 addresses used.

2.   A. Routers use the same process steps when routing IPv6 packets as they do when routing IPv4 packets. Routers route IPv6 packets based on the IPv6 addresses, listed inside the IPv6 header in the IPv6 packets, by comparing the destination IPv6 address to the router's IPv6 routing table. As a result, the router discards the incoming frame's data-link header and trailer, leaving an IPv6 packet. The router compares the destination (not source) IPv6 address in the header to the router's IPv6 (not IPv4) routing table and then forwards the packet based on the matched route.

3.   D. If you are following the steps in the book, the first step removes up to three leading 0s in each quartet, leaving FE80:0:0:100:0:0:0:123. This leaves two strings of consecutive all-0 quartets; by changing the longest string of all 0s to ::, the address is FE80:0:0:100::123.

4.   B. This question has many quartets that make it easy to make a common mistake: removing trailing 0s in a quartet of hex digits. To abbreviate IPv6 addresses, only leading 0s in a quartet should be removed. Many of the quartets have trailing 0s (0s on the right side of the quartet), so make sure to not remove those 0s.

5.   A. The unabbreviated version of an IPv6 address must have 32 digits, and only one answer has 32 hex digits. In this case, the original number shows four quartets and a ::. So, the :: was replaced with four quartets of 0000, making the number have eight quartets. Then, for each quartet with fewer than four digits, leading 0s were added so that each quartet has four hex digits.

6.   C. The /64 prefix length means that the last 64 bits, or last 16 digits, of the address should be changed to all 0s. That process leaves the unabbreviated prefix as 2000:0000:0000:0005:0000:0000:0000:0000. The last four quartets are all 0s, making that string of all 0s be the longest and best string of 0s to replace with ::. After removing the leading 0s in other quartets, the answer is 2000:0:0:5::/64.

Chapter 23

1.   C. Unique local addresses begin with FD in the first two digits.

2.   A. Global unicast addresses can begin with many different initial values, but most commonly begin with either a hex 2 or 3.

3.   D. The global routing prefix is the address block, represented as a prefix value and prefix length, given to an organization by some numbering authority. All IPv6 addresses inside the company have the same value in these initial bits of their IPv6 addresses. Similarly, when a company uses a public IPv4 address block, all the addresses have the same value in the network part.

4.   B. Subnetting a global unicast address block, using a single prefix length for all subnets, breaks the addresses into three parts. The parts are the global routing prefix, subnet, and interface ID.

5.   D. Unique local addresses begin with a 2-hex-digit prefix of FD, followed by the 10-hex-digit global ID.

Chapter 24

1. A. The one correct answer lists the exact same IPv6 address listed in the question, with a /64 prefix length and no spaces in the syntax of the answer. Another (incorrect) answer is identical, except that it leaves a space between the address and prefix length, which is incorrect syntax. The two answers that list the **eui-64** parameter list an address and not a prefix; they should list a prefix to be correct, although neither would have resulted in the IPv6 address listed in the question.

2. B. With the **eui-64** parameter, the router will calculate the interface ID portion of the IPv6 address based on its MAC address. Beginning with 5055.4444.3333, the router injects FF FE in the middle (5055.44FF.FE44.3333). Then the router inverts the seventh bit in the first byte. Mentally, this converts hex 50 to binary 01010000, changing bit 7 so that the string is 0101 0010 and converting back to hex 52. The final interface ID value is 5255:44FF:FE44:3333. The wrong answers simply list a different value.

3. A and C. Of the four answers, the two correct answers show the minimal required configuration to support IPv6 on a Cisco router: enabling IPv6 routing (**ipv6 unicast-routing**) and enabling IPv6 on each interface, typically by adding a unicast address to each interface (**ipv6 address...**). The two incorrect answers list nonexistent commands.

4. A. With an **ipv6 address** command configured for a global unicast address, but without a link-local address configured with an **ipv6 address** command, the router calculates its link-local address on the interface based on its MAC address and EUI-64 rules. The first half of the link-local address begins FE80:0000:0000:0000. The router then calculates the second half of the link-local address value by taking the MAC address (0200.0001.000A), injecting FF FE in the middle (0200.00FF.FE01.000A), and flipping the seventh bit (0000.00FF.FE01.000A).

5. B. FF02::1 is used by all IPv6 hosts on the link, FF02::5 is used by all OSPFv3 routers, and FF02::A is used by all EIGRPv6 routers. FF02::2 is used to send packets to all IPv6 routers on a link.

Chapter 25

1. A and C. With an IPv6 address on a working interface, the router adds a connected route for the prefix (subnet) implied by the **ipv6 address** command. It also adds a local host route (with a /128 prefix length) based on the unicast address. The router does not add a route based on the link-local address.

2. A and C. The two correct answers show the correct subnet ID (prefix) and prefix length for the two connected subnets: 3111:1:1:1::/64 and 3222:2:2:2::/64. The answer with the /128 prefix length is shown in a local route, but those routes are not displayed by the **show ipv6 route connected** command. The other incorrect answer lists the entire IPv6 address with a /64 prefix length, and the entire address would not be displayed as a prefix when using a /64 prefix.

C

3. A. All four answers show examples of commands that use an outgoing interface. The two commands that begin with **ip route** define only IPv4 routes; the commands would be rejected because of the IPv6 prefixes listed in the commands. The two commands that begin with **ipv6 route** are syntactically correct, but the command should list the local router's interface (an interface on the router on which the command is being configured). R5 needs to use its local S0/1/1 interface as the outgoing interface.

4. B. All four answers show examples of commands that use a next-hop router IPv6 address. Two of the answers list R5's own IPv6 address (unicast or link-local), which is incorrect; the answer should be an address on the neighboring router, R6 in this case. For the two answers that list addresses on Router R6, the one that lists R6's global unicast address is correct. The one that lists R6's link-local address would also require R5's outgoing interface, so the answer that lists FE80::FF:FE00:6 would be rejected as well.

5. C. IOS will add a new static route to the IPv6 routing table if, when using a next-hop global unicast address, the router has a working route to reach that next-hop address and there is no better (lower administrative distance) route for the exact same subnet. So, the correct answer identifies one reason why the route would not appear. The answer that mentions a better route with administrative distance of 110 is a valid reason for the static route to not appear, but the question states that no route for the subnet appears in the routing table, so clearly that competing route does not exist.

The other two answers are incorrect about the **ipv6 route** command. This command can use a link-local next-hop address but does not have to do so. Also, when using a global unicast address as next-hop, the command does not also require an outgoing interface parameter.

6. A and B. The output shows two static routes, as noted with the "S" code on the far left. Both were added to the IPv6 routing table because of **ipv6 route** commands. Both have an administrative distance of 1, which is listed as the first number in brackets.

For the two incorrect answers, note that the **ipv6 address** interface subcommand does cause IOS to add connected IPv6 routes to the routing table, and the phrase "directly connected" with one route might make you think this is a connected route. However, the "S" in the far left identifies the source of the route. Likewise, the answer that mentions an IPv6 routing protocol is incorrect because both routes have a code of S, meaning static.

7. B. PC1 needs to discover PC2's MAC address. Unlike IPv4, IPv6 does not use ARP, instead using NDP. Specifically, PC1 uses the NDP Neighbor Solicitation (NS) message to request that PC2 send back an NDP Neighbor Advertisement (NA). SLAAC relates to address assignment, and not to discovering a neighbor's MAC address.

8. A and C. The NDP RA lists the router IPv6 address, the IPv6 prefixes known on the link, and the matching prefix lengths. When using DHCPv6, the host learns the IPv6 address of the DNS server through DHCPv6 messages. For MAC addresses of on-link neighbors, hosts use NDP NS and NA messages.

Chapter 26

1. C. The IEEE 802.3 standard defines Ethernet, while 802.11 defines Wi-Fi.

2. B. WLANs require half-duplex operation because all stations must contend for use of a channel to transmit frames.

3. C. An AP offers a basic service set (BSS). BSA is incorrect because it is a Basic Service Area, or the cell footprint of a BSS. BSD is incorrect because it does not pertain to wireless at all. IBSS is incorrect because it is an Independent BSS, or an ad hoc network, where an AP or BSS is not needed at all.

4. B. The AP at the heart of a BSS or cell identifies itself (and the BSS) with a Basic Service Set Identifier (BSSID). It also uses an SSID to identify the wireless network, but that is not unique to the AP or BSS. Finally, the radio MAC address is used as the basis for the BSSID value, but the value can be altered to form the BSSID for each SSID that the AP supports.

5. B. A workgroup bridge acts as a wireless client, but bridges traffic to and from a wired device connected to it.

6. B. In a mesh network, each mesh AP builds a standalone BSS. The APs relay client traffic to each other over wireless backhaul links, rather than wired Ethernet. Therefore, Ethernet cabling to each AP is not required.

7. D and E. Wi-Fi commonly uses the 2.5- and 5-GHz bands.

8. C and D. In the 2.4-GHz band, consecutively numbered channels are too wide to not overlap. Only channels 1, 6, and 11 are spaced far enough apart to avoid overlapping each other. In the 5-GHz band, all channels are considered to be nonoverlapping.

Chapter 27

1. A. An autonomous AP can operate independently without the need for a centralized wireless LAN controller.

2. B. The Cisco Meraki APs are autonomous APs that are managed through a centralized platform in the Meraki cloud.

3. C. On a lightweight AP, the MAC function is divided between the AP hardware and the WLC. Therefore, the architecture is known as split-MAC.

4. B. An LAP builds a CAPWAP tunnel with a WLC.

5. A. A trunk link carrying three VLANs is not needed at all. A lightweight AP in local mode needs only an access link with a single VLAN; everything else is carried over the CAPWAP tunnel to a WLC. The WLC will need to be connected to three VLANs so that it can work with the LAP to bind them to the three SSIDs.

6. C. A unified WLC deployment model is based around locating the WLC in a central location, to support a very large number of APs.

7. A. The local mode is the default mode, where the AP provides at least one functional BSS that wireless clients can join to connect to the network. Normal and client modes are not valid modes. Monitor mode is used to turn the AP into a dedicated wireless sensor.

8. D. The SE-Connect mode is used for spectrum analysis. "SE" denotes the Cisco Spectrum Expert software. Otherwise, an AP can operate in only one mode at a time. The local mode is the default mode.

Chapter 28

1. D. For effective security, you should leverage authentication, MIC, and encryption.

2. C. A message integrity check (MIC) is an effective way to protect against data tampering. WIPS is not correct because it provides intrusion protection functions. WEP is not correct because it does not provide data integrity along with its weak encryption. EAP is not correct because it defines the framework for authentication.

3. D. WEP is known to have a number of weaknesses and has been compromised. Therefore, it has been officially deprecated and should not be used in a wireless network. AES is not a correct answer because it is the current recommended encryption method. WPA is not correct because it defines a suite of security methods. EAP is not correct because it defines a framework for authentication.

4. C. EAP works with 802.1x to authenticate a client and enable access for it. Open authentication and WEP cannot be correct because both define a specific authentication method. WPA is not correct because it defines a suite of security methods in addition to authentication.

5. A. The TKIP method was deprecated when the 802.11 standard was updated in 2012. CCMP and GCMP are still valid methods. EAP is an authentication framework and is not related to data encryption and integrity.

6. C. WPA2 uses CCMP only. WEP has been deprecated and is not used in any of the WPA versions. TKIP has been deprecated but can be used in WPA only. WPA is not a correct answer because it is an earlier version of WPA2.

7. B. The Wi-Fi Alliance offers the WPA, WPA2, and WPA3 certifications for wireless security. WEP, AES, and 802.11 are not certifications designed and awarded by the Wi-Fi Alliance.

8. A and C. The personal mode for WPA, WPA2, and WPA3 is used to require a pre-shared key authentication. Enterprise mode uses 802.1x instead.

Chapter 29

1. A. A lightweight AP requires connectivity to only a single VLAN, so access mode is used.

2. B. An autonomous AP must connect to each of the VLANs it will extend to wireless LANs. Therefore, its link should be configured as a trunk.

3. D. You can use HTTP and HTTPS to access the GUI of a wireless LAN controller, as well as SSH to access its CLI. While HTTP is a valid management protocol on a WLC, it is usually disabled to make the WLC more secure.

4. C. Controllers use a link aggregation group (LAG) to bundle multiple ports together.

5. D. A dynamic interface makes a logical connection between a WLAN and a VLAN, all internal to the controller.

6. C and D. A WLAN binds an SSID to a controller interface so that the controller can link the wired and wireless networks. Although the WLAN ultimately reaches a wired VLAN, it does so only through a controller interface. It is the interface that is configured with a VLAN number.

7. C. You can configure a maximum of 512 WLANs on a controller. However, a maximum of only 16 of them can be configured on an AP.

8. A and C. The SSID and controller interface are the only parameters from the list that are necessary. The VLAN number is not because it is supplied when a controller interface is configured.

C

GLOSSARY

NUMERIC

10/100   A short reference to an Ethernet NIC or switch port that supports speed of 10 Mbps and 100 Mbps.

10/100/1000   A short reference to an Ethernet NIC or switch port that supports speeds of 10 Mbps, 100 Mbps, and 1000 Mbps (that is, 1 Gbps).

10BASE-T   The 10-Mbps baseband Ethernet specification using two pairs of twisted-pair cabling (Categories 3, 4, or 5): one pair transmits data and the other receives data. 10BASE-T, which is part of the IEEE 802.3 specification, has a distance limit of approximately 100 m (328 feet) per segment.

100BASE-T   A name for the IEEE Fast Ethernet standard that uses two-pair copper cabling, a speed of 100 Mbps, and a maximum cable length of 100 meters.

1000BASE-T   A name for the IEEE Gigabit Ethernet standard that uses four-pair copper cabling, a speed of 1000 Mbps (1 Gbps), and a maximum cable length of 100 meters.

2-way state   In OSPF, a neighbor state that implies that the router has exchanged Hellos with the neighbor and that all required parameters match.

802.11a   The IEEE standard for wireless LANs using the U-NII spectrum, OFDM encoding, and speeds of up to 54 Mbps.

802.11b   The IEEE standard for wireless LANs using the ISM spectrum, DSSS encoding, and speeds of up to 11 Mbps.

802.11g   The IEEE standard for wireless LANs using the ISM spectrum, OFDM or DSSS encoding, and speeds of up to 54 Mbps.

802.11n   The IEEE standard for wireless LANs using the ISM spectrum, OFDM encoding, and multiple antennas for single-stream speeds up to 150 Mbps.

802.1Q   The IEEE standardized protocol for VLAN trunking, which also includes RSTP details.

802.1x   An IEEE standard that defines port-based access control for wired and wireless networks.

A

AAA   Authentication, authorization, and accounting. Authentication confirms the identity of the user or device. Authorization determines what the user or device is allowed to do. Accounting records information about access attempts, including inappropriate requests.

AAA server   A server that holds security information and provides services related to user login, particularly authentication (is the user who he says he is?), authorization (once authenticated, what do we allow the user to do?), and accounting (tracking the user).

ABR   *See* Area Border Router.

access interface   A LAN network design term that refers to a switch interface connected to end-user devices, configured so that it does not use VLAN trunking.

access layer   In a campus LAN design, the switches that connect directly to endpoint devices (servers, user devices), and also connect into the distribution layer switches.

access link   In Frame Relay, the physical serial link that connects a Frame Relay DTE device, usually a router, to a Frame Relay switch. The access link uses the same physical layer standards as do point-to-point leased lines.

access point (AP)   A device that provides wireless service for clients within its coverage area or cell, with the AP connecting to both the wireless LAN and the wired Ethernet LAN.

accounting   In security, the recording of access attempts. *See also* AAA.

ad hoc network   *See* independent basic service set (IBSS).

address block   A set of consecutive IPv4 addresses. The term is most often used for a classless prefix as defined by CIDR but can also refer to any subnet or IPv4 network.

adjacent-layer interaction   The general topic of how, on one computer, two adjacent layers in a networking architectural model work together, with the lower layer providing services to the higher layer.

administrative distance   In Cisco routers, a means for one router to choose between multiple routes to reach the same subnet when those routes were learned by different routing protocols. The lower the administrative distance, the better the source of the routing information.

ADSL   Asymmetric digital subscriber line. One of many DSL technologies, ADSL is designed to deliver more bandwidth downstream (from the central office to the customer site) than upstream.

all-nodes multicast address   A specific IPv6 multicast address, FF02::1, with link-local scope, used to send packets to all devices on the link that support IPv6.

all-routers multicast address   A specific IPv6 multicast address, FF02::2, with link-local scope, used to send packets to all devices that act as IPv6 routers on the local link.

alternate port   With RSTP, a port role in which the port acts as an alternative to a switch's root port, so that when the switch's root port fails, the alternate port can immediately take over as the root port.

anycast address   An address shared by two or more hosts that exist in different parts of the network, so that by design, the routers will forward packets to the nearest of the two servers, allowing clients to communicate with the nearest such server, not caring which particular server with which the client communicates.

Area Border Router (ABR)   A router using OSPF in which the router has interfaces in multiple OSPF areas.

ARP   Address Resolution Protocol. An Internet protocol used to map an IP address to a MAC address. Defined in RFC 826.

ARP table   A list of IP addresses of neighbors on the same VLAN, along with their MAC addresses, as kept in memory by hosts and routers.

ARPANET   The first packet-switched network, first created around 1970, which served as the predecessor to the Internet.

ASBR   Autonomous System Border Router. A router using OSPF in which the router learns routes via another source, usually another routing protocol, exchanging routes that are external to OSPF with the OSPF domain.

asymmetric   A feature of many Internet access technologies, including DSL, cable, and modems, in which the downstream transmission rate is higher than the upstream transmission rate.

asynchronous   The lack of an imposed time ordering on a bit stream. Practically, both sides agree to the same speed, but there is no check or adjustment of the rates if they are slightly different. However, because only 1 byte per transfer is sent, slight differences in clock speed are not an issue.

authentication   In security, the verification of the identity of a person or a process. *See also* AAA.

authentication server (AS)   An 802.1x entity that authenticates users or clients based on their credentials, as matched against a user database. In a wireless network, a RADIUS server is an AS.

authenticator   An 802.1x entity that exists as a network device that provides access to the network. In a wireless network, a WLC acts as an authenticator.

authorization   In security, the determination of the rights allowed for a particular user or device. *See also* AAA.

autonegotiation   An IEEE standard mechanism (802.3u) with which two nodes can exchange messages for the purpose of choosing to use the same Ethernet standards on both ends of the link, ensuring that the link functions and functions well.

autonomous AP   A wireless AP operating in a standalone mode, such that it can provide a fully functional BSS and connect to the DS.

autonomous system   An internetwork in the administrative control of one organization, company, or governmental agency, inside which that organization typically runs an interior gateway protocol (IGP).

auxiliary port   A physical connector on a router that is designed to be used to allow a remote terminal, or PC with a terminal emulator, to access a router using an analog modem.

B

backbone area   In OSPFv2 and OSPFv3, the special area in a multiarea design, with all non-backbone areas needing to connect to the backbone area, area 0.

back-to-back link   A serial link between two routers, created without CSU/DSUs, by connecting a DTE cable to one router and a DCE cable to the other. Typically used in labs to build serial links without the expense of an actual leased line from the telco.

backup designated router   An OSPF router connected to a multiaccess network that monitors the work of the designated router (DR) and takes over the work of the DR if the DR fails.

backup port   With RSTP, a port role in which the port acts as a backup to one of the switch's ports acting as a designated port. If the switch's designated port fails, the switch will use the backup port to immediately take over as the designated port.

band   A contiguous range of frequencies.

bandwidth   A reference to the speed of a networking link. Its origins come from earlier communications technology in which the range, or width, of the frequency band dictated how fast communications could occur.

basic service set (BSS)   Wireless service provided by one AP to one or more associated clients.

basic service set identifier (BSSID)   A unique MAC address that is used to identify the AP that is providing a BSS.

binary mask   An IPv4 subnet mask written as a 32-bit binary number.

bitwise Boolean AND   A Boolean AND between two numbers of the same length in which the first bit in each number is ANDed, and then the second bit in each number, and then the third, and so on.

blocking state   In STP, a port state in which no received frames are processed and the switch forwards no frames out the interface, with the exception of STP messages.

Boolean AND   A math operation performed on a pair of one-digit binary numbers. The result is another one-digit binary number. 1 AND 1 yields 1; all other combinations yield a 0.

BPDU   Bridge protocol data unit. The generic name for Spanning Tree Protocol messages.

BPDU Guard   A Cisco switch feature that listens for incoming STP BPDU messages, disabling the interface if any are received. The goal is to prevent loops when a switch connects to a port expected to only have a host connected to it.

bridge ID (BID)   An 8-byte identifier for bridges and switches used by STP and RSTP. It is composed of a 2-byte priority field followed by a 6-byte System ID field that is usually filled with a MAC address.

bridge protocol data unit   *See* BPDU.

broadcast address   Generally, any address that represents all devices, and can be used to send one message to all devices. In Ethernet, the MAC address of all binary 1s, or FFFF.FFFF.FFFF in hex. For IPv4, *see* subnet broadcast address.

broadcast domain   A set of all devices that receive broadcast frames originating from any device within the set. Devices in the same VLAN are in the same broadcast domain.

broadcast frame   An Ethernet frame sent to destination address FFFF.FFFF.FFFF, meaning that the frame should be delivered to all hosts on that LAN.

broadcast subnet   When subnetting a Class A, B, or C network, the one subnet in each classful network for which all subnet bits have a value of binary 1. The subnet broadcast address in this subnet has the same numeric value as the classful network's networkwide broadcast address.

C

cable Internet   An Internet access technology that uses a cable TV (CATV) cable, normally used for video, to send and receive data.

CAPWAP   A standards-based tunneling protocol that defines communication between a lightweight AP and a wireless LAN controller.

cell   The area of wireless coverage provided by an AP; also known as the basic service area.

centralized WLC deployment   *See* unified WLC deployment.

certificate authority (CA)   A trusted entity that generates and signs digital certificates.

channel   An arbitrary index that points to a specific frequency within a band.

Channel-group   One term Cisco switches use to reference a bundle of links that are, in some respects, treated like a single link. Other similar terms include *EtherChannel* and *PortChannel*.

CIDR   Classless interdomain routing. An RFC-standard tool for global IP address range assignment. CIDR reduces the size of Internet routers' IP routing tables, helping deal with the rapid growth of the Internet. The term *classless* refers to the fact that the summarized groups of networks represent a group of addresses that do not conform to IPv4 classful (Class A, B, and C) grouping rules.

CIDR mask   Another term for a prefix mask, one that uses prefix or CIDR notation, in which the mask is represented by a slash (/) followed by a decimal number.

CIDR notation   *See* prefix notation.

cladding   In fiber-optic cabling, the second layer of the cable, surrounding the core of the cable, with the property of reflecting light back into the core.

classful addressing   A concept in IPv4 addressing that defines a subnetted IP address as having three parts: network, subnet, and host.

classful IP network   An IPv4 Class A, B, or C network; called a classful network because these networks are defined by the class rules for IPv4 addressing.

classful routing protocol   Does not transmit the mask information along with the subnet number and therefore must consider Class A, B, and C network boundaries and perform autosummarization at those boundaries. Does not support VLSM.

classless addressing   A concept in IPv4 addressing that defines a subnetted IP address as having two parts: a prefix (or subnet) and a host.

classless interdomain routing   The name of an RFC that defines several important features related to public IPv4 addressing: a global address assignment strategy to keep the size of IPv4 routing tables smaller, and the ability to assign public IPv4 addresses in sizes based on any prefix length.

classless prefix   A range of public IPv4 addresses as defined by CIDR.

classless prefix length   The mask (prefix length) used when defining a classless prefix.

classless routing protocol   An inherent characteristic of a routing protocol, specifically that the routing protocol does send subnet masks in its routing updates, thereby removing any need to make assumptions about the addresses in a particular subnet or network, making it able to support VLSM and manual route summarization.

CLI   Command-line interface. An interface that enables the user to interact with the operating system by entering commands and optional arguments.

clock rate   The speed at which a serial link encodes bits on the transmission medium.

clock source   The device to which the other devices on the link adjust their speed when using synchronous links.

clocking   The process of supplying a signal over a cable, either on a separate pin on a serial cable or as part of the signal transitions in the transmitted signal so that the receiving device can keep synchronization with the sending device.

cloud-based AP   A wireless AP operating much like an autonomous AP, but having management and control functions present in the Internet cloud.

cloud-based WLC deployment   A wireless network design that places a WLC centrally within a network topology, as a virtual machine in the private cloud portion of a data center.

collapsed core design   A campus LAN design in which the design does not use a separate set of core switches in addition to the distribution switches—in effect collapsing the core into the distribution switches.

collision domain   A set of network interface cards (NIC) for which a frame sent by one NIC could result in a collision with a frame sent by any other NIC in the same collision domain.

command-line interface   *See* CLI.

configuration mode   A part of the Cisco IOS Software CLI in which the user can type configuration commands that are then added to the device's currently used configuration file (running-config).

connected   The single-item status code listed by a **switch show interfaces status** command, with this status referring to a working interface.

connected route   On a router, an IP route added to the routing table when the router interface is both up and has an IP address configured. The route is for the subnet that can be calculated based on the configured IP address and mask.

console port A physical socket on a router or switch to which a cable can be connected between a computer and the router/switch, for the purpose of allowing the computer to use a terminal emulator and use the CLI to configure, verify, and troubleshoot the router/switch.

contiguous network A network topology in which subnets of network X are not separated by subnets of any other classful network.

convergence The time required for routing protocols to react to changes in the network, removing bad routes and adding new, better routes so that the current best routes are in all the routers' routing tables.

core In fiber-optic cabling, the center cylinder of the cable, made of fiberglass, through which light passes.

core design A campus LAN design that connects each access switch to distribution switches, and distribution switches into core switches, to provide a path between all LAN devices.

Counter/CBC-MAC Protocol (CCMP) A wireless security scheme based on 802.11i that uses AES counter mode for encryption and CBC-MAC for data integrity

crossover cable An Ethernet cable that swaps the pair used for transmission on one device to a pair used for receiving on the device on the opposite end of the cable. In 10BASE-T and 100BASE-TX networks, this cable swaps the pair at pins 1,2 to pins 3,6 on the other end of the cable, and the pair at pins 3,6 to pins 1,2 as well.

CSMA/CD Carrier sense multiple access with collision detection. A media-access mechanism in which devices ready to transmit data first check the channel for a carrier. If no carrier is sensed for a specific period of time, a device can transmit. If two devices transmit at once, a collision occurs and is detected by all colliding devices. This collision subsequently delays retransmissions from those devices for some random length of time.

CSU/DSU Channel service unit/data service unit. A device that understands the Layer 1 details of serial links installed by a telco and how to use a serial cable to communicate with networking equipment such as routers.

D

data VLAN A VLAN used by typical data devices connected to an Ethernet, like PCs and servers. Used in comparison to a voice VLAN.

Database Description An OSPF packet type that lists brief descriptions of the LSAs in the OSPF LSDB.

DCE Data communications equipment. From a physical layer perspective, the device providing the clocking on a WAN link, typically a CSU/DSU, is the DCE. From a packet-switching perspective, the service provider's switch, to which a router might connect, is considered the DCE.

DDN *See* dotted-decimal notation.

Dead Interval In OSPF, a timer used for each neighbor. A router considers the neighbor to have failed if no Hellos are received from that neighbor in the time defined by the timer.

decimal mask   An IPv4 subnet mask written in dotted-decimal notation; for example, 255.255.255.0.

de-encapsulation   On a computer that receives data over a network, the process in which the device interprets the lower-layer headers and, when finished with each header, removes the header, revealing the next-higher-layer PDU.

default gateway/default router   On an IP host, the IP address of some router to which the host sends packets when the packet's destination address is on a subnet other than the local subnet.

default mask   The mask used in a Class A, B, or C network that does not create any subnets; specifically, mask 255.0.0.0 for Class A networks, 255.255.0.0 for Class B networks, and 255.255.255.0 for Class C networks.

default route   On a router, the route that is considered to match all packets that are not otherwise matched by some more specific route.

default VLAN   A reference to the default setting of 1 (meaning VLAN ID 1) on the **switchport access vlan** *vlan-id* **interface** subcommand on Cisco switches, meaning that by default, a port will be assigned to VLAN 1 if acting as an access port.

designated port   In both STP and RSTP, a port role used to determine which of multiple interfaces on multiple switches, each connected to the same segment or collision domain, should forward frames to the segment. The switch advertising the lowest-cost Hello BPDU onto the segment becomes the DP.

designated router   In OSPF, on a multiaccess network, the router that wins an election and is therefore responsible for managing a streamlined process for exchanging OSPF topology information between all routers attached to that network.

DHCP   Dynamic Host Configuration Protocol. A protocol used by hosts to dynamically discover and lease an IP address, and learn the correct subnet mask, default gateway, and DNS server IP addresses.

DHCP client   Any device that uses DHCP protocols to ask to lease an IP address from a DHCP server, or to learn any IP settings from that server.

Dijkstra Shortest Path First (SPF) algorithm   The name of the algorithm used by link-state routing protocols to analyze the LSDB and find the least-cost routes from that router to each subnet.

directed broadcast address   *See* subnet broadcast address.

disabled port   In STP, a port role for nonworking interfaces—in other words, interfaces that are not in a connect or up/up interface state.

discarding state   An RSTP interface state in which no received frames are processed and the switch forwards no frames out the interface, with the exception of RSTP messages.

discontiguous network   A network topology in which subnets of network X are separated by subnets of some other classful network.

distance vector   The logic behind the behavior of some interior routing protocols, such as RIP. Distance vector routing algorithms call for each router to send its entire routing table in each update, but only to its neighbors. Distance vector routing algorithms can be prone to routing loops but are computationally simpler than link-state routing algorithms.

distribution layer   In a campus LAN design, the switches that connect to access layer switches as the most efficient means to provide connectivity from the access layer into the other parts of the LAN.

distribution system (DS)   The wired Ethernet that connects to an AP and transports traffic between a wired and wireless network.

DNS   Domain Name System. An application layer protocol used throughout the Internet for translating hostnames into their associated IP addresses.

DNS Reply   In the Domain Name System (DNS), a message sent by a DNS server to a DNS client in response to a DNS Request, identifying the IP address assigned to a particular hostname or fully qualified domain name (FQDN).

DNS Request   In the Domain Name System (DNS), a message sent by a DNS client to a DNS server, listing a hostname or fully qualified domain name (FQDN), asking the server to discover and reply with the IP address associated with that hostname or FQDN.

dotted-decimal notation (DDN)   The format used for IP version 4 addresses, in which four decimal values are used, separated by periods (dots).

DSL   Digital subscriber line. Public network technology that delivers high bandwidth over conventional telco local-loop copper wiring at limited distances. Typically used as an Internet access technology, connecting a user to an ISP.

DSL modem   A device that connects to a telephone line, using DSL standards, to transmit and receive data to/from a telco using DSL.

DTE   Data terminal equipment. From a Layer 1 perspective, the DTE synchronizes its clock based on the clock sent by the DCE. From a packet-switching perspective, the DTE is the device outside the service provider's network, typically a router.

dual stack   A mode of operation in which a host or router runs both IPv4 and IPv6.

duplex mismatch   On opposite ends of any Ethernet link, the condition in which one of the two devices uses full-duplex logic and the other uses half-duplex logic, resulting in unnecessary frame discards and retransmissions on the link.

duplicate address detection (DAD)   A term used in IPv6 to refer to how hosts first check whether another host is using a unicast address before the first host uses that address.

E

EAP Flexible Authentication by Secure Tunneling (EAP-FAST)   A Cisco authentication method that is based on EAP and uses a PAC as a credential for outer authentication and a TLS tunnel for inner authentication

EAP Transport Layer Security (EAP-TLS)   An authentication method that uses digital certificates on both the server and the supplicant for mutual authentication. A TLS tunnel is used during client authentication and key exchanges.

EIGRP   Enhanced Interior Gateway Routing Protocol. An advanced version of IGRP developed by Cisco. Provides superior convergence properties and operating efficiency and combines the advantages of link-state protocols with those of distance vector protocols.

EIGRP version 6   The version of the EIGRP routing protocol that supports IPv6, and not IPv4.

electromagnetic interference (EMI)   The name of the effect in which electricity passes through one cable as normal, inducing a magnetic field outside the conductor. That magnetic field, if it passes through another conductor, like a nearby cable, induces new electrical current in the second cable, interfering with the use of electricity to transmit data on the second cable.

embedded WLC deployment   A wireless network design that places a WLC in the access layer, co-located with a LAN switch stack, near the APs it controls.

enable mode   A part of the Cisco IOS CLI in which the user can use the most powerful and potentially disruptive commands on a router or switch, including the ability to then reach configuration mode and reconfigure the router.

encapsulation   The placement of data from a higher-layer protocol behind the header (and in some cases, between a header and trailer) of the next-lower-layer protocol. For example, an IP packet could be encapsulated in an Ethernet header and trailer before being sent over an Ethernet.

encryption   Applying a specific algorithm to data to alter the appearance of the data, making it incomprehensible to those who are not authorized to see the information.

enterprise mode   802.1x EAP-based authentication requirement for WPA, WPA2, and WPA3.

enterprise router   A term to describe the general role of a router as a router at a permanent site owned or leased by the enterprise, like an office building, manufacturing facility, branch office, or retail location. These sites typically have enough users to justify separate routers, switches, and wireless access points, and are more likely to justify private WAN services, in comparison to SOHO routers.

error detection   The process of discovering whether a data-link level frame was changed during transmission. This process typically uses a Frame Check Sequence (FCS) field in the data-link trailer.

error disabled   An interface state on LAN switches that can be the result of one of many security violations.

error recovery   The process of noticing when some transmitted data was not successfully received and resending the data until it is successfully received.

EtherChannel   A feature in which up to eight parallel Ethernet segments exist between the same two devices, each using the same speed. May be a Layer 2 EtherChannel, which acts like a single link for forwarding and Spanning Tree Protocol logic, or a Layer 3 EtherChannel, which acts like a single link for the switch's Layer 3 routing logic.

EtherChannel Load Distribution   The logic used by switches when forwarding messages over EtherChannels by which the switch chooses the specific physical link out which the switch will forward the frame.

Ethernet   A series of LAN standards defined by the IEEE, originally invented by Xerox Corporation and developed jointly by Xerox, Intel, and Digital Equipment Corporation.

Ethernet address   A 48-bit (6-byte) binary number, usually written as a 12-digit hexadecimal number, used to identify Ethernet nodes in an Ethernet network. Ethernet frame headers list a destination and source address field, used by the Ethernet devices to deliver Ethernet frames to the correct destination.

Ethernet frame   A term referring to an Ethernet data-link header and trailer, plus the data encapsulated between the header and trailer.

Ethernet Line Service (E-Line)   A specific carrier/metro Ethernet service defined by MEF (MEF.net) that provides a point-to-point topology between two customer devices, much as if the two devices were connected using an Ethernet crossover cable.

Ethernet link   A generic term for any physical link between two Ethernet nodes, no matter what type of cabling is used.

Ethernet over MPLS (EoMPLS)   A term referring specifically to how a service provider can create an Ethernet WAN service using an MPLS network. More generally, a term referring to Ethernet WAN services.

Ethernet port   A generic term for the opening on the side of any Ethernet node, typically in an Ethernet NIC or LAN switch, into which an Ethernet cable can be connected.

EtherType   Jargon that shortens the term *Ethernet Type*, which refers to the Type field in the Ethernet header. The Type field identifies the type of packet encapsulated inside an Ethernet frame.

EUI-64   Literally, a standard for an extended unique identifier that is 64 bits long. Specifically for IPv6, a set of rules for forming a 64-bit identifier, used as the interface ID in IPv6 addresses, by starting with a 48-bit MAC address, inserting FFFE (hex) in the middle, and inverting the seventh bit.

extended ping   An IOS command in which the **ping** command accepts many other options besides just the destination IP address.

extended service set (ESS)   Multiple APs that are connected by a common switched infrastructure.

Extensible Authentication Protocol (EAP)   A standardized authentication framework that is used by a variety of authentication methods

F

Fast Ethernet   The common name for all the IEEE standards that send data at 100 megabits per second.

fiber-optic cable   A type of cabling that uses glass fiber as a medium through which to transmit light.

filter   Generally, a process or a device that screens network traffic for certain characteristics, such as source address, destination address, or protocol, and determines whether to forward or discard that traffic based on the established criteria.

firewall   A device that forwards packets between the less secure and more secure parts of the network, applying rules that determine which packets are allowed to pass and which are not.

flash memory   A type of read/write permanent memory that retains its contents even with no power applied to the memory, and uses no moving parts, making the memory less likely to fail over time.

floating static route   A static IP route that uses a higher administrative distance than other routes, typically routes learned by a routing protocol. As a result, the router will not use the static route if the routing protocol route has been learned, but then use the static route if the routing protocol fails to learn the route.

flood/flooding   The result of the LAN switch forwarding process for broadcasts and unknown unicast frames. Switches forward these frames out all interfaces, except the interface in which the frame arrived. Switches also flood multicasts by default, although this behavior can be changed.

forward   To send a frame received in one interface out another interface, toward its ultimate destination.

forward delay   An STP timer, defaulting to 15 seconds, used to dictate how long an interface stays in the listening state and the time spent in learning state. Also called the forward delay timer.

forward route   From one host's perspective, the route over which a packet travels from that host to some other host.

forward secrecy   A key exchange method used in WPA3 that prevents attackers from being able to use a discovered pre-shared key to unencrypt data that has already been transmitted over the air

forwarding state   An STP and RSTP port state in which an interface operates unrestricted by STP.

frame   A term referring to a data-link header and trailer, plus the data encapsulated between the header and trailer.

Frame Check Sequence   A field in many data-link trailers used as part of the error-detection process.

full duplex   Generically, any communication in which two communicating devices can concurrently send and receive data. In Ethernet LANs, the allowance for both devices to send and receive at the same time, allowed when both devices disable their CSMA/CD logic.

full state   In OSPF, a neighbor state that implies that the two routers have exchanged the complete (full) contents of their respective LSDBs.

full update   With IP routing protocols, the general concept that a routing protocol update lists all known routes.

fully adjacent   In OSPF, a characterization of the state of a neighbor in which the two neighbors have reached the full state.

fully adjacent neighbor   In OSPF, a neighbor with which the local router has also reached the OSPF full state, meaning that the two routers have exchanged their LSDBs directly with each other.

G

Galois/Counter Mode Protocol (GCMP)   A strong encryption method used in the WPA3 wireless security model.

Gigabit Ethernet   The common name for all the IEEE standards that send data at 1 gigabit per second.

global routing prefix   An IPv6 prefix that defines an IPv6 address block made up of global unicast addresses, assigned to one organization, so that the organization has a block of globally unique IPv6 addresses to use in its network.

global unicast address   A type of unicast IPv6 address that has been allocated from a range of public globally unique IP addresses, as registered through IANA/ICANN, its member agencies, and other registries or ISPs.

H

half duplex   Generically, any communication in which only one device at a time can send data. In Ethernet LANs, the normal result of the CSMA/CD algorithm that enforces the rule that only one device should send at any point in time.

HDLC   High-Level Data Link Control. A bit-oriented synchronous data-link layer protocol developed by the International Organization for Standardization (ISO).

header   In computer networking, a set of bytes placed in front of some other data, encapsulating that data, as defined by a particular protocol.

Hello (Multiple definitions)   1) A protocol used by OSPF routers to discover, establish, and maintain neighbor relationships. 2) A protocol used by EIGRP routers to discover, establish, and maintain neighbor relationships. 3) In STP, refers to the name of the periodic message sourced by the root bridge in a spanning tree.

Hello BPDU   The STP and RSTP message used for the majority of STP communications, listing the root's bridge ID, the sending device's bridge ID, and the sending device's cost with which to reach the root.

Hello Interval   With OSPF and EIGRP, an interface timer that dictates how often the router should send Hello messages.

Hello timer   In STP, the time interval at which the root switch should send Hello BPDUs.

history buffer   In a Cisco router or switch, the function by which IOS keeps a list of commands that the user has used in this login session, both in EXEC mode and configuration mode. The user can then recall these commands for easier repeating or making small edits and issuing similar commands.

hop count   The metric used by the RIP routing protocol. Each router in an IP route is considered a hop, so for example, if two other routers sit between a router and some subnet, that router would have a hop count of two for that route.

host   Any device that uses an IP address.

host address   The IP address assigned to a network card on a computer.

host part   A term used to describe a part of an IPv4 address that is used to uniquely identify a host inside a subnet. The host part is identified by the bits of value 0 in the subnet mask.

host route   A route with a /32 mask, which by virtue of this mask represents a route to a single host IP address.

hostname   The alphanumeric name of an IP host.

hub   A LAN device that provides a centralized connection point for LAN cabling, repeating any received electrical signal out all other ports, thereby creating a logical bus. Hubs do not interpret the electrical signals as a frame of bits, so hubs are considered to be Layer 1 devices.

I

IANA   The Internet Assigned Numbers Authority (IANA). An organization that owns the rights to assign many operating numbers and facts about how the global Internet works, including public IPv4 and IPv6 addresses. *See also* ICANN.

ICANN   The Internet Corporation for Assigned Names and Numbers. An organization appointed by IANA to oversee the distributed process of assigning public IPv4 and IPv6 addresses across the globe.

ICMP   Internet Control Message Protocol. A TCP/IP network layer protocol that reports errors and provides other information relevant to IP packet processing.

ICMP echo reply   One type of ICMP message, created specifically to be used as the message sent by the ping command to test connectivity in a network. The ping command expects to receive these messages from other hosts, after the ping command first sends an ICMP echo request message to the host.

ICMP echo request   One type of ICMP message, created specifically to be used as the message sent by the ping command to test connectivity in a network. The ping command sends these messages to other hosts, expecting the other host to reply with an ICMP echo reply message.

IEEE   Institute of Electrical and Electronics Engineers. A professional organization that develops communications and network standards, among other activities.

IEEE 802.1 AD   The IEEE standard for the functional equivalent of the Cisco-proprietary EtherChannel.

IEEE 802.11   The IEEE base standard for wireless LANs.

IEEE 802.1Q   The IEEE standard VLAN trunking protocol. 802.1Q includes the concept of a native VLAN, for which no VLAN header is added, and a 4-byte VLAN header is inserted after the original frame's Type/Length field.

IEEE 802.2   An IEEE LAN protocol that specifies an implementation of the LLC sublayer of the data-link layer.

IEEE 802.3   A set of IEEE LAN protocols that specifies the many variations of what is known today as an Ethernet LAN.

IEEE 802.3 AD   The IEEE standard for the functional equivalent of the Cisco-proprietary EtherChannel.

IETF   The Internet Engineering Task Force. The IETF serves as the primary organization that works directly to create new TCP/IP standards.

IGP   *See* interior gateway protocol.

inactivity timer   For switch MAC address tables, a timer associated with each entry that counts time upward from 0 and is reset to 0 each time a switch receives a frame with the same MAC address. The entries with the largest timers can be removed to make space for additional MAC address table entries.

independent basic service set (IBSS)   An impromptu wireless network formed between two or more devices without an AP or a BSS; also known as an ad hoc network.

infrastructure mode   The operating mode of an AP that is providing a BSS for wireless clients.

Integrated Services Router (ISR)   Cisco's long-running term for several different model series of Enterprise-class routers, intended mostly for use as enterprise routers and some use as SOHO routers. ISR routers first serve as routers but, depending on the family or specific model, support all current types of WAN connections (private and Internet), LAN switching ports, Wireless APs, VPNs, and other integrated functions supported in a single device.

interface bandwidth   In OSPF, the numerator in the calculation of an interface's default OSPF cost metric, calculated as the interface bandwidth divided by the reference bandwidth.

interface-local scope   A concept in IPv6 for which packets sent to an address using this scope should not physically exit the interface, keeping the packet inside the sending host.

interior gateway protocol (IGP)   A routing protocol designed to be used to exchange routing information inside a single autonomous system.

interior routing protocol   A synonym of interior gateway protocol. *See* interior gateway protocol.

Internal Border Gateway Protocol (iBGP)   The use of BGP between two routers in the same ASN, with different rules compared to External BGP (eBGP).

internal router   In OSPF, a router with all interfaces in the same nonbackbone area.

Internetwork Operating System   The operating system (OS) of Cisco routers and switches, which provides the majority of a router's or switch's features, with the hardware providing the remaining features.

Inter-Switch Link (ISL)   The Cisco-proprietary VLAN trunking protocol that predated 802.IQ by many years. ISL defines a 26-byte header that encapsulates the original Ethernet frame.

IOS   *See* Internetwork Operating System.

IP   Internet Protocol. The network layer protocol in the TCP/IP stack, providing routing and logical addressing standards and services.

IP address (IP version 4)   In IP version 4 (IPv4), a 32-bit address assigned to hosts using TCP/IP. Each address consists of a network number, an optional subnetwork number, and a host number. The network and subnetwork numbers together are used for routing, and the host number is used to address an individual host within the network or subnetwork.

IP address (IP version 6)   In IP version 6 (IPv6), a 128-bit address assigned to hosts using TCP/IP. Addresses use different formats, commonly using a routing prefix, subnet, and interface ID, corresponding to the IPv4 network, subnet, and host parts of an address.

IP network   *See* classful IP network.

IP packet   An IP header, followed by the data encapsulated after the IP header, but specifically not including any headers and trailers for layers below the network layer.

IP routing table   *See* routing table.

IP subnet   Subdivisions of a Class A, B, or C network, as configured by a network administrator. Subnets allow a single Class A, B, or C network to be used instead of multiple networks, and still allow for a large number of groups of IP addresses, as is required for efficient IP routing.

IP version 4   Literally, the version of the Internet Protocol defined in an old RFC 791, standardized in 1980, and used as the basis of TCP/IP networks and the Internet for over 30 years.

IP version 6   A newer version of the Internet Protocol defined in RFC 2460, as well as many other RFCs, whose creation was motivated by the need to avoid the IPv4 address exhaustion problem.

IPv4   *See* IP version 4.

IPv4 address exhaustion   The process by which the public IPv4 addresses, available to create the Internet, were consumed through the 1980s until today, with the expectation that eventually the world would run out of available IPv4 addresses.

IPv6   *See* IP version 6.

IPv6 address scope   The concept of how far an IPv6 packet should be forwarded by hosts and routers in an IPv6 network. Includes interface-local, link-local, site-local, and organization-local scopes.

IPv6 administrative distance   In Cisco routers, a means for one router to choose between multiple IPv6 routes to reach the same subnet when those routes were learned by different routing protocols. The lower the administrative distance, the better the source of the routing information.

IPv6 host route   A route with a /128 mask, which by virtue of this mask represents a route to a single host IPv6 address.

IPv6 local route   A route added to an IPv6 router's routing table for the router's interface IP address, with a /128 mask, which by virtue of this mask represents a route to only that router's IPv4 address.

IPv6 multicast scope   The idea of how far away from the sending host an IPv6 multicast packet should be forwarded, as based on the value in the 4th hex digit of the multicast address.

IPv6 neighbor table   The IPv6 equivalent of the ARP table. A table that lists IPv6 addresses of other hosts on the same link, along with their matching MAC addresses, as typically learned using Neighbor Discovery Protocol (NDP).

ISL   Inter-Switch Link. A Cisco-proprietary protocol that maintains VLAN information as traffic flows between switches and routers.

ISO   International Organization for Standardization. An international organization that is responsible for a wide range of standards, including many standards relevant to networking. The ISO developed the OSI reference model, a popular networking reference model.

K–L

keepalive   A proprietary feature of Cisco routers in which the router sends messages on a periodic basis as a means of letting the neighboring router know that the first router is still alive and well.

known unicast frame   An Ethernet frame whose destination MAC address is listed in a switch's MAC address table, so the switch will forward the frame out the one port associated with that entry in the MAC address table.

L2PDU   Layer 2 protocol data unit. Often called a frame. The data compiled by a Layer 2 protocol, including Layer 2 header, encapsulated high-layer data, and Layer 2 trailer.

L3PDU   Layer 3 protocol data unit. Often called a packet. The data compiled by a Layer 3 protocol, including Layer 3 headers and the encapsulated high-layer data, but not including lower-layer headers and trailers.

L4PDU   Layer 4 protocol data unit. Often called a segment. The data compiled by a Layer 4 protocol, including Layer 4 headers and encapsulated high-layer data, but not including lower-layer headers and trailers.

LACP   Link Aggregation Control Protocol is a messaging protocol defined by the IEEE 802.3ad standard that enables two neighboring devices to realize that they have multiple parallel links connecting to each other and then to decide which links can be combined into an EtherChannel.

Layer 2 EtherChannel (L2 EtherChannel)   An EtherChannel that acts as a switched port (that is, not a routed port), and as such, is used by a switch's Layer 2 forwarding logic. As a result, the Layer 2 switch lists the Layer 2 EtherChannel in switch MAC address tables, and when forwarding a frame based on one of these MAC table entries, the switch balances traffic across the various ports in the Layer 2 EtherChannel.

Layer 3 EtherChannel (L3 EtherChannel)   An EtherChannel that acts as a routed port (that is, not a switched port), and as such, is used by a switch's Layer 3 forwarding logic. As a result, the Layer 3 switch lists the Layer 3 EtherChannel in various routes in the switch's IP routing table, with the switch balancing traffic across the various ports in the Layer 3 EtherChannel.

Layer 3 protocol   A protocol that has characteristics like OSI Layer 3, which defines logical addressing and routing. IPv4 and IPv6 are Layer 3 protocols.

Layer 3 switch   *See* multilayer switch.

learning   The process used by switches for discovering MAC addresses, and their relative location, by looking at the source MAC address of all frames received by a bridge or switch.

learning state   In STP, a temporary port state in which the interface does not forward frames, but it can begin to learn MAC addresses from frames received on the interface.

leased line   A serial communications circuit between two points, provided by some service provider, typically a telephone company (telco). Because the telco does not sell a physical cable between the two endpoints, instead charging a monthly fee for the ability to send bits between the two sites, the service is considered to be a leased service.

lightweight AP   A wireless AP that performs real-time 802.11 functions to interface with wireless clients, while relying on a wireless LAN controller to handle all management functions.

Lightweight EAP (LEAP)   A legacy Cisco proprietary wireless security method.

link state   A classification of the underlying algorithm used in some routing protocols. Link-state protocols build a detailed database that lists links (subnets) and their state (up, down), from which the best routes can then be calculated.

link-local address   A unicast IPv6 address that begins FE80, used on each IPv6-enabled interface, used for sending packets within the attached link by applying a link-local scope.

link-local multicast address   A multicast IPv6 address that begins with FF02, with the fourth digit of 2 identifying the scope as link-local, to which devices apply a link-local scope.

link-local scope   With IPv6 multicasts, a term that refers to the parts (scope) of the network to which a multicast packet can flow, with link-local referring to the fact that the packet stays on the subnet in which it originated.

link-state advertisement (LSA)   In OSPF, the name of the data structure that resides inside the LSDB and describes in detail the various components in a network, including routers and links (subnets).

link-state database (LSDB)   In OSPF, the data structure in RAM of a router that holds the various LSAs, with the collective LSAs representing the entire topology of the network.

Link-State Request   An OSPF packet used to ask a neighboring router to send a particular LSA.

Link-State Update   An OSPF packet used to send an LSA to a neighboring router.

listening state   A temporary STP port state that occurs immediately when a blocking interface must be moved to a forwarding state. The switch times out MAC table entries during this state. It also ignores frames received on the interface and doesn't forward any frames out the interface.

LLC   Logical Link Control. The higher of the two sublayers of the data-link layer defined by the IEEE. Synonymous with IEEE 802.2.

local broadcast IP address   IPv4 address 255.255.255.255. A packet sent to this address is sent as a data-link broadcast, but only flows to hosts in the subnet into which it was originally sent. Routers do not forward these packets.

local mode   The default mode of a Cisco lightweight AP that offers one or more functioning BSSs on a specific channel.

local route   A route added to an IPv4 router's routing table for the router's interface IP address, with a /32 mask, which by virtue of this mask represents a route to only that router's IPv4 address.

local username   A username (with matching password), configured on a router or switch. It is considered local because it exists on the router or switch, and not on a remote server.

logical address   A generic reference to addresses as defined by Layer 3 protocols that do not have to be concerned with the physical details of the underlying physical media. Used mainly to contrast these addresses with data-link addresses, which are generically considered to be physical addresses because they differ based on the type of physical medium.

LSA   *See* link-state advertisement.

LSDB   *See* link-state database.

M

MAC   Media Access Control. The lower of the two sublayers of the data-link layer defined by the IEEE. Synonymous with IEEE 802.3 for Ethernet LANs.

MAC address   A standardized data-link layer address that is required for every device that connects to a LAN. Ethernet MAC addresses are 6 bytes long and are controlled by the IEEE. Also known as a hardware address, a MAC layer address, and a physical address.

MAC address table   A table of forwarding information held by a Layer 2 switch, built dynamically by listening to incoming frames and used by the switch to match frames to make decisions about where to forward the frame.

MaxAge   In STP, a timer that states how long a switch should wait when it no longer receives Hellos from the root switch before acting to reconverge the STP topology. Also called the MaxAge timer.

maximum paths   In Cisco IOS, a reference to the number of equal cost routes (paths) to reach a single subnet that IOS will add to the IP routing table at the same time.

MD5 hash   A specific mathematical algorithm intended for use in various security protocols. In the context of Cisco routers and switches, the devices store the MD5 hash of certain passwords, rather than the passwords themselves, in an effort to make the device more secure.

media access control (MAC) layer   A low-level function performed as part of Layer 2; in wireless networks, this function can be divided between a wireless LAN controller and a lightweight AP to form a split-MAC architecture.

mesh network   A network of APs used to cover a large area without the need for wired Ethernet cabling; client traffic is bridged from AP to AP over a backhaul network.

message integrity check (MIC)   A cryptographic value computed from the contents of a data frame and used to detect tampering.

message of the day   One type of login banner that can be defined on a Cisco router or switch.

metric   A unit of measure used by routing protocol algorithms to determine the best route for traffic to use to reach a particular destination.

Mobility Express WLC deployment   A wireless network design that places a WLC co-located with a lightweight AP.

Modified EUI-64   *See* EUI-64.

multiarea   In OSPFv2 and OSPFv3, a design that uses multiple areas.

multicast IP address   A class D IPv4 address. When used as a destination address in a packet, the routers collectively work to deliver copies of the one original packet to all hosts who have previously registered to receive packets sent to that particular multicast address.

multilayer switch   A LAN switch that can also perform Layer 3 routing functions. The name comes from the fact that this device makes forwarding decisions based on logic from multiple OSI layers (Layers 2 and 3).

multimode fiber   A type of fiber cable that works well with transmitters like LEDs that emit multiple angles of light into the core of the cable; to accommodate the multiple angles of incident, the cable has a larger core in comparison to single-mode fiber cables.

N

name resolution   The process by which an IP host discovers the IP address associated with a hostname, often involving sending a DNS request to a DNS server, with the server supplying the IP address used by a host with the listed hostname.

name server   A server connected to a network that resolves network names into network addresses.

NAT   Network Address Translation. A mechanism for reducing the need for globally unique IP addresses. NAT allows an organization with addresses that are not globally unique to connect to the Internet, by translating those addresses into public addresses in the globally routable address space.

native VLAN   The one VLAN ID on any 802.1Q VLAN trunk for which the trunk forwards frames without an 802.1Q header.

neighbor   In routing protocols, another router with which a router decides to exchange routing information.

Neighbor Advertisement (NA)   A message defined by the IPv6 Neighbor Discovery Protocol (NDP), used to declare to other neighbors a host's MAC address. Sometimes sent in response to a previously received NDP Neighbor Solicitation (NS) message.

Neighbor Discovery Protocol (NDP)   A protocol that is part of the IPv6 protocol suite, used to discover and exchange information about devices on the same subnet (neighbors). In particular, it replaces the IPv4 ARP protocol.

Neighbor Solicitation (NS)   A message defined by the IPv6 Neighbor Discovery Protocol (NDP), used to ask a neighbor to reply with a Neighbor Advertisement, which lists the neighbor's MAC address.

neighbor table   For OSPF and EIGRP, a list of routers that have reached neighbor status.

network   A collection of computers, printers, routers, switches, and other devices that can communicate with each other over some transmission medium.

network address   *See* network number.

network broadcast address   In IPv4, a special address in each classful network that can be used to broadcast a packet to all hosts in that same classful network. Numerically, the address has the same value as the network number in the network part of the address and all 255s in the host octets; for example, 10.255.255.255 is the network broadcast address for classful network 10.0.0.0.

network ID   A number that identifies an IPv4 network, using a number in dotted-decimal notation (like IP addresses); a number that represents any single Class A, B, or C IP network.

network interface card (NIC)   A computer card, sometimes an expansion card and sometimes integrated into the motherboard of the computer, that provides the electronics and other functions to connect to a computer network. Today, most NICs are specifically Ethernet NICs, and most have an RJ-45 port, the most common type of Ethernet port.

Network LSA In OSPF, a type of LSA that a designated router (DR) creates for the network (subnet) for which the DR is helping to distribute LSAs.

network number A number that uses dotted-decimal notation like IP addresses, but the number itself represents all hosts in a single Class A, B, or C IP network.

network part The portion of an IPv4 address that is either 1, 2, or 3 octets/bytes long, based on whether the address is in a Class A, B, or C network.

network route A route for a classful network.

networking model A generic term referring to any set of protocols and standards collected into a comprehensive grouping that, when followed by the devices in a network, allows all the devices to communicate. Examples include TCP/IP and OSI.

next-hop router In an IP route in a routing table, part of a routing table entry that refers to the next IP router (by IP address) that should receive packets that match the route.

NIC *See* network interface card.

nonoverlapping channels Successive channel numbers in a band that each have a frequency range that is narrow enough to not overlap the next channel above or below.

NVRAM Nonvolatile RAM. A type of random-access memory (RAM) that retains its contents when a unit is powered off.

O

open authentication An 802.11 authentication method that requires clients to associate with an AP without providing any credentials at all.

Organization-local scope A concept in IPv6 for which packets sent to an address using this scope should be forwarded by routers inside the organization but not over any links connected to other organizations or over links connected to the Internet.

OSI Open System Interconnection reference model. A network architectural model developed by the ISO. The model consists of seven layers, each of which specifies particular network functions, such as addressing, flow control, error control, encapsulation, and reliable message transfer.

OSPF Open Shortest Path First. A popular link-state IGP that uses a link-state database and the Shortest Path First (SPF) algorithm to calculate the best routes to reach each known subnet.

OSPF version 2 The version of the OSPF routing protocol that supports IPv4, and not IPv6, and has been commonly used for over 20 years.

OSPF version 3 The version of the OSPF routing protocol that originally supported only IPv6, and not IPv4, but now supports IPv4 through the use of address family configuration.

outgoing interface In an IP route in a routing table, part of a routing table entry that refers to the local interface out which the local router should forward packets that match the route.

overlapping subnets An (incorrect) IP subnet design condition in which one subnet's range of addresses includes addresses in the range of another subnet.

P

packet   A logical grouping of bytes that includes the network layer header and encapsulated data, but specifically does not include any headers and trailers below the network layer.

PagP   Port Aggregation Protocol (PAgP) is a messaging protocol defined by Cisco that enables two neighboring devices to realize that they have multiple parallel links connecting to each other and then to decide which links can be combined into an EtherChannel.

partial mesh   A network topology in which more than two devices could physically communicate but, by choice, only a subset of the pairs of devices connected to the network is allowed to communicate directly.

passive interface   With a routing protocol, a router interface for which the routing protocol is enabled on the interface, but for which the routing protocol does not send routing protocol messages out that interface.

patch cable   An Ethernet cable, usually short, that connects from a device's Ethernet port to a wall plate or switch. With wiring inside a building, electricians prewire from the wiring closet to each cubicle or other location, with a patch cable connecting the short distance from the wall plate to the user device.

PDU   Protocol data unit. An OSI term to refer generically to a grouping of information by a particular layer of the OSI model. More specifically, an LxPDU would imply the data and headers as defined by Layer x.

periodic update   With routing protocols, the concept that the routing protocol advertises routes in a routing update on a regular periodic basis. This is typical of distance vector routing protocols.

personal mode   Pre-shared key authentication as applied to WPA, WPA2, and WPA3.

ping   An Internet Control Message Protocol (ICMP) echo message and its reply; ping often is used in IP networks to test the reachability of a network device.

pinout   The documentation and implementation of which wires inside a cable connect to each pin position in any connector.

point-to-point bridge   An AP configured to bridge a wired network to a companion bridge at the far end of a line-of-sight path.

port   In TCP and UDP, a number that is used to uniquely identify the application process that either sent (source port) or should receive (destination port) data. In LAN switching, another term for *switch interface*.

PortChannel   One term Cisco switches use to reference a bundle of links that are, in some respects, treated like a single link. Other similar terms include *EtherChannel* and *Channel-group*.

PortFast   A switch STP feature in which a port is placed in an STP forwarding state as soon as the interface comes up, bypassing the listening and learning states. This feature is meant for ports connected to end-user devices.

Prefix (prefix ID)   In both IPv4 and IPv6, this term refers to the number that identifies a group of IPv4 or IPv6 addresses, respectively. Another term for *subnet identifier*.

prefix length   In IPv6, the number of bits in an IPv6 prefix.

prefix mask   A term to describe an IPv4 subnet mask when represented as a slash (/) followed by a decimal number. The decimal number is the number of binary 1s in the mask.

prefix notation (IP version 4)   A shorter way to write a subnet mask in which the number of binary 1s in the mask is simply written in decimal. For example, /24 denotes the subnet mask with 24 binary 1 bits in the subnet mask. The number of bits of value binary 1 in the mask is considered to be the prefix length.

primary root   This term refers to the switch configured with the primary keyword on the **spanning-tree vlan x root {primary | secondary}** command. At time of configuration, this command causes the switch to choose a new priority setting that makes the switch become the root switch in the network.

private addresses   IP addresses in several Class A, B, and C networks that are set aside for use inside private organizations. These addresses, as defined in RFC 1918, are not routable through the Internet.

private IP network   Any of the IPv4 Class A, B, or C networks as defined by RFC 1918, intended for use inside a company but not used as public IP networks.

protected access credential (PAC)   Special-purpose data that is used as an authentication credential in EAP-FAST.

Protected EAP (PEAP)   An authentication method that uses a certificate on the AS for outer authentication and a TLS tunnel for inner authentication. Clients can provide their credentials through either MS-CHAPv2 or GTC.

Protected Management Frame (PMF)   A service provided by WPA3 that protects a set of 802.11 robust management and action frames, to prevent spoofing of AP functions.

protocol data unit (PDU)   A generic term referring to the header defined by some layer of a networking model, and the data encapsulated by the header (and possibly trailer) of that layer, but specifically not including any lower-layer headers and trailers.

Protocol Type field   A field in a LAN header that identifies the type of header that follows the LAN header. Includes the DIX Ethernet Type field, the IEEE 802.2 DSAP field, and the SNAP protocol Type field.

public IP address   An IP address that is part of a registered network number, as assigned by an Internet Assigned Numbers Authority (IANA) member agency, so that only the organization to which the address is registered is allowed to use the address. Routers in the Internet should have routes allowing them to forward packets to all the publicly registered IP addresses.

public IP network   Any IPv4 Class A, B, or C network assigned for use by one organization only, so that the addresses in the network are unique across the Internet, allowing packets to be sent through the public Internet using the addresses.

Public Key Infrastructure (PKI)   An enterprisewide system that generates and revokes digital certificates for client authentication.

PVST+   An STP option in Cisco switches that creates an STP instance per VLAN. Cisco proprietary.

Q–R

quartet   A term used in this book, but not in other references, to refer to a set of four hex digits in an IPv6 address.

RADIUS server   An authentication server used with 802.1x to authenticate wireless clients.

RAM   Random-access memory. A type of volatile memory that can be read and written by a microprocessor.

Rapid PVST+   An STP option in Cisco switches that creates an RSTP instance per VLAN. Cisco proprietary.

Rapid Spanning Tree Protocol (RSTP)   Defined in IEEE 802.lw. Defines an improved version of STP that converges much more quickly and consistently than STP (802.Id).

reference bandwidth   In OSPF, a configurable value for the OSPF routing process, used by OSPF when calculating an interface's default OSPF cost metric, calculated as the interface's bandwidth divided by the reference bandwidth.

Regional Internet Registry   An organization (five globally) that receives allocations of public IPv4 addresses from IANA and then manages that address space in their major geographic region, performing public address allocations to ISPs and assignments directly to companies that use the addresses.

repeater   A device that repeats or retransmits signals it receives, effectively expanding the wireless coverage area.

resident subnet   Each IP subnet contains a number of unicast IP addresses; that subnet is the resident subnet for each of those addresses—that is, the subnet in which those addresses reside.

reverse route   From one host's perspective, for packets sent back to the host from another host, the route over which the packet travels.

RFC   Request For Comments. A document used as the primary means for communicating information about the TCP/IP protocols. Some RFCs are designated by the Internet Architecture Board (IAB) as Internet standards, and others are informational. RFCs are available online from numerous sources, including http://www.rfc-editor.org.

RIP   Routing Information Protocol. An interior gateway protocol (IGP) that uses distance vector logic and router hop count as the metric. RIP version 2 (RIPv2) replaced the older RIP version 1 (RIPv1), with RIPv2 providing more features, including support for VLSM.

RIR   *See* Regional Internet Registry.

RJ-45   A popular type of cabling connector used for Ethernet cabling. It is similar to the RJ-11 connector used for telephone wiring in homes in the United States. RJ-45 allows the connection of eight wires.

roaming   The process a wireless client uses to move from one AP to another as it changes location.

ROAS   *See* Router-on-a-Stick.

ROM   Read-only memory. A type of nonvolatile memory that can be read but not written to by the microprocessor.

ROMMON   A shorter name for ROM Monitor, which is a low-level operating system that can be loaded into Cisco routers for several seldom-needed maintenance tasks, including password recovery and loading a new IOS when flash memory has been corrupted.

root bridge   *See* root switch.

root cost   The STP cost from a nonroot switch to reach the root switch, as the sum of all STP costs for all ports out which a frame would exit to reach the root.

root port   In STP and RSTP, the one port on a nonroot switch in which the least-cost Hello is received. Switches put root ports in a forwarding state.

root switch   In STP and RSTP, the switch that wins the election by virtue of having the lowest bridge ID and, as a result, sends periodic Hello BPDUs (default, 2 seconds).

routed port   A port on a multilayer Cisco switch, configured with the no switchport command, that tells the switch to treat the port as if it were a Layer 3 port, like a router interface.

routed protocol   A protocol that defines packets that can be routed by a router. Examples of routed protocols include IPv4 and IPv6.

Router Advertisement (RA)   A message defined by the IPv6 Neighbor Discovery Protocol (NDP), used by routers to announce their willingness to act as an IPv6 router on a link. These can be sent in response to a previously received NDP Router Solicitation (RS) message.

router ID (RID)   In EIGRP and OSPF, a 32-bit number, written in dotted-decimal notation, that uniquely identifies each router.

router LSA   In OSPF, a type of LSA that a router creates to describe itself and the networks connected to it.

Router-on-a-Stick (ROAS)   Jargon to refer to the Cisco router feature of using VLAN trunking on an Ethernet interface, which then allows the router to route packets that happen to enter the router on that trunk and then exit the router on that same trunk, just on a different VLAN.

Router Solicitation (RS)   A message defined by the IPv6 Neighbor Discovery Protocol (NDP), used to ask any routers on the link to reply, identifying the router, plus other configuration settings (prefixes and prefix lengths).

routing protocol   A set of messages and processes with which routers can exchange information about routes to reach subnets in a particular network. Examples of routing protocols include Enhanced Interior Gateway Routing Protocol (EIGRP), Open Shortest Path First (OSPF), and Routing Information Protocol (RIP).

routing table   A list of routes in a router, with each route listing the destination subnet and mask, the router interface out which to forward packets destined to that subnet, and as needed, the next-hop router's IP address.

routing update   A generic reference to any routing protocol's messages in which it sends routing information to a neighbor.

RSTP   *See* Rapid Spanning Tree Protocol.

running-config file   In Cisco IOS switches and routers, the name of the file that resides in RAM, holding the device's currently used configuration.

S

same-layer interaction   The communication between two networking devices for the purposes of the functions defined at a particular layer of a networking model, with that communication happening by using a header defined by that layer of the model. The two devices set values in the header, send the header and encapsulated data, with the receiving devices interpreting the header to decide what action to take.

secondary root   This term refers to the switch configured with the secondary keyword on the **spanning-tree vlan x root {primary | secondary}** command. At time of configuration, this command causes the switch to set its base priority to 28,762.

Secure Shell (SSH)   A TCP/IP application layer protocol that supports terminal emulation between a client and server, using dynamic key exchange and encryption to keep the communications private.

segment   In TCP, a term used to describe a TCP header and its encapsulated data (also called an L4PDU). Also in TCP, the process of accepting a large chunk of data from the application layer and breaking it into smaller pieces that fit into TCP segments. In Ethernet, a segment is either a single Ethernet cable or a single collision domain (no matter how many cables are used).

serial cable   A type of cable with many different styles of connectors used to connect a router to an external CSU/DSU on a leased-line installation.

serial interface   A type of interface on a router, used to connect to some types of WAN links, particularly leased lines and Frame Relay access links.

service set identifier (SSID)   A text string that is used to identify a wireless network.

shared Ethernet   An Ethernet that uses a hub, or even the original coaxial cabling, that results in the devices having to take turns sending data, sharing the available bandwidth.

shortest path first (SPF) algorithm   The name of the algorithm used by link-state routing protocols to analyze the LSDB and find the least-cost routes from that router to each subnet.

Simultaneous Authentication of Equals (SAE)   A strong authentication method used in WPA3 to authenticate wireless clients and APs and to prevent dictionary attacks for discovering pre-shared keys.

single-mode fiber   A type of fiber cable that works well with transmitters like lasers that emit a single angle of light into the core of the cable, allowing for a smaller core in comparison to multimode fiber cables.

site-local scope   A concept in IPv6 for which packets sent to an address using this scope should be forwarded by routers, but not forwarded over WAN links to other sites.

SOHO router   A term to describe the general role of a router that exists as part of the enterprise network but resides at an employee's home or at a smaller business site, possibly with a short-term lease compared to larger enterprise sites. These sites typically have few devices, so it makes sense to use one device that integrates routing, switches, wireless, and other features into a single device (the SOHO router) and are more likely to justify Internet access as the primary WAN access method.

solicited-node multicast address   A type of IPv6 multicast address, with link-local scope, used to send packets to all hosts in the subnet that share the same value in the last six hex digits of their unicast IPv6 addresses. Begins with FF02::1:FF00:0/104.

Spanning Tree Protocol (STP)   A protocol defined by IEEE standard 802.ID. Allows switches and bridges to create a redundant LAN, with the protocol dynamically causing some ports to block traffic, so that the bridge/switch forwarding logic will not cause frames to loop indefinitely around the LAN.

split-MAC architecture   A wireless AP strategy based around the idea that normal AP functions are split or divided between a wireless LAN controller and lightweight APs.

SSH   *See* Secure Shell.

standard access list   A list of IOS global configuration commands that can match only a packet's source IP address, for the purpose of deciding which packets to discard and which to allow through the router.

star topology   A network topology in which endpoints on a network are connected to a common central device by point-to-point links.

startup-config file   In Cisco IOS switches and routers, the name of the file that resides in NVRAM memory, holding the device's configuration that will be loaded into RAM as the running-config file when the device is next reloaded or powered on.

stateful DHCPv6   A term used in IPv6 to contrast with stateless DHCP. Stateful DHCP keeps track of which clients have been assigned which IPv6 addresses (state information).

stateless address autoconfiguration (SLAAC)   A feature of IPv6 in which a host or router can be assigned an IPv6 unicast address without the need for a stateful DHCP server.

stateless DHCPv6   A term used in IPv6 to contrast with stateful DHCP. Stateless DHCP servers don't lease IPv6 addresses to clients. Instead, they supply other useful information, such as DNS server IP addresses, but with no need to track information about the clients (state information).

static access interface   A LAN network design term, synonymous with the term *access interface*, but emphasizing that the port is assigned to one VLAN as a result of static configuration rather than through some dynamic process.

static route   An IP route on a router created by the user configuring the details of the route on the local router.

station (STA)   An 802.11 client device that is associated with a BSS.

STP   Shielded twisted-pair. This type of cabling has a layer of shielded insulation to reduce electromagnetic interference (EMI).

straight-through cable   In Ethernet, a cable that connects the wire on pin 1 on one end of the cable to pin 1 on the other end of the cable, pin 2 on one end to pin 2 on the other end, and so on.

subinterface   One of the virtual interfaces on a single physical interface.

subnet   Subdivisions of a Class A, B, or C network, as configured by a network administrator. Subnets allow a single Class A, B, or C network to be used instead of multiple networks, and still allow for a large number of groups of IP addresses, as is required for efficient IP routing.

subnet address   *See* subnet number.

subnet broadcast address   A special address in each IPv4 subnet, specifically the largest numeric address in the subnet, designed so that packets sent to this address should be delivered to all hosts in that subnet.

subnet ID (IPv4)   *See* subnet number.

subnet ID (IPv6)   The number that represents the IPv6 subnet. Also known as the IPv6 prefix, or more formally as the subnet-router anycast address.

subnet ID (prefix ID)   *See* subnet number.

subnet mask   A 32-bit number that numerically describes the format of an IP address, by representing the combined network and subnet bits in the address with mask bit values of 1, and representing the host bits in the address with mask bit values of 0.

subnet number   In IPv4, a dotted-decimal number that represents all addresses in a single subnet. Numerically, the smallest value in the range of numbers in a subnet, reserved so that it cannot be used as a unicast IP address by a host.

subnet part   In a subnetted IPv4 address, interpreted with classful addressing rules, one of three parts of the structure of an IP address, with the subnet part uniquely identifying different subnets of a classful IP network.

subnet router anycast address   A special anycast address in each IPv6 subnet, reserved for use by routers as a way to send a packet to any router on the subnet. The address's value in each subnet is the same number as the subnet ID.

subnet zero   An alternative term for *zero subnet*. *See* zero subnet.

subnetting   The process of subdividing a Class A, B, or C network into smaller groups called subnets.

summary LSA In OSPFv2, a type of LSA, created by an Area Border Router (ABR), to describe a subnet in one area in the database of another area.

supplicant An 802.1x entity that exists as software on a client device and serves to request network access.

switch A network device that filters, forwards, and floods Ethernet frames based on the destination address of each frame.

switched Ethernet An Ethernet that uses a switch, and particularly not a hub, so that the devices connected to one switch port do not have to contend to use the bandwidth available on another port. This term contrasts with *shared Ethernet*, in which the devices must share bandwidth, whereas switched Ethernet provides much more capacity, as the devices do not have to share the available bandwidth.

switched port A port on a multilayer Cisco switch or a Layer 2 switch, configured with the normal default interface setting of switchport, that tells the switch to treat the port as if it were a Layer 2 port, resulting in the switch performing switch MAC learning, Layer 2 forwarding, and STP on that interface.

switched virtual interface (SVI) Another term for any VLAN interface in a Cisco switch. *See also* VLAN interface.

symmetric A feature of many Internet access technologies in which the downstream transmission rate is the same as the upstream transmission rate.

synchronous The imposition of time ordering on a bit stream. Practically, a device will try to use the same speed as another device on the other end of a serial link. However, by examining transitions between voltage states on the link, the device can notice slight variations in the speed on each end and can adjust its speed accordingly.

system ID extension The term for the formatting applied to the original 16-bit STP priority field to break it into a 4-bit priority field and a 12-bit VLAN ID field.

T

T1 A line from the telco that allows transmission of data at 1.544 Mbps, with the ability to treat the line as 24 different 64-kbps DS0 channels (plus 8 kbps of overhead).

TCP Transmission Control Protocol. A connection-oriented transport layer TCP/IP protocol that provides reliable data transmission.

TCP/IP Transmission Control Protocol/Internet Protocol. A common name for the suite of protocols developed by the U.S. Department of Defense in the 1970s to support the construction of worldwide internetworks. TCP and IP are the two best-known protocols in the suite.

telco A common abbreviation for *telephone company*.

Telnet The standard terminal-emulation application layer protocol in the TCP/IP protocol stack. Telnet is used for remote terminal connection, enabling users to log in to remote systems and use resources as if they were connected to a local system. Telnet is defined in RFC 854.

Temporal Key Integrity Protocol (TKIP)   A wireless security scheme developed before 802.11i that provides a MIC for data integrity, a dynamic method for per-frame WEP encryption keys, and a 48-bit initialization vector. The MIC also includes a time stamp and the sender's MAC address

three-tier design   *See* core design.

topology database   The structured data that describes the network topology to a routing protocol. Link-state and balanced hybrid routing protocols use topology tables, from which they build the entries in the routing table.

trace   Short for traceroute. A program available on many systems that traces the path that a packet takes to a destination. It is used mostly to troubleshoot routing problems between hosts.

traceroute   A program available on many systems that traces the path that a packet takes to a destination. It is used mostly to debug routing problems between hosts.

trailer   In computer networking, a set of bytes placed behind some other data, encapsulating that data, as defined by a particular protocol. Typically, only data-link layer protocols define trailers.

transceiver   A term formed from the words *transmitter* and *receiver*. The hardware used to both send (transmit) energy over some communications medium (e.g., wires in a cable), as well as to process received energy signals to interpret as a series of 1s and 0s.

transparent bridge   The name of a networking device that was a precursor to modern LAN switches. Bridges forward frames between LAN segments based on the destination MAC address. Transparent bridging is so named because the presence of bridges is transparent to network end nodes.

trunk   In campus LANs, an Ethernet segment over which the devices add a VLAN header that identifies the VLAN in which the frame exists.

trunk interface   A switch interface configured so that it operates using VLAN trunking (either 802.1Q or ISL).

trunking   Also called *VLAN trunking*. A method (using either the Cisco ISL protocol or the IEEE 802.1Q protocol) to support multiple VLANs, allowing traffic from those VLANs to cross a single link.

trunking administrative mode   The configured trunking setting on a Cisco switch interface, as configured with the switchport mode command.

trunking operational mode   The current behavior of a Cisco switch interface for VLAN trunking.

twisted-pair   Transmission medium consisting of two insulated wires, with the wires twisted around each other in a spiral. An electrical circuit flows over the wire pair, with the current in opposite directions on each wire, which significantly reduces the interference between the two wires.

two-tier design   *See* collapsed core design.

U

UDP   User Datagram Protocol. Connectionless transport layer protocol in the TCP/IP protocol stack. UDP is a simple protocol that exchanges datagrams without acknowledgments or guaranteed delivery.

unicast address   Generally, any address in networking that represents a single device or interface, instead of a group of addresses (as would be represented by a multicast or broadcast address).

unicast IP address   An IP address that represents a single interface. In IPv4, these addresses come from the Class A, B, and C ranges.

unified WLC deployment   A wireless network design that places a WLC centrally within a network topology.

unique local address   A type of IPv6 unicast address meant as a replacement for IPv4 private addresses.

unknown unicast frame   An Ethernet frame whose destination MAC address is not listed in a switch's MAC address table, so the switch must flood the frame.

up and up   Jargon referring to the two interface states on a Cisco IOS router or switch (line status and protocol status), with the first "up" referring to the line status and the second "up" referring to the protocol status. An interface in this state should be able to pass data-link frames.

update timer   The time interval that regulates how often a routing protocol sends its next periodic routing updates. Distance vector routing protocols send full routing updates every update interval.

user mode   A mode of the user interface to a router or switch in which the user can type only nondisruptive EXEC commands, generally just to look at the current status, but not to change any operational settings.

UTP   Unshielded twisted-pair. A type of cabling, standardized by the Telecommunications Industry Association (TIA), that holds twisted pairs of copper wires (typically four pair) and does not contain any shielding from outside interference.

V

variable-length subnet mask (VLSM)   The capability to specify a different subnet mask for the same Class A, B, or C network number on different subnets. VLSM can help optimize available address space.

virtual LAN (VLAN)   A group of devices, connected to one or more switches, with the devices grouped into a single broadcast domain through switch configuration. VLANs allow switch administrators to separate the devices connected to the switches into separate VLANs without requiring separate physical switches, gaining design advantages of separating the traffic without the expense of buying additional hardware.

virtual private network (VPN)   The process of securing communication between two devices whose packets pass over some public and unsecured network, typically the Internet. VPNs encrypt packets so that the communication is private, and authenticate the identity of the endpoints.

VLAN   *See* virtual LAN.

VLAN configuration database   The name of the collective configuration of VLAN IDs and names on a Cisco switch.

VLAN interface   A configuration concept inside Cisco switches, used as an interface between IOS running on the switch and a VLAN supported inside the switch, so that the switch can assign an IP address and send IP packets into that VLAN.

VLAN Trunking Protocol (VTP)   A Cisco-proprietary messaging protocol used between Cisco switches to communicate configuration information about the existence of VLANs, including the VLAN ID and VLAN name.

voice VLAN   A VLAN defined for use by IP Phones, with the Cisco switch notifying the phone about the voice VLAN ID so that the phone can use 802.1Q frames to support traffic for the phone and the attached PC (which uses a data VLAN).

VoIP   Voice over IP. The transport of voice traffic inside IP packets over an IP network.

VTP   *See* VLAN Trunking Protocol.

VTP client mode   One of three VTP operational modes for a switch with which switches learn about VLAN numbers and names from other switches, but which does not allow the switch to be directly configured with VLAN information.

VTP server mode   One of three VTP operational modes. Switches in server mode can configure VLANs, tell other switches about the changes, and learn about VLAN changes from other switches.

VTP transparent mode   One of three VTP operational modes. Switches in transparent mode can configure VLANs, but they do not tell other switches about the changes, and they do not learn about VLAN changes from other switches.

W

WAN   *See* wide-area network.

web server   Software, running on a computer, that stores web pages and sends those web pages to web clients (web browsers) that request the web pages.

wide-area network (WAN)   A part of a larger network that implements mostly OSI Layer 1 and 2 technology, connects sites that typically sit far apart, and uses a business model in which a consumer (individual or business) must lease the WAN from a service provider (often a telco).

Wi-Fi Alliance   An organization formed by many companies in the wireless industry (an industry association) for the purpose of getting multivendor certified-compatible wireless products to market in a more timely fashion than would be possible by simply relying on standardization processes.

Wi-Fi Protected Access (WPA)   The first version of a Wi-Fi Alliance standard that requires pre-shared key or 802.1x authentication, TKIP, and dynamic key management; based on parts of the 802.11i amendment before it was ratified.

wildcard mask   The mask used in Cisco IOS ACL commands and OSPF and EIGRP network commands.

window   Represents the number of bytes that can be sent without receiving an acknowledgment.

Wired Equivalent Privacy (WEP)   An 802.11 authentication and encryption method that requires clients and APs to use a common WEP key.

wired LAN   A local-area network (LAN) that physically transmits bits using cables, often the wires inside cables. A term for local-area networks that use cables, emphasizing the fact that the LAN transmits data using wires (in cables) instead of wireless radio waves. *See also* wireless LAN.

wireless LAN   A local-area network (LAN) that physically transmits bits using radio waves. The name "wireless" compares these LANs to more traditional "wired" LANs, which are LANs that use cables (which often have copper wires inside).

wireless LAN Controller (WLC)   A device that cooperates with wireless lightweight access points (LWAP) to create a wireless LAN by performing some control functions for each LWAP and forwarding data between each LWAP and the wired LAN.

WLAN client   A wireless device that wants to gain access to a wireless access point for the purpose of communicating with other wireless devices or other devices connected to the wired internetwork.

workgroup bridge (WGB)   An AP that is configured to bridge between a wired device and a wireless network. The WGB acts as a wireless client.

WPA Version 2 (WPA2)   The second version of a Wi-Fi Alliance standard that requires pre-shared key or 802.1x authentication, TKIP or CCMP, and dynamic encryption key management; based on the complete 802.11i amendment after its ratification.

WPA Version 3 (WPA3)   The third version of a Wi-Fi Alliance standard introduced in 2018 that requires pre-shared key or 802.1x authentication, GCMP, SAE, and forward secrecy.

Z

zero subnet   For every classful IPv4 network that is subnetted, the one subnet whose subnet number has all binary 0s in the subnet part of the number. In decimal, the zero subnet can be easily identified because it is the same number as the classful network number.

Index

D

I

N

O

Q - R

U

REGISTER YOUR PRODUCT at CiscoPress.com/register
Access Additional Benefits and SAVE 35% on Your Next Purchase

- Download available product updates.

- Access bonus material when applicable.

- Receive exclusive offers on new editions and related products.
  (Just check the box to hear from us when setting up your account.)

- Get a coupon for 35% for your next purchase, valid for 30 days.
  Your code will be available in your Cisco Press cart. (You will also find
  it in the Manage Codes section of your account page.)

Registration benefits vary by product. Benefits will be listed on your account page
under Registered Products.

CiscoPress.com – Learning Solutions for Self-Paced Study, Enterprise, and the Classroom
Cisco Press is the Cisco Systems authorized book publisher of Cisco networking technology,
Cisco certification self-study, and Cisco Networking Academy Program materials.

At CiscoPress.com you can
- Shop our books, eBooks, software, and video training.
- Take advantage of our special offers and promotions (ciscopress.com/promotions).
- Sign up for special offers and content newsletters (ciscopress.com/newsletters).
- Read free articles, exam profiles, and blogs by information technology experts.
- Access thousands of free chapters and video lessons.

Connect with Cisco Press – Visit CiscoPress.com/community
Learn about Cisco Press community events and programs.

Cisco Press